THE BOOK OF DOW

GENEALOGICAL MEMOIRS

of the descendants of Henry Dow 1637, Thomas Dow 1639 and others
of the name, immigrants to America during Colonial Times

Also the allied family of Nudd

———

Written, compiled, edited i

ROBERT PIERCY DOW

of Laguna Beach, California,
and Claremont, N. H.

———

Published by

ROBERT P. DOW, JOHN W. DOW and SUSAN F. DOW
of Claremont, N. H.

———

Offered to all who are Dow by birth or ancestry or marriage; all imbued
with the honest pride of Dow; all interested in Massachusetts
Bay genealogy, in the study of heredity, or the
personal side of American History

1929

Another Quality Reprint of a Classic Book
by

The Apple Manor Press

Markham, Virginia

2016

Thousands of titles available at:
www.AppleManorPress.com

Book pages have been individually reproduced and processed by trained
Aritisans using uncompressed high resolution scanned images of the
original pages. Manually processing of the images allows proper attention to detail
not possible through inexpensive automated software.
Most low cost competitors use automated software with no human quality control
to process low quality compressed PDF files intended for internet viewing.

Manual processing each page allows for much better image and print quality

ISBN 13: 978-1-5421-0001-4 Part 1
ISBN 13: 978-1-5421-0002-1 Part 2

BOOK TWO

Descendants of Thomas Dow
of Newbury in 1639

BOOK TWO

DESCENDANTS OF THOMAS DOW

OF NEWBURY IN 1639

HERE beginneth the chronicles of a family of Dow, absolutely unrelated to the preceding, of unknown origin, possibly of different nationality, surely poor, much poorer than their average neighbor, actually suffering from lack of suitable food, illiterate (altho ability to read and write was not general in the colonies). On the new soil this family developed wonderfully,—one member in the second generation rising decidedly above the average in ability and prosperity. The fourth generation included very substantial men. The family progressed until its influence on the nation as a whole has been second to few. It has been distinctly a warrior race, sharing in the earliest fighting for preservation against the Indians, then for colonial defense, for independence, and in the Civil war. It is remarkable that among the home towns of this family,—Salem, Methuen and Plaistow, not one adult male Dow of good health remained at home during the Revolution.

In the list of original grantees of Newbury, Mass, 1639 occurs the name of Thomas Dow. The origin of Newbury is strangely absent from the records. Nothing is known of the vessel which carried them; none of them appear on other lists or in other places. There is a vague tradition that Thomas Dow came in 1637, but this seems error arising from the fact that Henry Dow came in 1637. The best presumption is that the founders of Newbury came together and in 1639, probably from some English seaport. All else is speculation without evidence. At all events he was in Newbury in 1639 with wife Phebe and at least one child. His house was in what is now called Newburyport, on the southerly side of Greenleaf's Lane (now State St) leading to Watt's Cellar. He next appears as being admitted a freeman by the General Court June 22, 1642. This does not imply any previous condition of non-freedom, indenture or lack of property qualifications. The term "freeman" was established in the first charter of the Massachusetts Bay Colony applied to such persons as took an oath of allegiance and were admitted by formal vote of the General Court. It lasted until the second charter changed the colony into a province. A freeholder was one who by grant, purchase or inheritance was entitled to a share of the "Commons," or undivided lands. The freeman alone could vote in the nomination of magistrates and deputies to the General Court. A freeholder need not be a freeman or vice versa. He might be neither, yet be qualified to vote in all town affairs. All inhabitants could vote on any question involving raising money. Thomas Dow was a freeholder from his arrival by reason of the original grant of his Newbury homestead; he continued a freeholder when he sold this and bought land in Haverhill.

There is probably no immigrant to America for whose antecedents more vigorous search has been made by professional and amateur genealogists. Yet, not the slightest trace has ever been discovered. At one time Richard Sylvester Dow bedebeje undertook the task, hoping to make the needed discoveries in time for a forthcoming history of Essex County. He himself could give no time to the work and employed professional aid. After sending an expedition to England and collecting a mass of data (all wholly irrelevant), and after spending several thousand dollars, his only reward was in proving that Thomas was none of the numerous of the name whom it was suspected that he might be. His professionals got together considerable material on the Dows here, but their work is often so misleading as to be rather worse than useless, no part of it usable without independent proof. The antecedents of Henry Dow, immigrant of 1637, being known, the searchers began by assuming that the two were brothers or near relatives. This gave them a pleasant outing in Norfolk Co with salary and expenses paid. They even failed to hit upon the item in Runham parish register showing that Henry Dow had a brother Thomas 14 years too old to fit the Newbury man and that this Thomas had a family and died on his inherited property in Runham. Moreover, they ignored the obvious fact that, while Henry Dow had more than average education, Thomas Dow could not read; that for five years Henry and Thomas lived in adjoining towns and for ten years thereafter they were but 15 miles apart, without the slightest evidence that one knew of the existence of the other.

The investigators next turned to Wiltshire, because one Francis Dow had come from there and returned there; but he had an only child, Peter. This made no difference; they searched for some kinsman Thomas, disregarding as before that our Thomas could not read and Francis was of the landed gentry and mayor of a city. To Stratford they next went, because a Thomas Dow of Stratford had a wife Phoebe. They did not hurry to weigh the patent evidence. Simon Fenn, clothier of Dedham, Essex, bequeathed money Jan 16, 1609, to his dau Phoebe, wife of Thomas Dowe of Stratford. Jan 10, 1615, Phoebe got another legacy from a kinswoman, being then called Phoebe Dow, wid. This Thomas Dow is about 40 years too old to fit and some curious searcher has since located all his family in Stratford. The investigators were then compelled to turn to a general search, published probate records being the most accessible field. They prepared lists of wills, over 200 of them, from every county in England, of Dow, Doue, Dove or any other similar spelling. Results wholly negative. They scanned every legatee, in hope that they might find from some parish rec that such had a son Thomas. They found of about right age a Robert Dowe of London, Bridget Dowe, wid of Thomas, legatees of their sister, Ann Colston, wid of Bristol 1620. They canvassed William Dowe and Mary, his wife, of 1620, she the dau of John Cossie of Baudsey, Suffolk. James Deowe is a new spelling; he was an appraiser May 1620 in Beamister, Dorset. Robert Dowe was a legatee in Exeter 1620. Thomas Dow, witness to a will in Newburye, Berks, 1620, raised their hopes from coincidence in name of place, altho presumptive age forbade. The number of Dow in Ireland can be imagined from the circumstance that 12 Thomas Dows were buried in Dublin in a single year. In Scotland during the 50 years preceding 1639 the number of recorded Thomas Dows could not be confined to a page.

One can only turn to evidence drawn from Thomas and Phebe themselves. There is nothing in the religion of either to afford a clue, for there was but one church in Haverhill, and Newbury. Thomas Dow was as religious as his neighbors, but this proves nothing except that he was a Puritan in Massachusetts. Could he be a Scotchman? The Scotch Dow were never an independent family; many of them were in Clan Buchanan, but there were some in almost every clan, indicating that the name was assumed by individuals without any concert whatever. The investigators did not look up any Scotch records; hunting would be like seeking a needle in a haystack. There was a Thomas Dow of Berriehell of Tullibagles, Methven Parish, near Perth, who made a will Aug 19, 1609, but he had no son Thomas; and there were a score of Thomas Dow within a few miles. There was no Scotch migration to America for many years after this, but this does not preclude the possibility of some individual getting from Scotland to England and joining a party to America. Moreover, any Scotchman joining a party of emigrants would be a marked man, living socially more or less apart.

An idea that our Thomas Dow of Newbury possessed a distinctive plaid or tartan is based wholly on a misunderstanding. Over 20 years ago a lady of Dow descent while visiting Edinburg was shown a Dow plaid and bought a quantity, distributing samples to such Dows as she knew or subsequently met. Some one who knew of the interest taken in the identity of Thomas Dow suggested that this might be his plaid and so the story grew. There are now some who assert positively that this plaid was worn by Thomas Dow of Newbury. This is absolutely untrue. It is well known that the canny Scotch manufacturers keep lines of plaid labelled to suit any name ever known in Scotland. There are plenty of retailers who will supply a plaid for any name and will swear that the Schmidts or O'Flahertys have worn it for a thousand years. The patterns are generally chosen with some care, so this particular plaid is a variant of the Buchanan. A few years ago experts looked at it once again. None admitted knowing it. Only a few were bold enough to call it a fake. One said plainly that it was a fabrication, not a true tartan, and was designed recently as resembling and varying from the Buchanan.

Whatever presumptive evidence there may be (and there may not be any) comes from the will of Thomas or the attached words of Phebe, his wife. Here and there a phrase faintly suggests the language or national canniness. Phebe's name was either Latly or Latty. The exact wording in the will seems to be "I, Phoebe Latly wife of Thomas." A photographic copy proves that latly begins with a small l. It also shows the cross bar of the t prolonged, as tho the writer began to write latty when his ink failed. The Author believes her name was Latty, because that is a name, while Latly is not. Perhaps this couple came from that part of the Highlands where Thrums might be, perhaps truth is stranger than fiction, perhaps Sir James Barrie is unwittingly a better genealogist than we, and Rob Dow, literary sawyer of Thrums and Aaron Latta, weaver of Thrums, are the true kin of this Newbury and Haverhill couple. This entails an unwelcome suggestion, as there was at the time no Scotch migration. Thomas, gillie, might have married Phebe. dairy maid, and had a son John; not liking his outlook, might have crossed the border and joined a Puritan party to America. In those days a runaway gillie was hauled back as ignominiously as a negro in 1850. If there was a runaway of this kind, it would be likely that the man would take a new name for concealment; if so, Dow was a common and general name, not attributable to any one clan or locality. The Author does not entertain this theory; merely cannot dismiss it until the truth comes out. Some day the marriage rec or birth of their son may be discovered, but if so, it will be by chance.

The American career of Thomas was neither obscure nor conspicuous. He was poorer than most of his neighbors, for his whole estate was appraised at less than £96. He lived 14 years in Newbury, during which time (as we shall see under bc) his children had not sufficient nourishment. The rec shows that his Newbury house was conveyed to John Bartlett May 29, 1660 (book 3, p 177, Ipswich series). Thomas was dead by this time so that the date must be of a belated recording. Norfolk rec I, p 122, shows: Richard Ormsby of Haverhill to Thomas Dow of Newbury, house and house lot cont 4 a more or less, with all appurtenances and 5 accommodations for two and fifty pounds, tenn shilling to be paid as appears by a bill of sale which the aforesaid Thomas Dow has given me under his hand. Dated 10 November 1653

Rec 18 May 1662

Richard Littlehale ⎱
John Clement   ⎰ wit

Here is a house and 9 acres of land for less than $260. Haverhill real estate was cheap, probably far cheaper than Newbury, it being a new town, on the frontier, a bulwark of the region of which Boston was the well protected center, soon to be the scene of the greatest amount of Indian fighting, where no one was safe and every one walked with gun in hand. Thomas did none of the fighting; he died May 31, 1654, "ae about 39." This must be nearly correct. It is also definitely stated that he was the first white adult to die in Haverhill. Not that Haverhill was an unusually healthy place, nor its inhabitants gifted with longevity. It was a new town; some one had to go first, and Thomas Dow happened to be the one, living there scarcely over 6 months.

His will is nuncupative, made two days before his death:

"The last will and testament of Thomas Dowe as it was delevered or expressed by him on the 29th day of May being in ye yeare 1654.

I, Thomas Dow, although weake in body yet of perfect memory i doe desire to submit my will, to God's will and to dispose of my estate to my wife and children as followeth, leaving my wife to be the sole executor at present of all my vesable and personall estate.

First I do give unto my loving wiffe Pheby my tow oxen that are now hers and mine and three young beastes beinge now one yeare and upwards ould and on cow and two swine and al my houseold goods to be at her disposinge for ever.

Also my will is that my oldest son John Dowe at the age of twenty and one yeare ould shall ingioy as his inheritance al the land and housinge that I have bought in Haverhill and to pay in to his other brothers thomas and Stephen and to his 2 sisters mary and martha as I shall apoynt the house and land being thought to be worth three score pounds; my second son Thomas shal reseave at his age of 21 ten pounds or 5 pounds at his age and 5 pounds when he is 22 yeares and for my son Steven he shall reseave at his age of 21: or 5 pounds at 21 and 5 pounds at 22; as to my will is that John my son shal pay to his sister Mary and his sister Martha at theyre age of 21 ten pounds or 5 pounds apeace at 21 and 5 pounds apece at ther age of 22; as there brothers reseave theres.

Also I Pheby latly wife to Thomas Dow doe joyne my consent to this will of my husband in each perticular and for my son John Dow I doe fully and freely resigne up al my wright in the house and land when my son shall come to the age of 21 yeares ould. wittness my hand prouided he shall pay to his brothers and sisters as his fathers will is.

        in witness hearof

                                The marke of

John Eaton (P)   Phebya (F) Dowe
Theo: Shatswell

This will was testified upon oath by ye witnesses in ye court held at Salisbury the (8) th off ye (2d) Mo: 1656.

John Eaton's mark resembles a P and that of Phebe an F, both showing unfamiliarity with the exact shape of the letters. Nevertheless, an effort was made to claim that this mark indicated her name was Fenn. The actual writing was done by Shatswell, of whom it may be said that he frequently spells a word twice the same way. It is quite clear that the first two paragraphs were composed by him and written down in advance as sure to meet the requirements. One can imagine the unction with which he put in the word vesable; it had a good sound, looked erudite, almost a legal term, and would add dignity to any will. The rest, which does not parse, was surely put down word by word as spoken laboredly by the dying Thomas. The last paragraph may have been dictated by Thomas, his wife assenting by a nod from time to time, but the final "prouided" is surely her own. A distinguished genealogist of Dow descent still claims that the mark of Phebe proves that her maiden name began with F and he reads: "I, Pheby, lately wife of Thomas." Now, Shatswell is just as liable to spell a name with a small as a capital letter, and it is inconceivable that Phoebe, just called "my loving wiffe," and sitting beside her husband, who lived two days longer, could call herself lately a wife.

Hers was not a vast dowry, the cattle and household goods worth less than £10. It is a pleasure to record that for seven years she had a home with her son John and that John made all the payments required in the will. After that, she married John Eaton, witness to the will. He was a cooper of Salisbury, who came to Haverhill 1646, was selectman 1648, thrice married, with 7 children, 6 surviving to become step children of Phebe Dow. They returned to Salisbury, where he d Oct 29, 1668, she Nov 3, 1672.

All the children d Haverhill; younger b Newbury:

    a   John, a minor in 1654, hence b later than 1633, presumably in Europe; not improbably 1638
    b   Thomas, probably b 1640 in Newbury
    c   Stephen b Newbury Mch 29, 1642
    d   Mary b Apr 16, 1644   e   Martha b June 1, 1648

John Dow ba d Nov 26, 1672, cooper of Haverhill; freeman 1666; on muster roll of Ensign Moses Higgins, assigned to sixth garrison. The sons of Thomas Dow were not strong, possibly early privations worked against them. John prospered moderately, for he made all payments charged to him in his father's will, kept his own land and was able to buy the allotment made in the fifth division to one Coffin. He and his brother Thomas appear as signers of the petition for the pardon of Maj Robert Pike, a high minded man always in trouble with the authorities for denouncing the witchcraft persecution and supporting the right of free speech by lay preachers in the absence of regular preachers. He m Oct 23, 1665, Mary Page b May 3, 1646, 4th child of John and Mary (Marsh) of Hingham, later of Haverhill. The improbability of relationship of John Page and Robert Page of Hampton is discussed under abc. Hist Windham states that John Dow ba was the ancestor of the Atkinson Dow family,—a *lapsus calami*, for that family is fully accounted for, coming from John Dow bcfi. John's children:

    a   Mary b and d Haverhill Apr 1668

b   Joseph b Sept 20, 1669; d Mch 16, 1688-9, unm
c   John b Nov 6, 1672; not mentioned in Hoyt's Old Families

John d intestate. Apr 3, 1673, wid Mary Dow swore to the inventory
of his estate (£174-1-0). July 14, 1673, she m 2nd Samuel Shepard.
Joseph Dow bab chose her brother Onesiphorus Page as his guardian in
1686. Apparently Joseph was entitled to some overlooked property,
for seven years after his death, May 4, 1696, Samuel Shepard and Mary,
his wife, formally refused to administer Joseph's estate. After considerable delay it was administered by his cousin Samuel Dow bcb and the
property divided among his surviving uncles and aunts (Essex Co Prob,
vol 305, p 128). This argues that John Dow bac was not living and had
no heirs, for such would be heirs-at-law. The matter needs more search,
for there is a Haverhill line still unconnected, whose most frequently
recurring name is John.

Mary (Page) Dow had 7 children by Samuel Shepard, of whom the
youngest m Samuel Dow adk.

———————

Thomas Dow bb, husbandman, d Haverhill June 21, 1676; will
probated Nov 14. He evidently shared the family lack of vital resistance.
He started toward prosperity; was able to buy land in 1662. It does not
appear that he was admitted a freeman. He m Dec 17, 1668, Dorcas
Kimball b 1649, dau of Henry and Mary (Wyatt) of Ipswich. Henry
was son of Richard Kimball who m 2nd Margaret (Cole) Dow a. A
statement has been printed that Mary Wyatt m 2nd her father-in-law.
This is obvious error, for Richard (1) Kimball d the same year as his
2nd wife. Richard (2) Kimball had two wives, both named Mary.
Hoyt gives the 2nd as Mary Gott (?). She must be Mary Wyatt Dow.
Titcomb, Early New England People, apparently started the widely
printed error that Thomas Dow m Elizabeth Duston (Dustin or Dunster).
Dorcas Kimball survived Thomas by eight years. Apparently she did
not serve as executrix, for the estate was administered by Henry Kimball,
another brother, and receipts for all legacies were made to him. Children:

a   Thomas b Oct 23, d Nov 4, 1669
b   Henry b Mch 5, 1670-1. In his will his father gave this child to Joan, wife of
    John Haseltine. This step must have had the consent of Dorcas. From
    Henry comes a large posterity,—roughly, one tenth of all the b Dow family
c   Dorcas b Feb 27, 1672; d Apr 3, 1673
d   Phoebe b Sept 20, 1674; m Jan 16, 1695, Samuel Smith (Topsfield rec). Chil-
    dren,—Phoebe; Mary m Aug 14, 1721, Thomas Demcy of Topsfield; Samuel;
    Susannah; Solomon; Joseph; and probably Priscilla bap Oct 2, 1715, m
    Mch 30, 1738, Robert Cragg, immigrant to Rowley

Hoyt, Old Families, suggests another, posthumuous, child, but gives
no evidence. Perhaps he, too, was looking for some ancestor for the
unconnected Dows of Haverhill.

Henry Dow bbb, brought up in the Haseltine family, m Apr 11,
1692, Elizabeth Colby of Rowley b Haverhill Oct 30, 1671, dau of Isaac

and Martha (Jewett). They had a farm on the Amesbury-Salisbury border, all rec in Amesbury. Henry does not appear at any time in any public capacity; he receipted in due time to Henry Kimball for his inheritance and did not sell his Haverhill land until after his marriage. Children:

a — b and d Oct 13, 1693   b Martha b Oct 1694
c Elizabeth b Oct 12, 1702   d Thomas b May 3, 1704
e Isaac b Jan 27, 1707   f Joseph b Aug 27, 1709
g Jerusha b June 17, 1713; m July 9, 1736, Samuel Stevens Jr b Nov 28, 1710, son of Samuel and Rachel (Heath)

Martha Dow bbbb m Amesbury Sept 17, 1718, Jonathan Davis of West Amesbury b Jan 8, 1695-6, son of John and Sarah (Carter); 2nd Amesbury Aug 21, 1746, Benjamin Wadleigh. Children, by 1st husband:

a Eleanor b May 25, 1721; probably d young
b Elizabeth b Aug 29, 1723; m her cousin, Solomon Copp, cordwainer
c John b Feb 7, 1725-6; m Hannah Wadleigh
d Ruth b Oct 23, 1727   e Hannah b Feb 18, 1729-30; d young
f Malachi b May 26, 1732   g Orpha b July 15, 1735
h Hannah b Mch 28, 1737

Elizabeth Dow bbbc. The mss prepared for Richard S Dow have her m 1719 Jonathan Copp of Amesbury b Oct 9, 1699, having son Solomon b Mch 3, 1720. It is too common a practice to conceal distasteful genealogical facts. Haverhill rec is clear: Solomon, son of Jonathan Copps and Elizabeth Dowe as she saith b Mch 3, 1720. Jonathan, son of Aaron and Mary (Heath), refused to father the child or marry the girl, fled the Mass jurisdiction. He afterwards married and had a family in New Hampshire. Oddly, his grandson m her granddau. Solomon was brought up by his aunt Martha Davis bbbb and m her dau.

In those days a slip made by a young girl was not long or seriously held against her. Elizabeth m (int pub Jan 15, 1725-6) Andrew Rowan (correct in Salisbury rec; Amesbury and Marblehead give Andrew Brown). They had children:

a Margaret b Feb 17, 1727-8   b Andrew bap July 7, 1728
c John bap Mch 1, 1729-30   d Elizabeth b Jan 18, 1731

Andrew Rowan Jr has been confused with his father; was a pioneer of Sanbornton with wife Phoebe. A brook, a hill, a cape in the pond, etc, are still his memorials, altho the name is mis-spelled Roen, Rohan, Rown, etc. As no Rowan genealogy has been prepared, we give his children:

Andrew enlisted 1777; d scurvy Mch 1, 1778
John, Rev veteran, m Sarah Hancock
Thomas d Nov 11, 1818, unm   Joseph d unm
Henry d Dec 8, 1809, unm   Sally m and moved out of State
Betsey, outlived all her kin; d in almshouse Sept 20, 1851, at great age

Thomas Dow bbbd presumably inherited the Amesbury homestead; m Aug 19, 1725, Sarah Goodwin, presumably dau of Samuel, shipwright of Amesbury, and Esther (Jameson). Thomas soon died, possibly the youngest child posthumous. Abstract of wills at Haverhill gives Sarah Dow, exr of Thomas, but without date. Wid Sarah Dow appears in Hampton Falls tax books for 1728-9 only. She seems to have sold the homestead; m 2nd 1736 John Pressey of Amesbury and outlived him. He b Dec 2, 1691, son of William and Susanna (Jameson), m 1st Feb 2, 1712-3, Elizabeth Weed; d Dec 13, 1737; had 5 children, the youngest b 1729. Children of Thomas:

    a Phoebe b Dec 21, 1726. Phoebe Dow m Sou Hampton Apr 23, 1752, Andrew
        Barnard. Anna, dau of Phoebe Dow, bap Haverhill May 6, 1759. Probably
        this is garbled and both apply here
    b Sarah b Jan 11, 1728-9

Sarah Dow bbbdb m So Hampton Apr 25, 1750, Timothy Huntington (Hunteton in rec). She d; he m 2nd 1764. Children:

    a Timothy b June 3, 1753   b William b June 6, 1756
    c Thomas d unm   d Mary b Aug 6, 1758; m —— Elliot of Concord

Isaac Dow bbbe is known only from Amesbury vital rec; m June 5, 1729, Jane Fowler, unplaced in Hoyt's Old Families. Children:

    a Jerusha b June 1, 1731; d in infancy
    b Simeon bap Mch 20, 1733   c Jerusha bap Apr 14, 1734
    d Henry bap May 30, 1739. Untraced

Simeon Dow bbbeb m Feb 23, 1758, Phoebe Sanders b Haverhill, d May 21, 1807, dau of Nathaniel and Mary (Bixby). In spite of mature years, he was a minute man from Methuen (unless see ahbc). After the war, the family moved to Hopkinton. He d Hopkinton Aug 15, 1827. Children:

    a Amos b July 7, 1758; d young   b Susanna b July 1, 1760
    c Simeon b June 4, 1761   d Isaac b Aug 25, 1763
    e Elizabeth b Aug 25, 1765. An Elizabeth Dow int pub Feb 20, 1795, to Moses
        Wodley of Hampstead
    f Nathaniel b Aug 25, 1768   g Amos b Amesbury Sept 26, 1770
    h Judith b Sept 12, 1772

Simeon Dow bbbebc of Hopkinton d, ae 98, Feb 12, 1860; m Nov 25, 1784, Phoebe Stevens b 1757, d Sept 13, 1823. Children:

    a Polly b Aug 21, 1785   b Joseph b Nov 19, 1787
    c Phoebe b Nov 19, 1787   d Zadick (Zadoc, rec) b Aug 10, 1789
    e Frederick b Dec 14, 1791; untraced   f Sally b June 12, 1794
    g Betsey (Betty, State rec) b Jan 7, 1797   h Ladd b Jan 7, 1797; untraced
    i Daniel b June 13, 1799; left a son Andrew J. Neither found in 1850 census

Joseph Dow bbbebcb of Hopkinton, land assessed $3,000 in 1850; m 1813 Hannah F French b Mch 21, 1789, d July 15, 1781, dau of Asa. The couple lived together 64 years. Children:

    a Caroline Gage b Dec 22, 1814; m Sept 21, 1848, John Herrick of Libertyville,
        Ill
    b Joseph French b Mch 10, 1817   c Horace Page b Feb 3, 1819
    d George Lovejoy b Feb 21, 1821   e Daniel David b Apr 22, 1823
    f Mary Jane b Aug 29, 1825; d May 5, 1831

g Arthur b May 13, 1828; d Oct 18, 1829
h Charles Stevens b Jan 23, 1831; d Apr 1, 1832

Joseph F Dow bbbebcbb, carpenter, d Hopkinton July 7, 1884.
D rec of dau gives wife as Maria T.   He must be the J French Dow who
m Mary J Perry b New Boston July 1, 1825, dau of Varnum and Dorothy
(French).   She m 2nd (his 3rd) Sept 13, 1892, John Philander Mudgett.
One child found:

a   Alice C d Hopkinton Jan 28, 1859, ae 12

Horace P Dow bbbebcbc d Jan 15, 1880; m Jan 18, 1844, Mary P
Emerson, both of Hopkinton; 2nd, Nov 3, 1857, Amanda J Hunt of
Providence, R I.   Children:

a   Mary P m Feb 29, 1872, Abner R Farnum of West Concord
b   Clara J b 1845   c   Harriet E b 1848

George L Dow bbbebcbd, farmer of Hopkinton, married, d Aug 18,
1863; wife Henrietta b Concord.   She was Henriette Hoyt b 1824, dau
of Enoch W who m wid Mary French.   Apparently Henriette was by
his 1st wife.   She m 2nd, Charles Stark of Fishersville. One child found:

a   Josephine B b Hopkinton Dec 14, 1859

Daniel D Dow bbbebcbe, retired machinist, d Concord July 22,
1902; m Nov 10, 1856, Betsey W Putnam, both of Hopkinton.   A d rec
gives Betsey B Dow, wid of Daniel D, b New Sharon, Me, Feb 18, 1832,
dau of Benjamin Blackstone and Betsey (Whittier).   One child sure,
altho rec not found:

a   Carrie J

Carrie J Dow bbbebcbea of Hopkinton m Dec 20, 1881, John
Herman Sargent, carpenter of Concord.   Children:

a   Lena M b Jan 4, 1885   b   Daniel Dow b Apr 18, 1886
c   Neal A b June 1897

Sarah Dow bbbebcf m Aug 17, 1811, Judah Bailey b Apr 7, 1789.
They moved to Iowa.   Children, b Hopkinton:

a   Caroline m Richard McAdams   b   Emeline m John Dennison
c   Eliza m John Edgar   d   Amanda m (his 2nd) John Edgar
e   Phoebe McKenzie m William Fenton of Aurora, Ill
f   Mellvilla d young   g   Thomas P D d young

Zadoc Dow bbbebcd is untraced.   One of the 3 brothers herein
untraced had a son b 1816.   One would think from dates it would be the
oldest.   Living descendants do not recall any facts prior to 1816, nor
if there were other children:

a   Simon b Hopkinton 1816; one rec gives Simeon, probably correct; he probably
      changed the name himself

Simon Dow bbbebcda is called in Hist Hampstead Lieut, for what
reason unstated.   Census 1850 gives him shoemaker of Hampstead,

realty $125. Hist Hampstead gives him a prominent place in the centennial celebration but attempts no genealogy and is not wholly accurate otherwise. He was popularly known as Dimon. State rec gives Hannah Poor m Sept 10, 1839, Simon Dow, both of Hampstead. A descendant writes that Simon's wife was Martha Rand. Hannah d Hampstead Dec 11, 1884, ae 69-8-9. Martha Rand must be right, but how to reconcile the data we do not know. Children; all b Hampstead:

    a   Martin V B b Nov 7, 1840
    b   George R b Aug 12, 1842. Undoubtedly the George R Dow enlisted Pembroke
        1861; d Baton Rouge, La, 1863, unm
    c   Mary; not found in 1850 census
    d   Simon Harvey b Aug 17, 1847   e   Orrin Boardman b Aug 3, 1853

Martin V B Dow bbbebcdaa m Hampstead Jan 17, 1864, Josephine W Dow bcfiibcc; neither now living. Children:

    a   George F   b   Annie E b Jan 1, 1870   c   Herman Wallace b 1874

George F Dow bbbebcdaaa m Mary A Quimby; d comparatively young. Two sons:

    a   Frank; left 2 sons, one named Harold   b   William b 1886

Will M Dow bbbebcdaaab of Haverhill m Melrose July 31, 1907, Jennie Alice Nicholson, ae 18, dau of Thomas and Sarah J (MacDonald).

Annie E Dow bbbebcdaab has the distinction of being the first child b in the city of Haverhill, a few minutes after the city was incorporated. Her mother was greatly interested in her family genealogy and recalled that Thomas Dow b was the first white adult d in Haverhill town. Unfortunately, Mrs Josephine W Dow left no written memoranda. Annie m Homer Littlefield; no children.

Herman W Dow bbbebcdaac appears in recent directory as clerk in Haverhill; m Oct 14, 1903, Maud Elizabeth Robbins, ae 24, dau of William S and Cora M (Clondman). Only child:

    a   Norman Robbins b Haverhill Feb 4, 1908; d young

S Harvey Dow bbbebcdad, shoemaker of Hampstead, m Apr 25, 1869, Martha A Newhall, ae 23, dau of Isaiah and Mary. She living 1923 with dau in Beverly. Only child:

    a   Ora M b Hampstead July 25, 1870; now Mrs Shapleigh of Beverly; had 1
        child,—Marion Dow now Mrs Hersey

Orrin B Dow bbbebcdae m Etta R Morrill b Poland Springs, Me; formerly restaurant keeper in Haverhill; in 1923 having restaurant winters in St Petersburg, Fla, summers, Salisbury Beach, Mass; has never replied to letters asking genealogical information. Children:

    a   Arthur H b 1889   b   Lewis M b 1892; both b Haverhill

Arthur H Dow bbbebcdaea, last maker of Lynn, m Mch 3, 1914, Lillie Cutter, ae 16, dau of Clarence A and Catherine (Domey).

Lewis M Dow bbbebcdaeb, teacher of Cambridge, m Feb 22, 1916, Harriet Smith, ae 20, dau of Frank T and Ida E (Fowler).

Isaac Dow bbbebd has so far appeared only in m rec of son. He settled in Warner; m Phebya ——. Probably other children, but only one appears:

    a Isaac b Warner Jan 15, 1793

Isaac Dow bbbebda, farmer of Warner, d Warner Aug 11, 1858; m Polly Watson b Salisbury Oct 8, 1797, d wid Warner Mch 24, 1888, dau of Abijah and Sarah (Quimby). Probably only 3 children:

    a Lendon C b 1819
    b Mary Ann b Warner Aug 23, 1821; d Alexandria, N H, June 8, 1914, unm.
       Hist Bristol gives b Boscawen Aug 27, 1821
    c Cyrus Benjamin b Warner 1835

Lendon C Dow bbbebdaa, draughtsman, d tuberculosis Manchester Nov 8, 1850; m Apr 9, 1849, Phoebe S Pierce, both of Lowell, Mass. Child:

    a Patience T b 1849

Cyrus B Dow bbbebdac, farmer of Warner, d Warner July 24, 1878, ae 43, m Nov 1864 Ellen M Couch, ae 21, dau of Albert J and Ruth (Sargent), both of Warner. She d Hopkinton Mch 15, 1899. Children, b Warner:

    a Gilford Q b Jan 16, 1866; d young   b George Albert b May 4, 1870
    c Guilford Q b Aug 1, 1871

Guilford C (sic in m rec) **Dow** bbbebdaca, farmer of Warner, moved to Webster; m Feb 20, 1895, Mary E Sanborn, ae 30, b Webster, dau of Ezra and Sarah F (Elliott). One child found:

    a Bernard Joseph b Webster Nov 6, 1899

George A Dow bbbebdacb settled in Bristol, farmer and meat dealer. Hist Bristol does not mention m or children.

Nathaniel Dow bbbebf settled in Boscawen. Vital rec of this town are in very bad shape and its Hist unsatisfactory in its genealogical aspect. Nathaniel was twice m and had a large family. Vital rec mention only those who d young. Those who survived are left to conjecture. Nathaniel d Boscawen Sept 11, 1837; m 2nd, Salisbury, Mass, Sarah Pettingell. A son named for her proves the Boscawen rec that wid Sarah Dow d Boscawen July 12, 1838. Known children:

    a —— d Sept 22, 18—, ae 13   b —— (sex?) d Feb 6, 1816
    c —— d Sept 1822, ae 3   d —— d June 26, 1825, ae 2
    e Pettingell d Feb 16, 1839

The four following are surely sons or nephews and a relative.

Lorenzo G Dow bbbebfg (Lorenzo S in census), farmer of Boscawen, realty $600, b N H 1821; m Oct 20, 1847, Maria A Story of Hopkinton b N H 1826. A child; no others in N H rec:

    a Betsey A b Boscawen Dec 5, 1849

Calvin Dow bbbebfh, unm pauper, d Boscawen May 16, 1872, ae 52.

Mehitable Dow bbbebfi m Hopkinton Dec 29, 1834, Collins Flanders, both of Boscawen.

Margaret Dow (Mrs) bbbebfj (also in rec Mrs Hannah Dow) of Boscawen or Warner, m (his 2nd) Concord Nov 8, 1842, William Danforth of Boscawen b Jan 22, 1780, son of William and Olive (Elliott).

Amos Dow bbbebg m Mary Brown of Amesbury; 2nd, Nov 14, 1804, Polly Holmes b Hopkinton 1787. Hopkinton 1850 census gives them with 1 child, presumably a grandchild. Presumably children b in the 14 year interval, but no trace of such:

    a Samuel Harris b June 10, 1818   b Rufus B b 1826

Samuel H Dow bbbebga, lumber dealer, d Warner Sept 6, 1894; m Sept 23, 1846, Harriet Story Currier b 1824, both of Warner; 2nd, May 5, 1852, Matilda S Currier, both of Warner; 3rd, Emily R Rand living 1908 with son Herman. Children:

    a Frances Currier b Nov 13, 1847; m Oscar L Rand; 3 children
    b Harvey S b Aug 16, 1849   c Herman Adelbert b Sept 8, 1858
    d Emily G b Jan 30, 1861; m Fred H Savory; children, Fred A, Miriam E

Harvey S Dow bbbebgab, lumber dealer of East Canaan, N H, m Dec 22, 1875, Bertha E Barney ae 19, dau of Eben and Emily of Grafton. She m 2nd, Jan 1, 1896, Albert L Hadley of Canaan. Harvey d Oct 8, 1890. Children:

    a Edith Marion b Jan 27, 1878; m June 25, 1898, Perley J Columbia of Canaan
    b Pearl Emeline b Jan 29, 1880   c Florence Bertha b Apr 28, 1883
    d Archie Samuel b Dec 3, d Dec 7, 1885

Herman A Dow bbbebgac farmer and lumber dealer of Warner appears in 1908 directory with sister and wid mother; m June 20, 1888, Stella M Wright, teacher, ae 22, dau of Henry P. Children:

    a Samuel Harris b Dec 13, 1890   b Harold Wright b Sept 27, 1897

Rufus B Dow bbbebgb of Hopkinton m Oct 14, 1845, Maria Bruce of Hopkinton. This family not found in 1850 census. One child by own rec, perhaps others:

    a Addie N (M in m rec) b Hopkinton, m Jan 1, 1868, Charles W Brown of Henniker; a son Harry R b Henniker 1876

Joseph Dow bbbf had a home of his own by 1735 in west parish, Amesbury, near the Haverhill line. Records of this line were very meager, but Alton L Smith of Worcester, whose wife is a descendant, made a study of it of remarkable completeness, seeming not to have overlooked a single deed or any other reference to him. He bought and sold real estate often and moved from town to town with a frequency very unusual in those days. A man of ability, he began a business which

reached its height under his grandchildren.   From deeds he appears as
a joiner in 1735, housewright 1739, inn holder, trader in 1754 and 1762,
shipwright 1767; moved from Amesbury to Kingston 1744; in Haverhill
most of the time 1760 to 1771; d Dec 8, 1780.   Oct 13, 1771, he and
wife were dismissed from Second church Amesbury to the new church in
Goffstown.   He m Amesbury Jan 12, 1731, Judith Butman (Bootman in
rec), dau of Joseph and (wid) Rebecca (Harris).   Joseph was son of
Jeremy of Beverly and Hester (Lambert).   Hester was dau of Richard
Lambert of Salem.   The oldest 5 children were bap together Nov 8,
1741, in west parish, Amesbury.   Probably this was due to the changing
sentiment in favor of infant baptism:

a   Joseph   b Judith   c Eunice   d Susanna
e   —— not named   f Benjamin bap July 4, 1742
g   Anna bap Apr 22, 1744   h Henry bap Apr 24, 1748
i   Mary bap Apr 24, 1748; unm in 1765   j Abigail bap July 8, 1750
k   Sarah bap Mch 25, 1853; probably the Sarah m Haverhill July 15, 1782,
        Ichabod Grindall
l   Lois bap Jan 9, 1755

Joseph Dow bbbfa m Haverhill Apr 20, 1768, Judith Emery,
whose sister Mary subsequently m his brother Henry.   This line is
not in Emery Gen.   They had a brother who moved to N Y State.
Another brother (or close relative) emigrated with the Dows to New
Brunswick and has a posterity now in that Province.   A grandson says
that his grandmother was Eliza Ann Emery, it is likely that Eliza was a
niece and a 2nd wife.   Judith's name appears in deeds until the family
disappears from Mass in 1771.   Joseph remained closely associated with
his father in shipwrighting and land speculation.   It is not easy to distinguish between them in deeds, as both had wives Judith.   The Chelmsford roster of troops for the 1760 Canadian campaign contains Joseph
Dow b Amesbury, 17, of Chelmsford.   For some campaign (probably
this one) he secured his cousin Gideon Colby as substitute.   In 1765 he
received land in Haverhill from his father, which he sold Jan 5, 1771, to
James McHard.   From this time he drops absolutely out of sight until
he reappears in New Brunswick 1801.   He had business interests in
Dracut and Goffstown and family tradition calls one of his sons Ipswich,
a suggestive name.

Prior to 1783 New Brunswick had almost no population and was
part of Nova Scotia.   In the spring of 1783 a large party of colonists
from Mass and adjoining States landed at the mouth of St John River
and took up lands.   They had been tories and this was their first opportunity to reach British soil.   Their lives had been made most unpleasant
since 1775 and many of them had lived in strict seclusion.   This party,
however, contained no Dow.

The Provincial government was liberal in the matter of granting land;
indeed it could well afford to be to get *bona fide* settlers.   Land had been
"squatted upon" and such was readily confirmed by Government title.

To William Dow bcdhd land was granted in Charlotte Co in 1791, on which his kin had settled possibly as early as 1772. William Dow, probably not identical, got York Co land by grant in 1815. On Deer Isl, N B, there is a place known for 150 years as Hannah Dow's Hill, origin of name uncertain.

The grants of land to the bbbfa line did not begin until 1803. A series of accidental discoveries have brought to light the movements of this family throughout. Joseph Dow and wife were in Boston 1774 and he took part in the so-called Boston Tea Party. Just when he was converted to the tory cause we do not know. The people of Boston had no chance to join the Federals at Bunker Hill. They had to look on in silence, whatever their sympathies. Joseph was a ship builder already; under the British occupation of the city he was the best man at that trade in the place. He was kept busy and well paid. Family tradition says that a son of Joseph was born in or near Haverhill 1783. This is absent in the well kept Haverhill rec, and is doubtful, unless the family was there in hiding. When the British evacuated Boston, the position of the tories was precarious. A fairly large party fled; among them was Joseph Dow and at least three members of the allied family of Emery. These subsequently followed Joseph to New Brunswick, where their descendants are plenty, some being quite prominent merchants in St John today. They took refuge first on the uninhabited island of Southport, just outside of Wiscasset, Me. Possibly Henry Dow bbbfh went there first. They traveled in a boat of Joseph's own making and were successful in taking all portable property, tools for ship-building being a prime necessity.

The stay at Southport lasted twenty years. Here Judith Emery died and Joseph took a second wife, Eliza Ann Emery. Here were born probably eight children. Here a ship yard was built and many vessels launched, mostly of the schooner type. It is a family tradition that Joseph built the first schooner known to Maine. Altho Southport had no money and needed none, except for taxes, no government existing for years, Joseph and his associates became comparatively wealthy, wealth consisting of vessels. They set up a coasting trade and their boats became well known from Halifax to Boston. St John, N B, was of course a regular port of call and the Dow vessels became well known to the Provincial government. The Governor himself, realizing that the Province lacked good builders, invited Joseph Dow to locate there, promising ample lands, virgin timber tracts and deep water. Joseph accepted, and the place chosen was at the junction of the St John and Oromocto Rivers. The first grant, in Sunbury Co, was made in 1803 to Aps Dow. This is Absalom bbbfaf. In 1810 John and William got additional grants. Joseph Dow Jr got a grant in 1810 and another in 1818. He was by this time Joseph Dow, as his father had joined the great majority. If our theory is correct, a 1st born of Joseph and Judith remained in Southport.   The rest developed the great ship-building business begun at Oromocto.   There was some sort of partnership, but how extensive or lasting is not known.   Very naturally, however, the whole family, wealthy and aristocratic, considered themselves tory of tories.   In Oromocto dwelt 6 sons, 1 dau:

x   Thomas; the son who elected to stay in Southport
a   Joseph, surely the grantee of 1810; genealogically untraced
b   John b Jan 12, 1783; regarded as the head of the family
c   William; a grantee but genealogically untraced
d   Daniel; not a grantee; genealogically untraced. Ipswich Dow seems to have been a nickname for one or the other of these brothers. He followed the sea.   Over 50 years later he visited the family in New Limerick, Me, and was the subject of good-natured railery because of a sailor's habit of throwing the fish bones on the floor
e   Henry m Mary McGonegal; a partner in the ship building plant
f   Absalom, probably older than John. Genealogically untraced
g   Eunice. Name recalled by posterity, but nothing else

JOHN DOW OF OROMOCTO AND
HIS DESCENDANTS

Contributed by Sterling Tucker Dow, Kennebunk, Me

FOR the benefit of the family and for the preservation of what information we have, there are gathered here the fragments of knowledge we have of John Dow. The records of some of his children are not easy to trace, even though they come within the ken of relatives now living. No written word of him, of his times and environment exists, so that our sole source of information is the stories and accounts which have been handed down by word of mouth. More than a century has passed since his departure from Haverhill, Mass, to (what must have been) the wilds of New Brunswick, and 65 years have rolled around since his death at New Limerick, Me. How quickly we pass on and are forgotten and how many difficulties bestrew the path of him who attempts to reconstruct the lives of those of his line who passed on but a few years before! How much of interest would be added to this meager narrative could we but know the characteristics of John Dow, who his associates were, what motives actuated him and why; in fact, a thousand and one things of human interest which would picture him to his descendants. No one of his 17 children is now alive, so that the opportunity for securing first hand information about his home and business life is gone and we are forced to rely upon the scraps—and few enough they are at that—which these children have passed along to the next generation.

Even the parentage of John Dow is obscure, and while it is believed that he had brothers and sisters, the records of his native Haverhill reveal the names of none of them. Possibly in course of time it will be established that there were such, through a search of the parish records of Oromocto. Family tradition says his father was an immigrant to Ipswich, Mass, in 1773, but does not give his father's name. The same source names two brothers, Absalom and Ipswich, and one sister, Eunice. We have the record of Joseph Dow and of his marriage to Judith Emery in 1768 in Haverhill. The name of Emery had been well known in Haverhill for a century and this representative of the family is described as a woman of very superior character and of great native worth. Our Genealogist assigns these two to John Dow as his parents and much color is given to the assignment because the name of Emery persists to this day in the family. Indeed, no name has been used more, as may be seen if you have the interest and patience to read on. Obviously Joseph Dow could not have been an immigrant in 1773 and married Judith Emery in Haverhill in 1768. Assuming, then, that Joseph Dow was the father of John, one naturally asks: "How much farther back can his ancestry be traced?" Here again we refer to our Genealogist, who writes:

"You are descended from Thomas Dow and Phebe, his wife, original grantees of Newbury, Mass, 1639. We do not know whence he came; he was a Puritan."

What then do we know about John Dow? No personal picture of him is extant, so that we know nothing of his appearance, manner, or traits of character. The reader can only deduce, however, from the following that he was a man of more than average intelligence and ability. He was born in Haverhill, Mass, Jan 12, 1783. If, as it is believed, he was the son of Joseph, it is altogether probable that other children preceded him in the 15 years since the marriage of Joseph and Judith Emery. In 1803 he went to New Brunswick. Family tradition steps in once more with a reason for this change—because he was a Tory. This may have been, although the large number of Tories left New England at about the time of the evacuation of Boston by the British in the War of the Revolution. Without doubt feeling against the mother country still ran high in 1803, and in going to a British province he might have let it be known that he had tory sympathies in order to secure peace in his new surroundings and to keep on good terms with his neighbors. It is not believed that he became a British subject as he afterwards held town office in New Limerick, Me. The lack of record of his brothers and sisters in Haverhill leads to the belief that they accompanied him to the Province. At the junction of the Oromocto River with the St John he settled and became a builder of ships. His business prospered and he became a man of substance and of local prominence at least. Several full rigged ships came from his yard, among which are remembered the names of three: the "Rival," the "Sir Howard Douglass," named for the Governor of the Province, and the "Phoebe," named for his wife. Some of the vessels he built he operated himself between the Province and British ports. The Phoebe was one of these and was lost on a voyage to Liverpool, with no insurance.

On his 26th birthday John Dow was married to Phoebe Smith in Watertown Parish, Queens Co, New Brunswick. She was but sixteen, the date of her birth being Aug 30, 1793. Miss Margaret A Swift of Brunswick, Me (her great granddaughter) writes thus of Phoebe Smith:

"Mother tells us that her grandmother Phoebe Smith Dow's father was a rich man, so she was well educated and brought up in affluence, with her own pony and carriage, etc.

Another extract:

"After which they came to New Limerick to farm and Phoebe went right into the work to help retrieve, is even said to have picked up stones for their boundary, and how she was a very busy woman, was very generous in helping every one and gifted in many ways. They finally built themselves a fine new house and were in readiness to move in when fire destroyed their possessions. She (Mother) remembers her grandfather as a very grand old man, had very beautiful white hair worn longer than usual, and was of a very religious turn of mind."

Here is another picture from the capable pen of Mrs Mary E Dow of Briarcliff Manor:

"—— used to tell me a great deal about the Dow family and I have a vivid impression of the patriarchal life in your great grandfather's family. Your grandmother told me that when she visited this large dignified house the farm laborers were all fed in a large basement dining room—often as many as sixty men at a time, and that your great grandmother, still young, very handsome and very "capable," managed the whole great establishment. She also found time in her leisure moments to hemstitch the ruffles for her little girls' white gowns and very possibly your great grandfather's ruffled shirts. I often wonder whether a large part of the good looks and great physical vigor of the Dow family did not come from her.

Here is portrayed a woman of no ordinary mould, and when it is remembered that seventeen children were born to her between 1811 and 1835 at Oromocto (eleven of whom reached adult age) our wonder increases. She is described as being of very slight physique but her strength must have been nothing short of marvelous. Just stop and review for a moment: brought up in affluence, married to a man who had his own way to make and whose successes and failures were large, the management of large establishments at Oromocto and New Limerick, the hardships incidental to life in a new country and the care of a family the size of which is well nigh unheard-of in these days, do you wonder that she lived to only 48?

John Dow prospered in his shipping business. His sons helped in rafting logs down the St John River to the mills which sawed them into lumber which constituted the outgoing cargoes of his ships. With increasing means came an increased establishment and we can readily understand why the family grew into the ways and habits of the well-to-do. Why should they not enjoy the fruits of their labor? One recorder reports that they became quite aristocratic, holding themselves in high esteem. We have all seen the like, have we not? About 1835 prosperity began to wane, due to two probable causes. The first was the loss of the good ship Phoebe uninsured [another vessel, the Eliza Ann (named for Eliza Ann Emery), is also spoken of as lost under similar circumstances]. No doubt this was a severe blow to the family finances. The second cause is given as the remission of duties on lumber entering British ports from the Baltic Sea, with which the provincial product could not compete. This put a quietus on the lumber export trade of New Brunswick, and, along with many others, John Dow failed.

The date of the departure of the family from Oromocto to found a new home at New Limerick is not known, but inasmuch as all but one of the children were born at Oromocto, it must have been very shortly after 1835. Knowing something of the farm he conducted there, it is inconceivable that his failure deprived him of everything. He had passed the age of 50 and had the numerous family hereinafter recorded. Some of the children were old enough to be of material help. We have read of the patriarchal home he and his able wife made for themselves at New Limerick, and it is difficult to believe that something was not saved with which to start it. The farm is known at this date as the Edward Hennigan place.

As Phoebe Smith died Nov 27, 1841, she did not live long after leaving Oromocto. John Dow lived on at New Limerick, his daughter Mary Frances taking the mother's place, and on Apr 21, 1852, surrounded by his family singing

When I can read my title clear

To mansions in the skies,

he passed on to the higher life.

The 1850 census finds John in No 5, Range 3, Aroostook Co, the place not yet having been officially named New Limerick. Two dau were then with him,—Mary and Eleanor

The children of John and Phoebe, record made by Absalom Smith Dow of New Limerick and copied by Margaret A Swift:

a	Eliza Ann b Feb 1, 1810	b	John Emery b Apr 13, 1811
c	Henry b July 14, 1812	d	George b Mar 7, 1814; d Oct 2, 1815
e and f	—— twins b Apr 18, d Apr 19, 1815		
g	Mary Frances b June 11, 1816	h	Elijah Smith b Feb 11, 1818
i	Absalom Smith b May 27, 1819	j	Phoebe Amanda b Mch 25, 1821
k	Eleanor Amelia b Feb 11, 1823	l	Margaret Taylor b Jan 12, 1825
m	Oliver Smith b Dec 3, 1827	n	Arthur b May 5, d May 6, 1829
o	Catherine Leonard b Apr 5, 1830; d young		
p	Catherine Annie b Mch 1, 1835	q	—— not named, b New Limerick

Eleven of these children reached maturity, and your recorder owns with considerable regret that his information regarding some of them is still only fragmentary. It is also a matter for regret that the statistics which follow are not enlivened by more anecdotes and incidents from the lives recorded. To make an account of this kind alive and interesting, and to make our forbears alive to us again, such incidents are vital.

Ann Eliza Dow bbbfaba. The tale is soon told. The sum total of our information is that she m Henry Bonnell and went to Digby, N S, to live. Inquiry of the postmaster as to Bonnells living there brings no response. Mrs Swift says there were a large family of children, among them:

Henry, Eliza, Frank, John, Helen

John Emery Dow bbbfabb d Apr 6, 1893; for a time his father's partner in Oromocto: m St John, N B, July 12, 1834, Sophia Jane Barlow b St John June 27, 1810. They made their home at Sheffield, not far from Oromocto, where all but the youngest of the children were born. Once more let us pay tribute to the wife. Mrs Mary E Dow writes thus appreciatively:

Perhaps you remember your grandmother as I so well remember you as a child in the house in Myrtle St—but you could not have understood the rare intelligence and innate refinement and absolute integrity of her character. I consider the really intimate friendship she gave me was a great honor.

Coming from a woman who has influenced the lives of so many women of America and has been such a power for good, this is indeed rare praise. Speaking of her determination that her sons should have all the advantages possible, Mrs Frederick George Dow writes:

But the strongest impression I have is that dear Mother Dow had the hardest kind of a life and but for her splendid effort her sons would never have had the opportunities they did.

Who is capable of estimating the value of a good mother? We Dows have been fortunate, nay blessed, in our wives and mothers, and Emery Augustus Dow is justified in his statement:

.... be that as it may, I have yet to meet a man or woman by the name of Dow who would not, it seems to me, bear inspection and give quite a respectable account of himself or herself.

Considering our ancestry how can it be otherwise?

The date and reason for the removal of John Emery Dow and his family from Sheffield to Portland, Me, are not known. It certainly antedated the Civil War, as his sons volunteered from Portland. Children:

a Edwin Barlow b June 20, 1835
b George Heyward b May 18, 1837; d July 1839
c Sophia Amelia b July 16, 1841   d John Emery b Aug 6, 1843
e Sterling b Sept 12, 1845   f Frederick George b St John Aug 24, 1851

Edwin B Dow bbbfabba was his father's partner before and, for a time, after the War, in Portland. He was the second commander of the 6th Me battery (known as Dow's Battery) and was brevetted Major for meritorious service at Gettysburg. His position there became isolated and was about the last obstacle to the Confederate sweep of the whole field. Made the center of fire by batteries and infantry charges, he and a small group of survivors returned an effective fire until the Union infantry re-formed, advanced and turned the tide of battle. A monument to the band has stood for many years on the spot. He is buried in the Arlington National Cemetery.

After the war he engaged in the insurance business, retiring finally 1907, living most of the time in N Y City; m Dec 24, 1857, Josephine Augusta Devereux of Charlestown, Mass, b Mch 9, 1840, d on her 2nd wedding anniversary; 2nd, Anna Margaret Granger of Boston b Hartford, Conn, Aug 2, 1843, d before him, a well known concert singer. He d June 29, 1917.   Children:

 a Gertrude Josephine b N Y Nov 30, 1859; d Sept 1860
 b (adopted) Fanny; now Mrs Gustav L Becker of N Y

Sophia Amelia Dow bbbfabbc never married and always lived at home. After her mother's death she became the comfort and support of her father. Through years of illness and suffering her patience and fortitude command our admiration. Always cheerful, never complaining, she indeed fought a good fight under adverse conditions. The writer will always remember and cherish with gratitude the memory of her affectionate regard, interest and solicitude. Naturally, perhaps, the writer retains keen recollection of the goodies always forthcoming whenever he chose to pay her a visit. She d Feb 19, 1917. (It was to Miss Sophia that the Author first appealed for information on the then absolutely untraced line of bbbfa and she inspired Sterling T Dow to undertake the study).

John Emery Dow bbbfabbd, grad Bowdoin and Harvard Law School, opened an office in N Y, his career starting with much promise. Health failing, he had to give up business in 1876; d May 7, 1878; m Jan 7, 1869, Mary Elizabeth Dunning, dau of George F and Annetta (O'Brien).   Children:

 a Annetta b Oct 21, 1871; d Dec 17, 1876
 b Lawrence b July 28, 1874; d Jan 24, 1879

Mrs Mary E Dow, bereft in three years of husband and both children, entered the teaching staff of Miss Porter's school for girls at Farmington, Conn; later founded the school for young women which bears her name at Briarcliff-on-Hudson, N Y. Respected, revered by her graduates the country over, her career makes a bright mark for the credit and pride of womanhood in America. She lives Briarcliff with a summer home in the Maine woods.

Sterling Dow bbbfabbe enlisted at 17 in his brother's battery and served throughout the war as quartermaster's sgt; afterwards engaged in fire insurance business in Portland up to the time of his death, June 30, 1892; m Oct 13, 1868, Mary Manning Tucker of Portland b Oct 13, 1847, dau of Daniel and Harriet (Vose).   Children:

 a Sterling Tucker b Nov 4, 1869   b Elizabeth Emery b Apr 26, 1876

Sterling T Dow bbbfabbea has always been in the service of transportation companies, first with the Maine Central at Bangor, accounting clerk, traveling auditor and freight agent; afterwards asst treas, then general manager of the Atlantic Shore Ry. He m June 5, 1902, Alice

Gertrude Verrill of Portland b Aug 28, 1871, dau of Byron D and Harriet (Robinson). Children:

  a   Sterling b Portland Nov 19, 1903; won Rhodes scholarship from Harvard
  b   Harriet b Portland July 22, 1906
  c   Elizabeth (Betty) b Kennebunk Jan 2, 1911

Elizabeth E Dow bbbfabbeb m Apr 26, 1896, Charles Baker Mitchell d June 1916. Child:

  a   John Emery b Sept 2, 1899; grad Harvard

Frederick G Dow bbbfabbf, grad Bowdoin and Columbia Law School, opened an office in N Y, his partner being Lewis R Conklin; member of the Congregational church; counsel for or member of the Century Association, Fulton Club (five years its secy), American Hardware Rubber Co., Hardware Board of Trade and others.   He lived Flushing; m Oct 4, 1876, Emily Schlesinger of College Point, dau of Auguste; d Dec 28, 1901, his wife surviving. Child:

  a   Harold Francis b July 17, 1877; d May 3, 1886

Henry Dow bbbfabc. Little is recalled of him. The writer knew him and well remembers his stories about hunting in Aroostook. For years he was a regular visitor at his brother Absalom's home in New Limerick, spending his winters in Florida; m Jane Hathaway of Sheffield; moved to Woodstock, N B; afterwards to Boston. Children:

  a Emma   b Mary   c Bessie   d George, d, prob unm
  e Julia

Mary F Dow bbbfabg. Here again our information is the smallest. It is believed that she never married, but lived at home, assuming charge of the household after her mother's death, living to be about 50. Miss Swift tells of having a sampler worked by her, but now so faded that the date is illegible.

Elijah Smith Dow bbbfabh, carpenter, d Gorham, Me, Mch 11, 1863; lived several places in southern Maine; m Jan 1, 1846, Caroline Elizabeth Merrill of Portland d Naples Dec 20, 1902, ae 90-11-15, dau of William and Mary (McClellan). Census 1850 shows him farmer of No 6, range 4, Aroostook Co, realty $400. Children, youngest b Gorham, rest Smyrna:

  a   John William b Jan 9, 1847   b   George Green b Nov 2, 1849
  c   Sophia Eliza b June 9, 1852   d   James Merrill b Sept 1, 1855

John W Dow bbbfabha, mechanic of Naples, m Nov 29, 1873, Bertha L Shaw of Sebago. He appears in comparatively recent directory as Hilbert Dow, farmer of Norridgewalk. Children:

  a   Charles Clarence b Sept 16, m 1877; d Naples May 9, 1900, photographer unm
  b   Maude Caroline b Dec 10, 1880; m May 28, 1913, Alphonso E Ward of South
      Portland
  c   Martha Lena b Aug 10, 1891; teacher, d Jan 3, 1915, unm

George G Dow bbbfabhb, blacksmith of Baldwin, m Frances Ellen Binford. Children:

    a George Wright b 1878   b Jennie Eliza b 1883; d Mch 25, 1885
    c Annie Ella b Feb 23, 1894

George W Dow bbbfabhba m while a dental student in Portland, Aug 28, 1900, Georgia C Harding, teacher, ae 20, dau of George H and Annie B (McKenney). Dentist of Rockland, later farmer of Bradford. Children:

    a Katherine b Nov 14, 1900; d Sept 29, 1901
    b —— son b Feb 8, 1905   c —— dau b Oct 6, 1906
    d —— son b July 19, 1909   e —— son b July 9, 1916

Sophia Eliza Dow bbbfabhc m Cyrus Noble of Baldwin.   Children:

    a Willard C, not living   b Queenie, not living
    c Cyrus L   d Ralph   e Louis H

James Merrill Dow bbbfabhd, blacksmith of Parsonsfield, m Nov 25, 1896 (her 2nd) wid Ada B Haynes, ae 38, b N S, dau of George b Eng and Sarah E (Crocker) Caldwell. She d May 12, 1906, ae 49-5-24. No children; he not living.

Absalom Smith Dow bbbfabi d Eastport Nov 12, 1901.   Named for his mother's brother, he went with the family to New Limerick. The writer remembers him with greatest respect and pleasure. With his bald head and patriarchal white beard, his was as kindly and fine a face as is often seen, indicative as it was of peacefulness with, and good will to, everybody. Somewhere, from a source not now remembered, the writer learned that Absalom was considered the student of the family, the one who turned naturally to the finer things of life. If his expression and bearing were any index to his character, this certainly must have been true. He m Mch 31, 1852, Loranah Sanborn Drew b New Limerick Nov 5, 1827, d May 1894. (New Limerick rec badly garbled, gives Lorana S Dow d June 27, 1894, ae 66-7-22, unm, dau of Moses b Limerick and Joanna (White) b N B. Another garble gives John Dow b 1804, married, d New Limerick May 29, 1897, ae 93-5-18. His name was Drew.)
Children of Absalom, all b New Limerick:

    a Phoebe Smith b Mch 22, 1853; m Sept 17, 1892, George W Armstrong of New
         Limerick; 2nd Aug 20, 1903, William Halverstadt of Waterville. No
         children
    b Absalom Smith b Apr 7, 1861
    c Harriet J b May 26, 1864; d July 29, 1872
    d Emery Augustus b Mch 8, 1867; m New Limerick Dec 8, 1888, Alice Eva
         Cole. No children. Much interested in Dow genealogy, he is our authority
         on New Limerick history
    e Emma Amelia b June 8, 1870; m Waterville May 1, 1902, James Jerome
         Pray. No children

Absalom Smith Dow bbbfabib lives Ft Kent; m New Limerick Apr 15, 1890, Catherine Elizabeth Mullen b July 7, 1871, d Apr 19, 1915. Children, all but eldest b Ft Kent:

    a John Rex b Apr 24, 1891   b Augustus Drew b Mch 10, 1895

c Phoebe b June 15, 1897   d Harold Mullen b Oct 27, 1899
e Lenora Dorothy b Mch 26, 1902   f Katherine Imogene b July 24, 1904
g Henry Smith b Nov 8, 1906; d 1926
h Doris June b June 8, 1909 i Margaret Elizabeth b Sept 14, 1912

Phoebe Amanda Dow bbbfabj d Topsham Oct 1890. Always alert, vivacious and interesting, she will ever be to the writer Aunt Amanda. Even in her later years she was remarkably fine looking and in her early days she must have been a beauty; m New Limerick Mch. 28, 1840, George Gardner Green of Topsham; 2nd, St Stephen's, N B, Henry Wilson Green of Topsham brother of her 1st husband. Children, by 1st husband:

a Caroline Amanda b May 24, 1841
b Kate Amelia b Jan 4, 1843   c Louisa b 1846; d 1847
A granddau is Miss Margaret A Swift of Brunswick

Eleanor A Dow bbbfabk d Edmundston, N B, May 17, 1901; m Cornelius McMonagle, widower, who d about 2 years later at Smyrna; 2nd John Balloch b Sept 14, 1814, d Mch 16, 1875; lived Edmundston. Children, by 2nd husband:

a Alfred Perry b Oct 24, 1854; d Aug 28, 1907
b Eliza b Aug 6, 1856; d Feb 8, 1896 c Caroline Matilda b Dec 20, 1858

Margaret T Dow bbbfabl d Ridley Park, Pa, Feb 27, 1906; m New Limerick May 22, 1845, by Parson Blake U S A, George William Merrill. Children:

a Mary Frances b Feb 27, 1846   b Eleanor Amelia b May 3, 1847
c Margaret Dow b Jan 13, 1849   d Amanda Green b Nov 29, 1850
e William John b Apr 22, 1852   f Thomas Leonard b Oct 10, 1854
g Henry Green b Mch 29, 1856   h Charles Henry b Sept 11, 1860

Oliver Smith Dow bbbfabm, of unerring eye and versed in forest lore, settled in Island Falls; d Feb 12, 1888; m Apr 18, 1853, Pauline Wentworth Sewall, sister of William W (Bill) Sewall, foreman on Theodore Roosevelt's Dakota ranch. Census 1850 shows him alone, realty $400, in No 6, range 4, Aroostook Co. He m 2nd, June 22, 1875, Mary J Bradbury d Oct 8, 1915, ae 72-3-11, dau of Samuel and Julia (True). Children:

a Wilmot Sewall b Aug 14, 1854   b Rebecca b 1857; d 1859
c Pauline Wentworth b 1860; d Dec 10, 1862
d Sarah Elizabeth b Dec 11, 1862   e Levi Sewall b Mch 5, 1865; d 1872
f Pauline Wentworth b Dec 27, 1867   g Oliver Smith b Apr 25, 1876
h Ralph b May 30, 1879   i Bradbury b Feb 28, 1884
j John Emery b July 27, 1885

Wilmot S Dow bbbfabma d May 21, 1891; m July 13, 1885, Elizabeth A Edwards. He was with his uncle on Theodore Roosevelt's ranch. His uncle writes: "Oliver's oldest son, Wilmot S, generally known as Will Dow, was my nephew. He was a blacksmith by trade, a very strong, bright man, a great hunter and fisherman. He and I were with Roosevelt on his ranch in Dakota. He and Roosevelt were great friends. Roosevelt says Dow was the best shot at game he has ever seen.

By kind permission of Col Roosevelt the following incident is copied from the Roosevelt Autobiography: The Elkhorn ranch house was built mainly by Sewall and Dow, who, like most men of the Maine woods, were mighty with the axe. I could chop fairly well for an amateur, but I could not do one-third of the work they could. One day when we were cutting down the cotton wood trees, to begin our building operations, I heard some one ask Dow what the total cut had been, and Dow, not realizing I was in hearing, answered: "Well, Bill cut down fifty-three, I cut forty-nine, and the boss he beavered down seventeen." Those who have seen the stump of a tree which has been gnawed down by a beaver will understand the exact force of this comparison.

In his note to the writer Col Roosevelt adds: "Will Dow was a natural born gentleman, and as fine a man in all ways as I ever met—and as staunch a friend."

Children of Wilmot S:

a Wilmot Edwards b Aug 12, 1886   b George Field b Mch 31, 1888
c Levi Sewall b Apr 4, 1890

Wilmot E Dow bbbfabmaa, drug clerk of Presque Isle, m June 14, 1911, Katherine M Stevens b Wis, ae 24, dau of Henry Coleman and Margaret (McGilton). Children:

a Wilmot Stevens b Mch 27, 1912
b Margaret Elizabeth b June 4, 1914   c —— dau b Mch 16, 1917

George F Dow bbbfabmab, laborer, m Dec 15, 1910, Ellen A Roberts, ae 23, dau of Richard and Mary (Thomas). No children.

Levi S Dow bbbfabmac, bookkeeper of Island Falls, m Feb 11, 1919, Rilla Merrifield (in son's rec Rillia Lizzie Merrihew), div, ae 23, dau of Bentley and Grace (Gould) Walls. Child:

a Levi Sewall b Portage Lake July 20, 1920

Sarah E Dow bbbfabmd m Oct 24, 1887, George W Stearns. Children:

a Rosewel b Aug 2, 1888   b Pauline b June 10, 1890

Pauline W Dow bbbfabmf m Nov 23, 1890, Ralph W Emerson. No children.

Oliver S Dow bbbfabmg, farmer of Island Falls and Crystal, m Oct 12, 1898, Ada M Lawler, ae 19, dau of John and Fannie (Mabbs). Children:

a Elizabeth b Aug 22, 1899   b —— son b June 19, d June 23, 1906

Ralph Dow bbbfabmh, laborer of Island Falls, m Amber Callis

(Corliss in rec, probably right), post office clerk, ae 23, dau of Willard C
and Annie E (Sherman). Children:

    a Marjorie Pauline b July 26, 1905   b ——
    c Ronald Edward b Aug 6, 1911

Bradbury Dow bbbfabmi, clerk, m Oct 21, 1913, Nora E Kimball,
ae 23, dau of Elbridge and Mary E (Cummings). Children:

    a Philip b Houlton Oct 7, 1914   b —— son b Millinickett Dec 16, 1918

John Emery Dow bbbfabmj, clerk, m Nov 27, 1908, Lena C Crage,
ae 21, dau of Robert T and Lillian E (Stimpson). Children:

    a Helen Pauline b June 19, 1912   b Robert Oliver b Feb 8, 1914
    c Mary Isabel b July 25, 1916   d —— son b May 1, 1917

Catherine A Dow bbbfabp. The writer remembers with much
appreciation the kindness of Aunt Kate upon his first visit to Aroostook.
She m Hodgdon Sept 18, 1852, Thomas Merrill Bradbury b May 30,
1820, d Nov 22, 1896. She d Houlton Apr 26, 1891. Children:

    a Frances Webster b Feb 24, 1854; d May 13, 1911
    b Jefferson b Apr 8, 1858   c Katherine Leonard b Feb 23, 1864
    d Frederick True b Jan 3, 1874; d Feb 13, 1894

Henry Dow bbbfae. His son in 1892 wrote to Edgar R Dow
what he could recall about his grandsire. We are certain of our identi-
fications because he and Absalom Smith Dow bbbfabi agree that their
grandfather was Joseph Dow and grandmother Eliza Ann (Emery).
This proves that Joseph m her prior to 1783. He is recalled as riding
each morning from his home to the shipyard, generally with a dau on the
saddle with him. He wore his pure white hair a little longer than was
customary, in a queue tied with a ribbon. His silver breeches buckles
are still a family heirloom. His son recalls that he was fond of expressing
his tory sentiments. It is evident that he himself established the great
shipyard, of which his son John became the head. What connection
Henry Dow had with it is not apparent. He m Mary McMonegal.
There was a dau, as well as a son:

    a Joseph Emery

Joseph E Dow bbbfaea m Annie E Morrell, who in 1923 survives
him; they came to N Y City. Oldest child:

    a Mary Emery b N Y 1869; m Elihu B Frost of N Y; div 1909; 2nd Hamilton
        Cary of N Y; 3rd Baron Emil de Cartier de Marchienne, Belgian Ambass-
        ador to U S; in 1923 one of the social leaders of Washington. No children.

Judith Dow bbbfb. Hist Hampstead errs calling her dau of bcf.
She went to Kingston with her father, who was an original incorporator
of Hampstead; m Kingston June 11, 1747, John Bond b Haverhill Jan
14, 1718-9, son of John and Martha (Mary?) Hale (Hall?). A physician,

he was an original incorporator of Hampstead, practiced there all his
life. Children:

    a John b May 9, 1753; m Mary Moulton; 7 children
    b Gilbert b June 19, 1756   c Nanny b Sept 17, 1758
    d Joseph b Nov 23, 1761   e Ammie Rhumah b Feb 26, 1764
    f Jonathan b Aug 6, 1776; m Abigail Rogers; 2 children

Susanna Dow bbbfd m Jan 28, 1751, John George of Salisbury;
renewed the covenant Amesbury 1753; bought land in Goffstown 1774;
moved there after 1778. Eleven children. His will dated Oct 26, 1798,
mentions Susanna and children,—Thomas, Austin, Ellis, Anna, John,
Alice, Henry. Amesbury rec give children not named in will, so presumably d before their father,—James, Mary, Hester, Susanna.

Eunice Dow bbbfc m June 15, 1757, Jonathan Hoyt b June 12,
1734, son of Timothy and Sarah. Children, oldest b Amesbury, others
Haverhill:

    Judith, Eunice, Anna, Benjamin, Sally

Thomas Dow bbbfax. His d rec gives him b 1768, and he was
surely an original settler at Southport. Thomas Dow bcdig is untraced
but was 9 years older. There seems no other place possible for Thomas
of Southport, and the more we cogitate, the more probable it seems that
our identification is correct. He was a man grown when his parents
moved to N B; his interests were at Wiscasset, his wife presumably
preferred it to the plan of pioneering all over again at Oromocto; moreover, he could not foresee the prosperity which Oromocto was to give.
He was a ship calker, about the hardest job in all ship building. His
wife was Nancy Hues d Belfast 1847, ae 87. Rec probably overstates
her age by ten years. The Haverhill family several times intermarried
with Dow appears as Hews, Huse, Hewes, but never Hughes. Presumably one or more of them were of the tory party pioneering at Southport. A great grandson says that the wife of Thomas was Nancy Thaxter.
This is possibly explicable by a 2nd m, for Thomas d Wiscasset Mch 1,
1813, ae 45. A family rec has it Mch 3, 1814, but the Wiscasset rec is
official. A family Bible exists giving all the children. The year that
Thomas d, the whole family moved to Pittson, where perhaps his wife's
people lived.

    a Mary Ann b Dec 1, 1799; d Pittston July 5, 1815
    b Henry b Feb 11, 1801   c Sarah b Dec 13, 1803; d Sept 1, 1811
    d Thomas b Dec 27, 1805; d Chelsea, Mass, Mch 13, 1841
    e Catherine b Apr 20, 1808; of Belfast m May 11, 1830, Gardiner Brooks of
        Bangor
    f Nancy b Dec 13, 1811; d Pittston Nov 18, 1829
    g William C b Pittston Aug 1, 1813; sea capt, d Belfast June 1838 (Family rec),
        better Mch 13, 1842 (official rec). Presumably unm

Henry Dow bbbfaxb, farmer of Pittston, living there 1851, m May 1,
1825, Hannah Jewett b Londonderry, N H, Sept 1797, d Pittston June
6, 1871. Children:

    a Hannah E J b Pittston Feb 15, 1826; d Dec 13, 1841

b Ann Maria b Mch 27, 1828; d in infancy   c Thomas H b Apr 11, 1829
d Ellen Augusta b Mch 18, 1833; m Jan 29, 1885, Nathaniel G McMahon; survived him; no children
e George Walter b Nov 23, 1835; farmer and hay dealer of Pittston, d Mch 17, 1905, unm

Thomas H Dow bbbfaxbc m Dec 24, 1857, Georgianna Rollins b Pittston Aug 5, 1839, d May 1, 1905, ae 65-8-26, dau of William and Cynthia (Richardson). At her death he went to East Pepperell, Mass, to visit his only surviving child, but d almost at once June 21, 1905. Children:

a Floreda M b Pittston Feb 28, 1860; m July 1, 1880, J Merritt McCausland; moved to East Pepperell; only child,—Harold
b Emma G b West Gardiner Jan 4, 1865; unm, living Farmington 1885

Thomas Dow bbbfaxd, sea captain, m Pittston Oct 27, 1833, Sarah P Rollins; she d Nov 5, 1838, ae 29, 5 mos, and he did not survive long. No children. The male line from bbbfax is extinct.

Benjamin Dow bbbff served under Capt Henry Young Brown May 4, 1761, to Jan 8, 1762, his brothers-in-law, David Kimball, Timothy Kimball, and Richard Simonds, in the same company. He bought (consideration named £6) lot 44 in Goffstown, which John Goffe of Derryfield had sold to Samuel Johnson of Hampstead for £33. Samuel Johnson was his father-in-law. Benjamin sold this lot Jan 9, 1767, to Timothy Kimball for £33, and it later belonged to John George, another brother-in-law. He bought a new home Oct 15, 1789, from Thomas Senter of Bedford, lot 123 near Piscataquog bridge. He sold part of this, with half the mills and water power for $1,000 to Thomas Parker and Joseph Buswell. Benjamin was apt at a land trade. He then bought land in Deering, which became the homestead. He intended to live there, but d Sept 5, 1798, poisoned by eating fish in Hillsboro. Nov 2, 1771, a remonstrance against setting off a separate parish was widely signed, including Hennary Dow bbbfh, Benjamin bbbff, Joseph bbbf, John George bbbfd, Joseph Dow Jr bbbfa, Job Dow bcfi. Seven other signatures duplicated these names with varied spelling, the document clearly being padded. Benjamin m Haverhill Oct 31, 1765, Hannah Johnson b Hampstead Dec 4, 1746, dau of Samuel, blacksmith. Census 1790 shows them of Bedford 3a, 2b, 5c:

a Joseph b Haverhill Aug 19, 1766   b Benjamin (rec not found)
c Samuel b Bedford May 19, 1778
d Amos (rec not found, order of children inaccurate, but left as per family rec)
e Hannah b Goffstown Nov 9, 1774; m Aug 8, 1793, Samuel Cogin of Bedford
f Susanna m Goffstown Mch 16, 1790, Eleazer Ordway. Mrs Alton L Smith is a descendant
g Margery   h Polly (or Mary); b rec of last three not found

Joseph Dow bbbffa m Mary Wells b Mch 4, 1768, d Nov 25, 1851, dau of Eleazer and Sarah. Joseph d Deering Dec 3, 1839; lived Deering, presumably having inherited the homestead. Children:

a Benjamin d Feb 3, 1816, ae 19   b Joseph d Mch 4, 1815, ae 16
c Roxanna d Oct 7, 1816, ae 15

d David b Nov 5, 1802; d Feb 15, 1872; d rec does not mention any wife
e Sarah b about 1804   f Freeman b Apr 14, 1807
g Lyman b 1809   h Daniel d Jan 28, 1816, ae 4
i Hiram d Dec 29, 1836, ae 23. Order of children clearly inaccurate

David Dow bbbffad, in 1850 laborer of Manchester, with $1,000 realty, m Lucretia —— b N H 1806. Children, by census:

a Martha b 1830   b Alfred b 1832
c Sarah b 1834   d Lucretia b 1845

Alfred Dow bbbffadb, in the railroad business, m Manchester Apr 22, 1853, Lydia Ann Brown (Eliza in rec of dau). Children:

a Mary Lucretia b Burlington, Vt, Sept 4, 1863; m Aug 23, 1889, Orin Henry
   Carpenter, lawyer of Malden, Mass
   Possibly the wife of O H Carpenter is bcbebbcd. It is a remarkable coincidence
   that two Alfred Dows should have wives Eliza and each a son George A.
   Age does not fit and they cannot be identical
b George Alfred b Bellows Falls, Vt, 1874; express messenger of Bellows Falls,
   m Jan 25, 1899, Catherine E Paxton, ae 25, b Alstead, N H, dau of Melville
   and Lizzie (Morrison)

Freeman Dow bbbffaf, farmer of Deering, assessed $3,000 in 1850, m June 20, 1829, Mary Alcock b Hillsborough 1813, d Deering Jan 15, 1890, dau of James and Mary (Stevens). Children:

a Scott F b Nov 23, 1844   b John Wells b 1849
c Mary b May 12, 1848

Scott F Dow bbbffafa, farmer of Deering, d Apr 24, 1900; m Nov 21, 1871, Stella V Brown, ae 17, dau of Stephen A and Hannah of Hillsborough. One dau found:

a Cora Belle b Deering Dec 11, 1883

Cora Belle Dow bbbffafaa of Deering m Arlington, Mass, Jan 23, 1907, Joseph Merrill Mann, ae 37, of Clarence, Mo, son of Jacob E and Carrie (Walde).

John W Dow bbbffafb, farmer of Deering, m Mch 2, 1901, Bessie Parnell, ae 35, div, b Nova Scotia, dau of Capt David and Catherine (Fault). In letter he made no mention of children.

Lyman Dow bbbffag, farmer of Antrim, d Aug 1, 1887; m Feb 11, 1836, Eliza Woods of Antrim d July 16, 1843; 2nd, Mch 12, 1844, Esther A Hadley of Deering. Children:

a Mary Jeannette b Feb 8, 1837; m Nov 4, 1860, George Eaton of Woonsockett,
   R I
b Sylvanus b Apr 7, 1844; unm in 1880 c Charles Lyman b Apr 21, 1846
d Esther A b Mch 21, 1849; m Nov 2, 1868, Arthur A Miller, both of Hillsborough

Charles L Dow bbbffagc, butcher, moved to Rhode Island; m Dec 30, 1875, Lizzie Merwin Sawyer b Mch 24, 1855, dau of Jacob and Mary; she m 2nd, George A Woodward. Child:

a Grace May b Nov 18, 1876

Benjamin Dow bbbffb was a giant, well remembered in Goffstown tradition; about 7 feet tall, weighing about 300, a mighty wrestler and by far the strongest man in the countryside. Hearsay from the Goffstown Dow was that he d about ae 30. This is error. He m Sept 10, 1795, Sarah Richardson of Goffstown and was living ten years later in Hooksett. Perhaps more children, but only one found:

    a Benjamin b Hooksett Apr 14, 1805

Benjamin Dow bbbffba d Hooksett of old age; was a blacksmith; lived in many places, including Norwich, Vt, Hanover, Manchester, Hooksett; m June 15, 1828, Sarah D Woodworth b P Q, both of Hooksett. Two children found:

    a Myron Edward b Hanover Mch 12, 1830 (Apr 14, 1829, family rec)
    b Olive Sarah b Manchester 1835; m Sept 15, 1855, Oren Dunning Carpenter of Reheboth, Mass, and Manchester
       An Abby C Dow m Oct 8, 1855, Hiram B McMurphy, both of Hooksett, does not belong here

Myron E Dow bbbffbaa, jack of many trades, good husband, good father, honest man, was in his way a genius; traveled many years as a peddler with span and wagon. He m Mch 16, 1849, Sophronia G Maxfield of Manchester b Exeter, Me, Mch 31, 1829, d Manchester July 13, 1866; 2nd, Feb 4, 1883, Ella Francena Johnson b Ossipee Aug 6, 1855, dau of Solomon and Lydia Ann (Gowen) Young. Five children by 1st wife.

About 1889 the couple received from Edgar R Dow his regular inquiry for aid to a Dow genealogy, with the usual blank forms for data. After they answered it succinctly, it occurred to them that a published genealogy of the Dow family would be a fine advertisement, as it might contain an extensive biography and notice of the business. So, each wrote at frequent intervals biographical notices, modified at each writing and extended. In the Edgar R Dow papers received by the Author in 1923 his photo was found, an unfixed proof. His wife forwarded his autograph, which she was sure would be needed; it was torn from the bottom of an old letter. She was autobiographic. She had married at 15 and had 3 children. After five years she got rid of a very undesirable husband and continued as a mill worker to support them. In fairness, it should be said that she did so and Myron Dow was always a good and high-minded step-father. She met her second husband when he was in her home town selling wares from the back of his team, playing the cornet to attract the crowd, wagon gaily painted, horses with much trapping. She proved a good wife and valuable helper.

He, in youth, had been apprenticed and learned plastering and masonry. He broke loose as soon as he could. In Manchester he put in all his time, when not out peddling, at building houses, being his own plumber, mason, carpenter, in fact, doing every bit of the work with his own hands. But, the peddler's wagon was the joy of his life. As a lecturer, he was sure he excelled; he spoke on astronomy or any other subject that came into his head. He was much better received, he said, than was Bob Ingersoll. Mrs Dow wrote graphically about their travels together; how the lecture lasted about 20 minutes and the selling began with 2-foot folding rules at 10 cents each. Then followed razors, patent medicines, anything, everything, until after 3 hours they had taken in $70 gross. We suspect that she herself composed an account which she says was penned by a friend: "I attended one of the evening entertainments given by Dow and Lady. They came into town about 4 o'clock; we heard music and looking out saw a Lady driving a span of blooded horses while a gentleman sitting beside her was not only making music but scattering bills while the Lady called our attention to the fact that the Open Air Lecture was for one evening only at 7:30. At 7:30 we all went out into the Square where the cart stood 3 large lights were lighted which for brilliancy excelled anything I ever saw the carriage was very fancifully painted and coverd with masonic and other emblems on a platform which let down from the back end of the cart stood the Lady and after Mr Dow had delivered a spirited lecture of about 10 minutes length he performed several jugglers' tricks very cleverly and exposed spiritualism to the great amusement of the crowd which grew larger and drew nearer untill every man woman and child in the place that could walk was there Mrs Dow then Address the people and Recitated several selections and the crowd grew more and more interested and exsited at her as she gave them with a perfect Dutch dialect the comical selection, Sockery setting a hen.

Human nature could keep quiet no longer and shout after shout rent the air. Three cheers were given for Dow & Lady and the business commenced—"

Mr Dow dwelled long with pride on the favorite nickname applied to him,—the Edison of the Peddlers.

Children, all by 1st wife:

a   George B N b June 15, 1850. Of him his father wrote: born in the middle of
      the century, middle of the year, middle of the month, middle of the day
b   Grace Hannah b Aug 24, 1852   c   Rose Lenna b 1859; d young
d   Fred Myron b Jan 12, 1864   e   Sophronia Bell b July 3, 1866

George B N Dow bbbffbaaa m Mch 31, 1868, Hattie Brown. Directory 1915 gave him of Manchester, inventor, justice of the peace; has 1 child.

Grace H Dow bbbffbaab m Feb 8, 1872, George H Lincoln b Hillsboro Mch 24, 1850, photographer of Hillsboro. Three children, of whom:

a   Lewis Perkins b Sept 29, 1876   b   Grace Sarah b Sept 16, 1879

Fred M Dow bbbffbaad, photographer and painter of Manchester m (Myron E in rec) Feb 17, 1886, Georgianna A Davis, ae 22, d Nov 3,

1896, dau of John and Sarah (Wheeler); 2nd, Apr 12, 1899, Louisa Adelia
Farnham, ae 19, dau of James E and Louisa Rice Wright (Chase); 3rd,
May 25, 1909, Ella V Wilson, div, ae 42, dau of Thomas and Olivia
(Brown) Flint.   At least 3 children:

   a Laura A b Lawrence, Mass, June 9 (1880 in rec obvious error); d Manchester
       Dec 9, 1907
   b Harold Fred b Chicago (by m rec) 1887
   c Leslie F b Manchester Aug 19, 1888

Harold F Dow bbbffbaadb, painter of Manchester, m Oct 6, 1917,
Caroline Augusta Theodora Larson, ae 24, d Denmark, dau of Capt
Theodor and Severene (Pelck).

Samuel Dow bbbffc settled in Deering; d June 29, 1857; m June
3, 1802, Mary McAllister b New Boston Dec 30, 1779, d Deering Aug 15,
1855.   Children:

   a Mary b Oct 1, 1804; d Goffstown Nov 13, 1806
   b Samuel b Aug 30, 1806   c Archibald b July 4, 1808
   d Benjamin b Sept 8, 1810   e Henry Johnson b Nov 15, 1813
   f Mary b Sept 20, 1816; d Henniker Aug 31, 1882
   g Eliza b Oct 31, 1818; d Manchester Feb 6, 1879
   h Robert Clark b Goffstown May 18, 1821

Samuel Dow bbbffcb, farmer and militia captain; assessed in
1850 $1,200; d Goffstown Dec 12, 1880; m Feb 2, 1830, Lydia Black b
Nov 30, 1806, d Sept 5, 1889, dau of James and Ruth (Wyman) of
Goffstown.   Wife and children, all b, m and d Goffstown:

   a Samuel J b Dec 5, 1830 b James b Feb 19, 1833; d Aug 26, 1853
   c Harriet b Nov 10, d Dec 16, 1834
   d Joseph b Dec 16, 1837; d Oct 8, 1845
   e Mary Jane b June 11, 1840; d Oct 8, 1845
   f Harriet Helen b July 6, 1844; d Aug 16, 1845
   g Lydia Ellen b June 23, 1847; m Jan 1, 1867, John C Hardy; lived Hooksett;
       a son Scott E m Hooksett 1893

Samuel J Dow bbbffcba d Dec 24, 1893; m Feb 28, 1857, Cyrene
Dunlap b Goffstown Apr 1, 1832, d Aug 7, 1898, dau of James and
Hannah (Coggin) of Bedford.   Children:

   a Joseph A b Sept 1, 1857; d Manchester Apr 21, 1912, unm; an interesting man,
       a constant general reader.   One of his activities was in assembling the
       genealogical data of his line
   b Hattie J b Sept 25, 1859; d Nov 6, 1910; m Feb 22, 1899, John Vining b Cam-
       bridge 1853; d Manchester Feb 9, 1900. A son George A was 1917 in
       Manchester high school
   c James E b Feb 1, 1862   d Charles B b Sept 24, 1864
   e Harry E b Mch 26, 1867   f Augusta M b Jan 1, 1870
   g Alice L b Dec 12, 1870   h Samuel B b Apr 21, 1873
   i George H b Oct 5, 1875; d Jan 19, 1896, accidental gunshot
   j Archibald W b Sept 30, 1877

James E Dow bbbffcbac of Goffstown m Oct 3, 1888, Lottie Page
b Goffstown Jan 24, 1862, dau of Isaac J and Jane R (Curtis from Thetford, Vt).   Children:

   a Elmer C b Oct 2, 1891; shipping clerk of Manchester, overseas 1918
   b Harlon F b Oct 22, 1896

Harlon F Dow bbbffcbacb m Manchester Dec 8, 1915, Cordelia E Sansoucie, ae 18, b Manchester, dau of Camille and Mary (Bonner). Child:

a   Alma Frances b Goffstown July 20, 1916

Charles B Dow bbbffcbad m Dec 19, 1900, Mary Foster of Manchester, dau of Thomas and Jane Ann (Pierce) of Devonshire, Eng; for over 27 years night watchman for Amoskeag Mfg Co.   Children:

a   Grace A b Oct 8, 1902; d Oct 11, 1915   b   Ethel E b and d Feb 5, 1907

Harry E Dow bbbffcbae appears in recent directory as farmer of Manchester, N H.   Some Harry E Dow m Lottie L and had:

a   Marjorie M Hewitt b Salisbury, Mass, Aug 3, 1901

Augusta M Dow bbbffcbaf m June 10, 1896, Charles H Fellows; lives East Deering.   Children:

a   Alice M b June 9, 1897   b   Flora C b Jan 22, 1899

Alice L Dow bbbffcbag m Goffstown Oct 16, 1895, Charles L Dodge, son of Ezra F and Mary (George of Goshen); live Riverdale, N H. Children:

a   George H b Goffstown July 5, 1896   b   Mary A b Jan 25, 1899
c   Arline G b Feb 25, 1900   d   Gertrude V b Jan 6, 1905

Samuel Bertram Dow bbbffcbah m Manchester Nov 23, 1904, Margaret Theresa Starr b San Joachim, Shefford, P Q, Aug 4, 1871, dau of Thomas and Gertrude (Kilroy); live Goffstown.   No children.

Archibald W Dow bbbffcbaj m Goffstown Feb 19, 1912, Annie W Starr.   Children:

a   Gertrude Margaret b Jan 24, 1913   b   Pauline M b Mch 24, 1915

Archibald Dow bbbffcc d Hillsborough June 16, 1885; m Newbury, Vt, Feb 4, 1833, Mary ——.   Perhaps more than 1 child:

a   —— b Manchester May 21; d June 29, 1851

Benjamin Dow bbbffcd appears in 1850 census farmer of Goffstown; wife Tabitha b N H 1819.   Family rec gives wife Tomson Willey b Sheffield, Vt, d June 19, 1890, dau of William.   This must be 2nd wife, m 1850-55.   Census gives here Eliza Dow b 1849, perhaps a niece. Children, older by census:

a   Tabitha b 1841   b   Frances A b 1847   c   Mary J b 1849
d   Albert J b 1855   e   Fanny Merrill, living Manchester 1917
f   William H b Goffstown Oct 13, 1860

Mary J Dow bbbffcdc.   Rec somewhat garbled: Jennie A Dow, dau of Benj, of Goffstown m June 24, 1869, J Carl Cheney of Manchester. A dau:

a   Edna M (dau of Fanny A and John K Cheney) m Manchester 1900 Benjamin Price

Albert J Dow bbbffcdd m Apr 27, 1879, Lena Merrill, ae 17; lived Manchester and Goffstown; not in recent directories; untraced.

William H Dow bbbffcdf, by recent directory wood worker of Goffstown, m Nov 27, 1884, Isabella T Brown, ae 22, dau of Robinson. Children:

a ——, son b Oct 16, 1885   b —— son b Warner Dec 13, 1890
c Ralph Harold b Nov 16, 1893   d Esther Belle b Jan 11, 1899

Henry J Dow bbbffce d Manchester Dec 26, 187–; m Feb 5, 1839, Pauline Taylor b Chatham, Mass, Jan 1, 1813, d Manchester Jan 12, 1889, dau of Barnabas and Susan (Atkins).   Children (perhaps others):

a Amos W b Goffstown May 16, 1841; machinist, d Manchester Feb·17, 1920, 60 years resident, unm. At same address 1915 were Frank P and Nellie M Dow, apparently not close relatives
b Georgianna F d Manchester Apr 25, 1849, ae 2, 4 mos

Mary Dow bbbffcf m Feb 4, 1839, John Sawyer Elliott b Boscawen Aug 14, 1804, d 1888, whose war service lasted 3 years, 1 mo, the oldest veteran in the State and 3rd oldest in the country.   Children:

a George W b Goffstown Sept 1, 1842; enlisted with father; d of wounds
b Mary Maria b Bedford Apr 2, 1844; m —— Davis; .2nd 1894 E Elmer Buchanan
c Eliza Jane b Manchester Sept 17, 1846; d Henniker Mch 21, 1863

Robert C Dow bbbffch, carpenter and machinist, assessed 1850 on $400 realty; organized and was capt of Co H, 3rd N H; resigned June 21, 1862; m Feb 25, 1847, Emeline Poor b Goffstown, d Manchester Dec 18, 1881, ae 57-1-24.   Children:

a Elizabeth Emeline b Feb 6, 1848
b Frank Johnson b Apr 23, 1850; killed by Indians Kan Sept 15, 1878, unm
c Martha Ida b Mch 4, 1852; unm in 1876   d Mary Ella b Dec 22, 1853
e Hattie Eva b May 24, d Oct 17, 1857
f Harry Robert b Derry Depot Feb 5, 1863; livery stable keeper, d Manchester July 9, 1901, unm

Elizabeth E Dow bbbffcha m June 10, 1869, John Pearson, son of Joseph and Evalena (Maban) (Scollay).   Children:

a Hattie Ella b Goffstown Aug 5, 1871
b Arthur Lincoln b Aug 11, 1875   c Lizzie Evalina b May 1, 1877

Amos Dow bbbffd m Durham, N H, Nov 29, 1809, Hannah Wheeler b Aug 2, 1788, dau of Benjamin and Joanna; moved to Bangor, Me; pioneers of Hampden, charter members 1817 of 1st Cong church; d Hampden Aug 7, 1872, ae 90. She d Aug 8, 1870, ae 80. Two children known:

a Sophronia b Hampden Aug 14, 1811
b Amos b about 1816   c (a guess) Joseph

Sophronia Dow bbbffda m Oldtown May 23, 1836, James Greeley b Garland Dec 30, 1813, son of Philip.   Children:

a Henry C b June 4, 1837   b Mary G b June 18, 1839; m Martin R Weeks

c David b Nov 4, 1841   d Sophronia G b Oct 23, 1844; d Mch 27, 1834
e Lucy W b July 19, 1847; d Apr 10, 1871
f Amos Dow b Sept 16, 1849; m Sarepta Sias   g   Charles F b July 7, 1855

Amos Dow bbbffdb, farmer, teacher, deputy sheriff 1856, d R I about 1892; m (int pub Feb 26, 1842) Roxanna Runnels b Garland Jan 3, 1818, d July 3, 1844; 2nd, Mary Holmes b Mch 25, 1824, d Sept 4, 1849, dau of Joseph and Sarah (Kenney); 3rd, 1872 Mary Dwelley of Dover d Oct 1904.   Children:

a Anna R b Feb 3, 1843   b   Mary b Aug 1849; d unm
c (by 3rd wife) ——, son, untraced; presumably went to R I

Anna R Dow bbbffdba d Winslow Aug 26, 1879; m Aug 31, 1865, Burnham W Hinds, son of Benjamin and Johanna Crosby (Wheeler). Children:

a Ulmer B b June 20, 1866; lived Iowa; m Jennie M Meyers
b William Amos b Dec 7, 1867; d accident July 1883

Joseph Dow bbbffdc, physician of Providence, R I, m Eliza F Turner b Hampden 1819. No children. Coincidence of places suggests guessing this identity.

Mary Dow bbbffh m Feb 9, 1815, Joseph George, apparently a 1st cousin, both of Goffstown.

Anna Dow bbbfg m Richard Simonds; 2nd, Mch 10, 1767, Timothy Kimball of Bradford, Haverhill and Goffstown, b Aug 16, 1741, son of Abraham and Hannah (Hazeltine). Timothy served 1760 and in Revolution. Children:

a Richard (Simonds)   b   Timothy d Goffstown, unm
c Richard b Dec 10, 1769; d Oct 26, 1827
d Hannah   e   Mary; neither in Kimball Gen
f Judith m —— Pherson of Goffstown   g   Sally d young

Henry Dow bbbfh d Wiscasset, Me, 1811. Our genealogists discovered at the outset that he m Haverhill June 5, 1771, Mary Emery, sister of Judith bbbfa, and that he became a pioneer of Wiscasset. Further search found him in Goffstown, N H, June 18, 1773, buying land from William McDoel. From that date nothing more was found until he turns up in 1790 census, of Topsham. Henry Dow served 14 days in 1776, Capt Thomas Coggswell, Col Loammi Baldwin, but this is just as likely to be the untraced bbbebd as it is our Henry.

The mass of correspondence of Edgar R Dow which he was unable to classify reached the Author in 1923.   In this was a letter from a descendant which proved identities, named all the children and gave other particulars. Henry's situation was much like that of his older brother; he was a tory. This does not disprove that he enlisted in the Federal army. Enoch Dow bcdgd served twice, yet became a pronounced tory. He may have changed his ideas or his enlistment may have been a matter

of policy. Howbeit, the reason that he took his family to the lonely
island of Southport, beyond Wiscasset, was to escape the persecution
meted out to those who disapproved of the Revolution. Mary Emery
d in Wiscasset. All children but the oldest were b Southport. It is
family tradition that the oldest was born Haverhill, but we doubt it.
Haverhill rec are as complete as any in New England. The census 1790
shows five young sons and three females. As there were three dau, the
mother was either dead by 1790 or one dau b later. Latter is presumably
the case. Extant stones in Wiscasset cemetery mark one son and three
of the grandchildren. It is an odd survival of a trivial circumstance
that in 1795 a letter to Henry Dow, Wiscasset, was advertised "not
found." Family rec give no dates for the children:

a Joseph. D rec says b Aug 20, 1785. One would expect the 1st born about
   1772
b Thomas; lived Wiscasset; m Mrs Nancy Webster
c Henry, probably 2nd born   d Robert m Sally Orne of Southport
e Moses drowned off Squam Isl, ae 45, unm
f John; lived to old age in Wiscasset; never m
g Catherine m Samuel Dunton of Westport
h Mary m Stephen Webster of Southport
i Edna m Eben Lundy of Southport

Another descendant wrote to Edgar R Dow that there were 9 sons,
another said 5 sons, 2 dau, both clearly in error.

Joseph Dow bbbfha, named for his uncle, is found in Wiscasset
cemetery; d Feb 2, 1831; m Charlotte Smith b Sept 28, 1791, d Jan 19,
1852. Three children found by gravestone rec; family rec gives all:

a Abigail b Apr 24, 1809; d Nov 2, 1828   b Mary E
c William P
d Betsey S. Gravestone says Elizabeth b Feb 16, 1815; d Mch 21, 1816
e George S   f Joseph   g Susan S   h John S
i Ann Maria
j Abby b Dec 20, 1829; d Apr 13, 1833

William P Dow bbbfhac lived San Francisco; in 1885 visited sister
in Vallejo, Calif. George S, Joseph, John S not living 1885; none traced
further.

Susan S Dow bbbfhag m —— Wright; living 1885 Woburn, Mass;
no children.

Ann Maria Dow bbbfhai m —— Housley; in 1885 long standing
resident of Vallejo, Calif.

Thomas Dow bbbfhb and **Henry Dow** bbbfhc remain undis-
covered, but one or the other had at least 3 sons:

a Robert b Me 1814   x Henry   y William

Robert Dow bbbfhba, found in Wiscasset 1850 census, farmer,

realty $200; wife Susan b Me 1821, either 2nd wife or m at 15.   Children,
by census:

  a   Mary b 1837   b   Hannah b 1842   c   Robert b 1844
  d   Martha b 1846
  e   Henry b 1848; unt.   Some one of this line moved to N B, lost sight of

Robert Dow bbbfhbac, farmer of Wiscasset, m Abigail Chaney b
Alna.   Children found only by own rec, hence perhaps others:

  a   Austin L b 1871   b   Saul H b 1878, both Wiscasset

Austin L Dow bbbfhbaca, mill man of Wiscasset, m Nov 27, 1907,
Olive Low b Lincoln, ae 39, dau of Daniel D and Vesta A (Doble).
Presumably no children.

Saul H Dow bbbfhbacb, railroader of Wiscasset, m June 13, 1903,
Gertrude B Jones, ae 21, dau of George E and Martha (Geddis).   Only
child:

  a   Henry Bickford b Wiscasset May 17, 1905.   This youngster took first prize
      at a baby show

Henry Dow bbbfhbx b Wiscasset had several brothers who continued
to live there.   One was Robert who had a son who went early to Calif.
Another was William, unt.   Henry became pioneer of Lee, Me.   Census
1850 shows him laborer, realty $100; wife Sarah Potter b Me 1809.
Census gives 4 children:

  a   Catherine b 1839   b   Sarah b 1841   c   Walter L b 1843
  d   Henry E b 1849; unt

Walter L Dow bbbfhbxc b Lee, laborer of Millinockett, m Zelma
White.   Four older children b Lee, others Forest City, only c, f and g
living 1923:

  a   Lettie   b   Nellie   c   Susan   d   Henry E b 1874
  e   Walter   f   Mary   g   Robert Earl b 1879   h   Minnie
  i   Abbie

Henry E Dow bbbfhbxcd, paper mill worker of Millinockett, d
acute alcoholism July 25, 1920; m Dec 24, 1903, Ella Gertrude Martin,
ae 16, dau of George and Rose (Inman).   Only child:

  a   Mabel b Apr 22, 1906

Robert E Dow bbbfhbxcg, mechanic of Millinockett, m Aug 16,
1903, Addie E Swazey, ae 18, dau of John F and Ella L (Reed).   Children:

  a   Gladys J b Sept 27, 1904   b   Earl B b Dec 5, 1906
  c   Ella M b June 2, 1909   d   Robert H b Mch 30, 1913
  e   Lewis H b Aug 7, 1919   f   Ralph b Aug 8, 1920; d young
  g   Ethel A b Feb 2, 1921

Catherine Dow bbbfhbxa m Henry Houghton; 3 sons, 4 dau; a
dau now of Forest City.

Sarah Dow bbbfhbxb m Stark Webster; only son drowned in young
manhood.

Henry Dow bbbfhc said by grandson b Wiscasset 1774, d Wiscasset Aug 20, 1825; surely correct. No rec of Abigail Cromwell, 1st wife. Hannah Jackson, 2nd wife b Wiscasset Aug 20, 1789, d Wiscasset Mch 11, 1885. Like his father, he was shipwright and calker. Four sons, 3 dau, of whom:

a ——— only child by 1st wife; probably d unm
d (a safe guess) John b Me 1809
f Walter Scott b Wiscasset Mch 1, 1820. Family Bible has curious error giving him b Feb 29, 1815
g Loring b Wiscasset Mch 22, 1823; dates suggest these two youngest

John Dow bbbfhcd was town clerk of Pittston 1851. Census gives him ship carpenter; realty $300; wife Mary b Me 1819. Census also gives a Henry Dow of Pittston, probably a missing brother. The only other unaccounted for Dow of Pittston 1850 is John R Dow, probably a cousin. One child by census:

a Susan b 1833

Walter S Dow bbbfhcf, farmer of Wiscasset, d Alna Dec 28, 1906, ae 86-9-28; m Frances McCormick b Eng, d Alna Dec 27, 1916, 75 years resident, dau of Patrick and Mary (Lewis). Children:

a George Sewall b 1851
b Clara M b 1852; m Roy R Marston, druggist of Wiscasset; left 1 son, Lawrence
c Walter Scott b 1854
d Ida M b 1856; d unm   e Leonard P b 1858   f Edgar S b 1858
g Ellsworth E   h Frank Adelbert b 1866
i ——— dau b 1868; m Angus George of Wiscasset; a dau Mrs Linwood Fossett of Wiscasset has Madeline and Francis
j J D Webster b 1871   k Theodore B b 1873   l Thomas A b 1874

George S Dow bbbfhcfa apparently m twice, for George S Dow ae 21, quarryman from Alna, Me, of Concord, N H, m Jan 1, 1874, Clara N Nichols, ae 18, b Charlestown, Vt. George S Dow of Pittston m July 7, 1882, Eva F Moody. One child by 1st wife:

a ——— dau b Oct 17, 1874
b Ada F b Jan 31, 1883; m ——— Allen of Gardiner; has Doris and Albert
c Edna E b July 6, 1884; of Pittston
d Ida E b Feb 20, 1886; now Mrs Gilbert of Portland

Walter S Dow bbbfhcfc, engineer of Kennebunkport, m Jennie M Hinckley b Eustis, d Augusta May 8, 1901, ae 38, 10 mos, dau of Enoch and Lizzie (Fuller); 2nd (giving ae 43) 1904, Florence Leach of Kennebunkport. Two children by 1st wife not found:

a ——— now Mrs Matthew Nicolson of Augusta; has Doris, Lora, Norman
d Linwood J b May 13, 1898
e Florence G b Mch 25, 1906, of Kennebunkport
f Marion M b Aug 10, 1912; of Kennebunkport

Leonard P Dow bbbfhcfe Kennebunkport m Dec 18, 1879, Clara Louise White b 1856, d Feb 2, 1891, dau of David and Sophronia; 2nd, Gertrude M Derry. Children:

a ——— b Dec 24, 1880; now Mrs Harold Alford of Newark, N J
b Hale Macomber b 1889

c —— b Feb 2, 1893; now Mrs Albert Hardman of Lowell, Mass
d —— now Mrs Frank McAllister of Mexico, Me
e Derry Walter Fogg b June 12, 1897   f Frances R b Oct 9, 1900
g Justin L b June 30, 1905   h Gertrude

Hale M Dow bbbfhcfeb, carpenter of Westport, m June 19, 1914, Henrietta Viola Houston teacher ae 24, dau of James H and Barbara J (Dinsmore).

Derry W F Dow bbbfhcfee, expressman and farmer, volunteer stationed at Ft Story, Boston, m Jan 20, 1915, Marion Warren Hutchings, ae 18, dau of Lester A and Barbara J (Warren). Children:

a Ninelle D b Aug 19, 1915   b Lester B b Dec 19, 1916

Edgar S Dow bbbfhcff, engineer of Augusta, drowned Oct 13, 1900; m Mary A Hamilton of Augusta. M rec of son gives mother as Mary Rockwood. Children:

a Walter S d Readfield Apr 25, 1905, ae 18, 3 mos
b Edgar, now of Augusta   c Fanny, now of Boston
d Genevieve, now of Boston   e Ella G b Augusta June 14, 1895

Edgar Leslie Dow bbbfhcffb, electrician of Augusta, m (both parents dec) Nov 22, 1916, Ina May Dow bbbfhcfgb, shoe shop worker.

Ellsworth E Dow bbbfhcfg of Vassalboro and Augusta, m Mary L Lowell of Vassalboro b Augusta. Vassalboro directory 1915 creates a little confusion by placing her name next that of William H Dow, station agent of E Vassalboro, then giving Elmer E and Elmer E Jr, but no Ellsworth. Children, earlier by directory:

a Elmer E b 1892   b Ina May   c Helen G b Oct 12, 1895
d Maud H   e Robert Emery b Oct 4, 1899   f Herbert Martin, twin
g Roy M   h Virginia Madeline b Aug 24, 1913

Elmer E Dow bbbfhcfga, railroad employe, later merchant, m Vassalboro Apr 6, 1918, Mary Lavina Colbath, postmistress ae 31, dau of Emery J and Hannah C (Pease). Children:

a Dorothy Alice b Dec 27, 1918   b Elmer E b Jan 26, 1920

Frank A Dow bbbfhcfh, farmer of Readfield, later liveryman of Kent's Hill, m Belle C Pullen b Palermo, 1863. Children:

a Blanche M, postmistress by recent directory
b Maynard Weston b May 19, 1893   c Carl B b Jan 25, 1897
d Harden (or Harlan) K b Oct 10, 1898

Maynard W Dow bbbfhcfhb m 1921 Caroline R Houston ahbabajcca, dau of Harry and Glencora (Lambert). They live Brunswick. Children:

a C Houston   b Gleneora Elizabeth

Webster Dow bbbfhcfj farmer of Alna, m June 29, 1896, Winnifred Hutchinson, dressmaker of Readfield, ae 23, dau of Willard and Calista (Herbert); moved back to Wiscasset.

Theodore B Dow bbbfhcfk hotel employe d Somerville, Mass, Nov 23, 1910, ae 33-4-23; m Maggie Rines.   Children, older b Wiscasset:

a Thelma b Aug 8, 1898   b Hilda A b Mch 20 1900
c Theodore B b Boston Jan 16, 1905
d Walter Scott b Somerville Oct 20, 1907

Thomas A Dow bbbfhcfl, cook of Wiscasset, m Ella Rines b Hancock ae 23, dau of Edward and Rachel (Rines).   Children:

a Roderick Thomas b June 19, 1900   b Vinton b Dec 22, 1902

Loring Dow bbbfhcg, farmer and trader, moved after 1857 to Newcastle; d Nov 20, 1906; m Mch 3, 1850, Ann Eliza Munsey b Wiscasset Oct 24, 1827, d Newcastle Jan 15, 1910, dau of David and Martha (Blagden). D rec of son gives mother as Elizabeth Poole, seemingly entire error.   Three sons:

a William b Wiscasset July 8, 1850; farmer and clerk, d lunacy Sept 11, 1909, unm
b Joseph b Sept 16, 1852
c Loring b Apr 15, 1857; of San Francisco unm in 1885

Joseph Dow bbbfhcgb, farmer of Newcastle, m Eudora R Potter b Newcastle (in rec of 7th child called Dora Patten).   Of 8 children:

f Loring J b 1891   g —— son b Nov 11, 1892
h Chester V b June 9, 1898

Loring J Dow bbbfhcgbf, lumber scaler and ship fitter, m Whitefield Sept 26, 1915, Velma F Bowman, nurse ae 18, dau of Ensign Dow and Bertha (Sprague).   Children:

a —— son b Whitefield Aug 8, 1916   b Gwendolyn b Bath Apr 23, 1920

As every disconnected Dow of Wiscasset is surely of bbbfh line, all are placed here for handy reference.

George R Dow bbbfhja of Bath, living 1915, m Adelia D Mason (or Nason) d Bath July 8, 1907, dau of John, farmer of Wiscasset.

John Huntoon Dow bbbfhjb, farmer of Wiscasset, m Rosilla Rines. Children:

a Susan Rena b Apr 16, 1883   c Earl b 1888
e —— dau b Oct 6, 1892   f Guy Trafton b 1893
i Lottie O b Sept 28, 1894   k Roy La Vaughn b June 29, 1899

Susan R Dow bbbfhjba m June 16, 1904, Elwell William Stimpson b Wiscasset Feb 26, 1875, son of William Elwell Parks and Etta Rachel (Wall).   Child:

a Edith Chaney b Nov 24, 1905

Earl Dow bbbfhjbc, clerk of Wiscasset, m June 28, 1911, Alice C Greenough ae 19 milliner, dau of Frank G and Mary C (Davis).

Guy T Dow bbbfhcjbf, farmer of Wiscasset, m Feb 26, 1913, Hazel Henwood Blagden ae 23, dau of Benjamin F and Hope E (McKenzie). Child:

a —— dau b Wiscasset Sept 21, 1916

Roy La V Dow bbbfhjbk, farmer of Wiscasset, m June 2, 1920, Olive Scott Weston Reed ae 18 b So Framingham, Mass, dau of William Edsel and Ethel C (Rogers).

Ann E Dow bbbfhjc appears in 1850 census, ae 22, presumably wid with child:

a William b 1850; unt

William S Dow bbbfhjd, sawyer, and **Samuel S Dow,** mail carrier, in recent Wiscasset directory.

George Dow bbbfhje, captain piloted a party of 25 in a brig to Calif 1849. It is said all hands returned safely to Pittston in a few years.

Millie W (possibly Nellie) **Dow** bbbfhjf int pub Pittston June 18, 1899 to Joel T Maine.

Rose M Dow bbbfhjg m Pittston Dec 18, 1880, John W Hunt.

Joseph L Dow bbbfhjh m Nancy ——. He may be the missing bbbfhaf. Child:

a Ruth A b Pittston May 21, 1865

Mary Dow bbbfi. Wiscasset rec gives Elizabeth Dow m Mch 18, 1783, John Graves. This was disconcerting, as no Elizabeth is known. Newcastle, N H, gives rec, of which Wiscasset is garbled copy: Mary Dow m Mch 13, 1783, John Grevis, both of Newcastle.

Abigail Dow bbbfj m Haverhill Apr 20, 1768, David Kimball, brother of Timothy, himself a veteran. Abigail d, by gravestone rec May 4, 1811, ae 57; by church rec May 10, 1812, ae 56. David d Haverhill Nov 25, 1817. Children:

a Abigail m Moses Gage; 2nd Amos Hazeltine   b   Henry bap Dec 5, 1773
c Sarah bap Dec 5, 1773   d   David bap Dec 17, 1776
e Joseph bap May 10, 1778; d Sept 1, 1816
f Nabby bap Oct 1, 1779   g   Mary bap June 14, 1782
h Moses b 1783   i John   j Benjamin

Jerusha Dow bbbg m Samuel Stevens Jr. At least 2 children:

a Jerusha b Haverhill Feb 13, 1739; m —— Dorien; moved to Pembroke
b Henry bap Amesbury Sept 13, 1741

STEPHEN DOW bc, admitted freeman 1668, lived and died in Haverhill. His parents being very poor, he was apprenticed at age of 9. When he was 15, in 1657, an interesting lawsuit throws more light than all other records on the status of this family. He was bound out to Thomas Davis and wife, who agreed to teach him the stone mason's trade, to read and write. The testimony of his mother showed that this was a verbal agreement and that finding a home for Stephen was a great relief to herself and her husband. A neighbor, she testified, had previously promised to take the boy but was dissuaded by his wife, who pointed out that the boy was weak, undersized and sickly, sure to become a burden. Kemp, the defendant to the suit, was charged with taking the boy away from Davis and attempted to justify his action by alleging that the boy was not properly treated. The neighbors were all agreed that the boy was unpromising, was unable to take off or put on his own clothes, and gave little promise of growing to manhood. The boy's own testimony is ingenuous and illuminative. He had run away a number of times but for no definite reason, except possibly once to see his mother, and always intended to come back. He admitted that his master and mistress were good and kind, but he did 'acknowledge that it was a good while before he could eat his master's food viz. Meate and milk or drink beer, saying he did not know it was good, because he was not used to eat such victuall, but to eate bread and water porridge and to drink water.'

While the food of the Haverhill pioneers was simple in the extreme, even bean porridge not to be freely used, an exclusive diet of bread and water was not the usual fare. It is not unlikely that the death of Thomas Dow at 39 was due to this undernourishment, coupled with hard work and other privation. The symptoms of little Stephen, unable to put on his own clothes, indicate conclusively an undernourished, rickety condition, and surely the future Indian fighter owed his life to the victualls, viz: Meate, milk and beer furnished by master and goodwife Davis, who seem to be worthy people. The jury took this view and there was no further complaint of Kemp's intervention or Stephen's runaways. Shortly afterwards Phoebe Dow m John Eaton and moved to Salisbury. Stephen's apprenticeship was to last until he was 18, and it probably did. Nothing more appears about him until he was 22, a healthy, vigorous man, able to do his fighting share. He soon came to own a goodly piece of land, his neighbor to the southeast being Capt John White. Its exact site has not been determined, but it was over the border, into what is now Plaistow. It faced the commons, and when that land was fenced in, he was ordered by the selectmen to erect a gate thereto by the side of his house. From 1690 to 1697 he was a minor officer in the 6th garrison, on what is now Mill St, its captain being John White. This blockhouse still stands.

He was a member of Haverhill first church; selectman 1682, 1685, 1690 and 1697; grand juror 1692. He d July 3, 1717, his will dated 2 days previously. His posterity includes a majority of all the Dow b family, the Dows of Plaistow, Salem, Windham, Atkinson, etc.

Stephen m Sept 13, 1663, Ann St—y d Feb 3, 1715, and must have been b by 1646. Altho the marriage is recorded in Haverhill, it is improbable that it took place there. If she had been a Haverhill resident, her parents would have been known. Next to Thomas Dow himself, no search in the family has been carried on with more assiduity than for Ann, and the results are far from conclusive. Her name appears many times but as Story and Stacy, about equally divided. Genealogical authorities do not give reasons for their choice. Hoyt, Old Families, gives: "Story (or Stacy)." Titcomb seems sure of Story, but that author took almost all her early data at second hand. Others have merely jumped at conclusions. As there *was* an Ann Stacy, most have used her name without searching for proof. A little investigation shows that no possible Ann Stacy is known. Simon Stace, immigrant, came with wife Elizabeth and children,—Thomas, Sarah, Ann and perhaps others. They located in Ipswich. Elizabeth was the survivor and Mch 1670 (probated Mch 29) made a nuncupative will,—"as reced from her own mouth by Simon Stace, Sarah Stace, Ann Stace," in which she left to "my daughter Ann in consideration of her care of me in my old age all my other household stuff." Ann Stacy, therefore, was of Ipswich, living with her mother seven years after Stephen Dow was married and set up his Haverhill home. A Susannah Stacy, probably dau of Simon, m Ipswich 1653 Joseph French (Edward 1) of Salisbury. Thomas Stacy, the first mentioned in the will, m Oct 4, 1663, Susannah, dau of Rev William Worcester of Salisbury. This couple moved to Salem, had 11 children, but none was named Ann.

While there are many Mass towns whose vital statistics have not been published, there is none whose records prior to 1675 have not been exhaustively studied. In none occurs any Ann, Anna, Anne, Annie, whose last name can be distorted into St—y. There are but two logical conclusions,—either she was b in Europe and her name is not found in any list of immigrants, or her b rec is not extant. We know that few early rec of Ipswich exist.

The Author's belief is that she was Ann Story. In the list of passengers of the Rose & Dorothy from Yarmouth 1737, incidentally shipmates of Henry Dow a, there is a Samuel Dix, with wife, two dau, two servants. One of these is William Storey b 1614. As Dix was a joiner, presumably Story was an apprentice in that trade. The Dix family has not been located. No other can well be the William Story, carpenter of Ipswich and Dover. He might have m a Dix; there was plenty of time to find a wife and raise a family in Ipswich, which has no rec until 1648. The children of William Story are not all known, so there might have been an

Ann among them. Dea Seth Story, a son, became quite prominent in Ipswich. William himself moved to Dover 1648, but Dover rec are as defective as Ipswich. He appears there in a deed as William Storer. He m 2nd, when both were too old for children, Sarah Starbuck of Dover. Incidentally it may be noted that Ann's oldest dau m a Dover man.

Stephen Dow m 2nd, in his 70th year, his youngest child being then a man of 41, Feb 7, 1716, Johannah Corliss b Apr 28, 1650, d Oct 29, 1734, dau of George and Johanna (Davis) and wid of Joseph Hutchins. Children:

a Ruhamah (spelled in 7 different ways in as many rec) b Haverhill Jan 24,
   1663-4. Note that some date is error, as Stephen m Sept 13, 1663
b Samuel b Jan 22, 1665-6   c Hannah b July 1, 1668
d Stephen b Sept 10, 1670   e Martha b Apr 1, 1673
f John b July 13, 1675

Ruhamah Dow bca m Jan 16, 1681, Moses Davis of Haverhill b Dec 30, 1657, son of John and Jane (Peasley). They moved about 1686 to Dover, where his father had been a pioneer about 1652. She was living 1717; her husband killed in the massacre of June 10, 1724. Children:

a John b Haverhill Jan 4, 1682; m 1703-6 Abigail Meader
b Moses b Nov 2, 1684; killed with his father June 10, 1724
c Joseph bap Mch 8, 1685-6, "grandson of Stephen Dow sen"; probably d young
d James bap Jan 27, 1722-3; m May 19, 1719, Mary Stevenson; 2nd Oct 4,
   1728, Elizabeth Dun (name blurred, may be Dam, Dame, Deen, Dean).
   He may be the fighting militia captain of 1712
e Jabez living 1726; built and commanded a small garrison house in Durham
f Solomon bap Apr 26, 1722; m Feb 4, 1724, Elizabeth Davis
g Ebenezer bap Nov 26, 1727; b June 10, 1702; presumably the Ebenezer who
   d Durham May 7, 1755
h Abigail bap Nov 26, 1727   i Samuel bap June 29, 1729; grew up and m

Samuel Dow bcb, lifelong resident of east parish, Haverhill, presumably inheriting the homestead, d Dec 30, 1749; served in Lieut Saltonstall's Snow Shoe Men, organized Haverhill 1710; m May 5, 1691, Ruth Johnson, dau of John and Eliza (Maverick), wid of Timothy Ayer. She had 3 children by 1st husband, 2 of whom lived with their step-father. Samuel was a substantial citizen, but does not appear in public life. Children:

a Ruth b Apr 21, 1692
b Abigail b Mch 1, 1694-5. Both were among the 11 petitioners for a woman's
   pew to be built in the meeting house
c Samuel b Apr 19, 1696   d Hannah b Oct 20, 1698; d Aug 29, 1721
e Timothy b May 10, 1700   f Hepzibah b Oct 16, 1701
g Ann b Mch 21, 1705-6; d May 19, 1706   h Peter b Jan 27, 1708-9

Ruth Dow bcba m Nov 10, 1715, Jonathan Haseltine b Bradford Apr 12, 1694, son of Abraham and Elizabeth (Longhorn); must be the wid Ruth Haseltine m Haverhill Nov 27, 1759, Cornelius Page. Seven children, all b Haverhill:

a Abigail b Aug 6, 1716   b Samuel b Nov 11, 1718
c Timothy b Oct 9, 1720; m Ann Hancock; 2nd Nov 2, 1762, Mrs Ruth (Wilson)
   Stickney. A deacon, settled 1752 in the Saco valley, Me, prominent citizen
   and pioneer; his posterity still in Saco

d Samuel b Dec 26, 1722   e Peter b Sept 14, 1725
f Abraham b June 14, 1728   g Joshua b June 23, 1729

Abigail Dow bcbb m John Hobbs b Dec 12, 1688, d No Hampton Mch 17, 1783, son of Morris and Sarah (Swett); lived North Hill, No Hampton; she d May 5, 1775. This family intermarried with the ab and ae Dows. Children:

a Joseph b Feb 21, d Sept 17, 1721   b John b May 13, 1723
c Joseph b Apr 2, 1726; d July 6, 1820; m Abigail Page abbja
d Abigail b June 7, 1728; m Samuel Chapman   e Samuel b Jan 24, 1731
f Mary b Nov 18, 1733; d Dec 9, 1832, unm
g Simon b May 7, 1736; d Aug 27, 1771; m Abigail Godfrey
h Benjamin b Feb 18, 1739; d July 16, 1825; m Judith Marden

Samuel Dow bcbc. Original manuscript of b lines, prepared for Richard S Dow gave him d May 28, 1722. This is complete error. Amesbury rec: Samuel Dow and wife Mary had:

a Jacob b June 24, 1723

Some wid Mary Dow m Haverhill May 7, 1745, Henry Herring. Perhaps a conscientious genealogist should leave this line here. Our policy, however, is to include in the volume every untraced line. There turn up Dow families in Malden and Pelham, of considerable importance, the origin of which is unknown. A careful survey fails to find any likely ancestor. We take it as our hypothesis that Samuel and wife moved to Pelham, leaving the homestead to be inherited by his brother Timothy. In this case, we must assume that there was another son:

b Samuel b anywhere from 1725 to 1730

Jacob Dow bcbca. There were two Dows of Malden who cannot be accounted for. We continue our guessing by assuming that Jacob Dow had at least two children:

a John presumably b 1745 to 1750   b Solomon, served from Malden.

John Dow bcbcaa must have been close to Haverhill, for he marched from there as a minute man to Lexington Apr 19, 1775, Capt James Sawyer, Col James Frye. He re-enlisted, was at the Battle of Trenton; in continuous service until mustered out Mch 17, 1779. He must have hastened home from New Jersey, for he m July 4 (int pub July 3), 1779, Mehitable Sargent of Malden b Jan 22, 1756, dau of David and Mehitable (Green). Apparently John Dow d leaving an only child. Wid Mehitable Dow m Apr 20, 1786, John Hancock of Malden. Child, Haverhill rec:

a Isaac b June 15, 1780. All that is known of him is from the 1850 census: farmer of Malden, with him Esther Nichols ae 84, Esther Nichols ae 54, Harriet Nichols ae 39. Quite possible he had m a Nichols and was a widower. No evidence of children

Solomon Dow bcbcab of Malden, private, Capt Nailer Hatch, Col William Bond, 37th reg, Oct 6, 1775. Some Solomon Dow, seaman, exchanged, Halifax to Boston, Oct 8, 1778. No further trace.

Samuel Dow bcbcb. There was a Samuel Dow of Pelham, N H, with wife Rebecca. Apparently he d soon after b of 2nd child, for Rebeckah Dow of Pelham m Jan 31, 1757, William Tarbox b Aug 23, 1732, son of Jonathan and Mary (Clough) of Boston. They continued to live in Pelham; had one son, John b June 23, 1758; m Mch 3, 1779, Ruth Butler of Pelham; 8 children. Samuel had 2 children; both b Pelham:

a John b Oct 7, 1752 b Samuel b Dec 21, 1755

John Dow bcbcba. Our proven knowledge of him ends with his birth rec in Pelham. He may be the veteran given herein as bcbcaa whose identity is merely guessed. On the other hand, we must find parentage for a James Dow who Hist Littleton, N H, says was b Barnet, Vt, 1780. This James had a posterity coming to Littleton from Barnet after 1860 and there was a kinship between this posterity and the bcbcbb family of Littleton. Now, it is more than doubtful whether any Dow was in Barnet as early as 1780. Hist Littleton has taken some hearsay for granted. To provide for an actual James, we continue guessing,—that John Dow bcbcba was the father of James and that James settled in Barnet some time after 1783. Another close search in 1927 just before the printer received the copy of this chapter tends to prove the correctness of our hypotheses. James Dow of Littleton and James Dow of Barnet both had fathers who were Revolutionary veterans. They were closely akin. They were acquainted. They probably were first cousins. Therefore,—we place as son of John Dow:

a James b Sept 23, 1780; as likely in Pelham as elsewhere

James Dow bcbcbaa. Hist Littleton's account is evidently contributed by a member of the family, apparently after a lapse of many years with imperfect recollections to go by. No wife, no particulars are mentioned, only the existence of 2 sons:

a Samuel b Barnet Aug 27, 1803; place, as well as date, undoubtedly correct
b Amos H b Barnet; m Jan 2, 1829, Phebe Wadley of Danville.

Samuel Dow bcbcbaaa gets brief mention in Hist Littleton but appears in 1850 census joiner of Greensboro, Vt, realty $300. He d Greensboro Apr 9, 1871; m Oct 1, 1829, Jennette Kingsley b Dec 9, 1803, d Dec 12, 1846, dau of William; m 2nd, Feb 18, 1847, Lovina Stevens of Goshen Gore (now Stannard) b July 13, 1827, d Nov 12, 1868. Children:

a William Kingsley b Barnet Oct 7, 1830 b James b Aug 2, 1832
c Mary b Jan 25, 1836; d Apr 12, 1855 d Samuel H b Apr 13, 1842
e Amos S b Feb 28, 1846
f Julia Jennette b Jan 10, 1848 (census gave Jenet G)
g Darius L b 1849 (sic census; Harry L probably correct b June 8, 1849)
h Lovina b Sept 14, 1852; d Sept 19, 1867
i Benjamin Franklin b Sept 18, 1856; living Greensboro 1926

William K Dow bcbcbaaaa store keeper of Clinton, Wis, later traveling salesman, d Lincoln, Neb, May 17, 1877; m Huldah Maria Farnsworth b Danville, Vt, May 26, 1828, d Clinton Nov 7, 1875, dau of Alden.   After her death the children returned to Littleton:

a   William K b Buffalo May 30, 1860, printer; m Mch 2, 1890, Minnie A Glover ae 18, tailoress, dau of F R, farmer; div; no rec of children. Littleton census after 1900 gives William K Dow laborer also a William Dow laborer, latter unplaced
b   Dexter D b Buffalo Jan 20, 1863. Grad Dartmouth 1889; studied law in Littleton, admitted to Bar 1892, appointed Clerk of Superior Court of Grafton Co 1893 and has retained that position ever since. His home is Woodsville, N H; pres Woodsville Guaranty Savings Bank; vice-pres Woodsville National Bank; trustee Public Library; K P A, F, & A M; Kt St Gerard Commandery, A A S R 32nd degree A O N M—Mt Sinai. Unm
c   Jennie A b Chicago Oct 9, 1866

Jennie A Dow bcbcbaaaac now lives Helena, Mont; m Oct 20, 1883, John Harry Henry b Boston Oct 28, 1858, driver of Littleton. Children:

a   Eliza Georgia b Sept 5, 1885; m William O Whipps of Helena
b   William Dexter b Nov 22, 1887; d Aug 20, 1889

James Dow bcbcbaaab by 1850 census joiner of Greensboro d Albany, Vt, June 8, 1918; twice m, two children by 1st wife:

a   George A; unt   b   Charles; not now living; unt
c   William W; now of McIndoes Falls, Vt
d   Flora E m Gerald Plunket   e   Robert M m; had 2 children

Samuel H Dow bcbcbaaad d Littleton June 2, 1913; enlisted 1861 in 4th Vt; invalided; re-enlisted, wounded 1862; again re-enlisted; mustered out 1865; returned to Littleton, auctioneer, merchant; m Oct 4, 1875, Mandanah Huntoon b Dec 11, 1847, dau of Carter, wid of Milo E Fullford.   No children.

Amos S Dow bcbcbaaae also enlisted 4th Vt; mustered out Aug 25, 1864; farmer of Littleton; m Apr 4, 1882, Mary Jane Huntoon b July 21, 1840, dau of Carter and Diantha (Parker).   No children.

Darius S Dow bcbcbaaag (sic in m rec of son, but called Harry L in family rec) lived Greensboro; m Martha Flanders. Apparently but one child:

a   Harry Leslie b Greensboro 1881

Harry L Dow bcbcbaaaga m Holyoke, Mass, May 20, 1903, Daisy McCray ae 16 b Manchester, Conn, dau of William S and Ella (Carpenter). Children:

a   William Sargent b Mch 1, 1904   b   —— dau b Chicopee Apr 3, 1905

Amos H Dow bcbcbaab appears but little in extant rec. Local history that he m Phebe Wadley may be error; more likely he m 2nd

Ellen Powers. for her name as mother appears in 2nd m rec of son. A
son reports three children in all:

a   John H b 1867; for many years teamster of Roxbury, Mass
b   Amos J; living 1926 Provincetown, Mass
c   Andrew; 1926 lumberman of Thurlock, Calif

John H Dow bcbcbaaba now night watchman in a Boston wagon
factory m 1st Nellie F Scrollins d Boston Dec 12, 1901, ae 29-5-9; 5
children of whom 1 now living; m 2nd (her 2nd) Jan 25, 1903, Margaret
(Connelly) Kennedy ae 35, dau of Daniel and Margaret (Driscoll), all
b Ireland. Children:

a   John H d Boston Apr 3, 1903, ae 7-2-27
b   Rose Edna m Peter Fitzpatrick; of 4 children 3 living,—Henry, Edna May,
    and Florence
f   Helen Louise b Nov 2, 1903; m —— Fitzpatrick, brother of foregoing; only
    child,—Clair
g   George Andrew b Jan 14, 1906   h   Alice Catherine d Jan 16, 1909
i   Elizabeth b 1909   j   Gladys b 1911

Samuel Dow bcbcbb, Rev veteran, pensioner, his wife surviving to
be comfortable on his pension until 1850. His posterity is inadequately
treated in Hist Stoddard, which gives no genealogy. The indefat-
igable Edgar R Dow got in communication 1885 with a grandson with
great success altho not able to establish the ancestry of Samuel himself.
Samuel was a private on guard Cambridge May 15, 1775, and was present
at Bunker Hill.   Possible but unlikely that he was the corporal Samuel,
said to be of Dunstable, in 27th reg, Capt Ebenezer Bancroft, Col Ebenezer Bridge, 3 mos, 10 days from July 24, 1775.   This does not conflict
with the presence of Samuel in Pelham, where he m Nov 30, 1775, Eunice
Kimball b 1756. She is not in Kimball Genealogy, but her mother was
a Wyman. Family rec that she lived to 106 is fanciful; she d ae 96.
Judging from b of fifth child, the couple continued in Pelham until
1786 or later, then moved Tyngsboro, Mass. Hist Stoddard is correct
that Samuel, veteran, appeared first in Stoddard tax list 1800. Peaceful
old age followed. Edgar R Dow had the original of a letter Samuel
wrote in 1829 to his grandson in N Y State, saying that, altho lame, he
could still work steadily at his carpenter's bench and made a comfortable
living. Seven children, Tyngsboro and Stoddard rec very defective,
third and fourth proven by family Bibles only:

a   Samuel b about 1776; doubtless in Pelham
b   Eunice b about 1778; m Tyngsboro July 2, 1799, Cyrus Alexander
c   John b N H 1780 (census rec); identity not found in any rec; proved by his
    nephew
d   Daniel b N H 1784; existence confirmed by family but particulars only from
    1850 census
e   Asa b Pelham Jan 15, 1786
f   Peggy b Feb 6, 1790; d Stoddard old age July 27, 1881; unm
g   James b Aug 3, 1792

Samuel Dow bcbcbba of Tyngsboro m (int pub Nov 2, 1797,
Sally Cheney, not in Cheney Gen); moved to Stoddard, presumably

his parents following. Hist Stoddard says some of his descendants still live there but fails to mention a single child. Following list is probably complete but is gathered from various m rec and a few family mentions:

a Sophia m Dec 25, 1823, Nathaniel Friend
b Fanny m Apr 4, 1831, Joseph Waugh
c Samuel b Stoddard Mch 11, 1811
d Persis L m Dec 29, 1836, Silas Cram; a dau Laura M m —— Lowell, 2nd 1886 Marshall G Priest of Marlow
e Laura (Dowe) m Jan 16, 1840, William Dole. State rec seems more reliable than Stoddard, gives Dow and Dale
f John Cheney; probably 1st born; not found in any rec but coincidence of names and places makes his identity reasonably certain

Samuel Dow bcbcbbac of Stoddard m May 31, 1836, Sarah Stevens of Goffstown b 1816, d Amherst May 11, 1855. They moved some time to Amherst, N H, he appearing first time on voting list 1843. Census 1850 shows them farmers, realty assessed $1,200. After 1855 Samuel took his family to Manchester, where he was a carpenter and m 2nd, for he d May 24, 1884, a wife surviving. Children by census rec:

a Levi B b 1838; unt   b Mary J b 1839
c Joseph S b 1843; unt   d Margaret A b 1844   e Henry L b 1846; unt

Margaret Ann Dow bcbcbbacd b Jan 25, 1844; m Aug 12, 1859, John Parker Manning of Manchester. Children:

a Henry Waldo b Nov 17, 1861
b Walter Everett b Dec 17, 1867; m Cynthia Moore
c Anna Dell b Apr 6, 1870; m Goffstown 1895 Alonzo Foote

John Cheney Dow bcbcbbaf moved to Newington, Conn, presumably with his uncle John bcbcbbc. His children appear mostly from gravestone inscriptions in Wethersfield, nearby. This place was the home of a c family of Dow, but none is known from Newington. As further evidence of correctness of identification we note the recurrence of name Churchill in bcbcbbc. John C Dow m Aug 23, 1825, Laura Churchill of Wethersfield d May 27, 1830, ae 27; 2nd, Oct 10, 1832, Martha McCarter d Nov 24, 1854, ae 41. Children:

a Samuel bap Feb 11, d Nov 9, 1827   b John bap Aug 13, d Sept 1830
c Laura C bap Aug 3, 1834; d Mch 29, 1853
d Martha Urania bap July 31, 1836; d Nov 27, 1859
e Mary Abilene bap Sept 30, 1838; d Nov 8, 1855
f John Newell bap Nov 15, 1845
g Luella (identity doubtful; parents not stated) d Aug 9, 1867, ae 14 (Wethersfield inscriptions)

John N Dow bcbcbbaff may have been b several years before baptism; was surely one or both of following: Newell Dow private 13th reg 1861, or Newell Dow of Wethersfield corporal 22nd reg 1862. Beyond this he has been found only from m rec of a son, wife being Margaret Clarke:

a Henry Francis b Newington 1877; m 2nd Roxbury, Mass, Oct 10, 1907, Susie Evelyn Parker b N B 1875, dau of William T and Elmira B (Bunnell). Living Methuen 1926

John Dow bcbcbbc is known to us mainly from the Andrews Genealogy. He bought a farm in Newington, Conn, and m June 17, 1806, Lucy Andrews (Andrus in rec) b Newington May 23, 1789, d Pa Feb 3, 1845, dau of Fitch and Lois (Goodrich). They sold the Newington farm, perhaps to his nephew, to buy land in the Holland purchase and settled in L'ee, Oneida Co, N Y. Andrews Gen says he was living 1871 with dau Almira and had 5 sons, 3 dau. The Author has not yet gotten a transcript of 1850 census of N Y State and has found only two children:

a   Almira b Lee July 25, 1811
b   John Churchill bap Newington, adult; unt

Almira Dow bcbcbbca m May 23, 1838 (his 2nd) Lemuel Wells Andrews, 1st cousin, son of Epaphras and Abigail (Wells), clothier of West Bethany. Child:

a   Lucy Maria b July 30, 1840; m Charles K Cummings

Daniel Dow bcbcbbd appears in 1850 census carpenter of Stoddard, realty $750; wife Edna b N H 1785. Census shows no children, but all are named in their grandfather's letter of 1829, given in that order:

a   William d before 1829, unm   b   Sally m Dec 31, 1837, John Barrett
c   Peggy   d   Elizabeth; both living 1829
e   Sophia (1st born unless date be wrong) m Feb 19, 1819, ——Smith of Londonderry

Asa Dow bcbcbbe, house builder, moved soon after m to Antwerp, Jefferson Co, N Y; in old age lived Lawrence; d July 30, 1871; m Wethersfield July 27, 1811, Sarah Cleveland b Wethersfield, May 24, 1786, d Antwerp Sept 21, 1859, dau of Joseph and Rebecca (Collins). Twelve children, of whom 11 married; 28 grandchildren by 1884. Children, older 6 b Lee, others Turin:

a   Nancy b Mch 26, 1812; living 1884, Mrs Conyne of Antwerp
b   Cynthia b Jan 18, 1814; d Fulton, Ill, Nov 1871; m —— Wilcox
c   Calvin C b Oct 4, 1815; d Antwerp Mch 23, 1842
d   James H b July 22, 1817; d Antwerp Aug 26, 1858
e   John Mason b July 22, 1817
f   Augustus L b Oct 24, 1819; d N Y City Mch 2, 1846
g   Henry S b Jan 5, 1822; d Nashville, Tenn, Oct 12, 1864
h   William b Jan 1, 1824; living 1884 at Bath on Hudson, N Y
i   Emily b Dec 25, 1826; m —— Wight; d Antwerp Jan 11, 1852
j   Delia b July 30, 1828; m —— Coe of Wampville, N Y; living 1884
k   David b Sept 25, 1831; d Turin Apr 28, 1833
l   Martin L b Sept 26, 1835; d Martensburg, Me. Every member of this family married, except David

John M Dow bcbcbbee, homeopathic physician of Potsdam and Hermon, d Dec 6, 1888; m Lowville Dec 29, 1841, Amy B Bosworth b Lowville Feb 6, 1815, living 1890. Children, all b Turin:

a   Amelia J b June 18, 1844; m 2nd Apr 1880 A Stott; no children
b   Mather B b June 29, 1847; painter of Nashua, N H, m Apr 21, 1880, Amelia B Stott, ae 25, b Canada, dau of John and Mary (Ward)
c   Alvin Ara b Nov 13, 1850; d June 17, 1851
d   Delia A b May 26, 1852; of Nashua unm in 1884

e Duane M b Apr 20, 1856; m Oct 17, 1875, Libbie Green; homeopathic physician, located in Hermon; died within a year; 2 children. He had built up
   such a practice that his father moved from Potsdam to succeed him
f Hattie S b May 5, 1859; m Feb 16, 1880, J B Fairburn of Hermon; 1 child by
   1884

Mather B Dow bcbcbbeeb and Amelia H Stott had:

a Amy N b 1882; m Athol, Mass, June 8, 1904, Chester E Morse, ae 22, son of
   Charles L and Mary F (Hawes)

James Dow bcbcbbg came to Littleton, N H, about 1810; d July
2, 1876; served as fifer 1814-5, disch on account of wounds; m Oct 29,
1811, Lydia Thompson b Francestown May 1790, dau of Luther and
Beulah (White).   Children, all b Littleton:

a Naomi Hews b Jan 25, 1816   b Luther Thompson b Jan 25, 1816
c Laura Brackett b Aug 18, 1817   d Lydia b Mch 19, 1819; d Oct 26, 1821
e Mary T b Dec 8, 1820; m Nov 30, 1846, Franklin I Gouch, tool manufacturer
   of Poughkeepsie
f Susan Hines b Nov 1, 1822   g Lydia b July 26, 1824; d Jan 16, 1846
h Caroline T b Mch 20, 1826; m Feb 13, 1851, Thomas Nichols of Littleton
i Seraphina Larned b Jan 8, 1828; d Oct 19, 1854; m Oct 24, 1853, Hezekiah H
   Noyes
j James b Aug 8, 1831   k Ann Amanda b Nov 6, 1829; d Apr 20, 1832
l Catherine Balch b Feb 27, 1833

Naomi H Dow bcbcbbga m Oct 12, 1831, David Page Sanborn b
Feb 8, 1810, d Mch 1, 1871, tool maker, major of militia, son of Levi and
Hannah (Durgin).   Children:

a Amelia Barber b Littleton Feb 20, 1833; d Sept 16, 1853
b Francis Davidson b Oct 26, 1834; m Caroline Smith; 2 children
c Laura Burnham b Aug 26, 1836; m Albert Tyler Johnson; 2nd John Smillie
   of Newbury, Vt
d Luther Dow b Dec 12, 1841
e Ellen Josephine b Worcester, Mass, Mch 4, 1847; m Minot Weeks
f Emma Electa b Littleton Mch 16, 1849; m Charles Ball
g Jennie Lindsey b Apr 28, d Apr 29, 1853

Luther T Dow bcbcbbgb, named for his father-in-law, evidently
a man of distinction, judging from the number of children named for
him, was a sash and blind manufacturer; in 1885 retired capitalist;
Congregationalist; d Feb 21, 1898; m May 1, 1843, Elvira Bonney
Fitch b Aug 30, 1822, d Littleton Dec 27, 1893, dau of Solomon and Susan
(Fuller).   Children:

a Arthur Flanders b July 14, 1849   b Robert Morrison b Mch 16, 1856

Arthur F Dow bcbcbbgba m Oct 30, 1872, Mary Allein Johnson b
Feb 10, 1850, d May 27, 1878, dau of Elisha; no children; 2nd, July 23,
1879, Emma Euphemia (Minnie E) McLean b Easthaven, Vt, 1858,
dau of Alexander F and Margaret.   He d July 30, 1893, partner in Dow
Bros. She m 2nd, May 14, 1898, George R Armthing of Littleton.
Children:

a Annie Elvira b Oct 27, 1881   b Mary Louise b Oct 7, 1883
c Robert McLean b Nov 24, 1891

Robert M Dow bcbcbbgbb, partner in Dow Bros, d Nov 4, 1890; Unitarian; m Nov 20, 1877, Ella Mabel Woodard b Douglass, Mass, Nov 20, 18—, dau of George F.   Child:

a   George Luther b Dec 8, 1878

George L Dow bcbcbbgbba, miller, later express driver of Littleton, m Tamworth Oct 12, 1904, Lutie E Mason, ae 24, dau of Nicholas W and Emma P (Dame) of Hope, Ark.   Child:

a   Katherine Woodard b May 12, 1906

Laura B Dow bcbcbbgc m June 1838 Elisha Burnham, son of Samuel of Bethlehem.   Children:

a   Cyrus Eastman b Dec 2, 1838
b   Elbridge C b July 24, 1840; d Feb 5, 1842   c   Henry Baxter b Feb 6, 1842
d   Ella Dow b July 8, 1845; d July 6, 1847
e   Frank Elmer b July 10, 1847; 1st Vt cavalry; m Oct 1, 1897, Clara E West
f   Charles Julius b Jan 1, 1850; d Sept 7, 1865
g   Stella Laura b June 18, 1853; d unm   h   Edward Elisha b Oct 11, 1855
i   Alice Louise b July 23, 1857; d Dec 27, 1862

Susan H Dow bcbcbbgf m May 24, 1826, Ellery D Dunn, son of Joshua, carpenter and builder, member of the Legislature.   Children:

a   Edwin F b May 31, 1847; d Sept 5, 1849
b   Henry b Aug 6, d Sept 20, 1849
c   Addie Mary b Dec 1, 1850; m Mch 11, 1874, Clarence Smith; div; m 2nd Mch 24, 1893, Walter J Bartlett of Worcester, Mass

James Dow bcbcbbgj, carpenter and joiner, Methodist, d Littleton Nov 2, 1906; m Dec 28, 1863, Emily Bonney Kilburn b Oct 17, 1833, dau of Josiah; div; 2nd, Oct 28, 1878, Ellen Melissa Hatch b Lebanon Dec 6, 1849, d Apr 25, 1910, dau of Philo Scott, farmer, and Laodicea (Nichols).   Children:

a   Edith May b July 14, d Sept 5, 1880   b   Ada Florence b Dec 26, 1881
c   Leslie James b Apr 25, 1885

Catherine B Dow bcbcbbgl m Albert H Quimby b Barnet, Vt, Dec 13, 1831, musician in 5th N H.   Children:

a   Frank Albert b Apr 4, 1858
b   Catherine Alice b July 8, 1864; m Sept 23, 1889, Charles Edward Wright, lawyer of Whitefield, son of Sheldon Carpenter and Mary Julia (Nagle)

TIMOTHY DOW bcbe had a farm on Sweet Hill, a pleasant spot with a wide outlook in east parish, Haverhill, transferred to Plaistow by the relocation of the State boundary; d July 22, 1777; m June 13, 1723, Judith Worthen b Feb 7, 1703-4, dau of Samuel and Deliverance (Heath), granddau of Ezekiel Worthen, grantee of Amesbury 1663.   Children:

a   Hannah b May 12, 1724   b   Samuel b Mch 12, 1727
c   Deliverance b Mch 6, 1729-30
d   Mary b Aug 4, 1734; m Moses Ordway; presumably who m 1st 1746 Ann Huntington, he son of James and Elizabeth
e   Elizabeth b Jan 2, 1736-7; m Jan 13, 1774, Jonas Leslie of Hollis
f   Timothy bap Mch 31, 1738-9   g   Joshua b Oct 22, bap Oct 28, 1744
h   Ezekiel b Plaistow Sept 27, 1747
i   Ruth b 1749.   Plaistow rec says 1732.   When Plaistow separated from Haverhill, a clerk copied from the Haverhill books the earlier vital statistics; later a separate copy seems to have been made.   Both transcripts are very prone to clerical errors, the earlier often using some vague year date only, and often wrong.   Ruth m 1770 Nathan Gile, cooper of Plaistow, son of Daniel and Joanna (Heath); one son

Hannah Dow bcbea m Feb 14, 1748-9, Amos Davis of Haverhill b May 11, 1727, bap Amesbury 2nd church, son of Ephraim and Hannah (Eastman).   He inherited his father's Haverhill homestead, but they were living 1757 in Amesbury, bringing a negro to be bap; both living Haverhill 1795.   Only child:

a   Judith b Haverhill Jan 2, 1749-50; bap Amesbury July 14, 1751

Samuel Dow bcbeb.   There have been a number of Dow genealogists in the b lines, but all of them have been confined to the bcde lines.   The one exception is Titcomb, who monographed the bcbeh line.   Strangely, this author never even alludes to the elder brother, heir to the homestead.   The present Author of this Book has had to reconstruct as best he could this whole line out of the extremely defective Plaistow records and not a single Dow has ever given aid, even in the 30-year search made by the late Edgar R Dow.   Samuel, his son Samuel and brother Joshua appear Oct, 1777, in Capt Gile's company.   The Rolls give no inkling of length of service.   He m Nov 25, 1749, Mary Davis of Amesbury b Aug 30, 1729, dau of Nathaniel and Sarah (Silver).   The 1790 census finds him in Plaistow 2a, 1b, 2c.   This indicates some son b after 1774 and him we do not find.

His son Samuel m "Molly," presumably another Mary Davis. This makes it almost impossible to separate the two sets of children. There is a gap of seven years between the 6th and 7th child.   To place the 7th child as 1st born of his son Samuel would make the latter a father at 17.   More likely that a son b 1779 is the one indicated in the 1790 census.

We shall assume this to be the case.   The 3rd child Samuel was his father's heir, so far as the homestead is concerned; this indicates only one older surviving brother. Children:

a ——. A gap of 4 years after m is improbable
b Timothy b Nov 1, 1753   c Samuel b Nov 17, 1756
d Hannah b Feb 24, 1760   e Mary b May 24, 1763
f John b Jan 30, 1765   g Jeremiah b Sept 2, 1773
h Moley (Molly) b Dec 19, 1775   i James b Feb 9, 1779

Timothy Dow bcbebb. Boughton, Hist Concord, notes a Timothy Dow there by 1780 and, not placing him, interpolates him among the children of Ebenezer Dow ahbg, not stopping to realize that, if he were right, Timothy would be a father at 9. His d rec was overlooked by Hist Concord; 1808, b Plaistow. Apparently Timothy sought fortune elsewhere and permitted his younger brother to be heir to the homestead. A Timothy Dow enlisted 1776 from Londonderry. This may be bcbebb or bcbef. Our Timothy came to Concord from Bow, m about 1779 Margaret Gott of Pembroke. Hist Pembroke gives: William Dow m Margaret Gault, dau of Andrew (2) and Molly (Ayer) of Londonderry. The spellings Gott and Gault are generally interchangeable in early dates. William must be a pen slip for Timothy, altho there was a William Dow of Bow at this time. The couple came at once to Concord. Census 1790 indicates 1 son and 1 dau more than are otherwise found. Hist Concord abandons the family early. An appeal by the Author, printed in the Concord Patriot, did not get a single answer from any descendant of bcbebb, nor from any one else, for that matter. Hist Concord gives list of children, confirmed by official rec:

a Polly b Mch 24, 1780   b Samuel b Feb 24, 1782
c Timothy b July 27, 1784   d Hannah b Apr 6, 1786
e Isaac b Dec 31, 1789   f William b Jan 14, 1793

Mary Dow bcbebba m Dec 10, 1806, Philip Carrigan Baker of Bow d Sanbornton May 10, 1837; she d June 28, 1865. Children:

a Clarinda b Bow Aug 3, 1808; m Fenner H Emerson
b Timothy Dow b May 17, 1810   c Amos Morgan b Sept 25, 1815
d Mary Ann b Dec 6, 1819; d Bow, ae 7   e Mary Ann b Feb 28, 1827

Samuel Dow bcbebbb of Concord m Jan 13, 1806, Mary Ann Baker b Bow Nov 17, 1779, dau of Joseph and Mary Ann (Moore); she d Feb 1823; he m 2nd, Nov 20, 1823, Sally Harney (Hardy in rec, error). Children:

a Margaret b May 29, 1810   b Hannah b Oct 1, 1814
c Joseph b Sept 10, 1817; untraced   d Samuel Harvey b Mch 30, 1825
e Mary Ann b Feb 28, 1827; m Edwin Flanders; 1 child b 1854

Margaret Dow bcbebbba m Nov 26, 1829, John Carter Jr, both of Concord. Child:

a Hannah D m —— Johnson; 2nd 1896 Reuben Batchelder, both of Concord

Samuel H Dow bcbebbbd, farmer of Hopkinton, m Mch 20, 1847,

Sarah E Hoyt of Hopkinton d Mch 27, 1872, dau of Moses and Betsey (Palmer); 2nd (her 3rd), Jennie M Walker, ae 44. Children:

a Georgianna b 1848   b Warren Hoyt b 1853
c Harvey M b 1859   d Oscar Samuel b May 28, 1862

Warren H Dow bcbebbbdb, blacksmith of Hopkinton, set up a shop before 1883 in Bennington, Vt; in 1908 farmer of Warner, N H; m Aug 21, 1881, Emma F Keyes b Milford, ae 19, dau of Horace W and Sophia H (Page). She d Bennington Dec 5, 1883; he m 2nd, Sept 5, 1885, Charlotte Payson (Peerson in d rec) b Sweden Feb 20, 1858, d Warner Apr 4, 1907, dau of Andrew and Charlotte; m 3rd, July 7, 1909, wid Hattie P Ayer, ae 50, dau of George A and Mary (Small) Pike. Children, list possibly incomplete:

a —— son b and d Concord Dec 11, 1881
b Eva Mabel b Mch 18, 1883 (rec in both Bennington and Hopkinton); d Kensington May 28, 1883
c —— son b Concord May 10, 1889; untraced
d Emma Charlotte b Dec 26, 1892; at home Warner 1909

Emma C Dow bcbebbbdbd m Hudson, Mass, Dec 29 1908 (his 2nd) William Hanley, ae 29, both of Concord, Mass, son of Peter and Annie (Martin).

Harvey M Dow bcbebbbdc, farmer of Hopkinton, m Aug 28, 1881, Lydia J Austin, ae 20, dau of John and Lucy J (Webster); div; m 2nd, giving himself b 1862 (a man invariably lies about his age at 2nd m), Feb 22, 1892, Delia Webster, ae 16, dau of Frank D and Nettie (Dow b Hopkinton); div; m 3rd, June 25, 1906, Alice Etta Sweatt, ae 40 (her 3rd), wid b Locke. Hopkinton 1909 census gives them with 1 dau:

a Blanchie

Oscar S Dow bcbebbbdd, farmer of Hopkinton, m June 30, 1879, Augusta A Young, ae 22, of Manchester, dau of Robert and Jennie (Dow, unplaced).

Timothy Dow bcbebbc (called Capt in d rec) d Concord July 1833; m Sept 13, 1808, Margaret Sawyer (Sanger in one rec) of Concord. Children, list probably imperfect:

a Timothy   b Albert G   c —— d 1814; probably in infancy
d Alfred. A guess to accommodate an unplaced Alfred

Timothy Dow bcbebbca, 1st Lieut 7th N H, resigned Aug 22, 1863; m Mch 30, 1843, Martha J Hoyt of Concord b 1823. She m 2nd (Martha J A) Henniker Apr 11, 1868, Edward Gove Clark akecx. This rec gives her dau of Amos and Betsey Hoyt. They had a child,—Mittie F m Henniker 1892 Frederick A Gould. Children, list possibly incomplete; younger b Henniker:

a William Edward b Concord May 12, 1844
b Clara A b 1847; living 1850   c Sarah E b Dec 25, 1850

d   Byron T b Oct 28, 1853; d in infancy   e   Byron S b Jan 15, 1856
f   Charles A b 1858 (date given by himself at 2nd m)

William E Dow bcbebbcaa, railroad man, widower, d Concord Oct 7, 1915; m Sept 23, 1888, Mary A Derby b Saranac, N Y, d Aug 16, 1894, ae 52-11-7, dau of Martin and Almira (Kimball). In m rec, occupation hostler.   Probably only child:

a   Lillian A b Sept 25, 1895, Orlando L Caswell of Concord

Charles A Dow bcbebbcaf is presumably the Charles Dow b Concord, farmer of Hopkinton, m Mettie Currier b Hopkinton.   Child:

a   —— dau b Hopkinton July 9, 1879

He is surely Charles A of Concord m 2nd, Lebanon Nov 28, 1886, Jennie C Neal b Norwich, Vt, Sept 17, 1872 (sic; 1862?), d Manchester Oct 17, 1901, dau of James L b Unity and Mary (Warrener) b Hartford, Vt.

Albert G Dow bcbebbcb, farm assessed $2,500 in 1850, m May 19, 1846, Esther M Abbot d Concord Aug 19, 1893, ae 68-10-30, dau of Reuben and Mercy.   He d Concord (rec giving father Timothy b Plaistow and mother Margaret Sawyer) Mch 20, 1909.   Perhaps more than 1 child:

a   Esther E d Concord Sept 27, 1883, ae 32, 1 mo

Isaac Dow bcbebbe appears 1834 as surveyor of highways Concord; m Concord Nov 14, 1816, Perney (Pernley and Pernal in rec) Gill d 1825, ae 31, 2nd (called Isaac Jr to distinguish him from ahbgh), Dec 15, 1825, Nancy Austin, both of Concord. A carpenter, he moved to Fishersville; d Feb 24, 1878.   Both appear in 1850 census, he carpenter of Bedford, she b N H 1805.   Children, by census:

a   Asenath b 1830   b   Annette b 1833   c   William b 1836
d   Augusta b 1842

Asenath Dow bcbebbea b Bedford, m Sept 3, 1857, Franklin A Abbott b Fishersville.   A child:

a   Mary S m Concord 1888 Charles B Clark

William Dow bcbebbec, b Bedford, cabinet maker of Concord, m Lora M Baker b Grafton 1841.   A child, no other in State rec:

a   Frederick Herbert b Concord Nov 22, 1869; untraced

William Dow bcbebbf, member of Legislature 1836, m Sept 14, 1818, Hannah Austin; lived Fishersville, perhaps returning to Concord. One child known, 2nd a guess:

a   Henry E b Fishersville May 5, 1827   b   Lorenzo

Henry E Dow bcbebbfa, blacksmith, d Hopkinton July 7, 1892; m Feb 13, 1851, Charlotte A Boutelle b Hopkinton July 18, 1847, d Hop-

kinton Dec 28, 1900, dau of Calvin and Charlotte (Fisk). At least 4
children:

    a Frank P b Hillsboro 1853 (a guess)
    b William H b Hillsboro June 28, 1854   c Samuel O b Hopkinton 1862
    d Lizzie D m Mch 2, 1880, Walter H Colby, both of Hopkinton
    e Jennie S m May 31, 1882, Willie A Currier, both of Hopkinton

Frank P Dow bcbebbfaa, painter of Hillsboro, later farmer of
Croyden, m Helen Josephine Conger b Ohio (another rec gives Hopkinton).
Children:

    a Walter E b Hillsboro Bridge 1876   b —— dau b Croyden Oct 2, 1877
    c Ellsworth b Feb 8, 1883   d Clarence L b (both Sunapee) Apr 4, 1891

Walter E Dow bcbebbfaaa, farmer of Springfield, Vt, m July 15,
1902, Alice M Batchelder b 1881, dau of Henry and Fannie (Angell).
Children:

    a Marion Lucile b July 14, 1903   b Merwin b Feb 28, 1905
    c Dexter b July 9, 1907   d —— son b June 24, 1908
    e Helen Frances b Oct 16, 1910

Clarence L Dow bcbebbfaad, painter of Sunapee, m May 21, 1914,
Celia L Sullivan, ae 24, dau of John H and Stella M (Woods).

William H Dow bcbebbfab, stable keeper of Suncook, m Aug 18,
1874, Priscilla A Elliott, ae 22, dau of William Plummer and Amanda S
(Sanborn). He d tuberculosis Hopkinton July 18, 1878; she m 2nd, Oct
30, 1880, William D Harwood of Henniker.

Samuel O Dow bcbebbfac, farmer of Concord, m Grace M Wood b
Pepperell, Mass, 1870. Children:

    a Arthur Warren b Hopkinton 1893
    b Ernest Clyde b Hopkinton Aug 26, 1895
    d Marion Emma b Oct 30, 1902   e Lillian Lucy b Concord Oct 11, 1905

Arthur W Dow bcbebbfaca, valve cutter of Concord, m Nov 24,
1915, Blanche Evelyn Mills, ae 20, dau of Charles and Annie Louise
(Baker). Child:

    a Albert Arthur b Jan 8, 1917

Ernest C Dow bcbebbfacb, belt maker of Concord, m Aug 21,
1916, Carrie Gilman Baker, ae 19, dau of Gilman H and Mary (Matthews).

Lorenzo Dow bcbebbfb must be he who m Olive Lane and date
1839 of rec is error for 1849. They went from Hillsboro to Manchester.
Two children found; one date being obviously error:

    a —— dau b Hillsboro July 16, 1852
    b George Morrison d Manchester July 17, 1853, ae 1-4-15

Alfred Dow bcbebbcd. There was an Alfred Dow who m Eliza
and had a son. The only mention found of them is in rec of son, but the

family connections are such that it is reasonably certain he was of bcbebb line. His present position is in what seems the only likely vacancy

    a   George A b (by son's rec) 1848

George A Dow bcbebbcda, blacksmith of Concord, m about 1868 Christina Maria Barnes. One rec gives her b Concord 1849. It is certain that they were in Concord from 1870. Children, probably complete:

    a   Arthur A b 1869 (by m rec)
    b   Frank b Concord Nov 16, 1870; m wid Eva M Spaulding, ae 23
    c   Edwin Coburn b Concord Jan 23, 1873
    d   Clarence W d Concord Nov 18, 1882, ae 5 mos, 14 days
    e   Webster b 1883; blacksmith of Concord, not in recent directory
    f   Walter Scott b 1886   g   Carroll d Apr 11, 1888, ae 2-5-26
    h —— d Mch 26, 1888, ae 5 days   i —— b and d Aug 5, 1889
    j —— b and d Oct 9, 1892   k —— dau b Mch 26, 1888 (date?)

Arthur A Dow bcbebbcdaa, blacksmith of Concord, div, m 2nd, Jan 25, 1904, Agnes Knights, ae 36, div, b Scotland, dau of Andrew and Elizabeth (Holmes) Scrimenger. Child:

    a   Hattie Bell d Concord Nov 12, 1907, ae 3-5-12

Frank Dow bcbebbcdab, laborer of Concord, according to rec of child m Eva M Sullivan, so perhaps wid Spaulding nee Sullivan, or, more likely, error in rec. One child found:

    a   Madeline Sarah b Apr 17, 1906

Edwin C Dow bcbebbcdac, laborer, m Dec 18, 1893, Alice Bell Baker of Pembroke b Oct 20, 1874, dau of John B and Mary A (Abbott). She d Concord July 11, 1911. Recent directory gives him painter of Manchester. Children:

    a   George Edward b Feb 12, 1895   b   Raymond Scott b Feb 2, 1897

George E Dow bcbebbcdaca, laborer of Manchester, m Aug 13, 1913, Alice Mary Milne, ae 18, dau of John J and Mary A (Carney) b Ireland. Child:

    a   Christina Ruth b Sept 22, 1914
        Manchester rec has Edward Joseph Dow, son of John and Ruth (Milne), b
        Sept 22, d Sept 29, 1913. This seems garbled

Raymond S Dow bcbebbcdax, tool sharpener of Concord, m June 9, 1904, Lillian St John, ae 19, dau of George and Meline (Martin). She d July 11, 1911; he m 2nd, June 5, 1916, Laura Ellen Hall, ae 24, dau of Augustus B and Sarah (Currier). Children:

    a   Walter George b Mch 26, 1905   b   Harold Frank b Sept 11, 1906
    c   Earl Clarence b June 10, 1908   d   Kenneth Fred b Oct 12, 1909
    e —— son b and d June 19, 1911

Samuel Dow bcbebc, yeoman of Plaistow, had Revolutionary service, as stated previously, and inherited the Plaistow farm. Rec of children always give Samuel and Molly. She is presumably Mary Davis of Amesbury b Nov 25, 1753, dau of Timothy and Judith. They appear in 1790 census 2a, 2b, 3c. Unless the census taker erred, he had then a son over 16, arguing him married by 17. As said previously, Samuel father and son each m a Mary Davis and we cannot positively distinguish between the two sets of children. Arbitrarily, then:

a Moses b Mch 17, 1781; d Sept 30, 1784
b Susanna b July 20, 1783   c Peter b Sept 24, 1786
e Lucy b Mch 16, 1791   f Charles W b about 1794, a guess
g Levi b 1800, another guess. Plaistow rec are particularly defective about this
   time

Susanna Dow bcbebcb m Nov 7, 1816, Ezekiel Sargent d Jan 10, 1845, son of Ezekiel and Betsey (Kelly). Children:

a Darius b Mch 25, 1820   b Erastus b Apr 10, 1823
c Calvin b Dec 9, 1828   d and e d in infancy

Peter Dow bcbebcc int to Mary Davis of Amesbury pub 1819. Some Mary Davis of Amesbury m 1823 Charles W Dow. Not sure she was identical. It is said Peter m and had children. Even at that he may have d and she m 2nd his brother.

Lucy Dow bcbebce int pub Sept 14, 1809, to James Davis (Davice, rec) of Amesbury.

Charles W Dow bcbebcf d Sept 7, 1846, ae 60; m 1823, Mary Davis of Amesbury, not improbably she who was banned to his brother Oct 20, 1819. They moved from Haverhill to Amesbury. Children:

a Charles White b Haverhill Aug 2, d Amesbury Aug 19, 1823
b Mary Elizabeth b Aug 13, 1828

Levi Dow bcbebcg. Evidence for his identity is limited. That he belongs near here seems proven by the fact that a son named Darius and grandson Darius Augustus (names of his cousins) came. He is unknown until m rec; m Apr 27, 1824, Catherine Haynes. Hist Lexington gives his posterity, but is incomplete:

a Darius b Sudbury Jan 11, 1825
b Nancy. Sudbury gives Nancy, ae 21, m Nov 16, 1848, Benjamin O Farwell.
   Concord, N H, gives Mary m Oct 4, 1848, Benjamin O Farwell of Concord
c Josiah b 1836 (census of 1850. This shows Levi farmer of Sudbury, realty
   $3,000; wife Catherine b Mass 1805). Hist Lexington says Josiah killed
   Jan 1, 1835, by upsetting of a cart. This errs in date, at all events, probably
   correct otherwise
d Levi b 1830 (known from census only)
e James b 1836 (census)

Darius Dow bcbebcga m Oct 14, 1851, Abbie Lovewell of Weston b Nov 8, 1830. They settled in Lexington about 1853. Children:

a Darius Augustus b Waltham Dec 28, 1852
b George H b 1854   c ——— d young   d Henrietta J b Mch 6, 1862

Darius A Dow bcbebcgaa d Dec 2, 1905; m Mch 21, 1879, Carrie

Viola Fletcher b Billerica Apr 6, 1855, dau of Charles G and Harriet Proctor (Blood). Only child:

  a Edna Josephine b Oct 30, 1880; from 1917 onward cashier Hotel Clark, Los
     Angeles, Calif

George H Dow bcbebcgab m Apr 3, 1880, Sarah P Wing b Marion, Mass, dau of Jabez and Abby. Children, b Boston and Lexington:

  a George Otis b Feb 18, 1882   b Harry James b May 12, 1885
  c Herbert W b and d Sept 20, 1893

George O Dow bcbebcgaba m Winnifred G Cleveland b Winchester dau of John and Catherine (Clark). Children, b Lexington:

  a George Alonzo b May 17, d Sept 10, 1908
  b Kenning Wing b May 18, 1909   c Cleveland Otis b Dec 28, 1911

Harry J Dow bcbebcgabb m Florence Alice Tibbets b Aug 2, 1889, dau of Henry Eugene and Celia Jennie (Webber). Child:

  a Marion Hattie b July 18, 1907

James Dow bcbebcge d Sudbury Apr 28, 1905, ae 69-0-14. No other data, except parentage, in rec.

Hannah Dow bcbebd. We are probably correct in our unproved identification that Hannah accompanied her brother to Bow, m Pembroke Jan 24, 1786, David Lufkin, both of Bow. It is quite possible that the unplaced William Dow and Richard Dow of Bow, contemporaneous, are overlooked members of the bcbe line, but it would be unwise to guess farther.

John Dow bcbebf. The first transcript of Plaistow rec give him m Plaistow about 1793 Mary Colby, his niece. Second transcript gives John Dow m Oct 30, 1788, Molly Colby, both of Plaistow. Now, John Dow signed in 1794 for Molly, his wife, a quitclaim on real estate of Stephen and Elizabeth (Maxfield) Colby. If Molly Colby were dau of Stephen, she could not possibly be niece of John Dow. If a granddau of Stephen, it would necessitate an unknown brother of John Dow. Probably the entry "niece" is wholly error. The couple lived in Plaistow until after 1810, then moved to a farm in Londonderry. Their tombstones say John b 1763, d Feb 12, 1831; Mary, his wife, b 1778, d Nov 21, 1845. Children, all but youngest b Plaistow:

  a Samuel b June 13, 1794   b Polly b July 27, 1799
  c Betsey E d Londonderry Feb 5, 1877, ae 77-6-15, unm
  d John b May 19, 1803. Untraced   e Isaac b Mch 7, 1806
  f Jacob b Mch 2, 1808
  g Hezekiah b July 13, 1810; d Londonderry June 4, 1827
  h Belinda P b Manchester Apr 13, 1884, ae 70-1-10, unm

Samuel Dow bcbebfa appears twice, once in 1850 census, shoemaker of Londonderry, realty $1,400, then by Londonderry gravestone

d July 25, 1859.   He m Dec 28, 1823, Mary Watts b Feb 29, 1792, d
Feb 18, 1859, both of Londonderry.   No rec of children

Isaac Dow bcbebfe d Apr 2, 1878; m Elizabeth S Savory, both of
Londonderry, b May 10, 1810, d Feb 25, 1884, dau of Thomas, cabinet
maker, and Grisel (Holmes).   One child found:

    a   John Clark b Londonderry May 1, 1850

John C Dow bcbebfea, shoemaker, d Aug 1, 1875; m July 1, 1875,
Laura Z Powell, ae 21, dau of John and Jane of Londonderry.   Issue
improbable.

Jacob Dow bcbebff d Sept 29, 1841; m June 14, 1838, Esther Smith,
both of Londonderry; she m 2nd, Aug 20, 1849, George Aiken of Londonderry.

Jeremiah Dow bcbebg of Plaistow m Nov 7, 1816, Martha Nichols
b 1774, d Haverhill Dec 17, 1849, dau of Phineas and Mary.

Molly Dow bcbebh is presumably the Polly Dow m Plaistow May
7, 1803, Ephraim Davis Jr of Amesbury.

James Dow bcbebi.   An uncle of the same name lived in Warren,
N H, hence some confusion.   He m about 1795 Hannah Merrill of Plaistow b 1777, who returned to Plaistow, a wid, d Dec 27, 1855, ae 79.   He
lived Warren until 1811, judging from rec that all younger children b
Warren.   Nevertheless, he appears as a founder in 1810 of the First
Free Will Baptist church of Warner.   If this last date be 1812, no
confusion would be left.   In Warner, he was a miller and man of prominence. He was quite positive in opinions, argued strenuously that witches
existed, giving Biblical authority.   He held it impossible that the earth
should revolve on its axis, "else, why doesn't my mill pond spill out?"
On other authority, he wore his stockings inside out to cure ague and laid
his boots bottom up to ward off rheumatism.   Seven children found to
"James and Hannah":

    a   Susanna b Plaistow June 21, 1796
    b   Sally b Warren (all younger b Warren) Dec 24, 1798
    c   Betsey b Dec 5, 1801
    d   Stevens M b Nov 29, 1804. Hist Warner, brief, ungenealogical, unsatisfactory,
        calls him Col but gives no authority; was a subscriber 1870 to the Book.
        It does not mention m or children
    e   Ezekiel b Apr 1807   f   Jonathan M b (by d rec) 1809
    g   Lorenzo b Sept 12, 1811

Ezekiel Dow bcbebie taught school in Warner prior to 1840, then
went to Concord, entered first Congregational church and the ministry.
Upon the upstate spread of Universalism, he joined that denomination
and held a pastorate near Newport, coming back as pastor of the First
Universalist church of Concord.   Altho quite successful, he announced
unexpectedly from his pulpit a recantation and rejoined the Congre-

gational church. He subsequently held pastorates in Andover, Loudon, So Wellfleet, Ipswich, Nelson, Huntington, Becket. He d Warren Feb 5, 1784, unm. Clergyman of New Hampshire says he m Hannah Merrill; this is error for his mother.

Jonathan M Dow bcbebif d Warren Sept 9, 1893, ae 84, 6 mos. Census 1850 gives him farmer, realty $3,000; wife Betsey b N H 1803. This was 1st wife. His 2nd, Louisa M Hall, b Warren Nov 15, 1814, d Warren Sept 25, 1893, dau of Daniel and Betsey. Census shows 1 child:

    a   Jane b 1837

Lorenzo Dow bcbebig is not found in 1850 census. He is clearly recalled by kinsfolk, who say he lived Warren or Orange, nearby, m Margaret French and had dau Hannah M and Jennie B. Various records confirm this but other rec indicate that he moved to Concord, unless there is a remarkable coincidence of two Lorenzos. Concord rec give Lorenzo, shoemaker, d Nov 6, 1889, b Feb 21, 1811 (slight discrepancy); m Dec 11, 1857, Abbie C French, both of Concord. Probably Margaret d and he m 2nd her sister or niece; apparently 2 children by 1st wife did not go to Concord:

    a   Hannah Merrill d Grafton May 12, 1914, ae 74-9-12; m John H French, 4th child of John and Polly (Brown). No children
    b   Jennie B b Warren; d about 1912; m May 14, 1866, Brewster French, brother of foregoing; lived Natick, Mass; no children
    c   Estelle E (to Lorenzo and Abbie C) of Concord m Mch 30, 1881, Fred W Clough of Bow
    d   Nellie A (dau of Lorenzo) of Fishersville m Concord Apr 20, 1882, Charles M Abbott of Boscawen

JOSHUA DOW bcbeg, lifelong resident of Plaistow, d May 21, 1802; served 1779, Capt Ezekiel Gile; probably he is the Joshua (James Dow in same company) under Capt Smith Emerson, 2nd N H. for N Y campaign. He m Nov 22, 1769, Achsah Harriman. Census 1790 gives 2a, 2b, 5c. Children:

 a Moses b May 7, 1771; d in infancy b Moses b May 10, 1773
 c Deliverance b 1774; often called Delia. State rec gives b Dec 9, 1773, impossible if Moses is right. She m Aquila Dow bcdbee
 d Anna b Feb 6, 1776
 e Judah b 1778. State rec gives Judith b Apr 27, 1778, probably correct
 f Ruth b June 7, 1780 g Joshua b Dec 20, 1781
 h Timothy b Feb 21, 1784 i Rebecca b June 25, 1789
 j Achsah b May 7, 1794

Moses Dow bcbegb is confused often in print with Moses bcfigd, also of Plaistow. He moved to a farm on the Sunapee road, Newport, N H. Six or more independent Dow families have lived in Newport. He m Feb 23, 1800, Sarah Bradley of Haverhill b May 16, 1782, d Newport Mch 4, 1824, dau of Benjamin and Sarah (Noyes). Moses Dow m Oct 17, 1830, Sarah Kimball, both of Newport. This 2nd m is overlooked by Hist Newport. Children:

 a Harriet b Sept 14, 1800; d Sept 19, 1823
 b Betsey b Oct 17, 1801; m June 20, 1824, Syene Hale M D, grad Dartmouth; sons Moses and Parker became prominent physicians of Chicago
 c Sarah B b June 16, d Aug 24, 1803 d Achsah Philena b Feb 22, 1816
 e Lydia Millicent b Feb 2, 1820

Achsah P Dow bcbegbd m 1838 Lowell Fairbanks; moved to Illinois; d Newport Oct 7, 1890. Children:

 a Charles Dow b July 27, 1839; physician of Englewood, Ill; m May 28, 1868, Jennie M Opdyke
 b Elizabeth Philena b Hillsboro, Ill, Apr 15, 1842; m May 18, 1859, W W Whitney
 c Frances Mellisant b Fredonia, Ohio, Mch 1, 1845; d Feb 1, 1849
 d Mary Ellen b Delaware, Ohio, Nov 8, 1848; d unm

Lydia Millicent Dow bcbegbe m 1840 Francis Bryant. Children:

 a Augusta b 1841 b George Dow b 1843; d Fredonia Jan 20, 1864

Anna Dow bcbegd m Newton, Mch 22, 1804, Stephen Currier of Amesbury, son of Nathan and Miriam (Buzzell) of Plaistow. Children:

 a Anne b Apr 30, 1807 b Azubah Harriman b Nov 19, 1810
 c Rebecca Dow b Jan 4, 1813 d Mary Noyes b Aug 18, 1815
 e Cyrus Buzzell b Sept 1, 1817

Ruth Dow bcbegf m Oct 18, 1806, Nathan Currier Jr, brother of Stephen; moved to Newport, N H. Children:

 a Oliver b Feb 9, 1808 b Mary b June 24, 1812

Joshua Dow bcbegg m Oct 19, 1829, Miriam Walton, both of Newport. Hist Newport does not mention this, nor him. If he was of

Newport at all, it was for a brief time, as he was of Plaistow by 1831. Plaistow rec of son misnames her Miriam Watson. His next rec is that of 2nd m, July 1, 1841, Lettice (Lettie and Leathe in rec) Sargent of Goffstown, dau of Joseph and Sally (Blaisdell). He d farmer married Goffstown Dec 30, 1861. Census 1850 names 3 children, if there were others, presumably d young:

a   George Whitefield b Plaistow Mch 9, 1831
b   Sarah E b Plaistow Apr 10, 1843; saleswoman, d Manchester Dec 5, 1911, unm
c   Joseph N b Goffstown Oct 1847; untraced

George Whitefield Dow bcbegga m Ann M Child, by whom 1 dau found; must have m very young if Plaistow date is correct. Far from certain that he is the George W Dow railroad employe of Salem, Mass, with wife Olivia A Smith b Kingston. Child found only by own m rec:

a —— dau b Plaistow Sept 30, 1851   b   Charles E b Salem 1862

Charles E Dow bcbeggab clerk of Salem m Portland, Me, Jan 6, 1892, Nellie Cunningham of Salem ae 25, dau of James b Halifax and Kate (Copeland) b Eng, of Gloucester. Her d rec gives: d Salem Aug 14, 1902, ae 35-9-9, dau of James and Catherine (Murphy). Probably older children:

x —— b Salem Aug 14, 1902

EZEKIEL DOW bcbeh inherited part of the homestead farm in Plaistow and subsequently bought much adjoining land; d Plaistow Apr 4, 1832; m Sarah Merrill of Plaistow. Census 1790 gives him 1a, 3b, 6c. A published monograph of this line says there were 5 sons, 8 dau, but names only 6. Our list is sadly incomplete:

a James b Apr 23, 1775
b Elizabeth b 1778; m 1800 Henry Tucker of Kingston; son Ezekiel m Betsey Minot
c Hannah b Sept 4, 1780; m 1802 Samuel Noyes of Plaistow
d Francis W b Mch 13, 1782   e Frances b Apr 13, 1783
f Susanna probably never existed, confused by monographer with bcbebcc
g Sarah b Jan 2, 1786; m 1809 James Eaton of Plaistow
h Ezekiel b Nov 26, 1789   i Stephen, untraced, probably d young

James Dow bcbeha m Jan 19, 1796, Ruth Williams of Hampstead; moved to Warren, N H. Here his wife d Aug 28, 1900, leaving an infant dau. James returned to Haverhill; d Jan 31, 1839. The dau:

a Ruth Williams b Warren Aug 25, 1800

Ruth W Dow bcbehaa m June 13, 1819, George Eaton b Nov 14, 1797, farmer of Plymouth, son of King. Children:

a Amos b Mch 23, 1822; shoe manufacturer of Haverhill
b Moses Williams b Apr 23, 1824   c Ruth Ann b Jan 2, 1826
d Mehitable Williams b Apr 3, 1829   e Betsey b July 4, 1831

Francis W Dow bcbehd spent his young manhood in Boston; m about 1811 Betsey Farmer b Boston June 7, 1780, d Newton, N H, Oct 20, 1865. He returned to Plaistow; d Dec 4, 1826. Children:

a Elizabeth H b Plaistow Sept 11, 1812
b William Farmer b Mch 3, 1815
c Ruth Owen b Mch 18, 1818; d Sept 1839
d Darius A b May 22, 1820
e Betsey Ann Moody b Oct 26, 1822; d June 6, 1868; m Feb 20, 1842, George Henry Mears of Boston

Elizabeth H Dow bcbehda m Apr 25, 1836, Jacob Bartlett, farmer of Newton, b July 5, 1810, d June 20, 1854. Her mother lived with her during 41 years of widowhood. Children:

a Lewis F b Feb 18, d Apr 15, 1838
b Frank D b Nov 23, 1842; lived Amesbury; m Oct 2, 1866, Ruth B Jones
c William L b Mch 30, 1840; lived Newton; m Apr 7, 1861, Emma S ——

William F Dow bcbehdb, grad Brown Univ, moved to New Bedford; m Ann Lathrop; d June 20, 1866. Census 1850 gives him no occupation, but $4,500 realty; Ann b Mass. Census omits all dates

a Sarah   b John   c Thomas, both in school, 1850
d Mary; *fide* Titcomb, Early Families

Darius A Dow bcbehdd, division surgeon during the war, physician of Hyde Park, Chicago; m Feb 23, 1847, Mary G Quigg b Litchfield, N H, Apr 15, 1826, dau of Abel G.   Children:

a   Nellie M   b   Annie J
c   Goodrich Quigg b Chester, N H, Dec 3, 1848; druggist of Hyde Park; untraced

Ezekiel Dow bcbehh inherited the Plaistow homestead but years later sold it and bought a farm in Hopkinton, conducted as a model, taking first prize as the best farm in the county.   This he exchanged for real estate in Chelsea, Mass, but finally went back to Plaistow; for several years helpless from paralysis; an ardent prohibitionist, Baptist; m 1807 Elizabeth Bradley b 1790, d Oct 30, 1872, dau of John and Elizabeth.   Children:

a   Luther b Mch 7, 1808; d July 10, 1809
b   Elizabeth b 1811; kept house for her parents; their mainstay in old age
c   Elvira, her twin, m 1831 Joshua Merrill of Bedford
d   Martha Bradley b Dec 19, 1813   e   Jesse b Jan 13, 1816
f   Sarah Bradley b Feb 9, 1818   g   Luther Bradley b Apr 26, 1820
h   Catherine b June 23, 1822   i   John Calvin b Nov 9, 1824
j   Gilbert Bradley; known as George; bap on his death bed
k   Harriet A b Dec 30, 1828; teacher of Plaistow, d Dec 14, 1882, unm
l   Jane d young   m   Julia A b 1833

Martha B Dow bcbehhd d 1846; m Rev George W Bailey of Springfield, Vt, b June 19, 1816, several years member of Legislature, supt of schools.   Child:

a   George Byron b 1842; d 1848

Jesse Dow bcbehhe, manufacturer of Cambridgeport, d Jan 10, 1856; m Emeline Patten.

Sarah B Dow bcbehhf d Springfield, Mass, Feb 10, 1877; m June 30, 1839, Louis Frederick Titcomb b Pelham July 8, 1808, son of Pierson and Annie Maria De C (Derniere) of Northfield, Mass.   Four children, of whom:

a   Sarah Elizabeth b Lowell June 26, 1840; d Boston Apr 15, 1895

Luther B Dow bcbehhg, manufacturing confectioner of Portland, Me, d Sept 4, 1854; m Jan 11, 1846, Sarah Ann Lane b Hampton, N H, Dec 25, 1882, d Portland May 28, 1856.   Children:

a   Ida Evelyn b Sept 25, 1849; m Sept 20, 1882, Wales L Edgerton b Langdon,
      N H, Sept 8, 1825, restauranteur of Somerville, Mass
b   Luther Bradley b Portland Sept 20, 1854

Luther B Dow bcbehhgb always followed the sea with home ports Portland, Brooklyn and Boston; for many years treasurer American Association of Mates and Pilots; m July 29, 1876, Lizzie Caroline Bennett b Buckport, Me, May 28, 1854.   He d 1927.   Children:

a   Ethel Viletta b Portland Jan 4, 1878
b   Luther Bradley b Feb 24, 1879; lived Ridgewood, N J; has a family
c   Wilbur Edgerton b Brooklyn Apr 13, 1883

Catherine Dow bcbehhh m 1850 Arnold Otto Waldeck son of O Waldeck, a large land owner in Waldeck, Bavaria. He bought a large tract in Cordova, Ohio, and took his family thither.

John C Dow bcbehhi, trader of Lawrence, Mass, m Dec 3, 1850, Mary Ann Fenno b Boston July 10, 1830, dau of John and Ann Fawcett (Grafton), descendant of Rev John Woodbridge and Gov Joseph Dudley of Mass Bay. Children:

    a   George Grafton b Lawrence July 25, 1852; d Oct 3, 1861
    b   John Calvin b Apr 4, 1854; of Liverpool, Eng. Untraced
    c   Henry Bradley b Apr 8, 1857; d Mch 3, 1859
    d   Frank Prescott b Dec 9, 1859; of Mexico City; unm in 1884
    e   Charles Fenne b Oct 9, 1862; grad Tufts; later of Hanover, N H.   Untraced
    f   Fred Grafton b Feb 27, 1870; electrician and engineer of Lawrence; d Brooklyn,
            N Y, 1893; presumably unm

Gilbert B Dow bcbehhj went to Muscatine, Iowa, many years conductor on the Rock Island; later merchant; m Feb 23, 18—, Mary Ellen Greendycke b Oct 4, 1842, dau of Asa and Louise (Currier). He d Oct 4, 1873; she m 2nd, Mch 10, 1876, Alfred Bishop Brown of Muscatine. Children:

    a   Harriet Augusta b Feb 28, 1862
    b   Edward Harrington b Aug 10, 1866; d Nov 7, 1877
    c   Charles Silverman b Dec 10, 1872

Julia Dow bcbehhm m George Martin Blaker, son of Jesse and Hannah (Woodley); they went south to live.

Peter Dow bcbh, farmer of Plaistow, m Nov 12, 1730, Susannah Page b Haverhill Jan 10, 1709-10, dau of Benjamin Jr and Elizabeth (Lewis). Census 1790 gives 1a, 1c, probably himself and wife, all the children grown up and gone. All the sons who are traced appear in Maine. Plaistow rec give probably all:

    a   Abigail b July 6, 1731   b   Benjamin b Feb 9, 1732-3
    c   Miriam (Meriam, rec) b Mch 31, 1735   d   Peter b Sept 16, 1737
    e   Lydia b Dec 8, 1739
    f   James b Apr 4, 1742; presumably the James serving with other Plaistow men
            1779, Capt Ezekiel Gile; untraced
    g   Joseph b April 4 1742 (Joses, rec)
    h   Susannah b Apr 29, 1744; m 1764 Joseph Treadwell; 2nd Michael Smith
    i   Jeremiah b Mch 31, 1747; presumably the Jeremiah under Capt Kimball taken
            prisoner Ft Washington Nov 16, 1776.   Otherwise untraced
    j   Samuel b Jan 20, 1750; untraced   k   Hephzibah b Apr 26, 1752
    l   Rachel b Dec 14, 1754

Abigail Dow bcbha. She is probably the Abigail m July 17, 1758, Abiel Somerby, both of Newbury. Hampstead gives Abel Somersby. Newbury rec show 4 children:

    a   John b July 16, 1759   b   Abigail b Mch 15, 1762
    c   Rebecca b Feb 7, 1764   d   Abiel b Apr 15, bap Sept 11, 1771

Benjamin Dow bcbhb. As vital rec were not kept in Maine until recently, to have gone as a pioneer thither in Colonial times was to be genealogically lost. Few early church rec are extant. The census returns and an occasional family Bible are all that can be used in tracing lines. Happily, the preservation of a family Bible by Mrs Burroughs bcbhbfba proves the identity, the 1790 census adds and Benjamin's own diary amplifies an account. Family tradition says that Benjamin came from England; we note that a similar tradition runs widely through the b lines, wherever an ancestor becomes untraceable. The family Bible gives Benjamin b Feb 9, 1732, date coinciding exactly. That he served in the Revolution is sure, altho Mass rolls do not give him, nor his son Benjamin, also a veteran, nor, in fact, any Benjamin Dow. Family rec give him in the 4th Me infantry. This last must be error, as there was no Maine, all troops registered from Mass. In 1830, when Benjamin was 98, he applied for a pension, but one would presume this was for an increase. He was then of Penobscot Co. The 1790 census finds him of Vassalboro 1a, 4b, 2c. His son Benjamin was also of Vassalboro 1a, 3b, 2c. From a diary, extracts of which have reached the Author through the miscellaneous papers of Edgar R Dow, he calls himself Benjamin Dow of Lancaster. An entry: "July 17, 1774: the first blow was struck today to fell a tree. We call it Jones Plantation. With me are—Clark, Bely Burrell, Job Chadwick, Michael Norton."

A son of Benjamin Dow served in 1812 under a son of this Job Chadwick. Jones Plantation has become successively Harlem, Fairfax, Ligona, China. It became the home of a family of Benjamin's cousins, mill owners coming from Jefferson. Benjamin was an energetic man. He describes building for himself the first gristmill in the town. The only tools he had were an "old gun-barrell & an adze, and a hollow log composed the floom."

The Author knows no way after the passage of over 20 years of finding the original diary. Presumably it would mention his family, his first and second wife. He m Plaistow about 1754 Deliverance Haseltine, by whom 2 children, perhaps 3. Of his 2nd m nothing appears. We know the oldest child was b 1755, the youngest 1798, the span too great for any woman.

At least 1 more child than here appears:

a Moses b May 12, d Sept 30, 1755
b Abigail b Aug 1, 175-, both Plaistow
c Benjamin b 1763 (date from census) d Jacob
e David. Both known only from mention in family rec. Several families of interior Maine, now unconnected, may have come from them
f Moses b Jones Plantation Dec 8, 1784; rec from his son, hence reliable; was 4th child by 2nd wife
g Isaac b 1798 according to family rec, but date surely earlier, as he was veteran of 1812

Benjamin Dow bcbhbc is little known; of Vassalboro 1790 with wife, 3 sons and a dau. Persistent family tradition says he was also a Rev pensioner, but no such rec. Hist Eliot gives a Benjamin, surely he, m 1782 Elizabeth Moulton. Date seems too early. About 1830 in tax list of Union, family of 4, no names given; in 1850 of Union ae 87 living with Gowen family, presumably with married dau. Beyond much doubt at least two disconnected families of or near Vassalboro belong here.

Moses Dow bcbhbf grew up and married in China; soon after moved to the nearby towns of Albion and Winslow. His son writing 1884 does not give his mother's name. Laborer and carpenter of Winslow, he d May 2, 1864. In 1850 census of Winslow, realty $400; wife Mercy b Me 1790. She proves to be Mercy Lancaster. Census gives 2 children, rest from list given by one of them:

 a Hartwell d in infancy b Mary (Polly b 1812, in census)
 c Dolly living Bangor 1881, Mrs D C Holman d Aaron, untraced
 e David drowned 1889, June 2; body found 2 weeks later; probably lived
  Bangor. Untraced f Elvira living 1881, Mrs Keay of China
 g John Orr b Jan 28, 1822 h Lois B i Isaac J b Winslow Oct 1827

John O Dow bcbhbdfg b Albion, carpenter and school teacher, m Mercy Lancaster, relationship to his mother not stated. They moved to Smyrna, Jefferson Co, Ind. His letter of 1881 gave the above list of brothers and sisters. Children:

 a David Atwell b Litchfield Sept 2, 1852; d Oct 2, 1869
 b John Weston b Apr 17, 1860; horse car conductor Boston, Mass, m Mch 6,
  1883, Emma Alice Sawyer b Charlestown, Mass, Dec 31, 1860. Two
  children, untraced

Isaac J Dow bcbhbfi, cooper of Ashland, Winslow and other nearby towns, d widower Unity Pl Jan 23, 1899, ae 71, 3 mos; m Rosena Trask b Oakland. Doubtless more family than here appears; 3 sons found from own m rec:

 a Andrew Jackson b 1871 b Charles H b 1873
 c Lorenzo Edwin b 1878

Andrew J Dow bcbhbfia, farmer of Albion, m June 30, 1905, Clara A Ridlon, ae 16, dau of Wesley of Albion. He living 1915. Children, all b Albion:

 a Harry Merrill b Aug 15, 1895 b L M (dau) b Oct 9, 1897
 c Rosa Evelyn b Mch 3, 1900 d Wilbur Edward b Sept 18, 1903
 e Ralph W b Feb 7, 1907 f Edwin Cecil b May 27, 1912
 g Irvin Scott b Nov 5, 1914 h Bernice Mattie b Dec 4, 1916

Harry M Dow bcbhbfiaa, laborer of Albion, m May 4, 1918, Doris A Tuttle of Albion, ae 19, dau of Harry E and Agnes (Thompson). Child:

 a Merrill Tuttle b June 20, 1920

Charles H Dow bcbhbfib, fireman of China, m Jan 16, 1908, Grace May Keveen, ae 21, b Rocklanb, dau of John L and Emma A (Pelton).

Lorenzo E Dow bcbhbfic, farmer of Francestown, N H, m June 18, 1902, Gertrude Agnes Colby, ae 24, dau of Daniel A and Mary M K (Hoyt). Children:

 a Arthur Jackson b Aug 25, 1903 b Irene b Nov 15, 1904

c Alice May b Nov 23, 1906   d Carroll Colby b Feb 23, 1909
e Nellie b Sept 16, 1916

Isaac Dow bcbhbg, veteran of 1812, Capt Chadwick 34th Me, m in Maine Jan 2, 1822, Melinda Comstock d Aug 1852. Before 1830 the so-called Holland purchase in western New York was attracting settlers from all New England. About this time Isaac took his family to East Randolph, N Y, thence to Coldspring. Coincidently, a Dow family of bcdec chose the same towns. Isaac m 2nd, Sept 25, 1854, Phebean Cook, by whom 3 children. He d Coldspring Aug 6, 1863. Children:

a Minerva E b Nov 7, 1822; d Mch 23, 1835
b Maryett b Nov 23, 1824   c Nancy H b Oct 3, 1826; d July 1, 1850
d S Harlow b July 1, 1828
e Melinda b Apr 6, 1830; m —— Fisher; d Neb Apr 3, 1865; son,—Addison
   Edward b May 13, 1864, d Apr 6, 1867
f Hannah b Sept 1, 1833; d June 21, 1861
g Orville C b Dec 11, 1835; d Wyoming June 11, 1902; enlisted 9th N Y Cav
   Oct 21, 1861; disch for disability 1862
h Emily L b June 11, 1838; d Nov 22, 1862
i Lyman Giles b Jan 1, 1841; enlisted with his brother; d Nov 19, 1863; bur
   Arlington Nat Cemetery
j Samuel Allen b Apr 26, 1843; d Apr 12, 1862
k Mary E b June 15, 1856   l Frank C b Jan 11, 1859; d Apr 1861
m Agnes b Aug 22, 1862; d Nov 4, 1878

Maryett Dow bcbhbgb m —— Wilson. Two dau:

a Ellen J b May 26, 1850; m June 10, 1869, D S Burroughs; now of Riverside,
   Calif. Only child,—Carrie M b Sept 16, 1874, m Jan 1, 1901, Harry A Mac-
   Clyment, son David b Oct 2, 1906. Mrs Burroughs furnished the line of
   bcbhbg
b Mary Elizabeth b July 26, d Sept 24, 1851

S Harlow Dow bcbhbgd, always known as Harlow, lost his life Apr 20, 1902, on the City of Pittsburg in the Ohio River; m Philadelphia 1853 Carrie May Porter; moved 1853 to Memphis, Tenn. Children:

a Frederick Porter b June 12, 1854; d Salt Lake City 1901; m 1881 Lena Gray.
   No children
b Frances Boyer b Mch 28, 1859

Frances B Dow bcbhbgdb m 1879 Samuel S Savage of Ashland, Ky, d 1902. Children:

a Harlow Dow b 1880; m 1908 Edna Stanhope Wood of Clarksville, Va; 4
   children
b Carrie Porter b 1882; d 1900   c Samuel Stephenson b 1883; d 1884
d Patty Shelby b 1885
e Virginia McCready b 1886; d 1911; m 1907 Edwin Flye Poage; 1 child
f Frances b 1887
g Elizabeth Means b 1889; m 1914 Walter C Nash of Micanite, Colo; 3 children
h Sarah Margaret b 1891

Mary E Dow bcbhbgk m 1874 Newel Barnes. Children:

a Clare Dow b May 6, 1876
b Marie B b Nov 19, 1879; m Robert Payne; 1 child
c Elva Agnes b May 19, 1896

Peter Dow bcbhd enlisted in the 2nd foot company for the Lake George Expedition and drew pay 28£ May 19, 1755. He m Hampstead

Oct 30, **1759**, Elizabeth Huse. First born was at Plaistow; then the family disappears from the place. Hist Essex Co notes a tradition that a Dow was an original settler of Jefferson, Me, but knows no name. It has been printed that this was a son of ahbc, but it has been finally proved otherwise. A great grandson wrote 1889 to Edgar R Dow giving proof that the Jefferson settler was Peter from Plaistow. Years later the Jefferson town clerk reported to the Author that the first mention of Dow there was Peter who had 14 children. This proves to be a son. Census 1790 clinches matters, giving in Ballston Peter Dow Sr 1a, 2b, 2c and Peter Dow Jr 1a, 1b, 2c. Finally, the great grandson gave definitely the names of 3 sons, saying there were other children. It is evident from the census that 2 sons were born later than 1774. Two sons were **gone by 1790 and must be added:**

a Follansbee b Plaistow July 2, 1760 (both parents named in rec). He appears serving 14 days from May 1775, Capt Thomas Mighill, Col Loammi Baldwin, and receiving Nov 30, 1775, extra allowance for an overcoat. Nothing subsequent has appeared concerning him, and, altho there are a few early Dow of Jefferson still unplaced, it is unlikely that he came to that town
b Peter b Feb 17, 1766 (family Bible rec)
c Joshua. A great grandson of Peter gave this name, but he is not definitely known, if at all
d Jeremiah, original settler of Whitefield
e Thomas b 1778, in Jefferson according to above authority. Author doubts that the family reached Me by 1778, too many British ships harassing even coastwise navigation
f ——. A dau is called for in census

Peter Dow bcbhdb is progenitor of almost every Jefferson Dow. He m Mary Kennedy, a Scotch Presbyterian, doubtless an immigrant after 1783. As she was a woman of much character, all descendants agree about her identity. As to dates, children, etc., there is much disagreement. Jefferson town clerk informed us long ago that there were 14 children. In 1918 a descendant was found who named 7 of them. In 1920 another descendant named 4, added some local color, but confused the wife and added a son Joshua. This Joshua, if existent, must be the uncle or an unknown cousin. In 1922 Jefferson vital statistics were published and it is found that the original town clerks were careful and complete. The d rec of Thomas K Dow bcbhdbo says that his father was Peter b China, Me, and was a paper manufacturer, and that Mary Kennedy d China Sept, 1826, ae 60. Obviously this last is error, as she had a child by 1789. A descendant James M Dow wrote in 1881 that Peter was a rake maker of Vienna, d there 1851. A son of Thomas K Dow wrote in 1907 that Peter was b China and had 2 brothers, 4 sisters. However, we can depend on the official rec for the children, noting in each case the discrepancies introduced by descendants:

a Thomas b Nov 23, 1789.
b Elizabeth b Jan 14, 1791. Census 1790 calls for a dau. Possibly Elizabeth is meant and the census taker kept open books for a few extra months. Some dau of Peter m Noah Farnham of Jefferson, but which we do not know
c Jane b Aug 21, 1792. Some dau m —— Costello of Richmond. W N Dow says Jane m —— Newton

d Mary b May 18, 1793 (date impossible). One descendant says she m Joe
    Gazette; another says m —— Barney
e John Kennedy b Mch 1, 1795
f Rebecca b Feb 19, 1797; m Clark, as Rebecca Dow Clark d Jefferson Oct 3,
    1823
g Jeremiah b Nov 2, 1798; surely had middle initial G
h Nelly b Dec 2, 1801; seemingly identical with Eleanor m —— Woodson
    (*fide* W N Dow)
i Fanny b Dec 12, 1803; m Louis Saben, according to W N Dow
j Sally b Nov 28, 1804. Sarah m —— Tilton, according to W N Dow
k Susannah b Nov 21, 1806   l Rosannah b Jan 18, 1808
m Hannah b Aug 20, 1810; m ——Clarke, *fide* W N Dow
n William Newton b Feb 2, 1812; d July 26, 1896
o Thomas Kempis. W N Dow asserts he was younger than himself. This is
    correct. Thomas Dow bebhdba d young. W N Dow also says a sister
    Levina d ae 18.

John K Dow bcbhdbe appears in 1850 census as farmer of Washington, Lincoln Co, realty $1,300; wife Hannah b Me 1797. His son
James M Dow wrote to Edgar R Dow in 1881, at great length, but with
many statements which we cannot reconcile. It was he who gave us
the Joshua Dow of the 6th generation. He wrote that John Kennedy Dow
had had a first wife Comfort Ames who d Calais Jan 7, 1870, and who
bore him 4 sons and 2 dau. This is too circumstantial not to have some
basis of fact. John K Dow m Washington June 12, 1824, Hannah
Boyington, by whom the family hereinunder. To have 6 children and
a divorce at 29 is preposterous. Nor, could it refer to James M Dow
himself, whose m occurred at 25. Who or what is meant we do not know;
we feel sure it has nothing to do with this immediate branch of the family.
The children of John K and Hannah never were good correspondents.
They were alive in 1881, but, as James says, had not written for many
years:

a John b 1825 (properly John W)
b Ensign b 1827; joined the California gold rush in 1849; never came back; unt
c James Madison b Dec 9, 1831   d Leander Alphonso b 1831
    Census 1850 gives them both of Washington, but also gives (doubtless
    duplication) Warren: Madison Dow b Me 1829 and Linder Dow b Me 1831
e Alfred b 1833; living 1881 but never mentioned by any of our informants
f Julia d ae 2   g Phineas

This last name is given by Leander A Dow bcbhdbead, but as Phineas
m 1839, it is impossible, age forbidding. He must have been close kin.

Among the many statements of James Madison Dow in 1881 were
that Peter Dow was b Alna 1751 (both place and date impossible), that
he was a farmer of China, d China, that Polly Kennedy was b Jefferson,
that Uncle Thomas was alive in Mapleton, ae 92 (68!), that Uncle William
was of Minneapolis (true), that Aunt Hannah was of Fairfield (true).
He named 13 children of Peter and Polly (approximately correct), says
Jeremiah and Joshua, sons of bcbhd, both lived Alna. We hope this is
authentic news of Joshua; we know that Jeremiah was always of Whitefield.

John W Dow bcbhdbea d ae 64, m May 24, 1849, Jerusha Aver Hatch d June 3, 1865.   Children:

a   Helena A b May 15, 1852; d June 25, 1866
b   Ava Ann b Dec 30, 1856; d May 9, 1890; m —— Matthews; only child
    resumed name of Dow
c   Mary A b June 31, 1859; living 1926   d   Leander A b Apr 6, 1862

Harry Dow bcbhdbeaba, cooper of Rockport, d before 1926; in Dec 4, 1897, Annie M Carver d Rockport July 7, 1911, ae 39-8-2, dau of Willard G and Lucinda Ann (Shibles); 2nd, Mch 22, 1913, wid Martha Moody ae 55, dau of John and Lavina (Wood) Wood of Northport.   No children.

Leander A Dow bcbhdbead b Somerfield or Enfield (both in rec), interesting personality, lived many places, finally Rockland; followed many trades, preacher, cooper, farmer, laborer, operative; m Alice J Wyman b Waldoborough, d Auburn Dec 25, 1920, ae 5-2-13, dau of William and Lucy (Abbott).   In all 15 children:

a   Terence Powderly b 1888   b   Charles S b Rockland Jan 10, 1892
c   Maude E b Washington July 8, 1893; worker in sardine factory d Nov 8, 1917
d   —— dau b Mch 26, 1895   g   —— dau b Mch 4, 1896
h   Ruth b Rockport Apr 28, 1898
i   George Dewey b Rockville Apr 6, 1899; d Sept 4, 1900
j   Thelda S d Rockville Aug 21, 1900, ae 3 mos, 14 days
k   Leander Allen b Rockland Sept 12, d Sept 28, 1901
l   Bina May d Sept 27, 1903, ae 7 mos
n   Grace E b Rockland Mch 2, 1906   o   Eben C b Warren May 18, 1908

Terence F Dow bcbhdbeada clerk and laborer of Rockland m Sept 8, 1914, Lucy M Wellman, ae 23, dau of O A and Hannah (Athearn). 1st born:

a   Alden Augustus b Rockland May 19, 1916

James M Dow bcbhdbec located in Hartford, Conn, builder and real estate dealer; m Oct 14, 1856, Malleville E Benner b Waldoborough Oct 29, 1834.   Children:

a   Mary Ella b Minneapolis Nov 29, 1857
b   Lizzie M b Hartford Sept 2, 1862; both unm 1881

Leander A Dow bcbhdbed moved in young manhood to Minnesota and for over half his life neglected to communicate with his brothers. Aversion to writing family letters is not uncharacteristic of the whole Dow family and several instances are noted in this Book of sons failing for a score of years to communicate with parents.   Leander m 1857 Mary Louise Chapin; moved 1889 to Washington State; d 1915.   Children, all b Minn:

a   John Kennedy b Dryden Sept 21, 1861
b   Jessie b July 1863; m N C Berlin; lives Kent, Wash
c   Helen Augusta m William Whitaker of Palouse, Wash
d   Edwin of Malott, Wash; m Grace De Lance; has a son De Lance

John K Dow bcbhdbeda for many years well known architect of Spokane m Nov 11, 1885, Sarah Lydia Goodrich, 7th in descent from Capt Miles Standish, having 5 ancestors to support her D A R membership, member of Mass Society of Mayflower Descendants, and with Goodrich line proved to year 870.   Children:

   a   Leander Allen b Minneapolis Nov 9, 1886.   Remarkable coincidence that 2nd cousins, whose parents had never known each other, should bear exactly the same name and this not from any namesake
   b   Doris Stella b Spokane Oct 16, 1889

Leander A Dow bcbhdbedaa grad Mass Inst of Technology, architect of Seattle, m Arlington, Wash, Sept 11, 1921, Ellen Maghan. Child:

   a   Daphne Jean b Seattle June 18, 1925

Doris S Dow bcbhdbedab grad Smith College, m Chicago Aug 1917 Henry Linberger Potter, an editor of the Timberman, Portland, Ore, said by Secy Hoover to be the best informed man in the country on timber. Child:

   a   John Clarkson b Chicago May 15, 1921

Phineas Dow bcbhdbeg is said by Hist Thomaston b 1814, at which time John K Dow was but 19.   He was of Jefferson, moving to Thomaston in young manhood; m (int pub Feb 26, 1839) Delight Young b 1813, d Thomaston Mch 16, 1894, ae 81-6-0, dau of Gideon and Roxie (Reed). Hist Thomaston is brief concerning the family but agrees with census:

   a   Maria b Oct 7, 1839   b   Dana Y b May 4, 1841
   c   Israel b 1843; unt   d   Edwin b 1845
   e   Ebenezer S b Sept 3, 1846; d Sept 17, 1847
   f   Lucy b 1850   g   Emily b about 1854
   h   Ebenezer (called Eben) b about 1857 (Hist Thomaston) (earlier?)

Dana Y Dow bcbhdbegb enlisted 1861 from Thomaston; d Nov 9, 1903; stone mason; m Iantha P Kelly.   Children:

   a   Marian   b   Inez m —— Gillchrist of Brooklyn, N Y

Edwin A Dow bcbhdbegd, identity our guess, m Georgia E Hall; has appeared only in rec of son:

   a   Oliver M d Rockland sail maker unm May 2, 1904, ae 19-1-11

Eben Dow bcbhdbegh is a much less confident guess, for rec of children says b Hingham, Mass.   Traveling salesman of Portland, m Mary E Ross b Portland, d June 13, 1886.   Two children, found by own rec:

   a   Eben b Yarmouth 1874   b   Walter b Portland July 13, 1882

Eben Dow bcbhdbegha, clerk of Portland, m June 4, 1899, Ellen Augusta Elwell, ae 23, dau of Frank and Mary (Boynton).

Walter Dow bcbhdbeghb, druggist of Portland, m Apr 24, 1912,

Nellie Louise Drummond, ae 32, dau of Charles L and Louise M (Daniels).
Letters to both brothers returned 1922 to writer "not found."

Jeremiah R Dow bcbhdbg. All we know of him came from his
grandson and identity quite doubtful; said b N B and his home in Calais
suggests this. No room for him in bcdg family and he is just of age to
fit the missing Jeremiah G Dow. Farmer, his children, his wife said b
Eng:

  a John M b Calais July 1822
  b Lorenzo R pioneer 1849 of Alameda Co, Calif; surveyed and built after 1900
     some railroad line in Los Angeles; had a family; unt
  c Mary J m —— Wellman of Calais or St Stephen
  d Elizabeth m —— Moulton of Augusta
  e Sarah m —— Morrison of Calais or St. Stephen

John M Dow bcbhdbga farmer of Calais and Bowdoinham d Bowdoinham Oct 12, 1894; m Lydia A Smith b Ripley, d Gardiner Apr 1,
1910, ae 88-7-19, dau of Thomas farmer b Mass. Only child:

  a Jerry W b Ripley Mch 22, 1862

Jerry W Dow bcbhdbgaa mill man of Richmond and Gardiner m
Sept 9, 1893, Joanna McCurdy b Boston, ae 18, dau of Christopher and
Dorcas M (Small) of Bowdoinham. Children, b Gardiner:

  a Evilena b Dec 17, 1895   b —— son b Oct 5, 1901
  c Mildred Hazel b Feb 26, (rec says 1907)
  d Dorothy May b May 6, 1907

William N Dow bcbhdbn d Minneapolis July 26, 1896; m Feb 14,
1833, Sarah Wellman b Farmington May 26, 1808, d Mch 28, 1895, dau
of James and Sarah (Francis). James Wellman was for over 50 years
farmer of Farmington. Joseph Francis, father of Sarah, was a sea
captain. The couple moved 1854 to Newport, R I; in 1858 to Iowa City,
where for many years he supervised bridge construction; as bridge builder
served the Govt through the Civil War. The couple lived later years
and celebrated their golden wedding in Minneapolis. He originally a
carpenter, a Baptist and good singer; she a lifelong Methodist. Children, all b New England:

  a William Wellman b Farmington Jan 25, 1834
  b George Washington b Augusta Mch 9, 1835
  c Sarah Melvina b Augusta May 23, 1837
  d Charles Wesley Wellman b Augusta May 17, 1838
  e Mary Ann Rebecca b Lincoln, Mass, July 25, 1840
  f Hannah Frances b Boston Nov 10, 1842
  g Jacob Rollin Neal b Lynn Oct 23, 1845; d Sept 2, 1846
  h Melissa Neal, twin
  i Jacob Rollin Neal b Lawrence Dec 6, 1849

William (Frederick) W Dow bcbhdbna, confectioner, studied medicine and practiced many years in Somverille; d May 8, 1891; m 1st
Vershire, Vt, Apr 11, 1852, Mary Ann Kelly b Thetford Sept 15, 1832,
dau of Abner B and Sophia of Goshen, N H; m 2nd, May 10, 1876,

Sylvia Antoinette Griffin b Guilford, Me, Feb 24, 1844, d Guilford Sept 23, 1893, dau of John Hill and Rosamond (Cushman) Davis. Children:

a Georgiette Kelly b June 26, 1858; d with infant son Apr 13, 1890; m Dr George Stephens
b William Griffin b May 4, d Sept 27, 1877
c Willard Wellman b Sept 26, 1879

Willard W Dow bcbhdbnac grad Mass Inst of Technology; m May 27, 1903, Blanche Estelle Lincoln. Consulting accountant of Boston; res Malden and Waban. Children:

a Sylvia Lincoln b Malden Mch 12, 1904
b Marjorie b Malden Jan 3, 1906   c Willard b Cambridge June 23, 1916

George W Dow bcbhdbnb m 1856 Sarah Katherine Chappel of Newport, R I, d Worthington Apr 10, 1902, ae 64. Carpenter, bridge builder, millwright, he engaged some years in the fruit trade between Spanish ports and the Atlantic coast; in 1858 moved to Iowa City, thence to Kansas City as a dry goods merchant; took in 1873 a Govt homestead in Ransom Tp, Minn; moved 1889 to Worthington. Children:

a Mary Florence b Newport Jan 17, 1857
b Grace Wellman b Iowa City Mch 18, 1859
c Carrie Louise b Dec 10, 1861
d Katherine Estelle b Kansas City Nov 1, 1867
e Gertrude May b Ransom Jan 14, 1875; sang in Methodist choir; now of Modesto, Calif; unm
f Frank Arthur b Ransom Mch 1, 1877
g Fred b Ransom Jan 4, 1880; d ae 4 days

Mary F Dow bcbhdbnba m Herbert Belknap farmer of Ransom; moved to Osakis; d 1917, he soon afterwards. Three children:

a George b Nobles Co; m and has a ranch in Dak or Mont
b Charles; lives Osakis; has sons Harold and Floyd
c Willie d ae 9

Grace W Dow bcbhdbnbb m Worthington May 30, 1878, Frederick Avery Hubbard, son of Avery Douglass and Amy (Dickinson) of Sunderland, Mass. She d Carthage, Mo, June 18, 1916. Children:

a Bessie Agnes b Worthington July 30, 1879; d Carthage Nov 2, 1924; m H C Curtis; no children
b Fred Ernest b Ransom Oct 14, 1880; m Duluth Aug 22, 1914, Albra Griffin; now of Minneapolis; children,—Arthur Griffin, Grace Eugenia, Earl Ernest
c Emma

Carrie L Dow bcbhdbnbc m Apr 7, 1881, Frank Theodore Graves, farmer and county commissioner, b Kinderhook, N Y. He killed by train Mch 14, 1907. She lives Worthington with married dau

a Bertha Louise b July 25, 1882; m Oct 15, 1903, Isaac Alonzo Milton farmer of Ransom, b Belmont, Wis. Children; Edna Claire, Beth Ione
b Roy Edward b 1886; d 1889
c Anna Lois b Sept 26, 1891; grad Hamline univ; m William McKeon Parker. Children,—William Junior, Donald Graves, Burton Joyce
d Arthur Fred b Apr 1, 1893; m 1917 Mabel Nicklas of Worthington; moved to Tallulah, La. Children,—Frank Arthur, Robert Nicklas

Katherine E Dow bcbhdbnbd m Worthington Dec 1891 James W. Crandall, son of Edwin G and Laura (Willis); moved to San Diego, thence to Newkirk, Okla, now of Denver, Colo. He d Oct 26, 1913. Children:

   a Bertie Royce b Nov 15, 1893; m May 21, 1916, Douglas, Wyo, Mildred S Skelton. Auto salesman; has 1 son
   b Beatrice Estelle b Oct 26, 1895; m Cheyenne, Wyo, June 9, 1919, James Keating; now of Denver. Child,—James Crandall

Frank A Dow bcbhdbnbf m Worthington Dec 15, 1898, Mabel Harriet Dunham b Delevan, Wis, Sept 5, 1880. Now a miller of Sioux City. Eleven children:

   a Frank Howard b Worthington Sept 29, 1899; optician of Sioux City; m Elk Point, S D, Aug 30, 1920, Agnes Marie Corcoran b Cascade, Neb, Aug 3, 1905
   b Lloyd Ernest b June 25, 1901; broom maker of Sioux City; m Elk Point, S D, Sept 18, 1924, Laura Violet Washburn
   c Everett Verner b Mch 14, 1903; auto top trimmer of Sioux City; m Elk Point Nov 27, 1925, Helen Marguerite Corcoran b Omaha May 3, 1908
   d Louis Leland b Sept 2, 1904; brush maker of Sioux City; m Sioux City May 27, 1922, Florence Mae Clark b June 20, 1905. Child,—Louis Frank b Nov 15, 1923
   e Blanche Corinne b May 11, 1906; m Elk Point Apr 5, 1924, Robert Edward Bryans
   f Marguerite Georgia b Feb 11, 1908   g Grayce Viviene b Dec 14, 1909
   h George Wellman b Sept 23, 1911
   i Shirley Clarice b Jan 5, 1914; d Mch 28, 1915
   j Robert Neal b Nov 22, 1915   k Richard Claire b Feb 2, 1918

Sarah M Dow bcbndbnc m Nov 23, 1870, Wilson Shannon Atkinson professor of mathematics in Hiram College, Ohio, who entered journalism but d Minneapolis about 1879. She d June 16, 1926, ae 89. She and several sisters had unusually good voices and musical ability characterizes the whole bcbhdbn line. Children:

   a Frederick b about 1871; married, farmer of Amidon, N D
   b Frank b about 1873; d ae 19
   c Bertha; unm, of New London, Conn, Washington, D C, and Minneapolis; d 1921

Charles W W Dow bcbhdbnd learned the upholstering trade in the East but on coming west preferred a more adventurous life. He joined the gold rush to Pike's Peak 1858 and went with Gen John C Fremont in the transcontinental railroad survey. In 1859 he was campaigning against the Navajos in New Mexico. When the war broke out in 1861 he rode his pony 1,000 miles from Sante Fe, twice escaping the hostile Sioux, to Iowa City in time to join the 1st Iowa Cavalry. Made 1st sgt Sept 1, 1862. His command of a platoon at the famous moonlight midnight charge against Newton's reg at Jackson, Mo, brought promotion to 2nd Lieut July 18, 1863. A bullet wound in the head Apr 4, 1864, put him out of commission but a short time and he was promoted to 1st Lieut Feb 7, 1865. Policing service on the border kept him in service until Feb 28, 1866. While on leave he m Apr 30, 1865, Lucy Emeline North b Ohio May 18, 1844, dau of William from Hartford, Conn, and Welthy (Weed) from N Y State. She grad Univ of Iowa City. The day school in Nanchang, China, is named in her memory. In 1872 they took up a homestead in Nobles Co, moving 1900 to Worthington. At their golden wedding 12 of 13 children were present. She d Mch 20, 1919; he Oct 11, 1920. He had served under Fremont, Lyons, Siegel, Rosecrans and finally Custer. A mason and member of G A R, he served 4 years as judge of Probate and 33 years as justice of the peace. Children:

a Lounita Le North b Dec 10, 1866; d Apr 16, 1916
b William North b Jan 18, 1868; farmer, m Nov 29, 1899, Lizzie Florence Fengar b Conn Feb 24, 1873, dau of Thomas J and Mary Warner (Holt). Now shipping clerk of New London, Conn. No children
c Sarah Leona b Mch 20, 1869　　　d Ida Francois b Apr 15, 1871
e Minnie Myrtle b Minn Mch 26, 1873
f La Reina b Aug 1, 1875; graduate nurse; m Sept 14, 1916, Walter Davis, banker of Clarkston, Wash, d Oct 22, 1917. No children
g Cara Belle b Aug 7, 1877; school teacher, lived with her parents as long as they lived; now of Worthington, unm
h Don Carlos b Apr 26, 1879　　i Georgiette b Apr 3, 1881
j Cora May b Aug 22, 1883　　k Dora, twin
l Charles Fremont b Nov 4, 1885　　m Neal Ellis b Sept 21, 1890

Lounita L Dow bcbhdbnda teacher m June 22, 1898, Charles Edwin Boddy b Chicago Mch 15, 1870, grain buyer, chicken rancher, carpenter. Lived Rushmore. Children:

a Helen b Minneapolis July 25, 1908; d Mch 28, 1911
b Evelyn b Aug 13, 1909; in high school 1926

Sarah L Dow bcbhdbndc taught school until she m Feb 21, 1889, John Donald Pettit of Rushmore b Ill Dec 3, 1865, son of Joseph Addison b N Y and Mary Elizabeth (Miller) b Ill. Farmer, merchant, postmaster. He d Apr 3, 1924. She is now postmaster at Backoo, N D. Children:

a Pearl Florence b Apr 14, 1890; m Nov 26, 1914, Malcolm Greenwood of Crystal, N D. Seven children
b Ruby b Aug 13, 1891; m Oct 22, 1919, Lee Mountain Hillis of Backoo; 2 children
c Marian Lucille b Aug 4, 1895; m Oct 15, 1925, George Oscar Reck of Danube, Minn
d Leon Hartzell b Aug 20, 1897; m June 25, 1919, Ines Maud Harding; 3 children
e Wellman Donald b May 21, 1901; m June 13, 1925, Alice Grace Daby
f Marjorie Grace b Feb 1, 1913; d Feb 13, 1913

Ida F Dow bcbhdbndd taught and nursed until she m Nov 24, 1898, John Thomas Milton b Eng, d Dec 26, 1905, son of Isaac and Ellen (Cole), farmer and power house engineer. She m 2nd, June 2, 1913, Harry H Jackson farmer of Worthington, d June 29, 1918; m 3rd, Sept 2, 1920, George W James of Wagner, S D. Now of St Paul. Children:

a Verna b Aug 6, 1899; grad nurse; m May 18, 1915, Russell O Cooper. Dau, —Lois and June
b Lillian b May 15, 1901; m Dec 20, 1920, Arthur Woelfle, cheese mfgr; soprano singer; in 1926 completing hospital course in nursing; no children
c Floyd b Apr 14, 1904; farmer m Nov 20, 1925, Florence Larson of Worthington; 1 dau
d Florence, twin, m Mch 20, 1923, Elmer J Willson, grain solicitor. She and her sister are radio singers in Minneapolis

Minnie M Dow bcbhdbnde taught for 9 years; m Nov 11, 1903, Alexander Walker b Scotland Feb 24, 1852, son of Robert and Annie (Allenach). For 25 years he has been pres of Magnolia State Bank; 22 years treas and mgr of Farmers Elevator Co, County Commissioner, etc. She is church organist and has headed the Ladies' Aid Society since she organized it 23 years ago. No children.

La Reina Dow bcbhdbndf m 2nd, Jan 18, 1923, Clarence Hudson Old b Cornwall, Eng, May 1, 1871, rancher of Conrad, Mont.

Don Carlos Dow bcbhdbndh taught and worked his way through Univ of Minn; grad 1905; grad College of Law 1906; located Pullman, Wash; has been some years city attorney; m Mch 16, 1910, Elizabeth Thayer b Me, of Minn. Children:

    a Wesley Carlos b Nov 21, 1910   b Vernon Thayer b Feb 2, 1912
    c Glidden North b May 18, 1914   d Winnifred Elizabeth b Mch 20, 1917
    e Delmar Whitman b July 10, 1923

Georgiette Dow bcbhdbndi taught for a year; m June 27, 1900, Guy Otis Bigelow of Worthington b Conn, for 25 years engineer on the Omaha; of Pipestone, Minn. Both are accomplished singers. Children:

    a Guy Mercelon b Apr 28, 1901; grad Univ of Minn; m Sept 20, 1923, Dorothy
       Myers, dau of Rev M R and Lulu (Birkett); dau,—Jane Jaquelin and Janice
       Dorothy
    b Vera La Rene b June 24, 1903; m Sept 5, 1922, John C Hagge motor dealer,
       son of Thomas. Child,—Betty Jean
    c Willard Otis b June 18, 1905   d Abbie Irene b Jan 6, 1907
    e Lois Virginia b Apr 10, 1911   f Donald Vernon b May 6, 1918

Cora Dow bcbhdbndj taught for over 10 years; m Jan 21, 1914, Herman William Oesterreich b Stettin, Germany, Feb 24, 1883, son of Rudolph and Amelia. He is upholstery foreman at Superior, Wis. She is an artist and both are solo singers. Children:

    a Jean Barbara b Nov 16, 1914   b Cora Leona b Nov 29, 1917
    c Helen Joyce b Oct 1, 1919

Dora Dow bcbhdbndk m Jan 30, 1902, Walter Harold Paine, farmer of Worthington and teacher, son of James Monroe. Invalid 12 years, he d Aug 12, 1925. She now hospital nurse and caring for her own large family.

    a Cora Lucile b Sept 30, 1902; d Nov 26, 1908
    b Dora Jurene b Dec 25, 1903; d Jan 8, 1904
    c Doris Genevieve b Apr 27, 1906; teacher, high soprano radio singer
    d Wesley Walter b Dec 4, 1908   e Lyle Everett b Apr 16, 1909
    f Raymond Dow b Mch 2, 1913   g Fremont Howard b June 14, 1911
    h Dorothy Arlonine b Mch 8, 1916   i James Monroe b Jan 23, 1919
    j Hazel Marguerite b May 26, 1923

Charles F Dow bcbhdbndl grad Univ of Minn 1908; m July 14, 1914, Crystal Lehman b July 24, 1887, dau of August b Germany and

Helena (Bauer); now has a dairy and high grade Guernsey ranch at Downing, Wis.   Children:

a ——— b and d Oct 23, 1916   b   Willard Neal b Sept 14, 1917
c   Robert L b Sept 12, 1919; d Dec 28, 1923
d   Charles Wellman b June 15, 1921   e   Helen Lucille b Oct 31, 1924

Neal E Dow bcbhdbndm grad Hamline Univ and Univ of Minn Law School; served in coast defense 1918; practiced law in partnership with his brother in Pullman; now of Culver City, Calif, practicing in Los Angeles; m Feb 2, 1918, Bessie Elliott b Ogden, Ia, July 21, 1891, grad Hamline Univ, high school teacher and musician.   Children:

a   Doris Louise b Feb 22, 1919   b   Virginia Irene b Sept 27, 1921
c   Mary Jean b Aug 11, 1923   d   Evelyn Harriet b Jan 23, 1925

Mary A R Dow bcbhdbne d 1920; m Oct 29, 1859, Arthur William Briggs, merchant, who d; m 2nd, Frank M Ellis D D, Baptist clergyman of Tremont Temple, Boston, Brooklyn, Denver and elsewhere.   No children by 2nd m.   Dr Ellis has a dau by 1st m.   Children:

a   Charles Arthur b Feb 22, 1862; m Dec 18, 1889, Anna G Woods; now merchant
     of Oroville, Calif.   Child,—Frances Marion
b   Frederick F; now a Baptist clergyman of Baltimore

Hannah F Dow bcbhdbnf m Dec 25, 1862, Willard Abner Clarke of Iowa City.   He d, she now of San Diego, Calif.   Children:

a   Ralph Louis b Jan 25, 1864; electrician of San Diego; not now living; m Leah
     ———
b   Harry b Sept 7, 1866; d National City Calif, May 5, 1925; m ———
c   Gertrude; grad New England Conservatory of Music; m R L Edwards
d   Grace Estelle; actress; m ———

Melissa N Dow bcbhdbnh m May 3, 1863, John Boyd Haddock b Wilmington, Del, Mch 18, 1840, d Minneapolis Nov 20, 1922, banker and special insurance agent in Minn and Iowa.   Children:

a   Agnes b and d May 18, 1864
b   Lillian Agnes b Aug 15, 1866; m June 15, 1887, J Curtis Moore b Fairview, Pa,
     Dec 6, 1861, d Minneapolis June 17, 1919.   He was a reclaimer of the Florida
     everglades.   Children,—Lillian Marguerite, Bonnie Jean, Harold Barry,
     Robert Haddock, Grace Elizabeth
c   John Howard b Jan 1, 1869; m Kate Spiess McCann; only son d young
d   Anna Mabel b Sept 14, 1870; m Omaha Feb 6, 1894, Frederick A Savage.
     Children,—Elizabeth L m Harold Lovelace Kelley (4 children), Frederick
e   Royal Wellman b Dec 11, 1874; m Minneapolis Oct 9, 1897, Maude E Duffy;
     2nd Clara Emerich of Brooklyn; 2 children
f   Emma Theodora b Mch 29, 1876; m St Paul Nov 11, 1896, Louis C Beindorff
     of Omaha; 2 children
g   Mildred b Dec 22, 1880; d Jan 22, 1881
h   Robert Lightner b May 25, 1884; m Minneapolis June 3, 1906, Florence E
     Hedborg; 2 children; now of Earlington, Wash

Jacob R N Dow bcbhdbni, druggist of Minneapolis and Butte, d Butte Oct 11, 1889; m Minneapolis June 25, 1879, May A Drakeson b Fond du Lac, Wis, Aug 28, 1859.   Children:

a   Rollin Neal b Minneapolis June 1, 1880, grad Univ of Minn; m 1905 a Miss
     Horthy of Hibbing, Minn; has 2 children; a well known business man of
     Minneapolis

   b Sarah Melissa b Oct 26, 1881; grad Winona Normal School; teacher; m Paul
      Heard, son of Rev C M Heard of Minneapolis; 1 child
   c William Leonard b June 2, d June 20, 1886
   d Clarence Arthur b Jan 15, 1888; grad Univ of Minn; electrician of Minneapolis;
      m ——; 3 children

Thomas K Dow bcbhdbo moved to Mapleton, Newcastle or Vienna, all named in some rec or other. He d farmer of Newcastle Oct 16, 1897, ae 83-11-14. This agrees perfectly with the statement of his brother. Census 1850 showed him farmer of Vienna, realty $1,400, above the average. He m Pelma Clark b China, d Mapleton. Family rec says she d 1853, clearly wrong by at least a year. Census 1850 gave her Pelena b Me 1814. Census names 6 children, 7th by family rec:

   a Charles Edward (Edwin, census) b Vienna 1839   b Henry b 1840; unt
   c Mary b 1843   d Samuel b 1846; unt   e Lydia b 1848
   f Lavina b 1849
   g John B b Oct 20, 1854 (both China and Vienna in rec)

Charles E Dow bcbhdboa appears many times from 1892 in vital statistics as attending physician; served as army surgeon 1862-5; m Aug 1862 Clara E Spooner b Princeton, Me, d Melrose, Mass, Jan 27, 1911, ae 71-9-3. In 1907 he wrote briefly to Edgar R Dow, but made no mention of children.

John B Dow bcbhdbog, farmer of Castle Hill, m Ella L Smith b Charlotte, d Oct 14, 1900, dau of Isaiah and —— (Lakin). He d Nov 10, 1909, accident while sinking a rock. Older children not found, younger b Castle Hill:

   e Manley E b 1886   f Thomas E b 1888   g John H b about 1890
   h Joy E b Oct 2, 1893   i Percie M b Feb 25, 1897

Manley E Dow bcbhdboge, farmer of Castle Hill, apparently moved to Mapleton after 1913; m Dec 31, 1907, Ella May Ridgewell, ae 18 b N B, dau of Stephen and Izetta (Orphan). Children, 3 younger b Mapleton:

   a —— dau b Mch 31, 1909   b Evelyn Madeline b June 1, 1911
   c Muriel Pearl b Jan 26, 1913   d —— son b Nov 4, 1915
   e —— dau b Oct 21, 1917   f Edwin Stephen b Nov 11, 1919

Thomas E Dow bcbhdbogf, farmer of Castle Hill, seems also to have moved to Mapleton; m Elizabeth A (Isabella in one rec) Carter b 1887, dau of William E and Estella A (Foster). Younger children b Mapleton:

   a —— son b Mapleton Dec 4, 1906   c —— son b Feb 13, 1910
   d —— dau b Sept 27, 1912   g Thomas Russell b Jan 21, 1916
   h Delbert Warren b Aug 1, 1917   i —— son b Dec 23, 1918

John H Dow bcbhdbogg farmer of Castle Hill m Aug 31, 1912, Laura E Grindell, ae 17, dau of Henry and Emma (Casey). Children:

   a —— dau b Aug 27, 1913   b Biron Thomas b Nov 2, 1914

Jeremiah Dow bcbhdd apprenticed as a blacksmith, having mastered his trade, m Rebecca Glidden b Lincoln Co, and set up a shop in Whitefield, a place still known as Dow's Corner. Here they lived to old age. Census 1850 gives no help, the children m and gone. In 1918 a great grandson was found in Howland, who named 4 sons, reporting there were in all 9 sons, 4 dau. In 1926 the Author got a list compiled many years ago by a descendant, Rev Charles W Lowell, Methodist minister, then of Castine. This seems complete:

a	Moses b Dec 7, 1798	b	Alexander b Feb 2, 1800
c	Jeremiah b Feb 15, 1802	d	Thankful b July 28, 1803
e	Jonathan b Mch 12, 1805	f	William b Jan 31, 1807
g	Peter b Nov 7, 1808	h	Abigail b Mch 22, 1811
i	Rebecca b July 27, 1815	j	Hannah b Jan 27, 1819

Moses Dow bcbhdda, carpenter of Somerville and Argyle, d comparatively young; m 1st Thankful Shepard, of whom it was said that she was "educated." In fact, she had taught school and liked her books. She d leaving 5 children. He m 2nd, Rachel Hunt b Belfast 1807. In one rec she appears as Rachel Heath, clerical error. She lived to old age with her son Peter; appears in census 1850 as wid of Windsor, realty $250. Census gives the children, 3 dau having m or d young:

a George Washington b 1829; grad Brown Univ 1855; taught in Moline, Ill, then became manufacturer of writing fluids. For many years he corresponded regularly with the family in Argyle. Impression rests that he left no posterity

b Elizabeth b 1829; known from census only   c Thankful m ——

f Peter b Somerville 1833   g William Hunt b Mch 10, 1835

h Abigail b 1837; d unm   i John E B Whitefield 1839

j Mary b 1841; many years a dressmaker in Augusta; d 1907; m Leslie Weeks of Jefferson; no children

Peter Dow bcbhddaf came to Argyle for a year or two from 1866, but went back and spent the rest of his life at Cooper's Mills, a short distance from Dow's Corner. Farmer, he m Anne Elizabeth Benjamin b Whitefield. Children:

a Benjamin (family rec gives Beniar) (Beniah?) B Carpenter m, d tuberculosis June 1, 1896, ae 24-6-3. No children. Whitefield rec gives him A B Dow and does not mention wife

b Nellie May m R V Cary; only child,—Marion m ——

c Minnie Adelaide m George Fowles; only child,—Neota in high school 1926

d Winnifred Etta d Whitefield Sept 11, 1902, ae 23-4-28, unm

William H Dow bcbhddag settled in Orono the year the railroad was built, but came by stage because it was quicker; soon after moved to Argyle; m Mary Foster, who d leaving 1 child; m 2nd, Matilda Danforth b Argyle. The 200-acre Danforth homestead is still owned by her son. She d 1871; he m 3rd, Lucy Ballard; 2 children. Again a widower, he went to live with married dau in Old Town, d there June 11, 1916. Children:

a Abbie Inez b July 19, 1862

b Franklin Augustus b Argyle Mch 23, 1864

c d and e —— d in infancy   f Abner William

g   Nancy Jane m Edward G Fink; live Westfield, N J. Only child,—Inez M m
    Walter Baird Jr of Westfield, has a son,—Robert Lionel

Abbie I Dow bcbhddaga m Walter W Spencer; live Old Town, Me;
has given no little aid on her own line.   Children:

a   Winfield; lives Old Town; m Leila Dow bcbhddagbe
b   Walter A m Angie Wheeler; children,—Vaughn and Velma
c   William R, treas Fay & Scott Machine Shop, m Hazel Slater. Child,—Barbara

Frank A Dow bcbhddagb is also interested in his family history;
spent 2 years in N J and one in Gardner, Mass, but found better opportunities near his old home; moved 1918 from Argyle to Howland, Lumberman; m 1st, 1883, Mattie B Freeman; div; m 2nd, Dec 7, 1898, Maud
L Nason, ae 19, b N B, dau of Daniel and Nancy (Craig).   Children:

a and b —— sons d in infancy
c   Myra Mayfair b Dec 26, 1886; grad nurse Jefferson Hospital, Philadelphia;
    m Thomas Gillingham; now of Miami, Fla. Sons,—Gordon Dow, Dexter
    Davis
d   Fred Waldo d Oct 6, 1901, ae 11 mos, 2 days
e   William Franklin b Oct 21, 1901
f   Gardys Venona b Mch 20, 1904; m Albert Edward Bickford of Me; has,—
    Merl Edward b 1923 and —— dau b 1925
g   Wallace Gilmore b June 30, 1906   h   Thelma Dorothy b Aug 11, 1909
i   Herbert Russell b Old Town Jan 7, 1915
j   Walter Gillingham b Howland Oct 19, 1918
k   Inez Theresa b July 19, 1922

William F Dow bcbhddagbe m Bessie Agnes Curtis b Lowell 1901.
Children:

a   Verlie Veldine b 1921   b   Irene

William Abner Dow bcbhddagf of Westfield, N J, m Minnie Brown;
2nd, Nettie Hultz.   Two children by each:

a   William Edward b Apr 28, 1896; unm
b   Robert S b June 10, 1897; m and has 1 child; both live N J

John Erskine Dow bcbhddai farmer of Argyle d Aug 5, 1918; m
Lucinda Grant of Argyle d Apr 25, 1926.   Children:

a   Charles William b June 8, 1861; m Aug 30, 1884, Harriet Freeze, dau of
    Gilbert Warren and Martha A (Lowe). No children
b   Sewall E b July 8, 1866

Sewall E Dow bcbhddaib of Argyle, riverman, mail carrier, laborer,
farmer, runner, general agent, m Alice M Mann of Argyle d Aug 24,
1896, ae 25-1-5, dau of Isaac and Melissa J (Orr); m 2nd, Bangor, May
9, 1898, Mamie Judkins of Alton, ae 16, d June 10, 1908, dau of Hiram
and Eva (Hinckley); m 3rd, Old Town Dec 9, 1916, Dora Edna Jones,
div, ae 28, dau of Lester and Ada May (Tilton) Skillin.   Children:

a   Myrtie May b Feb 11, 1889   b   Florence Mabel b July 18, 1891
c   Alice Flora b Aug 21, 1896   d   George A b Aug 21, 1896; d Sept 28, 1897
e   Lila Fern b Apr 15, 1901; m Winfield Spencer bcbhddagaa; has made many
    additions and corrections to this line
f   Lloyd Elmer b Nov 21, 1903; m Nov 28, 1925, Paulina Walters of Milford
g   Arline Beatrice b Sept 19, d Oct 16, 1905

Myrtie M Dow bcbhddaiba m Nov 11, 1908, Merle Leon Stormann of Stillwater, Me. Children:

a   Florence Mae b Sept 2, 1910
b   Eugene Elmer b Jan 16, 1912
c   Clyde Dow b Aug 23, 1914
d   Phyllis Frances b Dec 27, 1918
e   Corinne Doris b Sept 12, 1920
f   Merle Leon b Oct 2, 1922
g   Lawrence Wesley b July 6, 1925

Florence M Dow bcbhddaibb m Apr 26, 1913, Manson Crosby of Howland. Child:

a   Sewall Elmer b Dec 7, 1913

Alice F Dow bcbhddaibc m Dec 7, 1915, Elmer L Bradford of Argyle. Children:

a   Vertilee Linda b June 4, 1917
b   George Lloyd b Apr 20, 1919
c   Lila Alice b Apr 15, 1921
d   Charles Edward b Sept 5, 1923
e   John Dow b June 16, 1925

Alexander Dow bcbhddb bought a farm near Palermo; m Susan Heald b Jefferson. Two children found from own rec; 3rd, a conjecture:

a   Alexander S b Palermo Feb 16, 1838
b   Weston W b Palermo 1845   c   James P b about 1848

Alexander S Dow bcbhddba, carpenter, spent his last 2 years in Gardner, coming from E Machias; d June 9, 1900; m Annie Leaman of Liberty; m 2nd, Great Falls, N H, June 13, 1875, Izoza Z Prescott b 1847, dau of Eben P and Susan of Liberty. Vital statistics were not collected in Me prior to 1892 and only sources of information are personal recollections, church rec or family Bibles. Whenever we say "one child found" it is possible that any number more were born:

a   Fred A b Providence, R I, 1873

Fred A Dow bcbhddbaa, carpenter of Waterville, m July 25, 1904, Martha J Bragg, weaver of Vassalboro, ae 24, dau of Samuel and Mary (Brown); div; m 2nd, Mch 31, 1917, Viva M Gordon, div, ae 24, dau of Robert and Helen (Gordon) Martin.

Weston W Dow bcbhddbb, blacksmith of Palermo, d married Washington, D C, Oct 10, 1910, ae 65-5-9; m Lizzie May (Mary Elizabeth) Fowler. One child found:

a   Earl Walden b 1876-7

Earl W Dow bcbhddbba, shoemaker of Randolph and Lewiston; m Feb 23, 1901, Ethel M Buker b Richmond 1880, dau of Melvin G and ·Maria (Alexander); div; m 2nd, Lewiston May 24, 1913, Gertrude Frances Pease b Lewiston 1880, wid, dau of Christopher and Frances (Gosson) b Eng. Children:

a   Melvin Buker b Richmond Nov 14, 1903
b   Gertrude Elizabeth b Lewiston Feb 18, 1920

James P Dow bcbhddbc m Susan L Belding b Palermo; moved to

Albion; later farmer of Chelsea, Mass; d about 1878. Children, by own rec:

 a   Fred B b Vassalboro June 14, 1873   b   Charles H b Albion 1874
 c   Ellen May b Vassalboro June 10, 1876; living Mass 1923

Fred B Dow bcbhddbca, barber of Wilmot, N H, d June 16, 1904; m Concord July 13, 1899, Delia M Hubbard, ae 23, of Worcester, Mass, dau of George and Lavina (Kenniston); left 2 dau, of whom:

 b   Marion P b Worcester Mch 14, 1902

Charles H Dow bcbhddbcb, mill man of Corinna, Me, m Oct 16, 1904, Addie F Burrill, ae 18, dau of Daniel S and Zetta (Robinson) of Bangor. Children, all but 1 b Corinna:

 a   Herbert E b Bangor Dec 15, 1904   b   George Fredora b Apr 13, 1906
 c   Charles Alton b Oct 14, 1907   d   Lillian Frances b Dec 30, 1909
 e   Ninette May b Nov 14, 1911   f   Levinia Adell b Sept 3, 1914
 g   Leslie James d Feb 9, 1919, ae 1-9-4   h   Carolyn Olive b Oct 19, 1920

Jeremiah Dow bcbhddc said by a granddau to be 9th child, settled near by; m Sarah Glidden. To them 9 children:

 a   Harry F
 b   Waterman L m Mary Place; no children; now has a hotel at Cooper's Mills
 c   Isaiah M; now farmer of Edgewood, Calif; m Roxana Dobkin; 1 child—
       Clarence
 d   Clara A m Lincoln Turner of Palermo d Jan 13, 1926. Children,—Waterman D
       d ae 2,   Mabel
 e   Hannah P d young   f   Addie A d young

Harry F Dow bcbhddca b Somerville, farmer of Jefferson, m Laura E Plummer d Jefferson Mch 24, 1907, ae 53-6-1, dau of William and Caroline (Eaton). Children:

 a   Florence b Dec 15, 1884, teacher, m Fred O Meserve; now have a hotel at
       Damariscotta Lake, Jefferson, wintering in Fla. One child,—Laura H
 b   Harold E b Sept 30, 1888   c   Clara E b May 7, 1893; unm

Harold E Dow bcbhddcab, farmer of Jefferson, m Jan 4, 1919, Berenice M Cunningham, ae 27, dau of William and Mary E (Cooper). Children:

 a   Edwina May b Washington Feb 3, 1919
 b   Winona Louise b Jefferson Aug 23, 1923

Thankful Dow bcbhddd m Dec 25, 1827, Charles Lowell of Alna, veteran of 1812, and for many years drew a widow's pension. Had considerable family. A grandson, Rev Charles W Lowell, took from the, family Bible a transcript of the children of bcbhdd.

Jonathan Dow bcbhdde may be untraced but is probably the Jonathan known only from son's rec,— b Pittston, laborer, m Jennie Hervey b Dallas Pl. Presumably other children:

 a   William S b Avon 1826; farmer, widower, d Avon Sept 10, 1910. Presumably
       a posterity

William Dow bcbhddf m Susan Plummer. Children:

a Isaac'd unm   b Jonathan d unm
c Charles m Melissa Heal; farmer d Jefferson Apr 11, 1905, ae 68-4-16; no children

Peter Dow bcbhddg lived some time in Pittsfield, then Damariscotta, finally buying a farm in Perham. Jefferson tradition mentions that some Dow went to Perham as a pioneer. It is still a mooted question whether a contemporaneous Henry Dow, pioneer of Perham, was akin. Peter d Perham Jan 4, 1896; m Mary Elizabeth Turner b N B, d Perham Feb 10, 1892, ae 74, dau of James b Eng and Eunice (Hanson). Children, not at all in correct order:

a Augustus   b Warren; unt   c Seth; unt
d Zimri; unt; probably all went west
e Stillman; in 1924 only living member of his generation; living Astoria, Ore, with Mrs Anna Ford, presumably his dau
f Victoria m —— Shaw of Victoria Corner, N B
g Octavia m —— Hanson; 2nd —— Tobie of Wade
h Abigail m —— Oliver of Perham   i Jessie, of Perham
j Rebecca m —— Roberts of Kennebeck Co

Augustus Dow bcbhddga b Calais, d Feb 10, 1895, farmer of Perham; m Mary E Rogers b N B, of Wade, d Perham Dec 19, 1919, dau of Amaziah and Lucy (Dickinson). Note how frequently these names occur in the bcdgd line of New Brunswick Dow. Two children, b Perham:

a Ruel A b 1881   b Walter E b 1883

Ruel A Dow bcbhddgaa, farmer of Wade Pl, m Laura Kidney b N B 1884, dau of James and Lydia (Howe). Children:

a Lillian Pearl b Nov 9, 1903   b Marion Louise b Aug 1, 1907
c Linwood Malcolm b Apr 23, 1909   d Kenneth Leroy b Feb 12, 1915
e Malcolm Ruel b Aug 29, 1922

Walter E Dow bcbhddgab, farmer of Woodland, moved to Washburn; m Aug 15, 1903, Harriet R Everett, ae 17, dau of Daniel and Persis (Bennett). Children:

a Elwyn E b Woodland Mch 15, 1904; now of Burbank, Calif
b Wilda Persis b Mch 13, 1908
c Avis Mae b Wade June 19, 1910   d —— dau b Dec 10, 1914

Hannah Lull Dow bcbhddj m May 10, 1834, Alexander Erskine b July 8, 1808, son of John and Margaret (Bryant). He lived Pittston until 1884; veteran of 1st Me Battery; d in the South (cf Erskine Gen). Children:

a Lloyd Quimby b Jan 3, 1835; vet of Civil War ; m Sarah A Savage
b Julia Maria b Mch 16, 1837
c Caroline Dow b Sept 1, 1839; m June 22, 1861, James Grover Jr of Wiscasset
d Fairfield b Feb 21, 1841; vet of Civil War
e Edward Alexander b Sept 16, 1842; d Sept 1843
f Rebecca Abbie b Dec 25, 1843; d Sept 1844
g John Franklin b Mch 7, 1845; d Detroit, Mich
h Alexander Edward b Nov 1847; d Towle, Calif
i Mary Ellen b Apr 23, 1849; lived Portland, Ore

> j Abbie Rebecca b Mch 31, 1850; m ——— Simpson
> k Cyrus Henry b Mch 11, 1852   l Isaac Austin b Feb 16, 1855; d Towle
> m Clara Belle b Mch 30, 1857; living Ore 1918
> n Sewall Rogers b July 31, 1858

Thomas Dow bcbhde m by 1803 Ruth Brooking, dau of Eben of Woolwich. His experience was one of the many which brought on the War of 1812. British frigates were then accustomed to recruit their seamen in complete disregard of whether or not they were British subjects, and few men thus shanghaied ever returned to tell the tale. Thomas was seized one day on shore by a press gang which included the ship's captain. His cries brought friends, but they had no weapons. Several friends took boats and rowed not far away. Thomas attacked the captain in his open boat, the crew either unable or unwilling to interfere successfully. Thomas either killed or disabled the captain, he never knew which, swam to a friend's dory and returned safe to his wife. They had the family usual to the time, list perfectly authenticated, all reaching maturity:

> a Eben m Martha Clark   b Peter m Eliza Whitehouse
> c Thomas m Hannah Rankin
> d Elizabeth m Charles Sidelinger   e Esther m Edward Monk
> f Cushing m Mary A Plummer; unt
> g Mary A b 1818; m Edward E Follansbee. This name has followed the bcbhd
>   line since 1760 (cf bcbhda)
> h Joseph m Eliza Merry   i John m Mary E King
> j Martha m John Dean   k Henry b 1826; living 1901

Eben Dow bcbhdea appears in Jefferson 1850 census, farmer, realty $700; wife Martha b Me 1803. If children, presumably m and gone by 1850.

Peter Dow bcbhdeb in 1850 census wheelwright of Newcastle, realty $200; wife Eliza b Me 1801. Census gives 3 children:

> a James Oliver Chase b 1834   b Anna b 1836   c Mary b 1843
> d Henry: not in census; name given by a nephew who reported his mother was
>   Nancy. Possibly Nancy was a 2nd wife and Henry b after 1850. [He lived
>   Me, had a family, some of his children going to Braintree, Mass

James O C Dow bcbhdeba d Boston 1917, ae 83-4-1. Probably only 2 children:

> a Fred A; now of Denver, Colo; wrote 1921 the bare facts as above
> b ———, Mrs J M Gibbs of E Livermore; did not answer at all

Thomas Dow bcbhdec appears in census mariner of Jefferson b 1810, no realty; wife Hannah b Me 1827. No mention of children

Mary A Dow bcbhdeg m E E Follansbee, then of Leominster, Mass; moved to Braintree, d Mch 26, 1849. She d Braintree Aug 30, 1897. Children:

> a Edward F b Aug 22, 1838   b Lucy J b Mch 26, 1849

Joseph G Dow bcbhdeh d Aug 1, 1869; m Eliza G Merry b Me 1822. Blacksmith of Warren; moved to Edgcomb. After his death his family returned to Jefferson. Census 1850 shows him of Edgcomb, realty $200. Children, from Hist Warren:

a   Joshua M b Oct 24, 1842; m Olive Dow bcbhdeka; cooper, married d Warren Dec 6, 1906. No mention of children
b   Henry b Warren June 28, 1843; possibly the Henry farmer d Jefferson Dec 8, 1920; m Susan Jones b Jefferson May 10, 1836, d Jefferson May 26, 1917, dau of Michael and Annie (Wright). No mention of children
c   George H b 1844; m Catherine Dow bcbhdekb; lived Jefferson. This by Hist Warren. Jefferson 1896 directory gave G H Dow farmer and cooper, wife Susan Kennedy. Perhaps not identical
d   Eliza E b 1846; m ——; lived Clark's Island
e   Oceana b 1848; m Seth Cole   f   Nathaniel Alford bap Warren Apr 1852
g   Alfred W   h   Emma   i   Edward; unt   j   Evena
k   Lizzie

Nathaniel A Dow bcbhdehf carpenter of Rockport m Aug 29, 1872, Clara E Spears b E Warren. Children:

a   Charles b Warren July 21, 1873; d Sept 1875
b   Sidney A b Oct 29, 1874; cooper of Rockport m Apr 21, 1908, Rena W Hall, ae 30, dau of Dodge and Sarah (Towney)
    Edith M b Warren May 13, 1876; m Boston Aug 13, 1902, Woodward A Perry ae 25, of Dover Point, son of George W and Georgia E (Cables)
d   Clarence farmer of West Rockport d Feb 16, 1900, ae 21-5-7, unm
e   Mary E; of Boston by 1893   f   Gracie; at home 1893
g   Lora O (sic 1893 directory) b 1885   h   Myrtle; living 1893
i   ——   j   —— dau b Rockport Mch 26, 1906

Loring O Dow bcbhdehfg expressman of Camden m Sept 2, 1913, Adelaide J Thomas, ae 28, dau of C E and Mary (Blood). Child:

a   Loring Woodman b Camden Mch 11, 1915

Alfred W Dow bcbhdehg b Warren, laborer and cooper of Warren; m Mabel E Plummer b Palermo. Older children not found:

c   Alfred P b Aug 13, 1900   d   George Raymond b Mch 28, 1910

John C Dow bcbhdei, carpenter of Jefferson, m (int pub Mch 15, 1854) Mary Ellen King b Chelsea, Mass, Feb 9, 1834, d wid Appleton Aug 10, 1915, dau of Moses and Mary. One child found by own rec:

a   A M b 1862; mechanic of Appleton m June 24, 1893, Edith H Burkett d Appleton June 9, 1910, ae 56-11-7, dau of Andrew and Eliza J (Leigh)

Henry Dow bcbhdek farmer of Edgcomb, later of Boothbay, d Oct 14, 1906, survived by 3rd wife; m Matilda Stover; 2nd, Sarah Stover; 3rd, Ellen A Page. Sons sure, dau a guess.

a   Olive m Joshua M Dow bcbhdeha
b   Catherine m George H Dow bcbhdehc
c   Eben T b June 1856, both Edgcomb and Boothbay in rec
d   Harry G b Boothbay 1881

Eben T Dow bcbhdekc inherited the Boothbay farm; m Nov 28, 1900, Flossie A Somes, ae 20, dau of Kiah B and Arabella (Sherman) of Edgcomb; d leaving wid Aug 1, 1913. Children, b Boothbay:

a   Otis R b Dec 28, 1901   b   —— dau b June 24, 1904

Harry G Dow bcbhdekd of Boston m Lynn Nov 16, 1904, May E
Lyons, ae 25, dau of Thomas E and Martha R (Black).   A child:

a   Harold Allen b Boston July 19, 1906

Rebecca Dow bcbhdf m Feb 4 (int pub Ballstown Jan 14), 1793,
Joshua Follingsby Little of Pittston.   In m rec she is called Mrs Rebeckah
so might be wid, but more probably is the missing dau of Peter Dow
bcbhd.

From the foregoing it may be seen that about half of the Dow tribe
of Jefferson have so far been genealogically placed.   Further search
locally will doubtless place many more.   Presumably all Jefferson Dow
belong to the bcbhd line, so all such are collected and indexed here for
easy reference.

Henry Dow bcbhdxa.   Jefferson annals mention that a Dow
became a pioneer of Perham, but it finally comes to light that this is
Peter Dow bcbhddg, who went there rather late in life.   Another Dow
was of Perham, but he is known only from rec of 2nd m of a son, which
says Henry m Ann Gallagher, both b N B.   There is surely no room in
bcdg line for him and probably none in the h family.   A much better guess
is of the bcbhd or bcbhb line and that the N B reference applies to Ann
but not to Henry.   One child found:

a   James H b presumably 1835 or so

James H Dow bcbhdxaa, farmer of Caribou, known only to us from
d rec of wives and m rec of children; m Mahala Jane Sands d Aug 6,
1905, ae 66-9-25, dau of Stephen and Millie (Post); m 2nd, Oct 27, 1906,
H R Adella Morse d ae 61-0-5, wid of —— Southerland and dau of Carleton and Julia (Howe) of Dixmont.   Six children found by own rec:

a   Stephen b 1862   b   Thomas b 1864   c   Daniel F b Woodland 1867
d   Effie E b 1868; m Lynn, Mass, Mch 17, 1901, Joseph A Clough, b Me, son of
     John and Electa (Partridge)
e   Susan b 1871; d Mch 3, 1895; unm   f   James H b 1874

Stephen Dow bcbhdxaaa, blacksmith of Stockham and Perham, in
1907 letter carrier; m Alice Langley b Jan 19, 1869, d May 2, 1900, dau
of James and Salome (Broen); 2nd, wid Mary E Ward ae 29, d Perham
Apr 22, 1911, ae 38-2-5, dau of John and Agnes (Miller) Miller of Caribou;
3rd, Perham June 3, 1911, Mrs Meedie Langley ae 39, dau of Jim and
Maude (Brown) Cochran.   Children:

a   Thomas b 1887   b   Herbert b 1891   c   Bennie b July 7, 1893; unt
d   Abby b July 4, 1894   e   Oscar b 1892   f   William b Apr 2, 1900
g   —— son b Apr 2, 1907   h   —— son b Perham Aug 1, 1909

Thomas M Dow bcbhdxaaaa, blacksmith of Perham, m Apr 24,
1909, Tonny (Tony, Toney in rec) Wilcox ae 14, dau of Hudson and
Hulda Brewer.   Had:

a   —— dau b Apr 15, 1911   b   —— son b Mch 26, 1914

c —— dau b July 20, 1916   d —— dau b Oct 31, 1917
e —— dau b Perham Nov 16, d Nov 18, 1918

Herbert Dow bcbhdxaaab, laborer of Washburn, m Nov 2, 1915, Nettie Langley ae 16, dau of Heuron and Almeda (Cochran).   Child:

a —— son b Jan 21, 1918

Oscar Dow bcbhdxaaae, laborer of Washburn, d a soldier Sept 20, 1918, ae 26; m June 19, 1918, Ethel T Griffin ae 21, dau of Arthur and Rose (Argent).   Posthumous child:

a Rosalie Blanche b Presque Isle Oct 6, d Mapleton Oct 9, 1918

Thomas Dow bcbhdxaab, in one rec said b Tobique, N B, blacksmith and veterinary surgeon, d Caribou Aug 21, 1910; m Mary Bonney b Woodland.   Older children guessed, younger by Me rec:

a Arden E   b Allison   c Elmer
e —— dau b Perham Nov 26, 1892
f Neal C b Mch 4, 1895   g —— b Mch 10, 1896
h Ralph Philip b Aug 18, 1897; d Caribou Aug 26, 1913

Arden E Dow bcbhdxaaba, laborer of Perham, m Jan 19, 1915, Ethel A Buzzell ae 18, dau of John and Annie (Marsh).   Children:

b —— son b Oct 19, 1917   c Anita Marguerite b Lincoln July 7, 1920

Allison Dow bcbhdxaabb, farmer, m Laura Buzzell.   1st born (?):

a —— dau b Caribou June 30, 1916

Elmer Dow bcbhdxaabc b Ft Fairfield, laborer of Caribou, m Lily Harris b Woodland.   1st born:

a —— dau b Caribou June 30, 1916

Neal C Dow bcbhdxaabf, laborer and blacksmith of Perham, m Jan 16, 1915, Ruby M Bradley ae 16, dau of George and Isabel (Bacon).   Children:

a —— son b July 13, 1915   b —— son b Jan 15, 1918
c Alma Isabelle b Lincoln May 7, 1919

Daniel F Dow bcbhdxaac, farmer of Caribou, m Ellen M Crock or Ellen Cyr, both in rec b Van Buren; probably identical.   Mother's names are much mixed in State rec. He m 2nd, Effie Langley; 3rd, June 4, 1904 (her 3rd; div) Sadie M Randall ae 27, dau of Elijah and Mary J (Jordan).   Children:

a Ainslee b Caribou 1889   b Dora d July 3, 1893, ae 3, 3 mos
c John d Sept 29, 1892, ae 2 mos   d Lewis Clifford b Woodland Dec 26, 1893
e Clarence E b Nov 7, 1895   f Freeman d Mch 29, 1915, ae 18
g Tom b May 13, 1899   h Henry b Jan 17, 1901
i Hewey b Apr 25, 1903 (called 7th in rec: 7th by 2nd wife?)

Ainslee Dow bcbhdxaaca, laborer of Woodland, m Sept 6, 1911, Annie Louise Abbott ae 23, dau of John A and Annie (McCubrey).

Lewis C Dow bcbhdxaacd, laborer of Washburn, m June 30, 1916, Nina J Geldert, ae 18, dau of John A and Laura B (Wilson). Children:

a —— dau b Sept 6, 1917   b Clayton Lewis b June 13, 1920

Asa Dow bcbhdxb. Little evidence that he belongs here; known only from 1850 census, farmer of Wellington, Piscataquis Co, b Me 1815; realty $200; wife Elizabeth b Me 1822. One child by census, others might be b later:

a Franklin b 1846; unt

Hiram Dow bcbhdxc is more probably of bcbhdb line; known only from rec of son; m Lydia Pierce

a Frank b Vassalboro; m 3rd Attleboro, Mass, May 21, 1903, giving ae 57, Mary A West [her 2nd ae 45, dau of Hugh and Mary (Drummond)]

Lucy Dow bcbhdxd appears in Jefferson 1850 census, apparently wid with son

a Charles b 1843; unt

Nancy Dow bcbhdxe d Jefferson June 16, 1832; no other data

William Dow bcbhdxf, farmer, b Corinth, m Emma Robbins b Corinth. Child by own rec:

a Ralph E b Mapleton 1882

Ralph E Dow bcbhdxfa, farmer of Mapleton, m July 15, 1903, Gertrude Porter, teacher, b Castle Hill ae 25, dau of Robert and Rachel (Foster) b N S.

Charles W Dow bcbhdxg b Newcastle Dec 11, 1881; about 1907 farmer of Newcastle, apparently moved to Amesbury, Mass; m Alice Bertha Cook b N S. Child:

a Lucy Alberta b Amesbury Apr 26, 1910

Samuel Dow bcbhdxh may be a Quaker line or bcdhdb line. Born China or nearby 1800 or later; he had at least 1 brother, the latter having a son George E Dow living Monarda 1902. Samuel m Polly Pinkham of China (Quaker name) and cleared a farm in Lincoln township. Children:

a John b Lincoln Oct 28, 1828
b Benjamin b Nov 30, 1830; d Oct 1, 1864
c Samuel b 1831; d Feb 20, 1905, unm. He and John shared the homestead
d Nahum P b June 14, 1834; d July 11, 1861
e Sarah D b June 16, 1838; d Apr 4, 1870

John Dow bcbhdxha d May 24, 1915; m Ann Russell Lowell d Lincoln Feb 27, 1905, ae 69-2-5, dau of Thomas Sr and Martha J (Smith). Only child:

a Harold C b 1865

Harold C Dow bcbhdxhaa, farmer of Lincoln, a well educated, progressive man, school supt of Lincoln, m Jan 9, 1915, Bertha T Wheeler ae 34, dau of Augustus and Sarah (Lane). She d; he m 2nd, Feb 12, 1919, Alberta Amelia Fenwick, div, ae 48, dau of Michael and Marguerette (McKeown) of Creighton, N B. He d suddenly Dec 4, 1923, the last of his line.

Joseph Dow bcbhdxi of Palermo m Jennie Sabine. He was born Joseph Evans but he legally changed his name, for reason not now known. In rec of 1stborn he appears as Joseph Evans and his wife as Mary J Dow. Possibly, then, he merely took his wife's name. His great grandson has been so helpful genealogically that we wish to keep him in the family. These children found by own rec:

a Charles B b 1816 (his own statement at 2nd m)
b Mary Jane b Palermo; d Palermo Apr 15, 1896, ae 76-6-25, unm

Charles B Dow bcbhdxia, carpenter of Passadumkeag; m 2nd (her 2nd), Dec 15, 1864, Eliza J Lancaster ae 36, dau of Timothy H and Nancy (Wadleigh). He d Bangor June 26, 1908, ae 93-1-5; b China or St Albans; his 1st wife Sarah H Goodwin b St Albans. Three children found by own rec:

a Percival Barton b St Albans 1851   b Charles W b Bangor Feb 8, 1856
c Freddie A b Jan 15, 1865

Percival B Dow bcbhdxiaa merchant of Brewer, widower; m 2nd, Apr 4, 1900, Susan McLawn, wid dau of Elijah and Caroline (Day) Bradbury. He d Brewer Jan 20, 1905, ae 54-4-11; she d Bangor July 5, 1909, ae 59.

Charles W Dow bcbhdxiab, laborer of Rockland, d Sept 23, 1919; m Sarah F Staples b Deer Isl, who survived, apparently moved to Rockland about 1882. Older children b Bangor, not found:

c Earl Charles b 1883   e Dana Irene d June 13, 1897, ae 7-9-11
f —— dau b July 2, 1892   g Geraldine b Warren

Earl C Dow bcbhdxiaba, nurse of Belmont, Mass, m Oct 13, 1906, Katherine Stanhope Banks ae 23 of Rockport, dau of Samendal and Frances R (Veazie); later street ry conductor of Rockport. Children:

a Francis Parker b Revere, Mass, Mch 29, 1907
b Earl Samuel b Rockport June 23, 1910

Fred A Dow bcbhdxiac is presumably the Fred Dow b Bangor, carpenter, m Cassie Ham b Winterport. Children:

a Clyde Hadley b Winterport Sept 7, 1897
b Norman C b Chelsea, Mass, Sept 3, 1902

Theophilus Dow bcbhdxj b Whitefield, farmer, m Lydia Dearborn b Monmouth. No dates given; known only from rec of dau Lottie b Cornville, d Skowhegan Feb 8, 1898, ae not stated.

Joseph Dow bcbhg appears in bap rec as Joses.　Apparently the family of Peter and Susannah Dow separated, one group going to Maine, another westward, some of the girls probably marrying and continuing to live not many miles from Plaistow.　In Maine we find a record which possibly belongs to bcbhg.　Joseph Dow, a cripple, was warned June 10, 1775, by the selectmen of Belfast to leave town, as they did not wish him to become a citizen, lest he eventually become unable to support himself.　He withdrew a short distance and took refuge for the night in a storehouse.　A party of British privateers came looking for loot and set fire to the place.　Joseph put out the fire and was subjected to much violence by the enemy, who did not kill him but left him apparently disabled.　They again fired the place and withdrew.　Joseph put out the fire again, made his way back into town and warned the troops. Whether the selectmen woke to a sense of shame history does not record and Joseph Dow is genealogically lost.

Hannah Dow bcc m Jan 5, 1686-7, Daniel Bradley Jr, both of Haverhill, son of Daniel, immigrant, and Mary (Williams).　Both were killed in the Indian massacre Mch 15, 1696-7.　At this time 37 in all were killed, mostly women and children.　It is called the Dustin massacre, from Mrs Hannah Dustin, whose escape from captivity is one of the most remarkable and best known episodes in Colonial history.　Children:

    a Ruth b May 5, 1688; m Nov 13, 1706, Thomas Johnson; killed by Indians Aug 29, 1708.　Her dau Lydia b Aug 23, 1707, m Jan 6, 1731-2, Ebenezer Gile, is the great granddau cared for by Stephen Dow bc and mentioned in his will

    b Daniel b Oct 28, 1690; captive in Dustin massacre; never returned

    c Mary b May 6, 1693　　　d Hannah b May 6, 1696; both killed

STEPHEN Dow bcd, carpenter, lifelong resident of Haverhill, d
June 17, 1743; appeared for the last time on the tax list Dec 10,
1741. The exact site of his house has not been determined, but
it must have been near, perhaps part of, his father's homestead, as Dec
5, 1723, he filed a petition for 5 additional acres "beyond Nicholas
White's." This in 1720 was the extreme northeast edge of the settlement,
land afterwards included in Salem, N H. He was 27 when the Dustin
massacre occurred and was with his father in garrison 6. The Indians
had a peculiar call, known to the colonists as "their whistle"; it was
made by placing both hands over the mouth. Stephen was the only
man in Haverhill who learned to imitate it. He used it to set up
ambuscades, but whether successfully or not does not appear in history.
He took part in a number of Indian fights, some away from Haverhill.
He m Dec 14, 1697, Mary Hutchins b Haverhill Mch 4, 1679, dau of
Joseph and Johanna (Corliss), his step sister. She d Oct 29, 1734.
Her father was on the muster roll of Capt John Osgood Mch 29, 1659, and
in the company of Capt Edmund Moore Nov 2, 1659-60. Children:

- a Timothy b Sept 4, d Sept 1698   b Nathaniel b Aug 11, 1699
- c Mary b Apr 18, 1701
- d Elizabeth b Feb 29, 1704; m before 1726 William Heath
- e Richard b Feb 15, 1705-6   f Johanna b Sept 26, 1709
- g David b Dec 25, 1714   h Jonathan b Sept 11, 1718
- i Stephen b Oct 13, 1722

Nathaniel Dow bcdb, cooper of Salem, was at Crown Point 1762
and won a Lieutenant's commission from the King. He and his family
anticipated the Revolution long before it came and were prepared for
it. Nathaniel used his own funds to prepare troops and in 1775 was
serving as a volunteer under Capt Henry Elkins in the hurried plans for
the defense of Piscataway. His commission as Lieut from the Continental Congress soon arrived, and he was later commissioned as Capt. All
three commissions are preserved as family heirlooms. In spite of his
age, he took the field, Capt Dearborn, Col Stark, and was Lieut under
Col Welch at the Battle of Bennington; was present at the surrender
of Gen Burgoyne. Apparently, he sold what land grant he received
under the act of 1783, for no descendant appears as having such land.
He d 1787; m Oct 4, 1726, Mary Hendrick b Mch 31, 1696, d Sept 20,
1776, dau of Israel and Sarah (Gutterson); m 2nd, ae 78, Susanna
—— b 1710, d 1794. Children:

- a Daniel b July 28, 1728   b Mary bap Apr 26, 1730
- c James b Sept 2, 1731; d Feb 3, 1737-8
- d Amos b Mch 12, 1734-5; selectman of Salem 1776; sgt of militia Newbury
    1777; in 1790 census 1a, 1c; d Salem Jan 20, 1820, married, but no children
- e Jeremiah b Mch 14, 1737-8

Daniel Dow bcdba of Salem d Jan or Feb 1758; m Nov 16, 1748,
Rebeckah Peaslee (Pesele, rec) bap Nov 1727, d June 2, 1757, dau of

Daniel and Rebecca. Presumably the three orphan children grew up with grandfather Dow. At all events, both boys learned the cooper's trade. Children:

a Phineas b June 16, 1750
b Olif b Nov 25, 1751; d Sept 25, 1753
c Zillah b May 30 (or 10), 1753
d Peasle b Sept 2, 1754. His name in Rev rolls and all subsequent rec is Percy

Phineas Dow bcdbaa appears in 1772 as cooper in Pittsfield, N H, unm. Not found in 1790 census. He must have married in 1772. judging from d rec of dau, the only sure mention found. Some Phineas Dow of Boston m Sept 2, 1804, Ann Wyman. No particular reason to think them identical; if so, it was 2nd m. The same Phineas Dow of Boston invented in 1810 a rather valuable machine for splitting leather. Many years ago a query in Boston Transcript for his parentage left an inference that he left posterity. In 1835 he was a machinist of Boston with store on Portland St. So far as we are concerned, he must be left untraced, except that he could not be far from Haverhill. Children:

a Martha. Haverhill rec gives her dau of Phineas, d dropsy Dec 17, 1849, ae 77

Zillah Dow bcdbac d Maumee City, Ohio, Sept 2, 1844; m Nov 26, 1773, Benjamin Woodbury of Salem b July 1753, d Apr 20, 1809, son of Jonathan; 2nd, June 2, 1814, Jonathan Pillsbury of Candia, N H. Children:

a Zillah b Sept 28, 1774; m —— Gay   b Jonathan b July 23, 1776
c Daniel b June 15, 1778
d Phineas b Nov 21, 1780; d Haverhill Mch 12, 1817
e Olive b Jan 11, 1783; m —— Seamans
f Manley Gates b July 12, 1785; lived Rochester, N Y
g Delia b Aug 13, 1787   h Roxana b Mch 27, 1790
i Benjamin b Aug 3, 1792   j Ira b 1794; d young

Percy Dow bcdbad, cooper of Salem, left his bride of a few months to serve as fifer under Capt Richard Dow bcde at Great Island from Nov 5, 1775; m Deborah Barker b Sept 24, 1752, d 1844, dau of Zebediah and Deborah (Merrill). Five years later they moved to Antrim, in 1782 to Londonderry; 13 years later to Newport, N H; where he d 1824. His posterity, numerically strong, disappeared wholly from Newport about 1890. Children:

a Rebecca b Sept 23, 1776; d Jan 24, 1805; m 1801 Matthew Adams b Dec 17, 1778, d Sept 10, 1828
b Hannah Peaslee b Feb 7, d Feb 8, 1778
c Daniel b Salem June 11, 1779; d 1812; presumably unm
d Zebediah Barker b Mch 10, 1781
e Deborah b Jan 2, 1783; d Feb 1833; m 1803 John Webster; 11 children
f Zillah b Antrim Mch 12, 1785; m 1805 Alexander Spinney
g Hannah Peaslee b Feb 8, 1787
h Polly Boyd b May 26, 1789; m 1809 Thomas Whittier of Newport; 8 children
i Elizabeth b Apr 27, 1791
j Anna Boyd b Apr 30, 1793. Hist Antrim, followed by Hist Newport, gives m 1813 Abram Henderson; probably wholly error
k Caroline M b Feb 10, 1796

Zebediah B Dow bcdbadd continued to live on the Croyden side of Newport; d 1863; m Nov 23, 1808, Asenath Smart of Croyden, suicide by drowning Dec 11, 1857, ae 66. The cooperage trade, inherited by 4 generations, developed in the next into an architectural ability marked in the whole family. B rec of children not extant, list doubtless complete and correct. Children:

a Hiram b 1809   b Rebecca b 1811   c Addina b 1813
d Hial b 1815 (Croyden rec, no month date)
e Asenath b 1817; m (Asenath Smart in garbled rec) of Nashua Apr 28, 1841, Joseph Packard of Nashua
f Edward b 1819   g Caleb b 1821   h Adalia b 1823
i Lucy b 1825   j Lorenzo b 1827
k Lucinda b 1830; some Lucinda m Windsor, Vt, July 5, 1852, Obed Parmenter of Greenfield, Mass
l Caroline b 1830-3   m Alphonso b 1836 (census rec)

Hiram Dow bcdbadda appears in Concord 1850 carpenter, realty $2,000; wife Eliza b N H 1810. Rec of child gives architect of Concord; wife Eliza B. Census mentions only 2nd child:

a William Auburn b Concord 1840; architect of Concord, m Oct 17, 1860, Ellen Marsh, ae 19
b Augustus unknown except from 1850 census

Rebecca Dow bcdbaddb d No Weare July 14, 1869; m Aug 1836 Nathaniel Brown Smith b Newport Nov 26, 1810, son of Chauncey and Abigail (Wheeler). He was a Methodist clergyman, joined the Free Will Baptists 1841; pastorates in Newport, Croyden, Weare, Deering, Newbury. Children:

a Asenath Dow m Weare 1857 Franklin H Peaslee
b Abbie H m Weare 1862 George W Dearborn

Hial Dow bcdbaddd had a joining and cooperage business in the Northfield section; built up a prosperous organization making butter tubs, etc; m Dec 30, 1841, Lura Powers b Croyden Dec 13, 1822. Children:

a Wallace L b Sept 21, 1845   b Wilbur A b Mch 21, 1848
c Isabel C b Jan 25, 1855; m Charles M Cummings

Wallace L Dow bcdbaddda formed the firm of W L Dow & Co, taking his father and brother into partnership, moved the factory nearer town, making many kinds of wood work, employing many hands. He drifted into architecture, moved to Sioux Falls, S D, became a leading architect, designing many public buildings in the Dakotas; d Sioux Falls July 8, 1911; m 1865 Lois M Whipple of Croyden. Children:

a Edwin W b May 6, 1869; living 1923 Sioux Falls; replied to a letter from the Author, promising to round out his family data
b Baron C b Nov 10, 1870; living 1923 Sioux Falls
c —— d June 22, 1873, ae 2   d Mason H b June 1, 1873; untraced
e Harry G b Aug 22, 1875; d Newport Apr 9, 1876
f Daisy Isabel b Mch 31, 1877   g Jessie b Aug 1, d Aug 9, 1880

Wilbur A Dow bcdbadddb moved to Gilman, Mont; living 1918;

never replied to repeated letters of genealogical inquiry; m 1868 Ellen J Gilmore, dau of William.   Children:

a   William b Aug 29, 1869   b   Eugene H b Nov 2, 1871
c   Arthur b Feb 1873   d   Josephine b Apr 10, 1875
e   George A b Aug 15, 1878   f ——— son b Feb 1, 1881; all b Newport

Edward Dow bcdbaddf, architect of Concord, d July 31, 1894; elected 1873 member of N H Historical Society; m Auburn, Mass, Oct 21, 1840, Lavina D Colby b Canandaigua, N Y, Feb 3, 1822, d Concord Feb 8, 1903, dau of Abner and Deborah (Gunnison).   He was 2nd Lieut of Berdan's Sharpshooters at the outbreak of the War; resigned July 16, 1862

Caleb Dow bcdbaddg of Hooksett m Nov 30, 1848, Rebecca J Rhoades of Alexandria

Lorenzo Dow bcdbaddj. The only likely candidate is Lorenzo Dow of Contoocook with wife Mary Ann; has only appeared in rec of a dau:

a   Annie of Contoocook m Hopkinton Feb 12, 1872, William P Bailey of Contoocook

Caroline J Dow bcdbaddl d Dec 18, 1881; m Aug 28, 1849, Charles Baker b Rochester, Vt, Oct 30, 1825, son of Rev Joseph and Mary (Austin); settled about 1862 in Andover, N H. He m 2nd Mary J Clark of Stratham.   Children:

a   Edison d in infancy
b   Carrie Eva b June 9, 1857; m Mch 6, 1878, Frederick C H Chappell; 2 children;
       m 2nd July 30, 1884, Jonathan Harvey Anderson of East Andover
c   Elmer Clarence b Mch 11, 1864; m Franklin July 6, 1901, Mahala D Emerson;
       3 children
d   Wilmer Clarendon b Dec 4, 1866; m July 25, 1891, Amelia R Wilson; 1 child

Hannah P Dow bcdbadg d 1837; m William Reed b 1787, d 1825, Capt in 1812; m 2nd 1828 Charles William Tennant, farmer of Ascutney-ville, Vt, son of John (sea capt from So Car) and Mary Ann (Hazard from N Y); moved to a farm near Fredonia, N Y.   Children:

a   Hamlin b 1811; d 1895   b   Darius b 1813; d 1911   c   Anson b 1815
d   Sarah b 1822; m 1847 Edwin Johnson, a dau Mary m George Hunt, lives
       Wa-Keeney, Kan, keenly interested in the family genealogy
e   Hannah b 1825; d 1850, unm   f   Caroline (Tennant) b 1829; d 1914
g   William b 1831; d 1905   h   Henry b 1833; d 1881

Anna B Dow bcdbadj d Jamestown, N Y, Sept 20, 1849. The statement that she m Abram Henderson is probably error by historian of Antrim, copied by Hist Newport. Her name was Dow when she m Ballston, N Y, Sept 20, 1819, Anson J Coates b Ballston Apr 23, 1799, d Jamestown Sept 20, 1868. Children:

a   Leroy Percy b Aug 16, 1822; d Jamestown Apr 5, 1895; m Matilda E Knapp;
       5 children
b   Lura Ann   c   Anson D   d   Laurel B   e   Jabez Valentine
f   Iva   g   Seneca Dow

Alphonso Dow bcdbaddm, carpenter of Concord, m Hopkinton Aug 19, 1860, Annie Augusta Currier, ae 17, dau of Sylvester and Mary. Further untraced. She is probably the Anna (Currier) Dow, div, who m 2nd Smith Glidden Dow adadhabb of Meredith.

Jeremiah Dow bcdbe d Salem Sept 10, 1826, ae 90. He obtained a captaincy in 1775 and served with considerable distinction in the N Y State campaigns. He was of New Salem when he m Bradford, Mass, May 1, 1766, Lydia Kimball b Jan 31, 1742, d Mch 12, 1826, dau of Isaac and Elizabeth (Jewett). Of them Mrs Ednah Dow Cheney writes: "—— how straight backed her grandfather was, and how venerable he looked with his long white hair, as he walked out of the church when the bass viol was brought in. He had a heart though like other men and fell in love with a gay young woman who delighted to tease him by performing the rites of baptism on the cats of the family. He prayed much over the question of marrying such an unregenerated young woman, but concluded it might prove for the good of her soul, and was greatly rejoiced when after her marriage she became regularly converted and joined his church." The 1790 census gives them 4a, 1b, 6c. Children: all b Salem:

   a Nathaniel b May 10, 1767
   b Mehitable b June 7, 1769; m Mch 6, 1793, Aaron Nettleton, first sheriff of Sullivan Co
   c Aquila b Apr 23, 1771   d Jeremiah b Apr 9, 1773
   e Lydia b May 7, 1776
   f Eliza b Feb 11, 1778; m Salem Mch 5, 1805, Joel Nettleton of Newport, brother of Aaron. Their father Jeremiah was a pioneer of Newport, coming from Killingworth, Conn
   g Hepzibah b Feb 26, 1782; d before 1826; m —— Crocker; left a dau,—Hepzibah
   h Fannie b Nov 2, 1784; m Pelham Apr 1, 1818, James Ayer 3rd of Haverhill
   i Amos b Jan 29, 1790; d Oct 12, 1793

Nathaniel Dow bcdbea located 1792 in Newport, N H, buying a farm in the east part. He d Newport Aug 15, 1844. Salem has a rec: Nathaniel Dow d Salem June 19, 1787, ae 19-1-19. This seems wholly error, no other Nathaniel of Salem known. He m Nov 11, 1792, Martha Buswell of Bow. Children:

   a Amos b Nov 18, 1793; d Sept 3, 1811
   b James B b Jan 26, 1796; went west; untraced
   c Matilda b May 18, 1798; m Bela J Sperry of Claremont. A son Anson Martin Sperry is a member of the Sons of the Revolution, but by some error his qualifying ancestor is given as Nathaniel Dow adaabc
   d Elizabeth b July 31, 1800; d Feb 16, 1854, unm
   e Hepzibah b Sept 19, 1802; m 1823 Daniel Straw of Hopkinton
   f Mehitable b Sept 16, 1804; m Newport Jan 5, 1830, Nathan Mudgett of Wendell
   g Martha B b Dec 23, 1806; m Samuel Garfield of Langdon; 2nd Seth Richards of Newport
   h Lydia Kimball b Nov 27, 1815; d Mch 7, 1818

Aquila Dow bcdbec, executor of his father's will, selectman o f

Salem 1833, moved 1836 to Exeter; d Salem Dec 28, 1837; m Dec 9, 1793, Deliverance Dow bcbegc.   Children:

   a   John b Mch 27, 1795; d July 16, 1796
   b   Phineas b Nov 28, 1796; by 1850 census farmer, insane; d Exeter Sept 21,
       1866, presumably unm
   c   John b Apr 17, 1799   d   Jeremiah b Mch 22, 1802
   e   Leonard Milton b Dec 30, 1805
   f   George Halleburton b June 4, 1807; d June 19, 1814
   g   George b Oct 18, 1818; merchant of Plaistow, d May 3, 1875, unm

John Dow bcdbecc d May 3, 1876; m 1824 Sarah Brooks Wade d Mch 16, 1883, ae 85, dau of John and Lydia (Le Bosquet) (census gives b 1800; family rec, 1793). Moving to Portland, Me, he built up the largest store in that city, devoted to general merchandise. His tax assessment 1850 was $20,000, very few larger in Portland. A fine home still stands. He and his brother Jeremiah were for many years prominent in Portland society and business. The male lines of each have been extinct for many years and only one granddau born Dow survives, unm. Children, from 1850 census:

   a   Jane Wade b 1825   b   John B b 1827; d unm
   c   Sumner b 1829; d unm
   d   Georgianna b 1831   e   George b 1833; d unm
   f   Ellen b 1835; m twice, d after 1900; of 3 children none survives

Jane W Dow bcdbecca m Gen Samuel Jameson Anderson, many years Collector of the Port of Portland. Reminiscences of Ednah Dow Cheney: "I must not forget my cousin and lifelong friend Jane W Dow of Portland. Her sparkling beauty and fascinating manners charmed young and old, but if she broke many hearts they were always finally healed and she remained friends with whom she had wounded. She had much talent for both music and poetry, and continued her studies in music after her seventieth year. She was full of wit and charming conversation which delighted her large circle wherever she went. She married happily Gen Anderson of Portland." Her children:

   a   Jeanie Campbell m Charles Mathewson of N Y; 1 son surviving 1923
   b   Samuel Jameson d in infancy   c   John d unm after 1900
   d   Susan Jameson m Frank Eliot Sweetzer; 8 children

Georgianna Dow bcdbeccd d 1900; m May 10, 1855, Charles Richardson 1903, son of Alford, Pres of Fame Insurance Co, Philad Children, b Phila:

   a   Georgianna Dow b Jan 2, 1857; unm. She wrote 1923 to the Author giving
       particulars of the bcdbecc and bcdbecd lines
   b   Charles Brooks b Jan 24, 1859   c   Alford Sumner b Dec 16, 1861
       All of Philadelphia. There is no third generation

Jeremiah Dow bcdbecd moved about 1828 to Portland; d Nov 20, 1886. Became secretary of a Portland insurance company; owned a farm outside the city limits, a show place about which Hist Portland has considerable to say; prominent in Portland social circles. He m Haverhill July 20, 1826, Polly Dow bcdedga; 2nd, 1835, Elizabeth ——. Children, all but oldest presumably b Portland, only rec found in 1850 census. No third generation.   Children:

a   Mary Frances b Haverhill Sept 21, 1826.   No evidence of identity with following.   Mary Louise Dow, dau of —— and Mary Frances Dow, b Worcester Aug 30, 1848.   Another rec: Martha L Dow of Exeter, dau of Jonathan and Elizabeth, m Dec 30, 1874, Frederick Blanchard of Tyngsboro. This lovely couple lived Brookline.   She, known as M Louise Dow, survived her husband, an accountant, very able amateur entomologist, prominent in the early days of the Cambridge Entomological Club.   No children
b   Carrie b 1828   c   Edward b 1830   d   Anna b 1836
e   Henry b 1838   f   Albert b 1840   All d unm

Leonard M Dow bcdbece, farmer of Exeter, assessed 1850 at $3,500; d Newport Dec 23, 1875; m Charlestown, Mass, Oct 5, 1829, Rebecca E Milliken d Nov 20, 1882, ae 79, 9 mos.   Children:

a   Carrie Delia b 1831   b   Harriet E b 1833
c   Charles Leonard b 1835   d   Walter Brooks b Portland July 6, 1838
e   Samuel Billings b Bangor Aug 27, 1839
f   Arabella b 1843; m 1866 Charles E Smith
g   Ella b 1843; m (as Edna Hathorne Dow) June 20, 1871, William H Hamilton of Hartford, Conn.   Their dau Edna Dow m Exeter 1900 Leonard D Hunt

Caroline D Dow bcdbecea m Alba C Taylor of Hampton b Apr 29, 1824, son of Samuel D and Phoebe (Stevens).   Children:

a   Charles Everett b Aug 12, 1850; d Feb 23, 1873
b   Ella M b Mch 8, d Apr 8, 1852
c   John b June 20, 1853; m Mrs Annie M Crane
d   Samuel D b Apr 11, d Dec 8, 1855
e   Ednah Dow b Jan 17, 1857   f   Belle b Jan 17, d Feb 1859
g   Arabella Stevens b Jan 17, 1860; m Samuel W Dearborn
h   George Dow b June 19, 1864; d Jan 5, 1870
i   Annie Clark b Nov 8, 1866; m Exeter 1894 William H Folsom

Charles L Dow bcdbecec, wholesale grocer of Louisville, Ky, had:

a   Samuel Russell, photo engraver of Chattanooga, Tenn
b   Leonard Milton, time keeper, Louisville
c   William, salesman, Denver   d   Bessie, clerk, Louisville

Leonard M Dow bcdbececb has children:

a   James Roger, tool maker, Louisville
b   Wallace H, commercial artist, Louisville and N Y City

Walter B Dow bcdbeced d Manchester, N H, June 5, 1903; m Sarah J Howard b Vermont, Me, 1844; in 1882 was shoemaker of Northwood.   Children, perhaps others:

a   Herbert W b Lynn 1863
b   Lewis S b Northwood Aug 28, 1868; m Tilton July 27, 1887, Jennie M Clark, ae 20, dau of Aaron
c   —— son b and d Northwood Feb 5, 1882

Herbert W Dow bcdbeceda m Nov 15, 1884, Nellie J Otis b 1862, d Tilton, N H, Oct 15, 1886, dau of Moses; div; m 2nd Oct 15, 1887, Addie L Simmons, ae 23, of Tilton.   Presumably he was the Herbert W Dow who m Boston Oct 12, 1905, Grace M Woods, ae 28, dau of Henry W and Ellen M (Town).

Samuel B Dow bcdbecee, brought up in Exeter, N H, became a merchant, later insurance agent of Knoxville, Tenn; is (1921) recorder of the local commandery, Knights Templar; m Feb 10, 1885, Marie Aebli b Switzerland May 28, 1863, dau of Casper and Magdalen (Oswald). Children, b Knoxville:

- a Sumner A b Dec 27, 1885; m Knoxville Ruby Harrison b Knoxville Oct 22, 1898; of Knoxville; no children
- b Peter Staub b Feb 11, 1887; not in recent Knoxville directory
- c Rebecca b Jan 13, 1889; m Lieut Commander J D Maloney, U S N, b Knoxville May 15, 1886. Son,—James Dodson b Manila, P I, Mch 11, 1921
- d Leonard Milton b Mch 16, 1892; unm
- e Magdalen b Apr 24, 1894; m Ernest R Fox b Knoxville Jan 29, 1881; dau,— Elizabeth Marie b Knoxville Apr 24, 1920
- f Edward Tuck b June 10, 1898; of Knoxville; unm
- g Dorothy b Aug 24, 1900; unm

Jeremiah Dow bcdbed d Exeter Oct 7, 1847; m Nov 27, 1797, Edna Parker b Bradford, Mass, Oct 18, 1776, d Exeter Feb 7, 1846, dau of Retire Hathorne and Ednah (Hardy). Of him Ednah Dow Cheney writes: "Grandfather Dow moved to Exeter where he carried on a large tannery. I remember that whenever we passed a tan-yard in our drives mother would say, as she inhaled the familiar smell,—there lives an honest man. After the fashion of children I pondered in secret but never inquired of the connection between hemlock bark and honesty." Children:

- a Edna Parker b Jan 18, 1799; m Exeter June 10, 1819, Sargent S Littlehale of Boston; their dau Ednah Dow m Seth Cheney, lived Boston, a well known writer for a long life span
- b Mary Frances b Jan 18, 1799   c Retire Parker b Mch 18, 1801
- d Hannah Park b Nov 1, 1808; m Nov 19, 1839 (his 2nd). Oshea Pinkham, cotton manufacturer of Exeter. No children
- e Jeremiah b Feb 5, 1813   f Elizabeth b Sept 18, 1816

Jeremiah Dow bcdbede, while untraced, seems to be Jeremiah m Sarah Rogers b Bozrah, Conn, Feb 12, 1815, dau of David and Lucinda (Gardner). No children.

Elizabeth Dow bcdbedf m Samuel Garfield Smith of Exeter, by whom 3 dau; m 2nd Rev Levi Washburn D D; 1 dau:

- a Ednah b So Berwick, Me, May 12, 1841; m Exeter June 4, 1862, Knight Dexter Cheney

Lydia Dow bcdbee of Salem m Oct 8, 1801, Daniel Ladd; went to Plymouth, N H; moved away 1813. Children:

- a George Williamson Livermore b June 21, 1802
- b Permelia b Dec 19, 1803; d Sept 4, 1805
- c Bela Orlando b Apr 23, 1805; m Dec 31, 1831, Elizabeth Robertson; lived Boston; 3 children
- d William H b Feb 12, 1807; m Hannah B Goodrich   e Charles

Hepzibah Dow bcdbeh d before 1826; m Dec 21, 1813, Stephen Crocker of Hampstead. Only child:

- a Hepzibah

The best of rules is occasionally honored in its breach. Space requires terminating female lines at the end of the second generation. Here is an exception, a line worked out by the distinguished amateur, the late Frank Hervey Pettingell of Los Angeles.

Mary Dow bcdc of Haverhill m Mch 24, 1718-9, David Roberts b Haverhill Sept 23, 1696, d Sept 1722, son of Ephraim and Dorothy (Hendrick). She m 2nd Haverhill Nov 5, 1724, Nathaniel Marble, and must be the wid Mary Marble m Obadiah Belknap, whose 1st wife Sarah Mitchel d Oct 27, 1742. All but two oldest by 2nd husband; all b and m Haverhill:

  a Ann bap July 20, 1721 (Robards, rec); m Nov 31, 1739, William Bailey of
       Haverhill
  b Sarah b Haverhill Apr 19, 1722
  c Rachel (Marble) b July 13, 1727; m Oct 3, 1751, James Davis of Methuen
  d Hannah b Oct 20, 1729; m Feb 4, 1747-8, Timothy Messer of Methuen
  e Abigail b Feb 1, 1731-2
  f Nathaniel b Mch 19, 1741-2; m before 1764 Ruth Hardey

Sarah Roberts bcdcb m Haverhill Sept 1, 1741, James Graves b Londonderry or Chelmsford Apr 22, 1714, bur So Hampton May 7, 1765, son of Samuel and Sarah (Perkins), great grandson of Abraham Perkins, father of Hampton. He bought 1761 a large farm in So Hampton and was an inn keeper. Sarah Graves bur Londonderry Dec 12, 1812. Children:

  a David b June 1, 1742; m Ruth Wadleigh; 8 children
  b Olive b Sept 10, 1743; m Benjamin Clough   c Samuel b Mch 27, 1745
  d William m Anna Currier; 5 children
  e James bur June 15, 1765, ae 17
  f Hannah m Samuel Goodwin of Newtown, N H
  g Phineas bap Hampstead Feb, 1753; m twice; 16 children
  h Sarah bap Jan, 1754; m May 4, 1775, Jonathan Currier of Salisbury
  i Abigail m William Ring of Salisbury
  j Martha m Feb 20, 1777, Jonathan Proctor of Kingston   k Lydia b 1759
  l Mary Elizabeth bap Oct 15, 1764; d Apr 23, 1767
  m Lucy b Aug 22, 1762; d So Hampton June 10, 1767

Lydia Graves bcdcbk d Newbury July 24, 1829; m 1775-6 John Smith, mariner of Newbury, either of Kittery, Me, or an itinerant sailor from England, marrying in Hampton and deciding to locate there permanently. He sailed from Newburyport Nov 15, 1776, on the privateer brig Dalton; captured by H M S Reasonable and taken to Plymouth; transferred successively to the prison ship Belle Isle, Tarbay, Burford, and after smallpox had broken out to the Blenheim. With others he was tried for high treason and committed to the Old Mill prison, Plymouth, suffering severely from filth and lack of food. Released Mch 15, 1779, he joined Com John Paul Jones' squadron, serving until June 7, 1780. It is said he then joined the infantry; received a wound in the leg which never healed. He lived in Newburyport, d July 11, 1811, ae given as 62. Children:

  a John b Dec 13, 1781; probably he who m Newburyport Mch 22, 1801, Mary
       Parsons

b Lydia b June 15, 1783; m —— Goodwin of Salem, Mass
c Lemuel b Oct 7, 1786; m Newbury Apr 28, 1814, Susan Stanwood
d Lucy b Dec 16, 1791; m So Hampton Sept 18, 1808, Cutting Pettingell; d
   Newburyport Jan 14, 1871. He d Sept 1, 1865. One of their children,
   Nathaniel Henry b Newbury Sept 11, 1835; d Newmarket, N H, Nov 12,
   1874

Nathaniel H Pettingell bcdcbkda m Newburyport Sept 6, 1863,
Mary Anna Felch b Newbury Sept 10, 1843, d Newburyport Aug 6, 1894.
Their son:

Frank Hervey Pettingell b Newburyport Jan 2, 1868, pres Cal
Genealogical Society, Society of Colonial Wars, etc.

Elizabeth Dow bcdd m William Heath b Jan 19, 1701-2, son of
John and Frances (Hutchins). Children:

a Elizabeth b May 5, 1726   b Mary b Sept 10, 1729
c Jeremiah b Dec 19, 1739
   Green, Hannah, Deliverance, children of William Heath, bap 1737 may or
   may not belong here

Richard Dow bcde was of Salem, his home close to that of his
brother Nathaniel, a locality first chosen by his grandfather Stephen;
m Nov 28, 1728, Phoebe Heath, his 2nd cousin, dau of Joseph and Hannah
(Bradley), granddau of Martha Dow be. Joseph and wife, both bereft
by the Dustin massacre, had 9 children b Haverhill 1698 to 1718, Phoebe
b June 25, 1705. Richard's first service was in the Indian campaign of
1746 under Capt John Goffe at Dover; 1758 enlisted as private, Capt
John Hazzens, against Ticonderoga and distinguished himself at Crown
Point. He gained a Lieut's commission from the Crown. He was one
of the many who expected the Revolution and prepared for it, financially
and otherwise. Thus, 3 sons and possibly the fourth were at Lexington.
He himself took a captaincy, serving and instructing recruits at Great
Island from Nov 5, 1775. In this company were ensign Jeremiah Dow
bcdbed, his own son Asa as sgt, Percy Dow bcdbad, fifer, and Isaac Dow,
private. The identity of this last is uncertain. Altho 70 years of age,
Richard advanced all his money to the town to pay soldier bounties and
equip troops, and was appointed to raise a new company for service in
N Y State. His oldest son had been crippled at Bunker Hill, his 2nd
already held a Lieutenancy. His 3rd son, Richard, was elected captain
of the new company and his commission confirmed by the Continental
Congress. The 4th son served throughout the war as sgt. This company
was assigned to the regiment of Col Nathan Hale of Coventry, Conn.
Richard himself retired to his Salem home; d Nov 17, 1786. There is a
vague tradition that he had 2 dau, but it is very doubtful. Sons:

a Reuben b Sept 7, 1729; bap Oct 25, 1730
b Oliver b July 28, 1736   c Richard b Oct 1, 1739
d Asa b Apr 5, 1743
e Stephen b Aug 26, 1745; d Sept 24, 1753

Reuben Dow bcdea m Salem Feb 8, 1753, Alidea (Leda, Lydia,

Ledea, Ledeah, Eleda, etc, in various rec) Jones b Methuen Apr 22, 1733,
d July 17, 1825, dau of Evan and Lydia (also spelled Ledah) (Ordway).
Lydia b Newbury July 14, 1693, dau of James Jr and Tirzah (Titcomb).
The Jones family descends from Evan Jones, immigrant from London, ae
19, May 21, 1631, of Amesbury and Salisbury.   Reuben and wife settled
1761 in Hollis, N H, two years later buying the homestead still owned by
his posterity.   This home beautifully located in as beautiful a village as
there is in New Hampshire now contains all his Revolutionary relics.
He entered at once the local militia company and was its 1st Lieut when
Lexington was fought.   The captain was temporarily incapacitated, so
Reuben marched to Lexington as acting Capt.   A month later he was
commissioned Captain, the commission to Reuben Dow, gentleman,
signed by Gen Joseph Warren, president pro tem of the Mass Provincial
Congress.   Hollis had been wide awake long in advance and the ordi-
narily peaceful militia had been carefully drilled for service. Nov 7, 1774,
Dea Stephen Jewett, Ensign Stephen Ames and Lieut Reuben Dow were
a committee to attend a county congress to arrange defense action.
The town then adopted a resolution,—"that we will at all times endeavor
to maintain our liberty and privileges, both civil and sacred, even at the
risque of our lives and fortunes, etc."   The march to Lexington was
made on foot and after a few days the Hollis company returned home to
prepare further for the next fight and await the call.   This came quickly,
so unexpectedly (so far as hours were concerned), that Reuben's little
son Daniel was left to unyoke the oxen from the plough.   Mrs Dow
made an equal division of the blankets in her store room and her mess
pork, one half going to the soldiers.   The company marched 69 strong,
all Hollis men, assigned on arival to Col Prescott's regiment.   It was the
second to arrive on the field at Bunker Hill and spent the night of June
16 digging trenches.   Next day they were on the firing line.   Reuben
was struck in the right ankle by a bullet, which shattered the bone.
Nevertheless, he made the retreat in good order with the troops.

On account of his disability he was continued for a short time on half
pay, later reduced to quarter.   In 1783 he was cited to appear before
the State authorities to show cause why his pension should not be dis-
continued.   A large number of witnesses were examined concerning
Reuben's ability to care for himself, and the verdict confirmed his pension
for life.   He d Feb 9, 1811; he and his wife buried in Hollis churchyard.
The homestead with all its Revolutionary relics is now owned by Charles
Jeremiah Bell bcdeabeaa.   The last Dow of Hollis disappeared about 1915
altho some of them still live in Pepperell, Framingham and other nearby
places.   Reuben's children:

    a Evan b Feb 6, 1754   b Stephen b Dec 30, 1757
    c Lydia b May 18, 1762; d July 14, 1825; m May 7, 1782, Oliver Lawrence;
       left a dau,—Lydia
    d Phoebe b June 22, 1766; m Oct 19, 1789, Ensign Daniel Merrill Jr; left 6
       children

   e Daniel b Dec 10, 1769
   f Lois b June 24, 1773; of Weare m Deering May 22, 1806, Moses Greenleaff

Evan Dow bcdeaa was a private under his father at Bunker Hill.
There are four instances of a Dow grandfather, father and son being in
Revolutionary service at the same time. Evan reported sick Oct 6,
1775, with 2 mos, 22 days service to his credit. He re-enlisted, mustered
out R I Aug 1778, Capt Daniel Emerson, Col Moses Nichols, receiving
£ 11-0-10. He was living 1785 in Deering, but may have come earlier.
His family settled in Weare between 1792 and 1794, and Hist Weare
depends much on hearsay about them. He m (date and place not in rec)
Sally Philbrick, dau of Jonathan and Beulah (Hardy). The genealogy
prepared for Richard S Dow is hopelessly wrong about their children,
and Hist Weare quite defective. Deering rec supply partial data. We
reconcile contradictory statements as best we can:

   a Evan b about 1783 (1780, Hist Weare)   b   Sarah b Deering May 31, 1785
   c Reuben b Deering June 11, 1787; d unm
   d Hannah b Deering Oct 23, 1789; m Jonathan Cram
   e Lydia b Deering Jan 29, 1789 (sic in rec, probably 1791; m Dec 31, 1812,
      Lowell Cram); a dau Aurelia m Joseph N Gove of Deering
   f Amos b Sept 24, 1794 (Weare rec, but overlooked in Hist Weare), son of Evan,
      farmer, and Sarah; untraced

There are three Weare rec, liable to be confused:

Stephen Dow b 1770, m Hannah Cram. If date is wrong he may
be adgfbde.

  —— **Dow** m Thomas Cram, brother of foregoing. He b about 1781,
son of Thomas and Sarah (Mudgett). She had 3 children; he m 2nd
wid Rebecca Collins.

  Phoebe Dow m Sept 14, 1819, Leland Cram b about 1785, 3rd
child of Thomas and Sarah (Mudgett). They moved to Ohio; she d and
he m 2nd. A son, Cleveland C, returned to Weare, m in 1850 and 1867.

Evan Dow bcdeaaa appears in subsequent family rec always as
Evans; m Jan 1, 1811, Nancy Balch of New Boston b June 10, 1789,
dau of Robert and Sarah (Dodge). They seem to have followed their
son to the Western Reserve, which presumably accounts for the in-
accuracies in Hist Weare. Children, list complete:

   a John b Nov 4, 1811; d Apr 5, 1867   b   Franklin b 1815; d 1870
   c Lucretia b 1817. The careers of both are unknown to the present living members
      of the family

John Dow bcdeaaaa moved to the Western Reserve and never
returned to New England; m Mch 1, 1835, Harriet Butterfield. Their
posterity are among the few who have a Revolutionary ancestry of
father, son and grandson. Children:

   a Adaline b Dec 25, 1835; not now living
   b Augusta b Feb 17, 1837; d Jan 25, 1858; m Bruce Shankland; only son Will,
      now of Benton Harbor, Mich
   c Wilder Butterfield b Dec 13, 1838; d Jan 18, 1921

d Nancy Lucretia b Feb 4, 1842; d Jan 1, 1910, M Frank Viets. A dau is now
    Gertrude Dow Titus of Minto, N D
e Joseph Edgar b Feb 5, 1844; d 1913
f Charles Evans b Jan 2, 1845
g Henry b Dec 24, 1850; d Oct 1, 1897
h Alice b May 25, 1854; d Sept 10, 1858
i Fremont b Mch 5, 1856   j Eva b Mch 27, 1858; d Oct 11, 1926
k John Jr b Mch 4, 1860; d Feb 8, 1922

Adaline Dow bcdeaaaaa m Edwin Herriman. Children,—Addie,
Ira, Fred, Frank and others, one being now Mrs Fred Moore of Brookfield, Mo

Wilder B Dow bcdeaaaac m Nov 8, 1877, Belle Marsh. Children:

a J Neal b Mch 11, 1879; d Sept 26, 1916
b Louise b July 7, 1887; m G A Funkey of Chicago; only child,—John Wilder
    b Feb 9, 1914

Joseph Edgar Dow bcdeaaaae m Kate Marsh. Only son:

a Jerry M b Feb 3, 1879; now of Long Beach, Calif

Charles E Dow bcdeaaaaf m Minnie Hewitt. Only child:

a Nellie b Dec 10, 1874; d Dec 10, 1899

Henry Dow bcdeaaaag m Delia Kent. Children:

a Frank Alvin b Aug 8, 1875; not now living
b Joseph Fremont b Aug 16, 1876; now of Los Angeles, Calif

Fremont Dow bcdeaaaai is spoken of as Colonel; m Hila Space;
2nd —— McMicheal; 1 child by each:

a —— now Mrs Della Dow Armstrong of N Y City
b John Fremont; unt

John J Dow bcdeaaaak was a well known citizen of Muncie, Ind;
m Lena Gregory; no children.

Hannah Dow bcdeaad m Mch 30, 1809, Jonathan Cram of Weare
Center, son of Nathan and —— (Nason). He was for many years drum-
mer in the town militia. Children:

a Lorenia b 1810; m 1832 Elijah A Leathe
b Nathan b Jan 2, 1813; m 1840 Mary Chase; 3 children
c William b 1815; m Mary Morse
d Cynthia b 1820; m 1840 John L Cheney of Lowell, Mass
e Jane b 1830; m —— Bamford

Lydia Dow bcdeaae m Lowell Cram b July 25, 1792, son of Ezekiel
and Mary (Kinson), who had moved to Weathersfield, Vt. Children:

a Selinda m Gilbert Lovering; lived Medford, Mass
b Amelia m Joseph Gove of Deering; 1 child,—Henry

Stephen Dow bcdeab lived in Deering, moved 1811 to Landgrove,
Vt; d Hollis Nov 1, 1839; m June 17, 1784, Abigail Jewett b Mch 17,
1763, d June 24, 1843, dau of Jacob and Mehitable (Mitchell). He served

a few days 1777 in the start for Ticonderoga, but in 1780 was at West
Point, Capt William Barron, Col Moses Nichols.   Children:

a   Lois b Deering Feb 2, 1786; m Dec 27, 1814, Christy Duncan of Hancock
b   Stephen b July 14, 1787   c   Hannah b Apr 28, 1790
d   Nathaniel b Aug 22, 1793   e   Jeremiah b Jan 5, 1795
f   Abigail b Aug 22, 1797   g   Elizabeth b Dec 24, 1800; d young

Stephen Dow bcdeabb m Mehitable Hall, both of Hollis, b Apr 24,
1789, d July 9, 1841, dau of Willis. He was later farmer of Deering. By
1850 he was farmer of Reading, Vt, realty assessed $3,000. He moved
finally to Woodstock; d Feb 18, 1876; m 2nd wid Mary Stowell of
Windsor b Mass 1789. She had 6 children of her own. Children:

a   Mehitable Elvira b Dec 1812; lived Landgrove, Vt; d Wrentham, Mass, Dec
      27, 1843; m 1833 Ebenezer Batchelder Parker; children,—Fannie,
      Elvira m —— Russell, Willard
b   Willard Hall b June 2, 1814   c   William Dexter d young
d   William Dexter b Sept 5, 1826; adopted the spelling Dowe
e   Caroline Abigail b Dec 17, 1831

Willard H Dow bcdeabbb of Landgrove d Woodstock Aug 6, 1877;
m Jan 1, 1840, Esther B Green; only child Sarah Mehitable m Charles
Cawl Buck.

William D Dowe bcdeabbd, grad Dartmouth 1855, practiced law
in Wilmington, Del; d Melrose Heights, Mass, Mch 17, 1902; in 1878
a director of the N J Historical Society and the Del Historical Society;
m Jan 11, 1866, Abbie Jennings Childress b Apr 10, 1840. Children:

a   Rebecca Reed b May 27, 1867; d Aug 23, 1868
b   Harriet Hall b June 4, 1868
c   Ellen Crate b July 6, 1869; d Jan 10, 1870

Hannah Dow bcdeabc d old age Jan 11, 1877; m Feb 2, 1814,
Simeon Spaulding b Hollis Feb 7, 1782, d Dec 28, 1839; moved to
Weston, Vt.   Children, all b Weston:

a   Simeon Dow b Feb 19, 1816; m Aug 17, 1843, Dorothy M Lawrence; son;—
      Melvin L; m 2nd Eliza B Work; dau, Mary A E d Weston Jan 5, 1907
b   Hannah C b May 27, 1818; d Nov 21, 1877, unm
c   Lucy M b Sept 1, 1820; m June 11, 1840, James M Taylor b July 11, 1818;
      children,—Lucella, Abbie, James H, Duane S, Romaine K, Nettie M. Ro-
      maine K Taylor has son Raymond of Weston, excellent genealogist
d   James G b Sept 21, 1822; d Nov 18, 1913; m Feb 29, 1844, Sophia A Hull;
      no children
e   ——
f   Lydia L b Feb 26, 1828; d Oct 20, 1851; m Aug 24, 1847, Dr M Martin; 2
      children, both d young
g   Eliza Ann b May 1, 1830; d Jan 22, 1851, unm
h   Mary Annette b Oct 21, 1834; d Sept 28, 1852

Caroline A Dow bcdeabbe m Rufus E Townsend of Reading, Vt;
2 children,—Abigail, Stephen Dow, now of Rutland.

Nathaniel Dow bcdeabd m Mch 13, 1817, Mary Ames b 1795, d
Mch 28, 1866, dau of Burpee and Anna (Cummings); settled in Hancock,

N H, for several years selectman; realty assessed in 1850 at $4,000. He d May 26, 1862. Children:

a Oliver Lawrence b Sept 1, 1818
b Lydia Lawrence b July 19, 1821; m Sept 2, 1857, Capt Asa Simons Jr of Hancock
c David Brainerd b Aug 16, 1826   d Caroline b 1827; d young, Hancock
e Hannah Abigail b May 21, 1830
f Jeremiah Ames b Jan 5, 1838; d Sept 23, 1839

Oliver L Dow bcdeabda m Apr 5, 1848, Mary Ann Eastman b Apr 29, 1821, d Dec 13, 1879, dau of Alpheus and Betsey of Hollis; realty assessed Hancock 1850 at $3,500; moved to Nelson, thence to Stoddard; d Keene Aug 1, 1886. Children:

a Mary Ames b Nov 12, 1851   b Hattie E b Dec 16, 1857

Mary A Dow bcdeabdaa m Stoddard Apr 1, 1874, Blanchard Bicknell, son of Ralph A and Emily (Irish); div; m 2nd Keene Apr 29, 1892, Henry Harvey Colburn, Congregationalist clergyman, b Groton Oct 3, 1833, son of Ezekiel and Joanna (Bartlett). Child:

a Mabel G b May 8, 1875; m —— Snyder of Lenox

David B Dow bcdeabdc of Hancock d Jan 13, 1857; m Mch 18, 1851, Caroline, wid of Jeremiah Ames, dau of Thomas and Sally (Proctor) Cummings. She had a son Jeremiah by 1st m. David's child:

a Lizzie d Jan 14, 1857, ae 2, 9 mos. Father and dau buried in s ame grave; mother followed Apr 12

Hannah A Dow bcdeabde m Jan 6, 1858, Gilman P Fletcher of Greenfield; d June 28, 1868, leaving son,—George I b May 6, 1861

Jeremiah Dow bcdeabe (Capt), farmer of Hollis, realty assessed 1850 at $10,000, d Nashua Mch 21, 1875; m Feb 25, 1818, Sarah Eastman d Feb 3, 1892, ae 92, 5 mos, dau of Joseph F and Abigail (Blanchard). Child:

a Sally A b Hollis Mch 26, 1819

Sarah A Dow bcdeabea d Apr 28, 1872; m June 18, 1844, John Charles Bell, machinist of Hollis. Children:

a Charles Jeremiah b June 2, 1845; heir to Reuben Dow's homestead
b Frank b Sept 8, 1847; dentist of Oswego, N Y

Abigail Dow bcdeabf d Oct 31, 1832; m Dec 28, 1813, Timothy Wyman b Nov 25, 1773, son of Timothy and Elizabeth (Shattuck); lived Hillsboro Bridge. Children:

a Lot b Dec 13, 1816; d Feb 4, 1833
b Stephen Dow b July 31, 1821; d Aug 29, 1900; m Ursula R Forsaith

Daniel Dow bcdeae is dismissed in the R S D ms as having sons Jefferson and Luther and being ancestor of the Pepperell Dows. He was a lifelong farmer of Hollis; d July 31, 1854; m Aug 20, 1794, Sally Lovejoy b Hollis June 26, 1775, d May 20, 1850, dau of Daniel and Sarah (Wyman). Children, all b Hollis:

a Daniel b Nov 27, 1794   b Sally b June 14, 1796
c Luther b May 1798   d Mark b Mch 15, 1800
e Polly b Nov 18, 1802; d ae 25, unm
f Thomas Jefferson b Feb 9, 1804
g Lydia b Sept 8, 1805; m Apr 8, 1834, Ezekiel Bradley, both of Hollis
h Lucy b June 5, 1807
i Indiana b July 5, 1815; m Apr 25, 1833, Moses Proctor of Hollis
j Hannah d unm   k Elizabeth d unm

Daniel Dow bcdeaea and his brother Thomas J are ancestors of all the Dow of Pepperell. He m Jan 28, 1818, Charlotte Farley of Hollis; 2nd Lucy Smith. Census 1850 gives him farmer of Hollis, realty $5,000, but no wife. Surely two children by 1st wife, but two others apparently quoted in error by a kinswoman, confused with children of bcdeaef:

a William, probably is bcdeaefc. Census 1850 surely correct gives Daniel F
      b Mass 1821, carpenter, realty $700; otherwise unt
b Jefferson d without children, probably d young
c Charles   d Mary; both surely error for bcdeaef
e Leonard Brooks b Sept 29, 1830   f Luther Henry b Aug 25, 1833
g John Albert b Dec 13, 1836

Leonard B Dow bcdeaeae, farmer and miller, located Northfield 1869; moved to Springfield, Mass 1898; d Mch 10, 1899; m Feb 21, 1869, Sarah J Pierce b Pepperell May 16, 1834, d Jan 25, 1918, dau of Calvin and Jane (Elliott). She spent 14 widowed years in Pepperell. Children:

a Lucy Jane b Milford Apr 14, 1870; teacher of Springfield, m George H Cushing
b Harriet Pierce b May 8, 1873; teacher of Springfield

Luther H Dow bcdeaeaf d Pepperell Aug 13, 1897; m June 9, 1861, Nellie M (family rec and directory give Marinda A) Divoll b Pepperell Sept 5, 1836.

John A Dow bcdeaeag d Pepperell Nov 17, 1888; m Mch 19, 1863, Josephine E Divoll. Only child:

a Meretta Josephine b May 30, 1866, d Sept 10, 1882. Very shortly before her
      sudden death she became engaged to Charles Morris Blood of Hollis, who
      continued to be looked upon as a member of the family. Seven years later
      he m Meretta's widowed mother and they have lived devotedly together
      ever since

Luther Dow bcdeaec d Hollis Jan 26, 1871; occupied his father's homestead, a greatly respected high-minded man, thorough believer in education; m Oct 18, 1841, Matilda Sophronia Newton of Nashua (Newborn, error in rec) d Medford Nov 13, 1904, dau of Asa and Mary (Stowe). Children:

a William d ae 5   b Daniel killed railroad accident ae 21 unm
c Frank Albert b Feb 20, 1854

Frank A Dow bcdeaecc d suddenly of heart disease Concord Dec 20,

1901; m Dec 31, 1879, Emma Louise Gilson of Dunstable, teacher of music. Only child:

a Ida Ellen b Hollis Feb 22, 1881; began musical education at 4; her mother
   lived with her in Boston, where she was soprano soloist, teacher and manager
   of her own concert troupe; unm. She rendered great assistance to the Author
   in clearing up the bcdeae lines. Her untimely death occurred in 1926

Mark Dow bcdeaed m Apr 13, 1830, Charlotte Blood b 1805, both of Hollis. Their farm assessed 1850 at $5,000. Children:

a Noah b Feb 23, 1831   b George b Apr 19, 1834, both Hollis

Noah Dow bcdeaeda, farmer of Hollis, d widower Hollis Apr 25, 1905; m Apr 11, 1854, Mary Jane Patch d June 4, 1897, ae 62-3-12, dau of Richard. Children:

a Melvin M b June 22, 1855; not now living
b Marietta b May 7, 1858; d Nov 18, 1888, unm
c Frank P b Hollis Feb 3, 1860

Melvin M Dow bcdeaedaa. Recent Framingham directory gave Mrs Mabel Dow stenographer, Frank M Dow purchasing agent, Flora I Dow, but letters of genealogical inquiry were never answered. Therefore items picked from vital rec may be incomplete. He m Flora L Cheney and apparently lived Hopkinton before settling in Framingham. Sons, found by own rec:

a Frank Melvin b Hopkinton 1882
b Perley Alvah b Framingham; m Holliston, Mass, May 23, 1909, Elsie May
   Bassett ae 23, dau of Edgar and Sarah
c Arthur B m So Framingham June 7, 1907, Laura Lunnell (spelling?), dau of
   Walter and Laura (Rogers)

Frank M Dow bcdeaedaaa, purchasing agent of Framingham, m Framingham Jan 12, 1903, Mabel E Taylor ae 19, dau of Frank A and Evelyn M (Lewellen). Two children found:

a —— b and d Framingham July 3, 1903   b Melvin Ernest b Aug 24, 1904

Frank P Dow bcdeaedac, farmer of Hollis, d of heart disease comparatively young; m Dec 29, 1885, Nellie H Parker ae 22 of Merrimac, dau of John R and Henrietta (Farley). No children. She m 2nd, Jan 4, 1898, Charles A Hale of Hollis; now wid living Los Angeles.

George Dow bcdeaedb, farmer and cooper of Hollis, d retired Nashua Aug 19, 1904; m Nashua Feb 28, 1872, Levy M Draper ae 35, dau of Thomas J and Mary J Avery. In rec of dau she appears as Lucy P b Lyndboro, N H. Two dau, of whom:

a Mary Frances b Hollis Jan 17, 1873; m Feb 20, 1892, Frank M Emery of
   Nashua; 2nd July 6, 1896, Liliola C Danforth of Boston

Thomas J Dow bcdeaef, born in the original homestead on the Hollis-Pepperell road, d 1879; m Rachel Elliott b Mass Dec 26, 1804. Census 1850 gives him farmer of Pepperell, with wife and two children:

a Charles b Sept 26, 1827   b Mary A b Oct 27, 1831
c William Prescott b Pepperell Dec 27, 1841

Charles Dow bcdeaefa, not found in 1850 census, of Pepperell d between 1884 and 1887; m Sarah E Miller d Pepperell July 1, 1903, ae 75-8-3, dau of Samuel and Sarah E. Dau in law mentioned 4 children only, but 5th distinctly credited in Mass vital statistics to Chas and Sarah (Miller) Dow:

 a Lizzie A m Charles Sartelle of Pepperell; no children
 b Frank M b Pepperell 1855
 c George H m Ada Morse; no children; now of Portland, Me
 d William W b 1865
 e Charles F b (by own m rec) Pepperell 1880 (mother then 52); m Haverhill Mch 27, 1907, Nettie Grant Belmer ae 16, dau of Andrew and Henrietta A (Herriman)

Frank M Dow bcdeaefab, not now living, m Nashua Nov 26, 1884, Lillian J Nutting. In Saugus, where they lived, she appears in rec as Sarah Lillie Josephine Nutting b 1866, dau of Charles P and Sarah J (Manley). Children:

 a Annie Ezzie b Pepperell 1886; m (Annie Lizzie) Ayer Mch 30, 1904, Alfred Thomas Hill ae 20, son of Thomas and Emma F (Durant); now of Pepperell
 b Ella F b Pepperell 1887; m Pepperell Apr 11, 1906, Lucius E Stark ae 21 of Hollis, son of George H and Hattie R (Hamilton); now of Fitchburg
 c Frederick; of Nashua; unm in 1923
 d George m Elizabeth Brownell; lives Niagara Falls
 e Marion E m Lester Terry (Torrey); lives Nashua
 f Charles Franklin b June 25, 1909; of Pepperell

William W Dow bcdeaefad of East Pepperell d since 1923; m June 18, 1897, Alice Maud Stevens ae 32, dau of Hiram P and Nancy (Tufts). Children:

 a Clarence R; now of Holden, Mass; m Emma Hodgkins. Has,—Violet and Clarice
 b Edith A; now Mrs Morse of Pepperell
 c Leonard Wilson b Apr 28, 1902 d Harry Jefferson b Feb 22, 1905

Mary A Dow bcdeaefb m Silas Stone. Children:

 a Anna; now Mrs Charles Walker of Greenwood, Ind b Kate
 c Frank

William P Dow bcdeaefc d Buffalo, N Y, Oct 4, 1918; m Mishawaka, Ind, Mch 31, 1870, Mary A Wilhelm Miller b Mishawaka May 20, 1848, d Buffalo May 30, 1905. Only child:

 a Harry Prescott b South Bend, Ind, July 25, 1871

Harry P Dow bcdeaefca, many years resident of Buffalo, member of Sons of Revolution, m July 29, 1901, Florence Virginia Hearn b Erie, Pa, Sept 22, 1872. No children.

Lydia Dow bcdeaeg m Ezekiel Bradley; had

 a Louisa m May 6, 1862, Silas M Spalding of Hollis; no children
 b George, of Milford, N H; m Maria Colburn Hudson; 2 children
 c Mary E m July 20, 1874, Stephen T Smith of Hollis; 3 children

Lucy Dow bcdeaeh of Hollis m Nov 2, 1829, Capt Leonard Blood. Children:

 a Dexter m Dec 11, 1862, Cornelia A Lovejoy of Amherst; no children
 b Amos m —— Eastman; no children
 c Lucy Ann m 1869 Isaac Pierce of Pepperell; 1 son

U NEQUAL fortunes attended the four sons of Richard Dow bcde, who at the beginning of the war had been a comparatively well to do man. He had advanced all his money and used his credit to support the town military measures. When this money came back to him it must have been in terms of Continental currency, soon dwindling to nothing. All four sons elected other permanent homes, altho the second returned to the old homestead three years after his father's death.

Oliver Dow bcdeb, saddler, m 1757 Hannah Pattee b Dec 7, 1737, d Mch 11, 1820, dau of Seth and Dorcas of Salem; moved 1773 to Hopkinton. That he was in Salem early in 1775 was due either to a visit or in the expectation of hostilities. He was at Bunker Hill and July 9, 1776, was a 2nd Lieut, Lieut Col Thomas Stickney. It would be remarkable for a commissioned officer to re-enlist as a private, but some Oliver Dow served 21 days in the R I campaign, Capt Daniel Emerson, Col Moses Nichols, mustered out Aug 1778 and we know of no other Oliver. About 1790 the family moved back from Hopkinton to Salem. Census gives him 3a, 2b, 4c. Ill health pursued him. In 1804 the town voted to abate his taxes until his health was better. He finally retired to his son's home in Waterville, Me; d Dec 18, 1824. Children:

a Phoebe b Mch 14, 1758   b Hannah b July 18, 1762
c Oliver b Apr 24, 1764; d in infancy   d Ellice b Sept 1, 1768
e Levi b Mch 25, 1771   f Simeon b June 22, 1774
g Oliver b Hopkinton Apr 24, 1776   h Phene b Feb 21, d Oct 3, 1777
i Lavinia (or Levina) b 1779; m Feb 1, 1809, John Farmer; 7 children, 5 d in infancy

Ellice Dow bcdebd d Londonderry; m Mch 24, 1791, Benjamin Leach of Salem. Children:

a Benjamin b July 12, 1796; m June 10, 1832, Sarah Cram of Weare; d Litchfield, N H, Oct 3, 1875
b Ira   c Simeon   d Hannah

Levi Dow bcdebe of Hopkinton moved to Boston and in 1833 to Waterville, Me, where he was an inn keeper; d Waterville Mch 27, 1849; Universalist; m Jan 19, 1802, Catherine Whipple d June 8, 1818; 2nd July 18, 1819, Elizabeth McClure Horton b Apr 7, 1791, d Oct 11, 1864, dau of Benjamin and Mary (McLane) of Boston. Children:

a Levi Albertus b June 10, 1802; d young
b Catherine b Feb 21, 1804   c Charlotte b Apr 21, 1805
d Charlotte Augusta b Nov 9, 1806
e Charles Austin b Boston Nov 17, 1808   f William H b July 14, 1810
g Elizabeth b Nov 1, 1812; d Jan 30, 1899; m Benjamin Mirick
h Thomas Augustus b Jan 17, 1814; unt
i Mary Marshall b Feb 29, 1820   j George Sylvanus Cobb b Oct 24, 1821
k Marshall Adams b Aug 16, 1823; d Mch 7, 1825
l John Randolph b July 18, 1825; d Sept 29, 1864; m Apr 23, 1850, Margaret A Thayer; unt
m Albert Marhall b Jan 1, 1830; d June 9, 1853

Charles A Dow bcdebee, farmer of Waterville, d Dec 23, 1891; m Dec 13, 1829, Philomela Ann Getchell b Waterville Sept 3, 1803, d May 16, 1880, dau of Nehimiah Jr, sea captain. Children:

a Nehimiah Getchell b 1831   b Levi A b 1835
c —— dau (not in census), now Mrs Fox of Waterville

N Getchell Dow bcdebeea m Oct 18, 1877, Ella Watson Edwards b Augusta Dec 26, 1854; moved to Los Angeles, Calif, map maker, surveyor. His wid m 2nd Fred Howe and moved to San Diego. Children, known as Howe, later resumed the name Dow:

a Helen Edwards b Los Angeles Mch 30, 1879; m De Forest Howry d 1920
b Ralph Getchell, accountant, Los Angeles; m Shirley Jenkins; 1 child

Levi A Dow bcdebeeb, farmer of Waterville; sgt 21st Me vols; m Oct 3, 1858, Josephine E Richardson b Winthrop Apr 5, 1840. Children:

a Cadde E b Oct 20, 1859; d Dec 12, 1864
b Charles C b May 5, 1861; d Oct 23, 1861
c Lizzie Drury b July 4, 1864; d Mch 21, 1892, unm
d Louise S b July 2, 1866; d July 7, 1868
e Evelyn Piper b Aug 16, 1868; d Skowhegan May 12, 1917, pianist, unm
f Ellen D b May 14, 1870; d May 26, 1874
g Josephine M b Jan 6, 1872
h Eldridge G b Oct 1, 1875; d Apr 6, 1881   i Levi R b Apr 13, 1881; unt

William H Dow bcdebef, b Boston, lived Waterville; d Aug 23, 1857; m June 19, 1834, Delia A Williams d June 25, 1895, ae 80-10-8, dau of Col Fernald Johnson and Elizabeth (Sanborn). Children:

a Alice E b Mch 25, 1835
b Ada Bradbury b Mch 10, 1839; d Apr 14, 1840

Alice E Dow bcdebefa d Newport, R I, Jan 13, 1900; m Apr 22, 1868, Capt Charles C Churchill, veteran of Mexican and Civil Wars.

Mary M Dow bcdebei d Minneapolis, Minn, Oct 17, 1904; m Aug 28, 1846, Paul Langdon Chandler of Fryeburg, son of President of Harvard College. Children:

a George Langdon b Waterville Jan 25, 1849; m Boston Nov 23, 1873, Emily Phipps
b Lizzie Langdon b Dec 23, 1850; d Sept 28, 1851
c Sewall Messenger b Dec 23, 1853; m Aug 1879 Eva Gee Putney of Duluth, Minn
d Philip Marhsall b Apr 27, 1856; of Minneapolis

George S C Dow bcdebej d Delaware Water Gap June 23, 1888; m Dec 5, 1843, Elizabeth Charlotte Sylvester b Norridgewalk Aug 29, 1825, d Bangor Oct 1919, dau of Samuel and Charlotte (Heald). Unitarian; lived Waterville, Boston, Davenport, Iowa, N Y City, Bangor; dry goods merchant, lawyer, banker, large real estate operator, and general capitalist. Having large affairs at the Corbin Banking Co of

Iowa and N Y, he met there and was more or less connected in business with R K Dow adggdcca. Children:

a   Ada Horton b Mch 6, 1846; of Bangor, unm
b   Herbert George b Brooklyn Aug 22, 1854; d Mch 13, 1878; grad Swarthmore; had entered Columbia Law School
c   Richard Henry Sylvester b Davenport May 2, 1863

Richard S Dow bcdebejc, LLB, Boston University, lawyer, financier of Boston, with home in Marion, Mass, essayed a genealogy of the Thomas Dow line, but, depending on professional work, failed utterly to locate its origin. The ms of later generations has been a great help and a great hindrance, unsafe to take any of its statements for granted. Unitarian, he m Oct 12, 1886, Abbie Jenness Rawson b Feb 17, 1865, dau of James F and Sarah D of Boston. Children:

a   George Herbert b Aug 7, 1887   b   Rawson b Aug 7, d Aug 21, 1887
c   Marion b Bangor July 17, 1888
d   Dorothy b Boston Dec 24, 1890; m Leslie Hastings of Boston; dau,—Dorothy
e   Elsie b Boston Jan 25, 1898

Marion Dow bcdebejcc m Mch 9, 1911, James G Blaine 3rd of N Y City; active 1920 in Government finance. Child:

a   Elizabeth b May 3, 1913; d Marion Oct 7, 1917

John R Dow bcdebel appears in Waterville 1850 census, b 1820, realty assessed $5,000; wife Margaret b Me 1825; no children, but mother Elizabeth living with them.

Simeon Dow bcdebf d Boston June 11, 1827; m Jan 10, 1799, Elizabeth Burns McClure b Boston 1780, d Milton Sept 1843; owned a wood wharf in Boston. Children:

a   John R b 1799; m Jan 4, 1833, Hannah Kendall; stock broker of Boston. Untraced, but possibly a son: Moses M d Meford Oct 1, 1842, ae 4 mos
b   Simeon b Aug 31, 1801   c   Albert b 1803; unt
d   Josephine Theresa b Nov 22, 1804; d Boston Sept 23, 1852; m David Coolidge Ballard
e   Elizabeth b about 1808
f   Emeline A b about 1809; m —— Kendall of Blue Hill, Mass
g   Joseph Warren b June 17, 1814

John R Dow bcdebfa. As we have noted already, the professionally compiled genealogy of the b lines is not to be trusted without corroboration. We find that Mary E White, wid of John R Dow, d Boston Mch 24, 1902, ae 82-10-7. Perhaps he never left Boston; perhaps he made a 2nd m.

Simeon Dow bcdebfb, cooper of Medford, d Aug 13, 1883; m Dec 29, 1824, Lucy Hatch Young b Marshfield June 23, 1799, d Medford Dec 8, 1870. Children:

a   John R b Boston Sept 24, 1825
b   Angeline M b July 28, 1827; d Aug 12, 1864; m George M Baxter
c   Charles H b July 7, 1829; d Shanghai, China, unm
d   Benjamin H b Wellfleet Oct 6, 1831   e   Albert F b Sept 24, 1833
f   Abbie C b Apr 21, 1836; m Perry Colman of Washington, D C

g   Simeon A b Oct 14, 1839; unm in 1881
h   Lucy A b July 12, 1842; d June 29, 1861, unm

John R Dow bcdebfba, cooper of Medford, m Oct 3, 1847, Philena S Lord b Portland, Me, Apr 21, 1825. Children:

a   Georgietta b Dec 3, 1848; d Jan 25, 1852
b   Charles A b Aug 1, 1850   c   Frank W b Sept 3, 1852, both Boston
d   Theodore W b Oct 20, 1858; of Medford unm in 1881

Charles A Dow bcdebfbab, in 1900 clerk of Medford, m Nov 15, 1876, Emma F Jaquith b Lynn Oct 22, 1850. No children in 1881.

Frank W Dow bcdebfbac, expressman of Exeter, N H, d Dorchester, Aug 25, 1903; m Nellie A Clark; 2nd Sept 3, 1878, Mary J Catherell, ae 29, b Nova Scotia. Original ms of b lines gives her Mary Casano, probably error.

Benjamin H Dow bcdebfbd, brass moulder of Watertown, served in Civil War 1862 to its close; wounded in thigh; m Elizabeth M Lord b Portland, Me, Apr 1, 1833

Albert F Dow bcdebfbe, ship carpenter of Chelsea, served 3 years in 39th Mass; wounded in head; m Emily N Dyer; 1 son, 1 dau.

a   Albert T d Medford Jan. 26, 1928, ae 68; bur Dorchester

Joseph W Dow bcdebfg, banker in Illinois, later Plymouth, Wis; m Nov 23, 1837, Alice B Champney b Charlestown, Mass, Jan 15, 1815. Children:

a   Sarah E b Earlsville, Ill, July 25, 1838; m Aug 17, 1874, ——
b   Josephine T b Aug 25, 1840; m Dec 24, 1861, —— Barnes of St Louis
c   Susie B b Jan 8, 1845; d Aug 13, 1846
d   Alice b Ottawa, Ill, Feb 21, d Feb 26, 1848   e   Edward A b Apr 1, 1853

Edward A Dow bcdebfge, pres of State Bank, Plymouth; m Dec 25, 1876, Ida J Hotchkiss b Plymouth Oct 5, 1855. Children:

a   Edith Alice b Sept 24, 1877; d Jan 5, 1878
b   Florence b July 14, d July 22, 1879
c   Robert W b Sept 25, 1881; in 1922 broker of Milwaukee
d   Edward H b Dec 23, 1883; d July 25, 1884

Oliver Dow bcdebg, farmer, moved from Salem to Hudson, N H; d Dec 25, 1845; m Mch 22, 1801, Susan Thayer b Nov 3, 1777, d Apr 19, 1833. Children:

a   Thayer b Jan 22, 1802   b   Elbridge b Mch 3, 1804
c   Eliza b Apr 6, d Dec 15, 1808   d   Lorenzo b Nov 24, 1809
e   Lovina (Lavinia, State rec) b Oct 26, 1812; d Mch 31, 1886; m 1848 James M
     Davis; moved to Whitewater, Wis; dau,—Susan R b 1845, thrice m, thrice
     wid; 3rd husband Edson Hollister, veteran of Civil War, d Sept 1909
f   Joseph G b Dec 18, 1814; d Aug 1, 1818

Thayer Dow bcdebga m 1822 Rachel Lawrence b Hudson Mch 25, 1804; d 3 hours apart Mch 31,-Apr 1, 1873; bur in same grave; shoemaker, moved to Chemung Co, N Y, 1837; to Dunkirk, Wis, 1845, later to Weyanwega, becoming farmer.   Children:

  a Oliver Parker b Hudson Sept 13, 1823
  b Eliza Lawrence b Jan 18, 1825; d July 31, 1880
  c Adeline b July 31, 1826; d Oct 22, 1898; m Edward Rogers of Indian Ford,
     Wis
  d Susan b July 17, 1828   e John Thayer b Jan 12, 1831
  f Hosea Ballou b Jan 15, 1833   g James L b Nov 20, 1838
  h William H b Jan 16, 1841
  i Lavina b June 2, 1843; d 1863; her dau m Joe Brockway of Whitewater

Oliver P Dow bcdebgaa, merchant and editor of Palmyra, Wis; d May 1901; m Aug 19, 1846, Mary B Boss b Smyrna, N Y, Dec 11, 1822, d June 15, 1859; 2nd, Mch 20, 1861, Emerett Sophronia Graves b July 11, 1837, dau of Lester.   Children:

  a Catherine L b Nov 20, 1847; m —— Phillips of Meridian, Miss
  b Herbert L b Aug 21, 1850; d Mch 29, 1852   c Everett E b July 7, 1853
  d Mary Delphine b Mch 29, 1856; m Charles Bishop
  e Oliver L b June 13, 1857   f Nellie E b Jan 3, 1862
  g Clifford L b Aug 8, 1864   h Birney T b Mch 24, 1866; d Sept 20, 1867
  i Lura J b June 1, 1869
  j Alice Cary b Feb 3, 1871; m William B Schultz
  k Bertha B b Sept 7, 1873; m Charles W McIntyre of Ft Atkinson, Wis

Everett E Dow bcdebgaac, breeder of registered Jersey cattle, Whitewater, m Dec 17, 1877, Kitty Bishop; has watched with keen interest the progress of this Book.   Children:

  a Harry L b Feb 1, 1879   b Herbert J b Jan 26, 1881
  c Agnes N b Mch 15, 1883   d Florence b Jan 12, 1888; d Nov 1907
  e Everett J b June 23, 1891   f Parker B b Apr 16, 1896
  g Marian b Oct 26, 1898

Harry L Dow bcdebgaaca m July 1905 Maud Hayes.   Children:

  a Katharyn A b Aug 29, 1907   b Harry H b Apr 21, 1916

Herbert J Dow bcdebgaacb m Aug 1907 Margaret Barlow.   Child:

  a Robert T b Jan 8, 1911

Agnes N Dow bcdebgaacc m Feb 9, 1910, W J Baker.   Children:

  a Alberta M b Jan 8, 1911   b Florence b Aug 28, 1912
  c Elsbeth M b Oct 2, 1915

Everett J Dow bcdebgaace m Nov 20, 1913, Emena Briggs.

Oliver Leslie Dow bcdebgaae of Portland, Ore, m Edna Malcolmson; she d; he m 2nd Minnie Specht.   Children:

  a Evalyn b Dec 19, 1894   b Edna b Dec 14, 1898; d 1907

Clifford Lincoln Dow bcdebgaag of Savannah, Ill, m Bridget McGraw

Eliza L Dow bcdebgab m Hiram Kuehn.   Children:

  a Elvira Hartsen m Robert Charley of Palmyra
  b Susan Watson m James W Congdon of La Crosse
  c Frank Watson of Minneapolis, m Agnes Swinton
  d Ada Martina m Frank Reddell; 2nd David Wescott of Minneapolis

Susan Dow bcdebgad m Sumner Wilson; 2nd George Wrighton. Children live Sioux Falls, So Dak:

a Ella (Wilson) m Irving Fisher   b Jessie (Wrighton) m —— Hubbard
c George, not living

John T Dow bcdebgae of Madison, Wis, d 1917 of old age; m Jane Irish. Children:

a Elva Jane m Edgar A Gilman; children,—Leila O, Edgar Dow
b Leila Eileen, of Madison
c Myrtle Irene m Perry Wern of London, Eng

Hosea B Dow bcdebgaf moved to Buffalo, N Y; later for many years dry goods merchant of Little Rock, Ark; m Josephine ——. Children:

a Kitty m Lester C Stevens of Buffalo   b Cornelius

Cornelius Dow bcdebgafb m Matie Burton; neither living 1921. Children:

a Burton   b Matie

James Lawrence Dow bcdebgag d Kansas about 1912; banker of Fredonia, So Dak; m Sept 25, 1866, Mary Brooks b Canada. Children:

a Viola Maud b Dane Co, Wis, July 16, 1867; m Albert A Stoddard d before 1921; lives Manhattan, Kan. Children,—Albert, Frank, Jessie, Delia, Lola, Mary, James, Ida, Lawrence d in infancy, Lawrence, Gladys, Ula, James, Hollis, Carol
b Percy James b Dec 31, 1870
c Zada Mary b Mitchell Co, Iowa, Feb 22, 1873; m Carl August Hedberg of Palian, Kan. Children,—James, Hollis, Carol
d Ada Jessie b Feb 23, 1876; m John Sandberg
e Ula May b Feb 1, 1880; now a college instructor, Cambridge, Mass, unm
f Jay Lawrence b Koto, Dak, Sept 30, 1884
g Odessa Della b Oct 30, 1887; of Manhattan, Kan
h Jane Mary b May 3, 1893; m Harold A Thackrey of Manhattan

Percy J Dow bcdebgagb of Duluth, Minn, m Nina Norton. Children:

a Gladys   b Ula

Jay L Dow bcdebgagf m Olga Korup. Children:

a Alvina Margaret   b Dorothy Jane

William Harrison Dow bcdebgah of Minneapolis, served 4 years in Civil War; m Sept 1, 1871, Charlotte E Janney b Weyanwega May 24, 1854. Child:

a Irene H b Weyanwega Nov 24, 1873; not now living

Elbridge Dow bcdebgb, for many years postmaster of Hudson, N H, d Apr 6, 1856; m June 24, 1830, Anna Davidson Robinson b Dec 17, 1804, d May 13, 1842, dau of David and Martha (Anderson); 2nd, June 29, 1843, Mary K Abbot of Sutton b 1816. Children:

a David Anderson b May 30, 1830; d June 27, 1849
b Elbridge Gardiner b Aug 28, 1832   c Martha Ann b Dec 9, 1835

d Lovisa Crosby b Jan 7, 1839; d Sept 7, 1858
e Dura F b 1844; sharpshooter in the army, d typhoid, ae 17
f Zetta A b 1848; d ae about 18   g Ella d ae 2
h Ada M b June 13, 1852; d Nashua May 10, 1920, unm
i Frank P b May 23, 1854

Elbridge G Dow bcdebgbb, wholsesale crockery dealer in Greenwich St, N Y City, m Josephine Theresa Chambers of Bridgeport, Conn. He is buried in Trinity churchyard, 155th St. Youngest child posthumous:

a Louis b 1850; d 1864
b Josephine Theresa b N Y June 30, 1862; now teacher of domestic science' Technical High School, Montreal
c Richard Frank b N Y Sept 8, 1864

Richard F Dow bcdebgbbc, expert accountant of Hartford, Conn, m 1888 Ida May Heath Marshall, both now living. Only child:

a Ada Louise b Apr 13, 1892; fatally burned Dec 11, 1907, while making Christmas gifts of burned wood

Frank P Dow bcdebgbi, overseer in a Nashua mill, m Apr 7, 1880, Ellen A Raymond b Feb 26, 1844, d Nashua Sept 21, 1913, dau of and Hannah S (Melvin).

Lorenzo Dow bcdebgd, teamster of Manchester, m 1837 Harriet M Jones b 1816; moved to Whitewater, Wis; d Apr 2, 1879. Children:

a Francina b 1838; m July 4, 1859, Daniel M Garland of Martin's Ferry, N H; left 3 children
b Newman J b 1841   c Alonzo C b May 23, 1843   d George d in infancy
e Harriette b about 1846; m Arthur Taylor d after 1900; lives Delavan, Wis

Newman J Dow bcdebgdb m 1861 Marana Kuehn; d leaving young children:

a Newman J lives Beloit, Wis; fireman; no children
b Lulu R m James Waugh; 6 children

Alonzo C Dow bcdebgdc m Apr 9, 1864, Frances A Powers now dead; moved many years ago to Neb; thence to Glenwood Springs, Colo. Children:

a Rosina B b May 12, 1857; d Apr 1, 1886   b Minnie b Nov 17, 1872
c Elton b Aug 5, 1875. Recent Glenwood Springs directory gives Alonzo C, laborer, and E A Dow, carpenter

---

Richard Dow bcdec left four young children to march to Lexington; enlisted 1776 in Col Joshua Wingate's reg for Canadian service. Next year he was elected captain of the Salem company organized by his father and was attached to Col Nathan Hale's reg. After the war he settled in Bow, N H. An abler man of business than his brothers he accumulated considerable property; d 1798. Apparently d intestate. All family rec give him but four children. He m 1765 Mary Saunders, rec not found, and probably not in Salem. There were five Dow families in Bow about this time and the records are sadly imperfect. Census 1790 gives him 2a, 4c and lists his oldest son separately. Obviously, then, there was a dau not appearing in family rec:

a   Solomon b Feb 11, 1766   b   Betty b Oct 1767.
c   Olli b July 17, 1770
d   Isaiah b May 17, 1774

Some Richard Dow of Bow, perhaps identical (no disconnected Richard is suitable) had children, Bow rec, mother not stated:

e   Sarah b May 11, 1779 (census calls for some dau)
f   Stephen b Jan 13, 1783. Unknown; if bcdecf, surely d before 1790

Solomon Dow bcdeca was known as Capt, altho the title is not mentioned in his son's autobiography. He must be the Solomon who enlisted June 15, 1780, Capt Samuel Paine, Maj Benjamin Whitcomb, for the defense of the western frontier, altho he was but 14. He m Phoebe Buzzell of Bow, dau of Dea James, selectman, revolutionary veteran, subsequently capt of militia, certainly a follower of the church militant. Date of m not found; list of children from son's autobiography, does not tally with 1790 census, which gives a young son. He settled in Plainfield, N H, between 1795 and 1801, living on the "Plain" in a house which has been torn down but recently. He was a man of no small ability, combining merchandising with his farming and having capital to lend. While in Plainfield he lost without apparent embarassment $1,600 by the failure of a local merchant. In 1811 he moved across the river to Hartland, Vt, buying what was considered the finest place in town, a large white house on land sloping toward the river. It had a large upstairs room in which the masonic meetings were held, he being lodge master. In 1812 he made a horseback trip to Ohio to inspect living conditions and decided to take his family there. The outbreak of the war delayed his plan, especially as a son enlisted promptly, and fought throughout the war. In 1816 the family started toward Ohio, but halted for the winter on the main Buffalo road nine miles west of Batavia. By spring he had decided to stay permanently and bought a cleared farm with the best log house in the region. An itinerant cooper once gained shelter at the house and was met with a proposition to stay, Solomon buying a new set of tools and backing the business. Becoming himself proficient, he always did more or less coopering. He d of ague 1822, ae 56. While opportunities for education were limited, he had the highest idea of the value of it and impressed it on his children. All his daughters at one time or another taught school. While at Batavia there occurred the mysterious disappearance of one Morgan, who had written a book "exposing" masonry. It was widely believed he had been killed by the masons. As Solomon was then lodge master, he found himself in something of a storm center. A national anti-masonic political party was started, which existed for several years.

His wid, who d ae 54, m 2nd Rev —— Gross, Universalist clergyman, editor of a religious paper and principal of a college preparatory school, who is spoken of very highly by his stepson.   Solomon's children:

a   Sarah b Bow May 29, 1789; m Wheaton Mason
b   Mary b June 5, 1793; m Benjamin Nutting
c   Richard b Bow Apr 18, 1795
d   Eliza b Feb 10, 1797; m Martin Montgomery
e   Caroline b Plainfield Dec 1, 1801; m Nathan Sawyer
f   Nancy b July 5, 1804; m Gaylord Harper
g   Hannah b July 20, 1806   h   Albert Gallatin b Aug 1808
i   Amos b Hartland May 22, 1811
j   Phoebe b Aug 3, 1813; m Abram Dinsmore

Richard Dow bcdecac served through the War of 1812, stationed at Lake Ontario, and returned home, but did not accompany the family westward.   His brother's autobiography makes no further mention of him, and, for some reason not explained to the Author, he was regarded as the family black sheep.   He lived to old age; m Cynthia Woodworth. Two children, of whom:

a   Chester Perry, b presumably about 1825

Chester P Dow bcdecaca lived to old age in Eaton Rapids, Mich; m Clara Trask.   Three children:

a   —— dau m and living 1921 in Eaton Rapids
b   Edward Everett d Toledo, Ohio, after 1902; a member of the Sons of the Revolution
c   ——, a son, unt

Hannah Dow bcdecag m 1827 Thomas Wilder b Winchendon Mass, July 6, 1800, school teacher of Madison and Attica, N Y, who entered the hardware business in Randolph, N Y, with his oldest son. He d Apr 1, 1864.   Children:

a   Henry Fayette   b   Delia E   c   Sarah D
d   Abel b Aug 18, 1835; d Jan 13, 1837   e   Mary b May 13, 1838
f   Thomas Eugene   g   Helen T b Jan 13, 1852

Albert Gallatin Dow bcdecah, in some ways the most remarkable man mentioned in this Book, d after preparations had been begun for the celebration of his 100th birthday, May, 1908.   His father had been tall and lanky, he was but 5 feet, 4.   He never had a sick day in his life until his last illness, and never missed a day from his office, vacations excepted, for over 50 years.   He complained one afternoon of a little difficulty in breathing and decided to go to bed.   Next day he died of the painless dissolution which is the normal end of human life, altho not occurring once in 10,000 cases.   He had never taken any particular care of his health, never shirked unlimited work, never denied himself anything he was particularly fond of, never used liquor, enjoyed cigars but abandoned smoking for "the latter 75 years of my life."   He always rose at 6 A M and devoted one to three hours to miscellaneous reading, seldom on any fixed plan or subject.

His schooling was the ordinary of the time.   His father dying while he was yet young, he had to go early to work.   While at school two

daughters of Wheaton Mason attracted his attention. "I remember
that Nancy's toes touched the floor but Lydia Ann's did not." Nancy
became his 1st wife, Lydia Ann his 2nd. His early career was typical of
the region and the time, coupled with a definite ambition to become a
merchant. For his first farm work he received $6 a month, soon to be
raised to $8, half cash, half notes. It was hard work, farming, for trees
had to be felled and land cleared. With his savings of a year he rode to
Ransom's Grove, where he had the promise of a clerkship in a general
store, but he found the store closed by the sheriff the very day of his
arrival. Instead of going back, he rode to Batavia, where Wheaton
Mason lived. Here he tended grocery store and harvested potatoes
three miles away. On the side he learned the shoe trade so that a year
later he felt competent to go into business for himself. He moved with
the Masons to Silver Creek, where Mason bought a hotel and he began a
shoe and leather jobbing business. He soon took a year off to learn the
tannery business. Oct 4, 1829, he m Freelove (Nancy) Mason, whose
mother was Octavia Belden and whose stepmother was his sister Sarah.
He bought a house at once and was never thereafter without a home of
his own and a reasonable amount of land nearby. At Silver Creek he
was tax collector, constable and justice of the peace. In middle life he
was an assemblyman and for 2 years state senator, refusing a re-election
which would interfere with his business. In 1840 he took his first railroad
journey, going by stage to Syracuse to make better time. The track was
of strap iron laid on timbers. The train was off the track two or three
times before it got to Albany, but the passengers alighted and pushed it
back on again. At Albany hill a rope was tied to the train, which was
thus pulled up the incline by a stationary engine. From Albany he
proceeded to New York by steamboat.

He started various stores, generally with an agent to conduct each.
He sold his dry goods store in East Randolph to his brother Amos.
Stoves were a novelty and to his mind presented great possibilities. He
bought in New York and, as the Erie R R to Randolph was abandoned
just about that time, he established wagon routes for deliveries over
several counties. Currency was scarce in the southerly counties; he
gave long credit and secured as long, so it became necessary to add a
banking business to his other activities. He was extending credit all the
way to Pittsburgh. His own bank in Randolph was opened in 1860, and
three years later he abandoned his merchandising. He subsequently
controlled the National Chatauqua Co Bank and became a stockholder
in many other financial institutions. He was a leading spirit in the
Chatauqua movement. A Universalist, he attended the Congregational
church and generally taught a Bible class. His 1st wife dying Aug 21,
1847, he m 2nd, Apr 26, 1850, Lydia Ann Mason d June 11, 1891. Children:

    a   James b July 1, 1830   b   Warren b Jan 15, 1833

c Sarah b Jan 22, 1837; d Feb 6, 1840   d Mary b June 13, 1842
e Albert Gallatin b Apr 17, 1844   f Charles Mason b Aug 1, 1853

James Dow bcdecaha d Feb 15, 1859; m Lucy O Stevens of Rochester; one son d young.

Warren Dow bcdecahb was the first pupil of Randolph Academy; clerk for his father 5 years; then partner until 1863 in A G Dow & Co; then went into business in Detroit; sold out; with his cousin started Dow & Co, bankers of Bradford, Pa, financing oil enterprises; next cashier of the Salamanca Nat Bank; m Sept 1, 1858, Josephine Guernsey, dau of John J and Susan (Thorne).   Children:

a Louise b Mch 13, 1864; m George E Allen of Plainfield, N J; children,—
   Josephine, Louise
b Jennie b May 1, 1867; m Allen Falconer; children,—Eleanor, Janet

Mary Dow bcdecahd m James G Johnson of Randolph, where her home still is. Children:

a Marc Dow b June 23, 1866; editor of the Randolph Register
b Willoughby Dow b Jan 26, 1868, d Dec 1868
c Grace Dow b May 8, 1870; d July 22, 1905
d Ruth Dow b May 14, 1876   e Daisy Dow b Feb 8, 1880; d Mch 22, 1884

Albert Gallatin Dow bcdecahe has always preferred Randolph as his home; served through the war; disch 1865 from 64th N Y Vol Inf as 1st Lieut and Adjutant; m 1868 Frances A Sheldon, dau of George A and Margery, d Apr 19, 1916. He has devoted many years to the community in which he lives; long treas of the board of trustees of Chamberlain Institute, pres of the board of water commissioners; supt of Randolph cemetery, founded and owns the Albert G Dow Free Library for the benefit of the public at large. No children.

Charles Mason Dow bcdecahf succeeded to the business of his father and was one of the best known bankers in the State; Congregationalist; republican, but never actively identified with politics; grad Oberlin College, BA 1869, MA 1871; studied law in Randolph 3 years; LLD from Bethany College 1914 and Niagara University 1915; from 1879 to 1884 partner in Dow & Co, Bradford, Pa; vice pres of Salamanca Trust Co since 1880; pres Jamestown Nat Bank 1888 to 1899; then pres of Nat Chatauqua Co Bank; vice pres 1903-4 of Title Guarantee & Trust Co, N Y City; trustee since 1903 of American Surety Co.

His best known service was in connection with the preservation of Niagara Falls; member of the State Board of Reservation 1898 to 1914 and its pres since 1903. In 1915 he published a volume, A History of the State Reservation at Niagara. He had previously published, 1913, A Century of Finance & Commerce, and many contributions to magazines. Pres of Jamestown park board since 1900 and director of Letchworth Park and Arboretum. This foundation is preserving the beauty of Portage Falls and is attempting to grow every species of tree adaptable to the climate. Trustee of American Scenic and Historical Preservation

Society; vice pres New York State Forestry Association; trustee for Preservation of the Adirondacks, and American Civic Association. He was a member of the N Y State constitutional convention of 1915, chairman of the conservation committee.

He m Jan 12, 1876, Eleanor Jones of Randolph, dau of E L. He d rather suddenly 1920 and his wife d soon after. Children:

  a Alberta b Apr 29, 1877
  b Charles Mason b Sept 25, 1878; grad Yale 1900; Harvard Law School 1903;
       d Dec 27, 1907, without issue
  c Howard b Aug 15, 1880; m June 30, 1917, Mary Campbell, dau of Peter of
       Newark, N J

Alberta Dow bcdecahfa m Oct 10, 1907, Fletcher Goodwill of Jamestown. Children:

  a Eleanor b Aug 7, 1908   b Charlotte b Sept 6, 1910

Amos Dow bcdecai d Apr 25, 1903; was 20 when his father d, and went to live with his uncle, Martin Montgomery, a substantial farmer and land owner of Attica, N Y. Here he learned the shoemaker's trade and tanning; then joined his brother in Silver Creek, buying a tannery and establishing a general store. He did well, and in 1854 bought from his brother the dry goods store of East Randolph. This he conducted until 1880. In 1872 he entered the banking business also, buying out the Thomas J Chamberlain Bank. In 1874 he bought the present bank building in East Randolph. To the private banking house of Amos Dow he admitted his son Charles as partner. The latter soon sold out to Seth W Thompson, and the firm became Dow & Thompson until 1881, when Amos bought out the Thompson interest. The business was then bought by the People's State Bank, of which Amos became a large stockholder. His only political office was as supervisor. Universalist, whig, later republican. While not as prominent as his brother, he was always one of the foremost men of the county, successful in business and energetic in public affairs. He m 1838 Eliza Ann Gates b Homer Oct 2, 1816, d 1895. Children:

  a Frank b Silver Creek Sept 1, 1839   b Rollin b Mch 31, 1846
  c Helen b Oct 22, 1848; m S C Jones; lives Tacoma, Wash; 2 children
  d Charles b Silver Creek Dec 12, 1850
  e Harriet b Sept 3, 1860; m John F Thompson, son of Seth W, his father's
       partner. He was a vice pres of Bankers Trust Co, N Y City. They were
       divorced on account of incompatibility, and he m 2nd. One child

Frank Dow bcdecaia m Anna Sawyer; served as private 9th N Y cav; returned to Silver Creek, broken in health; d 1865.

Rollin Dow bcdecaib, banker and merchant, d East Randolph Mch 18, 1908; m Dec 11, 1867, Nellie E Gates b Dec 16, 1846, dau of Jonathan and Diantha of Pike, N Y. Children:

  a Dora m Edwin Robbins of Cortland, N Y
  b Frances m Ward Snyder; 2nd E P Nicholas; lives Houser, N Y

Charles Dow bcdecaid entered Williams College, but stayed only a few weeks. His business career was varied and in many places, but never long in any one thing and ever restless. From college he went to Detroit with Warren Dow, his cousin, engaging in wire cloth manufacturing, screens and hardware. He soon returned to East Randolph and entered the banking house of his father, first as cashier, then as partner. Two years later he sold out and went to Minnesota, where he had interests in wheat elevators, junior partner of Hurd & Dow. His next move was operating a spice mill in Detroit, with a wholesale tea, coffee and spice business on the side. He sold this out and again joined Warren Dow as Dow & Co, Bradford, Pa, then center of the oil industry. He next undertook business ventures in Florida and Cuba until 1878, when he returned to Bradford and became an oil producer. This lasted six years, then he came back to East Randolph as cashier for Amos Dow, but resigned 1888, succeeded by his brother Rollin. In 1882 he and Rollin had started the banking house of Dow Bros, Richburg, and bought 300 acres of oil bearing land, which developed some good and profitable wells. He was for a time in the oil business in Warren, Pa. After leaving his father's bank he went to N Y City, becoming a bookkeeper, then asst cashier in the Gansvoort Bank, but in 1889 abandoned this, going to Michigan to care for his father's business interests. He was back in N Y City by 1891 with a position in the Bell Telephone Co. He later returned to East Randolph, where he now lives. He never married.

Much more difficult to trace has been the posterity of the younger children of Capt Richard Dow bcdec, the fourth child buying land located in Hinesburg, Vt, already the home of the adacea Dow family. The chief difficulty lay in the family Bible of Isaiah Dow bcdecd, wherein his birth date did not coincide with the Bow official rec. When the 1850 census was consulted, it was found to agree and prove the family Bible wrong.

Betty Dow bcdecb m Nov 24, 1786, Peter Manwell, Revolutionary veteran and pioneer of Jericho, Vt. It seems that some member or members of the family visited Vt soon after 1783, selected the land and possibly made plans for staying. It is probable that Betty had children.

Olli Dow bcdecc probably did not locate in Vt until she went there with her brother. She m Richmond Aug 6, 1815, Jesse Gloyd of Jericho. No children, she was his 2nd wife.

Isaiah Dow bcdecd, clothier, from the time of his marriage never lived more than five years in one place. He d Duxbury, Vt, Mch 11, 1826; m 1798 Abigail Messer of Piermont, N H, b 1781, d Sept 13, 1863. The family came to Hinesburg between 1807 and 1809. Census 1850 shows 7 children. A family rec insists there were 10. A grandson says 9, with only 4 sons. Family rec insists that Andrew was the 1stborn and this is stated in Hist Addison Co. It is probable that a dau preceded him, dying young. B dates are vague and from census:

a —— dau, probably d young. Some Achsah Dow of Hinesburg, b 1801, m 1820 Peter Palmer of Jericho. Identity is denied by our informant on this line and she may not belong here
b Andrew b N H Nov 17, 1803. There is room for two older than he and it is not unlikely that there were 10 children in all
c Eliza b N H 1805; m May 14, 1828, Justin Gloyd of Jericho, farmer. In 1850 her mother, wid Abigail Dow, and sister Mary were living with them

In Jericho at this time were several Dow b Canada, all farm laborers, probably none of any American family. These were,—Joseph Dow ae 65, Mary Dow ae 55, perhaps his wife; James ae 35, Joseph ae 28, perhaps their children; Joseph ae 28 (evidently a different Joseph).

d Mary b N H 1807   e Stephen b Vt 1809
h Daniel b Vt 1820   i Albert b Vt 1822

Andrew Dow bcdecdb is stated to have lived once in Londonderry, N H, probably in childhood. He was permanently located in Johnson, Vt, by 1832. His father had bought a cloth dressing plant in So Duxbury and died owing $800 on it. Young Andrew worked until he had paid off this debt, then bought a woolen mill. This was successful and was operated by his son and grandson, the firm finally being I and J G Dow. He was for several years judge of probate for Lamoille Co. In 1882 he was retired, living in Hinesburg. He d Oct 25, 1882; m May 1830 Mary Gloyd d Apr 29, 1851, dau of Jesse. She seems to be his sister's step dau. He m 2nd Dec 17, 1840 (sic in rec; 1860?) Sarah Ann Dodge. Hist Addison Co says 1 child by each wife. If correct, latter is unknown:

a Isaiah b Johnson Feb 7, 1832

Isaiah Dow bcdecdba d Hyde Park Oct 3, 1895. In 1887 he wrote to Edgar R Dow, stating that his father was one of nine children. Achsah Lorenzo and Lewis L not being included. Our other informant is apparently wrong and these three are probably members of adacea. Isaiah gives names of his aunts, in addition to those stated previously, as Orpha, Olla and Lavina. Nothing has been learned of their careers. Isaiah, woolen manufacturer, m Feb 1, 1855, Sarah Newland, by whom 2 children; 2nd Dulcena Benedict, dau of Levi Franklin and Olla V (Manwell). Sarah b Hyde Park Mch 8, 1829, d Sept 6, 1862; Dulcena b Hinesburg Aug 28, 1832, m Nov 30, 1862. Children, all b Hinesburg:

a Justin G b May 25, 1856   b Vernon b Dec 24, 1859; d Aug 21, 1860
c Anna Sarah b June 28, 1863; m Nov 19, 1884, John R Rollins of Hinesburg and Bridgeport, Conn. Child,—Anna Dow b Sept 25, 1885; m George Clark MD of Neligh, Neb; has children,—Richard b Aug 1912, Janet b Feb 1914, Barbara b Jan 6, 1918
d Andrew b Oct 5, 1865   e Frank Benedict b Aug 12, 1867
f Mary Olla b May 26, 1873

Justin Gloyd Dow bcdecdbaa of Hinesburg m Dora Baker. Only child:

a Isaiah b May 2, 1884

Isaiah Dow bcdecdbaaa appears in recent directory as clerk of Burlington; m Julia Collins. Children b Burlington:

  a George Andrew   b Helen

Andrew Dow bcdecdbad m Luella Blackburn; moved to Elwood, Neb. Children:

  a Donald b Mch 16, 1895; in gas and flame corps France 1918; d by 1923
  b Dorothy b June 26, 1899

Frank B Dow bcdecdbae of Hinesburg m Kate Challicone. Children:

  a Vernon T b Hinesburg July 3, 1893; m Nov 26, 1917, Elizabeth Chalmers; in 1918 2nd Lieut of engineers, France; about 1916 teacher in Burlington
  b Florence D b Gibbon, Neb, Apr. 21, 1899
  c Doris b Hinesburg Apr 16, 1902

Eliza Dow bcdecdc m Justin Gloyd. Children:

  a Mary A b 1829   b Jessie b 1832   c Edwin b 1841

Stephen Dow bcdecde, associated with his brother in business in Johnson, m Hinesburg Nov 17, 1841, Fannie Kenyon of Hinesburg. Children:

  a Levinice b 1842; d unm   b William; lived Jericho and Johnson; unt

Daniel Dow bcdecdh, associated with his brothers in manufacturing, m Johnson Aug 3, 1845, Eliza A Dodge of Johnson.

Albert Messer Dow bcdecdi, harness maker of Johnson, m Fannie Minerva Gates b Stanstead, P Q; many years later he sold out and moved to Boston; d Boston. Children:

  a Edgar Albert b Stanstead Oct 7, 1850   b —— a dau

Edgar A Dow bcdecdia, teamster of Boston, later shipper of Charlestown and Everett, m Mch 7, 1884, Katie Marian Fogg b Westmore, Vt Nov 3, 1861. Children:

  a Arthur Albert b Charlestown Aug 30, d Sept 17, 1885
  b Gladys Helen b Aug 17, d Oct 25, 1886

WITH the exception of a few casual comers, all the numerous Dow family of Windham and Bath, N H, are of Revolutionary ancestry from Capt Richard Dow bcde and his son sgt Asa Dow bcded.

Asa Dow bcded was at the very outset of the war a sgt in his father's company. When the new Salem company was organized in 1777 Asa continued as sgt under his brother Capt Richard and fought in this rank until the war ended. At its conclusion he returned to Salem. He had m 1769 Mary Wheeler b Sept 21, 1850, d 1835, dau of Benjamin and Rebecca (Pingue). In 1785 they bought the old Isaac Cochran farm in Windham and moved thither. Here Asa was at one time selectman. He d 1825, judging from date of his will. Children:

a	Eunice b Oct 20, 1770	b	Cyrus b June 7, 1772
c	Caleb b Apr 22, 1774	d	Abel b Apr 30, 1776
e	Benjamin b May 29, 1778; killed by lightning Medford June 18, 1801		
f	Richard b Oct 11, 1780	g	Jonah b Jan 20, 1782
h	Amos b Sept 22, 1783 (State rec, 1787)		
i	Sibbel b Apr 5, 1785; d Amesbury 1845; m Silas Wheeler		
j	Moses b Sept 19, 1789; d Jan 7, 1819		
k	David b Dec 18, 1792	l	Jonathan b Dec 18, 1792

Eunice Dow bcdeda d Windham Feb 7, 1814 (?); m (his 2nd) Apr 19, 1794, Robert Morrison b Feb 6, 1748, d Apr 1808, son of Samuel and Martha (Allison). By 1st wife he had a dau Elizabeth m Abel Dow bcdedd. Children:

a   Asa b Feb 10, 1795; d June 3, 1871; m Feb 1820 Lydia Allen d Jan 28, 1828; 2nd Nancy Scully
b   Nancy b Aug 17, 1796; m Abraham Dow Merrill, a 2nd cousin, son of Maj Joseph; d Jan 29, 1860, leaving 1 dau
c   Ira b July 18, 1798; d Braintree Mch 10, 1870; m Sophia Colby b Mch 3, 1801; 2 sons, 2 dau
d   Mary b Mch 25, 1800; m Jonathan Cochran bcdedha; 4 sons, 1 dau
e   Benjamin b July 22, 1802; d Mch 31, 1815
f   Leonard b May 5, 1804; d Apr 26, 1875; m Apr 8, 1827, Elizabeth Bennett; 1 son, 1 dau
g   Alva b May 13, 1806; d May 28, 1879; m July 11, 1830, Myra Southworth b Mch 3, 1810; 4 sons, 3 dau

Cyrus Dow bcdedb d Bath 1850. Hist Windham gives him m 1797 Polly Tulloch b 1770, d 1841, and this has been widely reprinted. Lynn rec: Silas Dow of Bath int pub to Mary Tillett; Tyrus Dow m Jan 7, 1796, Mary Tillett of Lynn, dau of Magnes. Cyrus and his brother Caleb were pioneers of Bath, carrying their chattels on an ox cart, walking alongside. The tax list mentions him in 1796, 2 acres of mow land, 48 wild land, a cow, 13 sh. He m 2nd, Feb 9, 1822, wid Abigail (Corey) Mellen b 1782 of Littleton, who came to Bath for her wedding with her goods on an ox cart driven by herself. His farm assessed 1850 at $3,000. Children:

a	Asa b 1798	b	Benjamin b 1801	c	Alden b Sept 15, 1804
d	Reuben	e	Polly b 1806; m Abram Hall of Lisbon		

f Sally m Mch 15, 1820, Daniel Moulton of Lyman
g Lucy m Mch 3, 1835, George Cargill of Morgan, Vt
h Eunice b Dec 9, 1841, Charles Cargill of Morgan

Asa Dow bcdedba m Bath Nov 9, 1820, Betsey Moulton b 1800, dau of John and Mary.   In 1850 she was living with her son.   Of **7 or more** children, b, c, d and f are in correct order.   Local rec very defective from 1820 on.   Children:

a Catherine m Lyman Dec 15, 1841, George W Presby
b —— dau b July 4, 1825; some dau m —— Thorne, had a dau Cora H m Eugene E Dow bcdedbbaa and m 2nd Albert Reed of Woodsville
c Robert M b Lyman Apr 26, 1827   d Webster M b Lyman July 1, 1829
e Asa b May 27, 1831; m Littleton Feb 18, 1869, Ellen B Smith of Lyman. Author doubts this name, unless she was wid, for Ellen B Dow b Littleton, dau of Mason Aldrich, d Lisbon Mch 18, 1882, ae 45-1-28
f Betsey C b Mch 5, 1833; must be the Betsey of Lyman m June 28, 1849, Henry Presby of Lyman
g Charlotte C m July 20, 1862, Ezra (Herod S in m rec) Gilman, both of Lyman. At least 3 children,—Nettie T m Lyman 1899 Clarence A Chase, Gertie m Lyman 1892 Robert Lynde, Frank L m Lisbon 1900

Robert M Dow bcdedbac, carpenter of Lisbon, assessed 1850 at $900, m Jan 19, 1859, Larestine B Parker, ae 17, dau of Samuel D and Lucinda (Presby).   She m 2nd, Sept 4, 1865, Johnson G Kimball of Lancaster.   Presumably only 2 children:

a Charles b Lisbon June 10, 1860; unt.   Some Charles Dow, said in d rec b Lisbon June 26, 1861, d Haverhill Almshouse Sept 8, 1910, unm
b Robert E b Lisbon 1862

Robert E Dow bcdedbacb, farmer of Whitefield, m Sept 15, 1890, Etta Baron, ae 25, dau of Levi and Eliza (Weare); 2nd, Oct 10, 1900, Edna Richey, ae 18, dau of Joseph and Mary (Hubbard).   Children:

a Maria b Dalton Nov 17, 1901   b —— dau b Whitefield Aug 25, 1904
c —— dau b Whitefield Oct 11, 1905

Webster M Dow bcdedbad, farmer of Lyman, m Nov 22, 1856, Priscilla Lewis of Lyman, b Bethlehem, d Lyman Apr 25, 1894, ae 69-7-29. At least 3 children:

a Albert W b Lyman Feb 1, 1857
b Corett (son) b Lyman Jan 11, 1859; unt
c Charles A b Lyman Apr 18, 1861-2; untraced but cf bcdedbaca

Albert W Dow bcdedbada, farmer of Lyman, m Mch 29, 1878, Mary T Sherman b 1858, dau of Samuel of Cornish (Duplicate says dau of Samuel Chamberlain).   Another rec gives Mrs A W Dow b Croyden, dau of —— Squires and Harriet (Farrington), d Lyman July 15, 1899, ae 42-2-1.   Still another gives her ae 33 (obvious error).   Albert m 2nd Dec 23, 1913, Lider A Allen, ae 35, div, dau of Arthur and Lizzie (Swett) Kelley.   Perhaps other children:

a Lawrence A b Jan 4, 1887; d Sept 26, 1900

Benjamin Dow bcdedbb of Lyman m June 10, 1825, Orinda Stickney of Lyman.   They were living in Lyman 1828 and 1850, but between they seem to have been in Vt. Rec of children not extant, but a granddau says there were 4 sons and 4 dau, but does not name the dau. There is a Lyman rec of a George Dow, farmer of Lyman, m Catherine —— b Lyman and had a 7th child b Lyman 1859. As no eligible occur in Lyman disconnected Dows, this may be garbled beyond recognition. At all events Benjamin had no son George. Children:

b   Jonathan b Lyman Oct 28, 1828 (perhaps a 1stborn d in infancy)
c   Horace b Feb 1836   d   Alden A b Lunenburg, Vt, 1840
e   The census 1850 gives in Lyman six Dows of whom the 4 dau of Benjamin
       surely belong: Mary b 1837; Margaret b 1838; Laura b 1836; Daniel b
       1840 (not found since); Charlotte b 1842; Loveron (sic) b 1848
f   Merrill. He d unm while home on a furlough during the Civil War

Jonathan Dow bcdedbbb, veteran of 5th N H, farmer of White-field, d May 15, 1903; m Apr 3, 1849, Phebe L Moulton; 2nd, May 15, 1855, Mary B Moulton (Morton in rec error). Ten children:

a   —— dau b Nov 25, 1851; d in infancy
b   Elsie Adaline b Feb 11, 1853; in 1923 Mrs Hodgkinson of Whitefield
c   Julia Ann b Aug 12, 1857; d 1895; m Aaron Stalbird b Eng; left 3 dau; one
       Douzetta m Concord 1895 Raymond M Bean
d   Phoebe O b Dec 19, 1858; d 1901
e   Maryett b Dec 25, 1860; in 1923 Mrs S J Richardson of Minneapolis
f   Edmund Eugene b May 25, 1869
g   Lillian Louise b Apr 19, 1871; in 1923 Mrs M W Lindsay of Lakeport; 1 son
h   Flora Osilla b Sept 6, 1873; m C H Verrill of Tilton; no children
i   Ada Belle b July 6, 1878; m E F Eaton of Whitefield; she furnished list of
       children of bcdedbbb
j   Herbert Linwood b Jan 22, 1881

Eugene E Dow bcdedbbbf, clerk of Whitefield, became merchant of Manchester; m June 5, 1893, Elva D Morton, ae 18, dau of William and Emma (Martin bcdedbebc) of Lancaster; div; m, 2nd, May 30, 1900, Cora H Thorne bcdedbaba ae 24. By 1st wife:

a   Berenice Mildred b Manchester June 26, 1897

Herbert L Dow bcdedbbbj, painter of Whitefield, m Nov 19, 1908, Helen A Stevens, ae 19, dau of Charles H and Annie (Montgomery). Children:

a   Dorothy Ida b Feb 17, 1909   b   Linwood Earl b Nov 29, 1911
c   Paul Eugene b Nov 9, 1913   d   Mary Anna b 1918   e   Elsie b 1919

Horace Dow bcdedbbc d Lancaster Mch 24, 1915; veteran of Civil War and served faithfully. Some confusion has been caused because some person giving the name of Horace Dow became a bounty jumper of Cornish, N H, in 1864 and later had trouble with the G A R of Coos Co. Horace lived some years in Vt but from 1880 until death was of Lancaster. He m 1862 Laura Moulton b Jefferson, d May 8, 1877, ae 36, dau of Eli; m 2nd Mary Dame b St Johnsbury, Vt, whose name given by a niece as Mary Reynolds. One son by 2nd wife:

a   Benjamin E b Whitefield 1867; laborer of Lancaster m Oct 9, 1889, **Dora**
       Hodge b Northumberland, ae 16, dau of Damon and Eliza. A son b Lan-
       caster May 9, 1891. They now live in the Canadian northwest
b   George b Lyman, coachman d Lancaster Jan 10, 1891, ae 22, 6 mos

c McClellan   d Orrin May d Lancaster Apr 3, 1876
e Alice Marble Maud b June 1, 1879; d Aug 15, 1880
f Arthur b Sept 4, 1885; in U S Navy at Portland, Me, unm at latest accounts

McClellan Dow bcdedbbcc of Springfield, Mass, m Nora Thompson of Chicopee. Probably more children:

a Mary b Northampton May 15, 1902. Mary Gladys dau of McClellan either b or d Northampton Aug 9, 1903

Alden A Dow bcdedbbd served in 14th N H; m Cynthia Stalbird, dau of Benjamin and Cornelia (Leighton); evidently div, for she m Lancaster Apr 11, 1885, Royal Hicks of Whitefield; he m 2nd, Dec 11, 1883, Annettie Stilling, ae 43, dau of Damon Hodge (wid or div; cf bcdedbbcc); m 3rd Bertha Eliot b Maidstone, Vt, 1877, d Dec 18, 1915. He lived Guildhall, Vt, coming to Lancaster by 1877. Seven children by 3rd wife, the youngest when he was past 75: D rec of a son mentions those who survived in 1920:

a Merrill Franklin b Guildhall 1867   b Irwin; d before 1923; left 1 son, unt
c Ernest b July 19, 1877; veteran of 14th Minn 1898; of Minneapolis 1920; unt
d Elbridge d Lancaster Oct 3, 1879, ae 4
x Gertrude m Feb 4, 1893, Willie Kimball of Lancaster; no children
e —— son b Lancaster Mch 28, 1901   f —— son b May 23, 1903
g —— dau b Aug 4, 1904   h Wilson Eliot b Jan 13, 1913
i —— son b Dec 14, 1915

Merrill F Dow bcdedbbda, farmer of Guildhall, moved to Lancaster; later farmer of Sheffield, Mass; for his last five years cared for a large estate in Sheffield; d June 17, 1921; m Abbie Freeman b Lancaster, who survived. Obituary gave 5 surviving children:

a Flora; now Mrs O'Keefe of Brooklyn, N Y
b Lulu; unm of Hartford, Conn
c Blanche; now Mrs Cowin of Windsor, Conn
d —— son b Lancaster Sept 17, 1897. A son is Hollis, now of Sheffield
e —— son b Lancaster Oct 4, 1899. A son is Freeman now of Sheffield
f Chase b July 29, d Aug 5, 1901, Lancaster
g Clarence F b Aug 3, 1901; d Apr 14, 1902

Irving A Dow bcdedbbdb, b Lancaster 1869, railroad man, m Grace M Cook b Chateaugay, N Y, 1872. Children b Concord:

a Gladys Evangeline b Dec 16, 1892; d Pembroke, Mass, Jan 15, 1901
b —— son b Nov 11, 1898; living 1923

Alden Dow bcdedbc inherited the Bath homestead; d suicide Aug 27, 1849; m Apr 12, 1826, Laodicea Cobleigh of Littleton b Jan 28, 1806, d Apr 12, 1848, dau of John and Mary (Polly) (Stanford), granddau of John Cobleigh d Chesterfield 1826; m 2nd, Apr 6, 1847 (sic in rec; 1849?), Sarah Martin, both of Bath, sister of bcdedbcb. Children:

a Reuben b Mch 9, 1827   b Emeline b Oct 8, 1828
c Benjamin b Nov 15, 1830   d Betsey b Jan 1, 1833
e George b Feb 10, 1835; d Lyman Sept 20, 1881; no children
f Mary b Feb 9, 1837   g Harriet
h Laura b Nov 8, 1842; d Mch 19, 1866   i Frances b Jan 14, 1844

Reuben Dow bcdedbca inherited the homestead, d Amherst, Mass May 28, 1903; m Jan 14, 1858, Laura Weeks Powers b Aug 3, 1832, d Dec 20, 1900, dau of Martin E and Mary W (Weeks).   Children:

a —— d July 10, 1860, ae 2 mos   b —— dau b and d Dec 23, 1861
c Alice Maria b Aug 18, 1863
d —— d Mch 18, 1869, ae 2   e Alberto b Mch 11, 1871; d Mch 17, 1873

Alice M Dow bcdedbcac of Bath m Oct 3, 1900, William Arthur Reed b Nov 15, 1859, son of Joshua Curtis and Lois Beaman (Cummings) of Amherst, Mass.

Emeline Dow bcdedbcb d Charlestown, Mass, July 26, 1894; m Bath May 6, 1847, Ira Foster Martin of Bath, later expressman of Charlestown, b Jan 28, 1823, d Bradford, Vt, Jan 26, 1876.   Children:

a Frances Eliza b Feb 26, 1848; m Apr 16, 1863, Octavius Theodore Rand
b Jahiel Hale b Feb 22, 1850; m Sept 21, 1871, Charlotte Ann Trefethan
c Emma Josephine b Aug 21, 1853; m William Morton
d Mary Ella b Feb 16, 1855; m Jan 29, 1875, Frank Lord
e Almina b Mch 3, 1858; m Sept 8, 1884, Daniel Chapin
f Ira Foster b July 10, 1860; m Nov 19, 1882, Sarah Collins
g Helen Gertrude b Sept 26, 1865; m June 12, 1887, Frederick K Jennings
h Edwin Walter b Apr 2, 1868; m Aug 28, 1895, Elizabeth Austin

Benjamin Dow bcdedbcc left home at 18 and established himself as a master teamster in Boston; 15 years later settled in Lyman, drover and shipper of cattle to Boston; representative to Legislature 1875-7 and widely known through the section; moved 1879 to Woodsville, near Haverhill, N H; breeder of fine cattle; held various town offices; d Dec 5, 1909; m Lyman Dec 24, 1861, Sarah Elizabeth Moulton d Nov 1, 1920, dau of James Madison and Sarah (Titus).   Children:

a Gilbert Moulton b Apr 5, 1865
b Eugene Madison b Lyman Aug 29, 1876

Gilbert M Dow bcdedbcca, railroad man, d Apr 11, 1894; m Dec 5, 1888, Cynthia Ranstead Cheney b Woodville July 11, 1862, dau of Joseph Young and Juliette (McNab). From 1894 she and her mother-in-law kept house together in Woodville.   Children:

a Shirley Cheney b Feb 25, 1890; now teacher of Laconia
b Norma Elizabeth b Apr 13, 1892; now stenographer of Boston

Eugene M Dow bcdedbccb, grad Dartmouth 1901, lives Brighton; teacher in Boston; pres of Educational Society; m 1907 Frances W Burditt, dau of Charles and Charlotte (McGregor) of Middletown, N S.   Children:

a Alleyn Moulton b Oct 26, 1909; d 1910   b Virginia b 1911
c Norman McGregor b 1915

Betsey Dow bcdedbcd m Apr 11, 1855, Andrew Jackson Flanders of Landaff, later of Bath.   Children:

a Charles Robert b Apr 9, 1857; m Bath 1900
b Frederick M b Apr 14, 1859; d Sept 23, 1866
c Mary Esther b Mch 19, 1861; m Oct 19, 1889, Ezra Chandler Burbank

d Arthur Eugene b Jan 31, 1863
e Andrew Perry b Aug 15, 1865; m Mary Eliza Mason; lives Adams, Mass
f Etta Frances b Nov 18, 1868

Mary Dow bcdedbcf of Charlestown, Mass, m Sept 2, 1858, Edward Rolliff Classon Murray, carpenter, b May 2, 1828, son of William and Eliza (Holland). Children:

a Edward Alden b June 27, 1859; not now living
b Gilbert Herbert b Aug 28, 1869; lives Charlestown; has children and grand-children

Harriet Dow bcdedbcg d Sept 22, 1861; m June 18, 1857 (duplicate rec gives May 20, 1858), Eben McAlpine of Lyman. Children:

a George Willis b Mch 18, 1859   b William Henry b 1861

Frances Dow bcdedbci lives Lyman; m Dec 31, 1867, Solon Rufus Titus, farmer, b Jan 18, 1831, son of Calvin and Sarah. Children:

a Edwin Calvin b Oct 19, 1874; d Sept 1, 1892
b Ernest Dow b July 5, 1878; of Laconia   c Sarah Elizabeth b Aug 4, 1884

Caleb Dow bcdedc, pioneer of Bath, d Apr 9, 1843; revisited Windham and took home a wife June 1802, Jennie Cochran b Aug 18 1779, d Feb 17, 1839, dau of James. Children:

a James b Bath Oct 27, 1802   b Cynthia b Feb 26, 1804
c Harriet b Nov 28, 1805; d Aug 26, 1852
d Richard b Sept 2, 1807; d Providence, R I, Apr 1, 1858; m 1830 Mary Brooks. No rec of children
e Rufus b May 14, 1809   f Jonathan b Oct 2, 1810
g Asa b May 5, 1812   h Caleb b Oct 21, 1814
i Osman b May 2, 1816; d Apr 9, 1841   j Cyrus M b Dec 25, 1817
k Erasmus b Nov 21, 1819; d July 20, 1820
l Edward Dean b Sept 20, 1821

James Dow bcdedca d Londonderry Dec 21, 1844; entered the Methodist ministry and gave promise of a brilliant career. His appointments were: Stratford 1832, Bethlehem 1833, Barton, Vt, 1834, Walden 1835, Barton 1836, Bristol, N H, 1837, Haverhill 1838, Tuftonborough and Brookfield 1839, Wolfboro 1840, Gilmanton 1841-2, Londonderry 1843. At Gilmanton he trebled the church membership and was almost equally successful elsewhere. He m Nov 3, 1831, Mary Aspinwall b Bradford, Vt, Aug 27, 1803, d Newbury, Vt, Sept 25, 1856, dau of John and Hannah (White). Children:

a Mary Jane b May 31, 1833   b Marcellus b 1837; d 1841

Mary J Dow bcdedcaa m Aug, 1853, Harvey Webster Emery of Lisbon, son of Moses and Eunice (English), d in the army Oct 13, 1862. She lived then Newbury, Vt, moving to Millersville, Pa. Children:

a Evelyn b Aug 19, 1859   b Harriet b May 5, 1861

Cynthia Dow bcdedcb d Warrensburg, N Y, Feb 14, 1843; m 1825 Rev Josiah Scarret. Children:

a Atkins   b Erasmus   c Charles   d George   e Cynthia
f Harriet   g Emma   h Ellen

Rufus Dow bcdedce d Piermont, N H, Jan 14, 1852; m May 21, 1835, Maria Louisa Bonaparte Bedell b Burlington, Vt, Sept 24, 1813, d Portage, Wis, Jan 15, 1886.   He was a clothier.   Children:

  a Charles Carroll b Piermont June 2, 1836   b —— dau d in childhood

Charles C Dow bcdedcea, capt of 2nd Wis vols, later county clerk at Portage, m Dec 16, 1867, Anna E Jones b Mt Savage, Md, Apr 3, 1845. Children:

  a Will Corning b Madison Feb 18, 1872
  b Carrie Louisa b Portage Sept 6, 1876; m Marcus Sandstein of Everett, Wash; only child,—Marcus in high school 1922
  c Charles Homer b July 1, 1878; drowned in boyhood

Will C Dow bcdedceaa was in the army of occupation Porto Rico 1898; railway mail clerk of Sheboygan and in recent years Milwaukee; mother living with him; m twice; 2 sons by 1st wife:

  a Charles Carleton b Portage Aug 15, 1901; in 1921 minor officer U S S Oklahoma; boxing champion of the ship
  b William Leonard b Sheboygan July 9, 1903; also on U S S Oklahoma

Jonathan Dow bcdedcf, farmer of Bath, d Lisbon Oct 12, 1888; m Aug 10, 1840, Abigail Cole b 1816, living Lisbon 1887, dau of Isaac and Hannah (Atwood).   Children:

  a Henry S b June 18, 1841
  b Jennie W (bap Jane Ursula) b Mch 16, 1843
  c James A b Dec 18, 1844   d Marcellus Irenaeus b Mch 16, 1847
  e Julia E b May 4, 1849
  f Eliza A b Nov 25, 1851; m Feb 22, 1877, James Watson of Cambridge, Mass; dau,—Mabel D
  g Charles E b July 3, 1855; went to N Y City, newspaper correspondent for a number of leading western dailies, one of the first writers who syndicated his articles; untraced since 1887

Henry S Dow bcdedcfa, 2nd Lieut 3rd N H, enlisted from Lisbon; promoted to 1st Lieut, then Jan 1, 1864, to Capt; mustered out Oct 7, 1864; moved to Bay City, Mich, editor of the Lumberman's Journal; d Detroit Dec 6, 1875.

Jennie W Dow bcdedcfb m Feb 23, 1864, John B Atwood of Lisbon. Children:

  a Henry D   b Fannie m 1888 Frank E Buck
  c Herbert K m 1899 ——   d Alice E m 1889 George E Parkinson
  e Kate E   f Josie L   g Jennie M m 1899 Leon E Noyes
  h Ethel B

James A Dow bcdedcfc, physician of Cambridge, began practice Windsor, Vt; m Mch 26, 1868, Alice L Lincoln b Windsor Aug 30, 1849. Ten grandchildren helped celebrate their golden wedding.   Children:

  a Esther A b Windsor Aug 2, 1869; m Harry Ball of Brooklyn, N Y
  b Clifford Wallace b June 8, 1872; m Mch 22, 1900, Grace E Stone, dau of Uriah
  c George Lincoln b Cambridge Dec 9, 1878; now real estate operator of Cambridge
  d Arthur Newton b Dec 9, 1878; not now living

Clifford W Dow bcdedcfcb and Grace E Stone have children; 2 elder b Cambridge, younger Newton:

a Kenneth Cushman b Nov 7, 1901   b Alice Lincoln b Dec 2, 1904
c James Arthur b Aug 7, 1907   d Marjorie Stone b Sept 3, 1910

George Lincoln Dow bcdedcfcc m Oct 11, 1905, Ethel Dora Appleton, ae 23, dau of John H and Dora (Shearer). Child:

a George Lincoln b Cambridge July 4, 1909

Marcellus I Dow bcdedcfd, druggist of Cambridge, m Apr 5, 1871, Eva A Temple b Landaff, N H, Dec 7, 1848. He was still active in business 1923. Children:

a Leslie G b 1872; unt
b Ethel M b 1874; now Mrs Frank Stubbs of Newton

Julia E Dow bcdedcfe m Mch 22, 1871, John D Child, farmer. Children:

a Aline E m 1895 Raymond M Lang   b Edith M   c Dwight P

Asa Dow bcdedcg d Lisbon Sept 23, 1878; m Jan 10, 1837, Caroline Buck. Children:

a George H b 1842
b Carrie L m Nov 10, 1869, Harvey Knight of Haverhill

George H Dow bcdedcga, harness maker, d widower Dalton July 15, 1903; m Aug 23, 1866, Jennie Gordon of Lyman. She by d rec is Hannah J Dow, dau of Andrew and Hannah G (Smith) Gordon, both b Lyman, d Lisbon Nov 5, 1900, ae 53-7-25. Children:

a Hattie E of Bath m Oct 21, 1880, Austin B Northy of Lisbon
b Irene L b Lisbon Feb 21, 1869; m July 10, 1890, Gilbert H Noyes

Caleb Dow bcdedch, grad Wesleyan University 1841, became principal of Portchester, N Y, Academy. Becoming Episcopalian, he was ordained priest 1849; rectorates Portsmouth and Paducah, Ky; Ascension, St Francesville, La; Natchez, Miss; Alexandria, La; Griffin, Ga; St Joseph, Franklin, La; he d Griffin Nov 29, 1890; m Joanna Hubbard of Middletown, Conn; 2nd Mrs Flora Felicia George d Feb 13, 1873; an only child m Dr Davidson.

Cyrus Marcellus Dow bcdedcj, teacher and physician of Memphis, Tenn, d Apr 2, 1845, unm.

Edward Dean Dow bcdedcl, editor of Central New Jersey Times of Plainfield 1868-71; moved to Knoxville, Tenn, as a general agent; d June 10, 1901; m 1843 Susanna L Hart b N Y City Feb 6, 1823. Children:

a Leonard E b Plainfield May 3, 1844; d Apr 1, 1868
b Edward S b July 19, 1846; d June 9, 1868
c Myra b Mch 5, 1849; d June 9, 1868
d Aline b Oct 15, 1852; d Jan 4, 1869
e Clara Hart b Sept 15, 1857; d May 20, 1864

f   Celeman Hart b July 15, 1861, unt
g   George Herbert b Jan 15, d, 1863

Reuben Dow bcdedbd.   This rec is left as it came to the Author in the original b ms.   Dateless and too close to older and younger, he probably never existed,—confused from bcdedbca

---

Abel Dow bcdedd became a nail manufacturer of Windham, but, losing his health, moved to Hooksett; in 1815 he returned, buying a farm from his father-in-law; d Oct 23, 1824; m May 5, 1811, his sister's stepdau, Elizabeth Morrison b Windham Dec 12, 1783; d Sept 28, 1865, dau of Robert and Agnes (Betton).   Children:

a   Alva b Windham Feb 13, 1812
b   Robert Morrison b Dunbarton Sept 3, 1813
c   Nancy Betton b Mch 30, 1815   d   Lucinda b Oct 22, 1816
e   Betsey b June 26, 1818   f   Philena b Sept 8, 1820
g   Hannah b Dec 27, 1822; d Sept 1842   h   Abel b Dec 12, 1824

Alva Dow bcdedda moved in middle life to Marseilles, Ill; d Nov 7, 1877; m Nov 30, 1836, Sarah Rumney b Biddeford, Me, Dec 5, 1820, d Mch 7, 1877.   Children:

a   Vermelia C b May 19, 1838   b   Gilman Corning b Jan 4, 1840
c   Sarah E b Feb 18, 1844
d   Charles A b Sept 21, 1846; d Apr 30, 1856
e   Emma F b July 6, d July 19, 1855

Vermelia C Dow bcdeddaa d Marseilles, Ill, July 28, 1878; m Sept 28, 1856, Nelson Rhines.   Children:

a   Ella Mary b Dec 31, 1858
b   Sadie Bell b Sept 12, 1859; d Aug 15, 1870   c   Alva Dow b Oct 10, 1871

Gilman C Dow bcdeddab d Lynn Mch 12, 1901 (rec giving parents Aliah and Sarah (Remey); shoemaker of Salem, moved to Lynn, where family now are; m Dec 16, 1865, Hannah Jane Kelley b Mch 5, 1848. Children:

a   Alva N b Oct 8, 1866; unt   b   Millie C b Apr 23, 1870
c   Francis H b Nov 16, 1872; recent Lynn directory gives Frank H Dow, grocer
d   —— son b and d Sept 26, 1874   e   Lillian A b Aug 23, 1877

Frank H Dow bcdeddabc m Dec 25, 1902, Ina Belle Haskell, ae 24, dau of Frank and Clara (record).   Children b Lynn:

a   Lenora Thompson b July 10, 1903
b   Marion Harriet b Feb 28, 1905   c   Herbert Gilman b Apr 21, 1908

Lillian A Dow bcdeddabe of Lynn m June 21, 1904, Leon Russell, ae 27, son of William O and Mary E (Glass).   Child:

a   William Ellsworth b Lynn July 11, 1908

Robert M Dow bcdeddb was the first of the family to move to Marseilles, Ill; later bought a farm in Bellevue, Neb; sold it and became hotel keeper in Omaha; m Oct 3, 1841, Ann W Bennett of Salem b Aug

9, 1813, d June 10, 1850; 2nd, May 4, 1855, Emily R Lane b Mch 2, 1827.
Children:

a Olive H b Marseilles July 12, 1842
b Robert H b May 19, 1844; d Apr 1, 1865
c Willard W b July 20, 1846   d —— infant d July 10, 1850
e Lizzie J b Aug 31, 1856   f Jessie F b Jan 13, 1858; d Oct 30, 1865
g Cora L b Aug 13, 1860; d Nov 11, 1885   h Nellie C b July 18, 1862
i —— infant d Dec 3, 1863   j Jessie L b Aug 23, 1865

Willard W Dow bcdeddbc m Jan 31, 1872, Mary J Jarvis. Child:

a Mary A b Jan 10, 1873

Lizzie J Dow bcdeddbe m Jan 8, 1875, M J Hamilton. Children:

a Mamie b July 27, 1876   b Edna B b Sept 15, 1878

Nancy B Dow bcdeddc d Apr 18, 1875; m Dec 31, 1835, Jonathan
Massy, farmer of Salem, later of Morris, Ill, b Jan 10, 1809, d June 16,
1866. Children:

a Stillman E b Oct 28, 1836; m July 31, 1872, Miriam F Barstow of Morris
b Adeline P b June 12, 1841; m Oct 18, 1861, John H Raymond; children,—
     Edward S b Aug 12, d Aug 18, 1863; Howard b Feb 18, 1865, of Morris
c Myra S b June 1, 1844: m June 30, 1873, Joseph H Pettitt of Morris; child,—
     Muriel b June 11, 1876
d Horace S b Aug 16, 1851   e Lizzie H b Sept 24, 1852

Lucinda Dow bcdeddd d Haverhill, Mass, Dec 27, 1838, Gilman
Corning of Haverhill b Salem. Child:

a Albion James b Nov 7, 1841; druggist, m Nov 12, 1871, Margaret Shepard
     Woodside of Baltimore, Md. Children,—John Woodside b Dec 10, 1872;
     Albion James b July 27, 1876

Betsey Dow bcdedde d Windham Dec 27, 1854; m (his 2nd) Aug
29, 1849, Ebenezer T Abbot b May 27, 1804; d Mch 2, 1853, farmer, one
time selectman of Windham. Child:

a Jacob b June 7, 1850; d Sept 20, 1857

Philena Dow bcdeddf d Sept 7, 1880; m Dec 26, 1839, Samuel
Carter Jordan of Morris, native of Kennebunkport, Me, d Apr 7, 1880.
Children:

a Elizabeth Hannah b May 15, 1841; d Jan 1, 1844
b Alva Reynolds b Dec 13, 1842; m June 18, 1869, Sarah D Parmalie; lawyer
     and county judge of Morris

Abel Dow bcdeddh d Mch 4, 1905; farmer, representative to
Legislature from Windham 1877-79-80; m Sept 28, 1849, Rhoda Ann
Plummer b Apr 9, 1833, living Salem Depot 1917, dau of Samuel and
Louisa (Morse) of Haverhill. Children:

a Martha Morrison b Dec 15, 1850; d Aug 27, 1852
b George Plummer b Nov 3, 1852; untraced
c Charles Allison b Dec 24, 1854   d Willard Elbridge b Oct 6, 1856
e Lizzie Lucinda b July 27, 1859
f Marion Louise b 1876; m Jan 12, 1899, Owen A Kenefick of Lawrence. Chil-
     dren,—Marion, Louise, Elizabeth

Charles A Dow bcdeddhc of Salem m Dec 24, 1878, Ada Dow Colby bcdedfic d Windham Oct 9, 1920.   Children:

a   Charles Abel b Mch 15, 1880   b   Lura Edna b Apr 24, 1881

Charles A Dow bcdeddhca writes 1923 from Canobie Lake, N H, signing Charles A Dow Jr; m June 23, 1903, Eva M Sykes, ae 20, dau of William, b Eng, and Helen (Winter) b Eng.   Children:

a   —— son b and d Dec 11, 1905   b   —— son d 1916, ae 2
c   Charles Allison b Apr 4, 1915

Lura E Dow bcdeddhcb m June 26, 1899, Fred Sanford b July 12, 1876, son of Charles O and D Louise (Webster).   Children:

a   Mabel Peasley b Sept 4, 1900; m 1917——   b   George Kittridge b Sept 24, 1901

Willard E Dow bcdeddhd, inventor, established and is treasurer of the Dow Mfg Co of Braintree, Mass, a very successful organization; m Dec 14, 1880, Alice Heath Fairbanks b Philadelphia July 11, 1861, dau of Lorenzo Sayles and Sarah E P (Heath).   Her father, wrote, her husband published the Fairbanks Gen.   Children:

a   Alice Rebecca b Dec 8, 1881; m Jan 1, 1905, George Lewis Anderson b June 1,
        1863, son of Charles J and Mary L (Joy)
b   Alva Morrison b Windham Sept 8, 1883
c   Clarence Willard b Nov 5, 1887

Alva M Dow bcdeddhdb of Braintree m June 23, 1909, Carrie Gertrude Hilliard b Sept 7, 1885, dau of Aubrey B and Anna (Morrison). Children:

a   Alva Morrison b Dec 8, 1910   b   Joseph Willard b Jan 10, 1912
c   Robert b July 23, 1914

Clarence W Dow bcdeddhdc m Sept 20, 1910, Cora May Turner b Apr 23, 1889, dau of Azro and Georgietta F (Litchfield).   Son:

a   Turner Fairbanks b June 9, 1914

Lizzie L Dow bcdeddhe d Feb 2, 1893; m Dec 20, 1880, Albert Onslow Alexander b Windham May 22, 1857.   Children:

a   Hannah May b Dec 14, 1882
b   George Howard b May 20, 1886; d Oct 25, 1895
c   Annie Marion b Nov 30, 1892; m and has a child

Richard Dow bcdedf came to Windham 1785; d Oct 2, 1846; succeeded his father on the East Windham farm and nail factory; enlisted 1812, Capt John Godfrey; m Apr 13, 1819, Phoebe Kelly b Dec 14, 1796, d Mch 10, 1872, dau of Richard and Sybil of Salem. In 1850 the family lived Methuen.   Children:

a   Lorenzo b Jan 9, 1820   b   Adaline b Apr 22, 1821
c   Homer b Jan 26, 1823   d   Virgil b Jan 26, 1823
e   Amos b Jan 13, 1825   f   Elizabeth Ann b Nov 8, 1826; d Oct 12, 1872
g   Phoebe b Feb 22, 1828   h   Susan Adams b Dec 31, 1829; d young
i   Frances Emeline b Dec 3, 1832   j   Esther b Mch 3, 1834; d young
k   Oliver Kimball b July 7, 1838; d Jan 24, 1869; unm

Lorenzo Dow bcdedfa, woolen mill superintendent of Lake Village, Lawrence and Methuen, d Nov 24, 1876; m May 14, 1850, Hannah E Frye, dau of Francis and Lydia (Whittier) of Methuen. Child:

a   Nannie F b Sept 27, 1852

Adaline Dow bcdedfb d Methuen June 14, 1900; m Oct 10, 1844, James Whiting Bailey b Brooklyn, Pa, July 9, 1818, d Bradford, Mass, Apr 24, 1891, woolen manufacturer of Windham, Salem, Tilton, Laconia, son of Col Frederick and Polly (Witter). Children:

a   Charles M b Jan 29, 1849; m July 1, 1874, Susie E Vance; 2nd Fannie Ramsey
b   Sarah M b Apr 22, 1851; d in infancy
c   Sarah B b Apr 22, 1851; m Nov 8, 1888, Peter Carrow of No Troy, Vt; now wid lives Methuen, an accomplished genealogist, contributing much detail to this Book
d   James B b Oct 27, 1858; d Sept 17, 1877

Homer Dow bcdedfc, farmer of Methuen, m Apr 24, 1851, Parmelia Potter b Nov 29, 1827, d Jan 2, 1871, dau of Samuel and Parmelia (Stevens) of Concord, N H; 2nd Feb 6, 1778, Mary A Titus b May 9, 1826, dau of Martin and Clarissa (Prouty) of Chesterfield, N H. Children:

a   Loren Stevens b Salem Nov 6, 1854
b   Harriet Sanders b Atkinson Oct 4, 1858; d Sept 27, 1878, unm
c   Frank Merton b Methuen Jan 30, 1864; d 1880

Loren Stevens Dow bcdedfca was railroad freight agent of Lawrence; moved to Pittsburgh, Pa, in a similiar capacity; married rather late in life a widow from Indiana. In 1919 he was sent by the U S Govt as a transportation expert to Constantinople. There he contracted an illness from which he d Pittsburgh Jan 14, 1920. No children.

Virgil Dow bcdedfd, farmer of Methuen, d Aug 16, 1899; m Dec 12, 1850, Sarah Kimball b Feb 20, 1827, dau of Reuben and Sally (Maynard) of Concord, N H. Children:

a   George William b Sept 23, 1851   b   Harry Robinson b Feb 12, 1862

George W Dow bcdedfda d Lawrence Nov 21, 1922, having practiced medicine there for 40 years, the senior member of the profession there. Grad Colby Academy, Brown University 1877, the first Brown pitcher to employ a curved ball. Grad Harvard Medical School 1881. He sang in the church choir for over 20 years and for 20 years was medical examiner for the county. He m Oct 15, 1885, Ella Truell, dau of Ira Whitcomb and Ruth Ann (Phillips) of Lawrence. She survives, member of D A R. Only child:

a   Harry Edward b June 5, 1891; now of Malden, Mass; m Aug 15, 1922, Laura Cleaves, dau of G H of Unionville, Me

Harry R Dow bcdedfdb, grad Harvard 1884; Harvard Law School; member Lawrence Common Council 1891-3, its pres 1893; representative 1898; special justice of police court; appointed 1898 Judge of Probate

& Insolvency for Essex Co; lives No Andover; m Sept 28, 1892, Harriet
B Robinson b Deerfield, N H, Nov 8, 1863, dau of James and Eliza
(White). Children:

    a Harry Robinson b Oct 12, 1896   b James Kimball b Dec 28, 1900

James K Dow bcdedfdbb, grad Harvard 1923, engagement
announced Sept 3, 1926, to Marion Pruden Tichenor of Montclair, N J,
dau of Halsey Taft

Amos Dow bcdedfe, woolen manufacturer of Methuen, killed by
accidental gunshot Sept 2, 1855; m Apr 26, 1849, Maria Elizabeth
Morrison b R I Nov 16, 1828, d Dec 22, 1859, dau of Leonard and Elizabeth (Bennett). Children:

    a Alvin Edson b Salem Mch 15, 1852, d 1852
    b Maria Lizzie b Salem Nov 10, 1853
    c Lura Amanda b Methuen Mch 15, 1856

Maria Lizzie Dow bcdedfeb m Sept 19, 1875, George W Adams of
Newbury. Children:

    a Raymond Morris b Oct 30, 1876; Episcopal clergyman at No Brookfield Mass
    b Eva M b May 21, 1884

Lura Amanda Dow bcdedfec m Charles W Hollis; four children.

Phoebe Dow bcdedfg m Dec 28, 1849, John A Wheeler, farmer of
Salem, b Aug 19, 1826, son of John A and Mary A (Stevens). Children:

    a Mary Azilla b Oct 16, 1851; d July 1, 1862
    b William Rust b Salem Jan 20, 1854
    c Ethel May b Dec 3, 1872; m Arthur Nye; dau b July 13, 1916

Frances Emeline Dow bcdedfi m 1855 William Greenleaf Colby of
Salem b Jan 27, 1820. Children:

    a William b Windham June 19, 1856; a sailor
    b Alva E b Salem Oct 3, 1857; d June 10, 1879
    c Ada Dow b Oct 7, 1860; m Charles A Dow bcdeddhc
    d Ida b Oct 7, 1860; m Dec 24, 1878, Hon Wallace W Cole; 8 children, one a dau
       Mabel b Jan 26, 1880
    e Emma L b Feb 18, 1863; m George Hayes
    f Evelyn M b Feb 16, 1866; m Walker Haigh   g Sarah B b Sept 15, 1871
    h Gertrude W b Jan 17, 1873; d Dec 24, 1873
    i Charles E b Apr 28, 1878; d May 9, 1879

Jonah Dow bcdedg. The original ms, professionally prepared,
gave Jonah as going to Maine, having nine children, then going west,
but not mentioning any children, dismissing the line. Now, a wise
prophet is soon forgotten, but a man thrown overboard as a trouble maker
lives long. Any victim named Jonah has a right to change his name.
There was in Haverhill a John Dow of just the right age, belonging
surely to the b lines, who went late in life to Portland, Me, and who had
exactly nine children. The Author believes that Jonah discarded his
name and took its similarly sounding John, regardless of the fact that
disconnected John Dow are more numerous than any others and that there

are about 200 of them. John Dow, whoever he may be, m Haverhill
Sept 27, 1804, Polly Plummer, dau of Silas, cordwainer, and Joanna
(Barker) of Rowley, Bradford and Haverhill. Children:

    a   Polly b Aug 3, 1805; m Haverhill July 20, 1826, Jeremiah Dow bcdbed; moved
        soon to Portland
    b   John Plummer b June 27, 1807. Untraced, presumably went to Maine
    c   Sarah Ann b Feb 27, 1809   d   Caroline b Mch 10, 1811
    e   Moses b May 6, 1813; unt
    f   Albert b Apr 4, 1815; d Aug 7, 1817
    g   William Henry b June 5, 1817   h   Elizabeth b Aug 1, 1819
    i   Harriet Scott b Mch 28, 1822; d Apr 7, 1840

Caroline Dow bcdedgd m Aug 23, 1836, John Barnett Dinsmore of
Lowell, her father's apprentice, b Apr 15, 1810, d Feb 8, 1882. She d
consumption June 18, 1843. Children:

    a   Caroline b Nov 5, 1838; m Mch 11, 1868, Dexter N Foster; children,—Mabel
        Dow, Jessie Pratt, Robert
    b   Mary Ella b Aug 19, 1840   c   John William b Oct 19, 1842

William H Dow bcdedgg, painter of Haverhill, m Clementina
Augusta Getchell m 2nd Jan 27, 1856, Alphonso J Haughton of Hartford.
We have already the name Getchell in Waterville, Me. Children:

    a   Charles Henry b Feb 27, 1846; unt
    b   Frank Augustine b (Haverhill rec) Mch 16, 1849 (m rec gives 1848) (dup rec
        gives Frank A b Anson, Me)

Frank Augustine Dow bcdedggb, veteran of 4th Mass heavy
artillery, shoe contractor, Universalist, m Mch 28, 1874, Geneva Kimball
Frost b Upton, Me, Sept 10, 1853, dau of Simeon Ford and Maria
(Abbott). She lives wid, Haverhill. Child:

    a   Maud La Von b Upton, Me, 1879, m Haverhill Nov 12, 1907, Harry Fogg
        Doe, ae 30, son of Parsons and Lavina B (Fogg)

Amos Dow bcdedh m 1818 Nabby Dustin, dau of Simeon; in
middle life he moved to Michigan, thence to a farm near Council Bluffs,
Iowa. Perhaps more children than here appear:

    a   Asa b Hopkinton about 1820
    b   Elbridge b Hopkinton 1822. These three dates inherited from the original
        b ms are probably too early. Elbridge is unt

Asa Dow bcdedha m Emily Jane Cochran, dau of Dea Jonathan
bcdedad of Windham; went to Mich, thence to Iowa; was located before
the Civil War in Chicago; became president of the Board of Trade. M
rec not found. At least two children:

    a   Alice Cochran b about 1851; m —— Allison. Her son, Brent Dow Allison
        presents a curious reversion from the type of his ancestry, martial and brave
        to the last degree; his experiences as a slacker 1917 onward are well known
    b   Harold Cochran b about 1853; unt

David Dow bcdedk went to New Haven, Ohio; fought at Ft Meigs
under Gen W H Harrison; d struck by lightning while inspecting land

in Neb May 20, 1834; m Feb 19, 1822, Louisa Beymer d Jan 30, 1877, m 2nd, June 2, 1836, William Lisle.   David's children:

    a Alvin b Nov 30, 1822   b Cyrus b Jan 18, 1825
    c Mary b Mch 14, 1828   d Leonard b June 9, 1831
    e Wealthea b Feb 13, 1833; d Sept 15, 1848

Alvin Dow bcdedka m 1st Olive Bragdon; m 2nd, June 21, 1849, Dorcas Carey b Feb 2, 1830, d Aug 1, 1909, dau of John and Dorcas (Wilcox).   This family came from Virginia and founded Carey, Ohio. Children:

    a Annie b about 1844; m B F Schwartz of Catasauqua, Pa
    b John Carey b about 1850;   untraced
    c Alice   d Rose   e Walter, unt
    f May   g Minnie W   h Dorcas

Cyrus Dow bcdedkb of New Haven d May, 1878; m 1st about 1850 Maria Dark of Plymouth, Ohio; m 2nd about 1855 Elizabeth Lawrence of Benton, Ohio.   Children:

    a Charles b about 1851;   untraced
    b James, unt   c Lawrence, unt   d Libbie, unt

Mary Dow bcdedkc m Mch 4, 1845, Elias C McVitty b Shirleysburg, Pa, Mch 4, 1824; moved 1882 to Nashville, Tenn.   Children:

    a Cyrus Cook b New Haven Feb 9, 1846; d Jan, 1849
    b Louisa b July 24, 1848
    c Frank D b Sandusky Sept 24, 1850; m Feb 23, 1881, Kate G Giers of Nashville,
         Tenn.   William McVitty of Norwalk, Ohio, seems their son
    d Willard D b Benton Mch 24, 1857

Leonard Dow bcdedkd of New Haven d Sept 12, 1874; m Mch, 1864, Belle Mulford.   Children:

    a Cyrus Marion b Jan 20, 1865   b Edith b Dec 28, 1867; d unm
    c Arthur b Feb 17, 1869; d unm
    d Grace b Nov 23, 1871; d unm
    e Leslie b Apr 23, 1875; lived Shirleysburg, Pa; d 1898 from injuries received
         in the Spanish War, unm

Cyrus M Dow bcdedkda, orphaned in childhood, lives West Toledo, Ohio; m Bowling Green Oct 10, 1895, Anna Kahler b Germany Apr 7, 1874.   Children:

    a Jennings b Bowling Green Jan 2, 1897; midshipman U S N 1918
    b Dewey M b Apr 2, 1898; machinist's mate Brooklyn Navy Yard
    c Leonard J b July 3, 1902   d Walter K b Dec 26, 1904
    e Cyrus Marion b Toledo June 28, 1906; these 3 junior naval scouts

---

Jonathan Dow bcdedl appears in the original ms of the b line as a preacher and farmer of western N Y State, with no rec of m or children. N H church directory gives him as free will Baptist with pastorates in Portland, N Y, 1802-5 and Pomfret, N Y, 1835-41, giving nothing for the 30 years interim.   Some Jonathan Dow (we know of no other possible) of Bath m Mch 7, 1841, Abigail Towne of Lisbon d wid Lisbon Mch 25, 1897, ae 79-5-5, dau of Joseph, farmer, and Mehitable (Cole), both b

Lisbon.   From similarity of names and places, the Author infers that this was a 2nd m and that he had a son by 1st wife:

a   Marcellus of Pachate, N Y, m Nov 1, 1843, Susan Young of Bath.   Further
     untraced

Johanna Dow bcdf m Aug 18, 1727, Moses Tucker of Salisbury b Mch 28, 1704, d Jan 6, 1769, son of Joseph and Phoebe (Page) of Kingston. A saddler, he served as captain in the French War; pioneer of New Ipswich as early as 1747, its first selectman.   Children:

a   Mary b Jan 3, 1728-9   b   Parker b Jan 11, 1730; d May 7, 1736
c   Phebe b Mch 6, 1735   d   Moses b Mch 16, 1736-7
e   Sarah b Mch 13, 1739   f   Elizabeth b Apr 8, 1741
g   Hannah b Sept 22, 1743   h   Reuben b June 19, 1747
i   Joseph b Oct 22, 1748   j   Mary b Oct 9, 1751; d 1812; m George Start

DAVID Dow bcdg. A posterity of any of the three younger sons of Stephen Dow bcd has been difficult to trace. In all the genealogical efforts previous to that of the present Author, the lines have been dismissed after the bare collection of such ·vital statistics as survive in Salem, Methuen and Plaistow. No direct descendant was found in forty years of search. Every item of the lines bcdg, bcdh and bcdi was dug out by the present Author. The vital statistics of Haverhill were well kept from the beginning, but from about 1740 that part of old Haverhill which became other towns, containing almost all the homes of Dows of the b line, was very poorly managed. The records of Methuen are less than 50 per cent complete. Not 25 per cent of old Salem records are extant, if ever made. The vital data of Plaistow were copied from one book to another and such wholesale errors in dates, names and other particulars were made that one doubts even the good faith of the copyist.

Nothing of bcdg would ever have been found, had not the Author obtained the mass of old letters which Edgar R Dow had been unable to identify. Among them were two from a very old man of Canterbury, N B, written in 1885. The ink was home made and faded almost to illegibility. The writer showed that at one time his knowledge of his family was great but forgetfulness and confusion had attacked his mind. He dwelt upon the names David and Enoch, but occasionally transposed them. However, they were father and son. He mentioned Majorfield as their home before coming to Canterbury. Both names were favorites in the family in every later generation. There were discrepancies in the narrative, many pages long, which at first seemed unsurmountable when the Author took as a working hypothesis that David was the missing bcdg. So, the Author began a series of letters, one to every person named Dow who could be found in New Brunswick. Finally, in 1924 one of these reached William Segee Dow of Old Town, Me, who had from boyhood taken deep interest in the progeny of David, but who had not even hoped to find out who David was. The correspondence following has been constant. The Author gave his hypothesis with every scrap of information bearing upon it. Thereupon W S Dow revisited Canterbury, redoubled his efforts, revised every paper obtainable, searched the memory of every elderly kin, recopied every grave stone. David's grandsons had themselves been interested in finding out who they were genealogically. Another letter was found written by one of them, in which the statement was clear that Enoch was son of David and had a brother Nith and a brother William. This is proof of identity, when one refers back to the Plaistow records. Nith is a unique name. William is found to be not a brother but the orphaned nephew of David and cousin of Enoch. Finally, the birth date of Enoch

of Plaistow coincides with that given in his death record.   From this
start, little by little, we have been able to reconstruct David and his entire
posterity, a most important happening for this Book, because his posterity is by far the largest of any Dow and is probably not exceeded by
any man in this country.   It is not often that a man has fourteen children and one of his sons has seventeen, almost all surviving to procreate
another generation.

Let us hasten to the reconstruction.   David Dow m Jan 28, 1736-7,
Abigail Kelley, both of Salem.   Next entry is: Mary, wife of David
Dow, d Salem Jan 1, 1743.   Abigail Dow d Salem Dec 29, 1743.   David
Dow, yeoman of Methuen, m Salem Apr 10, 1744, Mary Brown b
Jan 9, 1725-6, dau of Caleb of Bradford and Elizabeth.   There were
children by both wives.   By referring to the birth records of the children,
it is easy to see that Mary, wife of David, is a clerical error in re-copying
for Abigail Kelley Dow, and that David promptly remarried.   Of the
children three have parents specified in rec:

a   Abigail, dau of David and Abigail, b Salem Sept 12, 1737; presumably d Dec
    29, 1743
b   Hannah b Sept 4, 1740.   A land mark near the mouth of St John's River is
    Dow's Hill, said by legend to be named for some Hannah Dow (confirmatory
    of the Port Arthur Settlement of 1761-2?)
c   Mary, dau of David and Abigail, b Dec 17, 1743; must have d in infancy, as
    a younger sister is also Mary.   Apparently her birth cost her mother's life
d   Enoch b Methuen Nov 26, 1744
e   Nith, son of David and Mary (Brown), b Mch 20, 1748.   Proven to have
    returned from New Brunswick to the States in 1803, but further untraced
f   Mary b Oct 3, 1749.   Some Mary d Sept 20, 1770.   Some Mary d unm Salem
    Jan 1, 1844.   Alternative presumption is that Mary accompanied her
    parents to N B
g   Elizabeth b Apr 20, 1753

Localities prove that the family lived in Salem up to 1753.   It
then disappears until 1770, date of birth of a grandson to David.   Family
tradition gives the place as Majorfield, but we do not believe Majorfield
was founded until about 1783.   No evidence that David served in the
French wars, in which three of his brothers gained distinction.   In 1776
some David Dow of Cumberland, N S, receipted in Boston for pay 1
mo, 5 days, Capt Jabez West, Col. Jonathan Eddy.   This company
was raised mostly in N B and Nova Scotia, and age almost precludes that
the enlister was our David.   In the same company was a John Dow,
unknown to us, hailing from St John.   Probably a member of the g Dow
family.   It is interesting to note that the Canadian coast furnished
about an equal proportion of Federal sympathisers as the 13 colonies
furnished tories.

Unmistakable family tradition says that David came to N B
from Newburyport.   In 1785 he was living in New Brunswick, an avowed
tory, as were all his neighbors.   It was in Newburyport, then, the sea
port for all the Haverhill region, that David learned of lands beyond
seas, lands which could be had, not for the asking, merely for the pre-
empting.   Two of his sons were Canadian-born according to tradition.

It is not impossible that David was more or less at home there as early as 1772. Nevertheless, he might have been of Berwick, Me, in 1776 (cf bcdgg). The great influx of former tories to N B came in 1783, a single expedition. In 1785 surely David was of Majorfield, a pioneer in a region of rich timber alongside the St John River and much below Canterbury. Many of his companions later came to found Canterbury, all well known Mass Bay names, all tories. We believe that David, who knew the N B coast from 1772, led the party to Majorfield. He was elderly when he d there, a tree which he was chopping falling upon him. Curiously, his grandson David years later was killed under exactly the same circumstances. One account has it that Majorfield was abandoned between 1785 and 1788, but this seems error. In 1796 land in that county was granted to William Dow, whom we identify as the orphan bcdhd. In 1815 land near where Canterbury now is was granted to William Dow. This entry we do not understand for bcdhd never went to Canterbury but returned to U S in 1803. Most likely the 1815 date is wrong and that bcbhd got that land prior to 1803 and quit-claimed it to his cousin. The Majorfield colony had a hard time. All the clearing and the homes were close to the River. The industry was in floating timber to tidewater and selling it. Three times the Spring freshets assumed great proportions and swept away all the homes in Majorfield. Thereupon the colonists became utterly discouraged. Nith Dow, William Dow and others returned across the border. Enoch Dow bcdgd decided to remain and formulated a plan to move upstream to a safer shore and used for his purpose the Canterbury land grant. A dozen or so families went with him. They built a large flat boat and poled it up the river. The forest was trackless and so remained many years. The migration was in 1803,—this date is positive. About 100 miles north they stopped and chose the right bank for the new settlement. Some years later Dow's Settlement was founded across the stream and about 4 miles higher up. Still another 4 miles up the Lane was settled, another Dow home.

Enoch Dow bcdgd had a wife Ruth, m before 1770. There was no clue to her identity, but Sally Hull, Enoch's great granddaughter, who had lived with her grandfather, maintained that she had known who Ruth was but had forgotten. As Mrs Hull was over 90, this is not strange. W S Dow, trying to jog her memory, ran over various names until he came to Norton. A John Norton was a pioneer of 1803 and was the first to be buried in what is now the great Dow Cemetery. The second interment therein was David Dow, killed by a falling tree, while he was clearing the Sullivan Creek hill road. Mrs Hull brightened. Surely, the missing Ruth was Ruth Norton, John's sister, both pioneers from the States.

Almost the first act of the settlers was to build a church and lay out the Dow Cemetery, which is about a quarter mile below. With few exceptions every one now in this large cemetery was a Dow by birth or marriage and in 1926 it was planned to double its size. Enoch Dow was a Baptist and every descendant was of that denomination, with only three exceptions,—who turned Mormon and went to Utah. Enoch and sons did most of the building of the new church and Enoch Jr was its lay minister for years. Enoch was a lumberman both at Majorfield and Canterbury. That was the only wealth-giving occupation of the region. He d Sept 23, 1813. He was outspoken as a tory, altho 2 of his uncles and 8 cousins had careers as fighters on the Federal side. Some Enoch Dow enlisted 1776 for the Canadian campaign. Some Enoch Dow was a private at Winter Hill 1777. If these are not our Enoch, we do not know who they were. It is quite possible that both were our Enoch, who later recanted. If so, he never in after-years admitted service.

There is a homogeneity of the enormous posterity of Enoch Dow worth noting, the family being by far the largest of any Dow and perhaps the largest in America. It is rare that a man should have 14 children, almost all maturing, and that one of those children should have 17, almost all producing a posterity. There is not a single instance in this posterity of death from tuberculosis or cancer. Average longevity is remarkably great, but a majority become almost crippled from rheumatism in old age.

Moses Dow, a grandson, gave the first list of children in 1885 and from this the Author arranged his letter key. Moses declared that Jesse was 1st born in Majorfield 1770. William S Dow in 1926 found Jesse's tombstone, which gave 1772 as birthdate and found that John b 1770 was 1st born. We have not changed the letter key and one other pair of children does not accord with William's recent discovery. However, the text is perfect and the children:

b John b 1770; d 1832   a Jesse b 1772; d 1867
c David, d unm, 1773-1794 (gravestone rec)
d Amos m Anna Teed. Jesse m her sister Mary. This name appears in the various generations as Tid, Tidd, Teed, etc. It is rightly Tidley. Salaveras Tidley, their father, was a Rev veteran who had an eye shot out in battle. In spite of his sinister appearance, he managed to have very comely daughters
e Enoc (Enoch, of course) b 1777; d 1845; m Basha Cronkite; first preacher in Canterbury; baptized more people in St John's River than any five subsequent preachers
f Mary b 1778; d 1843; m Amos Brooks
g Rhoda b 1786; d 1877; m John Porter   h Ester m —— Watson
i Ruth m —— Estey   j Hannah m David Phillips; was not the youngest

A reading of the galley proofs of this Book by members of the Canterbury family and others has provoked a lively search into the political opinions of the pioneers, as well as the origin of the various families of early New Brunswick. It is a majority verdict that Enoch Dow was not so much of a tory, after all. Moreover, the Author clings to his original opinion that Enoch saw service in the Federal Army.

There is no way of knowing what families accompanied Enoch from Majorfield to Canterbury. It is certain that the Nortons came with him. The Majorfield party had to scatter rather widely, as Enoch's land grant was a large one. It had about two miles on the river front and extended about 3-1-4 miles inland. This tract was divided by Enoch among his sons and they, in turn, divided among all their sons. The Nortons, who were never tories, were their nearest neighbors. The Teeds sprang from a Federal soldier. They and the Dickinsons settled in Lower Woodstock. The Brooks family pioneered Southhampton; the Phillips Northhampton on the east side of the river. The Kearneys took land in Northhampton; the Ways and the Hillmans in Temple, four miles below. The Tompkins, in spite of name, were a German family and came later, as did the Lutwicks. The original Hartley farm was in Southhampton. The Marstons of Canterbury descended from a British soldier of 1812. The Yerxas settled at Kesewick, 20 miles from Fredericton. The Cronkites were of Lower Southhampton; the Porters of Lower Woodstock.

William Segee Dow, whose knowledge of early New Brunswick history is profound, disagrees with the Author on the whereabouts of David Dow's family on various dates. There was a settlement, he explains, by Newburyport people at Port Arthur (now St John) as early as 1761-2, and David was among them. He asserts that Enoch was married in Majorfield and his 1st born was there in 1770. He thinks the family were American sympathizers, altho after the war it was more politic to display tory convictions. The first tories from the States came in 1783 and the influx lasted several years.

Asa and Moses Dow, grandsons of Enoch, thought that Majorfield was abandoned and Canterbury founded about 1783, the Dows squatting there for some years. Surely David Dow 2nd died 1794 in Canterbury. His gravestone is legible now. Solomon Dow was born Canterbury 1802, Jesse Dow married there before that date. The gravestone of John Norton is not extant, but he was the first to be buried in Dow Cemetery, the date being 1794 or previously.

Jesse Dow bcdgda, farmer and lumberman, is, of course, bur Dow Cemetery, his stone giving 1772-1867. Mary Tidley, his wife, appears as Tid, b Mch 25, 1782, d Canterbury Mch 27, 1869. Beyond doubt he had more lineal descendants at his funeral than any other Dow in history, altho Phoebe (Green) Dow, Quaker, d ae 102, with 250 surviving descendants. Moses Dow, Jesse's son, in 1885 gave the list of children and the details as given below:

a   Solomon 1802-1895; m Martha Wright 1816-1882; 12 children, 30 grand-
     children; 2 great grandchildren
b   Jacob 1804-1872; m Fannie Yerxa 1809-1884; 7 children; 20 grand
c   Rhoda 1807-1869; unm
d   Ruth 1809-1901; m Elias Brown (properly Brawn); 2nd Jacob Cummins
     (Cummings is interchangeable spelling); 7 children, 17 grand
e   Betsey (properly 3rd child) b 1805; d before 1885; 7 children, 32 grand
f   Samuel 1810-1886; m Mahala Yerxa; 17 children, 50 grand
g   Aaron 1812-1888; m Lydia Cummings; 15 children, 38 grand, 1 great grand
h   Olive m Moses Hillman; 6 children, 32 grand, 5 great grand

i   Moses; 11 children, 25 grand
j   Esther, convert to Mormonism; moved to Utah, became plural wife; 2 chil-
    dren; never after communicated with her family
k   Ephraim 1820-1874; m Mary Blake; 2nd Eliza Knowles (both N H tory
    families); 7 children, 7 grand
l   Lydia 1824-1915; m Amos Knowles; 2 children
m   Mary (properly older than Ephraim) m Charles Grant; 4 children, 3 grand
n   Jesse 1826-1899; m Susan Wright; 10 children, 9 grand

Solomon Dow bcdgdaa m July 25, 1833, Martha Wright. He and his brother Jacob had river front farms, but, undertaking some unusually large lumbering operations, became financially involved and lost their farms. Solomon moved to "The Lane" and, of course, is buried in Dow Cemetery. Children:

a   George b June 20, 1834; m Obergill (sic) Bartlett (N H family)
b   Sarah b Sept 29, 1835; m David Farrel
c   Hezekiah b Oct 20, 1837; m Mahala Dickinson; 2nd Hulda Brown, nee
    Dickinson
d   Olive b Jan 2, 1840; d Apr 6, 1843
e   Jesse Rue b Oct 19, 1841; m Jane Prescott (a tory Prescott came to N B in
    1783)
f   Damaris b Oct 30, 1843; d Mch 16, 1853
g   Serepta b Oct 30, 1843; d Jan 15, 1860
h   Talmon b Aug 22, 1845; d May 22, 1846
i   Charles A b May 1, 1847; m Margarette Dickinson
j   Huldah b Aug 24, 1849; m Isaac Adams (another tory family from Mass)
k   Mordica b Sept 5, 1853; m Sarah Dickinson
l   Jeremiah b Sept 5, 1853; m Hulda Miller
m   Clarissa M b 1857; m Clarence Jameson

George Dow bcdgdaaa, mill operative of Milltown, later of Calais, d "laborer" Sept 1, 1899. In Me vital statistics the word laborer is used for brevity to include almost any employe of any capacity. Abigail Bartlett d Calais May 26, 1911, ae 73, dau of William and Annie Greenlaw. List of children possibly incomplete:

a   Amos, unm   b   George Fred b N B 1871
c   William J b St Stephen 1872
d   Hugh b Calais Aug 21, 1875   e   Catherine

George F Dow bcdgdaaab, millman of Calais, m Nov 18, 1893, Victoria A Glover, ae 18, dau of William and Sarah (Conkley). Letter 1924 returned "not found." Children, State rec:

a   William Leslie b Apr 19, 1895   b   Allan M b Jan 23, 1901
c   —— son b Apr 29, 1903

William L Dow bcdgdaaaba baggage master of McAdam Jc, m Bangor Aug 2, 1917, Edna L Shea, ae 22, dau of Eli and Margaret (Hanlan), both b N B.

William J Dow bcdgdaaac married, laborer, of Rumford d Feb 12, 1915, ae 43-8-1; otherwise untraced.

Hugh Dow bcdgdaaad, laborer of Calais, d May 20, 1919; m Calais July 2, 1904, Bella Kidder, ae 21, dau of Frank and Mary (McLaughlin). Child:

a   —— son b Baileyville Dec 13, 1906; d Mch 17, 1907

Sarah Dow bcdgdaab m David Farrel. In 1926 they and all children living at North Lake, N B:

a Stephen b 1858; m Ida Cropley; 8 children
b Caroline b 1860; m Moses E Dow bcdgdakb; 2 children
c William b 1862; m Martha Anderson; 5 children
d Emery b 1872; m Nellie Foster; 2 children
e Amanda b 1872; m David Graham; 6 children
f Elmer b 1876; m Anna Foster; 2 children

Hezekiah Dow bcdgdaac, farmer, buried in the Lane. One child by 2nd wife:

a Manzer b 1862; m Julia Wright   b Clarence Albert b 1864
c Celeste b 1866; m Henry Dow   d Robert Washington b July 15, 1868
e Adrian Ellsworth b 1873; m Jennie Robinson
f Stewart m Sarah Anderson

Manzer Dow bcdgdaaca, farmer of Scott's Siding, became much interested in the news of his ancestry. Children:

a Clarence b 1902; d 1908   b Alton b 1903
c Harold b 1906   d Gertrude m Archie Dow
e Helman b 1912

Clarence A Dow bcdgdaacb m Charlotte G Flight; moved to Houlton, where for many years he has been railroad employe. Children:

a Eileen Mae b Oct 15, 1895; m Nelson Wing
b Smith Emery b Dec 1, 1897; now of Houlton; m Rena Mae Gray
c Frances Elizabeth b Aug 31, 1899; m Frank Johnson; twins Eileen Grace and
      Cecil Philip b Mch 21, 1921
d Earl Edison b July 1, 1901; m 1927 Eunice Victoria Burden, dau of Isaac
e Cecil Flight b Dec 16, 1903
f Bertha Alfreda b Aug 6, 1905; m Oct 25, 1926, Beryle Shirley, son of Oscar
      of Houlton
g Arthur Putnam b Oct 16, 1906   h Emma Florence b Oct 20, 1909
i Donald Edwin b July 22, 1911

Earl J Dow, storekeeper, later section hand of Houlton, is not bcdgdaacbd, is as yet unplaced; m Clara Wasson b Windsor, N B. Children:

b —— dau b Feb 26, 1915   c —— dau b Jan 8, 1918
d Evelyn Ruth b May 27, 1920

Celeste Dow bcdgdaacc m Henry Dow of Canterbury Station, son of John and Eliza (Webberly). This John Dow was a hunter by profession and was American-born. There seems no room for him anywhere in the bcdg line and his family is considered under bcdgdi.

Robert W Dow bcdgdaacd m Annie M Price b Feb 18, 1871; moved to Methuen, Mass, where he served in the State Legislature, representing the home town of his great great grandfather. Children:

a Alton Lester b Jan 5, 1894   b Inez Celeste b Sept 10, 1896
c Kenneth Robert b Jan 16, 1898   d Bessie Frances d July 26, 1900
e Ruby Mae b Dec 22, 1901   f Merle Price b Oct 24, 1903
g George Ellsworth b Sept 26, 1906   h Evelyn Anna b Mch 17, 1912

Alton L Dow bcdgdaacda, m Ernestine Emerson. Child:

a Donald Alton b Sept 3, 1922

Inez C Dow bcdgdaacdb m Leslie Brooks Day of Norfolk Downs. Children:

a Robert Edwin b 1922   b Stephen Leslie b Dec 27, 1924

Kenneth R Dow bcdgdaacdc m Jennie E Appleyard. Child:

a Betty Constance b July 7, 1923

Adrian E Dow bcdgdaace, railroad engineer of Calais, m June 20, 1901, Jennie Augusta Dow (her 2nd) b Calais, ae 28, cotton mill operative, dau of George E and Mary (Leavitt) Robinson. Family living 1926 at Milltown. Children:

a —— dau b Apr 26, 1902   b —— dau b Mch 26, 1904
c —— son b Sept 15, 1906. State rec defective. Ruth, Muriel, Clarence are names of some of these
f Lois L b July 29, 1916

Stewart Dow bcdgdaacf m Sarah Anderson; live farmers at Scott's Siding. Children:

a Pearl b 1912   b Helen b 1914   c Edna 1915-1918
d Agnes b 1916   e Mary b 1918   f Clara (?) b 1921

Jesse R Dow bcdgdaae m Jane Prescott; moved many years ago to Lawrence, thence to Methuen, Mass, unwittingly returning to the home of his great great great grandfather. Children:

a Mary; in 1915 directory milliner of Methuen; now of Russell, Pa
b Martha d young in Methuen; bur beside her parents
c William d young in Methuen   d Henry
e Thomas b N B 1876
f Emily; in 1915 directory music teacher of Methuen; now Mrs Calvin E Wilson of Russell, Pa
g Robert Frederick b N B 1881; m Watertown, Mass, Sept 21, 1908, Mary Edith Griffith, b N B, ae 30, dau of James E and Charlotte (Ketchum)
h George A; now of Vacaville, Calif

Henry Dow bcdgdaaed m Lucy Price (Prior in one rec), both b N B. He is now in post office Edmonton, Alberta. Children:

a Gladys Phoebe b Methuen Apr 9, 1903
b Bertha b Haverhill Jan 19, 1908

Thomas Dow bcdgdaaee m Methuen July 25, 1903, Martha L Sargent, ae 28, dau of Edmund P and Louisa (Webster); in 1915 directory blacksmith of Methuen; now builder of wagon and auto truck bodies in Methuen. No children.

Charles A Dow bcdgdaai had but two children; his wid b 1855, dau of Elijah and Elizabeth (Jameson) m Mass Sept 4, 1905 (his 2nd) John Stapley, ae 65.

a Elizabeth m Tyler Maxon; 1 son; now of Fredericton   b Ruby, unm

Huldah Dow bcdgdaaj m Isaac Adams; living McAdam Jc. Children:

a   Lorenzo 1875-90   b   Almeda m Robert Bennett
c   Charles m Fannie Williams   d   Byron m ——   e   Pearl m ——

Mordeca Dow bcdgdaak had an only child:

a   Ira; left Canterbury long ago; untraced

Jeremiah Dow bcdgdaal m (by her d rec) Hannah Miller of Haverhill, Mass, b Canterbury, d Old Town Oct 16, 1916. Their old age was spent with a son in Old Town. Children:

a   Martha Anne b Sept 26, 1887; m George Harman
b   Stanley James b May 8, 1889   c   Charles E b Aug 27, 1891
d   Cecil Reed b Jan 9, 1900; m Laura Spitnor; no children

Martha A Dow bcdgdaala m Geo Harman, farmers near St Stephen. Children:

a   Margaret Isabell b June 15, 1907
b   Helen May b May 29, 1908   c   Robert A b Mch 17, 1910
d   Ralph E b Feb 10, 1912   e   Lillian E b Feb 14, 1914; d 1919

Stanley J Dow bcdgdaalb, laborer of Old Town, m Aug 28, 1911, Louisa Lewis Orono, full blood Indian, ae 21, dau of Frank Lewis and Rosella (Gray); div; m 2nd, May 12, 1917, Winnifred Kelley, ae 21, dau of Freeman b Plaistow, N H, and Mary (Winters). Sic State rec, but W S Dow reports he m Hazel McGiggen. No children.

Charles E Dow bcdgdaalc, laborer of Old Town, built a merry-go-round, with which he traveled through Me; m Old Town July 30, 1913, Celia M De Chaine, ae 18, dau of Joseph and Sally (Servis) of Old Town. Children:

a   Gladys L b Jan 2, 1914; d Mch 21, 1915
b   Pauline Annie b Jan 27, 1915   c   Annie Mary b Dec 3, 1916
d   Lawrence Joseph b Sept 15, 1917   e   Thomas J b Aug 2, 1918
f   Arthur E b Jan 8, 1920   g   Lucinda A b Dec 23, 1924

Clarissa Dow bcdgdaam m Clarence Jameson; moved to Lyndon, Wash. Children:

a   Mildred b Mch 28, 1885   b   Hugh E b June 6, 1891
c   Mary Pauline b June 21, 1895

Jacob Dow bcdgdab m Fannie Yerxa, descendant of a loyalist of Dutch descent from N Y State. The Kearney who came with him was also a tory refugee of the family which founded Kearney, N J. Jacob was a lumberman with his brother on a tract by the river, which they lost through over extended credit. It may be remembered that at this time the British government suddenly withdrew its preferential tariff on lumber in favor of its colonies. Scandinavian lumber then poured in, bankrupting many of the strongest firms of New Brunswick. The bbbfa Dow family were thus reduced from millionairedom to ruin. Jacob moved back to Dow's Settlement, near his brother Samuel and cousin David. In 1847 he built a log house there, still standing and occupied. The solid log house of the period was not built because it was cheaper, but because it resisted cold better than any other. Jacob's children:

a   Sampson b 1837 (1842 by own m rec) farmer of Canterbury d childless 1919; m Houlton July 2, 1892, wid Adelaide Dibble, ae 48, dau of Joseph and Mary (Dickerson) (Dickinson?) Wright
b   Sarah b 1839; m William Hull, immigrant from north of Ireland. A son Edward m Florence Hayes and is a plumber of Salt Lake City
c   Rhoda 1841-1888; m James McGibboney
d   Allan J b Apr 12, 1843   e   Nelson 1845-6, measles
f   Zebulon b 1847-1922; m Florence Kearney, sister of Ambrosine
g   Wellington 1848-1911; m Adelia Dow bcdgdeaj

Allan J Dow bcdgdabd lives 1927 with dau in Meductic; in excellent health, went alone in 1927 to visit a son in Saskatchewan; returned successfully; has written many times to the Author in firm clear hand on family history. He m Ambrosine Kearney 1850-1922. Fortunate in his children and proud of them:

a   William Segee b Oct 5, 1871   b   Homer b Oct 4, 1873; d Nov 29, 1875
c   Ethel Margaret b May 14, 1875; m Sept 7, 1904, Hurd M Edwards of Meductic; no children
d   Harry Kearney b Feb 7, 1878   e   Herbert L b Sept 13, 1881

William S Dow bcdgdabda, boss dyer, went from mill to mill in many New England towns, but now for many years overseer of dyeing in Old Town Woolen Co. His taste for family history began in childhood and through correspondence and personal effort he built up a remarkable list of the posterity of bcdgd. The Author was able to furnish the ancestry of bcdgd, since then the correspondence has been constant. The entire bcdg line was genealogically unknown until 1924.

He m Mch 28, 1902, Elsie Severance b Hollis, Me. This old Quaker family occurs first herein through m to adab. Children:

a   Hazel Vilmer b Buxton July 5, 1903; d Sept 1922
b   Allan Ambrose b Hollis Jan 15, 1905; in college 1926
c   Neal S b Dexter Aug 23, 1906; now asst boss dyer of Old Town
d   Florence Maxine b Old Town Nov 19, 1912

Harry K Dow bcdgdabdd m 1909 Alexandria Frazier; now wholesale coal dealer of Regina, Saskatchewan. Children:

a   Paul b 1910   b   Herbert b 1912   c   Seth b 1915

Herbert L Dow bcdgdabde, overseer of dyeing, American Woolen Co at Yantic, Conn; m Tilton, N H, 1919 Mary Louise De Chaine of Old Town. Children:

a   Mary Louise b July 4, 1920   b   Dorothy Helen b 1922

Sarah Dow bcdgdabb m William Hull; both living 1927 on a farm in Aroostook Co. Children:

a   Adelia b 1861; bur Dow Cemetery   b   Maria 1864-1883
c   Martha b 1867; m Abraham Marston; 8 children, all married. This Marston family descends from a British soldier of a regiment disbanded in N B after the war of 1812; originally spelled Masten

d Shepard b 1871; m Orie Hall of Easton, Me; 2 children
e Minnie b 1875; m —— Ross; 2 children
f Edward b 1877; m ——; 2 children; lives Colo
g Thomas 1881-1886

Rhoda Dow bcdgdabc m James McGibboney; lived St Stephen. Children:

a Elizabeth b 1869; m William Keating of St Stephen; 5 children
b Fannie b 1871; m —— Boober; lives Portland, Me
c Martha m George Dinsmore; lives St Stephen
d Florence m —— Newson; now a nurse in State Hospital
e Cassie m —— Mosher
f Mabel 1888-1921; m Harold Carter; 4 children

Zebulon Dow bcdgdabf left Canterbury 1888 for Gonic, N H; d there 1922. Name of wife often spelled Carney in rec. Children:

a Frederick 1875-1880; bur Dow Cemetery
b Nellie b 1878; m Clarence Pinkham of Old Quaker family of Dover
c Frances C b 1880; m Farmington, N H, Sept 22, 1900, Ralph A Newell of Springfield, Mass; div; m 2nd Gideon Gagnon; div, m 3rd Philip Haswell
d Franklin N b 1883; m Albena Coram; by recent directory drug clerk of Rochester
e Beulah Cora b Somersworth Apr 7, 1891; m Joseph Danforth

Nellie Dow bcdgdabfb and Clarence Pinkham live Dover. Children:

a Maurice b 1903   b Madelin 1905-1908   c Robert b 1908
d Harold 1910-1913   e Franklin b 1912   f Fannie Beulah b 1921

Fannie (Dow) Haswell bcdgdabfc lives Malden, Mass. Children (Newell):

a Frederick b 1901   b Florence b 1903; m George Adams

Beulah C Dow bcdgdabfe m Joseph Danforth; live Old Town. Only child:

a Paul D b 1921

Wellington Dow bcdgdabg, farmer of Dow's Settlement, d from fall from a roof which he was shingling. Children:

a Elmer b 1875; m Julia Johnson   b Daniel 1877-1886
c Estelle 1879-1905; m —— Shaw. No children. The Shaw family pre-Revolutionary from York, Me
d Clyde b 1882, m Hattie Shaw   e Allan 1884-1889
f Lena b 1886; m Frederick Johnson   g Velma b 1890; m Clarence Hatch

Elmer Dow bcdgdabga and wife are farmers near Hartland, Me. Children:

a Seth b 1902; unm
b Beatrice b 1904; m Silas Perkins (name from early Hampton, N H); sons,—Graydon b 1924, Reginald b 1926
c Willis b 1906; m —— Cox   d Hazel b 1914   e Leona b 1920

Lena Dow bcdgdabgf m Frederick Johnson, farmers of Dow's Settlement. Children:

a Wendall Allan b Aug 20, 1909   b Nellie Myrtle b July 19, 1911
c Vera Belle b Sept 22, 1913   d Alma May b July 11, 1915
e Robert Eugene b July 15, 1917   f Clifford Miles b Sept 24, 1919

Velma Dow bcdgdabgg m Clarence Hatch; live Dow's Settlement. Child:

a   Harry b 1919

Ruth Dow bcdgdad, bur Dow Cemetery, had 1 son by 1st husband:

a   Moses (Brown) 1836-1912; m Lena Edwards; 5 children; vet of Civil War; d Charlestown, Me
b   Silas (Cummins) b 1843; m Ellen Dow bcdgddec; lives Houlton
c   Mary b 1845; m James Teed; lived Forest City, Me; 6 children
d   Leonard b 1849; d Woodstock 1912; m Maria Graham; 2 children
e   George 1847-1904, unm

Betsey Dow bcdgdae m Thomas Edwards, a Scotchman; had a farm near Benton.   Children:

a   James m —— Mobury; kept the homestead
b   Blanche m Freeman Austin   c   Lena m Moses Brown; 4 children
d   Walter killed Civil War; unm   e   Robert m ——; lived Woodstock
f   Theophilus 1843-1911; m Eliza Jacques; 6 children
g   Eliza m —— Barker; 2 children lived and d in Montana

Samuel Dow bcdgdaf b Sept 25, 1810, m Mahala Yerxa b Mch 14, 1815, d 1889.   His farm in Dow's Settlement adjoins that of his brother and wife's sister.   Their children had more cousins living within a few miles than any other family in America. Of 17 children, no fewer than 7 survive in 1927:

a   Milan L b 1835; d 1918; m Olive Tompkins
b   Charles Perley b 1837; d 1909; m Caroline Dickinson
c   Emma 1839-1902; m Elias Yerxa; 2nd Enoch Gilbert
d   Gideon Yerxa b 1840; m Caroline Dow bcdgddeb
e   Amaziah N b 1841; m Adelaide Tompkins
f   Archie F 1842-1891; m Sarah Dickinson
g   Barbara 1844-1862; unm
h   Ruth E 1846-1902; m George B Dow bcdgddea
i   Joannah 1847-1899; m James Brittany
j   Jane L 1849-1924; m John Maxon
k   John Yerxa b 1850; m Ella Porter
l   Thurza (Theresa V) 1851-1897; m Charles Simpson
m   Samuel H 1853-1924; m Almeda Johnson
n   Alice E 1855-1917; m Farrel Maxon
o   Asa N b 1858; m 1st Ada Bishop
p   Frances L b 1860; m Dean Sawtelle; 2nd James Ramsdell; 3rd James McIntyre
q   Dudley J b 1863; m Mina Saunderson

Milan L Dow bcdgdafa and wife lived and d Meductic; bur Dow Cemetery.   Children:

a   Lorenzo D
b   Everett 1860-1925; m Katy St Clair; lived Montana; d Oakland, Calif; no children
c   Elizabeth 1862-1881; unm   d   Julia M b 1864   e   Corey b 1868
f   Jane b 1870   g   Samson M b Aug 9, 1872   h   Sarah b 1874

Lorenzo D Dow bcdgdafaa of Cranbrook m Sarah Scott.   Children:

a   Harold, unm   b   Olive m ——; lives Calif
c   Willard (Orville W); unm

Julia M Dow bcdgdafad m Amaziah Z Bragdon; moved to Lynn; returned to a farm in Bucksport, Me.   Children:

  a Pearl b 1895; m Arthur Gould; lives Danvers, Mass
  b Arthur b 1898, unm
  c Hazel b 1901; m Raymond Russell; lives Lynn; 1 child
  d Edith b 1903, m Harold Leonard Mead of Middleton, Mass
  e Evelyn Helene b Lynn Feb 23, 1907, unm

Corey Dow bcdgdafae, railroad man of Cranbrook, B C, m Ruth ——.   Children:

  a Ruth m ——; lives Edmonton   b John   c —— dau

Jane Dow bcdgdafaf m John Young, hotel keeper of Woodstock. Children:

  a Harold m ——; lives Lynn   b Stanley m ——; lives Houlton
  c Myrtle m John Mitchell of Smyrna Falls, Me   d Holly, unm

Samson M Dow bcdgdafag m Elois Taylor; live Meductic.   Children:

  a Faye b 1904; m Simeon Clows of Chipman; child,—Francis b 1925
  b Helen b 1909   c Milan b 1914   d Frederick b 1916
  e Lloyd E b Apr 13, 1916

Sarah Dow bcdgdafah m Joseph Belleveau; lives Lynn.   Children:

  a Gladys b 1898; m Kenneth Newhall of Miami   b Joseph b 1903
  c —— d young

Charles P Dow bcdgdafb m Caroline Dickinson; farmer at Scott's Siding.   Children:

  a Adelia (Delilah) m George Downey of Woodstock; children,—Grace m Gerald De Ware; Nellie
  b Althea m William Smith of Woodstock; 1 child d young
  c Ada d young   d Harvey Wood b Benton 1872
  e Edith; of Boston m Charles Smith; div; son Wilbur d young   f Ella

Harvey W Dow bcdgdafbd, train man of Van Buren, Brunswick, Bangor, Rumford Falls, lives 1926 Providence, R I; m Sept 26, 1897, Mary McFrederick b Benton, ae 22, dau of James and Mary (Knowles). Children:

  a Alice b Bangor Sept 26, 1898; m Pitman Hunt; lives Auburn, Me; 3 children
  b Dora Hazel b Feb 24, 1903; m William Costella; lives Providence; son Kenneth
  c —— son b Brunswick Apr 29, 1907; d young   d Eva, unm

Ella Dow bcdgdafbf m Theodore McKinney; live Woodstock. Children:

  a Pearl m Harry T Colpitts of Wakefield, Mass
  b Iva m Roy Smith; 1 dau
  c Estell m Karl H Healey of Auburn, Me; 1 surviving child,—Robert
  d Roy d young   e Allison d in infancy

Emma Dow bcdgdafc m Elias Yerxa; 2nd, Enoch Gilbert; lived Lower Woodstock.   Two children by 2nd m.

  a Samuel m Lela Sterling; 5 children   b Amaziah, unm
  c Henry 1865-1886

d   Ella m Tyler Brown; 1 child; 2nd Norman Yerxa, 4 children
e   Benjamin b 1872; m Celeste Stairs; lives New Haven, Conn; no children
f   Herman m — ; lives Salt Lake City; 2 children

Gideon Y Dow bcdgdafd now lives with a dau in Malden, Mass; locally said to have become quite well-to-do through lumbering and timber lands. In 1926 he made a long visit to his kinsfolk in N B, surprising everyone by his activity, strength and keenness of mind. Children:

a Lillian   b Alice   c Herbert, unm, printer of Malden

Lillian Dow bcdgdafda m Herbert McClellan; live Malden. Children:

a Geneva m ——   b Pauline m —— Currie; live Revere
c Spencer, of Boston, unm   d Phyllis, of Boston, unm

Alice Dow bcdgdafdb m John Moors; 2nd, Arthur Simmons; lives Franklin, N H; 5 children:

a Kenneth m Agnes ——   b Nellie m —— Thompson
c Eugene m Vivian Yates   d Neal m Jessie ——
e Alice Maud b 1908

Amaziah Dow bcdgdafe m Adelaide Tompkins; farmers of Lower Woodstock; he now lives with dau in Jacksontown. Children:

a Emma b 1865; m Charles Cummins
b Howard E b 1867; m Margaret Scott; 2nd Annie Temple
c Burden Elias b 1871; m Lela B Goff
d Tressa b 1873; m Wilmot Edwards   e Smith b 1876; m Hulda Miller
f Hulda m Horace Fitzgerald   g Burns 1880-1905; m Ada Deacon
h Gertrude m Judson Hillman

Emma Dow bcdgdafea m Charles Cummins, farmers of Dow's Settlement. Children:

a Chester m Emma Daugherty; 5 children
b Bertram m Elizabeth McLellan; 4 children
c Agnes m Stewart Darling; 1 child
d Teneriff m Burton Patterson; 4 children
e Frederick m Gertrude Tompkins; 2 children
f Smith m Verna Patterson; 3 children
g Hayward   h Sterling   i Vesta   j Gladys

Howard E Dow bcdgafeb, farmer of Lower Woodstock. Children, by 1st wife:

a Harry Ernest   b Joseph, unm   c Charles, unm

Harry E Dow bcdgdafeba m Dolphena Shannon. Children:

a Buster   b Alta Clara b 1922   c Ernest b 1925

Burden E Dow bcdgdafec, blacksmith of Meductic, m Easton, Me, Sept 23, 1899, Bessie L Groff, ae 20, dau of James E and Hannah E (Libby). Children:

a Beatrice m Cecil Dow bcdgdaghb; lives Dow's Settlement
b Hattie A m Arthur Ackers   c Fern W   d Willard B b 1906
e Burns C   f Vaughn

Tressa Dow bcdgdafed m Wilmot Edwards; lives Benton, N B. Children:

a Jessie E   b Helen   c Russel   d Bessie   e Mabel
f Arlene

Smith Dow bcdgdafee is a Baptist clergyman, at present at Marysville, N B. Children:

a Marie   b Ruth   c Burpee   d Grace   e Edward

Hulda Dow bcdgdafef m Horace Fitzgerald of St John, N B. Children:

a Eugene   b Donald   c George   d Elva   e Francis

Burns Dow bcdgdafeg, cook of Woodstock, m Houlton Dec 3, 1904, Ada Daken (sic rec), ae 21, dau of William and Mary (McIlroy). Child:

a Florence L b St Croix Dec 16, 1904; d young

Gertrude Dow bcdgdafeh m Judson Hillman, farmers of Jacksontown, N B. Children:

a Beulah   b Vernon   c Thelma   d Marion   e Smith
f Irma   g Glena

Archie Dow bcdgdaff m Sarah Dickinson; farmers of Scott's Siding; bur Lane Cemetery. Children:

a George 1870-1871   b Mahala 1871-1871   c Emma 1873-1873
d Henry b 1875; unm, of Houlton   e Bessie 1875-1895
f Augusta b 1879   g Odbur T 1881-1899
h Miles 1884-1884   i Maud 1886-1888

Augusta Dow bcdgdafff m Burton Hazlett; live Houlton. Children:

a Alton Grant b Boston Mch 25, 1902, unm   b Gerald   c Paul

Joannah Dow bcdgdafi m James Brittany. Only child:

a Laura m —— Cook; lives Calif

Jane L Dow bcdgdafj m John Maxon. Children:

a Tyler m Elizabeth Dow bcdgdaaia; live Fredericton; 1 child
b May m John Beardsley of Lower Woodstock
c Ernest m Edith Moors; 3 children   d Hedley m Joan White; 2 children
e Perry. Younger members all moved to Port Huron, Mich

John Y Dow bcdgdafk m Ella Porter; live Woodstock. Children:

a Norman L b 1875
b May b 1877; m Judson Kelley. Children,—Wilbert, Donald, Amy
c Electa m Burns Smullen; children,—Cecil, Thelma, Ella, Freda, Fred
d Prudence m Henry Smith; no children
e Addie m Roy Atherton; children,—Archie, Ruth
f Mahala m Claude Green; no children   g Kenneth, unm
h Harry, unm
i Rankin m Violet Smullen. Children,—Dorothy, Vivian, Bernard
j Annie m F C Tedford. Children,—Kenneth, Evelyn, Earle

Norman L Dow bcdgdafka, cook of Woodstock, m Houlton (rec gives b 1882) Apr 6, 1907, Lizzie J Astle b Houlton, ae 17, dau of Henry and Helen (Hannigan); div; m 2nd, farmer of Presque Isle, Inez Hinnison b Limestone; again div.   Three children by 2nd wife

a   —— dau b Houlton Nov 7, 1907
b   John Nelson b Sept 27, d Oct 29, 1909
c   —— son b Caribou Oct 29, 1909 (dates by rec) (identical?)
d   —— dau b and d Feb 4, 1911
e   Dorothea H d Aug 25, 1912, ae 4 mos   f   —— son b Oct 1, 1913
g   —— dau b May 12, 1918   h and i —— sons, Kenneth and Donald

Thyrsa Dow bcdgdafl; bur Dow Cemetery; m Charles Simpson. Child:

a   Della B b 1874; m Otis L Paige; live Springfield, Mass; 4 children, including
    Mabel Irene b Apr 7, 1901, George Otis b Apr 15, 1907

Samuel Howard Dow bcdgdafm m Almeda Johnson; lived Canterbury Station; bur Dow Cemetery.   Children:

a   Garfield, of Edmonton, Alberta; m Laura Darling; 4 children,—Francis,
    Marion and Basil surviving
b   Robert, of Canterbury Station; served in World War; m in Eng, Rose Newland.
    Children: Reginald b 1920, Ardean b 1921, Samuel b 1923, Dorothy b 1925
c   Jay N, veteran of World War; unm, teaches in St John High School
d   Hawley; lives Alberta; m Thelma (Annie) Jarvis; 2 children

Alice E Dow bcdgdafn m Farrel Maxon; moved to Wyo; d there. Children:

a   Maud m ——; 6 children   b   Beulah m ——; 1 child

Asa Norman Dow bcdgdafo of Lynn m 2nd, Apr 16, 1902, Minna Catherine Sternburg, ae 25, dau of Henry and Louise (Guttman); div; m 3rd, Alma Fitch; moved to Edmonton, Alberta.   Children:

a   William m Marjorie ——. Children,—Ada and Asa; enlisted in Alta reg,
    missing in action; wid lives Calif
b   Percy d young   c   Basil   d   Donald

Frances L Dow bcdgdafq, thrice widowed, lives Canterbury Station.

Dudley J Dow bcdgdafg m Mina Saunderson; moved to Edmonton. Children:

a   Vona m Joseph Clifford; 4 children: a Dorothy, b Muriel of Manitoba
b   Pacola m Philip Mohr; live Manitoba; only child,—Laurel
c   Dudley N m Maud Hale; live Manitoba; only child,—Mina
d   James m Annie Williams; live Edmonton; only child,—Melton
e   Melton 1897-1898   f   Barbara, unm

Aaron Dow bcdgdag m Lydia Cummings, their whole lives at Dow's Settlement. Their son Boardman carries on the homestead farm. Children:

a   Irene   b   Olive b 1845   c   Samuel Leonard b 1847
d   Judson d young   e   Rhoda m Ira Dow bcdgdeaab   f   Melvina
g   Doletta   h   Aaron Boardman
i   Belle   j   Cynthia   k   Sophronie   l   Ellen M d young
m   Jeannette   n   Edward d young   o   Josephine d young

Irene Dow bcdgdaga m John Patterson; lived Providence, where their children now live:

a Mary m W Allen   b Neal, unm   c Alonzo m ——
d Marion m Frederick Parkin   e Susie m ——

Olive Dow bcdgdagb m George Grant; live Houlton; she active in 1926, collected all the data of her father's posterity. Children:

a Mandy May   b Ada M
c Nellie J; all d young of diphtheria within a day of each other
b Minnie m Bruce Dickinson; 5 children
c Edith m Harry Johnson; 3 children
d Effie d young   e Weston m Mabel Dow bcdgdagca; no children
f Rankin m Ellen Hughes; 4 children   g Frederick, unm

Samuel L Dow bcdgdagc, carpenter of Houlton, d widower Sept 15, 1914; m Mabel Scovill. Children:

a Mabel m Weston Grant bcdgdagbe; lives Houlton
b Sophronie m Wallace Henderson; lives Paterson, N J
c Ira d young   d Arnum (adopted); unm, lives Paterson, N J

Melvina Dow bcdgdagf m Henry Watson; live Pittsfield, Me. Children:

a Essie m Ira Stewart; lives Pittsfield
b Harry m Elizabeth Pennock, teacher Pittsfield High School
c Gertrude m Albert Wiles   d Lottie m John Green
e Roy m Myrtle Elliott

Boardman Dow bcdgdagh, substantial farmer, m Jennie Lutwick. Me rec garbles this to Jane Lettrick; the origin of the name is, of course, Ludwig. Children:

a Maud m William Grant   b Harley R b 1891
c Cecil m Beatrice Dow bcdgdafeca   d Lester, unm

Maud Dow bcdgdagha and William Grant live Salem, Mass. Only child:

a Izona

Harley R Dow bcdgdaghb lives Patton, Me; laborer of Canterbury, m Houlton Mch 15, 1914, Hazel A Allen student ae 17, dau of Willlam and Agnes (Tompkins); 2nd Vera Stewart. Child, by 1st wife:

a —— dau b Apr 12, 1915

Cecil Dow bcdgdaghc and Beatrice have a farm at Dow's Settlement. Children:

a Madeline b 1921   b Dennis b 1923   c Bertha b 1925

Belle Dow bcdgdagi m Archie Patterson bcdgdeaaca; live Lewiston, Me. Children:

a Lydia B m Henry Kelley   b Mary J m Luther Grant
c Mina m Nelson Grant   d Aaron m ——   e Neal
f Kenneth   g ——; there were 7 children in all

Cynthia Dow bcdgdagj m Zebulon Grant; 2nd, Elbridge Hagerman; lived Temple, N B. Children:

a Nelson m Mina Patterson bcdgdagic   b Frank d young
c Allan m —— Ward   d Ward m —— Marlie   e Abner m ——
f Orilla m Todd Richie   g ——; there were 7 in all

Sophronia Dow bcdgdagk m John Crotters; their family live Providence, R I:

a Thomas m Mandy Dow bcdgdeaabc   b ——   c May m ——

Jeannette Dow bcdgdagm m James Scovill; lives B C. Children:

a Ada m —— Cummins   b Lena m ——   c May

Olive Dow bcdgdah m Moses Hillman, farmers of Temple, N B. Children:

a Neamiah (Nehimiah) 1837-1923; m Jane Grant; 5 children
b Jeremiah 1839-1914; m Sarah Tompkins; 8 children
c Mary 1844-1914; m Freeman Fox; 6 children
d John b 1847; m Adelia Carpenter; 5 children
e Warren b 1851; m Maria Hartley; 5 children
f Martha b 1849; m John Longstaff; 2nd Augustus Gillman; 5 children

---

Moses Dow bcdgdai, farmer, lived on the place inherited from his father; b Jan 3, 1816; m June 4, 1840, Nancy B Cummings b Fayette, Me, May 24, 1824. He started investigation of his family history, which his grandnephew afterwards developed. In 1885 the only information obtainable was from old letters, tombstone rec and personal memories. Moses had a large supply of these. Children, by his own list:

a Adna b Jan 13, 1841; d widower Lewiston, Me, Feb 26, 1918; 7 children
b Jerusha b Mch 8, 1843; m July 19, 1863, Edmund Hillman of Southhampton; 9 children
c Thankful P b Feb 24, 1845; m Sept 19, 1871, Samuel Grant of Canterbury; 1 child
d Alonzo C b Mch 31, 1847
e Aaron W b Feb 9, 1849; m Dec 23, 1873, Martha Cluff; 3 children
f Henrietta b May 15, 1851; m Frederick Brooks; d without children
g and h Edward and Levi d young
i Moses Roy b Apr 6, 1857; m Canterbury July 3, 1879, Tressie Tompkins
j Spurgeon b Feb 14, 1860; m Dec 3, 1884, Phebe Hillman
k July E b Apr 29, 1862; m July 7, 1880, Joel Tompkins; 1 child

Adna Dow bcdgdaia left Canterbury many years ago; settled in Lewiston, Me; in directory 1915, but never answered letters of genealogical inquiry. He m Gerusha Dickinson. Children:

a Georgia, lived Lewiston; m Samuel R Hoy; 1 son
b Azro Peter m —— Burr; 3 children. His family lives Vancouver while he spends most of his time in Wiseman, Alaska. An eccentric and apparently very likeable man, the amount of money he is supposed to have made in Alaska gold mining may be exaggerated. When in 1925 he made his annual visit to his family and his bankers in Vancouver the local daily papers gave the event a first page column and the circumstance was mentioned in newspapers throughout the country
c Grace m —— Chace; lives New Bedford, Mass
d Thursa (Theresa C) m —— Crowell; lives Rainy River, Ont

e Genora m Frederick Hewlett; farmers of Presque Isle, Me
f Alfonso d unm in Alaska

Lewiston directory gives an **E Waldron Dow** with Alice, clerk,
Eva, clerk, Eleanor W and Edna, apparently a wholly different and untraced family.

Jerusha Dow bcdgdaib m Edmund Hillman; lives Greenbush.
Children, all living N B:

a Annie m Jacob Cummins; 5 children
b Nelson m —— McLeod; 2nd —— Tompkins; 3 children
c Greely m Edith Marston; 5 children
d Moses b 1870; m Letha Patterson; 2nd wid Farnham; 6 children
e Belle m Abraham Cronkite   f Elsie; drowned, unm
g Jasper, unm   h Judson m Gertrude Dow bcdgdafeh
i Sylvia m Elijah Cameron

Thankful P Dow bcdgdaic m Samuel Grant. Dau:

a Edna m John Booth; lives Conn

Alonzo C Dow bcdgdaid, living Woodstock 1926, was farmer of
Canterbury; m May 3, 1877, Lucy A Dow bcdgdded. In good health,
he took a long tramp 1926 with cousin Allan J. Children:

a Ruby m Frank Cram; 2nd John Parker. They have a potato farm at Fort
   Fairfield, Me. Children, by 1st husband,—Eugene, unm, Mabel, Frank b
   1913
b Roy m Bessie Kearney; with Canadian Pacific at Vancouver. Children,—
   Mabel b 1911, Evelyn b 1913
c Iva; lives Woodstock; m Maurice Craig; dau,—Beatrice
d Harley   e Gladys m ——; d without children

Harley Dow bcdgdaidd, Baptist minister in 1926 of Hainesville,
Me, m Edmonton, Alberta, Florence Iblitson. Child:

a Alonzo John

Aaron W Dow bcdgdaie and wife celebrated golden wedding;
farmers of Northhampton, N B. Children:

a Newton S b 1874   b Jennie b 1876   c Guy F b 1883; m Jessia Graves

Newton S Dow bcdgdaiea appears as immigration inspector at
Vanceboro, Me, but went in 1914 to Rent, Wash. He m Elizabeth Gill,
both b N B. Me rec gives as 2nd child Lucille b Mch 26, 1915, but
family rec give as the children:

a Wilfred unm   b Edith m —— Rasmussan; 1 child
c Harold, unm   d Joyce, unm   e Hester   f Charles

Jennie Dow bcdgdaieb m Arthur Gibson; live Northhampton.
Children:

a Donald   b Douglas   c Mildred   d Anna
e Margarette

Guy F Dow bcdgdaiec and wife live Northhampton. Children:

a Margaret b 1914   b Clinton b 1917

Moses Roy Dow bcdgdaii, cotton mill worker, later shoemaker oᶠ Eel River, d at home of children, Salesville, R I; m July 3, 1879, Tressa E Tompkins b Dow Settlement Sept 22, 1857, d Calais Apr 25, 1905, dau of Jacob bcdgddae and Rhoda; m 2nd (her 2nd), May 29, 1907, Lydia M Irving, ae 47, d Calais Sept 30, 1911, dau of Samuel and Lydia M (Norwood) Grover; m 3rd, Helen Moses. Family brought up in St Stephen. Children:

   a Lena M b Feb 10, 1881; m Wesley McFarland. Calais rec that Lena M Dow
        d Oct 10, 1902, surely a garbled m rec. They live Salesville.
   b Hugh H b May 13, 1883   c Hadley J b May 10, 1885
   d Alma R b 1887   e Roberta V b 1889   f Violet O b 1892
   g Bertha P b 1895; m Newton Frost; live West Upton, Mass
   h Theresa E b and d 1897   i Albert V b 1898
   j Jennie M b 1901; unm   k Amy A b Mch 17, 1904; unm

Hugh H Dow bcdgdaiib, cotton mill worker of Calais, m **Aug 11, 1904**, Angie Townsend Knight, ae 18, dau of George A and Amanda N (Trafton); in 1908 paper mill worker of Baileysville; now of Worcester, Mass. Children:

   a Helen b Jan 26, 1907   b Dorothy b July 1, 1909
   c Muriel b Baileysville June 30, 1911

Hadley J Dow bcdgdaiic, cotton mill worker of Calais, m Apr 22, 1908, Dora E Bartlett, ae 20, dau of Seth and Minnie (Rogerson); now of Smithfield, R I. Children:

   a Sarah   b Fannie

Alma R Dow bcdgdaiid m Walter B Sprague; live Worcester, Mass. Children:

   a Dexter   b Frank

Roberta V Dow bcdgdaiie m John Acherson; live Salesville. Child:

   a Tressa

Violet O Dow bcdgdaiif m Howard Lee; live Calais. Children:

   a Francis   b Doris

Albert V Dow bcdgdaiii enlisted 42nd Batt R H C, Canadian Kilties; blown to pieces by a shrapnel. A square in front of Salesville Post Office has been named for him and his monument erected thereon.

Spurgeon Dow bcdgdaij lives on the original Enoch Dow grant at Canterbury Front. Children of Spurgeon and Phebe:

   a Harry   b Laura   c Zula   d Lois   e Philip
   f Effie   g Perley, unm   h Mildred, unm

Harry Dow bcdgdaija m Martha Grant; occupies the place descended from his great grandfather. Children:

   a Talmadge b Nov 23, 1913   b Evelyn b Apr 2, 1916

Laura Dow bcdgdaijb m Miles Grant of Canterbury. Child:

a   Hayward b Mch 12, 1911

Zula Dow bcdgdaijc m Charles Hall. Children:

a   Audry b Mch 24, 1912   b   Phyllis b July 22, 1914
c   Spurgeon b Dec 6, 1916

Elois Dow bcdgdaijd m Clyde McCloskey. Children:

a   Beatrice b Dec 18, 1914   b   Robert b Feb 25, 1916

Philip Dow bcdgdaije m Ida Brown; live Boston, Mass.   Children:

a   Barbara b May 28, 1923   b   Arlene b May 17, 1925

Effie Dow bcdgdaijf m Millard Wright of Jacksontown, N B. Children:

a   Laversa b Nov 30, 1913   b   Gordon b Mch 10, 1916
c   Maria b Mch 27, 1918   d   Philip b Sept 5, 1920
e   Elva b Apr 2, 1922

Julia E Dow bcdgdaik m Joel Tompkins; live Jacksontown, farmers. Children:

a   Alda M b Dec 19, 1883; m Thomas Kinney
b   Demie H b July 20, 1887; m Mabel Appleby
c   Herbert Smith b Mch 2, 1891; m Maud Grass
d   Coy b June 15, 1894; m Jennie Darling   e   Ira b Feb 23, 1900; unm

---

Ephraim Dow, bcdgdak, lumberman, always lived Canterbury; bur with both wives in Dow Cemetery. Children:

a   Henry Weed b 1850   b   Moses Charles b 1851   c   Edward L
d   Minerva C   e   George m ——— Goodsoe; no children; lives Benton

Henry W Dow bcdgdaka now lives with dau in Hollis Center, Me; railroad engineer of Gorham, m Annie McFrederick. Her d rec gives Rebecca A McFrederick d Mechanic Falls Oct 22, 1905, ae 43-6-20. Children:

a   Henry Howard b Hodgdon 1881   b   Albert, unm
c   Mary   d   Nellie

Henry H Dow bcdgdakaa, railroad conductor of Oakfield and Houlton, m Sept 28, 1909, Sarah Isabell Dorman, ae 25, dau of Leroy C and Christina (Clark). Children:

a   ——— son b Nov 20, 1913   b   ——— dau b June 8, 1917
c   Harold Raymond b Oct 28, 1919

Moses C Dow bcdgdakb, called Charles, also Moses Ephraim, now lives Saskatchewan; m 1st (Moses V) Jennie L Scott b Eel River; 2 sons; m 2nd, Newburyport, Mass,———; 4 or 5 children; m 3rd, carpenter of North Lake, Houlton, July 13, 1896, Caroline Verrill (Farrel in family rec seems the correct name), ae 29, dau of David and Sarah (Dow) bcdgdaab; 2 children:

a   George E b 1886   b   Walter Guy b Woodstock 1887
g   Theresa 1899-1921   h   Emery, unm

George E Dow bcdgdakba m Chelsea, Mass, June 29, 1909, Eva A Getchell, both b Waterville, Me, ae 21, dau of Daniel W and Mary E (Folger). 1st born:

a Ruth Dallas b Waterville Nov 5, 1910

Walter G Dow bcdgdakbb, by recent directory, electrician of Waterville, m Oct 17, 1914, Lena Parker, ae 19, b Eng, dau of James B and Nancy (Swallow).

Edward L Dow bcdgdakc, farmer of Bridgewater, Me, m Rosilla Bridges. Eight children:

a Clara Myrtle b Bridgewater 1880   b Elsie E d Mch 30, 1896, ae 14
c Kadie Laura   d Pearl m Nettie Hartley
f Earl Ephraim b Oct 3, 1893; d Jan 26, 1894
g —— twin d young   h Glenwood E b Apr 21, 1895

Clara M Dow bcdgdakca, m Chelmsford, Mass, Nov 26, 1902, George A Jameson, ae 23, son of John T and Azporah (Kilcollins); now farmers of Aroostook Co. Children:

a Ray   b Fay   c Nettie   d Howard   e Laura
f Ruby   g Edward   h Bertie   i Nanetta

Kadie L Dow bcdgdakcc m Leland Bockins; live Lynn, Mass. Children:

a Otto   b Leland   c Pearl   d Gilbert   e Rosella
f Elsie   g Earl   h Fay   i and j ——

Glenwood E Dow bcdgdakch, farmer of Bridgewater, m Oct 27, 1920, Fay Terrell, ae 19, of Balins, dau of Charles and Elizabeth (McKeen). Children:

a Llewellyn   b Laura

Minerva C Dow bcdgdakd m George Alexander of Sherman Mills, Me. Children:

a Lillian m Matthew Wilson   b Mary m Burns Bragdon

Nevers J Dow bcdgdakf, carpenter, has lived many years in Houlton; m Jennie M Hazlett. Children:

a Llewellyn L b 1888   b G Arthur b 1890   c Louise m Elmer Currier
d Phyllis m Raymond Cummings   e Marion m Alexander Duncan

Llewellyn L Dow bcdgdakfa, locomotive engineer of Houlton, m Sept 8, 1920, Lecta R Dickinson, ae 20, b Houlton, dau of Harvey and Clara (Wright).

G Arthur Dow bcdgdakfb, moulder of Houlton, later telegraph lineman, m Oct 27, 1915, Elizabeth G Donnelly, ae 21, stenographer, dau of William and Annie E (Hannigan), farmers of Littleton. Child:

a Helen Marion b Oct 15, 1920

Enos J Dow bcdgdakg, laborer of Benton, m Apr 7, 1898, Rose McPherson, ae 26, dau of William J and Mary (White) of Houlton. Now of Canterbury Lane and m wid Merithew.

Mary Dow bcdgdam m Charles Grant, farmers of Northhampton. Children:

a   Randolph   b   Allan   c   Moses m Martha Dow bcdgdanc
d   Mandy m Hugh Wright

Jesse Dow bcdgdan m Susan Wright b Canterbury, d Auburn, Me, Oct 11, 1903, ae 75, dau of Josiah. Ten children:

a   Lucretia m George Dinsmore; son William
b   Adelia b 1854; m Edmund Dickinson
c   Martha m Moses Grant of Houlton bcdgdamc
d   Mary b 1857; m Frank Mullen of Waltham, Mass   e   Asa
f   Annie m Jeremiah Grant of Waltham, Mass
g   Elizabeth M b Woodstock 1872; m Athol, Mass (his 2nd) Sept 4, 1902, William
     Stoddard Foster, ae 42, son of Charles and Lucy (Grimes)
h   Beecher b 1869; of Richmond; unm
i   Jesse Done b 1871; of Duluth; unm

Adelia Dow bcdgdanb m Edmund Dickinson, lived Richmond. Children:

a   Emerson N b 1877; m Clara M Crane
b   Theresa M b 1879; m Harry C Bennison
c   Alma V b 1881; m James E Holt   d   Helen E 1883-1901
e   Emily M b 1886; m Burton L Dunphy
f   Jessia H b 1888; m Lindsay E Seeley
g   Susie E b 1890; m George A Carpenter
h   Leslie P b 1892; m Florence I Grant

Asa Dow bcdgdane many years shoe worker, teamster, farmer of Auburn, Me, now farmer of Minot, m Hattie Patterson d Mch 24, 1893, ae 29-4-9, dau of Nathaniel and Isabel (Dow) bcdgdbafb; m 2nd, Mch 24, 1894, Elsie Shaw, ae 21, b Auburn dau of Stephen and Frances (Phillips). Children, all but two oldest b Auburn:

a   Robin Russell b 1888   b   Burton d June 21, 1893, ae 1-10-18
c   Gertrude L b Aug 27, 1895; m William Clifford
d   Ethel May b June 23, 1897; m Arthur Bean
e   Ernest Lee b July 3, 1899; shoemaker of Auburn, m Dec 18, 1918, Beatrice
     Ellis, ae 17, dau of Thomas b Ire and Emily (McLaughlin) b Can
f   Hattie b Sept 29, 1906   g   Earl b Apr 15, 1908
h   Fannie Louise b Mch 22, 1910   i   Ruth b Apr 15, 1915
j   Roger b May 15, 1916

Robin R Dow bcdgdanea, shoemaker of Auburn, m Apr 17, 1912, Clara Hazel Marston, ae 18, dau of George and Sarah (Mansfield). Children:

a   Russell Leroy b Feb 26, 1913   b   —— son b July 17, 1914

John Dow bcdgdb. Many years ago a grandson and a distant cousin furnished information of his personality, but from their distance were compelled to use much hearsay. W S Dow recently collected dates and exact facts. Primogeniture operated to make him the leading citizen of Canterbury, but his own ability had more to do with it. He was a magistrate for many years and for twenty years represented his home town in the Provincial Legislature. Hannah Brooks, his wife, may have been one of the original Majorfield party. He had all the characteristics of the sternest of New England Puritans. Like the whole community, he was a dogmatic and polemical Baptist. Twelve children:

a Enoch 1802-1883; always appears as Esq
b Hulda 1805-1878; m Amos Lewis; no children   c Mary d in infancy
d Mary m —— Scriver   e Asa 1810-1898
f Gertrude m —— Thomas   g Hannah m William Coulter
h and i Calvin, Luther, twins, d 1867 and 1870, unm
j Wesley J 1815-1894, unm
k Chloe d unm; said to have inherited a family Bible full of valuable data. This has not come to light
l Lydia d unm

Enoch Dow bcdgdba was easily successor to his father in ability and influence, the local magistrate for many years. He served as Capt in the Aroostook war of 1839 and his name is found in the Me official roster, altho he was always a Canadian of Canterbury. He m Mary (Molly) Jane Phillips d Canterbury Oct 18, 1875. Enoch was a stern magistrate and shared the intense religiousness of his father and grandfather, that type which seems to delight in regarding all pleasure as sin, and consequently his home was not a joyous place. One of his sons, unable to endure home life, ran away in early manhood and remained unheard-of for eighteen years. Enoch regarded his loss as a direct visitation of Providence rebuking him for his unworthiness, but it is not recorded that his home life became less stern. His children:

a Charles M 1829-1874; m Lydia Dickinson
b Jane m Alexander Kearney   c John Wesley m Hattie Tibbetts
d Maria m William Marston. One notes all through the bcdg line the tendency toward intermarriage with original Canterbury families,—very striking among members living far away from the old home. Half the marriages in this entire family are confined to a score of other families
e Augusta m Thomas Annis   f Chloe m Nathan Patterson

Charles M Dow bcdgdbaa, lumberman of Canterbury, d July 17, 1874; bur Dow Cemetery. Lydia Jane Dickinson, his wife, d Feb 25, 1903. Children:

a Robert M b Sept 2, 1850; d 1910; m Bertha C Titus b 1861
b Mahala J b June 14, 1852; d May 11, 1853
c Mary Jane b Mch 17, 1854; m Andrew Jameson; no children. In 1920 she visited Los Angeles and talked with the Author, but she had moved to Wash so many years ago that her family recollections were vague. Soon after she revisited Canterbury
d Luther M b Oct 1858 (1857?); d July 10, 1924; m Feb 5, 1883, Rebecca G Flight b Oct 23, 1859, d Apr 22, 1922
e Asa W, twin, d Sept 15, 1860
f Julia A b Apr 6, 1869; m Thomas Hagerman. Some one of this family m 2nd B H Sanborne of Robinson, Me
g Wilmot A b June 17, 1861; m Laura Grant
h John H b Sept 1, 1863; said went to Seattle, but not found by letter
i Maud M b Oct 4, 1866; m Benjamin Buxton of Woodstock
j and k Alpheus B and Lewis M, twins, b July 4, 1868, d May 6, 1869
l Charles M b Jan 14, 1870; m Abbie Young

Robert M Dow bcdgdbaaa, for 30 years conductor on the C P R, lived St Stephen; d married Presque Isle Apr 21, 1910. Children:

a Robert Percy b 1882. About 1915 he was for a fortnight substituting as telegrapher in a brokerage house at 25 Broad St, New York City. The Author, then of 15 Broad St, is Robert Piercy Dow. This caused great confusion in mail matter. The telegrapher left without complying with some formality with his union. The officials of the latter annoyed the Author for several years with their letters and never bothered to make personal investigation

b Pearl P (sic rec); properly Paul. For some reason the Canterbury clerk generally wrote Paul as Pearl

c Earl B b 1891   d Ralph W b 1898; located Montreal

Paul Dow bcdgdbaaab, telegrapher of Montreal, m Elizabeth Wilson b Moosehead. Child:

c —— son b Moosehead July 27, 1907

Earl B Dow bcdgdbaaac, mechanic, later garage owner of Brewer, Me, m Annie McAdams, both b N B. Children:

a Earl B b Aug 9, 1919   b Norma Ansten b Nov 25, 1920

Luther M Dow bcdgdbaad of Woodstock, 40 years an engineer of the C P R, d suddenly while on a visit to a dau in Boston. It is said that in eastern Me or western N B it is always safe to address any conductor or engineer as Mr Dow. The worst that may happen will be that the addressee will explain that his cousin, Mr Dow, is on vacation and he substituting the meanwhile. Luther's children:

a Smith Emery b July 1, 1884; d Mch 19, 1888   b Millard T b Jan 14, 1886
c Bessie M b Apr 6, 1887; m Feb 11, 1907, Charles G Kerrigan
d Mabel T b Mch 26, 1889; m July 2, 1919, Waldo O Millbury
e Guy S b Aug 8, 1890; d June 10, 1900
f James M b Apr 19, 1892; m Sept 23, 1918, Alice Harris
g Jennie L b Sept 23, 1894; d Mch 29, 1920; m Albert Sullivan
h Julia A b Sept 10, 1896; m Nov 27, 1915, Alphonso R Niles
i Mildred A b Jan 12, 1899; m Sept 26, 1923, John Millbury of Woodstock
j Hazel M b Jan 18, 1901; m Oct 15, 1919, Charles E Kilpatrick of Boston
k Lula G b June 14, 1905; m Sept 14, 1923, Purney E Taylor of Boston

Millard T Dow bcdgdbaadb lives Bangor; m June 1908 Abigail Getchell. Children:

a Luther M b Feb 16, 1921   b Elizabeth F

Bessie M Dow bcdgdbaadc m C G Kerrigan of Aroostook Jc, N B. Children:

a Mae L b Apr 9, 1907   b Clifford W b Aug 1, 1908
c Luther M b Apr 17, 1910   d Irvin William b Nov 15, 1911
e Jennie R b Nov 22, 1913; d Jan 21, 1914
f Florence M b Nov 25, 1915; d Oct 30, 1918
g Gladys B b Feb 17, 1918   h Alberta M b Nov 14, 1920
i Evelyn L b Dec 24, 1923

Mabel T Dow bcdgdbaadd m W O Millbury; live Oakfield Jc, Me. Children:

a James M b Mch 25, 1920   b Austin A b May 16, 1922

James M Dow bcdgdbaadf m Alice Harris; live Toronto. Child:

a John H b Aug 8, 1919

Jennie L Dow bcdgdbaadg m Albert Sullivan of Brownsville Jc, Me. Child:

a Jennie A b Nov 29, 1920

Hazel M Dow bcdgdbaadj m C E Kilpatrick of Boston. Child:

a Eugene L b July 28, 1920

Wilmot A Dow bcdgdbaag m July 15, 1886, Laura A Grant; live Temple, N B. Have:

a Ernest B b Sept 7, 1887   b Thursa A b Dec 25, 1889; d Nov 19, 1918
c Elva J b Mch 28, 1895; d Oct 7, 1918; both, nurses, d of "Flu."
d Lydia M b Aug 23, 1897, unm   e Vera V b Aug 30, 1899; unm

Charles M Dow bcdgdbaal of Woodstock is conductor on the C P R; m Abbie Young. Children:

a Jay m Georgia Brittain   b Maud M———   c Harold   d Gordon

Jane Dow bcdgdbab m Alexander Kearney; lives Northhampton. Children:

a William H; unm   b Ernest; unm; lives Honolulu
c Ella m ——   d Albert d B C unm e Howard m ——; lives on homestead
f Frank d young   g Maud m ——; lives B C   h Asa d young
i Augusta m ——; moved to B C

John W Dow bcdgdbac impatient at the pleasureless home life ran away to sea while yet in his teens, leaving his parents in ignorance for 18 years whether he was alive or dead. He shipped before the mast but in due time became first officer. He m Hattie F Tibbetts, sister of his captain, and made Pittston, Me, his home port. She b Boothbay Nov 19, 1841; m May 31, 1865. After the birth of a son John wrote home and soon after revisited Canterbury. A calf of considerable degree of fattedness was killed; Enoch enjoyed grandfatherdom and the two younger children were born in Canterbury. During school days the family lived in Boothbay. In middle life John bought a farm in West Branch, near Bay City, Mich, doing something in lumber business. For some reason not apparent his oldest son ran away from home and remained *incommunicado* for many years. His father deemed this a Divine rebuke for his own earlier sin. In 1887 he wrote to Edgar R Dow giving the salient facts of his own family. Children:

a Frank H b July 6, 1869; of Guadalajara, Mex; unm
b Mamie G b Apr 7, 1871   c Roscoe H b Jan 26, 1873

Mamie G Dow bcdgdbacb m Ralph Davison Miller, artist of Cincinnati; moved to Hollywood, Calif; living there 1924. Children:

a Mary Alice b 1900; m —— of Hollywood
b Carroll Bent; in High School 1920   c Norman Paul

Roscoe H Dow bcdgdbacc developed a successful lumber business in Bay City; m Oct 19, 1903, Nellie K Gillard; moved soon after to Santa Monica, Calif; was its Mayor 1911. Has a family.

Maria Dow bcdgdbad m William Marston; moved 60 years ago to Tobique, N B; their large family now live there.

Augusta Dow bcdgdbae m Thomas Annis. Children:

a Harry, farmer of Pittsfield, Me   b Maud

Chloe Dow bcdgdbaf m Nathan Patterson. Children:

a Nathan   b Hattie m Asa Dow bcdgdane

Hulda Dow bcdgdbb m Amos Lewis: no children.

Mary Dow bcdgdbd m —— Scriver; lived Northhampton, N B

Asa Dow bcdgdbe carried his religious fervor to an uncomfortable degree; a highminded man according to his lights but dictatorial and quite unbearable at home and elsewhere. His wife Irene Hartley soon left him; thereafter he devoted six days a week to money-making and became quite wealthy for his time and place; owned saw mills and grist mills at Eel River (now Meductic), conducted large lumbering interests. As he could not carry his money with him, he built and endowed the Asa Dow wing of Fredericton Hospital.

Gertrude Dow bcdgdbf m —— Thomas. Untraced, but there is reason for thinking they have posterity in N B.

Hannah Dow bcdgdbg m William Coulter; lived Canterbury Front. Children:

a John   b Dow; both grew up and m
c Gerusha m Abraham Collicutt

Amos Dow bcdgdd m Ann Teed, his sister-in-law. Farmer and lumberman, he took a prominent place in the early development of Canterbury. He d 1837. We note in his posterity the strongly marked tendency toward intermarriage with original Canterbury families. Children:

a David b July 14, 1801   b Charlotte m Matthew Lutwick
   Nancy m Elias Knowles   d Hannah m Daniel Randall
e John b 1810; d 1855-7   f Margarette m Benjamin Merrithew
g Eliza 1815-1921, longest lived of any Dow   h Mary Ann m —— Barker

David Dow bcdgdda, farmer and mill man, is really the founder of Dow's Settlement, altho the land belonged to his grandfather. He built a home and dam there, with a saw mill and grist mill. He m Mary R Way b Oct 5, 1799; after her death he spent the rest of his life with a son in Ludlow, Me. Children:

a Amos L b Nov 28, 1825   b Esther H b May 17, 1827
c John A b Oct 5, 1828   d Charlotte b Jan 24, 1830

e   Rhoda b Dec 15, 1832; m —— Tompkins; a son living Dow's Settlement 1922
f   Hannah M b Feb 4, 1835; m Thomas Condon
g   Mary Hope b Mch 3, 1837; unm
h   Walter Hay b Sept 25, 1839

Amos Lewis Dow bcdgddaa m Sophia Watson; in middle age moved from Canterbury to Ludlow; not a good correspondent, soon lost track of the old home. His children have all long since gone from Ludlow:

a   (George) Washington m —— Burch; moved to Toronto
b   David m Nancy Cummings of Bangor, b Ludlow. Had a child (sex or name not in rec) b Ludlow Mch 10, 1897. Soon after moved away; untraced
c   Amos m and moved to Gloucester, Mass; untraced
d   Sophia   e   Mary; both moved away long ago

Esther H Dow bcdgddab m William Watson; moved to Ludlow. Children:

a   Norris; unm
b   Henry m Malvina Dow bcdgdagf; now farmers of Pittsfield, Me; 5 children, a son Henry now teacher in Pittsfield High School
c   William; unm
d   David m Margaret Rogers, mail carrier of Houlton; 2 children

John A Dow bcdgddac moved 40 years ago from Canterbury Sta to Minneapolis; m Frances Outhouse. Children:

a   Albert, of Minneapolis, unm
b   Ellen m Horatio Grant; 4 children; div; moved to Minn
c   Elvie m George Harten; 1 child; lives Minn

Charlotte Dow bcdgddad m Dr Fred Watson, who practiced at Meductic, but moved to Ludlow; d there. Children:

a   Charlotte   b   Hannah m John Stephens
c   Mary m Charles Stephens   d   Manzer m Ida Stewart; now of Ludlow
e   Walter   f   Chick (sic in all rec) m —— Webb; 1 child

Rhoda Dow bcdgddae m Jacob Tompkins, farmer of Dow's Settlement; bur Dow Cemetery; children:

a   Joel b Nov 11, 1854; lives Jacksontown; m Julia Dow bcdgdaik
b   Tressa m Moses R Dow bcdgdaii; bur St Stephen
c   Frank b 1866; m Harriet Merrithew; 2 children; of Dow's Settlement
d   Arvid b 1868; m Jennie Dickinson; of Patton; 4 children

Hannah M Dow bcdgddaf moved to and d Fairfield, Me.

Mary H Dow bcdgddag unm, owned property in Bar Harbor and Miami, Fla; living 1922 with niece and namesake as companion.

Walter H Dow bcdgddah painter of Waterville, Me, d Dec 19, 1907; bur Canterbury Sta; m Angeline Norcross Cummings; 2nd, Annie A Anderson. She was burned to death trying to build a fire with kerosene. Children:

a   Mary Hope; taught school until 1919; then went to live with her aunt. Has now inherited hotels at Miami and Bar Harbor. She contributed the data of her own immediate line and interested a member of the bcfii line, who cleared up that difficult line
b   William Sheridan d ae 4
c   (2nd wife) Leverett Oscar b N B 1879

Leverett O Dow bcdgddahc entered a Waterville factory as laborer; its vice president and general manager; now owns a grocery store; m Dec 7, 1898, Dora Louise Soule, ae 22, dau of A P and Hattie L (Priest). Only child:

   a Mildred Hazel b Apr 4, 1900

Charlotte Dow bcdgddb m Matthew Lutwick; both bur Dow Cemetery. Children:

   a David, supt C P R at St John; bur Dow Cemetery
   b John m Ruth Dow bcdgdeag; live Dow's Settlement
   c Lorene m George Clenick; lives Fredericton with only child,—Mrs William
      Tompkins

Nancy Dow bcdgddc m Elias Knowles. Children:

   a Japhtha m —— Barker; lived near Fredericton; 6 dau
   b Amos m Lydia Dow bcgddal   c George
   d Eliza, 2nd wife of Ephraim Dow bcdgdak   e Charlotte

Hannah Dow bcdgddd m Daniel Randall, farmers of Dow's Settlement; a dau d young.

John Dow bcdgdde m Maria Brooks; lived on Enoch's original farm, where Spurgeon Dow now lives. Of course, bur Dow Cemetery. How closely everyone in this region is related to everyone else is shown by the marriages of his children:

   a George B m Ruth Dow bcdgdafh
   b Caroline m Gideon Y Dow bcdgdafd
   c Ellen m Silas Cummings, son of Ruth Dow bcdgdad
   d Lucy b Mch 21, 1855; m Alonzo C Dow bcdgdaid
   x and y Raymond and Eunice d in infancy

George B Dow bcdgddea now lives St Stephen; has m 2nd. Children by 1st wife:

   a Celia   b Hester   c Frank b 1869; unm
   d Cassie   e Gertrude

Celia Dow bcdgddeaa m John Bearsley; lived Lower Woodstock. Child:

   a Laura m ——; lives St Stephen

Hester Dow bcdgddeab m Ward McElroy, supt of railroad painting, Milo, Me. Children:

   a Cecil, teacher in Bangor High School   b Frank

Cassie Dow bcdgddead m Harry Burpee; live Eastport, Me. Children:

   a Harry   b and c —— dau

Ellen Dow bcdgddec m Silas Cummins; lives Houlton. Children:

   a Winifred m and lives Halifax   b Percy; unm of Bangor
   c Clara; unm of Houlton

Margaret Dow bcdgddf m Benjamin Merrithew, farmers of Canterbury Lane. Children:

a   John farmer of the Lane m Phoebe Dow bcdgdeae
b   Leonard m ———   c   Joan m Reuben Dow bcdgdeac
d   Hannah m Hammond Dow bcdgdead
e   Emma m Alfred Grant; lived Canterbury Sta

Eliza Dow bcdgddg m George Debec. Children b Canterbury. About 1860 the whole family with others of the original Majorfield settlement went by caravan to Eburn, near Vancouver, B C. Eliza, whose posterity is large, became the only centenarian in the Province and her birthday celebration was a notable event. She lived and retained her faculties six years longer. Without exception, the centenarian women mentioned in this Book had large families:

a   Ward m ———   b   Howard   c   Clarence
d   Mary Ann m Samuel Yerxa; 5 children
e   Genora m ———   f   Josephine m ———

Enoch Dow bcdgde m Basha Cronkite, whose family is untraced, but were probably of the Majorfield party. His services as lay preacher either brought no income, or at best, not enough for his support. He took up a farm 8 miles back from the River, near Canterbury Sta. He d 1845. Children:

a   Israel 1806-1881   b   Levy (Levi)   c   Hannah
d   Sarah m John Young   e   Olive m ——— Phillips
f   Mary m ——— Estey

Israel Dow bcdgdea m Harriet Dickinson; their farm at Grant's Crossing, Canterbury Lane. Children:

a   Enoch (3rd) 1831-1894   b   Catherine m John Wright
c   Reuben 1835-1902
d   Hammond   e   Phoebe   f   Ambrose   g   Ruth
h   Maria   i   Barrant b 1847
j   Adelia (twin) m Wellington Dow bcdgdabg

Enoch Dow bcdgdeaa, farmer of the Lane, m Sarah Ann Dickinson, who survived him many years; both bur Lane Cemetery. Children:

a   Irene   b   Ira   c   David b 1857
d   Enoch (4th)   e   Darius   f   John Wallace
g   George m Anna Anderson; unt
h   Eliza m James McMullen   i   Levy m Eva Patterson

Irene Dow bcdgdeaaa m Joel Young. Only child:

a   Elizabeth m Warren Wilcox

Ira Dow bcdgdeaab m Rhoda Dow bcdgdage, by whom 3 children; m 2nd, Bakey (Rebecca?) Dickinson; moved to Providence, R I; out of touch with Canterbury many years, altho the younger children came back

a   Percy   b   Eva m ———
c   Mandy (Amanda?) m Thomas Cotters; 2nd, John Flight
d   Roy; unm. Lives Harten Settlement, Canterbury
e   Elizabeth m ——— Berge; lives Bangor
f   Olin 1901-1924; unm   g   Gladys m Sanders Wright; lives Canterbury

Percy Dow bcdgdeaaba, motorman of Providence, m Houlton May 6, 1903, Marion Moors, ae 24, bookkeeper dau of Sylvester and Jane D (Manuel), both b N B.   Child:

a Jasper

David Dow bcdgdeaac m Doletta Dow bcdgdagg. She left him and many years later got a divorce and m his brother Enoch. David moved into Me. A family rec says there were children,—Rhoda, Atrume and Bertrume, but Me vital statistics show one:

a Ann J m Archibald Patterson bcdgdagi, her 1st cousin

Enoch Dow bcdgdeaad became farmer of West Peru, Me; m Dow's Settlement Mch 30, 1914, D Annette (Doletta) Dow. At m he gave himself b 1867, apparently the understatement a man usually makes at 2nd m. Said to have 1 child.

Darius Dow bcdgdeaae m Maud Grant by whom 1 son; div; lumberman of Houlton m 2nd, Mch 30, 1918, Eva May Dickinson, ae 25, dau of Bruce and Lucy (Hafford). At 2nd m he gave himself b Canterbury 1878, apparently underestimated.   Children, younger b Houlton:

a Clifton, unt   b —— son b Dec 29, 1918
c —— son b June 12, 1920

John W Dow bcdgdeaaf of Scott's Siding m Margaret Ferro; 2nd Selenda Dow bcdgdeada. Family by 1st wife:

a Fannie m Henry Dickinson   b Lottie m Charles Dickinson
c Hope m Harry Dow bcdgdi

Levi Dow bcdgdeaai m Eva Patterson; then disappears from Canterbury rec. Some Levi Dow, said b Hodgdon, lumberman of Warren, N H, m (ae 35) date missing in rec Nettie Annis, div, ae 35; further untraced.

Catherine Dow bcdgdeab m John Wright.   Children:

a Alfred   b Hattie   c Ambrose   d Mary m Thomas Harten
e John

Reuben Dow bcdgdeac m Joan Merrithew.   Children:

a Bertie m Sarah Dickinson, unt   b Lillian m Gordon Dickinson
c Adelbert; unm   d Annie; unm   e Reuben m Levina Dickinson
f Archie m Gertrude Dow   g Barrant; unm   h Lottie; unm

Reuben Dow bcdgdeace and Levina live Canterbury Sta.   Children:

a Elva m Beecher Russel; live Houlton   b Guy T b Canterbury 1894
c Lelia m Robert Carmichael; lives Houlton   d Otis W
e Kenneth (Rev), clergyman in Conn
f Stanley, machinist of New Haven, Conn
g Harold, machinist in Conn   h Ethel, of Scott's Siding

Guy T Dow bcdgdeaceb, railroad man of Brownsville Jc, m Nov 25, 1920, Clara E McLeod, ae 20, dau of John K and Katie (McClain).

Otis W Dow bcdgdeaced, now of Millinockett, then paper maker of Livermore Falls, m July 24, 1917, Lena Henry, dau of John B and Alphonsine (Nadeau).   A child:

a —— b Nov 11, 1917

Archie Dow bcdgdeacf m Gertrude Dow bcdgdaacad.   Children:

a   Emma b 1920   b   Vivian b 1922

Hammond Dow bcdgdead m Hannah Merrithew, farmers near Scott's Siding.   Children:

a Selenda m John W Dow bcdgdeaaf   b Loie
c Hope m Horatio Grant   d Leona ——   e Thursa m ——
f Luke J m Effie A Dibble   g Benjamin unm   h Miles; unm
i Odbur d young   j Hubert; unm

Hope Dow bcdgdeadc m Horatio Grant; live Canterbury Sta.   He m 1st Ellen Dow bddgddacb, who got a divorce and went west with her two children.   Hope had four

a   Ida   b   Dorothy; both went west
c   Percy b Bangor 1887; d Apr 20, 1919; m Mch 16, 1915, Stella M Ireland, ae
        18, dau of Graham and Clara (Fowler); lived Lincoln
d   Gladys m Andrew Cummins   e   Estelle m George Estey
f   Horatio Nelson m Grace McNally

Luke J Dow bcdgdeadf b Canterbury 1871, laborer of Houlton, m July 1897 Effie A Dibble, ae 19, dau of Nelson and Adelaide (Dickinson). Me rec errs giving his mother's name Hannah Merritt.

Phoebe Dow bcdgdeae m John Merrithew, farmers of Grant's Crossing.   Children:

a   John Allan m Clara Dickinson   b   Harriet m Frank Tompkins
c   Laura m Charles Dickinson   d   Nora m McLeod Mills of N S
e   Hannah m Benjamin McKenzie; 2nd Frank Leslie
f   Emma m John Ingraham of Houlton   g   Henry m Emma Mills
h   Frederick m Cora Bradscombe of Houlton
i   Frank m Leona Patterson

Ambrose Dow bcdgdeaf m Sarah Marston; lived Scott's Siding. Children:

a   Perley   b   Horace   c   Stewart Harold
d   Vata m —— Siggins

Perley Dow bcdgdeafa b 1878, farmer of Canterbury, moved to Littleton, Me; m Houlton Jan 7, 1904, Susan A Campbell, ae 36, dau of William b Ire and Jane (McLay).   Children:

a   Mary B b Mch 1, d Mch 11, 1905   b   —— son b June 21, 1907

Horace Dow bcdgdeafb m Bertha Wright.   Children:

a   Edith b 1912   b   Dorothy b 1915

Stewart H Dow bcdgdeafc in 1912 carpenter of Rangeley, 1916 laborer of Houlton, d Dec 27, 1918, ae 36-8-7; m Gertrude Edna Furrow

of Canterbury (sic Me rec, but Fenno by family rec presumably correct).
Children:

    a —— dau b Rumford Dec 21, 1910   b —— son b Rangeley Sept 26, 1912
    c —— dau b Houlton Jan 31, 1916

Ruth Dow bcdgdeag m John Lutwick; live Dow's Settlement.
Children:

    a George m Mary Dow; 6 children   b Izetta m William Lee; 1 child
    c Jennie m Boardman Dow bcdgdagh
    d David m —— Frederick; 6 children
    e Alonzo m —— Fox; 4 children
    f Laura m Henry Wilkins; 2 children

Maria Dow bcdgdeah m Howard Wright. Children:

    a Israel m Amelia Dickinson   b George m Hattie Wright
    c Saunders m Prudence Dickinson   d Clara m Harry Dickinson
    e Julia m Manzer Dow bcdgdaaca   f Herbert

Barrent Dow bcdgdeai, nicknamed Barney, m Victoria Adams,
farmers at Grant's Crossing. Children:

    a Elsie   b Prudence   c Amelia   d Ada   e Julia
    f Hattie   g Harry; unm

Elsie Dow bcdgdeaia m Frederick Wheaton. Children:

    a Berle m Henry Shean   b Ruth; unm

Prudence Dow bcdgdeaib m Stewart Darling of Canterbury Sta.
Children:

    a Robert   b Stewart

Amelia Dow bcdgdeaic m Charles Stitham. Children:

    a Cora; unm   b Vera m Hugh Fleming   c Florence; unm

Ada Dow bcdgeaid m Theodore Wilkins. Child:

    a Freeman

Julia Dow bcdgdeaie m Oscar Wilkins. Children:

    a Lillian   b Arthur

Hattie Dow bcdgdeaif m Roy McNally of Edmundston, N B.
Child:

    a Dorothy

Levi Dow bcdgdeb m Mahala Dickinson; moved about 65 years
ago to Wis; lost sight of. Children:

    a Henry   b Levi   c and d—— dau

Hannah Dow bcdgdec m John Dickinson, indirectly increasing the
Dow-Dickinson marriages by five:

    a Thomas; unm   b Julia m Hugh Jameson
    c Lydia J m Charles M Dow bcdgdbaa   d John; unm
    e Mahala m Hezekiah Dow bcdgdaac

f Caroline m Charles P Dow bcdgdafb   g Albert m Hulda Brooks
h Gerusha m Adna Dow bcdgdaia   i Sarah m Archie Jameson
j Stephen m —— Jameson

Sarah Dow bcdgded m John Young, nearby farmer. Children:

a Hezekiah m a Miss Patterson; 2nd Sarah Harris; 3rd wid Tremble; 4th wid
     Gilispie
b Joel m wid Gilispie; 2nd Irene Dow bcdgdeaaa; 1 child by each
c J W Saunders; became a Baptist minister, carrying on the work of Enoch
     Dow 2nd. He m Charlotte Hagerman, by whom 8 children; 2nd Mary
     Brooks; no children. One of his sons was John Young who m Jane Dow
     bcdgdafaf. Rev J W S Young officiated at a vast number of baptisms, but
     was more liberal in his localities than was Enoch Dow, using the St John
     River, a conveniently deep pool in Four Mile Brook, a body of water at
     Dow's Settlement, and one at the Lane. A son, Saunders Young Jr is at
     present carrying on his father's work in the sacred office which seems now
     well nigh hereditary

Olive Dow bcdgdee m Matthew Phillips, a son of Hannah Dow
bcdgdj. Over 70 years ago they left the neighborhood and it is vaguely
recalled that they joined the Mormons, taking with them their kinswoman Esther Dow.

————

Mary Dow bcdgdf m Amos Brooks; lived Southhampton, across
the River from Canterbury; both bur Dow Cemetery. Children:

a Dow m Mary Watson; 5 children
b Charles m Mary Wright; 6 children   c George m Nancy Clark
d Maria m John Dow bcdgdde
e Hester m William Brown (properly Brawn)

Rhoda Dow bcdgdg m John Porter; lived Lower Woodstock;
both bur Porter private cemetery. Their large posterity is at the present
time very numerous around Woodstock and if any one wished, could be
easily traced. Children:

a George m Rebecca Dickinson; 8 children
b John Dow m Emily Chapman; 7 children; 2nd Mary Irvine; 4 children
c Marjorie m Elijah Watson; 2nd Charles Trafton; 4 children by each
d Mary m Enoch Debec; 4 children
e Esther m Joseph Scott; 8 children
f Jacob C m Esther Dickinson; 10 children
g Mary (?) m Dr Charles Rice; 5 children

Esther Dow bcdgdh m —— Watson; apparently they moved out
of the neighborhood, perhaps toward Fredericton.

Ruth Dow bcdgdi m —— Estey; lived near Fredericton.

Hannah Dow bcdgdj m David Phillips, one of the pioneers from
Majorfield. Her gravestone is small and eluded notice until 1926.
She d 1816 ae 35. Absence of other stones indicates that if she had
children, they were elsewhere with her father.

One may easily realize that along the western border of New Brunswick over two-thirds of the population is closely akin with the posterity
of Enoch Dow bcdgd.

In the great mass of unconnected Dow data in possession of the Author there were many originating from N B. Most of these have slowly been proven and placed in order, but some remain and are placed here, index key letters for convenience. There have been almost no Dow immigrants to N B since 1800; all Dow in the Province seem either of the bcdgd line, bbbfa or the g Dow family spreading toward Me from Nova Scotia.

John Dow bcdgdk. A careful investigation in 1926 by W S Dow perhaps settles the question of the origin of this family, which before 1860 came to live at Carrol Ridge, about four miles back from Canterbury Sta, toward McAdam Jc. Neighbors who have lived there longest say that its founder was a John Reardon, Irishman, who for reasons not known to us took the name Dow. At all events, it was as John Reardon Dow that he m Rebecca McLaughlin. How much of a family they had we do not know. A son presumably b about 1835 was named for him. John Reardon Dow Jr m Eliza Webberly. She was a Canterbury girl and her identity is not hidden by the rec which gives Wobbly. Both these Dow were professional hunters and trappers. Well acquainted in Canterbury, the next generation married for the most part members of families identified with its original settlers. The many children are now widely scattered:

a   Henry m Celeste Dow bcdgdaac. The Harry Dow who m Hope Dow bcdgdeafc
    seems to be their son
b   Hannah m —— Tucker; sea capt at St Stephen
c   Fannie; now of St Stephen   d   Eliza moved long ago to Minnesota
e   May m George Lutwick; lives Dow's Settlement; our safest informant
f   Thomas m Charlotte Miller; 2nd Mrs —— Ritchie; had by 1st wife Victor
    and Georgia
g   John (John Reardon Dow 3rd) m Caroline Wright; 2nd Lottie Webberly;
    son Leslie by 1st wife
h   Richard   i   Alice   j   Minnie   k   Agnes
l   George; unt, but may be bcdgec   m   Rebecca

Richard Dow bcdgdkh, laborer of Orient, m Houlton Aug 17, 1892, Julia Tidd, ae 19, dau of James and Mary (Cummings). Rec says Richard b 1876, obviously error, but it is probably in m date. Fourteen years is too great a gap. Children:

a   —— son b Dec 13, 1906   b   —— son b Sept 23, 1908

Daniel Dow bcdgdl b N B farmer had a son:

a   Daniel b Amity 1833; d pauper unm Washburn Feb 18, 1908. Only possible
    place in bcdg line would be from one of the Majorfield party

John Dow bcdgdm b St John about 1800 might have same origin. A farmer, he m Isadore McKenney. A son:

a   William unm laborer d Mt Chase, Me, Aug 9, 1913

David Dow bcdgdn b Exeter, farmer, m Hannah Johnson b N B. Known only from d rec of son:

a   John H b N B; d m Calais Jan 7, 1896, ae 54

John H Dow bcdgdna appears only from rec of 4 children (may be others):

a Mattie E b Waite, Me, 1874; m Mass Nov 15, 1902, Clarence Robbins, ae 40, son of William and Polly (Chase)
b Custer b Talmage about 1877
c Frances E M b Calais 1882; m Falmouth Nov 24, 1906, Ernest Cliffton Crocker (his 2nd), ae 24, son of Augustus O and Isabel (Davis)
d Minnie A b Waite 1886; m Mass Nov 19, 1905, Stanley P Crocker, brother of above

Custer Dow bcdgdnab, shoe worker of Calais, m May 26, 1898, Jennie May Choate, ae 17, dau of Josiah and Nellie (Munson), both b N B. Firstborn:

a Hazel A b Calais Jan 5, 1899; d Lynn June 25, 1902

Alonzo C Dow bcdgdo, exact duplication of Canterbury name, b Enfield, Olomon, Greenbush, in various rec, farmer of Reed Pl, Me, m Mary Theriault b Houghton. Children:

c Willie Warren b June 15, 1900, laborer of Reed Pl, m Sept14, 1918, Mildred Howard, ae 18, dau of Henry and Edith (Irish)
d Wilfred B b Apr 26, 1905   f Edna M b Apr 5, 1910
g Charles R b July 24, 1910 (year?)

Robert Dow bcdgdp b St George, N B, m Margaret Craig, presumably g line; known only from m rec of son:

a Tobias G b St George 1852; by recent directory teamster of Lewiston, Me, m 2nd (her 2nd) Dec 28, 1897, Lucetta Martin, ae 42, dau of Christopher and Matilda (Rouix) of St George

Aaron Dow bcdgdq m Clara Wright (both names indicate bcdgd ļine). A son:

a Arthur S b 1871; div, m 2nd Newburyport Apr 1, 1907, Lula Peterson, div, of Salisbury, dau of Willam and Ella (Hughes) Lawrence

William Dow bcdgdr m Sarah A McKeen, both b N B (Scotch?). Known only from m rec of son:

a Lathrop H b N B 1848   b (a wild guess) m Ivan b about 1860

Lathrop H Dow bcdgdra, farmer of Caribou, d Oct 7, 1896, ae 48-7-10; m Rachel Jane Wark b N B, d Waterville Sept 19, 1916, dau of William and Rachel J, both b Scotland. At least 11 children:

a Issachar Hammond b Oct 22, 1882   b Wesley E b Dec 16, 1883
d Charles W b 1886   g —— son b Feb 18, 1894
h Faith b Feb 20, 1894   k Ivan Lathrop b June 15, 1897

Issachar H Dow bcdgdraa, farmer of Caribou, m Lillian Page. Children:

a —— dau b Aug 8, 1909   b —— dau b June 26, 1918
c Raymond Wesley b Presque Isle Dec 13, 1919

Recent Caribou directory gives above, also David Dow farmer, Bessie Dow dressmaker, Frank Dow station agent.

Charles W Dow bcdgdrad, farmer of Presque Isle, m Jan 4, 1917, Berle J Ayer, ae 25, stenographer, dau of Lester B and Mary (Arnold) of Boston.

M Ivan Dow bcdgdrak b N B is placed here solely because of recurrence of name Ivan. Insurance agent of Manchester, N H, m Carrie E——. Perhaps other children:

 a Harold R b Brighton, N B, 1889
 b Arthur Irvin b Manchester Mch 31, 1901

Harold R Dow bcdgdraka real estate agent of Melrose, Mass, m Nov 30, 1912, Mabel LaBelle, ae 22, dau of Alphonse and Josephine (Woodman). A child.

John F Dow bcdgds b Woodstock, car inspector of Lewiston, m Mary E Wilkins b Milltown. Firstborn:

 a John Hollis b Apr 1, 1910

Stephen Dow bcdgdt (perhaps bcbhdd line) m Mina Cochran b Woodland. Firstborn:

 a —— dau b New Sweden July 14, 1921

George N Dow bcdgdv m Alice J Williams, both b Calais. Children:

 a —— son b Crawford Jan 23, 1917 b Arnold b Jan 7, d May 3, 1918
 c Pearl L d Sept 9, 1920, ae 1-5-5 d Elna May b Dec 31, 1920

Sylvester W Dow bcdgdx of N B came to Seattle; was able to recall much about Woodstock, N B. A brother was killed on a gunboat during Civil War. A son:

 a Lorenzo, leading lawyer and legislator of Tacoma; has children,—Ethel, Mercedes, Janie, Lorenzo

Alfred D Dow bcdgdy, farmer of Houlton, Moro, Littleton, m Martha E Webberly, both b N B. Both names suggest bcdgdk. Five children not found

 a Francis A d Hersey Oct 18, 1896, ae 16-8-26
 c Martha N b Littleton Oct 19, 1893
 b Eliza Velma b Houlton dau of Alfred A and Martha E (Welleby), of Fall River m Aug 9, 1903, William Rufus Moses (his 2nd), ae 27, son of Andrew J and Susan (Dodge)
 h Alfred D b Moro 1897; d Mch 28, 1914

Abner W Dow bcdgdz, farmer of Argyle (sounds bcbhd), m Armenia L Brann b Cranford, N J. Firstborn:

 a William E b Apr 28, 1896

George W Dow bcdgea b N B, of Lewiston m Jennie Ferguson b N B; in 1912 appears in Boston as T George Dow, contractor. A son:

 a Guy S (Guy George in one rec) b Lewiston 1886

Guy S Dow bcdgeaa, box maker of Lewiston, m Mch 3, 1906, Grace J White, ae 19, dau of George b Malden and Flora (Vickery) b Auburn, Me; div; m 2nd, auto salesman of Boston, Dec 10, 1912, Mary Ann Harrison, ae 27, of Boston b Lewiston, dau of Patrick and Johanna (Shea) both b Ire. Child:

a Carrie May b Abington Jan 1, 1908

James Dow bcdgeb m Sarah Enright, both b Port Daniels (seems either Scotch or g line). Child:

a Edmund b 1877; m Oct 1, 1906, Ellen Madigan of Orono ae 32, dau of David and Bridget (White)

William Dow bcdgec of Rumford Falls m Alice May McLaughlin, both b St Stephen. Firstborn:

a Florence Annie b May 17, 1907

Mary Dow bcdged, wife or wid not stated, d Calais Sept 19, 1904, ae 87, dau of John and Nancy (Johnson) Brackett, both b Me.

Maggie Dow b St Stephen, mill worker of Calais, had:

a —— dau b Feb 10, 1898   b   James H b Oct 7, 1901; d May 4, 1902

Carrie Dow b Can, of Calais, had fifth child:

e —— son b Dec 6, 1902

Elizabeth Dow bcdgg. Some Elizabeth Dow m Berwick, Me, May 19, 1776, by Rev Jacob Foster, Robert Brawn. This name is correct, altho it also appears in rec as Brown and Bran. As already stated, we doubt much whether David Dow bcdg went permanently to New Brunswick as early as 1776. We know of no other Elizabeth of an age to fit this rec. Brawn is a very uncommon name; it occurs once more, an intermarriage with a Dow of this line in Canterbury, N B. It is quite possible that the bcdg family were of Berwick and that some Brawn, perhaps Robert and wife, were of the party which founded Majorfield, N B. Cf bcdg narrative. The Quaker Dow line of adab reached Berwick early and some Dow family reached Parsonfield, not yet identified.

Jonathan Dow bcdh, yeoman of Plaistow, m Haverhill July 8, 1745, Mary Haseltine b Feb 16, 1723-4, dau of Jonathan Jr and Mary (Simons). Plaistow rec of his d gives 1769, a copyist's error for 1759. Jonathan deeded land Apr 12, 1759; administration papers granted Dec 25, 1759, to Samuel Kimball of Plaistow, a kinsman, who was appointed guardian of his children. Wid Mary received her thirds Jan 22, 1762. Plaistow rec give all the children:

a Mary b Jan 6, 1746
b Phoebe b Feb 5, 1749 or Jan 28, 1748. Many hundred similar errors appear in the duplication of Plaistow rec
c Nathan b Oct 20, 1751   d   William b Feb 18, 1755

Nathan Dow bcdhc.   There is no proof whatever regarding the lives of the four half orphaned children of bcdh.   No marriages of the two girls are found in the well kept Haverhill rec.   As for Nathan we can only guess.   Some Nathan enlisted at Woburn in 7th company, Col Thomas Nixon, receipted for pay Feb 14, 1777, to May 4, 1778, and was in service Mch 3, 1779.   Some Nathan enlisted at Danvers, ae 28, 5 feet, 8, ruddy, and receipted for pay July 9, 1780, to Jan 6, 1781.   Nathan Dow enlisted at Danvers, but was 4 years younger.   This might be a very minor error.   No dates conflict and the three may be identical.   The pension list shows a Nathan Dow of N H in 1820, no particulars.   N H vital statistics has a Nathan Dow of Hebron with wife Susanna, also two children.   As Nathan was over 50 at this time, there might have been older children and Susanna might be a 2nd wife.   Children:

    a   Charlotte b Dec 28, 1801
    b   Lewis b Hebron Oct 10, 1803; d Dover Apr 23, 1852; no other data

William Dow bcdhd.   No room for doubt of the identity of the William Dow pioneer of Majorfield, N B, grantee of land 1793.   The family narrative is clear that, after the disastrous freshet of 1802, William and his cousin Nith bcdge returned to "the States."   Absolutely no trace further.   In 1802 there was only one State where an American could get land for the squatting and not encounter vital statistics.   That is Me.   We guess that William and Nith settled in Me and may have had posterity.   Many disconnected Dow were in Me from 1761 onward.

Stephen Dow bcdi, corporal under Capt John Hazzens, was at Crown Point 1758 in same company as his brothers Nathaniel and Richard; m Hannah Shepard, presumably dau of Lieut Samuel and Judith (Currier) of Amesbury.   Presumably their whole lives were spent in Plaistow, but they get no mention except in b rec of children:

    a   Hannah b Apr 21, 1745   b   Ruth b Jan 8, 1747; bap Jan 11, 1746-7
    c   Moses b Jan 30, bap Feb 5, d Mch 10, 1749
    d   Stephen b May 27, bap June 3, d Nov 21, 1750
    e   Susanna b Oct 28, bap Nov 3, 1751   f   Nabby bap Mch 10, 1754
    g   Thomas bap Mch 14, 1756.   Some Thomas Dow of Plaistow enlisted 1777; d
        same year.   Some Thomas Dow of Plaistow, corporal under Capt Ezekiel
        Gile, Col Stephen Peabody, dich R I Dec 30, 1778, service 10 mos, 24 days.
        Perhaps d rec is error and the two are identical; further unt
    h   Daniel bap Feb 26, 1758; unt, surely not in Rev rolls or 1790 census
    i   Mary b Apr 26, 1761; bap May 11, 1760.   Difference between old and new
        style dating does not apply here.   They say the Mormons have a practice
        of baptizing folks after they are dead.   This unique instance of baptizing an
        infant eleven months before birth is to be credited to some town clerk of
        Plaistow who has long since gone to his reward.

Martha Dow bce became 2nd wife May 17, 1697, of Josiah Gage, son of John and Anna, whose 1st wife was Lydia Ladd, dau of Daniel and Lydia (Singletary).   Lydia d childless Aug 14, 1796.   First edition Hist Haverhill says Martha was killed in Dustin massacre; this is error; she d natural death Haverhill Feb 10, 1716-7.   Josiah d 1717, mentioning in will that his wife was dead and he childless.

JOHN Dow bcf was with his father in garrison 6 at the time of the Dustin massacre and subsequently served with distinction in Indian fights. He was one time selectman and for many years a magistrate of Haverhill. He m May 23, 1696, Sarah Brown (almost always spelled Browne) b 25:11:1676, living 1733, dau of Abraham and Elizabeth (Shepard). Children:

a —— b and d Dec 29, 1696   b John b Apr 21, 1697; d June 9, 1698
c Joseph b Apr 21, d Aug 10, 1699
d Mehitable b June 2, 1700. Haverhill rec: Esther, spurious dau of Mehitable Dow, bap June 9, 1728
e Judith b Aug 11, 1701   f Abraham b Mch 18, 1703-4; d Apr 11, 1716
g Sarah Browne b Mch 31, 1705-6; d "old age" Jan 1793
h Elizabeth b Mch 31, 1706-7   i John b Aug 19, 1709
j Abiah b Sept 17, 1710; m Dec 27, 1739, John Cooper of Hampton
k Ann b May 7, 1715; m Haverhill Feb 27, 1733-4, John Maxfield

Judith Dow bcfe d Haverhill July 26, 1799; m Aug 20, 1723, John Whiting of Haverhill. Children:

a Jonathan b Oct 2, 1723
b Hannah b June 20, 1725; m Ezra Dodge of Beverly
c John bap Aug 21, 1728
d Sarah b June 22, 1730; m 1752 Charles Haddock
e Joseph b May 17, 1733   f Judith bap Apr 5, 1741
g Elizabeth (dau of John) bap July 24, 1743

John Dow bcfi, many years magistrate of Haverhill, was an original grantee of Goffstown, N H, but does not appear to have ever lived there himself, the property going to his son Job. He d Haverhill Jan 20, 1780; m June 3, 1728, Mehitable Haines b Jan 25, 1709, d Atkinson, Oct 23, 1783, dau of Thomas and Hannah (Harriman), granddau of Thomas Haynes of Amesbury, whose posterity has intermarried many times with Dow. A statement in a genealogical periodical, which seems complete error so far as Dow is concerned: John Dow m a dau b 1711 of John and Sarah (Harriman) Johnson of Haverhill. This couple and five daughters, all of whom married men named John, all being magistrates of Haverhill. These were John Johnson, John Morrill, John Webster, John Dow, and John Gage, widely known as the five Johns.

John and Mehitable had children:

a Abigail b Apr 3, 1729; d Oct 18, 1799
b Elizabeth b Feb 1, 1730; d Sept 11, 1737
c Abraham b Atkinson Feb 23, 1732   d John b Feb 20, 1736-7; d young
e Hannah b Sept 8, 1738   f Job b Oct 5, 1740
g John b Feb 10, 1742-3   h Moses b Feb 17, 1746-7
i James b Mch 13, 1754

Abraham Dow bcfic d Salem Mch 13, 1795; m 1751 Susannah Hoyt b Mch 7, 1729-30, dau of Micah and Susanna (Colby). His will mentions wife, all surviving children, brothers John and James. Abraham was an original grantee of Haverhill, N H, and apparently visited the place, later selling his interests to his brother Moses. He opened a mill in Atkinson, 1783, the event noted in the diary of Rev Stephen Peabody. Such were widely celebrated by great gatherings and much refreshment, chiefly liquid. Abraham was a successful man of business, many factories remaining today in the hands of his direct posterity. Children:

    a   Thomas b Aug 9, 1753 (other rec give Aug 19 and Aug 18, 1754)
    b   Susanna b 1756   c   Mehitable b Sept 8, 1761
    d   Mary b July 7, 1766

Thomas Dow bcfica d Atkinson Dec 22, 1825. Mass Rev rolls give only the beginning of his service, He enlisted as private Apr 29, 1775, Capt Jeremiah Gilman, serving 3 mos, 29 days. At the end of the war he emerged as Lieut; subsequently became Major of the 4th Mass. He m Dec 2, 1773, Elizabeth Jones b Dec 27, 1754. From soon after the war to about 1800 he kept a tavern in Salem and had some interest in the family manufacturing business. He appears as selectman 1794, representative to Legislature 1787, delegate to constitutional convention 1788, coroner 1790, a proprietor of the public library 1798, and on many committees until 1800. The 1790 census shows him of Salem 1a, 4b, 5c. He was an able man, always highly esteemed. His family of 18 children has been exceeded once and equalled once in the Dow family. Children:

    a   Thomas b and d Mch 15, 1774
    b   Abraham b Mch 10, 1775; d Aug 10, 1776
    c   Zelliah b Oct 7, 1775 (sic; must be 1776); d Nov 22, 1776
    d   Abraham b Oct 23, 1777
    e   Rachel b Feb 24, 1780; m (int pub Nov 15, 1804) Edmund Wright of Hamp-
           stead
    f   Evan b Dec 5, 1781; d 1846. Untraced, but a Concord, Mass, rec surely
           applies: Mary Dow, dau of Evan and Mary P, d Sept 23, 1835
    g   Zelliah b Aug 9, 1783
    h   Betty b Sept 9, 1784; probably d in infancy
    i   Elizabeth Jones b Sept 9, 1785; m Dec 15, 1813, Daniel Leonard Ware b Mch
           5, 1783, d Apr 30, 1850
    j   Susanna Hoyt b May 12, 1786   k   Amos b May 17, 1787; d 1820
    l   Moses b May 23, 1789; d 1870
    m   Relief b Mch 25, 1791; d Jan 23, 1792
    n   Jones b Apr 27, 1792   o   Hezekiah b June 18, 1794
    p   Relief b June 29, 1796; d 1836; m James Poor
    q   Louisa b Aug 18, 1798; d 1866; m Samuel Ketchum

Abraham Dow bcficad m Feb 27, 1800, Sarah Page of Atkinson. Children:

    a   Eliza b May 14, 1802; d Jan 25, 1869; m 1828 Thomas Huse Everett, b Feb
           6, 1799, d Mch 7, 1839, brother of Edward Everett
    b   Abraham b Oct 10, 1808

Abraham Dow bcficadb moved to West Newbury, farmer; m June 24, 1833, Henrietta Dana Carr b Jan 20, 1808, d Nov 25, 1845; 2nd Hannah W (Bunker) Heath b 1822, of Durham, dau of James and Lois (Foye). Children:

    a   George Carr b May 11, 1834   b   Abraham Arthur b Mch 3, 1836
    c   Henrietta Dana Carr b July 25, 1845; d June 5, 1846

George C Dow bcficadba d West Newbury Dec 19, 1877; m Hannah M Titcomb. Child:

a Eliza

Abraham A Dow bcficadbb, prominent in militia at Newbury, later returned to Atkinson; m Dec 27, 1867, Eliza Bastress b Oct 24, 1832, d May 9, 1908, dau of Samuel and Mary (Spange). No rec of children.

Rachel Dow bcficae m Edmund Wright, son of Jonathan and Ruth. Children:

a Edward
b George b Apr 2, 1813; had a son George Edmund of Atkinson

Elizabeth J Dow bcficai m Daniel Leonard Ware, son of Melatiah and Chloe (Man); lived Wilmington, Vt. Children:

a Horatio b 1814   b Elizabeth Jones b 1817   c Daniel b 1819
d Amos N b 1821   e William H b 1823
f Susan L b 1825

Susanna H Dow bcficaj (Susan and Sukey H in m rec; Susan H in b rec of son) m Aug 23, 1804 Robert Clendennin of Salem and Derry. Son:

a Robert b Sept 10, 1804; m Phebe Wyman Hale

Moses Dow bcfical, blacksmith of Atkinson, m Atkinson Dec 2, 1814, Clarissa Crawford of Bridgeport b 1798. This large family gets no mention in original ms genealogy of b lines. Hist Hampstead alludes to the large family but names only 3 children. No Dow of Atkinson has ever replied to repeated letters asking genealogical information. State rec give many children of "Moses" without specifying mother. Hence, list below may not be wholly reliable. Children:

a Moses b N Y City May 30, 1818; d Nov 1, 1819
b Louisa (Louezer, rec) b Atkinson May 31, 1820
c Mary Ann b Dec 13, 1823; m 1844 Sidney B Hadley of Manchester
d Moses C b Sept 21, 1825   e Amos b Dec 3, 1829
f Charles b Jan 14, 1832; shoemaker of Atkinson in 1850; unt
g Susan H b Apr 21, 1834; at home 1850
h Hezekiah b Jan 20, 1838; went to Calif. Recent Oakland directory has a Hezekiah Dow, presumably his son
i Clarissa J b July 23, 1843; m June 9, 1863, John W Follansbee of Atkinson

Amos Dow bcficale surely m Frances E —— b Portland, Me. Atkinson rec give 2 children and two adopted, but nothing about the man has appeared. There was later in Manchester an Amos Dow, whose age is about the same; he is probably wholly different, coming from Amesbury or Portsmouth and of the a line. This Amos had wife Susan E Wilson b Bedford 1826, a connection which suggests bbbff line. He d, printer of Manchester, Sept 9, 1894, ae 64-11-5. Children:

a Amos d Atkinson Nov 24, 1852   b —— dau b Nov 15, 1852, twin
c (adopted) George Willie d Atkinson Apr 21, 1873, ae 21 days; this may be garbled and identical with Willie (adopted) d Atkinson July 27, 1873, ae 1 mo, 27 days
d Arthur A b Amesbury 1857 (parents, dates, etc, from own m rec)

Arthur A Dow bcficaled, blacksmith of Portsmouth, N H, m Manchester Feb 1, 1883, E C Chapman, ae 27, dau of Anderson and Augusta (Gray); 2nd, Apr 22, 1900, Malvina Bougis b Sherbrooke, P Q, 1878, d Kittery, Me, July 15, 1900, ae 22-6-7, dau of John and Malvina; 3rd (2nd, by State rec) Aug 26, 1903, Annie E Simpson, ae 34, div, dau of Dennis and Julia (Lenihan) b Ireland.   No rec of children.

Jones Dow bcfican appears 1850 census as farmer of Schasticook, Me, assessed $800; m June 22, 1820, Catherine Page b Dec 15, 1800, d Jan 8, 1829; 2nd, Apr 17, 1833, Melinda Crowell b 1811, of West Waterville, Me.   Children:

- a   Charles Jones b June 12, 1821   b   William Cary b Oct 24, 1822
- c   Catherine Page b Mch 24, 1828; d Apr 29, 1893; m June 10, 1857, Richard Perkins of Boston
- d   Olive A b 1835; milliner, d Boston Feb 19, 1892
- e   Emily b 1836   f   Melinda Jones b 1837; living Foxburgh, Mass, 1900
- g   Mary b 1841   h   Joseph Henry b 1843   i   Ella b 1849

Charles J Dow bcficana of Boston d Brooklyn, N Y, Dec 10, 1859, m Dec 10, 1851, Rebecca Briggs Holmes b Mch 20, 1830, dau of George Bass and Maria (Holmes).   No children.

William C Dow bcficanb of Chicago m a Miss Sawyer; 2nd Marietta Van Wyck Adriance of Fishkill, N Y, dau of John b 1811 and Jane Ann (Van Wyck).   Dau:

- a   Jenny b Sept 7, 1866

Jenny Dow bcficanba m Apr 13, 1893, William Plate Harvey of Geneva, Ill.   Children:

- a   William Dow b Feb 3, 1894   b   Julia Plate b Aug 7, 1896

Joseph Henry Dow bcficanh.   Some Mrs J Henry Dow, married, d Cape Elizabeth Mch 13, 1893, ae 26, 8 mos.

Hezekiah Dow bcficao m Haverhill May 3, 1842, Lucy A C Foss b 1817, dau of James and Abigail; d·next year without children; she m 2nd (his 2nd) Thomas Dodge, carpenter, son of Thomas and Elizabeth.

Relief Dow bcficap m May 21, 1818, James Poor, son of Jonathan, he d 182-.   Children:

- a   Jonathan b Apr 14, 1819; m Eliza Currier
- b   Charles Augustus b Sept 9, 1820; m Persis Howard; 2nd Sarah Paine Wetherbee
- c   Benjamin Kimball b Jan 1, 1823; m Sophia Page Noyes of Atkinson
- d   Charles Herbert of Haverhill
- e   Ellen R m Rufus P Clement of Merrimack   f   Persis H d 1882, unm

Susannah Dow bcficb of Salem m John Spofford b Feb 20, 1742; moved to New Rowley, thence to Whitestown, N Y.   Children:

- a   Betsey d young   b   Thomas m Beulah Ransom
- c   Sarah m Dr Arnold   d   Isaac settled in N Y State
- e   Abram b 1782; m Betsey Brooks of Jaffray, N H   f   John settled in Pa

Mehitable Dow bcficc m Aug 23, 1789, Maj Joshua Merrill of Salem b Feb 13, 1764.   Children:

a   John Johnson b Sept 2, 1792; m Betsey Eaton
b   Hannah b Apr 2, 1794; m Brickett Bradley of Haverhill
c   Ambrose Dow b Mch 7, 1796; d Boston Apr 29, 1878; m Nancy Morrison b Feb 14, 1817, d Jan 29, 1860; 2nd Abigail T Hart; Methodist preacher in Salem and elsewhere; his portrait in Hist Windham

Mary Dow bcficd m Feb 26, 1782, Amos Mills of Hampstead; wid by Oct 25, 1795; went 1834 to Dunbarton with her son:

a   Ephraim b Jan 8, 1790

Hannah Dow bcfie m Capt Asa Pattee, son of Peter and Elizabeth (Scribner) of Salem; 3 children.   He m 2nd Mehitable Jewett, by whom 18 children; lived many places, including Concord and Canaan, N H. Of Hannah's children:

a   Asa b Sept 13, 1757   b   Moses b July 20, 1766, both Goffstown

ANY years ago Edgar R Dow, the first of Dow genealogists, got into communication with members of the bcfif line, most of whom had gone to Vermont, and with his customary patience followed the pursuit through family Bible after family Bible. Vt statistics are so imperfect that they do not give over a third of the material herein. About 20 per cent have been added by the efforts of the present Author.

Job Dow bcfif was a farmer but had the ability for manufacturing which was common to his family. He took up the land in Goffstown given to his father as an original grant. Here he opened a carding mill. The bridge near it is still known as Dow's bridge. He saw no service in the Revolution; d Atkinson Aug 15, 1809; m Feb 14, 1760, Hannah Pattee, sister of bcfie, b Oct 1739, d Atkinson Aug 7, 1806. Census 1790 shows them of Goffstown 4a, 1b, 7c. Children; all b Goffstown:

a   Peter b Feb 2, 1761   b   Polly b Feb 16, 1763
c   Abigail b Feb 19, 1765   d   Hannah b Dec 29, 1766
e   Mehitable b Aug 17, 1768   f   Job b June 23, 1770
g   Abraham b Mch 9, 1772; d Feb 11, 1776   h   Enoch b Sept 20, 1773
i   Elizabeth b Oct 2, 1775; m 1795 Thomas Worthley
j   Phineas Kimball b May 11, 1777   k   Anna b Aug 28, 1779
l   Nancy b Aug 28, 1780
m   Sally b Apr 17, 1781. These dates are incompatible
n   Achsah b Jan 11, 1783; d Jan 5, 1790
o   Nellie S b Jan 11, 1786; d Feb 27, 1873, unm

Peter Dow bcfifa moved to Methuen; m Dec 12, 1781, Martha Page of Goffstown; 2nd, May 27 (Mch 25, State rec), 1813, Phoebe Gault of New Boston b 1778, d Jan 30, 1748. Census 1790 finds them of Goffstown, but 3a, 4c does not fit well. Children:

a   Hannah b Apr 11, 1783   b   Polly b May 27, 1785
c   Henrietta b July 18, 1787   d   Abigail b July 11, 1791
e   Achsah b July 11, 1791; m Oct 24, 1821, Calvin Ferren of Goffstown
f   Martha Parker b Feb 12, 1798; m —— Currier
g   William b 1814; unt; d young

Polly Dow bcfifb d Goffstown 1836; m (his 2nd, 1st being Mary Hubbard, dau of Samuel) Jan 6, 1791, Dr Jonathan Gove of New Boston, a widely known physician, b Lincoln, Mass, Aug 22, 1746; d Mch 24, 1818. Children:

a   Clarissa b Mch 17, 1792; d Goffstown May 25, 1837; m William McQuestion d 1818; 2nd John Richards of Goffstown; 3 children by each
b   Charles Frederick b May 3, 1793; grad Dartmouth and Harvard Law School; m Mary Kennedy Gray of Nashua; no children
c   William Clark b July 8, 1796; d Aug 1832; m Mary Neal of Goffstown; 3 children, all d young
d   Lucretia b June 20, 1799; d Port Hope, Can; m Feb 15, 1816, Dr John Gillchrist; 6 children

Abigail Dow bcfifc m 1786 Nathan Barker Page. Children:

a   Job   b   Hannah b Oct 15, 1787   c   Nathan
d   Martha m Isaac Merrill of Danville, Vt   e   Isaac   f   William
g   Jane   h   Abraham d Barre, Vt; m Sarah Ann Clark
i   Abigail m Cyrus Heaton   j   Helen m Daniel Powers

Hannah Dow bcfifd m Aug 9, 1781, Thaddeus Ladd b Haverhill Jan 5, 1758, son of Nathaniel and Abigail (Bodwell); moved to Hopkinton; thence to Telford, Vt. Children:

a Heman b Feb 2, 1783; d in infancy
b Nabby (Abigail) b Nov 9, 1785; m Sylvanus Baldwin
c Polly b Mch 17, 1787; m Humphrey Currier
d Hannah b May 31, 1789; m James Abbott
e Achsah b May 23, 1791; m James Crocker
f Sally b Mch 17, 1793; m Lyman Smith
g Lucretia b May 12, 1795; m Royal Jackman
h Nancy b June 10, 1797; m John C Hammond
i Welcome D b Oct 1, 1799; d Jan 1881; m Abigail Hammond
j Jedediah P B b Mch 2, 1802; m Eliza Baldwin
k Sophronia b Apr 24, 1804   l Richmond b Aug 2, 1806; d in infancy
m Louisa b Mch 2, 1809; d Jan 1885; m Nov 22, 1836, George W Benton

Mehitable Dow bcfife d Aug 6, 1853; m Aug 9, 1791, William Thomas d July 2, 185–; moved to Big Bend, Wis. Children:

a Deborah   b John   c William Moody   d Caleb
e Abigail   f Job   g Enoch   h Mehitable
i Thomas Whittemore   j Hannah Dow   k Benjamin

Job Dow bcfiff moved to Waitesfield, Vt; d Sept 17, 1842; m Aug 27, 1791, Lydia Butterfield d Feb 22, 1795; 2nd, July 21, 1796, Elizabeth Colony of Goffstown; 3rd, July 21, 1822, Lois Stewart (Steward, Vt rec), wid of Moses. Children:

a Abigail b Goffstown Aug 27, 1792
b Lydia b Jan 25, 1795; m Sept 17, 1812, Jonathan Bell
c Nellie Eleanor b Waitesfield Feb 24, 1797
d Job b Dec 10, 1799   e Hannah b Mch 20, 1801
f James E b Mch 27, 1803   g John Butterfield b Mch 19, 1805
h Lydia Butterfield b Dec 24, 1807
i Maria b Jan 14, 1809; m May 10, 1826, James Hart of Middlebury, Vt; moved to Saranac, N Y
j Jonathan Gove b Nov 9, 1810; went to Canada; unt
k Moses b after 1810; d unm (family rec not very positive)

Abigail Dow bcfiffa d Waitesfield July 4, 1822; m Goffstown Oct 6, 1814, Robert Leach of New Boston. Children:

a Mary Abigail b Apr 25, 1820; m Nov 5, 1840, John Waterman of Waitesfield
b Lydia b June 22, 1822; m Cyron Joslyn

Nellie E Dow bcfiffc d Dec 30, 1882; m Dec 9, 1821, Simeon Farnsworth of Danville. Children:

a Eliza b Aug 23, 1822; d Sept 10, 1880; m Enoch Blair
b Mary Ann b June 30, 1825; d Danville Nov 10, 1893; m Eleazer Dole
c Simeon Dow b Walden Apr 30, 1827; d Prarie du Chien, Wis, 1868; m Oct 1, 1857, Jane Ambrose Eastman d Concord, N H, May 24, 1862

Job Dow bcfiffd of Peacham m Jan 10, 1838, Tamas Cross of Hardwick. Census 1850 shows him farmer of Cabot, taxed on $500; wife Tamer b Vt 1812. Children:

a Lydia b Vt 1839; m —— Foster; living 1922 in Middlesex with only son
b Kimball b 1842; m Jennie E Urie b East Craftsbury, dau of Robert and Elizabeth (Cunningham), d Jan 19, 1905, ae 41-0-29. He d 1907; no children
George b 1844

George Dow bcfiffdc of Cabot d 1913; m Lucy Pratt; 2nd Maria E Waterman, who lives 1922 in Cabot. Children, all by 1st wife:

a Myrtie H, now of Cabot   b Tyler T   c Burt K
d Ora L of Cabot m Mamie Smith; no children
e Eugene G of Medford, Ore, m Julia Dodge; no children

Tyler T Dow bcfiffdcb of Wallingford, Conn, m Kate Wales. Children:

a Arnold   b Vernon   c Leroy

Arnold Dow bcfiffdcba m Rena Wheeler. Children:

a Grace   b Hazel

Burt K Dow bcfiffdcc, physician of Willimantic, Conn, m Bessie Wells. Only child:

a Richard

Hannah Dow bcfiffe m 1826 Wright Page. Children:

a Mary   b Josiah   c Edwin   d Helen   e Elizabeth

James E Dow bcfifff of Waitesfield d Berlin July 8, 1877; m May 2, 1824, Levina Stewart (Steward, rec) b Feb 6, 1805, d Nov 26, 1847; 2nd Mrs Sarah B Pierce of Lowell, Mass. Children:

a Parna b Mch 19, 1825   b Fostean b Apr 10, 1828
c Fostina b Apr 10, 1828; d Newport, Vt, Jan 24, 1890; m Dec 5, 1850, Rufus R Root of Berlin
d Lydia E b Apr 22, 1832; m Jan 21, 1854, Charles F Collier of Coventry; moved to Cherokee, Iowa
e Hannah b Apr 21, 1836; d Sept 14, 1896; m 1857 Edwin Erving
f Katherine E b 1838; m June 26, 1866, Jason H Carpenter of Big Rock, Ill
g Eleanor Caroline b Feb 19, 1845   h Sarah L b Dec 12, 1848

Parna Dow bcfifffa m 1845 Samuel Gleason of Berlin, Vt. Children:

a Emeline m Arthur Stickney   b Louisa m Frank Barrett
c Augusta

Fostean Dow bcfifffb m 1848 Silas Smith of Aurora, Ill; left a dau.

John B Dow bcfiffg m Oct 8, 1834, Charlotte Hawley of Waitesfield; 2nd ——; moved to Gouverneur, N Y. Children:

a William b 1835; unt   b Mary Ann b about 1837
c Helen b about 1839

Lydia B Dow bcfiffh d May 31, 1897; m June 7, 1832, Harvey (Henry, Vt rec) Hawley. Children:

a Mary Elizabeth b Aug 24, 1836; m Henry O Skinner
b Avery Stone b June 2, 1839; m Emily Bucklin

Enoch Dow bcfifh, farmer of Goffstown, m Goffstown Nov 15, 1792, Phoebe Butterfield b Dec 9, 1776. He is said to have moved to Ohio, but if so it was late in life, and his wid returned to Goffstown, for she d Goffstown July 8, 1854. Census 1850 shows her of Goffstown, assessed $500. Children:

a Polly b May 11, 1794   b John Butterfield b Sept 15, 1796

c Elba b Nov 22, 1798; d Goffstown Aug 29, 1860, unm
d Naomi b Nov 8, 1800   e   Phoebe b Dec 8, 1802
f Hannah b Jan 14, 1805   g   Nellie b May 31, 1807; d July 3, 1810
h Enoch b July 29, 1809
i William b Dec 25, 1811.   Martha Dow, wid of William H (duplicate rec gives
     Samuel), b Goffstown 1815, d Milford Mch 20, 1906, dau of Joseph and
     Sarah (Plummer) Stevens.   If identical, is still untraced

Polly Dow bcfifha m Goffstown Dec 31, 1813, Daniel D Pattee d
July 22, 1831.   Children:

a James b May 3, 1815; d May 16, 1870; m Harriet Perkins d Mch 21, 1864;
     1 son, 3 dau
b Enoch Dow b 1817; d 1889; m Harriet A Jenkins; 4 dau
c Daniel b 1819; d 1878; m Mary ——; 2 sons, 3 dau
d Jesse b 1822; d 1889   e   William B b 1824; d 1858
f John b 1830; d in infancy

John B Dow bcfifhb d Oct 8, 1848; m 1842 Caroline —— d July
31, 1853, ae 49, 6 mos.   Children:

a Helen b 1834; of Goffstown by 1850 census
b Louise b 1837; m —— Lufkin of East Hebron, N H

Phoebe Dow bcfifhe m Nov 6, 1823, Moses Shepard of New London,
N H, b Jan 18, 1802, son of Jesse and Hannah (Page).   He d Bangor,
Me, June 6, 1860, Free Will Baptist clergyman with pastorates Corinth,
Hermon, Newburgh, Carmel, Me.   Children:

a Hannah b Sept 15, 1824; m —— Ham
b Mary P b Oct 10, 1826; d Beaver Falls, Pa, Oct 25, 1877; m James Emerson
c Henrietta D b Oct 10, 1828; d Aug 25, 1877; m —— Skillings
d Aurelia b Sutton Nov 22, 1830; m Frank Smith
e Phoebe Almanza b Corinth, Me, Mch 13, 1833; m Edwin Drew of Newton
     Highlands, Mass
f Jesse Turner b Dec 30, 1834; d Nov 29, 1836
g Elizabeth Merrill b Apr 23, 1837; m Charles Rackliff
h Theresa Louise b Hermon July 11, 1841; m Thomas J Thompson

Hannah Dow bcfifhf d May 19, 1851; m 1825 Samuel Stillman
Jackman Tenney b Goffstown 1804, d 1877, son of Samuel and Polly
(Jackman).   He m 2nd Naomi Dow bcfifhd.   Children:

a Caroline b 1834; m Daniel Tenney Butler; 4 children
b Orittie b 1836; m —— Noble; lived Cheslea, Mass

Enoch Dow bcfifhh, nail manufacturer, d Wareham, Mass, Apr 27,
1861; m Mch 1831 Ruexby Blake Bedge b Needham, Mass, May 29,
1814, d Nov 11, 1891; lived Wareham, Taunton, Weymouth.   Children
Weymouth rec:

a Ellen Frances b Nov 13, 1832; d Jan 29, 1833
b George William b Oct 23, 1834; d Feb 18, 1843
c Sarah E b Feb 4, d Feb 10, 1835
d Charles Henry b Salem Sept 15, 1837   e   Francis Lorenzo b Oct 10, 1839
f Ellen Augusta b Sept 15, 1843; m O B Besse
g Sarah Elizabeth Louisa b Goffstown Nov 28, 1848
h James Pattee b July 10, 1856

Charles H Dow bcfifhhd, shoemaker, m Aug 16, 1857, Frances M
Briggs of Brockton.   Child:

a Charles William b Wareham Oct 31, 1858

Charles W Dow bcfifhhda m Franklin, N H, Oct 4, 1882, Lucy Parsons Graves b Mch 30, 1852, dau of Arthur B and Lucy B of Salisbury. She survived him. He d Oct 23, 1926; was 17 years in the State tax division, finally supervisor of the southern district. Only child:

   a Helen Frances b Melrose May 18, 1884; m Clyde A Cutler of Cambridge

Francis L Dow bcfifhhe, chief of police of Taunton, m Celantha Baker. Child:

   a Ola Frances b July 30, 1871

Sarah E L Dow bcfifhhg m Henry Wass. Children:

   a Bertha Elizabeth b Dec 4, 1871
   b George Raymond b Nov 3, 1873; m Nellie Pierce; 1 son
   c Harry b Sept 7, 1880   d Fred Leslie b Aug 20, 1882
   e Ida Belle b July 24, 1884   f Gertie May b Dec 31, 1889
   g Roy Carlton b Dec 27, 1890

James P Dow bcfifhhh d before 1914; salesman, m Georgie E Webber. Children:

   a Mabel d ae 6   b Clarence Webber b Chelsea Mch 26, 1883
   c James Gilbert d ae 1

Clarence W Dow bcfifhhhb, musician of Chelsea, m Mch 4, 1909, by Rev David B Dow adgfcdgaa, Cora B Evelyn, ae 24, singer, dau of Samuel J and Frances Evelyn (Tompkins) of Ithaca, N Y, widower, m 2nd Portland, Me, Aug 16, 1914, Mabel F Libby, ae 26, dau of Frank J and Rose A (Cottle).

Andrew J Dow bcfifhk, harness maker of Bedford and Manchester, d Feb 28, 1886, at home of his son Solon; m June 15, 1837, Louise Harwell b 1818, both of Bedford. She d Melrose Feb 6, 1895. Children:

   a Solon b Bedford Jan 12, 1839; of Melrose. Recent directory gives a Solon Dow, but he failed to reply to letter of genealogical inquiry with return postage
   b Lewis b June 30, 1841; d Bedford Dec 12, 1845
   c Andrew Jackson b Bedford Sept 1, 1847; d Yonkers, N Y, Aug 13, 1897 (Manchester rec). No rec of m or children

Elizabeth Dow bcfifi, then of Londonderry, m Hillsborough, N H' Nov 26, 1801, Robert Danforth b Billerica, Mass. They worked northward from place to place through Vt into N Y State. Children:

   a Phineas Alpheus b Antrim Aug 20, 1802
   b Nason b Hillsborough Nov 26, 1804
   c Leander b Royalton, Vt, Jan 30, 1807; m Rochester N Y Oct 29, 1835 Eunice Kinsman Manning
   d Aurelia Anna b Livonia, N Y, July 26, 1810
   e Betsey Emma b Dec 21, 1812   f Adeline Luthera b Nov 3, 1815
   g Loemma Emmeline b Ogden, N Y, May 26, 1818
   h Robert Alonzo b Apr 16, 1821

Phineas K Dow bcfifj, mill wright, moved to Cabot, Vt; d about May 15, 1849; m Nov 16. 1797, Mary Gordon of New Boston d Cabot 1875, ae 90 ('). Children:

   a Abram b New Boston June 3, 1798
   b Jane Gordon (Janette Goodwin, Vt rec) b Ryegate Oct 19, 1799

c Nathan Barker Page b Apr 15, 1801   d Peter b Aug 22, 1802
e Phineas Kimball b Oct 7, 1804   f —— b Sept 25, 1806; d in infancy
g Sally A P b Cabot Aug 3, 1808
h Thaddeus Ladd b Feb 5, 1810; d young
i Mary b Sept 19, 1812; m Dec 5, 1833, Ebenezer K Cross of Peacham
j John Gordon b Feb 26, 1815   k Job b May 19, 1817
l Jonathan E b So Woodbury Mch 19, 1822; d young

Abram Dow bcfifja d West Barnet Feb 27, 1852; m Feb 27, 1821, Julietta Bradish of Winchester, Mass, b 1806, d May 1857.   Children:

a Diantha E b Mch 10, 1821; m Charles Matthewson; 2nd Philip Matthewson; 3rd Byron Smith
b Juliette b Mch 5, 1823; m Feb 1853 Malachai Langdon Richardson, farmer, b Sutton Apr 20, 1828, son of Jonathan and Nancy (Ingalls)
c Mary A b May 4, 1825; m Jonathan Eastman of Sutton, Vt
d Robert Bradish b Peacham Feb 17, 1827
e Zilphana b 1829; d ae 2, 6 mos   f Alexander b 1831; d ae 6 mos
g Thomas B b Apr 13, 1832   h Ellen b 1834; d 1837
i Phineas Kimball b Feb 20, 1837
j Nancy Jane b Jan 1, 1839; d Boston, unm
k William Henry Harrison b Jan 14, 1841; d Sept 1871, unm
l Orrin C b Feb 17, 1843

Robert B Dow bcfifjad, carpenter of West Barnet, m Jan 1, 1856, Aurora S Cudworth b Greenfield, N H, Oct 23, 1833.   Children:

a Aurora S b Woodbury Feb 21, 1857; d West Barnet; m ——; had,—Anna E, Julietta S
b Julietta E b West Barnet Aug 20, 1861   c Ada M b Sept 20, 1865
d Mattie J b Woodbury Oct 19, 1867   e Mabel E b Marshfield Nov 1, 1877

Thomas B Dow bcfifjag, jeweler, m Frances Coates; 2nd Frances Hill b Marshfield.   By 2nd wife:

a Jessie F, school teacher, d Husdon, N H, Apr 22, 1894, unm

Phineas K Dow bcfifjai, physician, moved to Wisconsin, thence to San Jose, Calif; m Jan 4, 1867 or 1869, Fannie O Hill of Varysburg, N Y. Living 1921, but letter of genealogical inquiry unanswered. Children:

a Mildred C b Spring Prairie, Wis, Sept 16, 1877
b Romanzo E b Jamesville, Wis, Nov 18, 1881; unt

Orrin C Dow bcfifjal appears in 1860 census as farm worker; 1870 (as Orange C) jeweler of Montpelier; m Sept 12, 1868, Ellen P Cutting b 1845.   One dau, rec not found.

Jane G Dow bcfifjb d Peacham; m Stuart Harvey d 1856.   Children:

a Emeline m Israel Cutting   b Lucy b Ryegate; m William Blood
c Mary Jane m Stephen Evans   d Duncan m Margaret Varnum
e Abigail d unm   f Margaret m Hiram Eaton   g Stewart L
h William m Rebecca Ruggles   i Harriet   j Lucinda
k Louisa

Nathan B P Dow bcfifjc d Cabot Mch 1862; farmer of Walden, in 1850, taxed on $200; m Phoebe Benjamin. No rec of children.

Peter Dow bcfifjd m Rhoda McDuffie; moved to Ponce, Neb. Children:

a Nancy   b Lucinda   c Louisa   d Lewis, untraced

Phineas K Dow bcfifje, farmer of Cabot, taxed 1850 on $500; m Lydia Cutting; wid mother lived with him. Children:
a Elvira; not in 1850 census   b Mary b 1833
c Henry b 1835, untraced
d Sarah b 1839; living 1923 Cabot, unm   e Kimball; not in 1850 census

Sally A P Dow bcfifjg m Dr Hiram Goodenough of Peacham; moved to Syracuse, N Y.

John Dow bcfifjj m Betsey Emerson, according to family letter to Edgar R Dow many years ago. List of five children named, but incorrectly, showing that writer was not in touch with this branch. He was John Gordon Dow, farmer and tool maker, lived one time in Williamstown. His wife was Betsey Cameron. He d 1878. Children:
a John Duncan b Marshfield, named for father and Duncan Harvey, a kinsman
b Henry A; living 1924   c Pilusa, by family letter; properly Philura M
d Myron E; d ae 13   e Sarah. This family not found in 1850 census

John D Dow bcfifjja living 1923; m Maryanne Wood, dau of Abraham and Permilley of Marshfield. The name Pamelia was very popular in New England for many years, but never is spelled correctly. Their children:
a Walter Abraham b Apr 26, 1861; of Keene, N H, 1924
b Lester Bryant b June 26, 1863; d 1923
c Nora Ruth b June 12, 1865; m George W Cole
d Fred Alsen b May 3, 1868; m Flora R McCloud
e Luella Blanche b Apr 14, 1871; m Mol—— McCloud
   Others d in infancy

Walter A Dow bcfifjjaa m Nellie J Remington. One dau

Lester B Dow bcfifjjab was civil engineer of Waltham, Mass; m Katie E Davis, who d soon after birth of only child:
a Lester Arthur b 1893; m 1916 Hazel Hester Haynes; now]civil engineer of Waltham

Henry A Dow bcfifjjb m 1871 Belle Luce of Williamstown. Children:
a Guy; unm 1924   b Lee m a Miss Horton of Cabot
c Myrtle   d Leon; unm in 1924

Philura M Dow bcfifjjc d recently; m Hosea Patterson of Peacham. Children:
a dau d in infancy   b Leon M d ae 9

Anna Dow bcfifk m Apr 3, 1899, Jesse Cross, both of Salem, son of Abiel; moved to New Salem. Children:

a   Nathaniel B b New Salem 1800; d Claremont, N H, 1903, the longest liver but one mentioned in this Book. For many years he carried the gold headed cane voted to the oldest man in town; left posterity in Wilmot
b   Jesse b New Salem 1802   c   Hannah m Eben Eaton of Newbury
d   Belinda m Thomas Dustin   e   David, killed in Civil War

Nancy Dow bcfifl d Apr 10, 1852; m Dec 1, 1799, John Chaffin of Claremont, N H, b Aug 19, 1776, d West Sumner, Me, Feb 6, 1852. After b of 1st child, they moved to Buckfield, Me. Children:

a   Henrietta De Albra b Nov 29, 1800; d Buckfield July 7, 1885; m Jonathan Buck
b   John b Apr 30, 1804; d Boston June 26, 1848; m Aris Maria Swain; 2 children
c   Anna b Buckfield Sept 16, 1807; d Cambridge, Mass, Aug 22, 1894; m June 10, 1830, Henry Prentiss Lewis, book printer, b June 21, 1807, d Oct 23, 1861, son of Edmund Jr and Abigail Bigelow (Prentiss) of Marblehead; 1 son, 2 dau
d   Rodney b Dec 12, 1810; d Portland May 11, 1886; m Mary G Waldron
e   Granville b June 30, 1812; d Feb 21, 1888; m Betsey Bonney; 2nd Bethiah Lathrop; 3 children by 1st wife, 1 by 2nd
f   Angeline M b Feb 25, 1816; m Apr 19, 1835, George W Furber b Feb 10, 1814, d Sept 23, 1874; 10 children
g   Adoniram b Sept 6, 1819; m Lydia Bean; 3 children

Sally Dow bcfifm m Jonathan Taggart. Children:

a   Jonathan b 1800   b   Nellie b 1801

Nellie L Dow bcfifo, known as the belle of Goffstown, either preferred single blessedness or refused one too many offers, for she d Goffstown Feb 26, 1873, an old maid.

John Dow bcfig moved from Haverhill to Atkinson, arriving as early or earlier than his older brother; d Atkinson Feb 21, 1815; m June 19, 1764, Anna Atwood b Haverhill Oct 14, 1744, d Nov 13, 1813. Children:

a   Elizabeth b May 5, 1765; d May 8, 1835, unm
b   —— son b and d Apr 26, 1767
c   Sarah b Oct 20, 1768; d Jan 9, 1838, heirs being brother Job and sister Anna
d   Moses b Atkinson Feb 4, 1771
e   Jesse b Apr 30, 1774; d Oct 9, 1794   f   Job b Jan 26, 1777
g   John b June 18, 1779; d Sept 6, 1817; presumably unm
h   Anna b Apr 27, 1782; d Dec 25, 1786
i   Joseph b Dec 25, 1783 or 1785; d Sept 6, 1817, presumably unm
j   Anna b Oct 31, 1788; d Aug 25, 1863; m Nathaniel Kelly

Moses Dow bcfigd, grad Dartmouth 1796, teacher Atkinson Academy 1796-7, entered Congregational ministry before 1800; pastor second church Beverly 1801-13, York, Me, 1815-30, Hampton Christian Baptist church 1803; moved to Plaistow; d May 9, 1837; m May 14, 1801, Hannah Knight b Atkinson Apr 14, 1777, d Plaistow Mch 1855, dau of Eliphalet of Atkinson. Children:

a   Louisa b Feb 21, 1804; d Dec 12, 1845, unm
b   Hannah Knight bap Feb 1, 1807 (Beverly rec says "a son"); m Hampton Falls by her father Oct 10, 1831, Josiah (or Isaiah) P Moody of Lowell
c   Moses Augustus b Mch 15, 1809

Moses A Dow bcfigdc, farmer, assessed 1850 for $1,500; for 9 years town clerk of Plaistow, d Mch 10, 1853; m Oct 1833 Julia Ann Bragdon b York, Me, Apr 10, 1810, d Plaistow Sept 26, 1877, dau of Benjamin Josiah and Nancy (Harris). Children:

a Ann Louisa b Plaistow Apr 8, 1835; for many years teacher in Plaistow; d unm
b Moses Bragdon b Jan 2, 1837
c Charles Augustus b Mch 24, 1839; private in 7th N H; d Texas 1867, unm
d Henry A b Jan 7, 1842; Co E, 1st Mass heavy artillery, d Andersonville prison Apr 1865

Moses B Dow bcfigdcb, carriage maker of Plaistow, representative to Legislature, d Nov 2, 1909; m Dec 25, 1878, Alice A Emerson b Portsmouth, N H, d Nov 6, 1896. His portrait in Hist Rockingham Co.

Job Dow bcfigf, farmer of Atkinson, d Oct 29, 1857; m Apr 4, 1806, Anna Atwood b Sept 25, 1777, d Apr 24, 1853. Atkinson rec gives Job Dow of Atkinson m Dec 25, 1806, Hannah Hazeltine of Haverhill. Int pub Nov 10, 1806. No other available Job is known; some error surely. Children of Job and Anna:

a Jesse b Sept 15, 1808   b Moses b July 10, 1810
c —— dau d in infancy   d John b Atkinson Jan 25, 1817
e Betsey S b 1819; at home 1850

Jesse Dow bcfigfa inherited the homestead; d Jan 28, 1861; m Betsey Sherburn b Feb 24, 1819, dau of Josiah and Abigail (Ferren) of Sandown. Children:

a Eliza Ann b Jan 31, 1846   b Sarah Atwood b Dec 4, 1846
c Abby b Nov 20, 1850   d John Milton b Feb 19, 1854; unt
e Mary Elizabeth b Apr 5, 1858

Moses Dow bcfigfb of Atkinson d Dec 26, 1868; elected deacon May 22, 1840; m May 28, 1835, Sally P Hanson b Haverhill Jan 22, 1808, d Feb 28, 1870, dau of Winthrop and Hepzibah (Mahany). Children:

a James Atwood b Nov 18, 1836; machinist, d Atkinson July 2, 1905, unm
b George Parsons b Aug 7, 1840   c Moses Augustus b May 31, 1843
d William Henry b July 20, 1845

George P Dow bcfigfbb, veteran of Civil War, d Atkinson Sept 28, 1910; long postmaster; m Julia A Carlton b Chelmsford. Children:

a Mary A b Sept 21, 1866; m May 3, 1899, William C Farley of Lawrence
b —— b and d May 24, 1880

Moses A Dow bcfigfbc lived Gilford, N H; m Dec 31, 1866, Eliza Ann Wheeler of Lake Village, dau of E H and Mehitable (Cole). Dau:

a Florence Lillian b 1867; m 1888 Fred W Stevens

John Dow bcfigfd d Geogetown, Mass Apr 19, 1894; m Aug 8, 1838, Matilda Putnam Atwood b Franconia Dec 20, 1814, d Atkinson Sept 26, 1882. He first entered the stove business in Salem, later clothier of Lawrence. He served creditably as adjutant and hospital nurse of 7th N H; disch on account of chronic illness; bought in 1864 a farm in West Chester, Pa; but soon returned to Atkinson. Children:

a Harriet Ann b Mch 24, 1839; m Nov 28, 1858, George S Weston of Georgetown
b Sarah Elizabeth b Apr 30, 1841; m Nov 10, 1864, Wyman B Knight; only son Frank B was in regular army 1887, stationed in Montana
c John b July 27, d Aug 5, 1843 d John b Dec 16, 1844
e Helen Matilda b Mch 27, 1847
f Emily Atwood b Lawrence July 25, 1849; d Oct 10, 1854
g Job Atwood b Atkinson May 27, 1852; in 1887 bookkeeper of Haverhill, unm

John Dow bcfigfdd of Atkinson moved to Lyme, N H. Atkinson rec: m Dec 25, 1870, Mary Phoebe Hale b Sept 1, 1852, dau of Nathaniel and Almira (Tewksbury). Poor gen gives Dec 23, 1869, Mary Phoebe Poor, dau of Nathaniel Hale. State rec is correct: m Mary Poor Little of Hampstead. Brother and sister m brother and sister. Children:

a Ethelyn Mary b June 29, 1872
b John Carlton b Dec 21, 1874; untraced c Frank E b 1882

A letter of inquiry to town clerk of Lyme brought reply that no member of this family was living there. The third son not in previous gen rec, but found by own rec.

Frank E Dow bcfigfddc b Lynn, Mass, m while a medical student Boston Sept 22, 1909, Marion Dole, dau of John W and Harriet H (Wilde) (see Who's Who in New Eng). Dau:

a Eleanor b Aug 4, 1910

Helen Matilda Dow bcfigfde m May 6, 1869, Frank Henry Little b Hampstead Oct 19, 1843, son of Nathaniel Hale, carpenter of Danvers, veteran of 11th N H vols. Children:

a Ernest E b Hampstead Apr 18, 1870
b Frank W b Haverhill Aug 26, 1872 c Helen J b Atkinson Nov 3, 1873
d John C b Lynn June 29, 1875; d Aug 29, 1877
e George H b Danvers Nov 28, 1876; d Aug 29, 1877
f Emma L b Mch 24, 1878 g Mary L b June 30, 1880
h Hattie A b Dec 23, 1882 i Henry C b Dec 12, 1884
j Minnie A b Oct 13, 1886

Moses Dow bcfih inherited his full share of the abilities of his father and grandfather, both magistrates of Haverhill; grad Harvard 1769, studied law. By 1774 he had located in Haverhill, N H, of which his brother Abraham was an original grantee. Moses certified to the list of Revolutionary soldiers from the place, adding that the town was not yet organized. He practiced law, helped organize the town, was for many years selectman. He fought long, locally and in the Legislature, to abolish the tax on all citizens to pay the minister's salary, holding that church members should do this without compulsion to outsiders. He was the second postmaster of Haverhill and for 30 years Register of Probate. He served as Major General of militia and as Gen on the Governor's staff. He was always subsequently known by this title. For many years judge of the court of common pleas. He was appointed to Congress 1784 but declined. Elected to the State Senate, he was its president 1791; later ran for Congress but was defeated.

He had a large farm 2 1-2 miles north of Haverhill Corner. His house was a large colonial structure, the finest for many miles around. Its dining room fireplace had a crane over 12 feet long and a child, standing in it, could see the sky. The house was burned 1900. A picture of it, and a sketch of Moses Dow is in Granite State Monthly July-Sept 1918. He was an organizer and large stockholder in the bridge built across the Connecticut and was identified with almost all local enterprises; an incorporator of Haverhill Academy, receiving A M from Dartmouth 1785. He was tall, with commanding manner and strongly opinionated.

He d 1811; m 1768 Phoebe Emerson b Mch 18, 1750-1, dau of Joseph and Mehitable (Haseltine) of Haverhill, Mass. Published rec generally call her Mrs Phoebe Emerson, wholly error. Hist Haverhill gives him 2 sons, 2 dau. Census 1790 gives 4a, 2b, 10c. This is impossible. List here is correct unless some child d in infancy. Children:

a　Mehitable b Nov 15, 1769; m Dec 29, 1793; moved to Newbury, Mass; John Hazeltine; a dau Phoebe Dow m Haines Johnson
b　Phoebe b Feb 17, 1772; m Sept 12, 1790, Moses Johnson. Hist Littleton gives her m Joseph Elliott, member of Congress
c　Kater b Jan 23, 1774; d Aug 16, 1779
d　Moses b Nov 5, 1775　　　e　Joseph Emerson b Dec 28, 1777
f　Lucy b May 12, 1780; m May 5, 1803, James Elliott of Brattleboro, Vt
g　Polly b Oct 13, 1784　　　h　Nancy b July 19, 1787; d Feb 3, 1802
i　Hannah b July 25, 1789

Phoebe Dow bcfihb m Moses Johnson b May 17, 1740. Children:

a　Moses b Dec 5, 1799; d Dec 20, 1812
b　Frank Phelps b May 19, 1805; d Aug 26, 1842; m Eleanor Ford Stevens

Moses Dow bcfihd studied law with his father; admitted to bar 1800; succeeded his father as Register of Probate and was postmaster, but removed by President Jackson. He figured in a widely gossiped breach of promise suit brought by a Miss Bell, in which the unrebuked statement was made in court: "Dow appears pretty well and generally has a ruffled shirt on, but it isn't always clean." The sympathies of the town were decidedly against him. He m Mch 17, 1825, Sally Young of Rumney. Two sons, 2 dau:

a　Moses Franklin b 1827　　　b　—— a son d young
c　Sarah m May 5, 1842, Voorannus B Keith of Haverhill; went south
d　Mary A m Mch 13, 1849, Nathaniel C Eastman of Newburyport, Mass

Moses F Dow bcfihda, grad Dartmouth 1849, taught school 4 years in Georgia; moved to Aberdeen, Miss, 1856 principal of a school; remained south during the war; d Smithville, Miss, Oct 1, 1878, presumably unm.

Joseph E Dow bcfihe, grad Dartmouth 1799, d Franconia Aug 25, 1857. A man of ability and fine mind, at first very successful. He gradually drank himself into poverty. He started practice 1803 in St Johnsbury, Vt; moved to Littleton, N H, the first lawyer in that town. In 1808 he became postmaster of Thornton, then had a local magistracy. His law dwindled to nothing and he retired to a farm. He m Mch 10, 1808, (1803?) Abigail B Arnold, dau of Hon Jonathan, member of Continental Congress from Rhode Island. Born late in her father's life, she was adopted by a relative. Joseph m 2nd, Oct 4, 1825, Nancy Bagley of Thornton b 1790, living 1850, who on one occasion got in the public eye when the sheriff, coming to serve an attachment, got from her a pail of boiling water. Children:

a Catherine b 1803; d young   b James Burrill b Littleton May 5, 1807
c Moses Arnold b May 20, 1810   d George Barber b 1813
e Charles Marsh b Franconia June 22, 1816
    A Hannah Dow b 1839 was living Thornton 1850 with wid Nancy, perhaps a niece

James B Dow bcfiheb went early to Boston and learned the printing trade; m Mary McBirney, who survived him, He gained control of the Christian Witness, an Episcopalian paper. It was in his employ that his brother, Moses A, conceived the idea of the Waverley magazine. James soon opened a store on Washington St, specializing in religious books. Beginning to dabble in real estate, he accumulated a fortune, sold out and traveled extensively. He d June 1878, of paralysis, leaving over $150,000 to his wid for life, then to pass to some charity of her selection. No children:

Moses A Dow bcfihec d Charlestown, Mass, June 22, 1886; came to Boston 1829; worked in his brother's printing shop, becoming foreman. The plant was small, his wages necessarily low, and he was not able to save much in 11 years. In 1850 he decided to start the Waverley magazine. For a few numbers it had many vicissitudes, barely keeping alive, from lack of capital, but before the end of its first year was well established. Its original idea was novel; his contributions were solicited from amateurs who wished to see themselves in print, even from school boys and girls. He figured that such material would cost him nothing and that friends of the contributors would buy enough magazines to make it pay. His judgment was correct. The Waverley is full of first effusions of writers who subsequently became more or less well known. It was helped much by contributions of George William Curtis, a cousin of the publisher. After the magazine was widely known, Moses employed an editor of standing to pass on contributions and build up its intellectual tone. He soon found, however, that rejected contributions hurt business. He discharged the editor and re-adopted most of his original idea. Upon this, the circulation, which had been cut by more than half, rose again, and all was well. Its circulation became (then unprecedented) 60,000, seldom falling below 50,000 copies. He sold out and the new owners soon failed. With the proceeds he built a fine hotel in Charlestown and dabbled in real estate. He made a large fortune; endowed the Dow Academy of Franconia. He m Oct 20, 1836, Elizabeth Taylor Houghton, dau of Thomas Jr and Betsey (Eckley). She d Brookline Nov 14, 1901, result of a carriage accident, leaving an estate estimated at $3,000,000. Children:

   a   James b 1837; d in infancy   b   Mary Elizabeth b Dec 22, 1844
   c   Emma J b Oct 15, 1846

Mary E Dow bcfihecb m Sept 27, 1870, Rev G W R Scott. Children:

   a   George Dow   b   Arnold   c   Mary Elizabeth d in infancy

Emma J Dow bcfihecc m Oct 7, 1869, Leonard F Cutter. Children:

   a   Arnold   b   Charles Winthrop   c   Irving Taylor

George B Dow bcfihed d Cambridge Oct 23, 1880; learned the hatter's trade in Plymouth, N H; came to Haverhill, Mass, becoming a manufacturer. He later had a meat market in Boston. An able man, ill health blocked his way always. He m Haverhill July 1, 1842, Hannah Eaton Emerson b Feb 5, 1813, d Enfield, N H, July 26, 1889, dau of Timothy b Haverhill and Lucinda Burdick (Morse) b Canaan, N H. Children:

   a   Abigail Arnold b Apr 20, 1843; m July 27, 1865, Andreas Zihn of Somerville:
       4 children
   b   James Charles b June 27, 1845; in 1882 a mariner, unm

Charles M Dow bcfihee learned the harness making business and came to Boston; d pneumonia 1841, unm.

Lucy Dow bcfihf m John James Elliott; settled in Newfane, Vt. A dau:

   a   Mary A b 1812; d Apr 2, 1896; m Wright Pomeroy

James Dow bcfii. In all the material received by the Author from earlier genealogists the only mention of James touched his birth and his being a beneficiary 1795 in the will of his brother Abraham. There seems to be no genealogical interest whatever in this whole line and it was reconstructed from the fragmentary and very imperfect vital statistics. Copies of the whole line were sent by the Author to William L Dow and Moses H Dow, both prominent shoe manufacturers of Haverhill, with earnest requests for family information, but no reply was ever received. Hist Haverhill, N H, mentions James casually as being there in 1790, but it was probably a passing visit. He was a resident of Atkinson, associated more or less closely with his brother Abraham in manufacturing. Census 1790 shows him of Atkinson 1a, 1b, 2c. He m Atkinson Nov 24, 1774, Sarah Young. Surely 2 children, but date of son or of marriage surely wrong. Children:

   a   Sally. Hampstead rec gives Sally Dow (parents not stated) d Apr 4, 1853,
       ae 75. If ae 73, she fits exactly as 1stborn

b Samuel T. In rec of a son he is called Samuel S. Atkinson has a rec: Samuel
Spofford Dow b June 22, 1792. A duplicate calls this man Samuel O. As
Samuel T had a son b 1813 and as James m 1775, there is either an
unplaced Samuel S Dow or some date is wrong. Hist Windham makes no
genealogical mention of this line, but mentions Caleb R Dow (see below) as
son of Samuel, son of Moses. This grandfather's name seems *lapsus calami*.
We must regard all these as identical

Samuel T Dow bcfiib, presumably lifelong resident of Atkinson,
m Atkinson Mch 5, 1812, Abigail Richards. Children, all b Atkinson:

a James Marsh How b Mch 8, 1813   b Caleb Richards b Aug 1, 1816
x Moses b N Y City May 30, 1818; this may be confusion with son of bcfical
c Francis Vose b Feb 27, 1820   d Peaslee Moody b Oct 22, 1822; unt

James M H Dow bcfiiba d Haverhill June 25, 1778 (father's name
given as Samuel Spofford Dow, mother's as Abigail Richards). Not
stated when or where he joined the ministry; a Methodist, but entered
the Congregational ministry 1843; pastorates in Dover, N H; Coventry,
R I; Washington, Pawtucket, Boston; then traveling evangelist in
Maine. He m Jan 21, 1834, Eliza Hovey Danforth d Apr 1867, dau of
Eliphalet and Mary (Hovey) of Londonderry; 2nd, June 9, 1868, Elinor
Lancaster Prible, dau of Abial and Sally (Haskell) of Machias, Me. In
Rhode Island more than half of all marriages for many years were per-
formed by him or Rev Daniel Dow ahcbg. One of his marriages estab-
lishes, we think, a record for elongated nomenclature: Alexander Philip
Socrates Caesar Hannibal Marcellus George Washington Treadwell to
Caroline Sophia Margaretta Maria Juliannes Worth Montague Joan
of Arc Williams, both American, of New Orleans.

Children of James M H Dow:

a James P (Popkins?) b Atkinson Nov 20, 1834; probably identical with a James
P Dow crockery dealer of Lawrence; unt
b Ann Eliza   c Gertrude   d Gaylord H
e Nellie M H b Boston 1875; of Littleton m Dec 16, 1902, John H Page ae 31,
son of Benjamin F and Caroline (Farr)

Gaylord H Dow bcfiibad m Alice Dennis (or Dennison, both in rec).
Children:

a Warren Preble b Boston Aug 1, 1902
b Walter Curtis b Cambridge Sept 1, 1906
c Herbert b Peabody Mch 6, 1909

Caleb R Dow bcfiibb of Atkinson was road commissioner 1847;
m Jan 20, 1842, Elizabeth H Cronk of Boston b 1824. No children in
1850 census.

Francis V Dow bcfiibc d Jan 7, 1893; m Nov 14, 1843, Mehitable
Hoyt b Sept 17, 1821, dau of Moses and Hannah (Williams). Beginning
in a small way he developed a very substantial shoe manufacturing
business, appearing at various times in Atkinson, Haverhill, Hampstead,
Chester and Derry. He occupies a prominent place in Centennial Hist
Hampstead, but that work (which, if a couple more years had been
given to its preparation, would have been one of the finest town histories)

fails to give his parents and gives only a few children. List as revised by a grandson probably complete. Children:

a Abbie Hannah b Atkinson Aug 26, 1844
b Ann Frances b Hampstead July 25, 1846
c Josephine Wallace b Aug 23, 1848; m Martin V B Dow bbbebcdaa (q v)
d Lizzie (probably error of Hist Hampstead and identical with next)
e Martha E (or Martha Lizzie) b Chester Mch 25, 1853
f Frank Peaslee b Derry Sept 7, 1855; d unm
g Lucy Richards b Hampstead Dec 5, 1857
h William Lowell   i Moses Hoyt b Jan 7, 1861

Abbie H Dow bcfiibca m Nov 16, 1862, William Alonzo Emerson b Atkinson Aug 28, 1844. Their children compose the firm of William A Emerson's Sons, shoe manufacturers of Haverhill:

a Daniel b Dec 2, 1863; m Esther Plunkett; 1 child
b Frank W b Jan 18, 1866; m Minnie E Stevens
c Arthur Mahlon b May 10, 1870; m May E Henwood; 2nd Alice M Hamlin; 4 children
d Myron E

Lucy R Dow bcfiibcg m George T Ordway. Only child:

a Edith Belle m Herbert C Little d without children

William L Dow bcfiibch, shoe manufacturer of Haverhill, m Emma Hamlin b Haverhill Mch 20, 1861. Child:

a Clifford D b Hampstead Aug 27, 1892

Moses H Dow bcfiibci, shoe manufacturer of Haverhill and Boston, d early in 1924; m Minnie O'Brien. Children:

a Moses Francis b Haverhill Sept 10, 1905
b William Moody. Wintering in Florida 1924, he met Mary Hope Dow bcdgddaha, who interested him in his own genealogy and induced him to write to the Author. Having learned that he came through James bcfii, instead of Abraham bcfic, as Josephine W Dow had supposed, he did excellent work on the data of the younger generations
c Margaret Virginia b Haverhill Nov 14, 1909

Mary Dow bd m Gilbert Wilford of Bradford, who moved to Haverhill, d July 1676; 2nd Haverhill Apr 2, 1679, Matthew Clarke. A statement in a genealogical periodical that Matthew was son of Elder James Clarke of Londonderry is obvious *lapsus*. Mary Dow was presumably stepmother of the Londonderry pioneer, and James Clarke, b before 1679, was probably grandfather of Elder James. At all events Elder James Clarke (sic) of Londonderry, b 1732, m Margaret Anderson and had,—James, Samuel, Matthew, John, Margaret, Mary, Elizabeth. Mary Dow had by 1st husband:

a Mary b Bradford Nov 18, 1667; m Haverhill Dec 17, 1684, John Corliss; 2nd Haverhill Jan 23, 1702-3, William Whittaker
b Martha b Jan 18, 1669; m Haverhill Feb 7, 1694-5, Joseph Greely
c Ruth b May 5, 1672; m Haverhill June 12, 1694, Thomas Ayer. He and dau Ruth killed by Indians
d Nathaniel b May 20, 1675; d Haverhill 1706, unm

Martha Dow be, whose posterity rejoined the line two generations later (Phoebe Heath beaa m Richard Dow bcde), surely endured vicissitudes tending to create a race of brave men; m June 27, 1672, Joseph Heath.   While carrying an unborn son, her husband was ambushed and killed by Indians on the Andover road Dec 1, 1672.   She m 2nd, Dec 2, 1673, Joseph Page b 1647, son of John and Mary (Marsh), and widower of Judith Guile.   He d a natural death Feb 5, 1683.   She m 3rd, Mch 19, 1688, Joseph Parker.   He lived in East Parish, Haverhill, and was killed by Indians while in his hay field Aug 3, 1690.   Thus Martha Dow was wid thrice before she was 43.   Many years later Joseph Heath in his will gave to his son Samuel land "set aside to my mother Parker as her right of dower in Joseph Page's estate."   Martha had 1 by 1st, rest by 2nd:

a Joseph (Heath) b Mch 23, 1673
b Phebe (Page) b Haverhill Nov 17, 1674; int pub Salisbury Oct 14, 1685, to
    Joseph Tucker, son of Morris
c Joseph b Nov 23, 1676; killed by Indians Aug 4, 1704; no children
d Hannah b Feb 5, or 12, 1678; m Nov 27, 1696, John Dow adb
e Martha b Feb 14, 1680; m Haverhill Dec 19, 1700, Matthew Herriman
f Thomas b Apr 12, 1683; d Haverhill June 5, 1683
g Ebenezer b May 9, 1684; soldier in Salisbury 1703; killed by Indians June 24,
    1707

THAT a Dow immigrant into Connecticut before 1664 existed has long been known, his name and marriage mentioned by all the classic pioneers in American Genealogy. It is only recently a discovery that he had a posterity in the male line. Savage, Genealogical Dictionary, mentions Samuel Dow of Hartford m Dec 12, 1665, Mary, dau of first George Graves of Hartford. Hinman, Connecticut Settlers, gives: Samuel Dow d 1690 and it explains the identity of George Graves, called first or senior to distinguish him from another of the same name in Hartford. George Graves, Hartford 1649, townsman, deputy in 1646, was in the land division of 1639; left children:

a John   b Josiah   c —— dau m —— Deming
d Mary m —— Dow   e Priscilla m —— Marcum

Samuel Dow c was a sailor, impecunious. Many such were on ships coming to America before 1700 and some remained here. How Samuel met and succeeded in marrying the dau of a very substantial Hartford citizen can only be surmised. He was home about the end of 1671, was at sea 1672-4. After that he may have settled down; he d June 2, 1690, in his Hartford home. That he had more than one child is evident from some court proceedings: A Generall Courte Held at Hartford Oct 8, 1674: Mary Dowe of Hartforde, informeing this Court that her husband being gone to sea and not being heard of for nearly two yeares, and leaving her destitute of supplyes necessary for the mayntenance of herself and children, she is fallen into debt and knowes not how to pay the same without it be by the sale of her house and lott, and therefore desired thie Court to empower her so to doe,—the Court considering the permises doe see good reason to grant her desire, and doe accordingly give her full power to grant, bargain and sell the sayd house and lott, and her deed therein shall be esteemed good and valid in the law.

Hartford District, Mainwaring, Probate Rec supply some more: 438: Dow, Samuel. Died June 2, 1690. Invt. £ 21-15-00. Taken 24 Oct. 1690, by George Graves Sen. and Thomas Olcott. Court Rec p. 19-5, Nov, 1690. Invt exhibited.

It is sure, then, that Samuel had little of his own and was more or less of a rolling stone. It is sure that he had "children." Only 1 is proved. There may have been more than 2:

a Sarah, the daughter of goodwife Dow (bapt) (Second Church, Hartford) ffebry 2, 1672. What became of her is unknown
b Edmund (based on evidence to follow, presumably b considerably later)

Edmund Dow cb is known only by rec of a son:

a George bap (2nd church) Aug 7, 1720, son to Edmund Dow. If this was an infant baptism, Edmund was surely very mature in 1720

At this point all proof of connection ends. We know that the

Connecticut Dows of early times were the brothers ahc, ahd and ahg, who came about 1715 and had large posterity. These lines have been so well studied that an overlooked member in Connecticut before 1775 is extremely improbable. There is a temptation, then, to place any unknown Dow of Connecticut in the c family. This is dangerous to accuracy, for little by little all such are found to be members of the a or b families and come from other New England states. Unless there was an immigrant Dow unknown, there are two families which still must be regarded as c.

Henry M Stiles, Ancient Wethersfield, has dug up so many Dows there that it seems impossible that they should be a or b people. To accommodate them, we suppose that the baptism of George Dow cba was as an adult. By such supposition, dates fit much better. We further suppose that George Dow cba settled in Wethersfield and had at least 1 child:

a   Edmund b 1728 (this from his d rec)

Edmund Dow cbaa d Wethersfield Mch 3, 1786, ae 58; m Dec 9, 1750, Sarah Sillman (that this name is really Stillman is argued from rec of a grandson (below). She is surely the wid Sarah Dow d Wethersfield Feb 21, 1800, ae 71. Wethersfield rec includes all their family:

a   Charles b Apr 25, 1751   b   Helen b Dec 1, 1752
c   Sarah b Apr 9, 1754; presumably the Sally Dow, adult, bap Wethersfield May 30, 1781
d   Edmonde b Jan 1, 1756
e   Polly. This is a guess to account for some Polly Dow of Wethersfield m Apr 22, 1779, Samuel Skinner of Hartford

To account for the next, we must presume that **Charles Dow** cbaaa had a family in Wethersfield:

a   Samuel bap Wethersfield Mch 15, 1795 (two years after his marriage)

Samuel Dow cbaaaa m Wethersfield Dec 12, 1793, Abigail Buckley. Children, town rec:

a   Samuel bap Jan 17, 1795; apparently d in infancy
b   Samuel Stillman (cf Stillman cbaa above) bap Feb 28, 1796. That he grew up and m is argued from the fact that Sarah Dow, wife of Samuel, bap May 6, 1821
c   Huldah bap Dec 21, 1797   d   William bap Mch 16, 1800

Edmonde Dow cbaad seems to Stiles to be the father of at least 3:

b   Huldah   c   Charlie, bap together Apr 29, 1781

To guess further regarding identities of Wethersfield Dows is wild and is done only for convenience in indexing.

Mehitable Dow cbaaf, adult, bap Wethersfield Oct 22, 1789

Sarah Dow cbaag m Jan 11, 1836, Solomon Wadsworth of East Hartford.

There was in Huntington, L I, from as early as 1761 at least one considerable Dow family, the individuals of which are as yet unconnectible with each other or with any line. It may be well to place them in the c line, with letter keys for indexing:

Joseph Dow cbba, ae 48, enlisted in Sea Fencibles from Huntington; he and Jacob appear in the list of refugees to Conn when the British overran the island.

Jacob Dow cbbb signed the Association Test Huntington May 8, 1775.

Jacob Dow cbbc, hardly possibly identical, appears in 1790 census of Huntington 1a, 2b, 2c. If he had sons older and was identical, it would follow:

  a Philip; known only from 1790 Huntington census, 1a, 1c
  b Samuel b presumably 1770 or before

Samuel Dow cbbcb m Huntington Apr 5, 1792, by Rev Joshua Hartt, Elizabeth (5) Burr b Commack about July 3, 1773, dau of Isaac and Mary (Baldwin). They moved to Elizabeth, N J. She was a devout Presbyterian; d Jan 3, 1858, ae 82, 6 mos. Only child:

  a Mary b 1796

Mary Dow cbbcba d Mch 20, 1866; m —— Dayton; 2nd Havilah Smith Halsey d Newark June 21, 1868. She was prominent in founding the Foster Home in Newark. No children. Cf Halsey Gen p 219.

Conn rosters contain Dow names which from localities suggest strongly c identities. So far, no living Dow has been found belonging to the line, but one cannot think it extinct. It is quite possible that the Huntington Dows did not return after 1783 but remained in Conn.

Henry Dow cca (this and subsequent lettered for convenience), no place given, served 1 week 1813.

Samuel Dow (Capt), no place, under Col Jared Strickland 1 mo, 8 days.

Thomas Dow (Capt), New London, served 5 mos.

William Dow, no place, service 1 mo, 3 days.

William Dowe, Groton, 1 mo, 7 days.

James Dow, Hartford, 25th inf, wounded Aug 18, 1814.

Henry G Dow, Wethersfield, private 22nd reg 1862; one naturally associates him with Newell Dow (bcbcbbaff) in same reg.

D FAMILY OF DOW

THIS line of Dow has neither beginning nor end; it occurs to meet the situation in Newington, N H, dating from 1683. In that year John Dow, an unmarried seaman, died at Piscataway, leaving a will. This mentioned no relatives. It might be supposed that he had been only a transient.

Some John Dow received a grant of land in Dover 1694; this has been supposed to be the well known John Doe of Oyster River. However, a rec is extant that to John Dow and Sarah were born:

    a Jonathan b 1695

This record reached the great Historian of Hampton, but he was never able to connect it. We find that John Dow (not Doe) was taxed in Portsmouth 1727. John Dow was admitted to Newington church Sept 15, 1736. Sarah Dow, supposedly his wife, was admitted Oct 17, 1736. Nothing further appears.

There are, however, in Newington and Portsmouth records of early dates not possibly attachable to any earlier family. We assume more children to John and Sarah:

    b Moses b by 1714, probably earlier. He appears but once: Moses Dow m Newington Mch 19, 1735, Sarah Phillips of Portsmouth. There is Moses Dow ahbb, b Newbury 1712 and not heard of again, but nothing is certain
    c Isaac b by 1720; no known Isaac can possibly fit

Jonathan Dow da had a wife Elizabeth. A child:

    a Mary bap Newington May 5, 1717; not heard of again

Barely possible that Jonathan had another, for:

    b Patience Dow of Newington m May 7, 1752, William Shackford. Not heard of again; cannot be the abcea family of Newington at a later time

Isaac Dow dc, might also be dab; certainly there is no room for him in a or b lines. He b Portsmouth, lived Newbury; d Jan 1779. He m Haverhill May 11, 1743, Lydia Foster, the only available Lydia being b Feb 28, 1712, dau of David and Lydia (Black). Presumably Isaac followed the sea. Children, Newbury rec:

a	Lydia bap Feb 26, 1743-4	b	Mary bap Aug 17, 1746
c	Abigail bap June 17, 1750	d	Isaac bap June 17, 1750
e	Hannah bap May 17, 1752; improbably the Hannah d Beverly May 25, 1833, at advanced age		

Isaac Dow dcd m Newburyport June 23, 1774, Abigail Merrill, presumably dau of Moses, bap 1750. Has not reappeared; may be the Isaac Dow exchanged, Halifax to Boston, Oct 8, 1778. Is probably the Isaac served 1775 under Capt Richard Dow bcde.

A SCOTCH family of Dow came to Philadelphia some time before 1760, probably to take part in the 1758 campaign. The known facts concerning them end in 1766.

James Dow e was clearly a man of gentle birth and of property, else he would not himself have been a British officer and been able to obtain commissions for three or four sons. He d in Philadelphia and a son's petition fixes the date as 1766. The three regiments in which this family served were Scotch. James Dow was a Lieut in the 60th reg up to the time of his death. Three sons are sure:

a   James, commissioned Lieut of 42nd reg May 24, 1758
b   John, commissioned ensign 60th reg May 4, 1757; Lieut May 24, 1758. His identity is unproved; he did not join in the petition signed by three sons; quite possible that he was a nephew
c   Archibald, commissioned ensign 60th reg Apr 6, 1759; Lieut Dec 12, 1760
d   Alexander, commissioned ensign 28th reg Nov 10, 1760; Lieut Mch 20, 1763

Some time after the end of the French war James, Archibald and Alexander Dow entered a petition for a grant of land, 2,000 acres to each on the west shore of Lake Champlain, by virtue of being sons of James Dow dec, late of the 60th reg. In a special petition dated 1766 James Dow Jr adds that his father had lately died. That something was done in the matter appears from some litigation many years later.

About 1790 a man who had lived since prior to 1782 on 400 acres of land near Whitehall, N Y, known as Dow's patent, was forced to fight in court for his title. By putting two and two together, the circumstances are fairly clear. At least 400 acres were granted to one or more of the sons of James Dow e. It is natural presumption that, if they remained in this country, they continued royalists and left before the actual outbreak of the Revolution. The logical way was over the Canadian border, as did vast numbers of tories. It matters little to us whether they made an effort to live on the land after 1766 or sold it at the first possible opportunity. British officers of the French campaign generally adopted the latter course. Being enemies of the United States, the land would be liable to confiscation. Hence the suit to oust the owner in 1790, perhaps an innocent purchaser. Its outcome has not been learned by the Author. The tale would end abruptly here, were it not for a striking coincidence.

James Dow eaa. About 1800 there crossed the border from the British provinces and settled in So Thomaston, Me, a Capt James Dow, a sea captain. Around him there is a well defined tradition that he had lived previously in the States and had had a military career. His name is one more reason for guessing him to be a son of one of the Philadelphia Lieuts. He m So Thomaston (int pub Mch 17, 1806) Elizabeth Coombs (adabb line). His posterity is very much American:

a   Abigail C m William M Hayden of So Thomaston
b   George C b 1808 (by census)   c   James

George C Dow eaab, sea captain, assessed 1850 on $500 realty, was for many years a trader and business adventurer between Maine and South America, with many exciting experiences and necessarily prolonged absences. At one time news of his death reached home, but many months later he arrived safely. Many years later he settled down for good in So Thomaston and d Apr 6, 1900, ae 92-3-9; m Dec 12, 1833, Catherine P Wade b Me 1811; 2nd, July 26, 1862, Mrs Sarah J (Packard) Fales. This maiden name from Hist Thomaston is probably error, for state rec gives her d Jan 23, 1907, ae 83-1-20, dau of David W and Eliza (Gleason) Piper. Children, by 1st wife:

a   Catherine L b June 26, 1835; m Charles Redman
b   George C b Aug 27, 1837; d Milbridge Mch 10, 1905, married, ae 66-6-17. A sea capt, he m July 26, 1862, Mary D Dyer of Thomaston. Hist Thomaston does not mention children
c   Emily E b May 20, 1840; d Sept 21, 1842
d   Octavia W b 1844   e   Mary Emma b 1846
f   Henry b 1849; known only from 1850 census; presumably d young

James Dow eaac, sea captain, m (int pub Aug 24, 1835) Julia Thorndyke; moved to Calif. Children, b Me, by census:

a   Helen b 1839   b   Frederick b 1843; unt
c   John B b 1845; d 1846   d   Caroline b about 1860

John Dow eb. If this officer were son of James, one would think he would have joined his brothers in their petition for a land grant. The facts that they were fellow Lieuts in the same regiment and together in Philadelphia surely argues kinship. John Dow m Anne McCall, an heiress of Philadelphia, b about 1739, dau of Samuel and Anne (McCall), 19th in descent from King Robert Bruce of Scotland by his 2nd wife, Lady Elizabeth de Burgh, dau of Richard, Earl of Ulster. That they had children is known, but the Author has no evidence that they remained in this country.

Archibald Dow ec is unknown except as already mentioned.

Alexander Dow ed is equally unknown. There are found at least one Alexander and one John Dow, wholly unplaced, who may best be disposed of here. Alexander Dowe, Lieut in Malcolm's reg, N Y, Apr 12, 1777, transferred to Flower's Artillery Artificers, promoted Apr 4, 1780, to Capt-Lieut, retired May 1, 1781, might be identical. One would think that if a Lieut in the British regulars espoused the Federal cause, he would have been started with higher rank. The 1790 census gives an Alexander Dow, no family, shoe manufacturer, Southwark, Pa, Front St, west side. This might be identical.

Alexander Dow edx m Plymouth, Mass, Jan 18, 1739, Sarah Duncan. Both names suggest Scotch. That the name is correct is indicated by the sequels. At least 1 child:

a   Alexander b Plymouth May 31, 1741

Alexander Dow edxa, whose dates might fit the Revolutionary officer or the Philadelphia manufacturer, but not possibly the true eda, m Plymouth Dec 4, 1766, Lydia Eames; further untraced.   No vacancies for this family seem possible in a or b lines. It is probable that some immigrant to Plymouth has been overlooked in original lists.

John Dow edg cannot be a Quaker and is absolutely unplaceable. **He** m Newport, R I, about 1742, by Rev Nicholas Eyres, Eliza ——. Untraced and possibly not a Dow at all.

F FAMILY OF DOW

F STANDS for the unknown and unnamed father of three brothers, who, according to a statement made by the grandson of one of them, came to N Y City in 1768, their trade being that of forgemen. Our informant supposes they were Scotch, but admits he was uncertain. One would be more inclined to look for iron workers in the industrial counties of England. It is probable that the ancestor is father of the William Dow whom the 1790 census shows in Canaan, N Y, with wife, dau and adult son. This William was necessarily b as early as about 1750. It seems highly probable that his earlier home was in Morristown, N J. A Mrs Dow was there 1774 to 1779, a school madame. We suppose her to be wife of William and it is natural that they should be where the boys started their iron forges. There is a church entry that Mrs Dow moved away. The three boys:

    a John   b Moses   c William b about 1750-8

John Dow fa built the first iron forge on Rockaway River, as early as 1795, perhaps before. The Swedeland forge at Milton was built 1797 by John Dow and Cornelius Davenport. John's partners in the first enterprise were Christian Straight, John Davenport and others. A third forge was built near by in 1800, or before. The Timber Brook forge near Greenville was built 1821-2 by John Dow, presumably the son of John fa. In all these enterprises the name of Moses Dow has not appeared. For his existence we have the word of a grandnephew, who relates that the son of William fc visited the son of Moses in Babylon, L I, about 1844, and that Moses Jr lived to very old age. It is also certain that the children of John Dow fa had own cousins in N Y City.

The region of the iron forges was the territory acquired subsequently by Cooper, Hewitt & Co, from which vast fortunes were made, the iron supply being for many years the largest in America. Perhaps John and Moses Dow sold out to that firm or their immediate predecessors. John Dow built a famous mansion in Belleville, N J, owned by a lineal descendant when the history of that town was written. A letter in 1922 was returned, no Dow living in town. There were two children, improbably more:

    a John   b Margaret, probably the older

John Dow faa left the regular church, being converted to Methodism by his sister. He himself combined afterwards preaching and iron forging, being for his time a wealthy capitalist. At least two children were left by him:

    a John Wesley, known as Squire Dow of Belleville
    b Abby m William Lee, a well known Methodist preacher

Margaret Dow fab was able to convert, also, her cousins in N Y City. She m (his 2nd) Rev William Holmes of N Y City.

William Dow fc was attracted by the cause of the Colonists and enlisted. Under the act of 1783 he received a grant of 160 acres, but apparently esteemed it of little value or too remote. He became a shipwright and settled in Milton, Ulster Co, where he d 1838 or 1839; his wife Sarah Fowler b Ulster Co, d Poughkeepsie.

After his death, his son and executor bethought himself of the soldier's land grant. Writing to Washington, he was informed, so a son says, that the 160 acres were where the heart of Rochester, N Y, now is. Some search of deeds was made in that county and it is claimed that no transfer was ever made from William Dow. For a few years there was a little excitement, but the heirs seemingly did not care to throw good money away on a wild chase.

The children of William:

a Job m Susan Vancuren; lived Poughkeepsie; probably a posterity
b Mariah m William Purcell of Milton   c Jane m David Purdy of Milton
d Caroline m William Johnson of Poughkeepsie   e Josiah Lacont b Ulster Co
f Hester m Sylvester Strong of Ulster Co
g Dorcas m John Wicklow of Ulster Co

Josiah L Dow fce, b Nov 8, 1808; d Aug 1, 1880; was a blacksmith; moved in middle life from Milton to Keyport, N J; m Aug 22, 1828, Fanny (Frances) Belinda Yelverton b Dutchess Co Aug 1, 1806, d Rockland Co Aug 29, 1881. Children:

a John William Henry b Milton May 11, 1829
b Sarah M b Nov 6, 1830; m June 22, 1854, William J Secor
c James E b Mch 25, 1831; m July 6, 1850, Amelia A Mott. One dau, 8 sons, unt
d George A b Nov 9, 1832; d Feb 5, 1917; m July 4, 1863, Sarah Polhamus
e Nelson b Apr 3, 1834; d Dec 21, 1914; m Oct 9, 1862, Maria Lenton. One son, 1 dau, unt
f Mary Ann b Mch 25, 1838; d June 9, 1840
g Caroline b Apr 3, 1839; d July 16, 1865; unm
h Josiah L b May 20, 1840; d Sept 9, 1888; m Jan 1, 1863, Jennett Halloway
i Stephen Y b Feb 18, 1842; d Oct 24, 1880; m Feb 15, 1855, Sarah Gilispe (sic in rec; Gillespie?)
j Andrew L b Jan 10, d Aug 8, 1845
k Royal S b Apr 5, 1846; m Dec 31, 1867, Dennaryous (sic in rec) Conk. One son, 1 dau, Gertrude, a nurse, m J Pierrepont Foster of New Haven, Conn
l Charles b Aug 9, 1849; d May 16, 1864

John W H Dow fcea was a road builder of Haverstraw, whose business soon required opening an office in N Y City. He d Nov 10, 1916; m Poughkeepsie Dec 15, 1849, Gertrude Myers b Jan 1, 1829, d Jan 21, 1906. Children:

a Sarah Frances b Nov 23, 1850; d Aug 24, 1852
b Henry Squire b Apr 16, 1852; living 1923
c Josiah L b Nov 10, 1853; d May 12, 1870
d Peter S b Jan 11, 1856; d Jan 27, 1857
e Alexander Pollard b Mch 20, 1859
f George A b Aug 4, 1860   g —— d at birth
h Julia Parkhurst b Keyport Oct 2, 1863
i John P b May 10, d Sept 30, 1866

Henry Squire Dow fceab m Oct 14, 1874, Amelia Frances Barker. Children:

a   Ralph H b Mch 18, 1876;   d July 29, 1898
b   Wilbur F b Nov 4, 1878; unt

Alexander P Dow fceae m 1892 Annie E Asper.   Children:

a   Percy A   b   Sarah   c   John H; all unt

George A Dow fceaf was in 1889 practicing dentistry in N Y City, now practicing in Keyport, N J; m Apr 3, 1889, Josephine Van Duzer. Children:

a   George H b Nov 21, 1894   b   Stanley M b Jan 17, 1897
c   Florence V b Mch 18, 1901

Julia P Dow fceah m Dec 15, 1884, Percy H Buckmaster of Iron Point, L I.   Children:

a   George A b Mch 5, 1886   b   Gertrude D b Aug 11, 1887
c   John W b Feb 28, 1889   d   Samuel K b Oct 8, 1891

FOLLOWING the conquest of Louisburg by the British and the expulsion of the French colonists from Acadia, strenuous attempts were made to recolonize the region, the immigrants being mostly Scotch,—hence the very name, Nova Scotia. Prior to 1750 there came one whose family spread into Maine prior to 1761. He was then a man grown. A vague family memory thinks his name might be Robert and he m a Miss Cook, but this may refer to his grandson. Climatic differences were important between the Nova Scotian coast and that of eastern Me, and the timber of the latter was much superior; hence a steady stream of migration. Few of this family remained permanently in Nova Scotia. From the time when facts replace vague family tradition, East Machias was the family headquarters. Members went as pioneers to Caribou, Columbia, Cherryfield. Still others went to Mass, where employment was more easily secured. Only one branch of the family has been traced and that due to the recovery of a family Bible. To the original immigrant we have two sons:

a   Jonathan b by 1750, perhaps quite a little earlier. Name does not sound
       Scotch, but locality indicates his identity
b   James b N S 1761 or earlier; identity certain

Jonathan Dow ga. All we know about him is from the 1790 census, in which he appears as farmer in section 13, 2a, 3c. This means he had a son of 16 or older, a wife and 2 dau, or, if no wife, 3 dau. Census also gives a Stephen Dow alone in section 13. We guess him a son of Jonathan who had taken up land of his own but had not yet married. We guess, then, he was not under 21, nor over, say 25, for men in that region married early. If, then, Stephen was born by 1770, his father was surely born considerably before 1750, or almost as soon as the immigrant reached Nova Scotia. One of the very few extant vital rec of Machias is: Eliza Dow d Feb 17, 1761. At this date Me did not have ten settlements. One guesses Eliza to be sister of Jonathan. The mother of his children must have been of later date. Children, by guess:

a   Stephen, mentioned above
b   A dau. Hist Machias, very fragmentary in its treatment of local beginnings,
       gives her without date m Eliphalet Huntley, son of Frederick and ——
       (Caldwell), pioneers of Machias. Hist Machias gives children: Oliver m
       Hannah Bab; Benjamin E m Delia Munson; 2nd, wid Trufton; Richard
       m a Miss Antone

It is an axiom with genealogists that intermarriages with some family never come singly. The recurrence of the name Huntley of Machias is very strong evidence of identities with the g line. There are similar recurrences in this line of the names Ackley and Worcester. found almost nowhere else.

Jonathan Dow gaax, index letters for convenience, must have been b about 1780; could not be son of Jonathan, else he would have appeared in 1790 census; could not be son of Stephen, for Stephen was too young. Our knowledge is confined to the d rec of son, in which parents' names are Jonathan and Judith (Worcester) both b Columbia. This last is more than doubtful. The son:

a   Richard far mer widower d Columbia Dec 1, 1910, ae 95, 10 mos.   Nothing more in rec.   We guess the next to be a son, probably a younger one.

Benjamin E Dow gaaxax is known only from m rec of son, b Columbia, of Cherryfield m Martha A Morse. One son proved, but almost any of the names following might be other sons:

a   Willie b 1879

Willie Dow gaaxaxa, laborer of Cherryfield, m Mch 4, 1901, Nancy H Matthews, ae 18, dau of E and Etta.   Children:

a ── son b Dec 25, 1902   b ── dau b Nov 25, 1904
c   Andrew killed by auto July 28, 1917, ae 7

Jordan Dow gaaxaxb b N F (if place is right he does not belong here), laborer of Columbia, m Georgia Worcester b Columbia.   Of children:

c ── son b Feb 8, 1914

Sewell Dow gaaxaxc, teamster of Cherryfield, m Vesta E Salisbury; both d before 1905.   A child found by own m rec:

a   Anson Cunningham teacher of Eden m Oct 26, 1905, Fannie Estee Coffin, ae 19, dau of Charles and Mary (Gray).   Not found by letter 1924

Snow H Dow gaaxaxd, laborer of Cherryfield, m Ellen Morse. Children:

a ── dau b May 20, 1894   f   Seward H b Feb 18, 1901

James Dow gaaxaxe of Cherryfield m Charity Hart. We note the very defective rec even after the compulsory registration law of 1892. Only 10th child found:

j   (guess) James Augustus b (say) 1883

James Augustus Dow Jr gaaxaxea, car repairer of Milo, Me, m Bertha May York.   Child:

e ── son b and d June 17, 1919

Azel S Dow gaaxaxf of Cherryfield m Hattie Davis.   Child:

b ── son b Apr 28, 1894

William E Dow gaaxaxg, laborer, m Inez Wood, both b Columbia Falls.   1stborn:

a   Mildred M b Columbia Falls Mch 28, 1894

Herbert Dow gaaxaxh b Columbia m Annie L Dow (maiden name?). Of children:

c ── dau b Columbia Nov 20, 1893   e   Annie G b Oct 1, 1897

Alvin Dow gaaxaxi of Cherryfield m Gertrude Davis. Of children:

a   Vera M d July 30, 1906, ae 8-1-14   d —— dau b Dec 6, 1902

George W Dow gaaxaxj of Cherryfield m Nellie Dow (maiden name?) of Columbia Falls. Child:

a   —— son b Nov 18, 1907

Ambros Dow gaaxaxk b Cherryfield, laborer of Mt Desert, m Edna Carter of Blue Hill. Child:

a   Emma Eleanor b Mt Desert Mch 12, 1915

Charles W Dow gaaxaxl of Cherryfield m Sara E Tabbitts of Columbia Falls. Of children:

g   —— son b Jan 1, 1894

Otto M Dow gaaxaxm m Cutler, Me, Nov 15, 18— (probably about 1890), Abbie J Ackley.

Henry W Dow gaaxaxn m Grace D Huntley b E Machias. Child:

a   Celia E b Brooks; d Lubec Oct 7, 1905, ae 2-0-1

A few Dow are found in Jonesport, Steuben and Lubec, almost surely of the g family. Immigration from Europe to the provinces of eastern Canada was rather heavy 1835 onward and about 50 families of Dow crossed the border to find more or less permanent homes in Maine. A majority were Scotch, several Irish and not a few were the second generation in America, coming from Newfoundland, Nova Scotia or Quebec.

———

James Dow gb. We know nothing of him except from a family rec, which names his sons. Presumably there were also dau

a   James b Oct 1791   b   William   c   Robert   d   Daniel

James Dow gba is definitely named in d rec of son and said b Nova Scotia. A ship carpenter, he seems to have settled in Machias 1825-8 and m there a 2nd wife, Rebecca Huntley. A family Bible begun at 2nd m is a fairly trustworthy guide, altho it gives Hartly instead of Huntley. Of 17 children 8 are said to be by 1st wife, which is certainly doing well for a man of 38. The list of them is very circumstantially given:

a   Elijah; lost at sea   b   Enoch   c   Robert   d   James
e   Joseph d East Boston, Mass   f   Esther m Robert O'Brien
g   Martha m John Wallace   h   Rebecca
i   William E b Oct 12, 1829; m Alma Ackley
j   Abbie b Apr 5, 1831; d about 1852
k   Andrew J b Lubec Feb 3, 1834
l   Jennette A b Mch 6, 1836; m Robert Hair
m   George W b Feb 6, 1839; m Hannah Stuart
n   John E b E Machias Aug 1, 1841; sea capt d Santos, Brazil, Aug 4, 1893
o   Lizzie b May 25, 1844; m A St John
p   Ruth b June 23, 1846; m John Bryant
q   James E b Sept 23, 1848; m Clara Sherman

William E Dow gbai (said in d rec b N S), stevedore of E Machias, d Feb 29, 1896; m Alma B Ackley d May 17, 1905, ae 74-6-25, dau of Nathan and Abbie (Bryant) of Cutler. Children, presumably more than 3, all b E Machias:

  a James E b 1850   b William b 1855   c Ernest E b 1879 (sic)

James E Dow gbaia, millman of E Machias, d Feb 27, 1915; m Abbie Beverly, who survived. Possibly other children:

  a Bion E b 1888; d Feb 27, 1915, unm
  b Hollis R b Feb 2, 1894; laborer of Machias m July 24, 1920, Ida May Dowling
      b 1897, dau of Edgar and Irene (Marston) of Whiting
  c Ethel A b Mch 28, 1899

William H Dow gbaib, laborer of Machiasport, d June 21, 1909; unt

Ernest E Dow gbaic, laborer of Machias, m 1st, July 23, 1903, Edith H Reynolds wid b 1878, dau of Silas and Nettie (Garnett) Harmon of E Machias; div; m 2nd, June 1, 1912, Gladys Garland, ae 19, dau of George and Clara (Young) of Bar Harbor. She d in hospital Concord, N H. Child by each:

  a Bertha M d May 16, 1905, ae 2 mos
  b William Henry b E Machias Sept 26, 1913

Andrew J Dow gbak d Bangor July 22, 1902; m Sarah A Bagley b E Machias Mch 30, 1833, d Jonesport Nov 26, 1912, dau of John and Sarah (Banks). They bought a farm and lived many years in No Billerica, Mass, returning to Me in old age. Children:

  a Clarena Jeannette b Mch 29, 1855; m Apr 1886 John B Wallace
  b Sarah Rebecca b Mch 7, 1857   c Emma Violette b June 27, 1860
  d Clarence Bertrand b Feb 19, 1861   e Charles Orris b Aug 24, 1863
  f Fred Hermon b Feb 5, 1865   g Clinton b Jan 6, 1868
  h Maurice Baily b Mch 10, 1873

Clarence B Dow gbakd, truckman, m Apr 6, 1884, Adana Amanda Boyden b Robbinstown Feb 2, 1860. Only child:

  a Clifton Wentworth b Eastport Oct 21, 1885; teamster of Eastport m July 19, 1913, Mary E Seward, ae 26, b Eng dau of Arthur

Fred H Dow gbakf continued to live Lowell, Mass; m Lilla P Ackley (Akerly by an erroneous rec) of Machias. Children:

  a Rena A b May 22, 1902   b Lila d 1903 ae 3 mos

Maurice B Dow gbakh lived some years in Lowell; returned and became a ship builder of Saco; m Bessie M Maker b Cutler or Lubec, d Jonesport Feb 10, 1910, dau of Job and Adeline (Bagley); m 2nd, her sister, Mch 10, 1918, Blanche B Maker, ae 40, teacher, b Cutler. One child found:

  a Theodora b Roque Bluffs June 28, 1905

James E Dow gbaq, farmer and policeman of Bridgewater, Mass, retired to E Machias; d Oct 1, 1920, married. D rec says b Sept 27, 1845, and does not mention children.

Still disconnected but surely of this family are several rec:

Leroy Dow gbea b E Machias m Josephine Wallace b Lubec. 1st born:

a　Ruth Wallace b Portland Dec 6, 1899

Frank W Dow gbeb b Machias m Ida M Barse b N S.　Child:

a　Earl Frank b Augusta Aug 21, 1908

Lilly Dow gbec b E Machias had:

a　Andrew E b E Machias Mch 11, 1897

Arthur A Dow gbed m Flora M Kelley b Addison.　Of children:

b　—— dau b Jonesport May 5, 1897

David Dow gbef, if of this family at all, might come from William gbb, Robert gbc or Daniel gbd, three untraced men whose names may not occur in order of birth.　He is known to us only from d rec of son. Presumably more than one child.　Rec gives him of Waite, Me, b Nova Scotia; wife Mary Blakely b N B.　Cf text and supplement sub adabbgaga.　Nelson Dow is therein given as identical.　Me rec are so defective that 18 years discrepancy is possible.　There is more than one untraced David Dow from Deer, Isl.　However, rec give a son to David and Mary:

a　Nelson A (also Nelson H in rec) b Waite 1844

Nelson A Dow gbefa, laborer of Waite, d Princeton Mch 21, 1916, ae 72-0-11, ten years a resident; m Josephine M Williams b Talmadge, d Feb 12, 1907, ae 55, 8 mos, dau of Hiram and Maggie (McFarland). At least 9 children:

a　Edward H b Waite 1875
b　Myrtie L d Dexter Feb 16, 1901, ae 25-7-7, unm
h　—— b Waite Feb 27, 1892

Edward H Dow gbefaa, laborer, then guide of Princeton, m Ada Belle Crosby of Princeton, ae 22, dau of Ephraim and Frances (Yates). Children, all b Princeton:

a　Vinal Curtis b July 30, 1903　　b　Doris E b Aug 29, 1904
c　—— son b May 30, 1909　　d　—— dau, his twin
e　Marguerite Williams b Sept 6, 1915
f　Winnifred b Aug 19, 1917　　g　Winona, twin

The following interesting family perhaps should not be considered Dow:

Hannah Dow, dau of Matthew of Amesbury, m 1651 Richard Harris.　This curious rec errs in at least two particulars.

There was a Fromabove Doue in England who had been in America and who owned land in Cambridge, Mass.　His brother-in-law, Mark Pierce of London, bequeathed in 1654 10s to Rebecca Doue and Ann

Doue, daughters of Fromabove. Presumably Fromabove was father of Matthew, who remained in America.

Matthew Doue was placed as a servant for four years, June 1, 1640, to John Blackleach of Salem, Mass. All his children were born in Salem, but, as has been frequently noted, an early town clerk of Amesbury-Salisbury was an enthusiast who entered any vital *datum* from anywhere, if he chanced to know one of the parties. He apparently knew Richard Harris. The children of Matthew:

a Hannah Elizabeth bap 10: 7: 1654. She was probably wife of Richard
    Harris, the right date possibly 1671
b Dorcas (dau of Matthew D Doue) bap 5: 8: 1656
c Bethiah bap 30: 3: 1658   d Daniel bap 20: 3: 1661
e Deborah bap 20: 3: 1666   f Matthew bap 10: 3: 1668

APPENDIX I

Census of 1790

The first Federal Census, that of 1790, aimed at little more than mere enumeration of the inhabitants. While parts of the records were destroyed by the British when they occupied Washington in the War of 1812, the losses in Dow names were few, if any. There are many heads of families recorded in this Book, which do not appear in the census, but this is probably chargeable to the inexperience or carelessness of the enumerators. The list has been well canvassed; nevertheless many are unidentified or doubtful. The letter key gives, at all events, the place where the identity is discussed. The sign ✻ denotes doubtful identity.

The census figures are in columns, the first being males of 16 or over. This includes, of course, the head of the family (except in case of a widow) and his grown sons. The second column is of males under 16; the third column is for females of all ages, including the mother (if living) and all daughters. The fourth column is for slaves (no concern to us, as no Dow of our lines ever owned a slave). Instead of ruled columns, we use the letters, a, b, c, d. Obviously, any one figuring in column b must have been born 1774 or later, any one in column a must have been born 1774 or earlier. We give the complete list of Dows with reference to the letter key, which is the equivalent of pagination throughout.

Jabez Dow	Standish, Me	1a, 2c	adkg
Joseph Dow	Standish, Me	1a, 2b, 2c	adkgd
Abner Dow	Standish, Me	2a, 2b, 2c	adkga
Henry Dow	Topsham, Me	1a, 5b, 3c	bbbfh
Jonathan Dow	Vassalborough, Me	1a, 1b, 1c	adbabb
Benjamin Dow	Vassalborough, Me	1a, 3b, 1c	bcbhb
Benjamin Dow, Jr	Vassalborough, Me	1a, 3b, 1c	bcbhbd
Jeremiah Dow	Little Falls, Me	2a, 2c	adgfb
Jeremiah Dow, Jr	Little Falls, Me	1a, 1b, 2c	adgfbe
Ebenezer Dow	Little Falls, Mc	1a, 2c	adgfd
Ebenezer Dow, Jr	Little Falls, Me	2a, 2b, 6c	adgfda
Samuel Dow	Little Falls, Me	1a, 2c	adgfcb
John Dow	Schumm Island, Me	1a, 4b, 3c	adabbg
Jonathan Dow	Machias, Me	2a, 3c	gaa
Moses Dow	Berwick, Me	1a, 3b, 3c	adbábg
Nathan Dow	Hancock Co, Me	1a, 1b, 3c	adabb
Nathan Dow, Jr	Hancock Co, Me	1a, 1b, 3c	adabbb
Peter Dow	Ballstown, Me	1a, 2b, 2c	bcbhd
Peter Dow, Jr	Ballstown, Me	1a, 2b, 2c	bcdhdb

Stephen Dowe	Machias, Me	1a	gaa
Job Dow	Goffstown, N H	4a, 1b, 7c	bcfif
Peter Dow	Goffstown, N H	3a, 4c	bcfifa
Aaron Dow	Henniker, N H	1a, 1b, 2c	adahc
Samuel Dow	Hampton, N H	2a, 2b, 4c	abbea
Joseph Dow	Hampton, N H	3a, 1b, 1c	abbee
Simon Dow	Hampton, N H	1a, 2b, 3c	abccb
Judah Dow	Hampton Falls, N H	3a, 1b, 3c	adaaaj
Zebulon Dow	Hampton Falls, N H	1a, 2b, 1c	adaij
Caleb Dow	Kensington, N H	1a, 1b, 4c	adked
Jabez Dow	Kensington, N H	1a, 1b, 3c	abdci
Jonathan Dow	Kensington, N H	3a, 3c	adadi
Abihal Dow	Kensington, N H	1a, 2b, 3c	abcfl
Nathan Dow	Kensington, N H	1a, 2b, 3c	abdce
Benjamin Dow	Kensington, N H	1a, 1c	abdceb
Reuben Dow	Kensington, N H	4a, 1b, 4c	adaaai
Joseph Dow	Kensington, N H	1a, 3b	adkdb
Josiah Dow	Kensington, N H	1a, 1c	adkd
Benjamin Dow	Kensington, N H	1a, 1b, 4c	adkdd
Jeremiah Dow	Salem, N H	4a, 1b, 6c	bcdbe
Oliver Dow	Salem, N H	3a, 2b, 4c	bcdeb
Amos Dow	Salem, N H	1a, 1c	bcdbd
Thomas Dow	Salem, N H	1a, 4b, 5c	bcfica
Abraham Dow	Salem, N H	2a, 2b, 2c	bcfic
Sarah Dow	Sandown, N H	1b, 2c	ahbx ✳
Ela Dow	Sandown, N H	2a, 1b, 3c	ahbcf
David Dow	Seabrook, N H	3a, 1b, 4c	adggb
Abraham Dow	Seabrook, N H	2a, 2b, 3c	adhch
Benjamin Dow	Seabrook, N H	3a, 1b, 5c	adhcd
Jacob Dow	Seabrook, N H	1a, 3b, 1c	adgxf
Moses Dow	Seabrook, N H	1a, 3b, 6c	adaie
Winthrop Dow	Seabrook, N H	1a, 1c	adhab
Winthrop Dow	Seabrook, N H	1a, 4c	adha
Zebulon Dow	Seabrook, N H	3a, 2b, 2c	adaij ✳

No Zebulon known except adaij and ahbaaa. We guess this Zebulon some other name.

Josiah Dow	Seabrook, N H	1a, 2b, 3c	adhad
Levi Dow	Seabrook, N H	1a, 1b, 2c	adaii
Israel Dow	Seabrook, N H	1a, 3b, 1c	adkea
Robert Dow	Seabrook, N H	1a, 4b, 2c	adgda
Nathan Dow	Seabrook, N H	1a, 2c	adggba
Asa Dow	Windham, N H	2a, 6b, 4c	bcded
Samuel Dow	Epping, N H	1a, 2b, 3c	adgcac
Daniel Dow	Epping, N H	3a, 3b, 5c	ahbab
Josiah Dow	Epping, N H	2a, 1b, 5c	ahbae
John Dow	Epping, N H	3a, 3c	adaab

Winthrop Dow	Epping, N H	2a, 4b, 6c	adadab
Zebulon Dow	Epping, N H	1a, 1b, 4c	ahbaaa
Benjamin Dow	Epping, N H	1a, 3c	ahbabc
Beniah Dow	Epping, N H	2a, 3c	adada
Perry Dow	Antrim, N H	1a, 1b, 5c	bcdbad
Benjamin Dow	Bedford, N H	3a, 2b, 5c	bbbff
Evan Dow	Deering, N H	2a, 2b, 3c	bcdeaa
Stephen Dow	Deering, N H	1a, 1b, 4c	bcdeab
Benjamin Dow	Gilmanton, N H	2a, 2b, 3c	adaaba ✳
Benjamin Dow, Jr	Gilmanton, N H		adaabac ✳

These identities discussed in situ.

Capt Noah Dow	Gilmanton, N H	1a, 3b, 3c	ahbac
Nathaniel Dow	Gilmanton, N H	1a, 2b, 3c	adaabc
			(ahbacb, supplement)
Jonathan Dow	Gilmanton, N H	2a, 3b, 4c	adabi ✳
Jonathan Dow, Jr.	Gilmanton, N H	3a, 3b, 3c	adadi
Jonathan Dow, 3rd	Gilmanton, N H	1a, 1c	ahbacb

To distinguish between the Jonathans seems impossible.

Eliphalet Dow	Sanbornton, N H	2a, 1b, 3c	ahbaba

Doubtless error for Lyford Dow.

Chandler Dow	Sanbornton, N H	1a	ahbabd
Winthrop Dow	Weare, N H	2a, 1b, 3c	adhah
David Dow	Weare, N H	2a, 3b, 4c	adhaf
Jedediah Dow	Weare, N H	2a, 3b, 4c	adhcc
Jonathan Dow	Weare, N H	5a, 1b, 6c	adhcb
Timothy Dow	Concord, N H	1a, 4b, 4c	bcbebb
Ebenezer Dow	Concord, N H	4a, 1b, 2c	ahbg
Ebenezer Dow	Meredith, N H	3a, 1b, 5c	adadh
Samuel Dow	Bow, N H	1a, 1b, 2c	aedaaa ✳
Richard Dow	Bow, N H	2a, 4c	bcdec
Solomon Dow	Bow, N H	1a, 1b, 1c	bcdeca
Emersay Dow	Bow, N H	1a, 2c	aedaa

This thinly disguises Amasa.

John Dow	Bow, N H	1a, 2c	adgcad ✳

An unplaced John.

Samuel Dow	Plaistow, N H	2a, 1b, 2c	bcbeb
Samuel Dow, Jr	Plaistow, N H	2a, 2b, 3c	bcbebc
Joshua Dow	Plaistow, N H	2a, 2b, 5c	bcbeg
Ezekiel Dow	Plaistow, N H	1a, 3b, 6c	bcbeh
Peter Dow	Plaistow, N H	1a, 1c	bcbh
Isaac Dow	Rye, N H	1a, 4b, 4c	abceab
James Dow	Rye, N H	1a, 1c	abceae
James Dow	Atkinson, N H	1a, 1b, 2c	bcfii
Lucy Dow	Pembroke, N H	1c	adai ✳

She herself is unknown.

Jesse Dow	Pembroke, N H	2a, 1b, 3c	adaia

226

Phineas Dow	Pembroke, N H	1a, 3b, 2c	adaig
Jonathan Dow	Pembroke, N H	1a, 3b, 2c	
Jeremiah Dow	Pembroke, N H	2a, 2b, 5c	

We cannot place these members of adai line who lived in Pittsfield.

John Dow	Pembroke, N H	1a, 4b, 6c	adaie
Jonathan Dow	Lee, N H	1a, 2b, 2c	adgfb
Jesse Dow	Fishersfield, N H	1a, 4b, 2c	ahbch
Perley Dow	Chichester, N H	1a, 2b, 3c	adgcae
Joseph Dow	Chichester, N H	1a, 2b, 2c	adgcad
Moses Dow	New Durham, N H	1a, 1c	adgfg
Levi Dow	New Hampton, N H	2a, 1b, 6c	abbege
Lemuel Dow	Hanover, N H	1a, 4c	ahgf
Lemuel Dow, Jr	Hanover, N H	1a, 1c	ahgfb
London Dow	Hanover, N H	5d	✳

No such man. Five slaves but not himself!!

Salmon Dow	Hanover, N H	1a, 2c	ahgfd
Moses Dow	Haverhill, N H	4a, 2b, 10c	bcfih
Reuben Dow	Hollis, N H	3a, 2c	bcdea
Richard Dow	Wakefield, N H	1a, 5b, 2c	adkde
Simon Dow	No Hampton, N H	2a, 3c	abccb
Simon Dow	Newmarket, N H	2a, 3c	abccdg
Thomas Dow	Enfield, N H	1a, 3c	✳

Probably not a Dow at all.

Gideon Dow	Plainfield, Vt	2a, 1b, 4c	adggd
James Dow	Leicester, Vt	4a, 1b, 3c	adace
Moses Dow	Leicester, Vt	1a, 5b, 2c	adacea
Thomas Dow	Danville, Vt	1a, 1c	ahbcab
Thomas Dow	Danville, Vt	3a, 4c	ahbca
Dow & Glines	Wheelock, Vt	2a	ahbcab
Nehimiah Dow	Salisbury, Mass	1a, 1b, 2c	adaaaa
Samuel Dow	Salisbury, Mass	1a, 1b, 2c	adfcc
Aaron Dow	Salisbury, Mass	1a, 3b, 4c	adkfb
Joseph Dow	Salisbury, Mass	2a, 2b, 4c	adgxc
Henry Dow	Nantucket, Mass	3a, 6c	adaaaf
Isaiah Dow	Western, Mass	2a, 1b, 3c	adacf
Isaiah Dow, Jr	Western, Mass	1a, 2b, 1c	adacfc
John Dow	Rowley, Mass	1a, 1b, 4c	adgff
Lydia Dow	Haverhill, Mass	3c	da
Moses Dow	Roxbury, Mass	1a, 1b, 3c	✳

Unknown. Can he be ahbb?

Samuel Dow	Chelmsford, Mass	2a, 2b, 3c	bcbcb
Samuel Dow	Boston, Mass	1a, 1b, 4c	adkgb
Jeremiah Dowe	Manchester, Mass	1a, 3c	ahfc
Jeremiah Dowe	Manchester, Mass	1a, 2b, 3c	ahfca
William Dowe	Manchester, Mass	1a, 1b, 2c	ahfch
Michael Dowe	Manchester, Mass	1a, 2c	ahfa

Jacob Dow	Manchester, Mass	1a, 1c	ahfci
John Dowe	Beverly, Mass	1a, 2c	ahfch ✗
Martha Dowe	Newburyport, Mass	2c	?
Miss Dow	Boston, Mass	4c	?
Stephen Dow	Marblehead, Mass	1a, 1b, 5c	?

No clue to these three.

Samuel Dow	Smithfield, R I	1a, 1c	ahgdb
Abel Dow	Ashford, Conn	1a, 1b, 2c	ahcbb
Cyrus Dow	Ashford, Conn	4a, 1b, 2c	ahcba
Abel Dow	Ashford, Conn	1a, 1b, 2c	duplicate
Benjamin Dow	Voluntown, Conn	2a, 1b, 3c	ahch
Ebenezer Dow	Voluntown, Conn	3a, 1b, 3c	ahcf
Nathan Dow	Voluntown, Conn	2a, 2c	ahchb
Ephraim Dow	Coventry, Conn	1a, 4b, 1c	ahgc
Levy Dow	Coventry, Conn	1a, 4b, 2c	ahgd
Calvin Dow	Coventry, Conn	1a	ahgi
Ephraim Dow, 2nd	Coventry, Conn	1a, 3b, 3c	ahgce
Humphus Dow	Coventry, Conn	2a, 2b, 5c	ahgh
Peletiah Dow	Coventry, Conn	1a, 7c	ahgg
John Dowe	Plainfield, Conn	4a, 1b, 6c	ahda
Samuel Dow	Plainfield, Conn	2a, 1b, 1c	ahdf
Aaron Dow	New York, N Y	3a, 3c	ahcg
Philip Dow	Huntington, N Y	1a, 1c	c
Jacob Dow	Huntington, N Y	1a, 2b, 2c	c
William Dowe	Canaan, N Y	2a, 1c	fa
Elijah Dow	Northern Liberties,Pa	1a, 1b, 2c	?
Samuel Dow	Philadelphia, Pa.	18a, 5b, 7c	

This name in the list of lodgers in a boarding house.

| Peter Dow | Fairfax Co, Va | 1a | |
| Robert Dow | Camden Dist, S C | 3a, 5b, 2c, 3d | ? |

Considered in Supplement. Was not a member of any family treated in this Book.

APPENDIX II

Revolutionary Rosters

In one form or another almost every State has issued volumes of data of its Revolutionary soldiers. New Hampshire has four very large volumes issued as a report of the State Adjutant, covering the Colonial as well as Revolutionary activities. The Massachusetts Rosters are much more voluminous and include its (then) province of Maine. While these have been carefully edited, they are mostly made up of enlistment rolls and pay rolls from time to time. These are necessarily very incomplete. They very seldom follow any career upon a promotion. For example: Major Thomas Dow of Salem appears as a corporal and no higher. Major Joseph Dow of Kensington appears as Lieut, but only in consequence of signing a payroll. In only a very few instances is there some description of an individual, some clue to his identity.

Moreover, the place of a man's enlistment may have no connection with his home. After the first enthusiasm at the Battle of Lexington, enlistments were made with some deliberation. An enthusiast looked over the field to find where a bounty was offered higher than in his home town. Naturally, he wished to provide as much as possible for the family left behind, if not for his personal gain. For this reason an Epping Dow enlisted in Haverhill, Mass, and an Andover, Mass, man went all the way to Gilmanton, N H.

Actual Revolutionary service was, no doubt, performed by twice as many as is shown in the various rosters. No roster, for example, contains the Epping company organized early in 1775 by Capt Clark. There were hundreds of companies formed by interior towns, partly as a preparation against possible invasion, which never got to the front and never figure.

It should be needless to remark that the proportion of Dows on these rolls which are identified is small. One is seldom absolutely sure of identities without the backing of family records or collateral evidence.

MASSACHUSETTS, including MAINE

Aaron Dow (akkfb)

Private at Winter Hill, Nov 11, 1777-Apr 4, 1778, Capt Samuel Huse, Col Jacob Gerrish

Abner Dow (adkga)

Enlisted (4th sgt) Portland May 12, 1775, Capt David Braddish; mustered out July 8, 1775. Rec as 3rd sgt. Sixth quartermaster, Capt Abner Lowell co of matross Falmouth, Jan 1, 1777-Mch 31, 1777. Lieut 34 mos from Jan 1, 1777, Col Timothy Bigelow's 15th reg; Capt from Oct, 1779; receipted West Point 1780

Daniel Dow (ahbab)

Private Haverhill, 5th reg, Capt Jeremiah Gilman, Col John Nixon, Aug 1, 1775; at Winter Hill Dec, 1775; two re-enlistments; disch Nov 30, 1777

David Dow (untraced, probably untraceable) see bcdg

Private St Johns, Capt Jabez West, Col Jonathan Eddy, company raised in Cumberland, N S; receipted Boston 1776 for 1 mo, 5 days

Ebenezer Dow (ahbg, but only a small part of his service)

Receipted 1 1-2 days Apr 19, 1775, Capt Joshua Holt 4th Andover co; sgt under Capt Samuel Johnson, Col Wigglesworth; re-enlisted 1777; receipted for travel allowance from Albany

Elijah Dow (adaaah, identity absolute)

Salisbury, 5 feet, 7, ruddy, 5 mos, 27 days, Capt Frothingham's artillery

Enoch Dow (bcdgd?)

Private, Winter Hill Nov 10, 1777-Apr 4, 1778, Capt Samuel Huse, Col Jacob Gerrish. Some Enoch Dow received £ 10 bounty for enlistment at Salisbury

Evan Dow (bcdeaa, absolutely certain)

Private Capt Reuben Dow (bcdea) 2 mos, 22 days from May 1, 1775; reported sick Oct 6, 1775

Follinsbee Dow (bcbhda, identity certain)

Private 26th reg, Capt Thomas Mighill, Col Loamma Baldwin, 14 days from May, 1776

Henry Dow (bbbfh?)

Private Feb-May, 1776, Capt Thomas Coggswell, Col Baldwin

Isaac Dow (Portsmouth, N H, presumably d line)

Seaman, exchanged, Halifax to Boston, Oct 8, 1778

Jabez Dow (abdci, absolutely certain)

Of Kensington, Capt William Hudson Ballard, Col James Frye, June 8-Dec 13, 1775. See in place for details

Jabez Dow (adkge, certain)

Private, 8 mos, 23 days from Feb 29, 1776, Seacoast service, Capt Benjamin Hooper; re-enlisted Aug 11, 1777

Jeremiah Dow (ahfca)

Manchester, 5 feet, 6, dark complexion, 6 mos, 3 days from Sept 19, 1775, Capt Joseph Whipple; re-enlisted for period of war; serving 1779 in Worcester Co

Jeremiah Dow (bcbhi?)

Under Capt Kimball, taken prisoner Ft Washington Nov 16, 1776

Jeremiah Dow (adgfb?)

Salisbury, in service July 12, 1781

Jesse Dow (ahbch, certain)

Blacksmith of Methuen, ae 21, 5 feet, 10, dark, enlisted June 6,

1775, 27th reg, Capt John Ford, Col Ebenezer Bridge; service 3 mos, 10 days. Re-enlisted Sept 25, 1775

John Dow (untraced, probably untraceable)

St Johns, N B, Capt Jabez West, Col Jonathan Eddy, Nov 14, 1776-Dec 16, 1776. Possibly brother of David (see above)

John Dow (bcbcaa)

Haverhill, minute man marched Apr 19, 1775, Capt James Sawyer, Col James Frye; re-enlisted; was at Battle of Trenton; continuous service to Mch 17, 1779

John Dow (untraced) ahf line

Of Marblehead, 6 feet, dark, ae 25, ship carpenter and officer of marines, brig Prospect, Capt John Vesey, June 20, 1781

John Dow (possibly adgff)

Newbury, private, ae 23, 5 feet, 9, dark, 5 mos, 26 days from July 7, 1780

John Dow (unknown)

Newburyport, private Aug 10-Nov 2, 1781, Capt Joshua French, Col Enoch Putnam

John Dow (adabbg?)

Corporal, expedition against Majorbagaduce Aug 1-15, 1779, Capt Nathaniel Fales

Joseph Dow (adkgd, certain)

Falmouth, private, Capt Benjamin Hooper; first entry Oct 2, 1776; possibly not identical with Joseph at Andover Mch 24, 1780

Joseph Dow (adacg)

New Braintree, corporal, 3 days, 1777, Capt Thomas Whipple, Col James Converse

Moses Dow (unknown) (cf 1790 census of Roxbury) ahf line

Morristown or Manchester, private 3 mos, 14 days from Dec 1, 1776, Capt Joseph Hooker, Col Williams

Nathan Dow (unknown)

Danvers, ae 28, 5 feet, 8, ruddy, July 9, 1780-Jan 6, 1781

Nathan Dow (or Nathaniel)

Woburn, private 7th co, Col Thomas Nixon, Feb 14, 1777-May 4, 1778; in service Mch 3, 1779

Nathan Dow (probably adabb)

Private, expedition against Majorbagaduce, Aug 3-27, 1779

Nathan Dow

Danvers, ae 24, 5 feet, 8, Aug 19, 1779; disch Apr 10, 1780

Nathan Dow (ahci?)

Artillery matross Nov 27, 1780-Apr, 1781, Capt Buckland, Col Cram; was at Verplanck's Point

Nathaniel Dow (perhaps Drown)

Engaged for Uxbridge, in artillery, ae 19, 5 feet, 9, July 9, 1780

Nehimiah Dow (adaaaac)

> Ae 18, 5 feet, 6, reported deserted Sept 25, 1781; but on pay roll Oct, 1781

Reuben Dow (bcdea)

> Capt May 25, 1775, 3 mos, 14 days; wounded at Bunker Hill but reported present at close of battle

Robert Dow (adgda, certain)

> Salisbury, at Cambridge private Capt Stephen Merrill, Col Caleb Cushing, Apr 20-Nov 13 (and later), 1775

Sampson Dow. Possibly a Doe of Oyster River

> Of Vassalborough or Dover, corporal, Col Gamaliel Bradford, Mch 3, 1777-Mch 8, 1780

Samuel Dow (adkf)

> At Bunker Hill. Perhaps identical with Samuel Dow, of Dunstable, corporal 27th reg, Capt Ebenezer Bancroft, Col Ebenezer Bridge, July 24, 1775, 3 mos, 10 days

Samuel Dow (adkgc)

> Falmouth, May 15, 1775-Aug 11, 1775; matross 4th gunner; quartermaster at Boston

Samuel Dow

> Of Salisbury, private Apr 20, 1775, Capt Stephen Merrill: in service Nov 20, 1776

Samuel Dow

> Private, on guard Cambridge May 15, 1775, Maj Loammi Baldwin

Samuel Dow Jr

> Salisbury, 3 1-2 days Apr 20, 1775

Seward Dow (ahfg)

> Private, Cambridge and Winter Hill 4 mos, 26 days from Apr, 1778; disch Dec 14, 1778, Capt Sam Huse, Col Jacob Gerrish

Simeon Dow (bbbeb) (ahbcf?)

> Methuen, 2 days Apr 20, 1775; 40 days Oct 2, 1777

Solomon Dow (bcbcx)

> Malden, private Capt Nailer Hatch, Col William Bond, 37th reg, Oct 6, 1775

Solomon Dow

> Seaman, exchanged Boston from Halifax Oct 8, 1778

Thomas Dow (bcfica)

> Atkinson, private Capt Jeremiah Gilman, 3 mos, 19 days, from Apr 29, 1775

Thomas Dow (ahbca)

> See service *sub* ahbca

William Dow (ahfec)

> Manchester, private, Capt Richard Dodge, Lieut Col Loammi Baldwin, May 1, 1775-June, 1776

William Dow
Private Oct, 1775, for one year, Capt Jonathan Drown
William Dow
Enlisted Dec 15, 1775, Capt James Perry
Jabez Dow (adkge)
Falmouth, private 2 days 1775
Nathan Dowe (probably identical with above)
Danvers, corporal 3rd artillery, Capt Samuel Shaw, Nov 27, 1780, for period of the war
Simeon Dowe (presumably bbbeb) see above
Private, Capt John Bedwell, 2 mos, 27 days, from Apr 2, 1778

NEW HAMPSHIRE

Benjamin Dow (adaabd) see below
Five days from July 1, 1777, turned back on orders, Capt Duncan, Lieut Col Moses Kelley
Benjamin Dow (abccdf)
Received £ 4-10-0 for enlistment, Kensington; in service 1781; received $182.60 allowance for depreciation of currency, Col Joseph Cilley
Benjamin Dow (adaabd) (Noah Dow ahbac in same company)
Started 1777 for Ticonderoga, Capt Nathaniel Ambrose, Col Welch of Moultonborough
Daniel Dow (bcdih?)
Plaistow; Capt Ezekiel Gile, Col Stephen Peabody, mustered out R I Dec 30, 1778, service 11 mos, 16 days
Daniel Dow
Plaistow; Col Gilman, July 15, 1779
Daniel Dow (surely not identical)
Mustered out R I Aug, 1778, service 23 days, Capt Nathan Brown, Col Jacob Gale
Daniel Dow (ahbab)
Corporal, Col Hercules Mooney, mustered out R I 1779, service 5 mos, 25 days. Received bounty Kingston July, 1779
Daniel Dow
Sgt, Capt John Emerson, Col Thomas Bartlett, at West Point 1780, service 3 mos, 17 days
Ebenezer Dow (ahbg)
Sgt, 3 mos, 27 days, Sept, 1777, Saratoga expedition, Capt Porter Kimball, Col Stephen Evans. He was at Lexington, Quebec, and elsewhere, with three or more enlistments
Ebenezer Dow (adadh)
Husbandman of Epping, Capt John Norris, Col Poor, paid June 15, 1775, 2 mos, 15 days; paid $4 forever coat; with Winthrop Dow

and Zebulon Dow, Capt Samuel Gordon, Col Tash, in N Y State, each receipting Sept 20, 1776, for £ 8-10-00

Ebenezer Dow (probably ahbg)

Drew pay £ 6-13-3, Col Gilman, Sept 12, 1777

Ela Dow (ahbcd)

Private, Capt Robert Crawford, Great Island Nov 5, 1775; of Sandown, enlisted for Saratoga Sept, 1777, Capt Robert Collins; receipted for £ 9-0-8; selectman of Sandown 1781

Elijah Dow

Strafford Co (apparently error), Capt Piper for defense of Portsmouth July 14, 1780

Enoch Dow (see bcdgd)

In an unspecified list 1780. Probably identical, Enoch Dow received £60 bounty Hampton Falls 1779, enlistment one year. Enoch Dow enlisted for Canada July 16, 1776, Capt William Harper, Col Isaac Wyman (this company was organized in Haverhill)

Evan Dow (bcdeaa)

Was with his father, Capt Reuben, at Bunker Hill; six months later reported sick; disch R I Aug, 1778, Capt Daniel Emerson, Col Moses Nichols; receipted for £ 11-0-10

Isaac Dow (d line?)

Private, Capt Richard Dow, Great Island Nov 5, 1775

Isaac Dow

Under Capt Ezekiel Gile, Col Stephen Peabody, mustered out R I Dec 30, 1778; receipted for 5 mos, 29 days

Isaac Dow

In company of Capt Jacob Webster, 1775

James Dow

Second N H inf, Capt Smith Emerson, for N Y State

Jabez Dow (abdci)

Kensington, enlisted for three years, Capt Robinson, Col Nathan Hale; reported deserted N Y City; 1775 in Col James Frye, Mass reg; allowed 1780 $182.60 for depreciation of currency, in 5th co 1780, Col James Reid

Jeremiah Dow (abccd)

Receipted for 3 mos Sept, 1775, Capt Henry Dearborn, Col John Stark

Jeremiah Dow (John Dow and Richard Dow in same co)

Under Capt Henry Elkins for defense of Portsmouth Nov, 1775. Unable to read or write, he receipted with "his mark."

Jeremiah Dow (bcdbe)

Ensign under Capt Richard Dow, Great Island Nov 5, 1775; Capt Apr, 1777; served with distinction, N Y State

Jeremiah Dow

Col Abraham Drake's N H Militia, receipted Dec 1, 1777, for £ 3-10-8

John Dow (abbeac)

Under Capt Henry Elkins, defense of Portsmouth Nov, 1775

John Dow

Capt Moody, Col Badger, N Y State 1776, receipted for £ 8-13-4

John Dow (of Poplin)

Received £ 40 bounty and travel expense, Col Gilman, July 19, 1779

John Dow (of Gilmanton) (ahbgb)

Enlisted for three years, Capt Bell, Col Badger

John Dow (of or near Loudon) of Epping?

Served 2 mos, 6 days, Capt Sias, Col Thomas Stickney

John Dow (adgff?)

Under Col Worthen, disch R I 1779, service 5 mos, 27 days

John Dow

Second co, Col Joseph Cilley, allowed $25.20 for depreciation of currency

John Dow

Enlisted for three mos Concord July 7, 1780, Capt Kinsman, Col Stickney

John Dow

Ar West Point 1780, Capt Ebenezer Webster, Col Moses Nichols

Jonathan Dow

In co of Capt Rand Mch 4, 1776

Jonathan Dow (abbeg)

Enlisted July, 1775, Capt Henry Dearborn, Col John Stark; paid in Sept for 3 mos, 3 days. Jeremiah Dow in same company

Jonathan Dow

Served 3 mos, 15 days, 1780, expedition to West Point, Capt Timothy Emerson, Col Thomas Bartlett

Jonathan Dow (adgfc)

Of Gilmanton (Nathaniel Dow and Benjamin Dow in same company) enlisted Kingston 1780. All three receipted West Point July, 1780, for half pint of rum

Joshua Dow (bcbeg)

Second N H reg, Capt Smith Emerson, for N Y State (James Dow in same company)

Joshua Dow

Of Plaistow (two Samuel Dows in same company) under Capt Ezekiel Gile, 1779

Josiah Dow (ahbae)

In Capt Clark's Epping Co 1775; served 26 days, R I, Aug 5, 1778, Capt Sias, Col Moses Nichols

Lemuel Dow (ahgf)

Started for Ticonderoga 1777, Capt Jonathan Chase. He served 73 days in Vt

Joseph Dow (adkdb)

Husbandman Kensington, ae 28, Capt Winthrop Rowe, June 3, 1775; promoted to corporal; $4 extra for overcoat; asst muster master, Capt Joseph Parsons, Col Senter, R I, 1777; promoted to Lieut

Joseph Dow

Capt Nathan Sanborn, 3 mos, 3 days, from Sept 8, 1777

Joseph Dow (adgcad?)

Of Chichester, enlisted Capt Sias, Col Dame, Sept 9, 1779; some Joseph Dow pensioner 1840

Joseph Dow

Discharged R I Aug, 1778, Capt Moses Leavitt, Col Moses Nichols, service 26 days

Moses Dow

Winthrop Dow of Epping in same company, Capt Nathan Brown, Col Nat Gale, disch R I Aug, 1778, service 23 days

Moses Dow

Of Exeter, paid bounty for a soldier, he himself not being liable for service

Nathaniel Dow (adaabc)

Of Gilmanton, received £ 10-5-6, Capt Moody, Col Badger, for N Y State, 1776; receipted in Crown Point campaign for £ 36-8-0. In same company with Benjamin Dow enlisted at Kingston for Worcester campaign July 6, 1780

Oliver Dow

Private, Capt Joshua Bayley, Col Kelly, disch R I Aug, 1778, service 21 days

Reuben Dow (adaaai)

Disch R I Aug, 1778, Capt Daniel Emerson, Col Moses Nichols, service 28 days

Richard Dow (bcde)

In company of Capt John Goffe, Dover 1746; capt at Great Island Nov 5, 1775. In this company were Ensign Jeremiah Dow, Sgt Asa Dow, fifer Percy Dow, private Isaac Dow

Richard Dow (adkde)

In Capt Henry Elkins company for defense of Portsmouth Nov, 1775

Richard Dow Jr (bcdec)

In Londonderry or Nesmith company, Col Joshua Wingate, for expedition against Canada, July 9, 1776

Noah Dow (ahbac)

Of Gilmanton, ensign 12th company, Col Badger, 1776; started for Ticonderoga 1777, all turning back, as not needed

Oliver Dow (bcdeb)
Second Lieut, Col Thomas Stickney, July 9, 1776
Phineas Dow
Private, received £ 9-18-0 and £ 6-8-0 for billet
Samuel Dow (bcbeb)
Of Plaistow, in Capt Gile's company Oct, 1777; Samuel Jr and Joshua Dow in same company
Solomon Dow (bcdeca was then 14)
Enlisted June 15, 1780, Capt Samuel Paine, Maj Benjamin Whitcomb for defense of western frontier
Stephen Dow
Receipted for £ 6, 1776, Capt William Read, Col Nahum Baldwin
Stephen Dow
Started for Ticonderoga 1777, Capt Daniel Emerson, service 3 days
Stephen Dow (bcdeab)
Of Hollis, started for Ticonderoga 1777; served 5 days; possibly identical with above
Stephen Dow
Under Capt William Barron, Col Nichols, West Point 1780
Thomas Dow (ahbca)
Under Capt John Calfe, Col T Bartlett, Sept, 1776
Thomas Dow
Of Plaistow, enlisted for 8 mos, May 7, 1777
Thomas Dow (bcdig)
Corporal of Plaistow, Capt Ezekiel Gile, Col Stephen Peabody, . disch R I, Dec 30, 1778; service 10 mos, 24 days
Thomas Dow
Enlisted 1777, Capt Benjamin Stone; received travel allowance to Charlestown £ 1-6-8; died same year
Winthrop Dow (adada)
With Zebulon Dow in Capt Clark's Epping company 1775; enlisted from Epping; paid £ 8-10-0 to Sept 20, 1776, for N Y State service, Capt Daniel Gordon, Col Tash (Ebenezer and Zebulon Dow in same company); mustered out R I, Aug, 1778, Capt Nathan Brown, Col Jacob Gile; service 23 days
Zebulon Dow (ahbaaa)
In Capt Clark's Epping company 1775; under Capt Daniel Gordon 1776; drew pay for a month, Saratoga 1777
Benjamin Nudd (akebc)
Enlisted private for Stillwater Sept 8, 1777, Capt Nicholas Rawlings, Col Abraham Drake; entered as deserter Oct 10, 1777
David Nudd (akebbc)
Aug 29, 1782, four men reported as deserted, enlisted to fill four vacancies, Capt Titus Salter. There is no rec of any such company. If David Nudd existed, he would be akebbc or akebca

James Nudd (akebd)

Private, Capt Moses Leavitt, Col Moses Nichols, disch R I Aug, 1778; served 25 days

John Nudd (akebe)

Enlisted Hampton Falls Mch 30, 1759, at half pay for Canadian campaign, same company as Ebenezer Dow adgf and Gideon Dow adgg

John Nudd   (probably also akebe)

Corporal, Pierce Island from Nov 5, 1775, Capt Nathaniel Hobbs, then Capt Moses Leavitt, Col Abraham Drake; served Stillwater 3 mos, 18 days from Sept, 1777. Barely possible that there were two Johns, one being son of Samuel Nudd akebb

Samuel Nudd   (akebb and akebba)

That there were two Samuels is proven by the fact that two receipted at the same time for $4 for an overcoat, and the original enlistments are June 26, 1775, for one and June 27, 1775, for the other. The elder was under Capt Richard Shortridge, Col Enoch Poor. One or the other, was, Nov 5, 1775, under Capt Thomas Berry, and at Pierce Island Nov 25, 1775, Capt Henry Elkins

Samuel Nudd (akebba)

His enlistment June 27, 1780, gives him of Greenland, ae 25, 5 feet, 7, dark. He or his father appears as enlisting Greenland July 4, 1780. He receipted West Point July, 1780, for a pint of rum and a pound of sugar

Simon Nudd (akeca)

Altho always known by his title Cornet, the Rev Rolls give him no service; he was one of the Hampton military committee from June 14, 1775

Thomas Nudd (akebbb)

That he is not akebf is proved by his enlistment from No Hampton July 29, 1780, ae 18. Thomas Nudd appears under Lieut Col Dearborn enlisting Apr 4, 1780; disch Dec 30, 1780; but it seems impossible that there should be two Thomas Nudds

William Nudd (akebba)

Got £30 bounty Hampton Falls July 19, 1779. In 1st militia June 27, 1780, he is given as ae 18, 5 feet, 5, dark, of Greenland. He was in the 3rd militia, Capt Samuel Runnels, Col Hercules Mooney, six months from July 5, 1779

INDEX

THIS index includes, errors and omissions excepted, the name of every person mentioned in the Book, including those to whom any incidental reference is made. Its form is unusual and, the Author believes, is the most informatory and most labor-saving of any ever used in a large genealogy. As the arrangement of the Book is alphabetical, the letter symbols are equivalent to pagination.

Let us suppose, for example, that a reader wishes to find some John Dow. There are about 200 such in this Book. If it had been indexed by pages, he would have to begin with the very first reference and wade along until luck brought him to the right John Dow. Most genealogies are arranged with a number to each person. If this were done here, the reader would have the same blind search to come upon his desired John Dow. In our system the index tells him at a glance that a particular John Dow is of the seventh generation, is the first born child of a 2nd born, of a 3rd born, of a 1st born, of a 6th born, of the 2nd born of Henry Dow, immigrant of 1637.

Now, that is a great deal of information to be packed into seven letters, is it not? It may require as much as 60 seconds to learn the method and *unless that method is learned, the whole index is absolutely useless.*

To each name in this Book a letter symbol is attached. The number of letters in each symbol is the number of the generation of its possessor. The twelfth generation of Dow is now on earth. The first letter of each symbol denotes the original Dow immigrant. This Book includes seven such:

    a   Henry Dow, immigrant of 1637 to Watertown;

    b   Thomas Dow, to Newbury 1639;

    c   Samuel Dow, to Hartford 1660;

    d   John Dow, to Portsmouth by 1693;

    e   Lieut. James Dow, Phila about 1750;

    f   the line of an immigrant to N. Y. about 1750;

    g   the line of a Scotch family to Nova Scotia about 1750.

Each of these sections is alphabetically placed.

The first born of Henry Dow, immigrant, is aa. The 2nd child of Henry Dow's 2nd child is abb.

The 5th child of the 4th of the 3rd of Thomas Dow, immigrant, must be bcde. Conversely, bcde can be no other than the 5th child of the 4th child of the 3rd child of Thomas. If a symbol has eight letters, its owner must be a member of the eighth generation. Look for him, then, in his alphabetical place.

The letter symbol attached to every one born a Dow attaches also to his wife (or her husband) and to every person incidentally mentioned in connection with that particular Dow.

Be alphabetical. Remember that bcdbax is placed before bcdbba.

The letter x or letter y often occurs within a symbol. This denotes that we do not know the order of birth of the person to whom the symbol belongs. Unknown quantities are denoted by x or y since algebra was invented. But, x and y are always herein put in true alphabetical position.

Suppose that the name we wish to look up is Jones Dow bcfiean. We look there, but for his birth, his brothers and sisters, we naturally look for the father of Jones Dow,—of course bcfica; and you will find him in true alphabetical order.

We may wish to inspect James Dow aba. As this lad died young, he had no independent career and gets no mention except as son of his parents,—ab. Few persons who died unmarried have independent articles devoted to them.

Immediately following this index is a supplementary chapter, followed by its own index. This chapter covers all data received too late for insertion in the body of the Book.

Preceding symbols beginning with an (a) are occasionally to be found, some beginning with an (x). This is to denote the English ancestors of Henry Dow, immigrant, and they in the Book precede the narrative of Henry Dow, who was both (a) and (xaaf). Concisely, Henry was the 6th born of 1st born of 1st born of John Dow d 1544, whose parentage is unknown. Henry Dow practically adopted his step-son, Thomas Nudd. For convenience we treat of him just after the family of Henry Dow himself; we give to Thomas Nudd the symbol (ak).

ABBOT—ACKERMAN

ABBOT, Asaph ahbgeg
David ahbgf
Ebenezer T bcdedde
Edward Wilson adaceafgb
Esther M bcbebbcb
Jacob bcdedde
James W adaceafgb
Maria Florence adaceafgb
Mary K bcdedgb
Mercy wife bcbebbcb
Reuben bcbebbcb
ABBOTT Ann Maria ahbaacxca
Annie Louise bcbhddfaca
Charles M bcbebigd
Elizabeth adacglb
Emily ahbcaa
Franklin A bcbebbea

Hannah adggdci
James bcfifd
Jacob Rev adkdbc, adkecf
John A bcbhddfaca
Lucy bcbhddkbx
Lydia Ann ahbaaheab
Maria bcdedggb
Mary A bcbebcdac
Mary S bcbebbea
Olive adkeb
ACHERSON John bcdgdaiie
Tressa bcdgdaiie
ACKERMAN Augustus D abccgael
Charles P abccgacl
Charlotte A abccgael
Emma F abceabdbb
Eva adiagbbabc

780

Freda adaigbbabc
George H abccgacl
J Warren abccgacl
James O abccgacl
John M abccgacl
Mary J abccgacj
Meshech S abccgacl
Volney adaigbbabc
ACKERS Arthur bcdgdafecb
ACKLEY Abbie J gaaxaxm
Alma gei
Alma B gbai
Lilla P gbakf
Nathan gbai
ADAMS Abigail adkc
Addie abbeacbda
Agnes L adgxfaacbc
Alice adggdcc
Almeda bcdgdaacj
Archelaus adkc
Archelaus Jr adkc
Betsey adkc
Byron bcdgdaacj
Caroline Goodwin ahgcheba
Charles bcdgdaacj
Charles E adgxfbeb
Claude E adgxfaacbc, adgxbeb, adgxb-
ebe
Edwin adgxfbeb
Elihu T dagxfbeb
Eliabeth adbabgd
Ephraim abbeacbd
Eva M bcdedfeb
George bcdgdabfc
George W bcdedfeb
Gertrude M adgxfbeb
Harriet Sophronia ahgcabc
Herbert Quincy adgxfbeb
Isaac bcdgdaaj
James Henry abbeacbdb
Jeanna K abbeacbd
Joseph adkc
Joseph Rev abccd
Kate ahbabjibb
Leon L adabiggdc
Lorenzo bcdgdaacj
Margaret adkebabbf
Maria adkgaa
Mary adkc, ahbabaac
Matthew bcdbada
Mercy adkc (bis)
Pearl bcdgdaacj
Raymond Morris bcdedfeb
Samuel adkc, adkcg
Sarah adkc, adkcg
Sarah A abbegba
Stephen adkc
Victoria bcdgdeai
Will adhadceb
William Rev adggdcc
Zilpha adkc
—— adijbd, adkef
ADDY —— adaceafkc
ADRIANCE John bcficanb

Marietta Van Wyck bcficanb
AEBLI Casper bcdbecee
Marie bcdbecee
AGER Charles ahgdcac
AIKEN George bcbebff
ALCOCK Eliza adhcba
James bbbffaf
*Mary bbbffaf
ALDRICH Ellen B bcdedbae
Mason bcdedbae
—— ahbabjce
ALEXANDER Albert Onslow bcdeddhe
Annie Marion bcdeddhe
Cyrus bcbcbbb
Elizabeth ahbgfe
Eugene C ahbgfe
George bcdgdakd
George Howard bcdeddhe
Hannah ahbgfe
Hannah May bcdeddhe
James ahbgfe
Lillian bdcgdakd
Maria bcbhddbba
Mary bcdgdakd
Maud ahbcaji
Nathaniel ahbgfe, ahbgfg
Samuel ahbgfe
ALFORD Harold bbbfhcfea
ALFRED the Great adggdcc
ALGER John adggefd
Ruby adhadce
ALLAN Elizabeth K ahggbdaa
Laura adacean
ALLEN Abigail adkd
Albert bbbfhcfab
Amelia adkgddhd
Amos adgfbegf
Charles Stanley adgfbgfaaf
Dorcas adhccb
Doris bbbfhcfab
Ethan (Col) ahchb
Isaac adhccb
George E bcdecahba
Harriet W ahcfjb
Hazel A bcdgdaghb
Horace E adkgddd
Ida M adadhcah
James Franklin ahcbfec
Joel adacedhg
Jonathan Leach ahcbfec
Josephine bcdecahba
Joslyn adbac
Lider A wid bcdedbada
Louise bcdecahba
Lydia bcdeda
Margaret ahcf
Martha E adaabfc
Mary ahcfja
Nathaniel abbegbb
Robert Hugh adgfbgfaaf
Sarah adbaa
Susan ahgfa
W bcdgdaga
William Rev abce

William bcdgdaghb
—— abbegbb, adaceddb, bbbfhcfab
ALLEY Mary E adgfbo
ALLISON Brent Dow bcdedhaa
Caroline Brown ahcbfec
Martha bcdeda
—— bcdedhaa
ALMSTEAD Harriet ahgchfh
AMAZINE Blanche ahbabahgb
John ahbabahgb
AMBROSE Alice ad
AMES Alfred adacefb
Alwilda adkefbbcc
Aratus adgfcja
Augustus adgfcja
Burpee bcdeabd
Burton J ahchfdd
Caroline wid bcdeabdc
Comfort bcbhdbe
Davis adgfcja
Edgar adgfcja
Elizabeth adgfcja
Ernest Harlan ahchfdd
Frances adgfcja
Frank Weber ahchfdd
George adaaaiedb
Helen adgfcja
Henry Dow ahchfdd
Horace adgfcja
Irvin Garfield ahchfdd
Jeremiah bcdeabdc, (Jr) bcdeabdc
Mayland P adadiabb
Mary bcdeabd
Nathaniel P adgfcja
Norman Burton ahchfdd
Orlo Wilder ahchfdd
Perley adgfcja
Sarah O adkgaeba
Stephen (Ens) bcdea
AMMERMAN —— adacgfaba
ANDERSON Anna bcdgdeaag
Annie A bcdgddah
Annie M adabbgbebc
Charles J bcdeddhda
George Lewis bcdeddhda
Hannah Elizabeth ahbgbac
Jeanie Campbell bcdbecca
John bcdbecca
Jonathan Harvey bcdbaddl
Martha bcdebgb, bcdgdaab
Margaret bd
Sabrina H wid adgfcdaa
Samuel Jameson bcdbecca
Samuel Jameson Jr bcdbecca
Sarah bcdgdaacf
Susan Jameson bcdbecca
ANDREWS William a
ANDREWS Cyrus adgfcdf
Ella R adgfcdh
Epaphras bcbcbbca
Everett D adgfcdh
Fitch bcbcbbc
Ida E adaabbgaige
Ida W adgfcdh

Isabella A adgfcdh
James F adgfcdh
John adhaj
Lemuel Wells bcbcbbca
Levi adgfcde, adgfcdh
Loretta adgfcdgaa
Lucy bcbcbbc
Lucy Maria bcbcbbca
Mabel wid adaceagci
Nelson Harrison adhaj
Oliver S adgfcdh
ANDRUS, see also Andrews
—— adaabacag
ANGELL Albert G adgfbed
Fannie bcbebbfaaa
Irere adgcacca
ANNABLE Mary P ahfcaab
Solomon ahcaab
ANNIS Harry bcdgdbae
Nettie bcdgdeaai
Roxanna adkehbh
Thomas bcdgdbae
William F adkehbh
ANTONE —— Miss gab
APPLEBEE Della J bcdedcfcc
John H bcdedcfcc
APPLEBY Mabel bcdgdaik
APPLETON Ethel Dora bcdedcfcc
John (Hon) ai
John H bcdedcfcc
Samuel (Capt) ah
APPLEYARD Jennie E bcdgdaaedc
ARBUCKLE Ina ahfcfcb
John ahfcfcb
Margaret wife ahfcfcb
ARGENT Rose bcbhddfaae
ARLIN Alice ahbaef
John abbegfgaa
Rhoda abbegfgaa
ARLON Judith akebdbb
ARMSTRONG Byron Wesley adhafagc
Edward Dow adhafagc
Emma Dow adhafagc
George D adhafagc
George W abbegbdd, bbbfabia
Helen Standish adhafagc
Hial ahdadc
Jabin ahdadc
ARMTHING George R bcbcbbgba
ARNOLD Abigail B bcfihe
Ann Elizabeth adbabgc
Benedict (Gen) adabc, ahbg, ahbga
Cyrus adbabgc
Francis Edwin adbabgc
Henry Clay adbabgc
Jonathan (Hon) bcfihe
Mary bcdgsad
Mary Gibbons adbabgc
—— (Dr) bcficb
ARTLIP Homer adacffd
—— adacffd
ASHER Alice adabc
ASHWORTH Nellie E adhafgcdb
ASPER Annie E fceae

782

242

ASPINWALL John bededea
Mary bededea
ASTLE Jerry bedgdafka
Lizzie L bedgdafka
ATHEARN Hannah bebhddkbxa
ATHERTON Roy bedgdafke
Archie bedgdafke
ATKINS Henry adgfbeea
Mary Esther adgfbeea
Ruth bedgdafke
Susan bbbffce
ATKINSON Bertha adaabdaba
—— bcbhdbne
ATWATER Mary adggdee
Robert adggdee
ATWELL Mary abbegfg
ATWOOD Abigail adheba
Adeline S adkgaeb
Alice E bededefb
Anna befig, befigf
Arthur S ahbgbba
Eliza adgcace
Ethel B bededefb
Fannie M bededefb
Hannah bededefb
Henry D bededefb
Herbert K bededefb
Jennie M bededefb
John B bededefb
Joseph adaceab
Josie L bededefb
Kate E bededefb
Matilda Putnam befigfd
Solomon adkgaeb
AUBURN Charles W adgfbeje
AUSTIN Amanda abbegg
David abdcebbeah
Edith Leslie abdcebbeah
Elizabeth bededbeb
Freeman bedgdae
Hannah bebebbf
John bcbebbbdc
Joseph ahcbba
Lulu adabbgaiea
Lydia J bcbebbbdc
Marsh ahcbba
Mary bedbaddl
Sally ahcbba
Nancy bcbebbe
Sarah adaha
AVERILL Abigail ahbgbeb
AVERY Jennie ahbaaheab
Lurinda Polina adacedde
Mary J bedeaedb
Sarah adggeiba
Wilber Bucklin adaceagb
AYER Berle J bedgdsad
Caroline S adgcadaaa
Hattie P wid bcbebbbdb
Helen Gertrude ahgchfea
James 3rd bedbeh
Joseph abdceblh
Lester B bedgdsad
Molly bcbebb

Ruth bcb, (wid) bd
Thomas bd
Timothy bcb
AYERS Margaret abdecb
AXTELL Betsey ahbabja
Hiram ahbabja
BAB Hannah gab
BABB Elbra A adadicfba
Elizabeth adkgddha
Ida Ann adkgddha
William S adadicfba
BABBIDGE Abigail adabbgbca
Stephen adabbgl
BABCOCK Almira Pullen adbabfec
Benjamin ahgb
Jemima akebic
May ahbabai
Rosetta adhafce
Samuel ahda
BABSON Lizzie B adabbgr
BACHELDER Theodate ab
BACHELLER Abbie C ahgfbdgbba
BACON Alice M ahbgilh
Beverly J ahbgilh
Charles Henry ahbghjc
Elsie M ahbgilh
Hannah Gould adkfbeb
Henry ahbghjc
Isabel bcbhddfabf
John A ahbgilh
Matilda S adgfdcd
Olia M ahbgilh
BADCOCK Jennie ahfch
John ahfcb
Lydia wid ahfca
BADGER Elizabeth L adkddcb
Mary (Ladd) ahgc
John (Col) adaabc, ahbaac
BADMINTON Naomi adgcacbjd
BAGGERLY Elizabeth Ann ahdaadd
BAGLEY Abel adfcdb
Adeline gbakh
Alice abbegbda
Alice Edith ahchfic
Amy Lucinda ahchfic
Charles Clarence ahchfic
Daniel abccgaci
David Daniel ahchfic
George L ahchfic
Henry Elisha ahchfic
John ade, adfcdb, gbak
John D ahchfic
John Washington abbegbda
Laura J ahchfic
Milton Aaron ahchfic
Nancy befihe
Sarah A gbak
Vivian Adelbert ahchfic
Walter E ahchfic
William Eugene ahchfic
William Leroy ahchfic
BAILEY Amos Cluff ahbgaa
Arabella Peck abbegbibf
Amanda bbbebcf

Caroline abbegbeae, bcbebbcf
Charles Fred ahbgaa
Charles Frederick ahbgaa
Charles L adggdaab
Charles M bcdedfb
David ahbcai
Edward Buxton ahbgaa
Eliza bbbebcf
Elizabeth Ryder ahbgaa
Emeline bbbebcf
Florence ahbabjed
Frederick (Col) bcdedfb
George Byron bcbehhd
George W bcbehhd
Hannah Maria adbabfg
James B bcdedfb
James Whiting bcdedfb
Jane wife adabiggf
John ahbga
Judah bcbebbcf
Lizzie adabiggf
Melvilla bbbebcg
Myry Dane ahbgaa
Nathan W adhcba
Phineas ahbgaa
Phoebe McKenzie bbbebcf
Samuel ahbabjed
Sarah B bcdedfb
Sarah M bcdedfb
Susan Esther ahbgaa
Susannah ahbga
Thomas abbegbibf
Thomas P D bcbebcf
True Morse ahbgaa
William adabiggf, bcdc
William P bcdbaddja
BAIRD Jane adaceald
Margaret adaidaeb
Robert Lionel bcbhddccf
Walter Jr. bcbhddccf
BAKER Alberta M bcdebgaace,
Alice Bell bcbebbcdac
Alice Mary adacgfea
Amos Morgan bcbebba
Annie Louise bcbebbfaca
Carrie Eva bcdbaddl
Carrie Gilman bcbebbfacb
Celantha bcfifhhe
Charles bcdbaddl
Clarinda bcbebba
Dora bcdecdbaa
Edison bcdbaddl
Elmer Clarence bcdbaddl
Elsbeth M bcdebgaacc
Elizabeth ahbgf
Elizabeth G adhe
Florence bcdebgaacc
Gilman H bcbebbfacb
J D ahdaadd
John B bcbebbcdac
Joseph bcbebbb, (Rev) bcdbaddl
Lora M bcbebbec
Lydia adgcacb
Maria ahbcacbbb

Mary adhafcj
Mary Ann bcbebba, bcbebbb, bebebbae
Philip Carrigan bcbebba
Sidney Ernest adacgfea
Timothy Dow bcbebba
W J bcdebgaacc
William R adacgfea
William Roberts adacgfd
William Taylor adgfbeh
Wilmer Clarendon bcdbaddl
—— adgfgabca
BALCH Nancy bcdeaaa
Robert bcdeaaa
BALDWIN Cora ahbcabeab
Eliza bcfifd
Loammi (Col) ahfcf, bbbfh, (Maj) bc-
    bcbb, bcbhda
Mary bbbcb
Miranda adacgfb
Sylvanus bcfifd
BALL Charles bcbcbbga
Elzada H ahbabaed
George William abbeebcaa
Grace A abbeebcaa
Harry bcdedcfca
William ahbabaed
BALLARD Arthur H abceabefd
David Coolidge bcdebfd
Jeremiah (Capt) adggdcca
Lucy bcbhddcc
William Hudson (Capt) abdci
BALLOCH Alfred Perry bbbfabk
Caroline Matilda bbbfabk
Eliza bbbfabk
John bbbfabk
BALLOU Isabelle adaabdabca
BAMFORD —— bcdeaad
BANCROFT Charles Foster adkdecehb
Ebenezer (Capt) bcbcbb
BANFIELD Charles adaigbbaba
BANFILL Charles O abcegbabb
BANGS Charles Edwin adaceaaj
Burr H adaceaaj
Daniel Eugene adaceaaj
Daniel Lee adaceaaj
Ella adaceaaj
Hattie adaceaaj
Henry Heman adaceaaj
Medora adaceaaj
Theodore S ahbcaa
BANISTER Lulu adaceddeb
BANKER Emma G adaceafk
John adaaaaccab
Mary A adaaaaccab
BANKS Ella Maria adkdeae
Henry Harms adkdeae
Jennie adkdeae
Jeremiah Harris adkdeae
Katherine Stanhope bcbhdqaba
Samendal bcbhdqaba
Sarah gbak
—— (Gen) adhccbb
BANNARD Jeremiah (Rev) adacea
BARBER A Chaser (Capt) adadabcc

Addie adabbgaigb
BARBOUR Fred abdcebeca
Mary Ann adabbhg
BARDWELL Flora aghdcagb
BAREFOOTE Walter ab, ad
BARKER Amelia Frances fceab
Charles F akecahj
Deborah bcdbad
Joanna bcdedg
John ahbca, ahbcg
Mary ahbca
Sarah J adaiiab
Zebediah bcdbad
—— ahbabg, bcdgdae, bedgddc, bedg-
ddh
BARLOW Elva adhadccd
Charles adhadccd
Lewis adacedded
Margaret bcdebgacb
Sophia Jane bbbfabb
BARNARD Adaline ahbabjbd
Andrew bbbda
Anna bbbda
Charles adaimag, (Jr) adaimag, ahba-
bag
Daniel adgffa
Ella ahfcaaag
Frank ahfcaaag
Fred ahfcaaag
Henry adaabfaam
J F adhccba
Mary Abbie adaimag
Rhoda adaaaacc
Samuel abcf
Thomas ad
—— adahx
BARNES Albert adgfcicd
B adgfcja
C adgfcja
Christina Maria bcbebbcda
Clara E adgfcicd
Clare Dow bcbhbgk
Elva Agnes bcbhbgk
Hester D adgfcdad
Lydia adhadce
Maria B bcbhgk
Melissa J abbccdaa
Nettie M abccgbada
Newell bcbhgk
Olive ahgfdac
Samuel W abccgbada
T adgfcja
Walter B adhafde
—— adggdcc, abcdebfgb
BARNEY Bertha E bbbebgab
Eben bbbebgab
Emily wife bbbebgab
BARNUM Mary ahche
Phineas T ahche
BARON Etta bcdedbacb
Levi bcdedbacb
BARRET Almira adaceafg
Alonzo adaceafg
BARRETT Cyrus adahdc

Edson A adacgfd
Florence ahbgdfe
Frank bcfifffa
John bcbcbbdb
John P ahchfijc
Oliver P ahbgdfe
Ruth Elizabeth ahchfijc
Sarah adadhaca
William T adhcbbfa
BARRON Eliz a
William (Capt) bcdeab
BARSE Ida M gbeb
BARSTOW Elva adhadccd
Grenville Edgar adaabdaea
Miriam F bcdeddc
BARTHOLOMEW Inez Ellen adgfbeg-
gaa
BARTLETT Abigail bcdgdaaa
Alcena M adgxfaaec
Almira C adaaaifaa
Caroline ahbabi
Charles Jr. adkgaebfa
Charles H ahbabjea
David S adkdebd
Dora E bcdgdaiic
Elizabeth adaaaaaa
Ella Jencks ahcbee
Elroy G adgfcdacaa
Emma S bcbehda
Ethel adkgaebfa
Evelyn B adgfcdacaa
Frank D bcbehda
George ahcbee
Gershom adaaaaaa
Hosea ahbabjea
Imogene ahcbee
Jacob bcbehda
Jeanna bcdeabdaa
John b
John F adkebca
Josiah ahbabji
Judith adkeba
Kate ahcbee
Lewis F bcbehda
Margaret F ahbcachcb
Obergill bcdgdaaa
Richard Jr. ahbabi
Sarah Ann adaaaacca
Sarah Elizabeth ahbabji
Seth bcdgdaiic
Smith Jencks C ahcbee
Stephen adaaaacca
Susan ahcbee
Timothy (Col) ahbca
Walter J bcbcbbgf
William bcdgdaaa
William L bcbehda
BARTON Addie adaimbbb
Ellen F adiamaabb
BASSET Eunice adhce
Isaac adhce
Mary wife adhce
Ploomy wife adaaid

785

245

BASSETT Arthur F adadagabc
Edgar bcdeaedaab
Elsie May bcdeaedaab
Hannah M ahbgdfe
Lydia adhcbbc
Sarah wife bcdeaedaab
BASTRESS Eliza bcficadbb
Samuel bcficadbb
BATES Ada ahbgfiba
Charlotte Reed abbegfjac
Herman M abbegfjac
Olive Winslow abbegfjac
Rufus abbegfjac
Rufus Edward abbegfjac
Ruth adkebgba
BATTERSON Harold abbegfjd
Hortense abbegfjd
Howard abbegfjd
Mabel abbegfjd
William abbegfjd
BATCHELDER Alfred Johnson akeca-
  hj
Alice M bcbebbfaaa
Amy H akecahj
Benjamin abbec, (Jr) abbec
Carrie adgfbecf
Comfort abbec
Deborah abdb
E Geneva adaceddca
Edwin Bradley akecafh
Elizabeth abbed, adbce
Ella M adhae
Ethel M adaceddca
George L akecafh
George Nathaniel akecafh
Henry bcbebbfaaa
Hannah abbec
J adabigge
J Udell adaceddca
Jane abcd
John abbec
Josiah abdcb, akecahj
Judith abbee
Leroy A adbabfiaa
Levi akecb
Louisa J adabigge
Lyman adgfbecf
M wife adgfbecf
Marcia A akecahj
Mary abbea, aeeacaa
Mary A akecahj
Mary Emeline akacahj
Mildred T adaceddca
Nathan adkehg
Nathaniel aeea, (Capt) akecafh
Reuben bcbebbba
Sally ahbabi
Samuel akecac
Sanborn akecafh
Sarah abbec
Thomas abbea, abbec
Warren M akecafh
Warren Woodbury akecafh
William adgfbecf

Willie adgfbecf
BAXTER Charles adggeica
George M bcdebfbb
BEACH Lucy wid adkebgac
Mary E adacedfe
BEACHAM Edward adaaac
BEADLEY Etta H wid adaimbcf
BEAL Arvilla adaimbbd
Herbert A adkgaee
Josiah C adkebde
Maud E adkgaee
Welcome B adkgaee
Winship adaimbbd
BEAN Arthur bcdgdaned
Daniel adadaba
David ahbaa
Ebenezer aedb
Edna May adadhacac
Emma abccgbada
George adadabgb
James ahfcaaa
Jeremiah adgxb
John adaabcea
Levi adgxb
Lydia bcfifl
Martha E adaabcea
Mary S ahfcaaa
Nancy abccgbab
Polly akebh
Raymond M bcdedbbbc
Richard adgxb
Somersette Hoyte adaceage
Warren M adadhacac
BEANE Abbie Whidden abceabcg
Cora adgxfdada
Ruel J abceabcg
Sarah wife abceabcg
BEARCE Calista R ahbabag
BEARDSLEY John bcdgdafj
BEARSLEY John bcdgddeaa
Laura bcdgdeaa
BECKMAN Charles A adaimbiab
Clara adaimbbb
Edgar adaimbiac
Eugene Hale adaimbbb
Evelyn adaimbiac
Francis adaimbbb
Frank adaimbbb
George adaimbbb
James Arthur adkddgj
John adaimbh
John M adaimcdd
Laura adaimbbb
Lemuel S adaimbbb
Leon E adaimbbb
Lillian adaimbbb
Louisa adaimbbb
Mary Abigail adaimbi
Mary E adkfbbj
Mary J adaimbaf
Polly Ann adaimbh
Robert adaimbf, adkddgj
BECKER Gustav L bbbfabbab
——— ahgcabab

BECKLEY Alice Josephine ahgchec
Edgar ahgchec
BECKWITH Laura ahghc
BEDELL Maria Louisa Bonaparte bed-
edce
BEEBE Caroline adggdcg
Fernn E adacffeha
Franklin Doremus adhcbbdc
Rufus adaceak
BEECHER Mary ahgdccb
BEEDE Ann wife adbabb
Huldah adbabb
Jonathan adbabb
Nathan adaabbdabd
Robert E adaabdabd
Rolla adaabdabd
Will adaabdabd
BEEMAN Ellen Sophia adhcbbh
BEERS Joseph Vowels adhcbbdc
John adhcbbdc
Mabel adhcbbdc
Nathan Lee adhcbbdc
BELCHER Alpha A adacgfac
BELDEN Jane E ahgcig
BELDING Susan bcbhddbc
BELKNAP Obiadiah bcdc
BELL Bertha Hazel adkfbedda
Charles Jeremiah bcdeabea
Frank Lester bcdeabea
Frank bcdeabea
Gladys bcdgdafh
Jonathan bcfiffb
John Charles bcdeabea
William adabibb
—— (Miss) bcfihd
BELLEVEAU Joseph bcdgdafah
BELMER Andrew bcdeaefae
Nettie Grant bcdeaefae
BELON Joseph J adgxffae
BELT Nelle Mrs adgfcdabf
BENEDICT Dulcena bcdecdba
F D adacgff
Levi Franklin bcdecdba
Robert ahcbba
BENJAMIN Anne Elizabeth bcbhddcb
Phoebe bcfifjc
BENNER Flora M adgfbgfca
Malleville E bcbhdbec
BENNETT Addie Cora ahchfie
Ann W bcdeddb
Elizabeth bcdeda, bcdedfe
Francis M adkehi
George adaidaa
Jane adgfbecj
Lizzie abccgcfi
Lizzie A ahbabadb
Lizzie Caroline bcbehhgb
Persis bcbhddaab
Robert bcdgdaacj
William O adkfbf
BENNISON Harry C bcdgdanb
BENSON Arthur M adkgaa
Elizabeth adkgaa
James adkgaa

Joseph adkgaa
Martha adkgaa
Mary adkgaa
Sarah adkgaa
BENSTER Halsey ahgdgaab
BENTLEY Charlotte adgfbgfa
Emily Louisa ahchfeb
BENTLY Alice adggdcdc
Louis adggdcdc
Wilbur adggdcdc
BENTON George W bcfifd
Jacob adhccbba
Luna ahgfb
Stephen ahgfb
BERCE Ray P ahbabacda
BERDAN —— (Col) bcdbaddf
BERGANSON Arthur adadicfbb
BERGE —— bcdgdeaabe
BERGOINE Charles adaabfaaa
Lida adaabfaaa
BERGSTRESSER Charles M ahcfjbc
BERLIN N C bcbhdbedb
BERRY Charity abce
Charles adgxfdabb
Charles E ahbgfiba
Christie adgxfdabb
Fred H adbabfbh
George akecad
Haven S adkebabbb
Jennie S akecafi
Jesse abcec
John C adhcdacd
Lydia adgcacbc
Nathaniel abce
Pearl Lillian ahbgfiba
Sarah adgcad, akecad
Thomas (Capt) akebb
William abcec, akecb
—— abdb
BERWISE P E adgfcjc
BESSE O B bcfifhhf
BESSEY Charles Dow adbabfiab
Earl D adbabfiab
Earle D adbabfiab
John Marcellus adbabfiab
Hattie Mrs adgfedgbb
Nannie L adgfcicdc
Rollins adgfbef
BETTIS Alonzo ahgfbdc
BETTON Agnes bcdedd
Welthy A ahgfbdc
BEVERAGE Alfred F abccgcfdc
Henry S abccgcfdc
BEVERLY Abbie gbaia
BEYMER Louisa bcdedk
BICKFORD Albert Edward bcbhddccbf
Anna adadabbc, wife adaigaaca
Anna C adadabb
Asa Jr adadabbc
Belinda Jane adadai
Benjamin adadai
Charles H adadabbc
Clara adadabbc
Dorcas abbegfa

787

Dudley adadai
Dudley D adadai
George adadai
James adadai
James E adadhaad
Jane adbabf
Martha adadai
Merl Edward bcbhddccbf
Moses adbabf
Moses F adaigaaca
Myrtie L adaigaaca
Priscilla wife adbabf
Samuel adadai
Solomon adadai
—— adkecebaga
BICKNELL Blanchard bcdeabdaa
Mabel G bcdeabdea
Ralph A bcdeabdaa
BIGELOW Georgianna adgfbegga
Timothy (Col) adkga
—— bcbhdbndi
BILL Mary adaabdabb
BILLINGTON Alice Lena ahbgbba
Caroline Dow ahbgbba
Charles ahbgbba
Enoch Melvin ahbgbba
Ida Anna ahbgbba
John Franklin ahbgbba
Mary Love ahbgbba
Orlando Bradford ahbbgbba
William R ahbgbba
Zachary Taylor ahbgbba
BILLINGS Charles adaaafa
—— adaaafa
BINFORD Frances Ellen bbbfabhb
BINGLEY Elizabeth adhaa, (wid) ad-
haa
BIRD Laura ahbabadc
BIRKETT Retta adhadceh
BIRNEY Thomas (Sir) xaa
BIRTWELL Charles W adaijbaa
Roger adaijbaa
BISBEE Charles adgfbef, (Jr) adaijbaa
Elma adgfbef
Fred adgfbef
Inezetta adgfbef
Josephine adgfbef
Minnie adgfbef
BISHOP Ada bcdgdafo
Charles bcdebgaad
Dorcas adaceaga
Ira adaceaga
Kitty bcdebgaac
Margaret wife adaceaga
Rebecca adggdcc
BITHER Ormandel M ahbabamf
Zophar ahbabmh
BIXBY Benjamin adaabfxb
Mary bbbeb
Moses Harman adaabfxb
BLACK Annie E abccgdcf
James bbbffcb
Lydia bbbffcb dc
Lyman adkfbeh

Martha E bcbhdekd
Mary abccgd
Mary Cinderella adbabfef
Polly abccgd
Wallace adkfbeh
BLACKBURN Luella bcdecdbad
BLACKMER Norbourn H ahgfdec
BLACKSTONE Benjamin bbbebcbe
Betsey bbbebcbe
BLACKWELL Alice M ahbabaead
BLAGDEN Benjamin F bbbfhjbf
Hazel Henwood bbbfhjbf
Martha bbbfhcg
W W abbegbdfc
BLAINE Elizabeth bcdebejcc
James G adhccbb
James G 3rd bcdebejcc
BLAIR Eliza bcfiffc
BLAISDELL Alonzo G adabibka
Ann Frances ahbgid
Benjamin T adadibdj
Calvin D adaimbiad
Clarence adaimbiad
Diana Pillsbury adkeck
Dolly adggei
Herbert G adabibka
Jacob ahbgid
John adggei, (Jr) adkeck
John L adkeck
Mary adaf
Nell adhafabaa
Sally bcbegg
BLAKE A Trask adadabgb
Abbie adadabgb
Abigail adfcdcb
Angelia W ahbabaef
Anna adadag
Asahel abccdf
Bessie Nelson ahgchebb
Betsey ahbabaec
David W adgxffae
Dorothy abbee
Dudley Dow adadae
Eliza Adeline abbegbdca
Elizabeth F abccgacl
George A adaimbha
George B adaimbha
George H adabibid
Hannah adacb
Hazel G adadhacab
Hortense D adabibid
James abbegba
Jedediah adadag
Jemima abbef, akebbc
John Lauris adadae
Jonathan adadae
Jonathan Jr adadae
Joseph L abccgacl
L M adadabgb
Marcy Norris adadae
Mary abccga adaidaa, bcdgdak
Mary Ann abbeebbc
Nathan abbeb, abbebc, abbee
Payne abbegba

Polly abbegbdd
Rachel adadabbd
Samuel abbf
Sarah adadabgb
Simeon W adadhacab
Tabitha abdceb
Thomas abcega
—— Parson U S A bbbfabl
BLAKELY Mary gbef
BLAKER George Martin bcbehhm
Jesse bcbehhm
BLANCHARD Abigail bcdeabe
Clara akebdbbgdd
Frederick bcdbecda
Edward K adaiiaba
Joe akebdbbgdd
Mary E adaiiaba
Mary Jane ahbcabcbb
Melinda adabbgq
Roxana adabbgq
Sarah A abccgcfc
Susan adaabfx
BLANEY Elizabeth ahfa
BLANDEN Mary E ahgdhd
BLAUVELT Martha ahggbba
BLAZE Martha akebfb
BLAZEDELL Hannah adaaah
Jacob adaaah
Mary wife adaaah
BLENDINGER Fred L adkebgad
BLICK Elizabeth ahbaad
BLISS Celia adgfbfba
Levi W adggege
BLODGET Nellie Rebecca adaceafgb
BLODGETT Maria abccgachb
BLOFIELD R S (Rev) xaaf
BLOOD Amos bcdeaeh
Charles adhafahc
Charles A ahbabaeab
Charles Morris bcdeaeaga
Charlotte bcdeaed
Clara adhafahc
Dexter bcdeaeh
Dora I ahbabaeab
Everett L ahbabaeab
Frank adhafahc
Frederick E adhafahc
Harriet Proctor bcbebcgaa
Ira L ahbabaeab
Leonard (Capt) bcdeaeh
Lewis I ahbabaeab
Lizzie M ahbabaeab
Luella C ahbabaeab
Lucy Ann bcdeaeh
Mary bcbhdehfg
William bcfifjb
BLOXAM Hannah Walton ahbabja
Thomas ahbabja
BLUE Lafayette ahchbc
BOARDMAN Charles ahfcfcg
BOCKINS Earl bcdgdakcc
Elsie bcdgdakcc
Fay bcdgdakcc
Gilbert bcdgdakcc

Leland, Leland Jr bcdgdakcc
Otto bcdgdakcc
Pearl bcdgdakcc
Rosella bcdgdakcc
BODGE Ruexby Blake bcfifhh
BODDY —— bcbhdbnda
BODWELL Abigail bcfifd
Samuel (Maj) ahbca
BOLLES David ahggd
Hannah ahcbf
Jesse (Dea) ahcbf
BOLLINGER Judge ahbaedca
BOND Abigail wid ahgfb
Ada Frances wid adaabdabb
Ammie Rhumah bbbfb
Emery F adaabdabb
Jane wife abdgcafac
Gilbert bbbfb
John (Dr) 3rd bbbfb
Joseph bbbfb
Jonathan bbbfb
Mary adaidaa
Nanny bbbfb
Norman J abdgcafac
Sarah Moody abdgcafac
Susetta M abceabdbb
William (Col) bcbcab
BONNELL Eliza bbbfaba
Frank bbbfaba
Helen bbbfaba
Henry, Jr bbbfaba
John bbbfaba
BONNER Mary bbbffcbacb
BONNEY Betsey bcfifl
J F adkebda
Mary bcbhddfab
BOOBER —— bcdgdabc
BOOTH John bcdgdaic
BOOTHBY Alice E adgfcdaceb
Catie Elizabeth adkgddd
Charles Wesley Jr adkgddd
Ella Frances adkgddd
Emma Elvira adkgddd
BOOTMAN see BUTMAN
BORCHERS Henrietta E adacgfc
BORLAND Polly ahbcabe
BOSS Mary B bcdebgaa
BOSTON Olive adkdeaca
BOSWORTH Amy B bcbcbbee
BOTTOM Daniel Long ahdd
BOUGHTON —— ahgcaba
BOUGIS John bcficaled
Malvina, Malvina wife bcficaled
BOUGOIS Mathilde adkecbaca
BOULTER Nathaniel a, ae
BOURGE Alfred ahbaacdac
Mary Jane ahbaacdac
BOUTELLE Calvin bcbcbbfa
Charlotte A bcbebbfa
Sally abbeacbd
BOUTWELL Helen Irene ahbabjecb
Howard Patterson ahbabjecb
William Dow ahbabjecb
William Thurston ahbabjecb

789

249

BOWDEN Jane abccgcfg
Fred abccgcfg
Josie May adabbghgb
Leonard abccgcfg
Oscar adabbghgb
BOWEN Catherine Frances adabbgag-da, adabbhfa
Hannah adaiiaag
John adabbgagda, adabbhfa
Mary J abbegfgaa
BOWERS Frank ahbabjg
George ahbabjg
Henry ahbabjg
BOWIE Melvin adgfcdgc
Nettie B adgfcdgc
BOWLES Elizabeth adbabfab
John L adbabfab
Mary K abdccbcd
BOWMAN Ensign Dow bbbfhcgbf
J A akecahj
Velma F bbbfhcgbf
BOYD Daniel adaimaah
Elizabeth adaimbd
Emogene adaimaah
John Newell adgxfdg
Lenora A adgxfaacaa
Samuel adgxfaaaac
Sarah wife adaimaah
Thomas adgxfadb
William L adgxfaacaa
BOYDEN Adana Amanda gbakd
BOYINGTON Hannah bcbhdbe
BOYNTON A adkebag
Alice adaabfaaj
Clara ahgfbdh
I W adgfbfe
John adaaba
Osias adaabfaab
Polly abbegbd
BOYSON Thomas a
BOZINE Donald bcdgddeae
Doris bcdgddeae
Edward bcdgddeae
BRACE Francis abbegfgaga
Frank A abbegfgaga
Marion Estelle abbegfgaga
BRACKENBURY David adahe
Huldah adahe
BRACKETT Anthony abcec
Della adgfbgfaab
Isaac abceabcd
John bcdgee
Love abcec
Mary bcdgee
Samuel abceb
Zipperah abdd
—— (goodman) ab
BRADBURY Elijah bcbhdqaa
Elizabeth ahggbh
Frances Webster bbbfabq
Frederick True bbbfabp
Jane adggf
Jefferson bbbfabp
Katherine Leonard bbbfabp

Lucy adkdea
Mary Ella adgfbea
Mary J bbbfabm
Mehitabel abdgcafa
Philinda adggefc
Samuel bbbfabm
Susan bcbhdqaa
Thomas Merrill bbbfabp
BRADFORD Alice adggdcc
Charles Edward bcbhddcebc
Elmer L bcbhddcebc
George B adkgaee
George Lloyd bcbhddcebc
John Dow bcbhddcebc
Leila Alice bcbhddcebc
Vertilee Mae bcbhddcebc
William (Gov) adggdcc, ahgchfea, ahggc
William (Maj) adggdcc
BRADISH David (Capt) adkga
Julietta bcfifja
—— (Miss) abcfl
BRADLEY Benjamin bcbegb
Brickett bcficc
Daniel, Jr, 2nd bcc
Elizabeth, wife bcbehh
Ezekiel bcdeaeg
George bcdeaeg, bebhddfabf
Hannah bcc, bcde
John bcbehh
Louisa bcdeaeg
Mary bcc
Mary E bcdeaeg
Ruby M bcbhddfabf
Ruth bcc
Sarah bcbegb
BRADSCOMBE Hardie adbabfefd
BRADSTREET Lillian M adgfbgeah
R Thomas adgfbgeah
BRAGDON Amaziah C bcdgdafad
Arthur bcdgdafad
Benjamin Josiah bcfigdc
Burns bcdgdakd
Edith bcdgdafad
Evelyn Helene bcdgdafad
Hazel bcdgdafad
Julia Ann bcfigdc
Olive bcdedka
Pearl bcdgdafad
BRAGG Abigail wid adaij
Albertia G adgxfaacc
Caroline adaiic
Charles C adkehcca
Daniel adgxfaaad, adgxfaacc
George abccgab
Hannah adgxfd
Julia A wife adgxfaaad
Martha J bcbhddbaa
Mary Lydia adgxfaaad
Olive adkehg
Samuel bcbhddbaa
—— adaieaaa, adgfcja
BRAINARD H H ahggbh
—— ahggcb

BRAN Jane Jackson adaabfd
Robert bcdgg
BRANCH Oliver E adhafaf
BRANN Armelia N bcdgeh
BRANSCOMBE Joseph abccgaca
BRASHERS Olive adgfgabcc
BRAWN William bcdgdf
BRAY Bessie adabbgabdh
Harriet adaceaebb
Lois A adadhebd
Lucy adabbbdc
Susan adabbgagc
Theodore H adabbgaicb
Walter ahbabaf
BRAZIER Lucy ahbabjiba
BRECK Samuel ahbgbadda
BREED Caroline Silsby adhcbba
Clarissa adhcbbc
Dana Farrar adhcbba
Eliza Frances adhcbba
Enoch adhcbba
Enoch 2nd adhcbbc
Ebenezer adhcbbc
George Newell adhcbbc
Hannah wife adbabgb
Hannah B adbabgb
Lydia Ann adhcbba
Mary C adhadb
Mary Dow adhcbba
Moses adbabgb
Stephen P adhcbba
BREWER Hulda bcbhddfaaa
Lucy adgfe
—— ahbcabja
BREWSTER Mary A abdccb
BRIANT Hannah aeda
BRICKETT Otis P adgxfax
BRIDGE Ebenezer (Col) ahbch, bcb-
cbb
Henry C adgfbgdced
—— Parson ahbea
BRIDGEMAN Elvira ahgfbdb
Joseph ahghb
Mary Frances ahgfdc
BRIDGES Rosella bcdgdakc
BRIER —— adgcagah
BRIGGS Amelia Ann adaceac
Anna H adgfcdg
Calphurnia adaceac
Elizabeth wid abceabd
Emena bcdebgaace
Frances M bcfifhhd
Frank adaceac
J H adgfcdgca
Lotica adaceac
Mary E abceabdb
Murray adaceac
Nabby adaceah
Royal adaceac
William abceabdb, adhadcce
BRIGHAM Charles R adggdaab
Caroline Edith ahgchea
Charles S ahgchea
Frederick Newton ahgchea

Herbert Dow ahgchea
Jennie A adggdaab
Nellie O adbabfei
—— adabib
BRITTAIN Georgia bcdgbaala
BRITTANY James bcdgdafi
Laura bcdgdafh
BROCK Susanna adgfcdgc
BROCKLEBANK Aurilla wife abbegf-
gaa
Napoleon abbegfgaa
Susan F abbegfgaa
BROCKWAY Adelbert adaceaaeb
Angie C wid ahbabai
Joe bcdebgai
BRODIE Mary Ella ahbgbbeaa
BROOKING Eben bcbhde
Ruth bcbhde
BROOKS Amoe bcdgdf
Betsey bcficb
Charles acdgdf
Dow bcdgdf
Eliza adacgfc
Frederick bcdgdaif
Gardiner bbbfaxe
Gardner T akebbf
George bcdgdf
Hannah bcdgdb
Henry C adkedh
Hester bcdgdf
Hulda bcdgdec
Inez adkedh
Maria bcdgdde, bcdgdf
Michael adabe
Mary adkdeb, bcdebgag, bcdedcd
—— adkgdbada
BROWN Abby adgfbee
Abiah abccd
Abigail wife adaaaa, adadia, wife ada-
ime, akeab
Abraham bcf
Abram adaimca, adaimea, adgxffc
Achsah A adgxfdab
Alan Francis aeeacca
Alfred Bishop bcbehhj
Alice B akebdbbgd
Andrew bbbc
Angelina abceabef
Ann Eliza abceabeb
Annie J adkehcca
Annie L abbeacf
Asa, Asa Jr ahchg
Bella A ahbcaji
Benjamin ad, adkeabba, adkeg, (Jr) ad-
keg, ahchg
Betsey abdcaa, adaigb
Betsey L adaime
Betty adhadb, wife adhafb
Caleb bcdg
Charles adaimbbdb
Charles Bell adaimaaaa
Charles C adgxffbbb
Charles F adkeabaf
Charles W bcbebbgba

Clara Augusta adaimae
Comfort abbeg
Cora Belle ahgfbdgbba
David abccgad, adhafb, (Jr) adkgg
David Mitchell abbegbdd
Dora adaimbbdb
Doris Julian aeeacca
Dorothy adgcaf
Edward A adai, adfa, adkfbbc
Elias bcdgdad
Elijah adhaa
Elisha abbeacf
Eliza adaabdah, adhafb, bbbffadb
Elizabeth wife bcdg
Elizabeth Ann abbeacf
Emeline Marilla ahchg
Emery adaimae
Emily adkecbaaa
Emma L wife adgxffbbb
Enoch adhafb
Eugene adaimae
Eugene Russell adaimaaaa
Eunice Carney adkecba
Frank C aeeaecca
Fred M adkebgc
Freeman abbeebbc
George adhafb
George Ballard adaiebac
Gertrude adaimbbdb
Hannah wife bbbffafa
Hannah J adgxffc
Harriet E adggeiba
Harry E adacglb
Harry R bbbebgba
Hattie bbbffbaaa
Henry adgxfaaaa
Henry J aeeaecc, ahgfbdgbba
Henry Young (Capt) bbbff
Hulda wid bcdgdaac
Ida bcdgdaije
Ira C ahbgaa
Isaac adgxfac
Isabella T bbbffcdf
Jacob abbegd, adfa
Jacob Dow adgxfac
James adabbgda
James N akecaec
Jeremiah abbeacf
Jeremiah W adaiebac
John adaaaa, adhaff, ahbcaf
John L adkehj
Jonathan abceaba
Joshua aeea
La Motte adggeid
Langdon abceabeb
Leroy M akebdbbf
Levi adhaga, abbeedc
Levi A abbeedc
Louisa A adadief
Lowell adggbaa, adhaff
Lucetta C adabbgda
Lydia Ann bbbffadb
Margaret adkehe
Margaret A adgxfaha

Maria ahgcaba
Marjorie Dow adaimaaaa
Mark akebdbbgd
Marriam adkehd
Martha A adhcdaeaa
Martha M akecahc
Mary abbec, adhaa, adhafb, adhafd, bb-
    bebg, bcbhddbaa, bcdg
Matilda L adhcbbd
Maude bcbhddfaa
Mildred Binford adgfbgfaad
Minnie bcbhddccf
Miriam H adkehd
Molly adbb
Moses abbeacf, bcdgdad, bcdgdae
Myra Amelia adkfbebc
Myra C adkeabba
Nathan abbec, abceaa, abceabef, (Capt)
    adadab, adaie
Nathaniel adfa
Nancy adaimbb, adgxfaaa, adkedeceb
Nancy M ahchfdc
Olivia bbbffbaad
Oliver Albert abbeacf
Otis Simon abceabeb
Patience adaaaa
Paul adkecba
Perez, Perez Jr adggeid
Perley William aeeacca
Phoebe M abccgbae
Polly bcbebiga
Rachel aeea
Rebecca adggb
Reuben (Capt) adkgg
Rhoda wid adgxfada
Robert bcdgg
Robinson bbbffcdf
Ruth abccgbab
Ruth Ann adgxfac, adgxffb
Sally adaimea, adgxfa
Salome bcbhddfaa
Samuel akecaa
Samuel A adgxffbbb
Sarah adahe, adka, agbcf
Simon abceabeb, adhafb, Jr adhafb
Stephen abccgbab, abdcg, adbae
Stephen A bbbffafa
Stella V bbbffafa
Susanna abdcib, adad, adggda
Susey akecaa
Thomas adaime, abccd
Tyler bcdgdafc
Volney P adggeiba
Walter Edward adaiebac
William adaijba, adbae, adhcbbfbc, ae-
    eaecc, bcdgdf
William H adaijba, adgfcibb
BROWNE Abraham bcf
Sarah bcf
BROWNELL Elizabeth bcdeaefcbbd
Stella adhafdgcc
BRUCE Anna abbegfgac
Eliza Marston abdgcafa
Hannah abbegfgac, adhcbbfba

Harvey ahgfbg
Henry abdgcaf
James abdgcaf
Jane Savage abdgcaf
Jesse S abbegfgac
Maria bbbebgb
Mary abdgcaf
Mary W ahgfbg
Matilda wife ahgfbg
Nancy Anna wife abbegfgac
Phineas abdgcaf
Robert (King) abdgcaf
Sarah Marston abdgcaf
William abdgcaf
BRUDY Mary A adabbgxc
BRYANT Abbie gbai
Augusta bcbegbe
Charles D abbegfcaa
Clark adkebb
Emma F abbegfcaa
Francis bcbegbe
Frank K adkfbbccb
George Dow bcbegbe
Hope ahbgbadeb
John gbap
Kenla Arvilla adacgfd
Margaret bcbhdi
May A adkfbbccb
Walter abccdf
—— adbac
BUCK Abby adhcbbhb
Caroline bcdedcg
Charles Cawl bcdeabbba
E Elmer bbbffcf
Edmund adgxfdada
Frank E bcdedcfb
Henry H adgxfdada
Jonathan bcfifl
Lucinda adaabdae
Oel A (Maj) adggegc
Percy (Dr) adaabdaega
Ralph A adaabdaega
Sary G adaabcf
BUCKLEY Abigail cbaaaa
BUCKLIN Emily bcfiffh
BUCKMAN Clarissa I wife adgxffcc
Estella M adgxffcc
James A adgxffcc
BUCKMASTER George A fceah
Gertrude D fceah
John W fceah
Percy M fceah
Samuel K fceah
BUCOR Jeanne akebdbbgdd
BUFFUM Elizabeth wife adbabc
Ellen M adbabfeb
Huldah D adbabc
John adbabc
Joshua adbabc
Peace adbabc
William N adbabfeb
Zerviah adbabc
BUKER Ethel M bcbhddbba
Melvin G bcbhddbba

BULL —— Dr. ahgha
BULLOCK Calista adaceaea
Mary Elvira abbegbeb
BUMP Ain ahbcajda
Bertha ahbcajda
Celia E ahbcajda
Charles Summer ahbcaja
Charlestown A ahbcajda
Cyrus adacebd
Eunice ahbcabf
Everett ahbcaja
Everett Hale ahbcaja
Harriet adaceaff
Henrietta Lydia ahbcaja
Lewis adacebc
Melissa ahbcaja
Mary ahbcaja
Ruth E ahbcajda
Shepard Charles ahbcaja
Thomas Parker ahbcaja
Thomas Wellington ahbcajda
BUNKER Elizabeth adaaafd
Hannah W bcficadb
James bcficadb
BUNNELL Alva (Capt) abbeebca
Elmira B bcbcbbaffa
Sarah Jane bcbcbbaffa
BURBANK Arthur J adaabclb
Caroline A adkebag
Ezra Chandler bcdedbcd
George H adaabclb
Hannah adkebag
Jason Charles adggdccab
John adkebag
Jonathan adgxb
Laura F adkebag
Mabel Ruth adggdccab
Marinda J adkebag, adkebagf
Matilda H adkebag, adkebagf
Nathan adkebag
Thomas adkebag
William Wirt ahbgdfc
BURCH Melinda adacgfgg
—— bcdgddaaa
BURCHARDT —— adaabdabb
BURCHSTEAD Allan ahfcibb
Franklin W ahfcibb
James ahfcibb
BURDEN William Alexander adacf-
ffeaa
Eunice V bcdgdaacbd
BURDICK Carrie adggdcdaa
BURDITT Charles bcdedbccb
Frances W bcdedbccb
BURGESS Lucinda abccgcab
R B ahbcabea
BURGOYNE —— (Gen) bcdb
BURKE Elizabeth A adaiiaaed
George W adaabdabeh
Henry adaiiaaed
John C adaabdabh
Julia Lillian adaabdabeh
Nora ahbcabej
Walter Scott adaabdabeh

BURKETT Andrew bcbhdeia
Edith H bcbhdeia
BURLEY Alice ahbaah
Edward ahbaahd
Mary wife ahbaahd
Mary A ahbaahd
BURLINGHAME Matilda wid abbeg-
  bda
—— adaceaha
BURLEIGH Alice Elsie ahbaaa
Benjamin ahbaae
Betsey ahbaae
Caleb ahbaae
Elsie ahbaae
Frank Pierce adkecbae
Gordon, Gordon Jr ahbaaa
John ahbaaa
Joseph ahbaaa
Joshua ahbaaa
Judith ahbaaa
Samuel Randall adkecbae
Sarah ahbaae
Sarah C akebdbd
Thomas ahbaae
BURNAP Susanna adaceba
BURNHAM Alice Louise bcbcbbgc
Charles Julius bcbcbbgc
Cyrus Eastman bcbcbbgc
Edward Elisha bcbcbbgc
Elbridge C bcbcbbgc
Elisha bcbcbbgc
Elizabeth adgfe
Ella Dow hcbcbbgc
Foss A adaabffa
Frank Elmer bcbcbbgc
Henry Baxter bcbcbbgc
John A adhafgba
Rebecca abbeh
Samuel bcbcbbgc
Stella Laura bcbcbbgc
BURNS Betsey adaida
Maud adabbhh
Philip abccda
William ahdaadd
BURNSIDE Calista E akebiq
BURPEE Harry, Harry Jr bcdgddead
BURR Elibazeth cbbcb
—— bcdgdaiab
BURRELL Bely bcbhb
BURRILL Addie F bcbhddcb
Daniel S bcbhddcb
BURROUGHS Carrie M bcbhbgb
D S bcbhbgb
BURSIEL William adaaaid
BURSLEY Estelle S ahbabajada
BURT Lizzie L adadagfb
Pierce L adadagfb
BURTON Adeline C adggea
Elizabeth ahda ahdab
Mattie bcdebgafb
Prudence ahdaba
BUSH Elizabeth ahgfbg
Fairbanks ahgfbg
Jennie W adabbgagc

Rose ahbcabejb
BUSK Hannah adhafdgca
Herman adhafdgca
BUSWELL Hannah aedaa
Hannah L adabibca
John adabibca
Joseph bbbff
Martha bcdbea
—— (Capt) adkfbb
BUTLER Benjamin F (Gen) adhccbb
Charles ahcbeb, ahcbed
Daniel Tenney bcfifhf
Charles Edward adgfbeed
Ellen F adaimbba
Ethel ahgcibca
George adgfbeed, ahbgbxaaa
Herbert ahcbeb, ahcbed
Howard Ellsworth adaimbce
John (Capt) ahbabi
James Madison adabbgbc
John Wesley adaimbce
Joseph ahcbed
Marian ahcbeb, ahcbed
Mary Ella ahbgbxaaa
Mary Jane adaimaa
Michael adaimaa, adaimbba
Polly True adbabi
Robert adaimbce
William Ellsworth adaimbce
Zelda ahcbeb
BUTMAN Annie E adabbgea
Charles adabbgea
Jeremy bbbf
Joseph bbbf
Judith bbbf
BUTTERFIELD Abigail Lydia adhadce
Annie Stearns adgfbfcc
Charles G adhae
Hannah wife adhae
James adhadcc
Lydia bcfiff
Mary adhae
Myrtie Alice adhae
Phoebe bcfifh
William adhae, Jr adhae, bcfiff
BUTTERS Lois adabbgdd
William Andrew adkehbd
BUTTERWORTH Abel S adgcadaff
Annie Stearns adgfbfcc
Eliza adgcadaff
George adgfbfcc
James F adhcbbjac
James Francis adhcbbjac
M..artha wife adgcadaff
BUTTLES Matilda adhadce
BUXTON Benjamin bcdgdbaai
Albert W ahbabjl
BUZZELL Aaron Jr adggefb
Blanche adadagad
Charles adaabcjh
Clementine A adkfbbcid
David adadagad
Elmer E adaabcjc
Ethel A bcbhddfaba

Hannah L adabibca
Henry Dow adadagad
Ida M adkehbha
Israel adadagad
James (Dea) bcdeca
Jennie adaabcjh
John adabibca, bcbhddfaba
Laura bcbhddfabb
Maurice A adkfbbcid
Miriam bcbegd
Phoebe bcdece
William adaabcjc
CABLES Georgie bcbhdehfd
CAHOON —— Mayor adhccbb
CAIN Will G adggdcid
CALDWELL Ada B bbbfabhd
Daniel adhafaa
Elizabeth adkgddha
George bbbfabhd
Herman ahgfbb
Louise abbegbeaa
Lucretia adhafaa
—— gab
CALEB Emma Sophia ahbabjbd
Jasper ahbabjbd
CALFE John (Capt) ahbca
CALHOUN John C adhccbb
CALKINS Louisa Lydia ahbcajb
Mary L adggeij
CALLAHAN Mary adaimbhcb
CALLIS Amber bbbfabmh
CAMERON Betsey bcfifjj
Elijah bcdgdaib
Elizabeth R adaceafge
Helen J adadhacac
Katherine Wilson adgfbgfib
N Z adaabd
Thomas adgfbgfib
CAMP Charles Franklin ahgfbdb
Cora Ella ahgfbdb
David ahgfbdb
F B ahbchda
Franklin ahgfbdb
Laura Esther ahgfbdb
Lida Elvira ahgfbdb
Lucy Maria ahgfbdb
CAMPBELL Abby M adhafdfb
Edith Mary adaigaaae
Margaret abhegbif
Margaret A ahbabaaa
Mary bcdecahfc
Mary Ann wife abbegbif
Peter bcdecahfc
Philip abbegbif
Susan A bcdgdeafa
T A D adacgff
Watson adaigaaae
William bcdgdeafa
CANDAGE Maria adabbgbe
Maude M adabbhj
CANFIELD Sarah adhafce
CANTRELL —— ahbcabeh
CAPEN Herbert H adkddceb
Ina F adkddceb

CAPRON Caroline W adggeib
Clark Lyman adggeib
CAREY Dorcas bcdedka
John bcdedka
CARGABLE —— adkeda
CARGILL Charles bcdedbh
George bcdedbg
James adacgfggc
CARLETON Margaret ahbabaf
CARMICHAEL Robert bcdgdeacec
CARNES Eliza J adhagbc
George adhagbc
Harriet adaigbba
CARNEY Mae ahbabjgc
Mary A bcbebbcdaca
CARNEYS Kate adgcaccah
CARPENTER Adelia acdgdah
Ann Amelia ahgcabcc
Betsey Matilda ahgdg
Comfort ahcbbc
Darwin Erasmus adkfbbcib
E C ahgcabcc
Ella bcbcbaaaga
Esther ahgb
George A bcdgdanb
George W ahcbbc
Gertrude adkfbbcib
Jason H bcfiffff
Luther adacgfd
Mabel Rose ahfcfdba
Mary A ahbcacba
Olive J adacgfd
Oren Dunning bbbffbab
Orin Henry bbbffadba
Samuel H ahcbbc
William Dow ahcbbc
CARR Abigail wife abbd
Adeline ahgdgb
Anna Caroline adhafgcda
Betty adabj
Elizabeth ahbcac
Elliott adabj
Eva C adggeibc
Frank H adhafgcda
Hannah adabj
Henrietta Dana bcficadb
Jemima bcficadb
John bcficadb
Mary F adhafaab
Nancy adgffa
Nanne adabj
Naomi adgd, adke
Nathan adabj
Rhoda adabj
Robert adabj
Samuel adaabca
Sarah adabj
Susannah ahbcad
CARLTON Jacob (Capt) adabbgh
Julia A bcfigfbb
CARRIER Emily ahgfbda
George Irving ahgdcafd
Ira R ahgdcafd
CARROLL Lucy adggdcf

795

255

CARROW Peter bcdedfb
CARRUTH Emma G ahbcachc
CARSON Betsey adaabfd
CARTER Abigail ahfcfc
Abigail Heath adgcadaf
Addie I adadagad
Betsey adgfcic
Calvin adkfbebf
Carlene Frances adgxffcca
Carrie E adhafabaa
Carrie L ahbgbxaa
Dorcas ahbghjc
Edna gaaxaxk
Elizabeth A bcbhdgagf
Ella M adabbgdda
Ellen ahbabaead
Ellen E abccgdfa
Emma F adkedl
Frank E adgxffcca
Fred O adkedl
Hannah D bcbebbba
Hannah E adgxfag
Harold bcdgdabc
Irene Agnes adgxffcca
Isabella bcbhdgagf
James abccgdfa
James P adhafabaa
Jane akebis
Jannie ahgfdd
Jeremiah adkedl
John adadagad, adgcadaf
John Jr bcbebbba
John D adkedl
Maria adadabbda
Martha J ahbcabed
Polly wife adadagad
Sarah bbbb
Sherman adkedl
Sherman J adkedl
Simeon Hackley ahbcabed
William E bcbhdgagf
CARTIER Emil de Marchienne, Baron
  bbbfaeaa
CARVER Annie M bcbhdbeaa
Willard G bcbhdbeaa
CARY Hamilton bbbfaeaa
Marion bcbhddcb
Mary Margaret adaidc
R V bcbhddcb
—— (Sen) adhccbb
CASANO Mary bcdebfbac
CASE Adele wife adacgfd
Charles Johnson adacgfd
Ella Louise adacgfd
Eloise adacgfd
Elom Treadwell adacgfd
Eva adacgfd
George William adacgfd
Horace Riley adacgfd
Julia Sallie adacgfd
Olive Abigail adacgfd
Philena Melita adacgfd
Robert Bruce adacgfd
Sophia Dimock adacgfd

Susan abdcebeaj
Virgil Tallman adacgfd
CASEY Emma bcbhdgagg
CASS Abbie A ahbgeda
Belinda abbegbib
Mary abc
Moses abbd, adadab
Samuel ad
Sarah adadab
CASSEL MARY C ahgdccb
CASSIDY Jane adaceafa
Nancy ahbgbx
CASWELL Bernice adaimbbe
Bertha adaimbbeb
Charles adkebb
Henry adaimbbeb
Nathaniel D adkebb
Orlando L bcbebbcaaa
CATE Daniel S N P adhafgcdb
Izetta W adhafgcdb
Lola Montey adadhcbg
William adadhcbg
CATHERELL Mary J bcdebfbac
CATLIN Fidelia Rosella abbegbdfc
CAVERLEY Benjamin adaabfdf
Mary wife adaabfdf
Mary Jane adaabfdf
CAWLEY Nancy abbegba
CESTELLA Henry aeeacaaaa
Susia A aeeacaaaa
CHACE James L adadhaaca
Josiah ahbabjb
Mary R ahbabjb
—— bcdgdaiac
CHADBOURNE Abigail abdceda
CHADDOCK —— adggdj
CHADWICK Frank L adbabfefb
Hannah G abdcib
Hugh Elden ahbabfefb
Job bcbhb
—— (Capt) bcbhbg
CHAFFEE Fred French adggegdb
Harold Ray adaabdabeg
John Willard adggegdb
CHAFFIN Adoniram bcfifl
Angeline M bcfifl
Anna bcfifl
Granville bcfifl
Henrietta De Albra bcfifl
John, John Jr bcfifl
Rodney bcfifl
CHALKER Joel ahbaaheab
Wealthy Emma ahbaaheab
CHALLICONE Kate bcdecdbae
CHALLIS David adaaab, adhada
Josiah Dow adhada
Lydia adhaa
Mary ada, adab
Philip (Lieut) ada
Ruth adhada
Samuel adhada
Sarah wife adaaab
Thomas ad, adaaab
CHALMERS Elizabeth bcdecdbaea

CHAMBERLAIN Abigail akebina
Dudley akebid
Ebenezer adaabcc, adaabfab
Eliza A akebid
Ernest ahbaahdd
Paul ahbaahdd
Samuel bcdedbada
Silas C ahbaahdd
CHAMBERS Josephine Theresa bcdebgbb
CHAMPNEY Alice B bcdebfg
CHANDLER Edna C ahbabajadc
Elizabeth adggeg
Fred D adaabcja
George Langdon bcdebei
Hannah adgfcie
Herbert H ahbabajadc
Judith W ahbddf
Lizzie Langdon bcdebei
Mary adabbgbeba, ahbabad
Mary A adhafgcda
Mary Laurinda adaabcja
Nathan ahbgdf
Paul Langdon bcdebei
Philip Marshall bcdebei
Sewell Messenger bcdebei
Susan F adgfcdgb
CHANEY Abigail bbbfhbac
CHAPIN Daniel bcdedbcb
Marie Louise bcbhdbed
Uriah ahgdha
CHAPLAIN Lavina Jane akebdbbi
Marquis D akebdbbi
CHAPLIN W W agbgbfc
William adkgdde
CHAPMAN Anderson bcficaled
Charity A ahgcib
Charles H ahbabadf
Charlotte F adbafc
David abbegd
E C bcficaled
Edward adabig
Edward B ahbgie
Elizabeth adabig
Emily bcdgdg
Leon adaceaaic
Millard adaceaaic
Sadie Verona adgfcdabd
Samuel bcbb
—— abbegd
CHAPPELL Frederick C H bcbdaddl
CHARLES Maggie S adgxfaabab
Mehitable adkgg
CHARLEY Robert bcdebgab
CHARPIE Eldon C ahgdccb
Harmon D ahgdccb
CHASE Abigail adaaaf, adhaa, (3) adhaa
Abial adbaa
Abraham adhcba
Alfred W adhafaf
Althea adhccbbc
Amos adahb, adhaa, adhadd
Anna adhaa

Anna Maud adaimbbea
Anna S ahbabahc
Aquila (1) adhaa
Belinda C adadhaac
Betsey adkfbe
Carrie M wid adaaaifaa
Charles adhcbbd
Charles F adhcdaea
Clarence A bcdedbag
Daniel adkddg
Daniel R adadhaac
David adkgddg, akecahc
Dolly adhaa, adhadd
Dudley adhcba
Eli adhafcad
Esther Ann wife adaimbbea
Esther Melissa akebdbbgd
Frank adadhcbe
Frank W adhafaf
Fred L adaimbaf
George adgxfde
George S adhafaf
George W abdcebbee
Gertrude akebjd
Green adgxb
Hannah adaha, wife adhafcad, adhafd
Hannah G adhadb
Harriet adhcbbd
Harriet A adadhaac
Harriet Augusta adgkddg
Helen S akecahc
Ivory W adaimbaf
J E (Dr) ahgfbdgcc
James (2) adhaa, adkfbe
Jane adggba
Jeremiah adaimbbea
John adgfcic, (3 & 4) adhaa, (2) adhaa, adhadb, adhafaf
John L adgfdabbd
John W adhafaf
Jonathan ahbaa, (Capt) ahgf
Jonathan Dow adhafh
Joseph ad
Josiah Dow adhadb
Judith adba
Lena M adaimbaf
Lilla A adaigaaa
Louisa Rice Wright bbbffbaad
Lowell A adaimbaf
Lydia G adhadb
Madison addahaac
Marcy adgfcic
Mary adaiic, adgfcic, adhae, adhafcab, bcdeaad
Mary C adgfgaba
Mary Eliza adhafca
Mary Frances adhcdaea
Molly adhadb
Nathan G adhadb
Nathaniel adhaa, adhafd, akebbf
Olive A adabibce
Phoebe H adhadb
Polly bcdgdmaa
Rachel adgge, adhaac

797

Roanna E adhafcad
Salmon P adhccbb
Sally adaha
Sarah adgcadaaaa, wife adkddg
Sarah A adkddg
Sarah E adhafaf
Sarah M adhafaf, adhafdie
Sarah Marian adgfdabbd
Susanna adhadc
Thomas ad, adahb, adaimbaf, (1) adh-
  aa, adhaa, (2) adhaa
Vittie M adadhaac
William adgfgabb
William T adaimbaf
Winthrop adhaa, adhaad, adhafh
CHAUNCEY Henry Israel adaieaaff
Lillian Gertrude adaieaaff
CHEEVER Charles A ahbaaaae
Clara Elmira adkfbedda
Durant ahbaaaae
Elizabeth S ahbaaaae
Gertrude ahbaaaae
John ahbaaaae
John Haven ahbaaaae
CHENEY Alice P adkfbbcid
Anna adgfbegc
Cynthia Ranstead bcdedbcca
Edna M bbbffcdc
Ednah Dow (Mrs) bcdbe
Eldora R ahbgbah
Flora L bcdeaedaa
J Carl bbbffcdc
James adgfbea
John K bbbffcdc
John L bcdeaad
Joseph Young bcdedbcca
Knight Dexter bcdbedf
Sally bcbcbba
Seth bcdbeda
—— adgcacae
CHESLEY Lois adhafcd
Walter L adadagfbb
CHICK J Arthur ahgfbdga
CHIFF —— (Capt) ahbcaj
CHILD Aline E bcdedcfe
Anne M bcbegga
Dwight P bcdedcfe
Edith M bcdedcfe
John D bcdedcfe
CHILDRESS Abbie Jennings bcdeabbd
CHILDS Elizabeth adggdc
CHIPMAN Annie adgfbi
Ralph adgfgabcd
CHIPNELL Sarah adaiiaaed
CHITTICK Lydia wife adabbgqb
CHOATE Charles adhcbbi
Daniel aia
Jennie May bcdgdmab
Josiah bcdgdmab
CHRISTIAN Anna Mrs ahfca
John adkfbbb, adgxfdb
Joseph adkfbbb, adgxfdb
Zelphia Ann adgxfdb
CHURCH Anna Woodman ahbgbbeaa

Candace adacebf
Charles ahgfda
Daniel Edward ahbgbbeaa
Edmond xa
Electa abbegfjba
Hannah wife ahgfda
Lucie xab
Mary L ahgfda
CHURCHILL Abbie J adgfcdgaa
Charles C (Capt) bcdebefa
Edsyl adaimbbb
Kingman adgfcdgaa
Laura bcbcbbaf
CILLEY Abraham B adkebb
Abraham B Jr adkebb
Cutting adkebb
Edward adaiee
Eliza A ahbabaec
Hannah adkebb
Isaac ahbabaec
John 2nd adkebb
John adkebb
Jonathan Elliott adkebb
Joseph P adkebb
Julia A adkebb
Mark Jr adaiia
Martha adkebb, adkebbf
Mary J adkebb, adkebbf
Mary Jane adkebb, adkebbf
Mehitable adgx, adhab
Naomi adkebb
Olive adkebb, adkebbg
Samuel B adadabbe, adkebb
Rebecca J adkebb
Thomas adgg, adgx
—— (Miss) ahbabk
CLAPHAM Foster L adaimbaj
CLAREY Charles adbabgada
Edith A adbabgada
CLARK Aaron bcdbecedb
Anna W ahbgbbeaa
Aruna ahgfbdd
Aurora adggej
Barbara bcdecdbac
Benjamin akex
Bethia abbd
Bion Ellis ahgfbdd
Carlos ahgfbdd
Carlton Leslie ahgfbdd
Caroline P adhccgab
Catherine bcbebcgaba
Charles A ahgdccab
Charles B bcbebbea
Charles M ahgfdaa
Christina bcdgdakaa
E B adabibe
Edna A ahbabal
Edward C adbgbbeaa
Edward Gove akex, bcbebbca
Edwin G abccgbabd
Eleanor ahbgf
Eliza ahghc
Elizabeth ahg, Elizabeth wife ahg
Elliott F adhccgab

Emma J akebdbbgda
Eunice adaabdaed, adhafdj
Fanny Robinson ahgfbdd
Frank akebdbbgda
George bcdecdbac
Grace ahbabaead
Grace L adgfbgeag
Hannah M abccgdfba
Horace Ernest ahgfbdd
Humphrey (Rev) ahg
Isaac ahbgbg
Isabella F adabbhf
Isabella Florence adabbgagd
James akebdbbic
Janet bcdecdbac
Jehiah ahgdhc
Jennie adkedl
Jennie M bcdbecedb
John abbeed, adaceaag
Josephine wid abbegfgaa
Leon Lewis ahgfbdd
Louisa Boardman adadhaab
Louise adaceaag
Lydia ahcbe
Maria abbeacf
Martha bebhdea
Mary adahxa, adhafcabd
Mary Elizabeth ahgfbdd
Mary J bcdbaddl
May abbeed
Mittie F bcbebbca
Nancy bcdgdf
Nellie A bcdebfbac
Oliver adggec
Pelma bebhdga
Prentis adggej
Rebecca ahc
Richard bcdecdbac
Samuel ahbgf
Samuel C adggej
Sarah Ann bcfifc
Stephen (Capt) adadab, adadhaab
Susan A ahbaacfba
Thomas abccgdfba
Willie Dowe ahgfbdd
Zilpha adacffec
—— (Capt) ahbaaa, ahbae
—— adggeeca, bcbhb, bcbhdbf
CLARKE Elizabeth bd
Fannie ahbabahcaa
Grace Maud ahbabaead
James, James (Elder), James Jr bd
John bd
Margaret bd, bcbcbbaffa
Matthew bd
Nathan W ahbabaead
Samuel bd
CLAY Henry adhccbb
CLEASBY Joseph, Joseph Jr ahbge
CLEAVES Frank Sidney adadhcbda
G H bcdedfdaa
Joseph S adadhcbda
Laura bcdedfdaa
Lydia adgfbge

CLEMENT Archie W adhagbe
Arthur adhagbe
Carlton adhcbf
Charles J adkgaede
Elizabeth Hurd adggdcf
Frances ahbabja
Fred Dow adhagbe
George adkgac
Grace W adkgaede
John adabigf, b
Jonathan Dow adhagbd, adhcbf
Julia Emma adhagbd
Keziah adhcbf
Loren Dow adhagbe
Moses Hanson adhagbd
Orison adhagbe
Richard, Richard Jr adhcbf
Rufus P bcficap
Solomon adggdcf
Squires S adhcbf
CLEMENTS —— adhccc
CLEMSON G M adkebgab
CLENDENNIN Robert bcficaj
Robert Jr bcficaj
CLENICK George bcdgddb
CLERMONT Clara wid akebdbbgdd
CLEVELAND Elmore E adgfcieb
Henry Elmore adgfcieb
John bcbebcgaba
Joseph bcbcbbe
Mabel Darling adgfcieb
Sarah bcbcbbe
Winnifred G bcbebcgaba
CLEWLEY Heber B adhcbbfa
CLIFFORD Abigail abbd
Albert akebdbbie
Arthur E adabibia
Benjamin abbd
Clarence, Clarence 2nd adabibia
Dorothy bcdgdafqa
Hannah abbd, ake
Israel abbd
Joseph abbd, adadibia, bcdgdafqa
Judith abbed
Maria B adadhaca
Martha H adadhaca
Muriel bcdgdafqa
Nathan adhccbb
Rachel abbd
Samuel, Samuel Jr abbd, adggbaa
Sarah abbd
Solomon M abbegbic
Sylvester adadhaca
William bcdgdanec
CLONDMAN Cora M bbbebcdaac
CLOON Cecil May ahbgbebd
Fred M ahbgbebd
CLOSE Louisa C abbegfja
CLOUGH Aaron adkef
Abel adkef
Abner adka
Anna adka
Arthur Francis adkfbdxc
Benjamin adkef, bcdcb

Charlotte ahbae
Cynthia adkef
Dahiel adka
Diana adaabdabe
Fred W bebebigc
Hazen adkef
Hiram adkef
Isaiah adka, adkef
John ahbaacx, bcbhddfa
Joseph adkef
Joseph A bcbhddfa
Jonathan adka
Josiah adka, adkef
Mary abccdgd, bcbcb
Mehitabel adka
Miriam adka
Peter adaf
Richard aedaaa
Robert adham
Samuel adaf, adka, (Jr) adka
Sally (Dow) ahbaacx
Sarah adka, ahbae
Thomas Van Buren adkfbdxc
CLOWS Francis bcdgdafag
Simeon bcdgdafag
CLUFF Esther ahbgaa
Martha bcdgdaie
COATES Anson D bcdbadj
Anson J bcdbadj
Frances bcfifag
Iva bcdbadj
Jabez Valentine bcdbadj
Laurel B bcdbadj
Leroy Percy bcdbadj
Lura Ann bcdbadj
Mary Mabel adhahea
Seneca Dow bcdbadj
COBB Abigail adbabg
Betsey ahbgb
Lydia adgfcdi
Mabel adaceagci
Olive adacgf
Perez adacgf
COBLEIGH John, John Jr bcdedbc
Laodicea bcdedbc
COBURN Adelaide akecaah
Adeline akecaah
Edward akecaah
Gertrude May ahbgade
Gridley akecaah
Joseph akecaah
COCHRAN Almeda bcbhddfaab
Arta I adggeijaa
Emily Jane bcdedbja
Isaac bcded
James bcdedc
Jennie bcdedc
Jessie McDowall adadagabf
Jim bcbhddfaa
Jonathan (Dea) bcdeda, bcdedha
Meedie bcbhddfaa
Mina bcdgdu
Susan adhafdic
CODDINGTON —— adkdeba

COE Eliza adggdcda
Fidelia adgfcid
James Lewis aeeaecb
—— bcbcbbej
COFF Florence adaigbbae
COFFIN Benjamin adadabbc
Charles gaaxaxc
David adkdee
Enoch adkde
Eunice Kelley adkecbae
Fannie Estee gaaxaxe
Lucia Ann March adkdee
Mercy adkde
Myra adkeabbad
Nancy abdccb
—— ba
COGGIN Hannah bbbffcba
COGGLESHALL Daniel ahga
Joshua Jr ahga
Luther ahga
Mary ahga
Rufus ahga
Serlema ahga
COGGSWELL George H adahdbb
Mary L wife adahdbb
Sarah R adahdbb
Thomas (Capt) bbbfh
COGIN Samuel bbbffe
COIT Samuel (J P) ahcf
COLBATH Emery J bbbfhcfga
Mary Lavina bbbfhcfga
COLBURN Ezekiel bcdeabdaa
Henry Harvey bcdeabdaa
Josiah B adhafgcbb
Neva adhafgcbb
—— adgffcb
COLBY Abner bcdbaddf
Ada Dow bcdedfic, bcdeddhc
Alva E bcdedfi
Belle S adhafgcbb
Charles E bcdedfi
Daniel A bcbhbfic
Dicy abbegbibe
Eldora wife abbegbibe
Elizabeth abbegba, bbb
Emma L bcdedfi
Evelyn M bcdedfi
Frank True Russell abbegfcb
Gertrude Agnes bcbhbfic
Gertrude W bcdedfi
Gideon bbbfa
Hazen adgffb, adhafcj
Ida bcdedfi
Ida Eldean abbegbibe
Isaac bbb
John G adkfbbi
Lavina D bcdbaddf
Louisa adhaff
Mary adhafgc, bcbebf
Molly bcbebf
Sarah B bcdedfi
Sophia bcdeda
Stephen bcbebf
Susanna bcfic

Walter H bcbebbfad
William bcdedfi
William Greenleaf bcdedfi
COLCORD —— abcgdceb
COLE Abigail bcdedcf
Alice Eva bbbfabid
Asahel ahchj
Conilla E adabbgdaac
Daniel B ahbchi
Elizabeth A ahgcif
George W bcfigbjjac
Emma N adgfbdba
Henry akebdbbfeb
Henry C abccgaccaac
Hettie F adgfdabbb
Isaac bcdedcf
Lora M abccgaccaac
Louisa wife akebdbbfeb
Lydia Thompson adkgdd
Margaret a, ae, bb
Mabel bcdedfi
Mehitable bcdedl, bcfigfbc
Oliver adgfdabbb
Pearl Ruby wid akebdbbfeb
Polly adacgfe
Seth bcbhdehe
Susanna adabbgdab
Thomas Jr ahbchh
Wallace W bcdedfi
William adabbgdaac
COLEMAN Mary adbabfee
COLGATE Abraham bcdgdbg
COLLIER Charles F bcfifffd
COLLINS Abigail adbg
Abigail Dow adabc
Abijah adbac
Amos adfccb
Ann adggdcc
Betsey adbac
Content adhce
Elijah adbg
Emily adaceafgea
Ephraim, Ephraim sr adabe
Esther adbac, adabc
Ezra adhce
George H adbabff
Hannah adbac, adfcca
Huldah adbac
Isaac adfccb
Jacob, Jacob Jr adfccb
James abbegbdff
John ad, adabc, adbac
Joshua, Joshua Jr adfcca
Judith adbac, (wife) adgxg, adbac
Julia bcdecdbaaa
Levi adabc
Lydia adbac, (wife) adgxff
Kesiah adgxfaac
Mary adbac, adada, adfccb
Mary Abbie ahbabjk
Moses akecad
Moses Norris ahbabjk
Nancy adhce

Nathaniel (Rev) adggdcc
Patience adbac
Paul adbabff, adbac
Peace adfcca
Phebe adbg
Rebecca wid bcdeaa, bcdcbbe
Reuben adfccb
Richard adabc, (Jr) adabc, adbg, ad-
  bga, Jr adbg
Rhoda adgxff
Robert adgxg
Ruth adfcca
Sally adgxfab
Samuel adbac, adgxfaac, adhcde, ad-
  hce, ahbaacxf, adkfbbdc
Sarah adbg, adfcca, bcdedbcb
Stephen adfcca
Tristram adbac, adgxfab, adgxff, ad-
  gxg
Warren Otis adbabff
Zachaeus adhce, Jr adhce, 2nd adhce
Zilpha Angeline adbabff
COLLYER Martha J adaceddb
Samuel B adaceddb
COLMAN Anna ad
Perry bcdebfbf
Sarah bcfiff
COLPITTS Harry T bcdgdafbf
COLSTON —— wid adggde
COLTHARP Mollie O ahchfij
COLUMBIA Perley J bbbebgaba
COMINGS Eliza Jane ahbabjecb
COMSTOCK Elva adaabdag
Emma B adabiggf
Eznona adabiggf
John M ahgchm
Lucius O adaabdag
Mamie E ahgchm
Mary L wife adabiggf
Melinda bcbhbg
Minnie R ahgchm
Orville adaabdag
Willard H adabiggf
Willie D ahgchm
CONANT George ahbgbaec
CONABY Etta M adabbgbccc
CONDON Thomas bcdgddaf
CONE Henry Franklin ahgchebaa
James Brewster ahgchebaa
CONERTY Ella M adaabdabc
CONGDON James W bcdebgab
CONGER Barbara Lois adgcacbada
Elizabeth adaceaa
Frank L adgcacbada
Helen Josephine bcbebbfaa
CONK Dennaryous fcek
CONKLEY Sarah bcdgdaaab
CONKLIN Lewis R bbbfabbf
CONLEY James H adkdececb
Samuel adkdececb
CONNELL Elizabeth Rebecca ahbgb-
  acb
Paul T ahbgbacb
CONNELLY Daniel bcbcbaaba

801

Margaret bcbcbaaba
CONNER Dorothy adha
CONNOR Clara A adadhcaic
Dorothy adaabac
J H adgcadaaaf
Jesse Crossman adbabfecc
Marion S adgcadaaaf
Mary J adbabfdb
CONVERSE James (Col) adacg
Mary A adaabdabca
Robert adaabdabc
CONWAY Elizabeth adkgddha
CONYNE —— bcbcbbea
COOK Alice Bertha bcbhde
Charles, Charles Jr adabbgbch
Ernest V adkgaeg
Grace M bcdedbbdb
Harvey adkebaac
Lewis J adgkaeg
Lewis W adkgaeg
Melvina adadhcahb
Minnie E adaabcjj
Phebean bcbhbg
Richard adadhcahb
Ruby May adkgaeg
Susan Chadwick adkebaac
William adaabcjj
—— (Miss) g
—— bcdgdafh
COOLE Margaret a
COOMBS Anthony (Lieut) adabba, ad-
  abbgagd
Betsey adabbgagd
Daniel adabba
David adabba
Elizabeth eaa
Jemima adabba
John adabba
Jonathan adabba
Joshua adabba
Judith adabba
Mary adabba
Nathaniel adabba
Sarah adabba
Stephen, Stephen (Lieut) adabba
COON Frank adggega
COONITY Mary adaabdabc
COOP Christopher x
Johan x
COOPER John bcfj
Mary E bcbhddiaab
COPE Winnogene ahbcabfea
COPELAND Florence akebcfac
Grace Mildred adacgface
Kate bcbeggab
Raymond Wallace bcbeggab
Wallace bcbeggab
COPP Aaron bbbc
Jonathan bbbc
Solomon bbbb, bbbca
CORAM Albena bcdgdabfd
CORBIN Aaron Johnson ahcbfea
E ahcbfea
COREY Abigail bcdedb

Charles D adacgfd
Mary abbegbifb
CORLISS Amber bbbfabmh
David Bailey adkfbedc
Johanna bcd
Johannan bc
George bc
John bd
Lucinda N ahbgai
Willard C bbbfabmh
CORNELL Mary adacedhca
CORNING Albion James bcdeddd
Albion James Jr. bcdeddd
Gilman bcdeddd
John Woodside bcdeddd
Samuel, Samuel Jr adggac
CORSON John F adkecbal
CORTLAND Sarah adbaa
COSGROVE Alice adacffec
COSTELLA Kenneth bcdgdafhdb
William bcdgdafhdb
COSTELLO —— bcbhdbc
COTTLE John ada
Rose A bcfifhhhb
COTTON Mary Jane abceabcb
Meribah Taylor abbegfcaa
Seaborn (Rev) a
COUCH Albert J bbbebdac
Ellen M bbbebdac
COULTER Dow bcdgdbg
Gerusha bcdgdbg
John bcdgdbg
William bcdgdbg
COURTLAND Miriam adhcbb
COWDEN John E ahbaaaae
COWELL Mabel L adgfbhada
Q C adgfbhada
COWIN —— bcdedbbdac
COX Benjamin adabba
Ida J adacgface
Minerva wid abceaba
—— adhcdaba, bcdgdabgac
COY Lucy abccgeh
Elizabeth wife adbd
George adbd
John adbd
CRABTREE Ida L adabbgta
Lucy ahbabja
CRAFTS Aurora Resina adhafdd
Emily Ann Webster adhafdd
Harrison adhafdd
Henrietta adhafdd
Mary Susan adhafdd
Melina Atwood adhafdd
Pliny Earl adhafdd
Warren Levi adhafdd
CRAGE Lena C bbbfabmj
Robert T bbbfabmj
CRAGG Robert bbd
CRAIG Beatrice bcdgdaidc
Margaret bcdgde
Mary Belcher ahbabcdb
Nancy bcbhddceb
Moses ahbabcdb

Rufus ahbaea
CRAM Abbie F adhagbf
Abigail adkebg
Amelia bcdeaae
Anna adkec
Aurelia bcdeaac
Benjamin adadabba
Charles Choate adhcbbe
Daniel adhcbbe
Cleveland C bcdeaa
Cynthia bcdeaad
Elizabeth abdc
Emma Dow adhcbbe
Eugene bcdgdaida
Ezekiel bcdeaae
Frank bcdgdaida
Hial Plumley adhcbbe
Hannah bcdeaa
Jane bcdeaad
John F adhagbf
Jonathan bcdeaad
Joseph adkgdef
Laura M bcbcbbad
Leland bcdeaa
Lorenia bcdeaad
Lowell bcdeaae
Mabel bcdgdaida
Melvin D adadabba
Moses adhagbf
Nancy adkeh
Nathan, Nathan Jr .Nathan 3rd bcdeaa
Ophelia P adkgdef
Sarah bcdebd
Selnida bcdeaae
Silas bcbcbbad
Thomas abdc, abcdeaa, Jr bcdeaa
William bcdeaad
CRAMER Aden W adacgfc
Ara B adacgfc
Belinda adacgfc
David adacgfc
David Amer adacgfc
Edward O adacgfc
Ezra adacgfc
George Dow adacgfc
Henry Abner, adacgfc
Julia adacgfc
Mary adacgfc
Olive adacgfc
Philena adacgfc
CRANDALL Walter S adkgaedb
CRANE Annie M wid bcdbecea
Clara M bcdgeanb
CRANFIELD —— (Gov) ab, ad
CRANTON Henry L adadhaca
CRAWFORD Clarissa befical
Robert (Captain) ahbcf
Harold adbabfecab
CREELE see Greeley
CREIGHTON David adaija
James adaija
——ahbaaae
CREOLE Rose adabbgabd
CRIDGE Alfred Denton ahgfbdg

CROCK Ellen M bebhddfac
CROCKER Augustus O bcdgdmac
Ernest Clifton bcdgdmac
Henry F R adkehbd
Hepzibah bcdbeg, bcdbeh
James befifd
Jane abccgcf
Oliver P adkehbd
Sarah abccgcfc
Sarah E bbbfabhd
Stanley P bcdgdmad
Stephen bcdbeh
—— bcdbeg
CROCKETT Charles adkgac
E D adacedfg
George adkgac
Josiah adabbc
Nelson H adkgac
—— ahbaea
CROFT Byron adacfff
Cyrus adacfff
Ezra, Ezra Jr adacfff
Dwight adacfff
James adacfff
Nancy adacfff
Sophronia adacfff
CROMMETT John ahbabaeac
Nora L ahbabaeac
CROMWELL Abigail bbbfhc
CRONK Arthur adhadced
Cora F ahfcfceg
Elizabeth H befiibb
CRONKITE Abraham bcdgdaib
Basha bcdgde
CROOK Anna S adhadccb
CROPLEY Ida bcdgdaab
CROSBY Ada Belle gbefaa
Emma ahbabamgc
Ephraim gbefaa
Gilman adggdcib
Manson bcbhddcebb
Nora E adggdcib
Sewall Elmer bcbhddcebb
—— adgcadaaae, adggdaab
CROSS Abiel befifk
Belinda befifk
David befifk
Ebenezer K befifji
Hannah befifk
Jesse, Jesse Jr. befifk
Lucy adkdeac
Nathaniel B befifk
Susie E ahbabaeb
Tamas befiffd
CROSSETT —— adgfbfccb
CROSSMAN Cynthia ahgca
Ebenezer ahgca
CROTTERS John bcdgdagk
May bcdgdagk
Thomas bcdgdagk
CROUCH James abbegbdf
Mary Ann abbegbdf
CROUSE Mary E abbeebba
CROWDER Emeline adkedc

Francis J adkedc
Mary adkedc
CROWELL Doris Elizabeth abdcebk
Herbert C abdcebk
Mabel L adgfbhada
Melinda bcfican
Nancy adgcacb
Timothy C adaimbbh
William Eaton ahbcai
—— bcdgdaiad
CRUFF Arthur Newcomb adacffeec
CRUMNEY John D adacgfaea
CUDWORTH Aurora S bcfifjad
Thaddeus adaceafi
CULVER Azubah adaabdab
CUMMINGS Adeline adhcbbfba
Angeline Norcross bcdgddah
Anna bcdeabd
Caroline bcdeabdc
Charles K bcbcbbca
Charles M bcdbadddc
Elizabeth adacg
Jeff adacffib
Lois Beaman bcdedbcac
Lydia bcdgdag
Mary bcdgdia
Mary E adgfdabba, bbbfabmi
Maurice adgfcdgcc
May Isabelle adgfcdgcc
Thomas bcdeabdc
CUMMINS Agnes bcdgdafea
Andrew bcdgdeadc
Bertram bcdgdeadc
Charles bcdgdeadc
Chester bcdgdeadc
Frederick bcdgdeadc
George bcdgdad
Gladys bcdgdafea
Hayward bcdgdafea
Jacob bedgdad, bcdgdatb
Leonard bcdgdad
Mary bcdgdad
Percy bcdgddec
Raymond bcdgdakfd
Silas bcdgdad, bcdgddec
Smith bcdgdafea
Sterling bcdgdafea
Teneriff bcdgdafea
Vesta bcdgdafea
Winifred bcdgddec
—— bcdgdagm
CUNNINGHAM Bernice M bcbhddiaab
Arthur Leslie abdcebk
Elizabeth bcfiffdb
Harriet G adaabffdc
James bcbeggab
Nellie bcbeggab
Richard abdcebk
William bcbhddiaab
CURRAN Nellie adadieaaa
CURRIE —— bcdgdafda
CURRIER Aaron Shute adaiiabb
Ann bcbegd
Anna adadhabb, bcdcb

Annie Augusta bcdbaddm
Azubah Harriman bcbegd
Betsey H abccgaea
Cyrus Buzzell bcbegd
Edmund ahbabam, ahbabcb
Eleanor adfa
Eliza bcficap
Elmer bcdgdakfc
Emily Augusta ahbabam
Harriet Story bbbebga
Humphrey bcfifd
James L bcbebbcaf
Jonathan bcdcb
Judith bcdi
Lavinia adkfbbcb
Louise adhafabaab, bcbehhj
Martha Jane akebdbbg
Mary ahbabdad, bcbegf, wife bcdbaddm
Mary Noyes bcbegd
Matilda S bbbebga
Merrill adkebf
Mettie bcbebbcaf
Nathan bcbegd, bcbegf
Nathaniel adfa
Oliver bcbegf
Oliver bcbegf
Philip adaaaicb
Polly adkebf
Rebecca Dow bcbegd
Samuel adadhabb
Sarah bcbebbcdax
Sarah E adaaaie
Stephen bcbegd
Sylvester bcdbaddm
Willie A bcbebbfae
—— adaieaaf, ahbabcg, bcfifaf
CURRILL Rachel wid abcflc
CURTIS Alfred abccgcaa
Amanda M adgfcdh
Bessie Agnes bcbhddccbe
Billdad ahgcg
Carrie adgfcicf
Carrie B adgcadae
Eliza adabbgaji
George William bcfihec
Jane R bbbffcbac
John abbegbeae
Marvin ahgcg
Philemon adkehba
Rebecca J adkehba
Sarah wife adkehba
Sarah M abbegbeae
CUSHING Benjamin adggbf
Caleb adg, (Col) adgda, adggbf
Frank adhcbba
George H bcdeaeae
John Newmarch adggba
Lucinda abccgba
Lydia adggbf
Maria A adkech
CUSHION see Cushing
CUSTER Olive ahdaadd
CUTLER Clara E adhafgcdc
Clyde A bcfifhhdaa

804

Henry R adaabdaed
James adhafgedc
Lydia adacfe
CUTTER Arnold befihecc
Charles Winthrop befihecc
Clarence A bbbebcdaea
Henrietta ahgchj
Irving Taylor befihecc
Leonard F befihecc
Lillie bcbebbcdaea
Rebecca adggehb
CUTTING Ellen P befifjal
Israel befifjb
Loving adacfdb
Lydia befifje
CUTTS Elizabeth abdcebed
CYR Ellen bcbhddfac
DAGGET David (Hon) ahcbc
DAGGETT Phebe ahbcaje
DAKEN Ada bcdgeafeg
William M bedgeafeg
DALE William bcbcbbae
DALTON Joseph abceaba
Mary abbegbdg
Moses ahbaa
Sam a
Sarah akecd
Timothy ak
DAME Emma P bcbcbbgbba
Mary bcdedbbc
Mary Caroline abbegbdg
DANA James (Rev) ahcbc
Katherine adaabdabea
Mehitable adkdeab
Sarah adggdc
DANFORD Rachel adkdbe
DANFORTH Adeline Luthera befifi
Albert Hallar adaabcba
Aurella Anna befifi
Betsey Emma befifi
Charles adaabcjh
Eliphalet befiiba
Eliza Hovey befiiba
Elizabeth ahbg
Hannah ahbg
Jennie abccgefcab
John ahbg
Joseph bcdgdabfe
Leander befifi
Liliola C bcdeaedba
Loemma Emeline befifi
Matilda bcbhddcc
Nason befifi
Paul D bcdgdabfe
Phinease Alpheus befifi
Robert befifi
Robert Alonzo befifi
William, William Jr. bbbebfj
DANIEL Eliza H abbegbebbb
DANIELS George S adgdcadaaaa
Louise M bcbhdhhb
Nabby ahbcab
Nettie M adgcadaaaa
DARK Maria bcdedkb

DARLING Alan Richards adgfbeggaa
Andrew McClary adgfbeggaa
Doris Lillian adgfbeggaa
Drusilla adgfcie
Hannah adgcaccafa
Henry M abccgbabc
Jennie bcdgdaik
Jesse adggdaac
Joseph Kimball adggdaac
Laura bcdgdafma
Polly ahbgbi
Reuben D adgfcie
Robert bcdgdeaib
Stewart bcdgdafea, bcdgdeaib
Stewart Jr bcdgdeaib
DART —— ahbcabba
DAUGHERTY Emma bcdgdafea
DAVENPORT Cornelius fa
John fa
DAVID Charles A ahbgbfaac
Charles Herbert ahbgbfaac
DAVIDSON Agnes R ahbcai
Christine ahgfbdac
James Wheeler abdcebcabd
—— (Dr.) bcdedcha
DAVIE Gregorie x
DAVIS Abigail bca
Abigail T adabbgh
Albert M ahbabajaf
Allen T abbegbibb
Alvin A ahbgbaed
Amanda M ahbaacda
Amos bcbea
Anna Augusta ahbgbaed
Benjamin adbabfdea
Betsey ahbaacd
Charles W ahbcacg
Daniel adkebgba
David Dow adhafe
Dolly wife ahbabje
Dolly D ahbabje
Ebenezer bca
Eleanor bbbb
Eliza Ann adhafgb
Elizabeth bbbb, bca
Ellen adgfcdgab, adgfcdgcb
Emily Adelia ahcabca
Ephraim bcbea, Jr. bcbebh
Ephraim Lemuel ahchea
Evelyn M ahbabajaf
Fannie adaimbbga
Frankie May adbabfdea
Gertrude gaaxaxi
Georgianna A bbbffbaad
Greeley ahchea
Hannah bbbb, bbbbh
Harry Putnam adhcbbfba
Hattie gaaxaxf
Horace gaaxaxf
Irene ahbabamgb
Isabell bcdgdmac
Jabez bca
James (Capt) abcc, adba, aee
James bca, bcdc, bcbebce

James M bcdebge
Johanna bc
John bbbb, bbbffbaad, bca
John D adhafe
Jonathan bbbb
Joseph bca
Judith bcbea, wife bcbebc
Julia M adaimbaj
Katie E bcfifjjab
Laurien abbegbibb
Levi M adhafe
Malachi bbbb
Manley ahbabajaf
Mary bcbeb, bcbebcm, bcbebcc, bcbebcf
Mary A adacedh, ahgdcac
Mary C bbbfhjbc
Mary E adkebgba
Mary Lake abbegbibb
Moses Moses Jr bca
Nancy wife ahbaacda
Nathaniel ahbaacda, bcbeb
Nellie adabbgra
Orpha bbbb
Philena R ahbcacf
Rosamond Cushman bcbhdbna
Ruth bbbb
Samuel ade, bca
Sarah A adaabcje
Silas ahbabje
Smith adaimbaj
Solomon bca
Sophia R wid adkddca
Susan E wife adbabfdea
Susan R bcdebge
Thankful ahdaab
Thomas adgffb, adhafe, Jr adhafe, bc
Timothy bcbebc
Walter bcbhdbndf
William ada
—— bbbffcf
DAVISON Mary akebc
DAWSE Abigail T adabbgh
DAY Caroline bcbhdqaa
Dolly adggee
Gertrude wid adabbgaig
Icy adabbgaa
Joseph adaabdc
Joseph R ahbaadea
Leslie B bcdgdaacdd
Lillian L ahbaahdea
Polly adggef
Robert Edwin bcdgdaaedb
Stephen Leslie bcdgdaaedb
DAYTON —— bcdgdaacdd, cbbcba
DEACON Ada bcdgdafeg
DEAL Edgar adaimaf
Ednah adgxfag
DEAN Alden adkgaea
Carrie ahbabajd
John bcbhdej
John P adgfbgfaag
Maurice adacedhca
Merriam ahchh
Minnie G adacedhca

—— wid ahbcab
DEARBORN Abigail abcd
Ann abbef, aeb
Betsey akecac
Comfort ahbabi
Cynthia adgcadad
Edward abdcib
Edward Harris abdcib
Elizabeth abcb, akeba
Ella Frances akebbce
Elmer W abbegbid
Esther wife abcb
Frances Ross adhcdaed
George Elvin akebbce
George Tucker adhcdaed
George W abbegbid, bcdbaddb
Godfrey ak
Hannah abcb, abccga, adgxb
Helen Towle adhcdaed
Henry (Capt) abbeg, abccd
Henry abcb, Jr abcb, adadh, ahbabkg
James akebbce, abbegfgaa
Jeremiah, Jeremiah Jr Jeremiah 3rd
  akeba
Joanna M abbegfgaa
John adhcdaed, aeb, 3rd aeb, Jr Dea
  aeb
John Blake akebbce
John Tilton adhdcaed
Joseph aeb
Joseph F akecac
Joseph Jewell abdcic
Josiah (Maj) akecac
Josiah R abbegbdcab
Lydia bcbhddd
Martha adgfdabbc
Mary abcb, abdcib, akeba
Mary Ann adaigaa, akecac
Melinda abdcib, abdcicb
Nathan W abbege
Nathaniel ahbabi
Olive akeba
Reuben abdb
Reuben Gore aea
Samuel abdcib, akeba
Samuel John abbegba
Samuel W bcdbecea
Sarah abcb, abcfb, ak, akeba (bis),
  akecac
Sarah A adkebab
Sarah Nudd akebbce
Simon abcb
Simon Nudd akecac
Susan wife ahbabi
Susanna adfcdcb, ahbaed
Thomas Horace adhcdaed
William ahbabjd
—— Lieut Col akebf
—— Capt bcdb
DEARDEN Annie Jane akebdbba
James akebdbba
DEBEC Clarence bcdgddf
Enoch bcdgddg
Genore bcdgddf

George bcdgddg
Howard bcdgddf
Josephine bcdgddf
DE BROCAS —— (Miss) adggdcc
DE BURGH Elizabeth (Lady) cb
DE CHAINE Celia E bcdgdaalc
Joseph bcdgdaalc
Mary Louise bcdgdabde
DECKER Alfred adacgfabc
DEERING Elizabeth adgxfaae
Annie adaidaea
DE GROOT Earl bcdgdafn
DE LANCE Grace bcbhdbedd
DELAND Ann A wid adkfbedb
DEMCY Thomas bbd
DEMERRITT Clara A ahbabjj
Davis adgfe
Samuel (Gen) ahbabjj
DEMING William adggdcc
William Sumner adggdcc
—— c
DEMMING Charles H ahgdcaga
Francis D ahgdcaga
DENMAN Melissa J adaidaee
DENNETT —— adaimbbb
DENNIS Alice befiibad
Helen V aeeaeccc
William O aeeaeccc
DENNISON Alice befiibad
Almira adkgaebe
John bbbebef
DENSMORE George bcdgdana
DENTON Nora (Mrs) ahchfih
DERBY Martin bcbebbcaa
Mary A bcbebbcaa
DERNIERE Annie Maria De C bcbe-
hhf
DE ROSE Rose Ann adaceddc
DERRY Gertrude M bbbfhcfe
DESCOTEAN Aime J adkeabbad
Desire adkeabbad
DESFOSSES Frank adabibcad
Rosa adabibcad
DEVEREUX Josephine Augusta bbbf-
abba
DEVINE Annie adhccfea
DE WARE Gerald bcdgdafba
DEWEY Chandler adaabdae
George (Adm) ahgfbg
Horace Pease ahgge
Jesse ahgge
Jesse Edson ahgge
John Nelson ahgge
Laura ahgge
Louisa adaabdae
Lovina adaabdae
DE WITT Abigail H adabbgtac
Della M adabbgpaa
Jeremiah adabbgpaa
Mary M adadagacc
DEXTER Mary A wid ahbabajd
DIAMOND Ruth adhafabe
DIBBLE Adelaide wid bcdgdaba
Effie A bcdgdeadf

Nelson bcdgdeadf
DICKENSON Lucy bcbhddaa
DICKEY George W ahbgbfh
Wilson abccgcab
DICKINSON Adelaide bcdgdeadf
Albert bcdgdec
Alma V bcdgdanb
Amelia bcdgdeah
Bakey bcdgdeaab
Bruce bcdgdagb
Caroline bcdgdafb, bcdgdec
Charles bcdgdeaafb, bcdgdeae
Clara bcdgdeaafb, bcdgdeae
Edmund bcdgdahb
Elijah bcdgdv
Emerson N bcdgdanb
Emily M bcdgdanb
Esther bcdgdg
Eva May bcdgdaae
Gerusha bcdgdec
Gordon bcdgdeacb
Harriet bcdgdea
Harry bcdgdeah
Harvey bcdgdakfa
Helen E bcdgdanb
Henry bcdgdaafa
Hulda bcdgdaac
Jennie bcdgdddae
Jessie H bcdgdanb
John bcdgdec
Julia bcdgdec
Lecta R bcdgdakfa
Leslie P bcdgdanb
Levina bcdgdeace
Lydia bcdgdbaa, bcdgdec
Maggie L acdgdv
Mahala bcdgdaac, bcdgdeb, bcdgdec
Margarette bcdgdaai
Mary bcdgdaba
Prudence bcdgdeah
Rebecca bcdgdg
Sarah bcdgdaak, bcdgdaff, bcdgdeaca,
bcdgdec
Stephen bcdgdec
Sarah Ann bcdgdeaa
Susie E bcdgdanb
Theresa M bcdgdanb
Thomas bcdgdec
DINGHAM Abraham adacgfaba
Nellie adacgfaba
DINGLEY Petsey ahbgb, ahbgbe
Jeremiah ahbgbe
Julia Ann ahbgbe
DINSMORE Abram bcdecaj
Barbara J bbbfhcfeb
Caroline bcdedgd
George bcdgdabc
John Barnett bcdedgd
John William bcdedgd
Mary Dow adgffcb
Mary Ella bcdedgd
William adgffcb
DIVOLL Josephine E bcdeaeaf
Marinda A bcdeaeaf

Nellie M bcdeaeaf
DIX Samuel bc
S Melvina adacgff
DIXON Lovina bcdgen
DIXSON Miriam ahchb
DOAN Leland I abbeebcaab
DOBLE Vesta A bbbfhbaca
DODGE Arline G bbbffcbag
Charles L bbbffcbag
Edmund T adbabfefd
Eliza A bcdecdh
Elizabeth wife bcficao
Ezra bcfe
Ezra F bbbffcbag
George H bbbffcbag
Gertrude V bbbffcbag
Hattie May adhabfefd
Henry L akecafh
Isaac ahgfd
Julia bcfiffdce
Marietta adaceafb
Mary A bbbffcbag
Richard (Capt) ahfcf
Sarah bcdeaaa
Sarah Ann bcdecdb
Susan bcdgegb
Thomas, Thomas Jr. bcficao
Tryphena ahgfd
DOE Alice abccgcfda
Bartlett abbecf
Charles Franklin abbecf
Harry Fogg bcdedggba
John d
Keziah adhcbf
Parsons bcdedggba
DOLE Eleazer bcfiffc
Frances wid abdf
John W bcfigfddc
Lydia C adaimbcf
Marion bcfigfddc
William bcbcbbae
DOLBEAR Israel abcd
DOLBEARE George B ahghe
Lucy ahghe
DOLLIFF Sarah adgfbgeb
DOLLOFF Betsey Burnham adadhaba
Daniel ahbaahde
Helen A ahbabajg
Lena M ahbaahde
Melissa Sally abbegbb
Sarah M wife ahbaahde
Stephen abbegfa
Thomas abbegbb
DOMEY Catherine bbbebcdaea
DONALD Edgar A ahbabajd
Edgar J ahbabajd
Wallace ahbabajd
DONLEY Irene Grace adaimaaaba
William W adaimaaaba
DONNELLY Elizabeth G bcdgdakbf
William bcdgdakbf
DONONGAL Henry adadibdk
DONOVAN Eugene adkddcac
DOOLITTLE G F adkfbeba

Martha ahchff
Mary ahchff
DOORE Jennie S ahbabahca
Lillian ahbabaeadd
Lillian A ahbabahcd
DOPP Philander adacgfee
DORIEN —— bbbg
DORMAN Richard ahgchc
Joseph ahgchc
Leroy C bcdgdakaa
Sarah Isabell bcdgdakaa
DORR Alice adabbgqdb
DORSEY John adhafgcbg
Thomas W adhafgcbg
DOUGHTY Alice adaimaaaba
DOUGLASS Bessie ahbabajab
Edward adbac
Elizabeth adadhaaac
Howard (Sir) bbbfab
John A adabbhp
Stephen A adhccbb
Susanna ahchf
William ahchf
DOW A B bcbhddcba
A M bcbhdeia
Aaron adahd, adaiea, adaif, adaigc, ad-
    gfbhc, adkfb, adkfbd, adl, ahcff,
    ahcg, ahchfi, bcbhbfd, bcdgdag, bed-
    gdl, bcdgdq
Aaron Boardman bcdgdagh
Aaron Morrill adkehcc
Aaron W adhafdgec, bcdgdaie
Abba ahbgbxe
Abbie adaabacaf, adabigf, adadibda,
    ahfcfdba, bbbfhbxci, gbaj
Abbie A adaidage
Abbie Belle adabbgbcac
Abbie C adaimbib, bcdebfbf
Abbie F. adgxfaacaab
Abbie Frances adggdcia
Abbie Hannah bcfiibca
Abbie Inez bcbhddcca
Abbie J adaimcdd
Abbie M abccgbadb
Abbie Mary aeeaecb
Abbie (Rogers) akebdbbd
Abbie S adkgeag
Abbott adaimaad
Abbott C adgxffag
Abbot Low adkdeceh
Abby adaabd, adaijbc, adgfbgbc, bbb-
    fhaj, bcbhddfaad, bcfigfac, faab
Abby Ann adaiebab
Abby B adkebad
Abby C ahbabaac, ahbgbxc, bbbffba
Abby F ahbgeac
Abby Frances, abbeebcd
Abby M adaabclb, ahbgdcb
Abel ahcbb, bcdedd, bcdeddh
Abi ahbcabedd
Abiah bcfj
Abial adbad, adhcf
Abial Blanchard adaabfxa
Abial Green adhac

Abiel Rolfe ahbgdfb

Abigail abbc, abbeaa, abbeb, abbegfa, abbegbg, abcff, abdca, abdcebk, ada. adaaaib, adabbba, adabbgha, adabbgsa, adabc, adaca, adadabe, adaigag, adbaf, wife adbe, adge, adgfa, adgfbda, adgfbgc, adhcf, adkeaa, wife adkebc, adkebgg, adkgaa, ahbabg, ahbabjk, ahbcabab, ahbcabeb, ahbcace, ahbchh, ahbcj, ahde, ahgff, bbbfhaa, bbbfj, bcbb, bcbha, bcbhbb, bcbhddah, bcbhddcd, bcbhddl, bcdeabf, bcdga, bcfia, bcfifad, bcfife, bcfiffa, dec.

Abigail Ann adbafaa

Abigail Arnold bcfihedb

Abigail C eaaa

Abigail Carter ahfcfca

Abigail G adadiabb

Abigail Lincoln adbabfh

Abigail Marion adgfbgfaaa

Abigail Moore abbegbdbf

Abigail O adkedd

Abigail Phillips adbafabb

Abihal abcfl

Abner adkb, adkga, adkgde

Abner Gilmore bcbhddcefd

Abner W bcdgeh

Abner William bcbhddcef

Abner Harris adadabbdaaa

Abra E adgfbhac

Abraham abbegfkc, adbafd, adadicd, adgfbc, adgfbfb, adhadd, adhafaa, adhahe, adhb, adhc, adhcbbb, adhccd, adhch, adhcha, bcff, bcfic, bcficab, bcficad, bcficadb, bcfifg

Abraham Arthur bcficadbb

Abraham Brown aeeae

Abraham C aeeacaaf

Abraham Greenleaf adkfbbcc

Abraham L adfcdcaaa

Abraham Lincoln ahbgbadf

Abram adaimaab, adhcdaa, adhcha, bcfifja

Abram C aeeacaaf

Abram H adgxffcb

Abram S adadhac

Absalom bbbfaf

Absalom Smith bbbfabi, bbbfabib

Achsah ahbchf, bcbegj, bcdecda, bcfifae, bcfifn

Achsah Philena bcbegbd

Ada adaaaieeb, adaabceac, adadibdi, ahgchhd, bcdgdafbc, bcdgdafoaa, bcdgdeaid

Ada Belle bcdedbbbi

Ada Bradbury bcdebefb

Ada F adabbgahba, bbbfhcfab

Ada Florence bcbcbbgjb

Ada Horton bcdebeja

Ada Irene ahgdhbcd

Ada J adkgaefa

Ada Jessie bcdebgagd

Ada Louise bcdebgbbca

Ada M ahbabaeaeb, bcdebgbh, bcfifjadc

Ada M W adgfcdgaac

Ada May adgfcadaffb

Adah Salisbury ahbghgb

Adalia bcdgaddh

Adaline bcdedfb

Adams ahbcabc

Adams George ahbcabcbf

Addie abbeacbda, bcdgdafke

Addie A abccdgcab

Addie B abccgbabd

Addie C adabibcca

Addie E adacedha

Addie F adkddcac

Addie M adkgddfb

Addie N bbbebgba

Addie V adaceafkb

Addie Ward adgfcicf

Addina bcdbaddc

Addison adadibde

Adine Crawford adabibicbb

Adna bcdgdaia, bcdgdec

Adrian Ellsworth bcdgdaace

Adrith ahbabcdf

Adelia bcdgdabg, bcdgdafba, bcdgdanb, bcdgdeaj

Adelaide Adelia adaimaab

Adelaide Arvilla adhcdacf

Adelaide G adggeim

Adelaide L ahbabald

Adelbert adaceaaib, bcdgdeacc

Adelbert C ahbabahcd

Adelbert F adabbgdab

Adeline wife adaabfe, adgfbgad, adgxfde, adkdccn, ahbabccb, bcdebgac

Adeline Cornelia ahgdgbab

Adeline E adbabfba

Adeline Marsh adkdecd

Adeline Robbins adhafcg

Aden adaabcef

Aden W adaabcef

Adyn adgfdga

Agnes adadageb, bcbhbgm, bcdgdaacfd

Agnes D adaaaieea

Agnes Jane adaceafkf

Agnes Louisa adkedjc

Agnes M abbegbifa

Agnes N bcdebgaacc

Agnes S adaimbiace

Agrippa ahgfbd

Ainslee bedhddfaca

Albert abccabec, adaabacaa, adabbgbebc, adgfbfba, adgfdabb, ahbabaeadh, bcdbecdf, bcdebfc, bcdecdi, bcdedgf, bcdgddaca

Albert Arthur bcbcbbbacaa

Albert Barnes adgfcicdc

Albert Dean adabbgaice

Albert E adadhaaad, adaiiabaab

Albert Edmund ahfcfceg

Albert F adhafagb, bcdebfbe

Albert Freeman adkfbbdb

Albert G abbegfgae, bcbebbcb

Albert Gallatin ahbghg, ahbghgf, bedecah, bedecahe
Albert H adaabfdfb, adgfbgeag
Albert Hall ahgfbga
Albert Henry ahchfdcc, ahbcachcc
Albert J adabiggde, bbbffcdd
Albert Jay adaceagcce
Albert John adaabdabb
Albert L adabbgaiea
Albert Lafayette adkdeec
Albert Littlefield adkgaedd
Albert M adgxfaac, adgxfaacab, adkehaa
Albert Marshall bedebem
Albert Neal adadabcfad
Albert Nelson adadabcfa
Albert Richard ahbcachc
Albert Smith ahfcfcc, ahfcfceh
Albert V bedgdaiii
Albert W abbegfjc, abbegfjca, adabbgbebad, ahbgdca, bededbada
Alberta bedecahfa
Alberta Emma adggegbaeb
Albertine Musa ahbgdcaa
Alberto bededbcae
Albina ahbcabfg, ahbcabha
Albion K Parris adhccfg
Albon A adadagaab
Alden bededbc
Alden A bededbbd
Alden Augustus bcbhddkbxaa
Alden Ball abbeebcaae
Alexander abccgdc, adacedhf, adgfcdaac, bcbhddb, bcfifjaf, ed, ex, exa
Alexander Clark abbegfgaa
Alexander P adkgaef
Alexander Pollard fceae
Alexander R. ahdaagf
Alexander S bcbhddba
Alfonzo bedgdaiaf
Alfred adadhacac, adgxfadc, adhafdgc, adhcbbb, bbbffadb, bcebbcd, bcbhdbee, bcbhdehg
Alfred A adkgdef, bedgdgb
Alfred Abijah adhcbbfb
Alfred C adacedhe, adhafdif
Alfred D bedgeg bedgegh
Alfred E adaimbhf, adgcacbka, ahbabajadab
Alfred Ellsworth adaimbhcaa
Alfred Frank adgxfadca
Alfred Jesse adggegbaca
Alfred Newell adaimbba, adaimbbebc, adgxffbb
Alfred P ahbabajad, bcbhdehgc
Alfred Perry adaabdabc
Alfred V adkgdefb
Alfred W bcbhdehg
Alfred Walter adhafdgca
Aliah bededdab
Alice adaabd, adaabffc, adgfbgdcg, adgfbq, adhccgac, bedebfgd, bededkac, bedgdabbda, bedgdafdb, bedgdaia
Alice A adgcaccai

Alice Adeline adhaheaa
Alice Amelia adhabfddc
Alice Azuza abbegbeaac
Alice B adabbgahbg, adkgdbaca
Alice Burleigh ahbaaaaac, ahbabjia
Alice C bbbebcbba
Alice Catherine bebebaabah
Alice Cary bedebgaaj
Alice Cochran bededhaa
Alice Denise adadhcafab
Alice E adaaaifba, ahgfbdgcc, bedebefa, bedgdafn
Alice Estella abbegbdfca
Alice Flora bcbhddcebc
Alice Gertrude adaimbhcba, adhcbcba
Alice J wife adaaaied, adaieaafca, ahdaaddg
Alice L adacgfea, adbabfiab
Alice Lincoln bededcfcbb
Alice Longworth adkfbbcdam
Alice Mae ahbabkbba
Alice Marble Maud bededhbce
Alice Maria adaabfaaa, bededbcac
Alice May adgfbgeahb, bcbhbficc
Alice N ahbabaeaee
Alice O adaaaiebc
Alice Osborn adkedjb
Alice Rebacca bededdhda
Alice V adadhaaaadb
Aline bededcld
Alison adacffice
Allan bedgdabge
Allan Ambrose bedgdabdac
Allan Bentley ahchfebc
Allan Clare abbegbdfdb
Allan J bedgdabd
Allan M bedgdaaabc
Allan Wade ahggbdaac, ahggdbdaaca
Allen adgfdgd
Allein abbegbibfa
Alleyn Moulton bededbccba
Allison bcbhddfabb
Allston Marden adbabfeaa
Alma abccgcfdca, abbegbdfbc, adaabddd, ahbcabedc
Alma B adaabcjh
Alma Frances bbbffcbacba
Alma Isabelle bcbhddfabfc
Alma M ahfcfdab
Alma R bedgdaiid
Almeda adhafch
Almedia H ahbcajcb
Almena adaabcee
Almer adgfbgdcf
Almira adadieab, wife adkebga, adkgdbc, ahbaeda, ahcbab, ahggcb, bcbcbbca
Almira Burton abbeebbbc
Almira L adadhcba
Almira W adkfbbdd
Almon adhafabf, ahbabaja
Almys Laforest adadiabf
Alonzo adabbgsb, adahddc
Alonzo C bedebgdc, bedgdaid, bedgdo

Alonzo G adabbgajd
Alonzo John bcdgdaidda
Alpheus B bcdgdbaaj
Alphonso ahgfdac, ahgfdb, bcdbaddm, bcdgdaiac
Alphonso Burns adaidaec
Alphonso L adkgddh
Alroy C adaimbbg
Alson adhadcba
Alta Clara bedgdafebab
Althea bcdgdafbb
Alton adaabcee, bcdgdaacab, bcdgdaacda
Alton C adgfbgfaaba
Alton Dennis adabbgaigha
Alton E adkgaefc
Alton F adaabceab
Alton Grant bcdgep
Alva adgfbhe, bcdedda
Alva Morrison bcdedhda, bcdedhdba
Alvah E adaabfdf
Alvah H adgxfdaf
Alvah Leroy adgxfaaad
Alvan adgfbgb
Alvenett adabbgdca
Alvesta adgfcjba
Alvin bcdedka, gaaxaxi
Alvin Ara bcbcbbeec
Alvin Edson bcdedfea
Alvin H. P. adhccfg
Alvin W ahgdhdhdaa
Alvina wife adaceam
Alvina Hayden adaabdaba
Alvira adbabib, ahbchi
Amanda abccgdch, adgfdfa, ahbchi
Amanda AJvina adadhcbe
Amanda E adggeid
Amanda F adgfdcf
Amanda Fiske ahbabjca
Amanda Jane adbabfee
Amarilla adacfdc
Amasa aeda, aedaa, ahgcab, ahgcabc
Amaziah aedaa
Amaziah N bcdgdafe
Ambros gaaxaxk
Ambrose bcdgdeaf
Amelia adkdeceg, bcdgdeaic
Amelia B ahbgeaa
Amelia J bcbcbbeea
Amherst adaabacaaa
Amherst W adaabacaa
Amoret Brown adggeibac
Amos abccgdba, abceabb, abceabbb, adgfbgd, adgfbgdb, bbbeba, bbbebg, bbbffd, bbbffdb, bcdbd, bcdbeaa, bcdbei, bedeaaf, bcdecai, bcdedfe, bcdedh, bcdgdaaaa, bcdgdd, bcdgddaac, bcficak, bcficale, bcficalea
Amos Alfred abccgdbah
Amos Angell adabbgai
Amos Chase adhafcab, adhafcabda
Amos Fulton adabbgaic
Amos G adaimbhb
Amos H bcbcbaab

Amos J bcbcbaabb
Amos I adabbhc
Amos L adabbgtaaa, bcdgddaa
Amos Leroy adabbgtaa
Amos S bcbcbaaae
Amos V adailaaf
Amos W bbbffcea
Amy ahgdcad, bcdgeca
Amy A bcdgdaiik
Amy Haslam adadagabbb
Amy N bcbcbbeeba
Amy Warren abbeebbbb
Anchen adgfbgb
Andrew adgfbge, bcbcbbbaac, bcdecdb, gaaxaxac
Andrew E adgxfah, bcdgei, gbeca
Andrew Elmer abbegbdfacb
Andrew Gregg adgcacbad
Andrew J bbbebci, gbak
Andrew Jackson abbegbdfc, adadhcbg, bcbhbfia, bcfifhkc
Andrew L fcej
Andrew S ahfcfccb
Andrin J adaimaabd
Andy P adgxfaaaca
Angelia adaimbbf
Angelia M ahbgbai
Angelina adkgaea
Angeline ahbabade
Angeline M bcdebfbb
Angeline Thurlow adaimaaca
Angie S ahbabadba
Anita Marguerite bcbhddfabac
Ann (wife) x, adgfe, adhai, ahbaach, bcbg, bcfk
Ann Amanda bcbcbbgk
Ann Augusta adkdeck
Ann C adhafcae, ahbabadc
Ann Catherine adhafdj
Ann E bbbfhjc
Ann Eliza adgfbecf, adkedje, bcfiibab
Ann Elizabeth adabibia
Ann Frances bcfiibcb
Ann J bcdgdeaaca
Ann Louisa bcfigdca
Ann March adkdeeb
Ann Maria adhafgca, bbbfaxbb, bbbfhai
Anna abbegbibca, abccdaa, abccgbd, adabbgf, (wife) adabbhc, adacc, adaceagac, adaceagdc, adacgb, (Currier div) adadhabb, adadiac, adbafc, adgfbed, adgfbffb, adgfcce, adhafh, adhaha, adhe, adhcbd, adhcg, adkdc, adkddb, ahbcg, ahgchff, bbbfg, bcbegd, bcbhdbnh, bcbhdebb, bcdbecdd, bcdeaeacba, bcfifj, bcfifk, bcfigh
Anna Augusta adkecbaab
Anna Boyd bcdbadj
Anna Evelyn adaimaaa, adaimbid, adaimbde
Anna G adadibdc
Anna H adabbgajg
Anna M adadhacb, adgxfaaada

Anna Maria adkdecea
Anna Prince adkdeced
Anna R ahbgdgb, bbbffdba
Anna Sarah bcdecdbac
Anne ahbgbbb, ahgfc
Annie adabbgaigb, adacgfabc, adadibb-
  aa, adgfede, bcdbaddja, bededkaa, be-
  dgdanf, bcdgdeacd, bedgdafkj
Annie Arnold adgxfaaae
Annie B adabbgahbf
Annie Belle adadagfaa
Annie C adaimbaj
Annie E bbbebcdaab
Annie Eliza adadhcaj
Annie Elizabeth ahbaaaae
Annie Ella bbbfabhbc
Annie Elvira bcbcbbgbaa
Annie Ezzie bcdeaefaba
Annie G adhccfeb, gaaxaxhe
Annie Hilton adbabicb
Annie J bcbehddb
Annie L gaaxaxh
Annie Lizzie bcdeaeafaba
Annie Lois adgfbgfaac
Annie Lowell adgxfaabaa, adgxfaba,
  adgxfbd, adgxfebc
Annie M ahbabahcca
Annie Maria adaceagce
Annie Marietta adadabcfb
Annie Marion abdcebeac
Annie Mary bcdgdaalcc
Annie May adgfbgfab
Annie Melita adacgfgf
Annie Newell adaimbbaa, adaimbbh
Annetta bbbfabbda
Annette adhcbbdb, bcbebbeb
Annette True adgxfaabb
Anson ahgdi
Anson Cunningham gaaxaxca
Ansonette adkebaaa
Anthony adgxfaaadb
Apphia F adkebae
Aquila bcdbec
Arabella bcdbecef
Archibald bbbffcc, ec
Archibald W bbbffcbaj
Archie bcdgdaacad, bcdgdeacf
Archie C adhafabaab
Archie Chase adhafdifa
Archie F bcdgdaff
Archie Samuel bbbebgabd
Ardean bcdgdafmbb
Arden E bebhddfaba
Arden K ahbcabcbba
Arland adadiad, adadiada,
Arlene ahbabajgca, bcdgaijeb
Arlene A adkecbage
Arline adgfcicdca
Arline Beatrice bcbhddcebg
Arlon Brownell adhafdgcca
Armena ahbgif
Armenia adabbgajh
Arnol adadiad
Arnold bcdgebb, bcfiffdcba

Arnum bedgdagc
Artemas adabigge
Arthur adabbgaige, adgfbegja, adgfd-
  abbd, adkehccaa, ahgfbdacb, bbbebc-
  bg, bbbfabn, bcdbaddbc, bcdedbbcf,
  bcdedkdc
Arthur A adacgfggb, adgcaccaf, bcdeb-
  bcdaa, beficaled, gbed
Arthur Albert bcdecdiaa
Arthur B adaigaaae, bcdeaedaac
Arthur C adkehcca, adkgaefb
Arthur Chase adggdada, adggdadab
Arthur E bcdgdaalcf
Arthur Flanders bcbcbbgba
Arthur Francis adaabffdd
Arthur G adacedhbc
Arthur Greenleaf adgfcdgccb
Arthur H bbbebcdaea
Arthur Henry adabbgbeg
Arthur Irvin bcdgdsbb
Arthur J adaiiaaee, bcdgdqa
Arthur Jackson bcbhbfica
Arthur L adabibcce, adkgddfc
Arthur M ahbcabbad
Arthur Malcolm abhegfjba
Arthur Newton bcdedcfcd
Arthur Park ahggccb
Arthur Putnam bcdgdaacbg
Arthur Sanborn adadhacaba
Arthur Stephen abbegbeaaa
Arthur W adaimbbdf, ahbcachcd, ahb-
  giih
Arthur Walter adhafgcda
Arthur Warren bcbebbfaca
Arthur Wesley ahfcaaba
Arvilla adabigd, adgfbecga
Asa adadieb, adahc, adkdee, ahbabe,
  ahbchg, ahcha, ahcfj, ahdaac,
  ahdaah, bcbcbbe, bebhddg, beded, bc-
  dedba, bcdedeac, bededcg, bcdedha,
  bedgdafoab, bcdgdane, bcdgdbe
Asa Day adggefa
Asa H adabbgaha
Asa Lee adgfbeggac
Asa Norman bcdgdafe
Asa Parsons ahbabal, adkdeaa
Asa W bcdgbdaae
Asahel abcfl, adggei, adggeih
Asahel C adggeij
Asbury adgfbgfh
Asel adacfe
Asenath ahbcabbe, ahgcaa, bcbebbea,
  bcdbadde
Asenath H wife adhafabb
Asher adaceaad
Atlanta E adgcagac
Atrude bedgdeaaca
Aubrey Douglass ahbabajaba
Augusta bcbebbed, bcdgdafff, bcdgdbae
Augusta A adaiecaa, adailaada
Augusta M bbbffcbaf
Augustus adabbbdceb, adabbhl, adaceaj,
  ahbaacg, ahgchh, ahgcibb, bcdhddaa,
  bcdbaddab

Augustus A adabbbdcf
Augustus Drew bbbfabibb
Augustus E adhccgabb
Augustus Francisco ahgchh, ahgchhb
Augustus L bcbcbbef
Augustus Storrs ahgfbdc
Aura A adhagbd, adkeabab
Auranda adggeid
Aurilla adggeeb
Aurora A ahbabalb
Aurora S bcfifjada
Austin A adacedfk
Austin Herbert ahfcaaae
Austin L bbbfhbaca
Austin V adacgjae
Avetta adaimaabca
Avis ahbcabedb
Avis M adaabaei
Avis Mae bcbhddaabc
Azel S gaaxaxf
Azro bcdgdaiaa
Azro Peter bedgdaiab
B Susan ahbabahfc
Baird adaidaebb
Barbara ahgfbdacba, bcdgdafg, bcdga-
fqf, bcdgdaijea
Barbara A ahbabaefbb
Barbara Elizabeth ahbgbadec
Baron C bcdbadddab
Barrent bcdgdeai, bcdgdeacg
Bartlett A adgfdabbb
Basil bedgdafma, bedgdafoc
Beatrice bcdgdabgab, bcdgdafeca
Beatrice E adabbgqdl
Beatrice L adabbhia
Beecher bedgdanh
Belinda P bcbebfh
Bell adaabacaac
Belle bcdgdagi, bcbhdbndg
Benair B bebhddcba
Benaiah S adaaaacc
Beniah adada adadagd, adgfcd, adgfcdg
Benjamin abda, abdcc, abdceb, abd-
cebec, abdcebl, adaabac, adaabaca,
adaabacaae, adaabd, adabbbdcy, ada-
bbgah, adaidab, adbabbbx, adbe, adgg-
di, adggdia, adgxfai, adhcd, adhcda,
adhcdae, adkdd, adkdda, adkddf, ad-
kddgh, adkded, adkehd, ahba, ahba-
aab, ahbaacb, ahbaah, ahbaaha, ah-
babae, ahbabc, ahbabkd, ahbcabj, ah-
bcaj, ahbcajg, ahbcx, ahch, ahchff,
ahchff, ahdaae, ahh, bbbff, bbbffaa,
bbbffb, bbbffba, bbbffcd, bcbhb, bcbhbc, bcbhddcba, bcbhdpc, bcdedbb,
bcdedbcc, bcdede, bcdgdeadg
Benjamin A adaaba, adkgdbf
Benjamin Ayer adkgddf
Benjamin Bradley adgfbecd
Benjamin Brown abccdf
Benjamin Capen adkddcebd

Benjamin D adabbgahd
Benjamin E bcdedbbca, gaaxax
Benjamin F adaigaab, adaigaacb, ahb-
abacc, ahbabala, ahbcabca, ahbcabfc
Benjamin Franklin adaigaa, adggeffa,
adggeib, adhcbbj, ahbghj, ahbghja,
bcbebaaai
Benjamin G ahbabeafe
Benjamin H bcdebfbd
Benjamin K adgfcdga
Benjamin L adkgdee
Benjamin P adgfbfe
Benjamin Pettingell ahbabaaa
Benjamin Prince adkdecek, adkdecem
Benjamin R adaigbbab
Benjamin Randall adabibi, adabibif
Benjamin Weymouth adaigbba
Benjamin Worthen adkddce
Bennie bcbhddfaac
Berenice E adkecbagb, ahbabaeadj
Bernice Mildred bcdedbbbca
Beriah B abccgbc
Bernard ahbaacdaca, bcdgdafkic
Bernard Charles adbabfeaaa
Bernard Joseph bbbebdacaa
Bernard Russell adhafgcbdc
Bernice abccgchaba
Bernice Eleanor ahbaahdeab
Bernice Mattie bcbhbfiah
Bert B adabbgbcaaa
Bert W ahbcabeac
Bertie bcdgdeaca
Bertie F adaimbih
Bertie L adabbgaici
Bertran L adabbheb
Bertha abbegbifb, adacedded, bedgda-
ghcc, bcdgdwb
Bertha Alfreda bedgdaacbf
Bertha Alma adbabfefb
Bertha B bcdebgaak
Bertha Beckley ahgcheca
Bertha C abccgdfca, ahbcajdc
Bertha F adkebaacc
Bertha Louise adadhcbda
Bertha M ahgdhdd, gbaica
Bertha Matilda ahgdgbc
Bertha McLane ahggbdaad
Bertha P bedgdaiig
Bertha Ula abbegbdfcc
Bertina Emma adkecbacaa
Bertrume bedgdeaace
Bessie adabbgbccc, ahchfiga, bbbfabcc,
bcdbececd, bcdgdaffe, bcdgdsa
Bessie Edith adbabfddf
Bessie H adgfbffca
Bessie L adaimbiad
Bessie Lola abccgdfcd
Bessie M bcdgdbaadc
Bessie May adaimbiacb, adhadcecb
Bessie Sadie adaimbifx

Betsey abceabf, abdcea, adaabacad, adaabcbb, adaabcc, adaabd, adaabfeb, wife adabbbb, adabbgaa, adabibb, adabigg, adaigba, adgcacd, adgcadb, adgfbb, adggdj, adgxfae, adham, adkecg, ahbabb ahbabca, wife ahbabkxy, ahbcacc, ahbcag, ahbchb, ahbgbaa, ahbgbd, ahbgda, ahfcad, ahgck, ahggbc, bbbebcg, bcbebic, wife bebebif, bcbegbb, bcdedbcd, bcdedde, bcdgdae
Betsey A adaimbfa, bcbebfga
Betsey Ann Moody bcbehde
Betsey Burns adaidaga
Betsey C bcdedbaf
Betsey D adggeia
Betsey E adgcagag, bcbebfc
Betsey F adaimcd, adgxffa, adgxffaa, adkebdd
Betsey Fitts adaaaig
Betsey G ahbabag
Betsey Goodwin adkfbc
Betsey J adaimbdk
Betsey Jane adaimbg
Betsey L adgxffe
Betsey M adggbeh
Betsey Maria adgfbegb
Betsey S bbbfhad, bcfigfe
Betty adgfcc, adggab, adggbb, adhafb, ahbabb, ahbchb, bcdecb, bcficah
Betty Locke abccgacg
Betty Low adaaaix
Beulah ahbcajee
Beulah Bradford ahfcia
Beulah Cora bcdgdabfc
Beulah Janet adhadceca
Beverley Abbott ahgcif
Beverly S ahbgilb
Bildad adah
Billey ahfaa
Billings Putnam adabbgaicb
Bina May bcbhddkbxl
Bion E gbaiaa
Birney T bcdebgaah
Biron Thomas bcbhdgaggb
Blackmer Orlando Cullen ahgfdec
Blake T adhabcdc
Blanche adaceaaic, bcdedbbdac
Blanche Hinman adgfgabcd
Blanche M adhafgcbf, bbbfhcfha
Blanchie bcbebbbdca
Boardman bcdgdeag, bcdgdagh
Borsha Ann adacedfd
Bradbury bbbfabmi
Burden Elias bcdgdefcc
Bryant Scott ahbgbadeba
Budd adaabfaai
Burns bcdgdafeg
Burns C bcdgdafecd
Burpee bcdgdafeec
Burritt Newell adaaaieed
Burt K bcfiffdcc, ahdadb
Burton ahdadb, bcdebgafba, bcdgdaneb
Burton S adacffica

Buster bidgdafcbaa
Byron A adgfbgdce
Byron Gove adhcbbgdac
Byron J adbabfbg
Byron Kendrick abbegfgaf
Byron S bcbebbcae
Byron T bcbebbcad
C C ahbgbjx
C Leroy ahbabamgd
Cadde E bcdebeeba
Caddie L ahfcfcea
Cajaolia adaabacaal
Caleb adkec, adkecb, bcdedc, bcdedch
Caleb Miles ahbgimda
Caleb Richards bcfiibb
Caleb Wells ahbgim
Calista M ahbabahl
Callie B adabbgaicg
Calvin ahgi, bbbebfh, bcdgdbh
Calvin Lawrence adggegbac
Carl A adgxbdabb
Carl B bbbfhcfhc
Carl J ahbgilic
Carl Plumer ahbabjibb
Carl Stephen adhcbbffb
Carlos ahgcibd
Carleton adaabbghg
Carlton adgcacbf, adabbgaigk
Caroline abccgcab, adaceaac, adacffd, adaiiaaeg, adgfbj, wife adggefe, adkdecehc, ahbabfab, ahbabfba, ahbgbbc, wife ahfeaaa, ahgdhbcb, bcddaddl, bcdeabdd, bcdecae, bcdedgd, bcdgdafd, bcdgddda, wife befifhb, eaacd, fcd, fceg
Caroline A adgfbgge, adgxfafa
Caroline Abigail adkdebb, bcdeabbe
Caroline Augusta adadhcad
Caroline Bell adggeibb
Caroline Coffin adkdebb
Caroline E adabbgaigc, adhafaae
Caroline Ellen adaimbbebb
Caroline Gage bbbebcba
Caroline J adkfbbdc
Caroline M bcdbadk
Caroline Louise adacedfa
Caroline T bcbcbbgh
Carolyn adkddcebg
Carolyn Eva adaabffdca
Carolyn Olive bcdhddbcbh
Carrie adgcadaaae, adgfbgeaa, ahbcabeaa, bcdecdb, bcdgep
Carrie Adelaide adbabgaab
Carrie Alpharetta adgfbegcb
Carrie Bell adaabfaam
Carrie C adkddgj
Carrie Delia bcdbecea
Carrie E adabbhe, adabbfahbc, wife bcdgdsb
Carrie Ella adggegda
Carrie Estella adacgfaca
Carrie Ethel ahbcajgg
Carrie Farrar ahbgbfaac
Carrie H adaimcdbi

Carrie J bbbebcbea
Carrie L bcdedcgb
Carrie Lillian adaaaifac
Carrie Louisa bcdedceab
Carrie May bcdgejaa
Carrie R ahgdcaga
Carrol Wells ahbgikb
Carroll bbbebbcdag
Carroll Colby bcbhbficd
Carroll Erwin adgxffbf
Carroll Lincoln adaabfaak
Carroll Webster adaimaaabc
Carroll Winfield adkfbeiaa
Cartez Newton ahgched
Cassie bcdgddead
Catherine abceabeh, adabbgse, adacfe,
  wife adgga adggac, adgxfaaeca, adk-
  fbbcl, adailaad, ahbabamd, ahcbeb,
  ahbabcdh, bbbfaxe, bbbfhbxa, bbb-
  fhg, bcbehhh, bcbhdehc, bcbhdekb, bc-
  debeb, bcdedbaa, wife bededbb, bc-
  dgdaaae, bcdgdeab, bcfihea
Catherine Annie bbbfabp
Catherine Balch bcbcbbgl
Catherine E ahbabdaa
Catherine Evelyn adkecbaae
Catherine L bcdebgaaa, eaaba
Catherine Lenore adbabfddi
Catherine Leonard bbbfabe
Catherine Page bcficanc
Cazacana abceabeh
Ceba H adhafci
Cecil bcdgdafeca, bedgdaghc
Cecil Flight bcdgdaacbe
Cecil Reed bcdgdaald
Cecile Caroline adabbgaiig
Celende Thompson adhcbbgc
Celeste bcdgdaacc
Celeste Emily ahgchhba
Celia bcdgdeaa
Celia E gaaxaxna
Celia Maria abccgdci
Celinda ahbabkg
Challis adabd
Chandler jahbabdad
Chandler J ahbabdad
Charity adabbgsc, adj
Charles abccgcfl, abdcebca, adaabacaai,
  adaabacab, adaabddd, adabbgp, ada-
  bbgq, adabibih, adacgfbb, adadhcak,
  adbabbaa, adgfbejb, adgfbg, adgfbg-
  ag, adgfbgfc, adgfbk, adgfcdbga, adg-
  gefc, adgxfbc, adgxffccd, adhafabe,
  adkddcb, adkedka, ahbaacdb, ahbabc-
  dbd, ahbabcfb, ahbcx, ahcfjb, ahfcf-
  cbb, ahgdcaca, bebecaaabb, bcbhde-
  fa, bcbhdja, bcbhddka, bcdeaeac,
  bcdeaefa, bcdecaid, bcdedbaca, bcd-
  edkba, bcdgdabdae, bcdgdafebc, bc-
  dgdaieaf, bcficalf, cbaaa, fcel
Charles A adaieaaff, adaimbhd, adgxf-
  bea, adgxffcea, adkddgdb, ahgfbdgb,
  bcbebbcaf, bcdebfbab, bcdedbadc, bc-
  deddad, bcdgdaai

Charles Abel bcdeddhca
Charles Alexander adkdecg
Charles Allison bcdeddhc, bcdedhcac
Charles Alton bcbhddbcbc
Charles Amasa ahgcabcab
Charles Ambrose adacgfacb
Charles Archie adaimbcf
Charles Arthur abbegbdfda
Charles Asher ahbgikc
Charles Augustus bcfigdcc
Charles Austin adaimbhba, bcdebee
Charles B adaabcjj, adabbgrb, ahbcaj-
  bd, bbbffcbad, bcdhdqa
Charles Byron ahgfdea
Charles Boynton abbegbdca
Charles C adggeibd, adkddgc, bcdebee-
  bb
Charles Carleton bcdedceaaa
Charles Carroll bcdedcea
Charles Choate adhcbbjc
Charles Clarence bbbfabhaa
Charles Clinton adkfbeddab
Charles Curtis adkfbei
Charles D adhccgaa
Charles E abccgbaba, abdcicbb, adad-
  agacc, adadagfa, adaigaaca, adaiiaad,
  adaiiaaea, adgcagab, adgfbecbc, adgx-
  faacb, ahbabahh, ahgbhbbb bcbeggab,
  bcdedcfg, bcdgdaalc
Charles Edmund adkecbaaa, ahbgbaed
Charles Edward bcbhdgaa
Charles Edwin abbeebbc, adbabfea
Charles Everett adhahecb
Charles F adabibca, adgxffbd, adhccfee,
  adkfbedb, adkfbef, bcdeaefae
Charles Farrington ahgchfea
Charles Fenno bcbehhie
Charles Fitch adhccfe
Charles Forrest adkddgcaa
Charles Francis adkfbebca
Charles Frank adkebgbaaa
Charles Franklin adgxfaha, bcdeaefabf
Charles Fremont bcdhdbndl
Charles G abdceblg, adadhaca
Charles Granderson adaidbb
Charles Guy adgfcdabc
Charles H abbegfcae, abbegfja, abccd-
  gca, abceabefc, adabbgagd, adabib-
  caa, adaceagdb, adacgjad, adgfbfcc,
  adgfbbhad, adhafdia, adkddcebb, ad-
  kgdbaa, ahcfjbc, bcbhbfib, bcbhdd-
  bcb, bcdebfbc
Charles H M adbabfbi
Charles Hallet adabbgagd, adabbgag-
  dab
Charles Hardy adabbpaa
Charles Harold adkfbbjea
Charles Hawes adkfbeg
Charles Henry abbegbdfd, abdceblfa,
  adabbgqdb, adacgja, adaigaac, adg-
  gdcda, adhafgcbc, ahbgbadd, ahbgbadd, ahdaagc, ahfcaaab, bcdedgga,
  bcfifhhd
Charles Homer bcdedceac

Charles Irving adgxfagc
Charles J abccdgcba, adaimbah, adgxf-
faf
Charles Jones bcficana
Charles Jonathan adhafgcdc
Charles K ahbaaheab, ahbabalf
Charles L abccgbada, adabbgaica, adk-
ebdf, ahbgdga, ahfcfced
Charles Larin adhafabaa
Charles Layforest adkddgcaa
Charles Lee adabbgagda
Charles Leonard abdbecec
Charles Leroy adkgaebc
Charles Libbey adgfcdace
Charles Lyman bbbffagc
Charles M adaabdfa, adgfbfcca, ahba-
acdad, ahbaahdc, bcdgdbaa, bcdgdb-
aal, bcdgdec
Charles Marsh befihed
Charles Mason bcdecahf, bcdecahfb
Charles Moses ahbgbbec
Charles N ahbcabej
Charles O adaimbhe, bcdgdec
Charles Orris gbake
Charles P bcdgdafb
Charles Pike adaabffdc
Charles R bcdgdng
Charles Richardson ahgchfh
Charles Robinson ahbgbad
Charles Ross adgfbgaae
Charles S abbegbibc, adgxfaae, adkf-
bbje, ahbcahcb, bebhddkbxb
Charles Sewall adadhcbd
Charles Silverman bcbehhjc
Charles Stevens bbbebcbh
Charles Sumner adggeild
Charles T adhccfeaa
Charles W adaaaaccab, adaaaifbb, ada-
bbgabdg, adabibca, adgfbdbb, adgfh-
ad, adgfbk, bebhde, bcbhdmd, bcbh-
dqab, bcbebcf, bcdgdsad, gaaxaxl
Charles Warren abbegbeaa, adadhcaf,
adadhcafaa
Charles Wesley adgxfaga
Charles Wesley Wellman bcbhdbnd
Charles White bcbebcfa
Charles William adgcacbjd, bcbhddcea,
befifhhda
Charlie cbaadb
Charlie S adhadcec
Charlie Wilbur ahbgbebc
Charlier ahbcx
Charlotte abbegfjd, adaabacae, wife ad-
aabdca, adaceale, adaimbbgb, adgf-
bgba, adgxfam, adkech, adkedb, ah-
babaeg, ahbabaha, ahbabea, ahbabkf,
ahbaeb, bcdebec bcdedbbd, bcdgddad,
bcdgddb, bcdhca
Charlotte A ahbaahac
Charlotte Augusta bcdebed
Charlotte Adell adabbgbcf
Charlotte Ann adgxfaaaa
Charlotte B adabbgagb, adabbgdaab
Charlotte C bcdedbag

Charlotte Elizabeth adkdebd
Charlotte Emeline ahgcabcb
Charlotte L ahbabkba
Charlotte Mabel adaabdaej
Charlotte Mahitable adgfcdacba
Charlotte T adgxffah, ahbaahac
Chase adggeg, bcdedbbdaf
Chase L adggeicb
Chellis adabibc
Chauncey ahbcabee, ahgchi
Chauncey Handel ahgdhd
Chester B adggegd, adgxfdah
Chester Key adaimbhbb
Chester Newman adabbgaghba
Chester Perry bcdecaca
Chester Robinson adggeilea
Chester V bbbfhcgbh
Chivey Chase adhadcc
Chloe ahggba, bcdgdbaf, bcdgdbk
Chloe T ahbcajdd
Christina adkehbaa
Christiania adaabffb
Christiania A adgfbeed
Christina ahbcank
Christina Ruth bcbebbcdacaa
Christine Cinderella adbabfefeb
Christopher xad, xb, ahgdcacb
Christopher E adgxfag
Christopher S C ahgdga
Cinda E adadibdj
Cinderilla adadibdj
Clara abccgdcm, adhafahc, adkgaeda,
ahbgdgc, bcgdaacff
Clara A adgfbegca, bcbebbcab, bcbhd-
did
Clara Adella adaabfaae
Clara Agnes aeeacaaab
Clara Augusta adgfbecbb, ahbgikd
Clara Benton ahgfbdh
Clara E adhaha, ahbgbfj, bebhddiaac
Clara Emma adacgfggc
Clara Hart bcdedcle
Clara J abccgaeaaa, bbbebcbcb
Clara Jane adaabdaec
Clara Jeannette gbaka
Clara M adgxfaabac, ahbabahcba
Clara Maria abccabefa
Clara Myrtle bcdgdakca
Clara Viola adabbgbebac
Clarck adaabacaab
Clare Lincoln adggeicb
Clarena Jeannette gbaka
Clarence adaceagda, adgfcdabg, bcdhd-
ehfc, bcdgdaacaa, bcdgdaacb, bcdgd-
aace
Clarence A adabbgqdj
Clarence Bertrand gbakd
Clarence E adabbgbebb, adadhcahb, bc-
bhddface
Clarence Eugene adabbgbebaa
Clarence F bcdedbbdag
Clarence H adabbhf, adabiggf
Clarence L adgfbgdch, bcbebbfaad
Clarence Lee adabbgagda, adabbhfa

Clarence Lorenzo adgfbeggae
Clarence P ahbabamgda
Clarence R bcdeaefada
Clarence Samuel adadabgaa
Clarence T adabbgabdc
Clarence W bcbebbcdad
Clarence Webber bcfifhhhb
Clarence Willard bcdeddhdc
Clarice bcdeaefadab
Clarinda ahggh
Clarissa adabibe, adacebg, adgfbfda, wife adggeb, adgxfadd, ahbgdb, ahcbff, ahchba, bcdgdaam
Clarissa H adhafaab
Clarissa J abceabbf, bcficali
Clark ahbgfb
Claud Lorain ahbcabbadc
Clayton Henry adhafgcbca
Clayton Lewis bcbhddfacdb
Clement adacffice
Clement Kimball adacffic
Clemetine adacefc, adgfbegf
Cleo Veronica adaabdaebb
Cleveland Otis bcbebcgabac
Clifford C adacedhca
Clifford D bcfiibcha
Clifford Jack adhahecaa, adhahecaaa
Clifford L adacedhca, bcdebgaag
Clifford Wallace bcdedcfcb
Clifton ahbabajagb, bcdgdeaaea
Clifton Osma adbabfefd
Clifton Wentworth gbakda
Climena A ahbgdcc
Clinda E adgxffae
Clinton adkddix, bcdgdaiecb, gbakg
Clinton Austin adkecbaach
Clinton Hunt adkfbdedda
Clinton Israel adkebaacd
Clinton John adaabcjf
Clinton Sanford adhadceh
Clitidia adgxffae
Clyde bcdgdabgd
Clyde Hadley bcbhdqaca
Clyde Walton adaimaabba
Clytie abccgdcfd
Coleman Hart bcdedclf
Coletta bcdgdagg
Comfort abbeae, abbegbc, abbegc, abbbegfb, abbegg, abbei, abdcb, abdg
Comi adaabfgf
Conrad W adabibcaea
Constan ahbaahaa
Constance adaabdabed, adaabffdda
Constant S ahbaahaa
Cora adacebfba, bcbhdbndk
Cora A adhadceb
Cora Belle bbbffafaa
Cora Caroline adkefbeic
Cora E adhccgaba, ahbabaefa, wife ahbabjeca
Cora Ella adacgface, adaimcdgc
Cora Ellen ahbgbaea
Cora F ahbaacdg
Cora L bcdeddbg

Cora M abccgcfdc, adaimiab
Cora Moore abbegbdcaa
Cordelia ahbabjbe
Corett bcdedbadb
Corey bcdgdafae
Cornelia adgfdcc
Cornelia Herriman adkdecehb
Cornelia M ahbabahfb
Cornelius adabbgbea, ahbabahc, bcdebgafb
Crockett E adabbbdce
Crystodell adaimbcc
Cummings adaceaec
Curtis L ahdadad
Cushing bcdhdef
Custer bcdgdmab
Cynthia adaabacaaj, adbabhb, adkehh, ahbcacg, ahgdha, ahghaa, bcbcbbeb, bcdedcb, bcdgdagj
Cynthia C adkehh
Cynthia H adhafcj
Cynthia P adkehh
Cyrus adadicda, adkfbda, ahcba, ahgcib, bcdedb, bcdedkb
Cyrus B adadicc
Cyrus Benjamin bbbebdac
Cyrus F adadiccb, adadiccd
Cyrus G adkfbdxa
Cyrus M bcdedcj
Cyrus Marion bcdedkda, bcdedkdae
Cyrus Marsh ahchbaa
D Annette bcdgdgg, bcdgdagb, bcdgdeaad
D Florantha adaabcfb
Daisy adaidaeg
Daisy D adabbgqik
Daisy Isabel bcdbaddaf
Daisy Louise adkgdegb, adkgdegf, adkdecc
Dana abbegfe
Dana Francis ahfcaabb
Dana Frederick adaimbhcbf
Dana Irene bcbhdqabe
Dana Young bcbhdhb
Daniel (Capt) p 4, abccgbab, abccgb, abccgdi, abbcacbd, adabibcc, adabibk, adaceald, adacgi, adaiga, adaimbbdca, adaimbbdd, adbabbf, adfh, adgcagc, adgfbgfd, adgfbgh, adgfbhd, adgfda, adgfdac, adgfdd, adgga, adggbc, adggdaa, adggde, adggef, adggeicae, aeea, aeeaca, aha, ahbab, ahbabaa, ahbabj, ahbabji, ahbabkxba, ahbabx, ahbcaba, ahbcabed, ahcb, ahcbf, ahcbfb, ahchf, ahchfd, ahchfib, ahdh, ahfb, ahgca, ahgcaba, ahcabacb, bbbebci, bbbfad, bbbffah, bcbcbbd, bcdba, bcdbadc, bcdeae, bcdeaea, bcdeedh, bcdedbbd, bcdgdabgb, bcdgdl, bcdgdjl, bcdih, gbd
Daniel B adabibcab, adgxffb
Daniel C adaimcdbb
Daniel Clark ahgcj
Daniel David bcbebbcbe

Daniel Eaton ahbabcdd
Daniel Ernest adaimbbeaa
Daniel F adgxffbc, bcbhddfac, bcdeae-
   aa
Daniel F W adaimbdb
Daniel Frederick ahbabjiba
Daniel Gilman adhafca, adhafcac
Daniel J ahgcabac
Daniel Lyford ahbabaab, ahbabcd
Daniel M adabbgz, aeeacaa
Daniel Milburn ahdaadde
Daniel Mitchell ahchfeb
Daniel O aeeacaaa
Daniel P adaigbb
Daniel R adhafaad
Daniel Sherman adadhacaab
Daniel V adhadcd
Daniel W adaimbbd, adaimbic
Daniel Weber ahchfde
Daniel Webster ahbabjcc, ahbabjib, ah-
   bcabed
Daniel Weymouth abccgacb
Damaris bcdgdaaf
Daphne adacgfaebc
Dardama adgfcdj
Darius bcbebcga, bcdgdeaae
Darius A bcbehdd
Darius Augustus bcbebcgaa
Darius Jerome adaabff
Darius L bcbcbaaag
Darius S do
David abccgdf, adaabacaba, adabbbb,
   adaabbbdb, adabib, adadibac, adaigb,
   adbabia adgd, adgfbej, adgfbfc, ad-
   gfbh, adgfcg, adgfcj, adgfdd, adggb,
   adggbaa, adggbe, adggee ,adhaf, ad-
   hafab, adhafc, ahbabka, ahbabkxb,
   aed, ahbcaba, ahbgbx, ahbgbxb, ah-
   fcaa, bbbffad, bcbcbbek, bcbhbe, bc-
   bhbfe, bcdedk, bcdg, bcdgdc, bcdgd-
   da, bcdgddaab, bcdgdeaac, bcdgdn,
   bcdgdsa, gbef
David Albert adkfbbdfab
David Anderson bcdebgba
David Atwell bcbhbfga
David B adaabdea
David Benjamin ahdaage
David Brainerd bcdeabdc
David Briggs adgfcdgaa
David C abdcebeaha, adaimcdbf
David Coffin adkdeea
David Crocker abdcebeah
David Elwyn abbegbebba
David F adaimcdb
David Francis ahfcaab
David Gove adadibd
David Greeley adadibd
David H adabbhe
David Hoyt adadabbdbba
David M adkfbbdf, aeeacaca
David Moore Russell abbegbeb
David Perkins adgfbegc
David Sewall adkddgi
David William adabbbbdca

Deborah adaabacaam, adacefb, aedb,
   ahbabak, ahbgbha, bcdbade
Deborah Jane ahbabahb
Deborah T adkgded
Deborah W adabbgef
Deforest George adacgfgga
Delbert Warren bcbhdgagfh
DeLance bcdhdbedda
Delia adaceaaea, ahgdhc, bcbcbbej, bc-
   begc, bcdbee
Delia A bcbcbbeed
Delia M adgfcieb
Delila adadabf
Delilah bcdgdafba
Delilah Frances adaijbb
Deliverance bcbec, bcbegc, bcdbee
Della Lucella ahgfbdca
De Milton ahbcabeaba
Dennis adaabacac, adaimbh, adggdcd,
   bcdgdagheb
Dennis Franklin adaimbhcb
Derry Walter Fogg bbbfhcfee
Dewey M bcdedkdab
De Witt C adabiggda, ahgdgaa
De Witt Canfield ahgcigb
De Witt Clinton adaabejfb, ahgcabacg,
   ahgcabad
Dexter bcbebbfaaac
Dexter D ahbgilg, bcbcbaaaab
Dexter De Witt adabbhja
Diadema ahbgfa
Diana adabbd, ahbgbfh
Diantha ahggca
Diantha E bcfifjaa
Dida abcflb
Dimmick adaceafc
Dimon bbbebcda
Dinah adabbd
Doletta bcdgdeaac
Dolly adaabd, adabif, adaigad, adgfbef,
   adhae, adhafe, bcbhbfc
Don Cameron adaceafgee
Don Carlos bcbhdbndg
Donald bcdecdbada, bcdgdafka, bedgd-
   afod
Donald Augustus adgfbgfcab
Donald Dwight adggegbacc
Donald Edwin bcdgdaacbi
Donald Holt ahgfbdaea
Donald Sherman adkgdefbaa
Donna E adgcaccaj
Dora adabbgbccb, bcbhbndj, bcdecaiba,
   bcbhddfacb
Dora E adgfcjbdd
Dora Hazel bcdgdafbdb
Dora M adgxfaacba
Dorcas adhahc, adhahfc, bbe, bcdedkah,
   fcg
Dorcas Neal adhafdd
Dorillus Winfield adkfbeia
Doris adaceaaibb, adkddcebbbc, bcdec-
   dbaec
Doris Belle ahbabahcab
Doris Crocker adabbbdced

Doris E gbfeaab
Doris June bbbfabibh
Doris Louise bcbhdbndma
Doris Mae adaimbaiab
Doris Muriel bcbhddccfc
Doris Stella bebhdbedab
Dorothea H bcdgdafkae
Dorothea Porter abbegbdcaca
Dorothy abbee, abbeeda, adaaaic, wife adabbbh, adaigbbaac, adailaaa, adgfdabbda, adhae, ahbcabfeab, bcdbeceef, bcdebjcd, bcdecbadb, bcdgdaiibb, bcdgdafmbd, bcdgdeafbb, bcdgdafkia
Dorothy A ahbabjecaa
Dorothy Alice bbbfhcfgaa
Dorothy Darling abbeebcaa
Dorothy Delsey adaimbaiaa
Dorothy E adadhacaae
Dorothy Elizabeth aeeacaaaaa
Dorothy G adgfbggx, adkfbbde
Dorothy Genevieve Marie adabibcadf
Dorothy Helen bcdgdabdeb
Dorothy Howard abbegfjcaa
Dorothy Ida bcdedbbbja
Dorothy Lillian adgfcdacca
Dorothy Louise adadhcafcb
Dorothy M adgcadaffaa, ahbabajadac
Dorothy May adaabdabeg, bcdgdpaad
Dorothy March adaimbhcab
Dova W adgxfaacba
Dove Glendora ahbgimdb
Drusilla adaimbha
Duane M bcbcbbeee
Dudley adgcagbb, ahbabkxbe
Dudley H adabbgabd
Dudley J bcdgdafq
Dudley N bcdgdafqc
Dura F bedebgbe
Dwight adaceaadd
E Ross, E Ross Jr adacfficc
E S (Rev) adabbghgb
E Waldron bcdgdaia
Earl adaidaeea, bbbfhjbe, bcdgdaneg
Earl B bbbfhbxcgb, bcdgdbaaac, Jr bcdgdbaaaca
Earl C abccgdfbaa
Earl Charles bcbhdqabc
Earl Clarence bcbebbcdaxc
Earl Edison bedgdaacbd
Earl Ephraim bcdgdakcf
Earl Frank gbeba
Earl H adgfbeggad
Earl J bcdgea
Earl Pevear adaabdaebaa
Earl Raymond adbabfefe
Earl Samuel bcbhdqabab
Earl W adaimbaia
Earl Walden bcbhddbba
Eben adadabbdb, adgfbff, bcbhdea, bebhdhh, bcbhdhha
Eben C bebhddkbxo
Eben Coe adadabbd
Eben S adabbgahe
Eben T bcbhdekc

Ebenezer adabbgcd, adadh, adadhaa, adadhce, adadibab, adgf, adgfbf, adgfbff, adgfd, adgfdab, adggdadc, ahbg, ahbga, ahbgab, ahbghd, ahc, ahcf, ahcfe, bcbhdhh
Ebenezer Lawrence adadhaaa
Ebenezer S bcbhdhe
Edd C adggeija
Edgar adgfcjd ahbabajh
Edgar A adacedhb
Edgar Albert bcdecdia
Edgar C adkgddhd
Edgar E ahgdccac
Edgar Everett adbabfefa
Edgar Leslie bbbfhcffb
Edgar P adkgdbac
Edgar R adgfcjbc
Edgar Randolph adkgaebe
Edgar S bbbfhhcff
Edison adacebab
Edith adaabfdfc, wife adabbgs adaigbbaba, bcdeafadb, bcdedkdb, bcdgdafbc, bcdgdaieab, bcdgdeafba
Edith A bcdeaeacdb
Edith Alice bcdebfgea
Edith Celende adhcbbfbc
Edith E ahbaacxaaa
Edith Hortense ahgchef
Edith J adadhcaic
Edith Josephine adhahcddc
Edith Louise adggebbag
Edith M bcbhdehfd
Edith Marion bbbebgaba
Edith May adkedjf, ahbabjcfa, bcbcbbgja
Edith Morrill abdcebeak
Edmond ahbabama
Edmond M adkgdca
Edmondo cbaad
Edmund xaf, adkddia, ahbgba, ahbgbae, ahbgf, ahbgfi, bcdgeka, cb, cbaa
Edmund Charles ahbgbabeb
Edmund Eugene bcdedbbbf
Edmund Everett adbabfefda
Edmund F ahbgfia
Edmund Leroy ahgchfi
Edmund M adailaae
Edmund Scott ahbgbade
Edmund Terry ahgfbdac
Edna adaidaeeb, ahchfdcab, bbbfhi, wife bcbcbbd, bcdebgaaeb, bcdgdaacfc, bcdgdaia
Edna E adhafdgea, bbbfhcfac
Edna Elsa ahchfdcd
Edna Frances ahgchebab
Edna Grace ahbaabeaba
Edna Hathorne bcdbeceg
Edna Josephine bcbebcgaaa
Edna M adkebaad, bcdgdnf
Edna Maria adgfcjbca
Edna May ahchfijc
Edna Orett abbegbdbga
Edna Parker bcdbeda
Edna V M adkgddgb

Edna W ahbcajde
Ednah Lavinia adgcacbadb
Ednah May adgxffcch
Edson ahggbg
Edson W ahbabajgaa, ahbabaji
Edward xaag, adaabfee, adabbgaicc, adgfbbfdd, adhafcabc, adhccbbb, adhcdab, adkfbbh, ahcfjbb, ahdk, ahfcfce, bcbhdeni, bcbaddf, bcdbecdc, bcdgdafeee, bcdgdaig
Edward A bcdebfge
Edward Albert ahbcabejb, ahbcabejba, ahgfbdgbba
Edward Amos adabbgaicbb
Edward Augustus adhcbbfg
Edward B ahbgilc
Edward Chase adhafcad
Edward D adgxffab, ahgdhde
Edward Daniel adabibcaba
Edward Dean bcdedcl
Edward Dearborn adgxfdf, adgxff
Edward E adabbgaheb, adgxfaad
Edward Emerson ahgfbdgbb
Edward Everett abbegbeaf, adgcaccah, bcdecacab
Edward Francis adabbgaiic
Edward French adhahedda
Edward H adkfbbcca ahgchj, bcdebfged, gbefaa
Edward Harrington bcbehhjb
Edward Hicks adgfbgdcaa, adgfbgdcaaa
Edward Joseph bcbebbcdaca
Edward L bcdgdakc
Edward Perry ahgfdeaa
Edward S adgfbgebb, bcdedclb
Edward Steele adhahed
Edward Tuck bcdbeceef
Edward Whitcher ahbcabfe
Edward Y H adabbgaie
Edwin adaabd, adaceahf, adadagec, adgfcdadb, adkgaeb, bcdhdbedd, bcbhdhd
Edwin A bcbhdhd
Edwin Augustus adgxfagb
Edwin B ahbaahda, ahbgida
Edwin Barlow bbbfabba
Edwin C adaceddcc, adhadcbb, adhadcca
Edwin Carlos ahgcibca
Edwin Cecil bcbhbfiaf
Edwin Clinton adgfcdad
Edwin Coburn bcbebbcdac
Edwin D adgfbegcc
Edwin Elom adacgfae
Edwin Francis adkgaebfb
Edwin Guilford adadhcai
Edwin H adkebaba, ahbgeda
Edwin J adaabcfbe
Edwin Jeremiah adbabfdg
Edwin Joseph adacgfaeb
Edwin O adabbgaiex, adbabfbgc
Edwin Otis adbabfbc
Edwin P adadhcahc
Edwin Ruthven adkfbebl

Edwin Stephen bcbhdgagef
Edwin Tyson adbcebcabc
Edwin W adkgaefd, bcdbaddaa
Edwin Weston abbegbicd
Edwina May bcbhddiaaba
Effie ahbcabia, bcdgdaijf
Effie E bcbhddfad
Effie F ahbabaeda
Egbert adgfcdacee
Eileen bcdgdaacb
Eileen Mae bcdgdaacba
Ela ahbcf
Elba bcfifhc
Elbridge adadhcac, ahbaacdfa, bcdebgb, bcdedbbdd, bcdedhb
Elbridge Chaplain akebdbbia
Elbridge G ahbaacdf
Elbridge Gardiner bcdebgbb
Elden Leslie ahfcaaad
Eldridge G bcdebeebh
Eldridge N adaceafkc
Eleanor abceb, adadhcf, ahbgfe, bcfigfddca
Eleanor Amelia bbbfabk
Eleanor C adgcacbe, ahbgbx
Eleanor Caroline bcfifffg
Eleanor Emerson ahbabjcd
Eleanor G ahbabaefea
Eleanor Haley ahbabjl
Eleanor Lambert abbegfjada
Eleanor M adaimcf, adhccfd
Eleanor Mara adaimbhcbh
Eleanor Milborough ahbgfaaba
Eleanor Pike adaabffdcc
Eleanor W bcdgdaia
Eleanor Welch adgfbeagb
Electa ahchhb, bcdgdafkc
Electa Ethel bcdgdaacbg
Electa Flora ahbgbfaaa
Electa M abbegbiba
Electa Wilder abbeebbbe
Eli J ahbcacaa
Eli S adaidbba
Eli Sawtelle abceabeg
Eli Stedman adaidbd
Elias abceabea
Elias B adggefi
Elias Coy abccgchc
Elias H adaimbdc
Elias Howe adaimaaab
Elihu adgx, adgxfab, adgxfb, adgxfbe
Elihu F adabibd
Elijah adaaaaa, adaaah, adbabbe, adgcagba, adgfbgfg, adkecd, adhafabc, adhafd, adhag, adhagbc, gbaa
Elijah Peaslee adadicb, adadicfb
Elijah Smith bbbfabh
Elijah W ahbabfa
Elinor xaba
Eliphaz adaf
Eliphalet ahbaba
Elisha adgfbega, ahchd, ahchfid, ahdaab
Elisha A ahchfida

Elisha B ahgdcc

Eliza abbegbh, abccgdcb, abccgdd, ab-
dcebg, adabbgah, adabibcd, wife adabbgah, adabigc, adbabha, adacffc,
wife adgfbde, adgfcdc, adggdcc, adgxfaab, adgxfdd, adkfbbb, adkfbbch,
aeeacb, ahbabfa, wife ahbabkxa ah-
babkxfa, ahbcabcca, ahbgxab, ahcb-
fg, ahcfjf, ahgdhe, bbbffcd, bbbffcg,
wife bcbebbcd bcdbef, bcdebgc, bcdecad, bcdecdc, bcdgddg, bcdgeaah, bcficada, bcficadbaa, wife edy, ga

Eliza A abbegbdbg, adabbbdcc, adabbghe, adabbhdb, adgxfaab, adgxfdd,
bcdedcff

Eliza Ann abbegbde, abceabba, abcea-
bcc, adaimcg, adgfbfcb, ahfcibb, bbbfaba, bcfigfaa

Eliza B ahgfbdb, wife bedbadda

Eliza Bradley adgfcicb

Eliza C adhagbe

Eliza E adabbgahbb, adabbgahc, bcdh-
dehd

Eliza Ellen ahbcabad

Eliza F adabbgabc

Eliza Irish adkgddd

Eliza J abccgbaa

Eliza Jane adadabcc

Eliza Lawrence bcdebgab

Eliza O adkedf

Eliza Velma bcdgegb

Elizabeth x, abbeace, abbegbebd, abcfg,
abcfi, abdi, adaaafb, adaaag, adaaaicb,
adaabab, adaabb, adabbgca, adab-
bgcb, wife adabbgce, adabbgh,
adacedb, adacgc, adacgic, adadabba,
adadhcbdb, adaib, wife adaie, adaim-
cda, adfcca, adgcacbc, adgcadae wife
adgfbde, adgfbdeb, adgfbgaa, adgfa,
adgfcdacef, adgfcicdcc, adgi, adgxfa-
hc, wife adkefbehj, adkfbbca, adhad-
ccda, wife adhcefga, aea, adhd, aeeaa, aeeacb, ahbaae, ahbabjecab, wife
ahbabkxb, ahbcb, ahbd, ahcbed, wife
ahcff, ahdadd, ahdac, ahgbba, ahgc-
hk, ahggd, bbbc, bbbebe, bbbfabb-
eac, bbbfabmga, bbbfi, bcbcbaabai,
bcbcbbdd, bcbee, bcbehb, bcbehhb,
bcbhdbb, bcbhddcx, bcbhddd, wife bcbhddg, bcbhded, bcdbadi, bcdbead,
bfe, bcdedgh, bcdgdaai, bcdgdafac, be-
dd, bcdeabg, bcdeaek, bcdebeg, bcde-
bfe, bcdedgh, bcdgdaai, bcdgdafac bcdgdafj, bcdgdeaafe, bcdgdpc, bcdgg,
bcfh, bcfib, bcfifi, bcfiga, wife da

Elizabeth A abbegfcac, adabiggb

Elizabeth Allen abccdb

Elizabeth Ann xa, abbegfgai, ahbabjf,
bcdedff

Elizabeth B adabbgahbd, adabbhm, ad-
adhcahca

Elizabeth C ahdaaddi

Elizabeth Chase adhaddb

Elizabeth Davis ahbabjea

Elizabeth Drury adabbgagdc

Elizabeth Edith adhcbbjab

Elizabeth Emeline bbbffcha

Elizabeth Emery bbbfabbeb

Elizabeth F bcdgdbaadbb

Elizabeth French abbeebcf

Elizabeth H ahchfic, bcbehda

Elizabeth Hinckley adkgad

Elizabeth Jones bcficai

Elizabeth L abccgaca, adbafaba

Elizabeth M bcdgdang

Elizabeth Nason adgfgabch

Elizabeth Plumer ahbaaaab

Elizabeth S abceabeb

Elizabeth Seavey abceabda

Elizabeth Sheldon adggdccah

Elizabeth Weare adkebeb

Elizabeth Wilson ahbghl

Ella wife adbabfdh adgfbgeab, adgfcd-
acea, ahbaacfc, ahgfdaca, bcdbeceg,
bcdebgbg, bcdgdafbc, bcdgdafbf, bc-
ficani

Ella Adelaide adbabfej

Ella F abceabefe, adkfbedba, bcdcfabb

Ella Forest ahbghje

Ella Frances adbabfbgda, adbabfbh

Ella Francilea adadagabd

Ella G bbbfhcffe

Ella M adaigbbae, adhafagd, bbbfhb-
xcgc

Ella Tucker adkgaebd

Ella V adacfaea

Ellen x, xa, abccgcfh, abdcebcaa, adaceddd, adadagea, adaiiaafc, adgcaged,
adgfbfbc, adgfbgah, ahbabkxcb, bcd-
beccf, bcdgdad, bcdgddacb, bcdgddec,
bcfifjah

Ellen A adaceaeaa, adkddcab

Ellen Almira adkedecfa, adkedecl

Ellen Augusta abdcebeab, adhcdacg, bbbfaxbd, bcfifhhf

Ellen Celende adhcbbdc

Ellen Crate bcdeabbdc

Ellen E ahbgbfi, wife ahbaahae

Ellen D bcdebeebf

Ellen Delilah adhcbbdc

Ellen Esther ahgfdeb

Ellen F wife adaabcec

Ellen Frances bcfifhha

Ellen H adacffed, adkgdegc

Ellen J adaabcfbc, adaabfgc

Ellen L ahgciba

Ellen M abccgdbd, adaceddca, adaiga-
aab, adkddgcc

Ellen Mandanah ahbabjce

Ellen Margaret ahfcfcegc

Ellen Maria adaabdaec, adaijba, adhcb-
bbb, ahbgdfc

Ellen Marie adhcbbgdb

Ellen May ahgdhbca, bcbhddbcc

Ellen S adaabfxc

Ellen Thompson adhcbbfa

Ellen Wales ahgfdagc

Ellice bcdcbd

Ellie **M** adadhace
Ellie **May** adggeila
Ellis **M** adkecbagh
Ellsworth bcbebbfaac
Ellsworth **E** bbbfhcfg
Elmer bcdgdabga, bcbhddfac
Elmer **A** adhafgceb
Elmer **Asahel** adggeijaa
Elmer **C** ahbabaeaec, bbbffcbaca
Elmer **Chase** adkfbebi
Elmer **E** abccgcfda, abccgcfdac, bbbfh-
  cfgh, bbbfhcfgab
Elmer **L** ahbaacdae
Elmer **LeForest** ahbgbaeb
Elmer **P** adabbgaiew
Elmer **Pearl** adabbgaiia
Elmer **S** adabbgabdh
Elmer **Ulysses** adaceafge
Elmira adgfdacc
Elmira ahbabkxab
Elmira **Luania** adcgfgb
Elna **May** bcdgebd
Elnora **T** adabbgbce
Elnore **H** ahbabahcaaa
Eloisa adacede
Elom **King** adacgfad
Elsie abbegbdfbb, adaabfh, adgfdgb,
  ahbcai, bcdebjce, bcdedbbbje, bcdgd-
  eaia
Elsie **Adaline** bcdedbbba
Elsie **B** adkfbbcdab
Elsie **E** bcdgdakcb
Elsie **Estella** adabbgbcaf
Elsie **Louise** adgfbgdceb
Elsie **M** adabbgaijg, ahbabjla
Elsie **Storrs** ahgfbdad
Elton bcdebgbdcc
Elva ahbgbbeb, bcdgdeacea
Elva **Jane** bcdebgaea
Elva **Leila** abdabfdec, adbabfefc
Elvie bcdgdsacc
Elvie **A** ahbabajadf
Elvira adfcdcc, ahbcajda, ahbgie, bcb-
  ehhc, bcbhbff, bcfifjea
Elvira **Gove** adhcdace
Elvira **J** ahbabajae
Elvira **Philena** adacgfga
Elvira **Rosetta** ahbgiia
Elvira **Walker** adggega
Elwin **L** ahbabaeaea
Elwin **Pitman** adadhcah
Elwood **Weston** adbabfei
Elwyn bcbhddaaba
Emeline abceabbd, adaabdad, adaabgbd,
  adaimag, adgcacbb, addcacbc, adkg-
  ddb, ahbcabfb, ahgcabb, bcdedbcb
Emeline **A** ahbgei, bcdebff
Emeline **Augusta** adkedl
Emeline **B** adaimci
Emersay aedaa
Emery bcdgdakbd
Emery **Augustus** bbbfabid
Emery **L** adabbgqdd
Emery **W** adhcdach

Emilia adggeea
Emily adacgld, adaigai, adailaaf, **adgf**-
  cdgd, adgfcjbb, adggefd, ahbeabdab,
  ahbcabbd, ahbcabfa, ahgcid, bcbcb-
  bei, bcbhdhg, bcdgdaaef, bcficane
Emily **A** ahbgeca
Emily **Atwood** bcfigfdf
Emily **E** eaabc
Emily **F** abceabdbc
Emily **Frances** ahbgdge
Emily **G** adkgaee, bbbebgad
Emily **Genevieve** ahgchla
Emily **Grenleaf** adadabcd
Emily **J** adieaafg
Emily **L** bcbhbgh
Emily **M** adadabbf
Emily **Robinson** adadabcfac
Emma adabbgahbb, adaceagaa, adgfc-
  ibd, adhcdaba, adkgaedb, bbbfabca,
  bcbhdehh, bcdgdafc, bcdgdafea, bcd-
  kdaffc, bcdgeacfa
Emma **A** adaimbii
Emma **Amelia** bbbfabie
Emma **Bell** adhafdifb
Emma **C** ahgdccad
Emma **Catherine** adkfbebf
Emma **Charlotte** bcbebbbdbd
Emma **E** adadhaaca
Emma **Eleanor** gaaxaxka
Emma **Elizabeth** adaigbbacx
Emma **F** adabiggdd, adgxffbg, bcded-
  dae
Emma **Farnsworth** adaabfaad
Emma **Florence** bcdgdaacbh
Emma **Frances** adkedja
Emma **G** bbbfaxbcb
Emma **H** adabbgaick
Emma **J** adhafagc, ahbabfac, ahbcajcd,
  bcfihecc
Emma **Jane** adaimbag
Emma **Josephine** adgxfaaea
Emma **K** adaabfda
Emma **L** abccgcfi, adhafdic
Emma **Lovina** adaabdaea
Emma **Luania** adacgfgh
Emma **M** adggeik, adgxfaaac, adkeabad
Emma **Maria** adhcbbk
Emma **Maynard** adhccbbc
Emma **Minette** adhcbbffc
Emma **Pearl** adaimbife
Emma **S** ahbcabcbd, ahbgide
Emma **Violette** gbakc
Emmabelle ahbcabaef
Enid **May** ahbcabbadb
Enoch adggefe, adkdeb, adkecc, bcdgd,
  bcdgdagg, bcdgdba, bcdgde, bcdgde-
  aa, bcdgdaad, bcfifh, bcfifhh, gbab
Enoch **C** abccgcfdb, abccgcfe
Enoch **Coffin** adkdeac, adkdeaca
Enoch **French** adaidagb
Enoch **Hoit** ahbgdf
Enoch **Smith** adkehcb
Enos adacgfb
Enos **J** bcdgdakg

Ensign bcbhdbeb
Ephraim abccgcd, abcflc, adabbbg, ada-
bbgb, adaabfde, adabib, adabibj, ad-
add, ahg, ahgc, ahgce, bcdgdak, bcd-
gddc
Erasmus bcdedck
Erastus ahbabadb, ahdadaf
Ernest bcdedbbdc, bcdgdafebac
Ernest Arnold adkecbaach
Ernest B bcdgdbaaga
Ernest Clyde bcbebbfacb
Ernest E adabbgbeba, gbaic
Ernest Elmer adgcacbga
Ernest Fairman adaabdaeba
Ernest G adadhcaia
Ernest Gerry abbegfgada
Ernest H adkecbagg
Ernest Henry adgfbeaa
Ernest Hillgrove adgfbgfib
Ernest Hinman adgfgabcb
Ernest L adabbgaicj, adaimbbea
Ernest Lee bcdgdancc
Ernest Linwood ahbcabfea
Ernest Lyford ahbabahcaa
Ernest R adkecbaaf
Ernest Stinson ahbgfiba
Ernest W (Rev) adaceafkc
Ernest Wentworth adgfgabc
Ernestine adgfgabcg
Ervin Franklin adaimbhcbb
Ervine Levinia adhadcee
Erwin Augustus ahgcibba
Erwin P ahgcibc
Erwin W adagibbaca
Eselle bcdgdabgc
Estelle A adhadcdb
Estelle E bcbebigc
Ester bcdgdh
Esther abcfk, abdccb, abdcd, abde, ad-
kead, ahgdb, bcbhdee, bcdedfj, bcdg-
daj, bcfda, gbaf
Esther A adabibccb, adaimbbb, bbbff-
agd, bcdedcfca
Esther Ann adacedhg
Esther Belle bbbffcdfd
Esther C adaabcja
Esther E adabbgaia, adaimbeab, bcbe-
bbcba
Esther Frances ahgdgbaaa
Esther H bcdgddab
Esther N adgfdgaad
Esther Powers adhafdgeb
Ethan A adaabfgb
Ethel adaigbbabb, adgfcdgaba, bcdgde-
aceh, bcdgefa
Ethel A bbbfhbxcgg, gbaiac
Ethel Burtina adgfbgfcaa
Ethel E bbbffcbadb
Ethel Gordon Wells adadhacaaa
Ethel J ahbabajgab
Ethel M bcdedcfdb
Ethel Margaret bcdgdabdc
Ethel May abbegbibec, adgfbeggaf, bc-
dgdaned

Ethel Mina adgcacbjb
Ethel Robinson adhcbbhba
Ethel Vara abbegfgafa
Ethel Viletta bcbehhgba
Ethelinda ahgfbb, ahghb
Ethelyn Mary bcfigfdda
Etta adadibaca
Etta A adaabceca
Etta Bernice adabfaal
Etta F adkfbbcia
Etta Frances adhahecc
Etta M adgfcdgbc, adkecebaga
Ettie Agnes adaabcjfa
Eugene ahbaacff
Eugene F adaiiaaec
Eugene G bcfiffdce
Eugene H bcbadddbb
Eugene L adgfbgdca
Eugene Madison bcdedbccb
Eugene Marsh adkedecc
Eugene T adabbhh
Eula Evelyn adgxfdada
Euletta Flora ahbgbfaaa
Eunice adgfbgbf, adkeci, adkehba, ad-
kehk, ahbabai, ahbabamc, ahdadab,
ahgcha, bbbfag, bbbfc, bcbcbbb, bc-
deda, bcdedbh, bcdgddex
Eunice Ann ahfcaac
Eunice Appleton abbeebce
Eunice Gould adkdeae
Eunice Norris adkdei
Eunice Stearns ahgfdaga
Eva adabbgaigh, adabbgaigj, bcdgdaf-
bdd, bcdgdaia, bcdgdeaabb
Eva Alferetta ahbcajbc
Eva Alice abbegbdfdc
Eva Augusta adbabfecc
Eva Covert adbabfddd
Eva Mabel bcbebbbdbb
Eva May abbeebbaa, adabibcadb, ah-
baaheabb
Eva Maud adkfbbcie
Eva Susie adaceafke
Evan bcdeaa, bcdeaaa, bcficap
Evangeline Augusta ahgfbdcb
Evans ahbchc
Evalina adgfcdgca
Evalyn bcdebgaaea
Evaline adaabfed, adabbgcea
Eveline Adelaide abecgack
Eveline Elizabeth ahgfbgb
Evelyn abccgcfdcb, adaimaaabaa, adad-
hcea, ahgfbdgbbab, bcdkdaacdg, bcd-
gdaidbb, bcdgdaijab
Evelyn G adabbgqdi
Evelyn Harriet bcbhdbndmd
Evelyn Hinman adgfgabcb
Evelyn L adabbgbebae, adaigbbabd
Evelyn Madeline bcbhdgageb
Evelyn Piper bcdebeebe
Evelyn Ruth bcdgead
Everett adgcaccahd, ahbaacf, bcdgda-
fab
Everett A adaiefba

Everett C adkfbedd
Everett Duane ahgchebac
Everett E bcdebgaac
Everett Elton ahgcheba
Everett Gardner adaimbcbc
Everett Howard adkfbbcic
Everett J bcdebgaace
Everett Milton adbabfef
Everett Newton adbabfed
Everett Richardson adadibcabb
Everett S adgxfdaba
Evilena bcdgdpaaa
Ezekell xa
Ezekiel abdc, abdcic, adadc, bcbebie, bcbeh, bcbehh
Ezra adailxxb, adhahf, ahbgdj
Ezra Abbott ahgcig
Ezra C adhahb
Ezra Lowell M adkehbh
Ezra Wilson ahbgdfe
Faith adabbgrf, bcdgdsah
Fannie abccgbb, adaceaaf, adaceac, adaceafa, adaceafabe, wife adacgfba adggdcb, ahbabjid, bcdbeh, bcdgdaiicb, bcdgeaafa
Fannie A adaaaifad
Fannie E adhafcadb
Fannie Ethel adaabfdfa
Fannie Evaline ahbgiifab
Fannie Gertrude ahbcachd
Fannie H adabiggx
Fannie Isabel adhahecg
Fannie Louise bcdgdaneh
Fannie M adkgdcaa
Fanny ahggbh, bbbfabbab, bbbfhcffc, bcbcbbab, bcbndbi
Fanny Elizabeth adhafdgecb
Fanny F adaabfdd
Fanny J agdcacbg
Fanny Merrill bbbffcde
Fanny Plumer ahbaaaaa
Fanny S ahbgfd
Fanny Sarah adgfcdabe
Farrington Lawrence ahgchfeaa
Faye bcdgdafaga
Fayette Brown adggeibab
Fern adgcaccahc
Fern W bcdgdafeeb
Fernando A ahbgbfab
Fidela ahbabkxca
Fidela M adgfcieb
Fidelia Merle adabbgre
Finando E adacffee
Flavil ahbabkxbc
Flora abceabefd, adaabfge, adaceaaha, ahgdgaab, bcdedbbdaa
Flora Alice adhadcce
Flora Ann adaabdaef
Flora E adggdcfa, bcbcbaaabd
Flora Inez ahfcaaag
Flora Jeannette ahgfbdab
Flora Mae adgfbgfcac
Flora May adgxffbda, adgxffbdb
Flora Osilla bcdedbbbh

Floreda M bbbfaxbca
Florence adaaaiedb, adacffeed, adacgfaebaa, adadabcfc, adgfcdaab, adggdadaa, adggdcgab, adkfbebla, bcbhddiaaa, bcdebfgeb, bcdebgaacd
Florence A adadiabg
Florence Adelaide adaceafgb
Florence Adele ahgdgbb
Florence Annie bcdgela
Florence Ardine adgfcdabdc
Florence Augusta ahbgaba
Florence Bertha bbbebgabc
Florence Blanche adaigbbacb
Florence D bcdecdbaeb
Florence Edna adkfbeiab
Florence Elgiva adacgfacg
Florence Elizabeth adggdcfbb
Florence Ethel adgfbgdcea
Florence G bbbfhcfce
Florence Gertrude adaabcefa
Florence L bcdgdafega
Florence Lillian bcfigfbca
Florence M ahbabalc
Florence Mabel bcbhddcebb
Florence Marsh adkdececeb
Florence Maxine bcdgdabdad
Florence Miriam ahggbdaaca
Florence S adabbgdaad
Florence Talbot adaimbiacf
Florence V fceafc
Flossie adhafgcdba
Flossie S adabbgw
Floyd adacffeab
Follansbee bcbhda
Folsom adadabga
Forest adabbgqc
Forest Arthur adgfbgeaea
Forest Edward adabbgqda
Forest N adabbghga
Forrest adgfbeb
Forrest F adaabfaaca
Fostean bcfifffb
Foster Seymore adaabdabga
Foster W adacedfb
Fostina bcfifffc
Frances xaad, adabbghj, wife adgfbgab, adgfbi, ahbcajeb, ahbgbxi, bcbehe, bcbhdbng, bcdecaibb, bcdedbci, bcdgdaacb, bcdgdafmaa
Frances A bbbffcdb
Frances Ann adaabcdb
Frances Belle adgcagaba
Frances Boyer bcbhbgdb
Frances C bcdgdabfc
Frances Currier bbbebgaa
Frances E abccgaccaab, adbabixx, adadhcbc, wife beficale
Frances E M bcdgdnac
Frances Eleanor adabbgaib
Frances Elizabeth bcdgdaacbc
Frances Ellen adggege, ahbgbed
Frances Emeline bcdedfi
Frances G adadhcaiba
Frances L bcdgdafp

Frances M adaceafa
Frances Mabel abdcebeaf
Frances May ahfcfcegb
Frances R bbbfhcfef
Frances S adkgdec
Frances T abceabcd
Frances Wheeler adggdccaea
Frances Winifred adkfbeiac
Francina bcdebgda
Francis adacealf, adacgfbc, adgfbgab, adkddf, adkdeci, ahbabajagc, ahbgbhd, ahgfda, ahgfdae, b
Francis A adgfbgfda, bcdgega
Francis Byron adgxfaaf
Francis E adadagabb
Francis H adabbgahb, bcdeddabc
Francis J adacebfa
Francis Lorenzo bcfifhhe
Francis Lyford adkfbed
Francis Orett abbegbdba
Francis P adkecbagf
Francis Parker bcbhdqabaa
Francis Randall adggdccac
Francis S adkfbeddc
Francis Vose bcfiibc
Francis W bcbehd
Francis William adadhcafb
Franfis abda
Frank abccgdcea, adacgfabd, adgfcifb, adhafcaba, ahbaacxa, ahbabajgb, ahbabcfaa, ahbabjie, ahbgbbed, ahgdgaaa, bbbebcdaaaa, bbbfhcfh, bcbebbcdab, bcbhdbnba, bcbhddha, bcdecaia, bcdgddeac, bcdgdsa
Frank A adkfbbccb
Frank Albert bcdeaecc
Frank Albertine ahbgbadb
Frank Allen adhccbbh
Frank Augustine bcdedggb
Frank B adaaaaccaa, adacedhd, adaigaaac, adadagff, adgfbgfca, adgxfaaba
Frank Bacon ahbgbaca
Frank Bryant ahbgimd
Frank C adbabfdha, adhafaec, adkdfbcdan, ahbcabeja, bcbhbgl
Frank Chenery adhcbbgdaa
Frank D ahgfbdgbc
Frank E adkgaeba, adkgdefc, ahbabjecc bcfigfddc
Frank Edwin ahbcajgf
Frank Fowler adggeiba
Frank G ahbgfib
Frank H adkebgba, ahgfbdgca, bcdgdbaca
Frank Harrison adadhacaag
Frank Hayden adacffeee, adacffeeea
Frank Hayes abbegfgac
Frank Henry adhcbbja
Frank Herbert adgxfaabab
Frank Howard adacgfacc
Frank Howland abbegfccdb
Frank Irving adadabbdab
Frank Johnson bbbffchb
Frank L ahbabaeaa, bcbhddga

Frank Lafayette adgfcdgcc
Frank Lowell adhcbbgd
Frank M adabibie, adbabgda, bcdeaefcb
Frank Manning adbabfdba
Frank Melvin bcdeaedaaa
Frank Milton adabbgqdg
Frank Morton bcdedfcc
Frank Newton R adbabfeab
Frank O ahbchcba
Frank Paul aeeacaaaa
Frank P adkfbbcda, aeeacaad, ahbabdadb, bbbffcea, bcbebbfaa, bcdeaedac, bcdebgbi
Frank Peaslee bcfiibcf
Frank Pierce adaidagf
Frank Prescott bcbehhid
Frank R adabbhee
Frank S ahbabaeaa, ahbgilf
Frank Tuttle abbegbdbe
Frank W adhafagf, bcdebfbac, gbeb
Frank Wells ahbgiid
Franklin adaieaaf, adbabgb, adgcagaf, adgfdaca, bcbhddga, bcdeaaab, bcdgdabfd
Franklin Augustus bcbhddccb
Franklin H adaieaafa
Franklin Henry ahbgdgd
Franklin I adkgdea
Franklin G abccgbae
Franklin L adgxfaacaaa, bcbhddga
Franklin Pierce adkfbbci
Fred abccgcha, adaabcead, adaabffda, adadhcbdc, adhafcabb
Fred A bcbhddbaa, bcbhdeba, bcbhdqac
Fred Alsen bcfifjjad
Fred Alexander abccgdcfc
Fred B adbabfbga, adhafgcbe
Fred Burton adbabfeca
Fred C ahbabdada
Fred D adabibcaf, bcbhddbca
Fred Eugene adkgaede
Fred Everett adadabbdaa
Fred F ahbabajgc
Fred Grafton bcbehhif
Fred Harold abccdgcbba
Fred Henry adggdcic
Fred Hermon gbakf
Fred Hudson abccgchabb
Fred L adaaaieec, adhafccf
Fred Leland adkebabba
Fred Myron bbbffbaad
Fred N adgfbgeae
Fred O adaceafkg
Fred S adgxffbf
Fred Todd adkgdegd
Fred W adgfbgdcj, ahgdcafa
Fred Waldo bcbhddccbd
Freda adgfbffcd
Freda L abccgchada
Freddie L adacedhi
Frederick abccdgcbc, adaceai, adggegbacf, bbbebce, bcdeaefabc, bcdgdabfa, bcdgdafagd, eaacb

Frederick Augustus adhcbbjb
Frederick Charles adabibic
Frederick Edward adaceagccg
Frederick Elmer adkddiab
Frederick George bbbfabbf
Frederick Herbert bcbebbeca
Frederick Irving adabibica
Frederick J ahbaacdab
Frederick Morris adggegba
Frederick Northrup ahchfebb
Frederick Neal adkfbeg, adhccbbe
Frederick Porter bcbhbgda
Frederick R adaigbbc
Frederick Thompson adhcbbfbd
Frederick W adaceaea, adgfbggba
Frederick Warren adadhcafc
Frederick Waterbury adggegbai
Freeman ahbaace, bbbffaf, bcdedbbdae, bcbhddfacf
Freeman Augustus ahbaacfd
Freeman H adabbgaji
Freeman J abccgdfc
Fremont Adrian adhahecac
Frieda Grace abbegbdfcf
Furber adkdbc, adkddgb
G Arthur bcdgdakfb
Galen M adabbgu
Galusha adgfcie
Gardner adadiae
Gardner Warren ahbabjed
Gardys Venona bcbhddccbf
Garfield bcdgdafma
Gaylord H bcfiibad
Geneva Florence adabbgagdd
Geneva Isabelle adabbgagdac
Genevieve bbbfhcffd
Genevieve Laura adhcbbjdb
Genora bcdgdaiae
George adaabdabg, adaaabdc, adaabfea, adabbgdbc, adacedda, adacfe, adacglc, adailxxa, adgcageb, adgfbma, adgfdacb, adggdcg, adgxfahb, adkddca, adkecbaacd, adkehbe, aeeaec, ahbabkxyc, ahbcabec, ahbcaddba, ahbgbxg, bbbfabcd, bbbfabd, bbbfhje, bcbehhj, bcbhddcebd, bcdbecce, bcdbecg, bcdeaefahd, bcdeaedb, bcdebgdd, bcdedbb, bcdedbbcb, bcdedbce, bcdgdaaa, bcdgdaffa, bcdgdake, bcdgdeaag, bcdgej, cba
George A adgfbgead, adgfbp, adhafcd, adkeabae, aeeacac, bcbcbaaaba, bcbebbcda, bcdbaddbe, fceaf, fced
George Agnes ahgdhbbe
George Albert adadagfbd
George Albion adhccfga
George Alfred bbbffadbb
George Allen ahbaaheae
George Alonzo bcbebcgabaa
George Alvah abdcebcaba
George Alvin adhafcabd
George Andrew bcbcbaabag, bcdecdbaaaa

George B adabbgagcf, ahbabaead bcdgdafh, bcdgddea
George B N bbbffbaaa
George Barber bcfihed
George Brown adkfbebce
George C adabbgabda, adgfciea, adgxfaacc, eaab, eaabb
George Carr bcficadba
George Churchill adggeibc
George Dewey bcbhddkbxi
George E adadagac, adadhacaac, adaiiabaa, adkeabbab, bcbhdp, bcdgdakba
George Edgar adkecbaa, aeeaecc, aeeaeccc
George Edward adhafdgd, ahfcfcba, bcbebbcdaca
George Edwards ahgcabace
George Edwin abdcebcab
George Elbridge adadhcag
George Elmer adaceafgc
George Ellsworth adgxfaaccb, bcdgdaacdc
George Eugene adkgaebf
George F adadagacca, adaiiaba, adgfbgea, adhcdacac, bbbebcdaaa
George Falls adaimea
George Farrington adkfbeibb
George Farwell adkedjd
George Field bbbfabmab
George Francis adkdececa
George Frank abccgbae, adkecbaacc
George Franklin adhedae
George Fred bcdgdaaab
George Fredora bcbhddbcbb
George Freeman abccgdcc
George Grafton bcbehhia
George Green bbbfabhb
George H abccgaeea, abdceblia, adadagf, adadhacd, adgfbecgb, adgfbgfa, adggdcfc, adgxfaaec, adhafgcba, adhccfh, bbbffcbai, bcbebcgab, bcbhdehc, bcdeaeafc,bcdedcga, fceafa
George Halleburton bcdbecf
George Hamilton abbeacbc
George Harlan ahchfdca
George Harold abbegbdfba
George Henry adbabgaac, adgfbgfa
George Herbert adggdcfba, bcdebejca, bcdedclg
George Heyward bbbfabbb
George Hubbard adaimaah
George Hudson ahgdcagb
George K adaigbbaa
George L abbegfcaa, adaimbid, adgxfaacaa, ahdadada, ahgcabacc
George Lee ahbgbxaaa
George Lenville ahbgbbea
George Lenville Jr, ahbgbbeaa
George Lewis adggdcga
George Lincoln adbabfcc, bcdedcfcc
George Lovejoy bbbebcbd
George Luther bcbcbbgbba
George M adgcadafc, adgfbma
George Millard abccgcfcaa

George Morrison bcbebbfba
George N bcdgeb
George Newell adaaaied, adadieaa
George O adabbge, adaceafk, aeeaec
George Orville adabbgagcxa
George Otis bcbebgaba
George P adgcadafa
George Parsons bcfigfbb
George Peck adacgfg
George Percy adaimeac
George Plummer bcdeddhb
George Price ahbcajge
George Prince adkdecec
George Quincy ahbaaaab
George R ahbabaeadc, bbbebcdab, bb-
   bfhja
George R S adaaaieda
George Raymond bcbhdehgd
George Russell adaimbiff
George S adaieaab, adaieaafc, adhccga-
   bc, bbbfhae
George Saphroneus adacgfacf, adacgf-
   acfa
George Sewall bbfhcfa
George Stanley adhafdgecc
George Stephen adhcbbffda
George Sylvanus Cobb bcdebej
George W abccdgcaa, abccdgdcb, abcc-
   gaea, abdceble, adaabfac, adabbgagc,
   adabibcb, adacgfba, adadhaaab, adgf-
   becg, adgfbgead, adkdgcab, ahbgecb,
   ahdaaddf, gbam
George W P adggeba
George W S adhafgcb
George Walter ahbaaheaeb, bbbfaxbe
George Washington abbegbdc, abccgcfc,
   abceabdc, adaabfaaf, adhafgcbcf, ah-
   baacxg, ahbgec, bcbhdbnb, bcbhddca
George West adaidagfb
George Whitefield bcbegga
George Willard adbabfdh
George William abbegbdfb, adabbgda-
   ac, adabibce, adkehbf, bcdedfda, bc-
   fifhhb
George Willie bcficalec
George Winthrop adhahea
George Worthington adkdece, adkdece-
   bc
George Wright bbbfabhba
Georgia bcdgdaiaa
Georgian bcdgdaiab
Georgianna adbceblh, adabibib, bcbeb-
   bbda, bcdbeccd
Georgianna B adkebcca
Georgianna F bbbddceb
Georgietta bcdebfbaa
Georgiette bcbhdbndi, bcbhdbnaa
Gerald ahbabajgaaa
Geraldine adabbgaiey, ahgfbdgbbaa, bc-
   bhdqabg
Geraldine S ahbabaefbc
Gershom ahchfia

Gertrude adaabcefa, adaabdabh, adac-
   ebfaa, adacfeec, adacgfacca, adaigb-
   baaa, adgxfadab, adkddgja, adkeba-
   bbab, bbbfhcfeh, bcdedbbdx, bcdgd-
   aacad, bcdgdafeh, bcdgdaib, bcdgdbf,
   bcdgddeae, bcdgdeacf, bcfiibac, fceka
Gertrude Bell adkfbeddaa
Gertrude C ahbcachca
Gertrude E adgfbffcc
Gertrude Elizabeth bcbhddbbab
Gertrude Ellen adhcbbjda
Gertrude Emma adgxfaacca
Gertrude Gove adhcbbgf
Gertrude Josephine bbbfabbaa
Gertrude L ahchfecc, bcdgdanec
Gertrude Margaret bbbffcbaja
Gertrude Melvina ahchfeg
Gertrude Moulton adabibid
Gertrude Thelma adabbgtaa, adabbguc
Gideon adgba, adgg, adggd, adggdea
Gideon Y bcdgdafd, bcdgddeb
Gilbert A ahbcacbab
Gilbert Parker ahbcacba
Gilbert Bradley bcbehhj
Gilbert F adgcadafb
Gilbert Moulton bcdedbcca
Gilbert T ahbaeddbb
Gilford Q bbbebdaca
Gilman adaaaie, adaabd, adadhx, ahb-
   aacc, ahbabaeh, ahbabajj
Gilman Corning bcdeddab
Gilman L adaaaieb
Gladis adhafdiaa
Gladys adaigbbabf, bcbcbaabaj bcdebg-
   agba, bcdgdaide, bcdgdeaafg
Gladys E adaabclca, ahbabajadd
Gladys Evangeline bcdedbbdba
Gladys Helen bcdecdiab
Gladys J bbbfhbxcga
Gladys L bcdgdaalca
Gladys Phoebe bcdgdwa
Gladys Winnifred adgfbgebba
Glen H adaabcleb
Glenwood W bcdgdakch
Glidden North bcbhdbndhc
Goodrich Quigg bcbehddc
Gordon A adabbgqdc
Gordon Sumner adkebabbaa
Grace adaabdaega, adacebfac, adkecba-
   acg, ahbabjecb, ahchfiea, bcdedkdd,
   bcdgdafeed, bcdgdaiac, bcfiffdcbaa
Grace A bbbffcbada
Grace E adabbhp, adgcacbkb, adkfbbj-
   de, ahgciacaa, bcbhddkxbn
Grace Eaton ahbgbadh
Grace Edna adgfbgdced
Grace Elida adbabfiaa
Grace Elizabeth adgfcdaaa
Grace Hannah bbbffbaab
Grace Josephine adhaheef
Grace L adadagfbc
Grace Lillian adaabffdb
Grace Maud ahbgbaee
Grace May adhadcek, bbbffagca

827

287

Grace P adgfcdacf
Grace Phyllis adgfcdaceh
Grace Plumer ahbaaaaad
Grace Ruth adadhacaeb
Grace Tappan adkdececb
Grace Waterbury ahgdhbbd
Gracie bcbhdehff
Gracie E adabbgajaa
Grant adaceddeb
Granville S adaimcb, adaimbifh
Greeley adaabda, ahbcaaa, adhafdc
Greeley Elijah adhafdg
Greenleaf Clough abceabcgb
Greenleaf G adgfcdgc
Grove Samuel adgfgabcc, adgfgabcca
Guilford C bbbebdaca
Gussie bcdgep
Gustavus adadha
Guy abbegbibe, bcfifjjba
Guy A ahbabamgc
Guy F bcdgdaiec
Guy George bcdgeja
Guy H ahbcabeda
Guy Linwood adaceafgf
Guy S bcdgeja
Guy Stuart adgfcjbcb
Guy T bcdgdeaceb
Guy Trafton bbbfhjbf
Guy W adhadcef
Gwendolyn bbbfhcgbfb
Gynan adaimaabcc
H ahbabkxbd
H Shailer ahbgbaddb
Hadley J bcdgdaiic
Hale Macomber bbbfhcfeb
Hallie Calvin adabbgtab
Hammond bcdgddf, bcdgead
Hannah abba, abbed, abbeeba, abbeedc,
abbegd, abbj, abcb, abcce, abcfe, wife
ada, adaaba, adabbbf, adabbgdf, ad-
abbgg, adabbgib, adabbhk, adabiba,
adabid, adabige, adadac, adadf, adadha, adadibdb, adadj, adahdba, adaidaa, wife adaicaa, adaigd, adaimbf,
adbabd, adbabfa, adbac, adbb, ade,
wife adgcada adgfba, adgfbei, adgff-
cd, adggdf, adgj, adgxa, adgxffb, adhae, adhafaf, adhafdb, adhaga, adhagb, adhai, adhcdb, adkebag, adkebgf,
adkebi, adkede, aeb, ag, ahbaacxf, ahbaaf, ahbabahj, wife ahbabfa, wife
ahbabkx, wife ahbabkxd, ahbaaf, ahbcaca, ahbcah, ahbgef, ahca, ahcfd,
ahdc, ahe, ahgcc, ahgchc, wife ahgei,
ahggf, bbbebfj, bbbfa, bbbfhbab, bbbffe, bcbd, bcbe, bcbebbbb, bcbebbd,
bcbehc, bcbhgf, bcbhdbm, bebhddn,
bcc, bcdeaad, bcdeabc, bcdeaej, bcde-
bb, bcdecag, bcdeddg, bcdgb, bcdgdbg, bcdgddd, bcdgdec, bcdgdx, bcdia,
bcfifaa, bcfie, bcfifd, bcfiffffe, bcfifhf, bcfihex, bcfihi, dcc
Hannah Abigail bcdeabde
Hannah Ann adacgfec

Hannah B adbabba
Hannah Bacon adkfbebd
Hannah E adaieaac, adgfcja
Hannah E J bbbfaxba
Hannah Jane adhafabaaa
Hannah Knight befigdb
Hannah Lull bcbhddn
Hannah M adaimbdj, bcdgddaf
Hannah Maria abbeebcb, adhcdaec
Hannah Merrill bcbebiga
Hannah Nora ahfcfceha
Hannah Park bcdbedd
Hannah Peaslee bcdbadb, bcdbadg
Hannah Pickering abceabdi
Hannah Phillips adhcdaca
Hannah S adgfbggd
Hannah Wales ahgfdah
Hannah Zea adaimbik
Hannibal Hamlin ahbgbadg
Harden K bbbfhcfhd
Harlan Albert ahchfdcac
Harlan K bbbfhcfhd
Harlan Page ahchfdc
Harland E abccdgdcc
Harley bcdgdaidd
Harley R bcdgdaghb
Harlon abbegbif
Harlon F bbbffcbacb
Harman abbegfcce
Harmon James adggdcica
Harold adaceaaiaa, adbabfdhab, bbbeb-
cdaaaaa, bcdgdaacac, bcdgdabgac, bc-
dgdafaaa, bcdgdaieac, bcdgdeaceg
Harold Allen bcbhdekda
Harold C bcbhdpaa
Harold Cochran bcdedhab
Harold E adabbgra, ahgdcage, bcbhd-
diaab
Harold Eugene adabbhha
Harold Francis bbbfabbfa
Harold Frank bcbebbcdaxb
Harold Fred bbbffbaadb
Harold L adabbgqdf
Harold Leslie adabbgra, adabbgua
Harold Mullen bbbfabibd
Harold Parcher abccdgcbbaa
Harold R bcdgdsba
Harold Raymond bcdgdakaac
Harold Russell ahbaacdaba
Harold Stanley ahbaacfda
Harold T abccgaccaac
Harold W adaabfaacd
Harold Wright bbbebgacb
Harrie Ellsworth adkecbagd
Harriet abbegbebc, wife abccgcb, abc-
cgdcl, wife adabbbg, adacealh, adacf-
fib, adacgjb, adgcacbc, adgfbggbd,
adgfbhab, agdfdcb, adggbea, adhcb-
bda, adhccbc, adkdecj, adkdeef, ah-
babkxbb, ahcbead, ahgfdab, bbbfab-
beab, bbbffcbc, bcbegba, wife bcdea-
aaa, bcdecaie, bcdedbcg, bcdedcc
Harriet A abceabei, wife adadhaac, ada-
aidagd, bcbehhk

Harriet Ann adabbgbcd, befigfda
Harriet Anna ahgcabcc
Harriet Augusta bcbehhja
Harriet B adhahfd
Harriet Benita adgfbgfaadb
Harriet E adäcgja, adaimbdg, adgfbffa, bbbebcbcc, bcdbeceb
Harriet Elizabeth ahgchfc
Harriet Hall bcdeabbdb
Harriet Helen bbbffcbf
Harriet J bbbfabic
Harriet J S adkgaebfc
Harriet Josephine adhcbbfc
Harriet Louise adkfbbdfb
Harriet M wife abbegfjca
Harriet Maria adgcacbcd
Harriet Matilda ahgcabaa
Harriet Melissa adhafcaa
Harriet Newell ahbchgb
Harriet Pamela adkdbed
Harriet Pierce bcdeaeaeb
Harriet Rounds adkgdda
Harriet Sanders bcdedfcb
Harriet Scott bcdedgi
Harriet Stilson adbabfbd, adbabfbca
Harriette bcdebgde
Harrison adaabfd, adacebaa
Harrison L adabbgajab
Harry abccgcfdaa, adaceaebbe, adgfcdabb, adgfcieab, adkfbedcd, bcbhdbeaa, bcdgdafkh, bcdgdaija, bcdgdeaafc, bcdgdeaig
Harry A adadhcaha
Harry Augustus ahgcibbb
Harry Barnes adgfcdadc
Harry Chester adkddgcac
Harry D adaimbbeb
Harry E adgxffbba, adkecbaaaa, bbbffcbac
Harry Edward ahbgiifb, bcdedfdaa
Harry Ernest bcdgdafeba
Harry F bcbhddiaa
Harry G bcbhdekd, bcdbadddae
Harry Goodger adggegbaa
Harry H bcdebgaacab
Harry Israel adkebgbaa
Harry J ahbgbebb
Harry James bcbebcgabb
Harry Jefferson bcdeaefadd
Harry Kearney bcdgdabdd
Harry L adabbgaiez, adhafdiea, bcbcbaaag, bedebgaaca
Harry Lee adgfbegga
Harry Leslie bcbcbaaaga
Harry M ahbaahde
Harry Merrill bcbhbfiaa
Harry Prescott bcdeaefba
Harry Raymond adacgfaeba
Harry Robert bbbffchf
Harry Robinson bcdedfdb, bcdedfdba
Harry S adkgddhe
Harry Walton adaimaaabb
Harry Weston ahbaahdeaa
Hartwell bcbhbfa

Hartwell Guy ahbgiifaa
Harvey abbegfccd, ahgdj
Harvey Anson ahgdgb
Harvey James adaabcda
Harvey L ahgdhda
Harvey M bcbebbbdc
Harvey Murray ahgdgbaa
Harvey S bbbebgab
Harvey Warren adacgjd
Harvey Weed bcdgdafbd
Hattie bcdgdanef, bcdgdeaif
Hattie A adiagbbaf, adggeica, ahbghjg, bcdgdafecb
Hattie Bell bcbebbcdaaa
Hattie Belle ahbgbebd
Hattie C adgfcdgaab
Hattie E adggdciba, bcdeabdab, bcdedcgaa
Hattie Eva bbbffche
Hattie F ahgfdaeb
Hattie I adgfbq
Hattie J bbbffcbab
Hattie L adgxfdaa
Hattie Long abbegfjbc
Hattie M adabbgqa, adgfcdgbb
Hattie May adkgdgdegb
Hattie S bcbcbbeef
Hattie Simpson abbegbeac
Hattie W aeeaecca
Hawley bcdgdafmd
Hawley D adabbghgb
Hazel abccgchadc, abdcebcadb, adaabfaace, adgfdgc, bcdgdabgad, bcdgdafob, bcfiffdcbab
Hazel A bcdgdmaba
Hazel Aileen adacgfaebb
Hazel Alice adaabdabcc
Hazel C adgcacahb
Hazel L adbabfbga
Hazel M bcdgdbaadj
Hazel Marie adhafcabdb
Hazel Vilmer bcdgdabdaa
Hazen adaabcf, adgcacbh
Helen abbeebcaaa, adaceama, adaidaeba, adgffcb, ahbabajadb, ahbcabfeac, bcdecaic, bcdecdbaaab, bcdgdaacfb, bcdgdafagb, bcdgdafmda, bedgdaiiba, bcfiffgc, bcfifhba, cbaab, eaaca
Helen A adhafc
Helen Augusta adkdeeca, bebhdbedc
Helen B abdceble
Helen Deborah adaijbaa
Helen E adaabfdc, ahbabaeaef
Helen Edwards bcdebeeaa
Helen F adgxbbdc
Helen Frances adadhcaiab, bcbebbfaaae, bcfifhhdaa
Helen G bbbfhcfgc
Helen Hall ahbghjd
Helen I adaigbbabe
Helen Jane ahgchee
Helen Jeannette adaceagccc
Helen Kate adgfgabca
Helen L ahfcfceca

820

Helen Laura adacffeecc
Helen Louise abbegbeaab, adggeibe, bc-
bcbaabaf
Helen Lovina adgcacbaf
Helen M adhcdaeaa, adkfbbjbe, ahbab-
ajgba
Helen Maria adadgaba, adgfciec
Helen Marie adgfbgfaag
Helen Marion bcdgdakfba
Helen Mary ahbabajm
Helen Matilda befigfde
Helen Merrill adgfcicdb
Helen Pauline bbbfabmja
Helen Pearl ahchfdce
Helen Ruth ahbabajlb
Helena ahbcabg
Helena C adadheahd
Hellen adggefca
Hellen Etta adabiggdad
Hellen Maria ahbabajc
Helmar bcdgdaacae
Hendrick ahcbc
Henrietta ahbabadf, bcdgdaif, bcfifac
Henrietta Dana Carr beficadbc
Henrietta J bcbebcgad
Henrietta P ahbabahm
Henry x, xaa, xaaf, a, ab, abcea, abce-
abd, abceabdd, abch, abdcebcd, abd-
cedb, adaaaf, adaabceaa, adaabced,
adabbbdcx, adabibcada, adadaga, ad-
adhcbi, adf, adfg, adgfbfbb, adggdeh,
adggeec, adhaheca, adkdeee, aee, ah-
cfjba, ahdaa, ahdaad, bbb, bbbed, bbb-
fabc, bbbfae, bbbfaxb, bbbfh, bbbf-
hbae, bbbfhbx, bbbfhc, bcbhddf, bc-
bhddfach bcbhdebd, bcbhdehb, bcb-
hdek, bcbhdgab, bcdbeede, bcdgdaa-
cc, bcdgdaaed, bcdgdaffd, bcdgdeba,
bcdgrach, bcdgdw, bcfifjec, cca, ea-
abf
Henry A befifjjb, befigdcd
Henry Abijah Thompson adhcbbffa
Henry Alfred adabbgbcaa
Henry Alvah abdcebcad
Henry Archie adaimbifd
Henry Austin adacgid
Henry B adadagacb, adaimbbdg, ahba-
ahab
Henry Bickford bbbfhbacba
Henry Bradley bcbehhic
Henry Cecil adabbgaiif
Henry Clay ahbcacfh
Henry Daniel ahdaadd
Henry E adaigbbb, adkfbbjab, ahdaa-
ddd, bbbfhbxcd, bbbfhbxd, bcbebbfa
Henry Edward adaceafgeg
Henry Elisha ahchfdb
Henry Eugene adaabdabeb, adaabdabf
Henry F adacgjac
Henry Francis bcbcbbaffa
Henry G adggein, cca
Henry H adkfbbja, ahbcacff
Henry Howard bcdgdakaa
Henry Johnson bbbffce

Henry Keith adabbgabdfa
Henry Kenneth adhcbbffaa
Henry Keyes adfcdcaa
Henry Kingman adgfcdgaaa
Henry L bcbcbbace
Henry Laurens ahcbea
Henry Neal adhccbbd
Henry O adbabfib
Henry Oscar adhcbbge, adhcbbjd
Henry Putnam ahbcacbb
Henry S adaceaga, adgfcdgb, bcbcbb-
eg, bcdedcfa
Henry Sewell abccgdcd
Henry Smith bbbfabibg
Henry Squire fceab
Henry Sylvester adadagabe
Henry T adkecbab
Henry W adkebdg, gaaxaxn
Henry Ware abdcicab
Henry Warren abbeebbba
Henry Weed bcdgdaka
Hephzibah ahfce, ahfd, bcbhk
Hepzibah ahbgeg, ahfcj, ahgcg, bcbf,
bcdbeae, bcdbeg
Herbert abdcebcac, adadibaa, adadiba-
bd, adaimbig, adkebaae, bcbhddfaab,
bcdgdabddb, bcdgdafdc, bcfiibadc,
gaaxaxh
Herbert Allen adgxfafg
Herbert Ancel ahbabajag
Herbert Beane abceabcga
Herbert Beeman adhcbbhb
Herbert C adaabdabcb
Herbert E adhafcada, bcbhddbcba
Herbert Edgar adadhaaac
Herbert G adggefga
Herbert George bcdebejb
Herbert Gerry abbegfgad
Herbert Gilman bcdeddabcc
Herbert Gruby adhcbbgg
Herbert Henry abbeebcaa
Herbert J adbabfbe, bcdebgaacb
Herbert L adhafdid, ahbabajga, bcde-
bgaab, bcdgdabde
Herbert Lester adaimaabb
Herbert Linwood bcdedbbbj
Herbert M adgfbgfaabb
Herbert Manchester adgfbgfaa, adgfb-
gfaab
Herbert Martin bbbfhcfgf
Herbert Russell bcbhddccbi
Herbert S adadhabcb
Herbert W adkgdbad, bcbebcgabc, bcd-
beceda
Herman adacffeag
Herman Adelbert bbbebgac
Herman Furness adacffeh
Herman L abccgcfdd
Herman Wallace bbbebcdaac
Hester bcdgdaieae, bcdgddeab, fcf
Hettie C adgfcdacd
Hewey bcbhddfaci
Hezekiah adgfbgac, bcbebfg, bcdgdaac,
bcdgdec, bcficalh, bcficao

Hezekiah Farrington ahgchfe
Hezekiah Richardson ahgchf, ahgchfb
Hial bedbaddd
Hilbert bbbfabha
Hilda A bbbfhcfkb
Hilda Elizabeth adhaheddb
Hilda Margaret abccgcfdec
Hildah adahb
Hildur A wife ahbaacfda
Hipsabeth adabbbd, adabbgaj
Hiram adacedg, adgfcii, adggdcf, bbb-
    ffai, bcbhddh, bcdbadda
Hiram Albertine ahbcabcba
Hiram Augustus adhccgab
Hiram H adhccga
Hiram Harvey adgfcicd
Hollis adaabdc, bcdedbbdad, bcdgdafmd
Hollis R gbaiab
Hollis T bcdgdafmdd
Homer bcdedfc, bcdgdabdb
Homer Eugene adggeijaaa
Hope bcdgdeaafc, bcdgdeade
Horace adabbgaiga, adaceahc, adgcag
    ca, bcdedbbc, bcdgdeafb
Horace A adgcadaaad, adgcadaaag
Horace Albert adkfbebk
Horace Davenport adbabgaaa
Horace E adgcaccag
Horace F adkfbeda
Horace Henry adkdecfb
Horace Holly adkdecf
Horace Lincoln adabbgdaa
Horace M adgcadaaa, adgfbgdci, adk-
    fbedc
Horace Page bcbebcbc
Horace Sackett adggeiic
Horace Smith abbeacbf
Horatio ahcix
Hortense Robinson adabibig
Horton adacffead
Hosea abbegbia, adabbghc, adbabx
Hosea Ballou bcdebgaf
Howard bcdecahfc
Howard B adabbghgba, ahgfbdgdc
Howard E bcdgdafeb
Howard E bcdgdafcb
Howard F adadhcaib
Howard Frederick adkebgbaab
Howard K adkgddga
Howard Malcolm abbegfjb
Howard P adggdcaa
Hoyt Eben adadabbdbb
Hubert bcdgdeadj
Hugh bcdgdaaad
Hugh Arnold abbegbdfcg
Hugh H bcdgdaiib
Hulda bcdgdafef, bcdgdbb
Hulda J ahbabahd
Huldah adbaa, adbabff, adbabx, adaim-
    aaabc, adgxfccd, bcdgdaaj, cbaaaac,
    cbaada
Huldah A adgxfaba
Huldah M adaimbfc, adgxfaacd
Humphrey Bean ahgh

Huse adgfcda
Huse Ard adgfcdabdb
Iceley ahbabkxfd
Ida adadibdh, adgfbecgc, ahbabjic
Ida B ahbaacdaa
Ida C adgfbgdcb
Ida E adacedfl, bbbfhcfad
Ida Ellen bcdeaecca
Ida Evelyn bcbehhga
Ida Frances bcbhdbndd
Ida L adaabcfbe, wife adhccfga
Ida M adgfcdgcb, adhafdig, bbbfhcfd
Ida May adaabdaee, adaceafgd, adace-
    dhh, adgcacbjc
Ida Santha ahbgimc
Imogene R adkgaebb
Ina abbegbdfbd
Ina L adabbhi
Ina M adaimaaaba, adgcadaaaaa
Ina May bbbfhcffb, bbbfhcfgb
Increase K ahbabaef
Indiana bcdeaei
Inez bcbhdhbb, bcdgdaacdd
Inez Gertrude adkecbacac
Inez L ahgdhbba
Inez Theresa bcbhddccbk
Insley adggda, adggdad
Iona abccgdbaa
Ipswich bbbfad
Ira adaabd, adaabd, adgfcib, ahbgdd,
    bcdgdaak, bcdgdagca, bcdgdage, bc-
    dgdeaab
Ira Benton ahbgiif
Ira F adailaad
Ira Luther adadieaaa
Irene adgcaccaa, bcbhbficb, bcbhddcc-
    beb, bcdgdaga, bcdgdeaaa, bcdgded
Irene E ahbaacdabb
Irene Goff ahbaacdabc
Irene H bcdebgaha
Irene L bcdedcgab
Irma E ahbabajgad
Irville Leslie ahgchec
Irvin Scott bcbcbfiag
Irving adadabbda, adadabbdaab, adha-
    fabi
Irving E adaigbbac
Irving Millis adabibicba
Irving W adgfbgeah
Irwin bcdedbbdb
Irwin J adaabcfbf
Isa (Isaiah?) adaabd
Isaac abbegfka, abcc, abceabc, abcea-
    bcg, abceabdb, adaceafb, adacef, ah-
    bc, ahbcach, ahbcacha, ahbcad, ah-
    bcd, ahbgfd, ahbgh, bbbe, bbbebd,
    bbbebda, bcbcaaa, bcbebbe, bcbebbe,
    bcbhbg, bcde, dc, dcd
Isaac C adabbgabdb
Isaac Carlton adabbgbca
Isaac J bcbhbfi
Isaac K ahgdccd
Isaac Lincoln adbabfe
Isaac Newton ahbcaje

Isaac R ahgdcd
Isaac Walker ahbghjf
Isaac Washington adbabfdb
Isaac White ahbgdc
Isaac William adabbgccc
Isaac Wilson ahbgha, ahbghga, ahbgik
Isaack ahgdcd
Isabel bcdgdane, bcdgdbafb
Isabel C bcdbadddc
Isabell adgxfbda
Isabella adaabdeaa, adgfbfd
Isabella Grant ahcbecc
Isabella J adaceaeab
Isabelle ahchfc
Isabelle Maria ahchfeh
Isaiah abbeec, adacf, adacfd, adacfdb, adaid, adaida, adaima, adimch, bcb-hddia, bcdecd, bcdecdba, bcdecdbaaa
Isaiah C adkebga
Isaiah Lincoln adbabfde
Isaiah M bcbhddiac
Isophene Kimball adbabica
Israel adabbgi, adkeb, adkebaa, adkebg, adkegb, adkehc, bcbhdhc, bcdgdea
Issachar Hammond bcdgdsaa
Iva bcdgdaidc
Ivan Lathrop bcdgdsak
Ivena bcbhdehj
Izyphena ahbgib
J C ahbabkxc, ahbabkxy
J D Webster bbbfhcfj
J Herbert adhafaed
J Louise adadicfbb
J Neal bcbhdnc
J Russell adkebabbf
J W ahbabkxcd
Jabette adaabacag
Jabez abd, abdcebe, abdci, adfcb, adg-cag, adgcaga, adkfbe, adkg, adkgdb, adkge
Jabez Stephen abbegbebb
Jackson P adhafgcd
Jacob abbegfg, adaaaaab, adaceaa, ad-gfbdb, adgxf, adgxfaa, adgxfbf, ad-gxfc, adgxffa, adkea, adkeabba, ad-keba, adkebab, adkehb, ahbged, ah-bgi, ahfcib, bcbca, bcbebff, bebhbd, bcdgdab, cbbb, cbbc
Jacob B adkebab
Jacob Flanders adaaaacca
Jacob Franklin adgxfaaca
Jacob H adgcacca
Jacob Hilton ahfcfcd, ahfcfd, ahfci
Jacob Neale bcbhdbnc
Jacob Trussell ahbgid
Jadah ada, adai
James abccgdbab, abceabe, adaabb, ad-ac, adace, adaceaef, adace, adaceb, adaceba, adacebac, adacfda, add, ad-gfbhb, adficdacb, adkddib, adkeab, ahbabkxfb, ahbabkxya, ahbgbj, ahc-bf, ahchfh, ahfcib, ahfciba, ahgchjd, bbbffcbb, bcbcbaa, bcbcbaaab, bcbc-bbg, bcbcbbgj, bcbcbcge, bcbebi, be-

beha, bcbhf, bcdbc, bcdecaha, bcded-ca, bcdedkbb, bcdgdafqd, bcdgek, be-fiheca, bcfii, cca, e, ea, eaa, eaac, g, gaaxaxe, gbad, gb, gba
James A adgfbgfi, adgfcdacb, bcdedcfc
James Arthur abdcebeai, bcdedcfcbc
James Atwood bcfigfba
James Augustus gaaxaxea
James B adkecbag, bcdbeab
James Bell adaabcl
James Buchanan adaabdabe
James Burrill bcfiheb
James C adabbgrc ahbgeab
James Charles bcfiheda
James Chase adkfbeb, adkfbebcb
James De Wolf ahbabahe
James E bbbffcbac, bcfifff, fcec, gbaia, gbag
James Edwin adadibab
James Elmer ahbaacdaea
James Everett adabbgea, adadabbdb
James G adhafdgb, adkfbdc
James Gilbert ahcbcb, bcfifhhhc
James Gilman ahbaab, ahbaai
James Glines adaaabdaa
James Gove adadiba
James H abceabdbb, adaabcda, bcbcb-bed, bcbhddfa, bcbhddfaf, bcdgep
James Henry abbeacbdb, abceabef, ad-hcbbfd, adkfbeib, ahchfef
James Hilman ahbgbag
James Irving adhafabh
James Jabez adkfbebc
James Jewett abdcebeg
James Kimball bcdedfdbb
James L abccgdcc, adkeabba, bcdebgag
James Leon abbegbdcac
James M ahbaacda, ahchfii, bcdgdbaa-df
James Madison bcbhdbec
James Marsh How bcfiiba
James Merrill bbbfabhd
James Monroe ahbghjb, ahbghk
James Morrill adkehca
James Murphy adaimbifj
James N bcbhdme
James Neal adbabhd, adhcbbh, adhcb-bha
James O adkeabac, ahbgbj
James Oliver Chase bcbhdeba
James Osgood adhahec, adhahecab
James Otis adadhcbf
James P adgxfca, abcbhddbc, bcfiibaa
James Pattee bcfifhhh
James Pierce adaigaaa
James Rice, abbegfjbd
James Richardson ahgchl
James Roger bcdbececba
James S adgfbecb
James W abceabecc, adaimbai, adaim-bif, adhafaeb
James Wallace abccgdbae, ahgchfg
James William Churchill adhcbbfe
James William Churchill Jr do

832

Jane abccgbaea, adaabedb, adabbgac, adabbgl, adadha, adaiiaaa, wife ad-aim, adaimd, adbabba, adgfcjc, adgxfaj, adgfcdf, ahbabkxed, ahbgbbd, ahfcha, ahgge, bcbebifa, bcbehhl, bcbhdbe, bedgafaf, bcdgdbab, bedgded, fcc

Jane A adhaheda
Jane D ahbcabaeg
Jane Gordon bcfifjb
Jane H adhccfc
Jane L bcdgdafj
Jane Mary bcdebgagh
Jane Pauline ahbabaeadca
Jane Ursula bcdedcfb
Jane Wade bcdbecca
Jane Wilson ahbgiib
Janet Sherman adhadccb
Janette Goodwin bcfifjb
Janie bcdgefc
Janna wife adaim
Jason adgfbgda
Jason F adaabcea
Jasper adabbgaijb, bcdgdeaabaa
Jay bcdgdbaala
Jay Adelbert adaceagci
Jay Henry adgcadaffa
Jay Lawrence bedebgagf
Jay N bcdgdafmc
Jean Irving adgfbhadb
Jeannette Latham adggdcdc
Jeannete Lucy adaceagcb
Jeannette Parker abccgcfcad
Jedediah adhcc, adhcce, adhccfa, adhccfea
Jefferson abccgca, ahbcabcc, bcdeaeac
Jemima adaba, adabba, adabbbh, adabf, adabic, adadad, adade, adgxh, ahbgbfb
Jenet G bcbcbaaaf
Jennette A gbal
Jennette B adggefea
Jennie adaceaaeb, adaiiaafb, adaimbie, adaimbifa, bcbebbbdd, bcdecahbb, bcdgdaieb
Jennie A bbbffcdc, bcbcbaaaac
Jennie Agnes adhcbbje
Jennie Augusta wid bcdgdaace
Jennie B adabibcac, bcbebigb
Jennie C adhadcea
Jennie Cutler adaabfaah
Jennie E ahbabajia
Jennie Eliza bbbfabhbb
Jennie Eugenia adaceagca
Jennie Evelyn adacgfacd
Jennie L bcdgdbaadg
Jennie Lincoln abdeebeca
Jennie Louise ahgcigc
Jennie M adabiggdb, bcdgdaiij
Jennie S adhafgbb, bcbebbfae
Jennie W bcdedcfb
Jennings B bcdedkdaa
Jenny adadh, adkfbf, bcficahba

Jeremiah abccd, abccda, abccdga, adabbbc, adadie, adg, adgb, adgfb, adgfbe, adgfbeg, adgfbegd, adgfbgf, adgfga, adgfgabe, adggbg, adggdc, adgge, adggeh, adkddgd, adkddi, ahbaef, ahdi, ahf, ahfc, ahfca, ahgdd, ai, bcbebg, bcbhdbg, bcbhdd, bebhddi, bcdbe, bcdbecd, bcdbed, bcdbede, bcdeabe, bcdgdaal

Jeremiah A abbegfga
Jeremiah Ames bcdeabdf
Jeremiah Burns adaidae
Jeremiah Dingley ahbgbea
Jeremiah K ahdada
Jeremiah Kendall adaigbbb
Jeremiah R bcdgdp
Jeremiah Smith abbegfgag
Jeremiah W adaabd
Jerome B ahgdcea
Jerome C adggefeb
Jerry W bcdgdpaa
Jerusha bbbea, bbbec, bbbg, bcdgdaib
Jerusha M ahbabhd
Jessamine E adgcacbkc
Jesse adaia, ahbch, ahbchd, ahgcb, ahgcd, bcbehhe, bcdgda, bcdgdan, bcfige, bcfigfa
Jesse Done bcdgdani
Jesse Elmer adabbgib
Jesse Erskine ahcbfe
Jesse Morgan adaimaabe
Jesse R bcdgdaae
Jessie adgcaccaha, adgfbejba, bcbhdbedb, bcbhddai, bcdbadddaj
Jessie A ahbcajbg
Jessie Anderson adggdcdad
Jessie B adgxfaacbc, adgxfbebe
Jessie F bcdeddbf, bcfifjaga
Jessie L bcdeddbj
Jessie Lee abbegbdbgb
Jessie R adkebgbab
Joan adkddcebe
Joanna adaabfb, adabj, adaceaffa
Joanna Morse abbegfgah
Joannah bedgdafi
Job ahbabaj, bcfif, bcfiff, bcfiffd, bcfifjk, bcfigf, fca
Job Atwood, bcfigfdg
Joel adaced, adacedc, ahbabkx, ahbabkxae, ahbabkxf
Joel A ahbabkxfe
Joel L adaabcfa
Johanna adfa, bcdf
Johannah adaaad, adaaak
John x, xae, abbeac, abbeacd, abbegbibcb, abbegfcd, abccdgcb, abdcebe, adaab, adaabaa, adaabe, adab, adabbbdc, adabbbe, adabbg, adabig, adabigg, adaceag, adacfe, adacffe, adadhcd, adahxaa, adaic, adaidb, adaied, adb, adba, adbabbb, adbabe, adbabf, adbaf, adbafa, adfcdd, adgcac, adgcaccac, adgcadaa, adgcagb, adgfbeb, adgfbeea, adgfbga, adgfbgae, adg-

fcjb, adgfcjbfib, adgfdb, adgff, adg-
ffe, adhafda, adkdeh, adkfbb, adkfbbcb, adkfbbd, adkfbl, adkfc, aedb,
ahb, ahbaa, ahbaaaa, ahbaac, ahb-
aaca, ahbaacfa, ahbaacx, ahbaacxa,
ahbaahe, ahbabad, ahbabdb, ahbabf,
ahbabkb, ahbacb, ahbcabh, ahbgb,
ahbgbb, ahbgbeb, ahche, ahchfe,
ahda, ahdaaf, ahdab, ahdadac, ahfad,
ahfcaaaa, ahfcfe, ahfch, ahgci, ahgde,
ahggbb, ahggc, ba, bac, bbbfab,
bbbfhcd, bbbfhf, bcbcaa, bcbcba, bcbcbbafb, bcbcbbc, bcbebbcdaca,
bcbebf, bcbebfd, bcbehdbb, bcbhdbea
bcbhddfacc, bcbhdei, **bcbhdgagg, bc-**
bhdpa, bcdbeca, bcdbecc, **bcdeaaaa,**
bcdedg, bcdgdaacc, bcdgdde, **bcdgdf,**
bcdgdi, bcdgdk, bcf, bcfb, bcfi, bcfid,
bcfig, bcfigfd, **bcfigfdc, bcfigfdd,**
bcfigg, d, eb, edy, **fa, faa**
John A adabigg, adabiggd, bcdgddac
John Albert adaabdabb, adkdeeeb, **ahf-**
caaac, bcdeaeag
John Aldrich adkedjda
John Alvin adhcdaea
John Anderson ahbgbacab
John B abccgdfa, adaidbf, ahbaacxaa,
bcbhdgag, bcdbaccb, eaacc
John Blaisdell adggeic
John Butterfield bcfiffg, **bcfifhb**
John C abccgbad, abccdgebb, adhadcb,
adhadccc, adhadccd, bcbhdei
John Calen adaabcec
John Calvin bcbehhi, bcbehhib
John Carey bcdedkab
John Carleton adkfbbdfac
John Carlton bcfigfddb
John Charles adadhcafa
John Chase adadhcca, **adgfdabbdb**
John Cheney, bcbcbbaf
John Chester ahchfece
John Chipman adaabdab, adaabdabca
John Chivey adhadcei
John Churchill bcbcbbeb
John Clark bcbebfea
John D adkeabaa, ahbgbac
John Dorrance adaidaee
John Draper adaceagd
John Duane adhagbf
John Duncan bcfifjja
John E adaabacaca, ahbaacfb, **ahfcfcef,**
ahfciba, gban
John Edward ahfcaaa, **ahfcfceg**
John Edwin abdcebea
John Eels, ahgdhb
John Emery bbbfabb, bbbfabbd, bbbf-
abbeba, bbbfabmj
John Emerson adaceafg
John Erskine bcbhddce
John F adaimcdg, adhafgce, **adkddgg,**
adkdeed, ahbaeddb, **ahbgbxb, ahda-**
add, ahdaafx, bcdgdt
John Francis ahfcfega
John Franklin adkgddfa

John French ahgfdag
John G adaabcbda, adadhacc, **adkehba,**
ahbcacfeb
John Gilman adaabcb
John Goodchild ahgchhca
John Gordon ahchfie, **bcfifjj**
John Gove adahdb
John Gustavus adbafab
John H abccgacca, abccabeca abdce-
blf, adabbbdcz, adaimbdh, bcbcbaaba,
bcbcbaabaa, bcdgdbaadfa, **bcdgdba-**
ah, bcdgdma, fceaec
John Henry abdceblfab
John Hollis bcdgdta
John Huntoon bbbfhjb
John J abccgachb, adkgdbg, **bcdeaaaai**
John Joseph adkfbbjba
John K ahbaahea, ahbgila
John Kennedy bcbhdbe, **bcbhdbeda**
John L abccgdcec, ahgcabaca
John Leighton adhafdfb
John Lincoln adgfbffc
John Lyford ahbaede
John M adacedfeb, adadhaba, adaimcdc,
ahbchcb, ahgdhba, bcdgdpa
John Manley ahggbb
John Marshall ahgcabcaa
John Mason bcbcbbee
John Meader adbabbbx, adbabfi
John Melmoth ahggbdaa, ahggbbbb
John Merrill adaimce
John Milton bcfigfad
John Mooney abbegbdbh, **abbegbdcb,**
abbegbde
John Moulton abbeebba
John N adaimbbde, adkeaea
John Neal adgfcdaced
John Nelson ahggcc, bcdgdafkab
John Newell bcbchhaff
John Oliver adbabfdd
John Orr bcbhbfg
John Osborn abccdgd, adkedi, adkedj
John P ahbabaeac, fceai
John Plumer adadagfe
John Plummer adaimaa, bcdadgb
John Quincy adhafaba
John R adadagf, adkeabae, bbbfhcd, **be-**
debfa, bcdebfba
John Randolph bcdebel
John Reneau adgfgabcf
John Rex bbbfabiba
John Robinson adkeaba
John Rogers ahbghge, ahbghi
John S adgfcjbe, ahbaeddbc, bbbfhah
John Snowman adabbgaih
John T abccgaccaa
John Taylor abccgac, abccgacc
John Thayer bcdebgae
John W adbabfda, adkfbbjd, **ahfcfeca,**
bcbhdbea
John Wallace bcdgdeaaf
John Ware ahbabcf
John Wells bbbffafb
John Wesley bcdgdbac, **faaa**

John **Weston** bcbhbfgb
John **William** adabbgbcad, adkfbej, bb-
bfabha
John **William Henry** fcea
John **William Walton** adaimaaa
John **Winthrop** adggdccae
John **Y** bcdgdafk
Johnson ahgciac
Jonah bcdedg
Jonas Edward ahbgiifa
Jonas Richardson adacedde
Jonathan abbeg, abbegbe, abbegf, abb-
egfd, abccgba, abccgd, abccgdb, ab-
ccgdcf, abcf, adaaba, adaabf, adab-
bgdc, adabbghb, adabi, adabih, adac-
ff, adadi, adadhab, adadia adadicf,
adbabb, adgc, adgcacc, adgcad, adgd,
adgfc, adgfcc, adgfcf, adgfci, adgfcif,
adhafg, adhafgc, adhcb, adhcbbd, ad-
hccf, adkgdc, adkebgi, adkgf, bcbhd-
dj bcdbecda, bcdedbbb, bcdedcf, bcd-
edl, bcdh, da, ga, gaax
Jonathan Bradish abcfla
Jonathan Bulcher adhccff
Jonathan Drake abceabea
Jonathan E adgfcibc, bcfifjl
Jonathan G abdcibc
Jonathan Gove befiffj
Jonathan Haskell adabbgag
Jonathan Horton adacffea
Jonathan M bcbebif
Jonathan Mahaffie adacffeah
Jonathan Nudd abbeebbb
Jonathan S adaidag, adgxffc, adgxff-
ccb
Jones bcfican
Jordan gaaxaxb
Jose K ahbgili
Joseph aba, abbb, abbee, abbeebc, abb-
egff, abbegi, ad, ada, adaa, adaceda,
adacg, adacgf, adacgfa, adadhcae,
adaijc, adaijcc, adgca, adgcad, adgcada, adgcadaf, adgfbde adgfcia, adgfcic, adgxc, adgxca, adkdb, adke, adkeac, adkebd, adkedb, adkfbbci, adkgd, adkgdd, ahbaahc, ahbabccd, ahbabda, ahbge, ahbgil, ahcbf, ahci, ahgch, bab, bbbebcb, bbbf, bbbfa, bbb-
faa, bbbffa, bbbffab, bbbffcbd, bbbffdc, bbbfha, bbbfhaf, bbbfhcgb, bc-
bebbbc, bcbhdeh, bcbndq, bcbhg, bcdecdc, Jr bcdccdc, 3rd bcdccdc, bcd-
gdafebb, bcfc, bcfigi, cbba, gbae
Joseph A adhchaaa, adkfbbj, adkfbbjb,
adkgdefd, bbbffcbaa
Joseph Addison adacgfab
Joseph B adgfbgfia, ahbabcdb
Joseph Boynton abbegbdfe
Joseph C P ahbaacxax
Joseph Clark ahcbec
Joseph E ahfcfcceb
Joseph Edgar ahcbeca, ahcbecb
Joseph Emerson bcfihe
Joseph Emery bbbfaea

Joseph Evans bcbhdqa
Joseph F adgcadafe
Joseph Fabyan abceabdf
Joseph Farnum ahbgea
Joseph French bbbebcbb
Joseph G bcdebgf
Joseph Godfrey abbegbdf, abbegbd
Joseph Henry abbeebca, bcficanh
Joseph Hilton ahbabjc
Joseph L adaceddc, adkgddha, ahbaedb,
bbbfhjh
Joseph Morse abbegfgab
Joseph N adkfbbj, bcbeggc
Joseph P ahbaahd
Joseph Perry adacgfgg
Joseph Plummer adhafgb
Joseph Robinson ahbabcc
Joseph Ross abbegbdfde
Joseph S adadhabc, adkebdj, bcbcbbacc
Joseph T adadagab
Joseph W adaigbbad, adgfbgff, ahgd-
cb, ahgdccc
Joseph Warren adkdbe, adkfbbj, bcde-
bfg
Joseph Willard bcdeddhdbb
Josephine adaabfgh, adacgfaba, adkfb-
bcf, bcdbaddbd, wife bcdebgaf
Josephine B bbbebcbda
Josephine Harper ahgchjb
Josephine Hazel adabbgagcxb
Josephine M bcdebeebg
Josephine Medea adhcbbjca
Josephine Olivia ahbabahk
Josephine Plummer adkddcea
Josephine T bcdebfgb
Josephine Theresa bcdebfd, bcdebgbbb
Josephine W bbbebcdaa
Josephine Wallace bcfiibcc
Josephine Z adabbgbeca
Joshua adabbbh, adkebc, adkeh, adke-
ha, ahbgbf, ahbgbfa, bcbeg, bcbegg,
bcbhdc
Joshua H adabbgaij
Joshua M bcbhdeha
Joshua R ahbgbah
Josiah abbeeb, abbeebb, abccgde, ada-
cgg, adfcd, adfcdc, adfcdca, adh, ad-
had, adhafah, adhagb, 2nd adhan, ad-
hca, adhccb, adhccbbg, adkd, adkdec,
adkdeceb, adkeae, adked, ahbabam,
ahbabamg, ahbae, ahbaedd, ahbaeg,
bcbebcgc
Josiah B ahbabahf
Josiah Coffin adkdecd
Josiah F adaiiaaf, adaiiab, adaimbia
Josiah Felch adaimac, adaimbad
Josiah H ahfcfda
Josiah L fceac, fceh
Josiah Lacont fce
Josiah N ahfcfdaa
Josiah Willis adkfbebj
Josie A adaabfaacb
Josie Belle adhcbbfe
Josie M adabbgbebab

Joy E bcbhdgagh
Joy Wheeler ahgchhc, Jr ahgchheb
Joyce bcdgdaiead
Judah adai, adaaaj, bcbege
Judith xa, wife adabbb, adabbf, adabb-
  gac, adbc, adfccb, adff, adhada, adhe-
  bc, adhce, ahbaaad, ahbaad, ahbghc,
  bbbebh, bbbfb, bcbege, bcfe
Judith L adabbgaid
Judith Phillips adhcbbc
Julette adaabacag
Juley E bcdgdaik
Julia adaabfdg, adabbgac, adailaab, ad-
  aimeaa, adgfdcd, adhcbbbc, adkddg-
  da, ahbabkxac, ahcbccb, bbbfabde,
  bcbhdbef, bcdgdaik, bcdgddae, bcd-
  gdeaie
Julia A adaijca, adaim, adgxfbed, ad-
  hafaaa, adkddgda, adkfbbcg, bcbeh-
  hm, bcdgdbaadh, bcdgdbaaf
Julia Amy adacedff
Julia Ann ahbcabja bcdedbbbc
Julia Augusta ahcbfec, ahgfbdd
Julia B adaabcji
Julia E adaimbbc, adhahedb, bcdcdefe
Julia Elizabeth abbegbdbi
Julia Emma adkfbebe
Julia F adkedg
Julia Frances adkfbebh
Julia Hodgdon adgfcice
Julia Jennette bcbcbaaaf
Julia M adkehf, bcdgdafad
Julia Malina adkedk
Julia O adaaaiec
Julia P ahbabale
Julia Parkhurst fceah
Julia Thompson adhcbbfe
Julian Ellis adhcbbfbe
Juliana ahbcaci, ahgb
Juliet Philene adaabceg
Julietta adkebaab
Julietta E befifjadb
Juliette befifjab
Jura adaimaaaba
Justin Edwards adaidba
Justin Gloyd bcdecdbaa
Justin L bbbfhcfeg
Justina adkehbaa
Justine O abcegcfm
Kadie Laura bcdgdakcc
Kate abccgdcfa, ahcbeab, ahgcica, ahg-
  dcca
Kate D adgfbgaea, ahgdccab
Kate E ahgdcce
Kate L adhccfha
Kate Lulu adhafced
Kate M abccgdckb
Kate Sumner adgfcjbga
Kater befihc
Katie H ahbabajaa
Katharyn A bcdebgaacaa
Katherine xac, xc, abccgdca, adaigbba-
  ab, adhal, adhcbbffba, ahbabam, ah-
  babcb, ahbabjibba, bbbfabhbaa

Katherine E befiffff
Katherine Evelyn adaimbiacc
Katherine Imogene bbbfabibf
Katherine Maynard adhccbbeba
Katherine Phippen adkdecebb
Katherine Scott ahbcacbabb
Kelsey ahbabjbd
Kenneth bcdgdaacdb, bcdgdafkai bcd-
  gdafkg, bcdgdeacee
Kenneth B adgfdabbba
Kenneth Brooks adabbghgbb
Kenneth Cushman bededcfcba
Kenneth Fred bcbebbcdaxd
Kenneth Irwin adggegbaea
Kenneth Leroy bcbhddaaad
Kenneth Rufus adkgddgac
Kenneth Wing bcbebcgabab
Kesia adgxg
Kilinda K adgxffae
Kimball adacffi, befiffdb, befifjee
Kitty bcdebgafa
L M (dau) bcbhfiab
L Cella ahchfecd
L Priscilla abceabbe
L Thomas ahbabajadca
Ladd bbbebch
Lafayette adaceafe
Lafayette F ahbcajb
Lafayette Frank adgfcdgcca
La Forrest abccgdfaa
Lali Ida adhadcel
Langdon abceabbg
Langdon H ahbabcda
Lansing Millis adabibicb
La Reina bcbhdbndf
Lathrop H bcdgdsa
Laura adabbgage, adaccaeg, adaimbce
  adkedh, ahcbbd, ahgdcab, bcbcbbae,
  bcdedbbd, bcdedbch, bcdgdaijb, bcd-
  gdakchb
Laura A adabbgagcd, ahdaaddc, bbbff-
  baada
Laura Ann adgfciba, adkfbbi, ahbaac-
  xab, ahgfbdg
Laura B abccgcfcae
Laura Brackett bcbcbbgc
Laura C bcbcbbafc
Laura E adabbgagca, adaimbaa
Laura Estella adkfbdxc
Laura M adabbghcg, adaieaafcd
Laura Mason adbbafddb
Laura P adkgdege
Laurance A adabbbdcea
Laurance Everett abccgdceca
Laurence P adkfbbjbd
Lavias adacffj
Lavilla adgxffad
Lavina wife adacglc, adaieaad, ahbaaa-
  ba, ahgcf, bcbhdgaf, bcdebgai, bcde-
  cdba
Lavina C adkebde
Lavinia wife adabbghb, bcdebge, bcde-
  bi
Lavinia Sennet ahbcajcc

Lawrence bbbfabbdb, bcdedkbc
Lawrence A bcdedbada
Lawrence Amos adabbgaiie
Lawrence Edward adgfbgebbd
Lawrence Joseph bcdgdaalcd
Lawrence Taylor abccgaccaad
Lawson Myrick adacgjc
Lawson Sedgwick adaabdac
Leander abdcebli
Leander A bcbhddkbx
Leander Abner adkgdeg
Leander Allen bcbhdbedea, bcbhddkb-xk
Lander Alphonso bcbhdbed
Lee bcfifjjbb
Lee Burton adaceafgea
Leila ahbabajgd, bcbhddcca
Leila Eileen bcdebgaeb
Leland Brown adggeibaa, adggeibaaa
Lelia bcdgdeacec
Lellen M abbegbibb
Lemira Farrar abbeebcg
Lemuel ahgf, ahgfd
Lemuel Algernon ahgfdeab
Lemuel F adaimbbdh
Lemuel S adabbgaja
Lena bcdgdabgf
Lena C ahbcabcbe
Leona E adaimbcbd
Lena Ellsworth abdcebeae
Lena F adabbgahea
Lena M bcdgdaiia
Lena Mary aeeacacaafa
Lena Woodbury adaimbbdb
Lendon C bbbebdaa
Lenoir A ahbgbfaa
Lenora Dorothy bbbfabibe
Lenora Grace ahbaaheaa
Lenora Thompson bcdeddabca
Leona bcdgdabgae, bcdgdead
Leon bcfifjjbd
Leon Chester adadhacab
Leon F adkfbedea
Leon Kelsey abccgcfia
Leon L adkehbha
Leon O adaceaebba
Leonard ahbcajgi, bcdedkd
Leonard Brooks bcdeaeae
Lonard C adacedh
Leonard E abccgcfj, bededcla
Leonard J adaimaabcb, bcdedkdac
Leonard Jasper adaimaabc
Leonard Milton bcdece, bcdbececb, bc-dbeceed
Leonard P bbbfhcfe
Leonard Wilson bcdeaefadc
Leonora Mary abbegbicb
Leroy abccgdck, bcfiffdcbc, gbea
Leroy E adgxffccc, adkecbagc
Leroy Edward ahgdcagca
Leroy Eugene adkgaebfa
Leroy P ahbabajada
Leslie bcdedkde
Leslie Alexander abccgcfcaac

Leslie F bbbffbaadc
Leslie G bcdedcfda
Leslie James bcbcbbgjc, bcbhddbcbg
Leslie M adkgddhf
Leslie W adacffice
Lester adabbhj, bcdgdaghd
Lester Arthur bcfifjjaba
Lester B bbbfhcfeeb
Lester Bryant bcfifjjab
Lester C abccgdfba, adabbgaicl
Lester K adgfbejc
Letitia ahghea
Letitia Gove adhcbbga
Lettie bbbfhbxca, bcbhddda
Lettie J adadibdk, adaimbhg
Lettie L adgxfahaa
Levantha Cordelia ahbcabcbe
Leverett Oscar bcdgddahc
Levi abbegb, abbegbi, abbegfk, abbeg-fkb, adaii, adaiia, adaiiaa, adaimbi, ahbabkxe, ahbabkxec, ahgd, bcbebcg, bcbebcgd, bcdebe, bcdgdaih, bcdgdeb, bcdgdebb
Levi A adaiiaae, bcdebeeb
Levi Albertus bcdebea
Levi B bcbcbbaca
Levi C adaimbifb
Levi H adaidbbb
Levi Hoit adhafdi
Levi J adaiiaaed
Levi Jeff adhafdifd
Levi Paul abbegbibfb
Levi R bcdebeehi
Levi Sewall bbbfabmac, bbbfabmaca, bbbfabme
Levi Smith abbegbibf
Levina adacgd, bcdebi
Levinia Adell bcbhddbcbf
Levy bcdgdeaai
Lewis adaceafh, adaceam, adadiab, ad-gfbegj, adggdc, adhafcc, ahgfbdf, ah-gfdacc, bcdhcb, bcfifhkb, bcfifjdd
Lewis A adgfbegj, adkecbac
Lewis C adafficb
Lewis Clifford bcbhddfacd
Lewis E ahbgbfabb
Lewis Frederick adacealk
Lewis H ahbabaeae, ahbabajac, bbbfh-bxcge
Lewis Hale ahbcajgh
Lewis Leroy adadiabe
Lewis M bbbebcdaeb, bcdgdbaak
Lewis Phillips adhcdacc
Lewis S bcdbecedb
Lewis Sylvester adadhacaa
Lewis W adaieaac
Libbie bcdedkbd
Lila gbakfa
Lila Fern bcbhddcebe
Lilla Azubah adaabdabd
Lilla J ahbgile
Lilla M adgcadaaac
Lillian adabbgahbe, adacffeaf, adkga-edc, bcdgdafda, bcdgdeacb

Lillian A adabbgaich, bcbebbcaaa, bcd-
eddabe
Lillian Augusta adgfbeggaa
Lillian E abbegfjbb
Lillian Frances bcbhddbcbd
Lillian Hayes adaimcdgaa
Lillian Isabel ahgdhbcf
Lillian Louisa abdceblfac
Lillian Louise bcdedbbbg
Lillian Lucy bcbebbface
Lillian Maria abbegbibc
Lillian Maud adaimbifc
Lillian Maude adggeilb
Lilliam May adggeilda
Lillian Pearl bcbhddaaaa
Lillian R ahbabamga
Lilly gbec
Lincoln H ahbabami
Linder bcbhdbed
Linwood Earl bcdedbbbjb
Linwood J bbbfhcfcd
Linwood Malcolm bcbhddaaac
Livinia ahgcf
Lizetta adadabbdaad
Lizzie adaabdaeh, adaabfgg, ahbgbaga,
ahbgaha, bcdeabdca, bcbhdehk, bcf-
iibcd, gbao
Lizzie A bcdeaefa
Lizzie Adella abbegbicc
Lizzie Allan ahggbdaaa
Lizzie D ahbabcdbb, bcbebbfad
Lizzie Drury bcdebeebc
Lizzie E adaigbbabc
Lizzie Ellen adaiebaa
Lizzie F adaimbdi
Lizzie G adaimcdbc, adaimcdf
Lizzie Inness adbabfddg
Lizzie J bcdeddbe
Lizzie Lucinda bcdeddhe
Lizzie M wife adaaaiee, bcbhdbecb
Lizzie S adkecbaf
Llewellyn adkfbbjbf, ahbabajf, bcdgd-
akcha
Llewellyn H adabbgta
Llewellyn L bcdgdakfa
Lloyd Alexander adaimaabea
Lloyd E bcdgdafage
Lloyd Elmer bcbhddcebf
Lloyd L ahbabamgba
Lloyd Luther adaabdabef
Loie bcdgdeadb
Loie adaih, adaiic, wid adgxf, ahfcac,
ahfcb, bbbfl, bcdeaba, bcdeaf, bcdg-
daijd
Lois B bcbhbfh
Lois H ahcbbc
Lois E adabbbha
Lois L bcdgdaacef
Lois Willard adhcbbffab
Lola Bessie adabiggdc
Lola May adaimbbeba
Lonnita bcbhdnda
Lora O bcbhdehfg
Loraine ahbcajed

Lorance E adabbgdaaca
Loren adaabacaag, ahchffa
Loren S adaceaebb
Loren Stevens bcdedfca
Lorena Maud adkgaeddd
Lorenzo abbegbdbb, adaabcbc, adacea-
eb, adaceagab, adacgfe, adahdca, ad-
ahddb, adahdxa, adbabic, adgcagae,
adgfbegh, adgfbhaa, adgfcdaa, adgfg-
ac, adkecbah, adkfbbg, ahbaaaad, ah-
bgbaj, ahdax, ahgfdaea, ahghe, bcbeb-
bfb, bcbebig, bcdbaddj, bcdebgd, bc-
dedfa, bcdgef, Jr bcdgefd
Lorenzo D bcdgdafaa
Lorenzo Edwin bcbhbfic
Lorenzo Everett adgfcdacc
Lorenzo F ahggcca
Lorenzo H ahbcajh, ahgdgad
Lorenzo G ahbabaea, bbbebfg
Lorenzo L adgfcdaceb
Lorenzo Nelson adacgfeb
Lorenzo Park ahggccba
Lorenzo R bcdgdpb
Lorenzo S bbbebfg
Lorenzo Truman ahbcajgb
Lorenzo Ware abdcica
Loreta adgfbegi
Loretta May adabiggfb
Lorilla adaimcc
Loring bbbfhcg, bbbfhcgc
Loring J bbbfhcgbf
Loring O bcbhdehfg
Loring Woodman bcdgdehfga
Lottie bcdgdeaafb, bcdgdeach
Lottie A adabiggeb
Lottie Florence adkebabbc
Lottie L bbbffcbae
Lottie M adabbgagcc, adkfbbdfc
Lottie May adacffeea
Lottie O bbbfhjbi
Louis adabbbdd, adkfbbjbf, bcdebgbba
Louis Fenner ahbcacbaba
Louis Hackett adhcbbffd
Louis S adaceaebb
Louisa adaceaab, adadhaabb, adaigaf,
adgcacbc, ahbaahf, bcficalb, bcficaq,
bififjdc, bcfigda
Louisa A adaabdaf, adaceaebd
Louisa Allen ahbabjcb
Louisa Dwight adhccbba
Louisa E adggeii
Louisa Jane abbeacbe
Louisa M ahchfif
Louise adgfcifa, ahbabkxyb, bcdeaaaaa,
bcdecahba, bcdgdakfc, bcfifhbb
Louise H adgxfaaeb
Louise M abccgdfcb
Louise S bcdebeebd
Louise W ahbabaefd
Loveron bcdedbbd
Loverna L ahbgilib
Lovina bcbcbaaah, bcdebge
Lovinice bcdecdfa
Lovisa Crosby bcdebgbd

Lowell B adgxfdag
Lowell Blaine adbabfddh
Lowell Brown adgxfaab, adgxfal
Lowell Jordan adgfbgdcha
Lucelia Eleanor adggdcibc
Lucella E ahbabamf
Lucia adggegc
Lucia Ann Coffin adkdebc
Lucia Caroline adggeicba
Lucia E adacedfc
Lucia H ahgchg
Lucia Maria ahgchfd
Lucien adadhaac
Lucille bcdgdaica
Lucille F adhafgcbcc
Lucinda adaabfga, wife adabia, adgfb-
    gga, adggdab, adggdl, adgxfdc, ad-
    keaba, adkebgd, ahbgfg, ahbghe, bc-
    dbaddk, bcdeddd, bcfifjdb
Lucinda A bcdgdaalcg
Lucinda E aeeacaae
Lucinda H adhagba
Lucinda J adadabbb
Lucius adaceahd, adggehb
Lucius Harmon adggdci
Lucius Kalapon ahcbcc
Lucretia adgfgabf, ahbabaeb, ahbabjn,
    ahbabl, ahbgbff, bbbffad, bbbffadd,
    bcdeaaac, bcdgdana
Lucretia H ahbaahdb
Lucy xaab, abccgdceb, abdb, abdcebj, ab-
    dch, adaabfdh, adadhx, adgffb, adgf-
    fce, adkebgac, ahbaahe, ahchea, ah-
    chg, ahga, ahgcie, bcbebce, bcbhdhf,
    bcbhdj, bcdbaddi, bcdeach, bcdedbg,
    bcdgdaid, bcdgdded, bcfihf
Lucy A adaabdda, adaceagf, adadiec,
    bcdebfbh, bcdgdaid
Lucy Adelaide adaimbaf
Lucy Alberta bcbhdea
Lucy Ann adhcdacb, adkehca, ahgdcaa
Lucy Dingley ahbgbec
Lucy E ahbcabbada
Lucy Ellen abbeebcc
Lucy Faber ahbcabejd
Lucy H adabbdcb, adkgdbd
Lucy J ahgdcafc
Lucy Jane adaijaba, adaijcb, adhchaa,
    bcdeacaea
Lucy Josephine adabiggea, adacedfj
Lucy M adabbgajc, adkfbeddd
Lucy Maria adabbgajf
Lucy Richards bcfiibcg
Luella adgcaccad, bcbcbbafg
Luella Almira abbeebbca
Luella Blanche bcfifjjae
Luella C ahbabaeaeg
Luella E adhafdfa, adhafdfc
Luke bcdgdeadf
Luke Whitcher adadhca
Luman adggehc
Luman Frary adggeil
Lula Cushing adbabfecab
Lula G bcdgdbaadk

Lula May adaimbhfa
Lula R bcdebgdbb
Lulu bcdedbbdab
Lulu Juanita ahbgikca
Luna ahgfbh
Lunetta F adgxffcce
Lura adaceaade
Lura Amanda abbegbibd, bcdedfec
Lura Edna bcdeddhcb
Lura J bcdebgaai
Lura Mae adggegbah
Lura Maude abbegbibee
Lurie May adaabfdi, adgfdaaae
Luther ahbgdfd, bcbehha, bcdeaeac, bc-
    dgdbi
Luther Bradley bcbehhg, bcbehhgb, bc-
    behhgbb
Luther Calvin adaabdae
Luther Henry bcdeaeaf
Luther M bcdgdbaad, bcdgdbaadba
Luther Morrill ahbcacbbb
Luther Osgood adgfgabaa
Luther Thompson bcbebbgb
Lydia abceabca, abdcebi, abdcf, abdd,
    abdcia, adaaba, adaabddb, adabbg-
    ba, wife adabbgi, adabbgqb, adabda,
    adabe, adabibda, adacd, adacec, ad-
    acge, adadica, adadid, adahdcb, wife
    adahdd, adaidbbc, adfb, adgfbfa, ad-
    gfbgb, adgfck, adgfdaba, adggbaa,
    adggbf, adggdac, adggdd, adggea, ad-
    ggf, adhahg, adkeck, ahbchca, ahdaf,
    ahdb, ahgfe, bcbcbbgd, bcbcbbgg,
    bcbhdgae, bcbhe, bcdeaae, bcdeac,
    bcdeaeg, bcdbee, bcdgdal, bcdgdbl,
    bcdgddc, bcfiffb, bcfiffda, dca
Lydia A adacgfed, adadicdb, ahbcaji
Lydia Adeline ahdaaddb
Lydia Ann adaabfab, adhahfb
Lydia Butterfield bcfiffh
Lydia E bcfifffd
Lydia Ellen bbbffcbg
Lydia Gove adhadda, adhcbbi
Lydia J adaimbac
Lydia Jane ahbgbacb
Lydia Julia ahbcajca
Lydia Kimball bcdbeah
Lydia Lawrence bcdeabdb
Lydia Locke adgxfbcb
Lydia M adgcadaaac
Lydia Maria adgfcig
Lydia Mary ahbcajgd
Lydia Metcalf ahbgiic
Lydia Millicent bcbegbe
Lydia Neal adbabhe
Lydia P abceabbe
Lydia S wife bcbhdbeda
Lyford ahbaba, ahbabah, ahbabamb
Lyford P ahbabahca
Lyford T ahbaedea
Lyman adgfbece, ahbaedg, ahgchja, bb-
    bffag
Lyman DeWitt adabbgpaaa
Lyman Giles bcbhbgi

Lyman **M** ahfcfcec
M A wife ahbabkxc
M Ivan bcdgdsb
M Mary abccgchadb
M Pearl adkgdbada
Mabel abccgdfbb, adacfficd, adgcacb-
ada, adkeabbad, ahchfige, ahgga, bb-
bfhbxcda, bcdgdagca, bcdgdafmdc,
bcfifhhha
Mabel Abigail adgfbhadad
Mabel Aurora adhafdifc
Mabel D ahbafdifc
Mabel E adgcaccafa, adhafdii, bcfifja-
de
Mabel Elizabeth ahbgbaec, ahgdhbcc
Mabel J adkebabbb
Mabel Katherine ahbaaheaea
Mabel L adkfbbjbc
Mabel Lillian abdcebcabd
Mabel M adacedded
Mabel T adgxfdae, bcdgdbaadd
Mabel True abccgdbaf
Mabel V adabbgabdha
Mabelle E adacedfea
Madeline bcdgdaghca
Madeline Adella adabbgagde
Madeline Sarah bcbebbcdaba
Madison bcbhdbec
Mae Barnes adgfcdadd
Magdalen bcdbeceee
Maggie D wife adkgddh
Maggie bcdgep
Mahala adabibf, bcdgdaffb, bcdgdafkf
Mahala J bcdgdbaab
Major John adhccfb
Malcolm Ruel bcbhddaaae
Malcolm Stoddard ahbabajadaa
Malinda adgffcaa
Malissa adahddd
Mamie adaimcdbf, adkfbbjaa
Mamie G bcdgdbacb
Mamie Newell adaimbbdc
Mandy bcdgdeaabc
Manfred Cotton adaimbhcbc
Manfred D adaimbhc
Manfred Lewis adaimbhca
Manley E bcbhdgage
Manzer bcdgdaaca, bcdgdeah
Marcella adggegbacb
Marcella Buyrl adggegbab
Marcella C adggegbb
Marcellus bcdedcab, bcdedla
Marcellus Irenaeus bcdedcfd
Marcellus John adbabfia
Marcia adkebdi
Marcia Cecil abbegbdfce
Marcus ahcbfd
Mareba L aedaac
Margaret xafb, abdcebeahb, adaceagad,
adaceak, adacealg, aeeaeb, ahbgbad-
da, ahbgiifbb, ahcfje, aia, bcbebbba,
Mrs. bbbebfj, wife bcdebel, bcdedb-
bd, bcdgdaieca, **fab**

Margaret Ann adkehbg, ahchfik, **ahda-
agb**, bcbcbbacd
Margaret Anna aeeaeca
Margaret B abccgaccaa
Margaret Carolyn adhafdgccb
Margaret D adkgdbae
Margaret Elizabeth bbbfabibi, bbbfab-
maab
Margaret Emma ahbabamgca
Margaret F adabbgaicf
Margaret Grace abbeebcaaf
Margaret Merriman adkdeceha
Margaet Hilton ahfcfb
Margaret Lenora ahbgbbeaab
Margaret M wid abceabbg
Margaret Nona adabbgqdk
Margaret Olive adabbgaicea
Margaret Rebecca ahbgbbeaab
Margaret Sylvester adkfbeddca
Margaret Taylor bbbfabl
Margaret Virginia bcfiibcic
Magaret Whitney adkfbebcg
Margarett abccdgb
Margarette bcdgddf
Margariete Augusta adaceagcci
Margery ahggg, bbbffg
Margret A adkfbbjdc
Margueretta Duffield adkdecef
Marguerite Ethel adadicfbaa
Marguerite Williams gbfeaae
Maria adaabcba, adabbgbb, adadagaca,
adkdecej, ahbabaee, ahbghf, ahcbeae,
ahgchd, ahgdcba, ahgdccb, bcbhdha,
bcdedbacba, bcdgdbad, bcdgdeah, bc-
fiffi
Maria C ahgdccaaa
Maria Cornelia adhccbbf
Maria Cornelia Durant Maynard adhc-
cbbea
Maria Elizabeth ahbghjc
Maria Hepzebah ahbghgd
Maria Lizzie bcdedfeb
Maria T wife bbbebcbb
Maria Wakefield adkfbeba
Mariah fcb
Marian adacffeae, bcbhdhba, bcdebga-
acg
Marian T ahbabaefba
Marianna adhafdgccc
Marie adhcbbgga, bcdgdafeea
Marie A abccgbc
Marie Emma adggegbacd
Marietta adadhcaa, adaimaaaa, adhah-
edc, ahcbec, bcdeaedab
Mariette adaceaag
Marilla adaceaebc
Mariol adacfff
Marion adhadcehb, ahfcaaaca, bcdeb-
ejec, bcdgdafmab, bcdgdakfe
Marion Addie adaceagcg
Marion Anastasia adabbgagdaa
Marion Clyde adkecbaacf
Marion Durant adhccbbec
Marion E bcdeaefabe

Marion Emma bcbebbfacd
Marion Eunice adbabfecaa
Marion Frances ahfcfcecb
Marion Francilla adhafcabdc
Marion Geraldine adgfbgfaabc
Marion Harriet bededdabcb
Marion Hattie bcbebcgabba
Marion Heal adaabffdcb
Marion Howard abbegfjbe
Marion J adgfcicda, ahchfdd
Marion Jewel adaceagcch
Marion Leslie ahgchebaa
Marion Louise adgfbgfiba, bcbhddaaab, bcdeddhf
Marion Lucile bcbebbfaaaa
Marion M bbbfhcfcf
Marion Mayfield adaabfaag
Marion P bcbhddbcaa
Marion Wallace adhcbbgb
Marjorie adaidaebc, bcbhdbnacb, bcdgdafoa
Marjorie M Hewett bbbffcbaea
Marjorie Pauline bbbfabmha
Marjorie Stone bcdedcfcbd
Mark abbegfj, bcdeaed
Mark Leslie adgxfaff
Marshall Adams bcdebek
Marshall Clinton adkgdefa
Marshall L adaceaai
Marshall Prouty ahgcabca
Martha adaabceb, adaabffa, adabbbda, adabbgca, adabbgdba, adacfb, adaha, adaieaafl, adbd, adgdab, adgfbgdcc, adgfcibb, adgfcica, aeeacaa, aeeb, ahbabccc, ahbcae, ahbcajbf, ahbcc, ahbci, ahcfc, ahdadc, bbbb, bbbffada, bbbfhbad, bcbhdej, bcdbaaa, bcde, bcdgdaaeb, bcdgdad, bcdgdanc, bee, be, gbag
Martha A wife abccgacc, abceabce, adadhcbb, adhaj, aeeacaab
Martha Ann abceabee, adhcdaeb, adkehbc, bcdebgbc
Martha Anne bcdgdaala
Martha B bcdbeag
Martha Bradley bcbehhd
Martha Brown abccgacf
Martha Custis abbegbdg
Martha E adaabcjd, ahdaagg
Martha Flavilla adabbgajj
Martha Follinsby adkfbec
Martha G adabbgabb
Martha Ida bbbffchc
Martha Irena adgfbege
Martha J ahbabcde
Martha Jane ahbabjg
Martha L bcdbecda
Martha Lena bbbfabhac
Martha Lizzie bcfiibce
Martha Locke abceaea
Martha Louise abbegbebbe
Martha Lucretia adgdcdb, adggdcie
Martha M ahbaea
Martha Matilda abbegbdfa

Martha McClaren abceabce
Martha Morrison bcdeddha
Martha N bcdgegc
Martha Parker bcfifaf
Martha Parsons abceabdg, abceabdh
Martha Rachel adaimbifi
Martha Sanborn adkgaec
Martha Smith abbeacbb
Martha Sophia adacglb
Martha Urania bcbcbbafd
Martha Williamson abdcebef
Martin adbabgab, adbabgd
Martin A adgcagad
Martin L bcbcbbel
Martin V B ahbgee, bbbebcdaa
Marvin Benjamin ahbcabbc
Mary xaaa, abbeab, abbec, wid abbegbdbg, abbegh, abca, abccf, abccgbac, abccgdcj, abceaa, abceabecb, abceb, abcfb, abda, badcca, ahdh, wife adaa, adaaac, adaaaifab, adaaaica, adaabcla, adaabfaab, adabbe, adabbgcc, adabbgdbx, adabbgn, adabdb, adabh, adabiba, adabibg, adacb, adaceafj, adaceahb, adacfa, (Dorr) adacfe, adacga, adadaba, adadabgab, adadae, adadhcaid, adadiab, adadice, adae, adahb, adaiea, adaiia, adaiiaaef, adailxx, adaimd, adbabba, adbabc, wife adbabfb, wife adbabfdde, adbabff, adbabhc, adbace, adbace, adbad, adbafb, adc, adfc, adfcda, adgbb, adgcagc, adgfbeca, adgfbek, wife adgfbma, wife adgfdae, adggbd, adggc, adggefb, adggefcb, adgxb, adgxf, adgxfac, adgxfag, adgxfdg, adhaa, adhafac, adhaff, adhah, adhan, adhcbbdc, adhcbe, adhcc, adhcca, adhci, adk, adkdbd, wife adkddf, adkdf, adkdh, adkedc, wife adkfbeb, af, aec, wife ahb, ahbaahb, ahbabajib, ahbabcdh, ahbabdac, ahbabja, ahbcaa, ahbcabcd, ahbcacba, ahbcacd, ahbcacfa, ahbcajbe, ahbcajea, ahbcxa, ahbe, ahbgaa, ahbgbg, ahbgbx, ahbgfh, ahbgih, ahbgij, ahcd, ahcfb, ahcfjd, wife ahd, ahdae, ahdj, ahgda, ba, baa, bbbebcdac, bbbfabcb, bbbffafc, bbbffca, wife bbbffec, bbbffef, bbbffdbb, bbbfhbaa, bbbfhbxcf, wife bbbfhed, bbbfhh, bbbfi, bcbc, wid bcbca, bcbcbaaac, bcbebba, bcbebcgb, bcbebe, bebed, bcbehdb, bchhbfb, bcbhdbd, bcbhddcf, bcbhdebc, bcbhdgac, bcdbb, bcdc, bcdeaead, bcdeaefa, bcdecab, bcdecahd, bcdeedc, bcdecdd, bcdedbbca, bcdedbbd, bcdedbcf, bcdedkc, bcdgc, bcdgdaacfe, bcdgdaaea, bcdgdaidba, bcdgdam, bcdgdand, bcdgdbc, bcdgdbd, bcdgddaae, bcdgdeag, bcdgdef, bcdgdf, bcdgf, bcdha, bcdii, bcficafa, bcficang, bcficd, bcfifjeb, bcfifji, bcfigd, bd, cbbcba, daa, bcb

Mary A abccgaeb, abccgcfb, adabbgbec, adabibcf, adadhaad, adgcaccae, adgfbecba, adhafaac, adkfbdxb, ahdaaddh, ahdaagh, bcbhdeg, bcdeaefb, bcdeddbca, bcfifjac, bcfigfbba, bcfihdd
Mary Abby aeeaecb
Mary Abigail adkehbb, adkeheb
Mary Abilene bcbcbhafe
Mary Adeline adhahece
Mary Akerman adaiebac
Mary Albertina adkecbaad
Mary Alice abdcebecb, adhafdgcd
Mary Almira adaceafggb
Mary Amanda abbegbice, abbegbid
Mary Amelia adkfbebcc
Mary Ames bcdeabdaa
Mary Ann abccgacd, abccgacm, adacgib, adahdbc, adbabge, adhafce, adhcdad, adkecaha, ahbaedf, ahbghgc, ahbghh, ahcbeaa, ahchbc, ahgfdaa, bbbebdab, bbbfaxa, bcbebbbe, wife bcdbaddj, bcdgddh, bcficalc, bcfiffgb, fcef
Mary Anna bcdedbbbjd
Mary Antoinetta ahgchea
Mary Anzolette adggdaac
Mary B adgcadaaaf, ahgchm, ahgdhdc, bcdgdeafaa
Mary Barker ahbcaja
Mary Barnard adkfbbda
Mary Belinda adacgfgd
Mary Buffum adbabfc
Mary C adaabcjb, adaabfc, adabbgac, adggbed
Mary Chase adhafde
Mary Coffin adkdef
Mary D adabbgm, ahbcabeh
Mary Delphine bcdebgaad
Mary E adabbbdcd, adabbgaba, adacffeg, adaimcdbf, adgfbq, adgfdh, adgfgabb, adggdadb, adhafaha, adhafgba, adhafgcf, adhak, wife adhccfg, adkddgcb, wife adkeabbaa, adkffbbja, adkfbbjc, ahbaacde, ahbabadbb, ahbabadd, ahbaedda, ahdadag, ahgdccb, bbbfhab, bcbhbgk, bcbhdehfe
Mary E D abceabdba
Mary Edith abccdgcaab, adbabgaae
Mary Eleanor abccgcfcae
Mary Eliza abccgbabb, adhcbbba, ahchfed
Mary Elizabeth abbegbdff, abdcebcb, adadiaba, adaidaea, adaijbd, adaabfdf, adbabfic, adggdadaba, adhahee, bcbebcfb, bcfigfae, bcfihecb
Mary Ella adggdcid, bbbffchd, bcbhdbeca
Mary Ellen adhcdaed
Mary Emery bbbfaeaa
Mary Emma adgfcdgaaaa, eaabe
Mary Ethel abbegbdcab
Mary Eunice ahbgiig, ahgdcafd
Mary Eva ahbcabeje
Mary Florence abdcebeag, adhafgchce,

Mary Florietta abbegbeba
Mary Frances adgfbgff, adkgaeh, ahfcfcg, bbbfabg, ahgfbde, bcdbecda, bcdbedb, bcdeaedba
Mary Gladys bcdedbbccb
Mary Green adhcbbe
Mary H ahbabjjb
Mary Hannah abbegbdbd
Mary Healey adkdbec
Mary Helen ahgfbdacc
Mary Hope bcdgddag, bcdgddaha
Mary Ida ahfcaaaf
Mary Isabel bbbfabmjc
Mary Isabelle ahgdhbbc
Mary J abccgdg, adaabddc, adabigh, adgfdca, bbbffcdc, bcbcbbacb, bcbhdq, bcdhdqb, bcdgdpc
Mary Jane adabibka, adacealc, adaceddba, adacgfggd, adaigae, adhahfa, ahbabjba, ahbaec, ahbgbada, ahbgbaf, bbbebcbf, bbbffcbe, bcdedcaa, bcdgdbaac
Mary Jane Boynton abbegbda
Mary Jean bcbhdbndmc
Mary Jeannette bbbffaga
Mary Kate ahbcacbba, ahgdhdhdab
Mary Katherine adhafgcbdb
Mary Kelsey ahbabjbb
Mary L adhafage, ahbabcdba
Mary L Hall adggeijaab
Mary Leonora ahbgbee
Mary Louise bcbcbbgbab, bcdbecda, bcdgdabdea
Mary Lucinda adhcdacd
Mary Lucretia bbbffadba
Mary M wife adaiiaa, adaimbbe, adggend
Mary Marshall bcdebei
Mary Morrill abdcebed
Mary O abccgacha, ahbabahi
Mary P adgcadafg, bbbebcbca, wife bcficaf
Mary Pickering adkdeceba
Mary R ahbcacbaa, ahbcacfa
Mary Rounds adkgdde
Mary S adgffcc, adhcdaeab, ahcbfea
Mary S S adaaaieba
Mary T adgfbhae, bcbcbbge
Mary True ahbabjia
Mary V adabbgdbb, ahbgbfc
Mary W adkddcc
Mary Wade ahggbdaab
Mary Windsor adggdccag
Mary Worthen adkddcaa
Maryett bcdedbbbe, bcbhbgb
Maryetta adgfbeje
Mason H bcdbadddad
Mather B bcbcbbeeb
Matie bcdebgafbb
Matilda adkgdbe, ahgcabacd, bcdbeac
Mattie adabbgbccf
Mattie E bcdgdmaa
Mattie J bcfifjadd
Maty adkdeba

Maud bcdgdaffi, bcdgdagha
Maud Annie adaceagcca
Maud H bbbfhcfgd
Maud La Von bcdedggba
Maud M adacedhcc, bcdgdbaai
Maude adaabdabec
Maude Caroline bbbfabhab
Maude E bcbhddkbxc
Maurice ahbabajadc
Maurice Baily gbakh
Maurice C ahbcabfeaa
Maurice Harmon adggdcibb
Maurice L adabbgaighb
Maurice R adabbgahed
May bcdedkaf, bcdgdafkb
May Charity adaceagccb
May E adkgdcba, ahgdcafd
May Electa adaceagch
Maynard Weston bbbfhcfhb
McLauren abceabcf
McClellan bcdedbbcc
McMorris Marshall adacffeha, adacff-
 ehaa
Mehitable abbg, abcfc, abcg, wife adg-
 cagb, adgfcdacec, adggec, wife adke-
 abb, adkebe, adkeca, adkeg, bbbebfi,
 wid bcbcaa, bcdbeaf, bcdbeb, befd,
 bcficc, bcfife, bcfiha, cbaaf
Mehitable Elvira bcdeabba
Mehitable L adaabfgd, adkebcb
Melicent abccgdbac
Melinda adgxfadaa, adkebge, bcbhbge
Melinda J ahfcfcee
Melinda Jones bcficanf
Melinda M adacebfc
Melissa adaimaaad, adaimbdf, adgfbg-
 gf, adgxfade
Melissa E adgxffcca
Melissa J adhafgaa
Melissa Neale bcbhdbnf
Melita adacgfd
Melmoth ahggbda
Melton bcdgdafqda, bcogdafqe
Melvin abdcebcadc, adadibdd, adgxfa-
 fda, ahbabcdbc
Melvin Buker bcbhddbbaa
Melvin Ernest bcdeaedaaaa
Melvin M bcdeaedaa
Melvina adadibdg, bcdgdaff, bcdgdagf,
 bcdgddabb
Melvina T adhafgaa
Melvina T adhafgaa
Mercedes bcdgefb
Mercy adabf, adga, adkc, adkgac, ad-
 kgh
Meredith M bcdgdbaagaa
Meretta Josephine bcdeaeaga
Meriam bcbhc
Meribah adgxfadb
Merl Hervy ahbabaeadg
Merla ahbgbfaba
Merle Eugene adgfcdabda
Merle Monroe adabbgtaab
Merle Price bcdgdaacdf

Merrill bcdedbbd
Merrill F adaabd
Merrill Franklin bcdedbbda
Merrill Neal adgfcdaced
Merrill Patch ahgchfa
Merrill Tuttle bcbhbfiaaa
Mertie May abbegfgaga
Merwin bcbebbfaaab
Meshech aedb
Meshech Weare adkdbf
Michael adaceaf, ahfab
Milan bdgdafagc
Milan L bcdgdafa
Mildred abccdgcaac, adabibcccb, bcd-
 gdaijh
Mildred A adbabfbgca, adhafgcbcb, bc-
 dgdbaadi
Mildred Arlene adaabidabeaa
Mildred C bcfifjaia
Mildred E adaigbbadb, adgfcdgcd
Mildred Hazel adhafcabdb, bcdgddah-
 ca, bcdgdpaac
Mildred L abbegfccda
Mildred Lillian ahbgiifba
Mildred Louise ahbabaeadl
Mildred M gaaxaxga
Mildred May adgfbgfaaf
Mildred Mercy adaceagccd
Mildred Stanley adaimbiacd
Mildred Stevens ahfcfceg
Miles bcdgdaffh, bcdgdeadh
Millard G abccgcfca
Millard George abccgcfcaaa
Millard T bcdgdbaadb
Millie ahchfigd
Millie C bcdeddabb
Millie E adabbhda
Millie W bbbfhjf
Milly adaceaaecb
Milton ahchfig, ahchfigc
Milton Edwin adbabfefea
Mima L adaimbae
Mina adabie, bcdgdafqc
Minah adabbgj, adadah
Minerva ahgfdc, bcdgdakd
Minerva A adkecbal
Minerva E adhafahb, bcbhbga
Minerva Monroe adaigbbacc
Minnie adabbgaigd, bbbfhbxch, bcde-
 bgbdcb
Minnie A bcdgdmad
Minnie B abccgcfcb
Minnie C adkddgcd
Minnie Clara ahchfdcga
Minnie E adadhabaa
Minnie L ahbgilh
Minnie Louise adhahecd
Minnie Maud adaimbij
Minnie Myrtle bcbhdbnde
Minnie W bcdedkag
Minnie Weber ahchfdcb
Mira J adkebgaa
Miranda adaceahe, adaceahfc, wife ad-
 gfbgac

Miranda J adhahfe
Miriam adacffh, adadai, adadibdf, adaiee, adgfbgaf, adgfbgfe, adgxd, aeeacab, aeeacc, acead, ahbf, bcbhc
Miriam F adadabbc
Miriam Jane adaimab, adaimba
Miriam L adkfbedeb
Mirza ahghc
Mittie A adgfcjbd
Molly adaabad, adabbge, adggbd, adkdbd, bcbebh
Monroe adaceah
Montreville adaceald
Moody ahbgd, ahbgdg, ahbgfc
Mordica bcdgdaak
Mortimer D adgfbejf
Moses adacea, adaceae, adaceaee, adaceala, adacealb, adacfe, adadabc, adadibb, adadic, adaie, adaieaa, adaieb, adbab, adbabba, adbabg, adgfbdc, adgfbha, adgfg, adhafcf, ahbb, ahbcacb, ahchi, ahfae, bbbfhe, bcbebca, bcbega, bcbegb, bcbhba, bcbhbf, bcbhddc, bcdedge, bcdedj, bcdgdai, bcdgec, bcdic, bcfical, bcficala, bcfiffk, bcfigfb, bcfih, bcfihd, bcfiikx, db, fb
Moses Abner adaieba
Moses Addison adadicfa
Moses Angell adabbgaig, adabbgaj
Moses Arnold bcfihec
Moses Augustus bcfigdc, bcfigfbc
Moses B adgfbha, adkebec
Moses Bragden bcfigdcb
Moses C bcficald
Moses Charles bcdgdakb
Moses D adgfcdgb
Moses E bcdgdaabb
Moses Emery adaibba
Moses Francis bcfiibcia
Moses Franklin adaicaaf, bcfihda
Moses Gove adhcbbg
Moses Hoyt bcfiibci
Moses J adgfcjbd
Moses M bcdebfaa
Moses R bcdgddae
Moses Roy adaceaff, bcdgdaii
Moses True adgxfafb
Moses W adbabbbx
Muriel bcdgdaace, bcdgdaiibc
Muriel Elizabeth adkdececca
Muriel H. R. adabiggdf
Muriel M bcdgdbaagab
Muriel Pearl bcbhdgagec
Murl Randolph adaimbhcbd
Myra abdcebd, bcdedcle
Myra Catherine adkfbebcf
Myra E abdcicba
Myra Mayfair bcbhddcebc
Myra McKeen abccgdbag
Myra P wife adkddia
Myron E bbbffbaad, bcfifjjd
Myron Edward bbbffbaa
Myron H adabbgaijc

Myrtie H bcfiffdca
Myrtie L gbefab
Myrtie Mabel Halliday adhafgcdaa
Myrtie May bcbhddceba
Myrtle ahbaacfdb, bcbhdehfh, bcdgdafmdb, bcfifjjbc
Myrtle Estelle abbegfgaj
Myrtle Irene bcdebgaec
Myrtle May adaceafkd
Mysan adaabacabb
N ahbabbkxaf
N D ahbabkxa
N Emerson adgfbfbaab
Nabby adaaaia, ahbchh, bcdif
Nabby McCrillis adaidbc
Nadine adhcbbggb
Nahum Morrill abdcebeb
Nahum P bcbhdpd
Nancy abbeacf, abbegbf, adaabdah, adabiga, adabigga, adacffa, adadie, wife adaiec, adaiecc, adailaa, adggdh, adgged, adhafad, adkddcd, adkddf, adkeac, adkebaf, adkebf, adkece, adkecj, adkeda, adkehg, adkfbaa, ahbabkxfc, ahbgbxb, ahcbfa, ahchbb, ahgcacab, ahgcabacf, ahgfdacb, bbbfaxf, wife bbbfhjh, bcbcbbea, bcbebcgb, bcbhdk, bcdecaf, bcdgdagd, bcdgddc, bcfifjda, bcfifl, bcfihh
Nancy Betton bcdeddc
Nancy Chase adkfbea
Nancy H bcbhbgc
Nancy J adgfcjbf, ahdaaga
Nancy Jane bcbhddccg, bcfifjaj
Nancy L adkebgh
Nancy Maria adgcacbd
Nancy May adgxffccg
Nancy S adadagfd
Nancy Sanborn adadagc
Nancy W adkehg, ahgfdad
Nancy Waterman ahbgike
Nannie F bcdedfaa
Naomi wife adabbgdb, adkebh, adkef, bcfifhd
Naomi (Carr) wid adke
Naomi Hews bcbcbbga
Napoleon Bonaparte adkfbbcd
Narcissa ahchfa, ahchfda,
Narcissa Chalista ahchfih
Nathan abccgc, abccgcb, abcfj, abdce, abdcebc, abdcec, adabb, adabbb, adabbbd, adabbbde, adabbgajb, adabbhk, adggba, ahbabkxeb, ahcc, ahchb, ahci, ahdaag, bcdhc
Nathan Barker Page bcfifjc
Nathan C adhafdf
Nathan Drake abbegbifc
Nathan H adabbha
Nathan Henry ahchhd
Nathan Moody ahbgdfa
Nathan T N adadhcbh
Nathan Thompson abdcedc
Nathan W ahbcajdb

Nathaniel xa, abcfa, adaabc, adggdadd, ahbabcca, bbbebf, bcdb, bcdbea, bcdeabd
Nathaniel Alford bcbhdehf
Nathaniel B adaabcd
Nathaniel Harland abbegbif
Nathaniel S adabigge
Neal (Gen) abbeebbc, adaabacaad, adgfgabce, adhccbb, adhccbbebb, adkaebcb, ahchfijb
Neal C bcbhddfabf
Neal E bcbhdbndm
Neal F adabbgr
Neal Francis adabbgrd
Neal L adacgfaebd
Neal Richard ahgfbdaeb
Neal S bcdgdabdac
Nehimiah adaaaa
Nehimiah Getchell bcdebeea
Neil K adabbgcde
Neil McAllister adgfbhadaa
Neil Ward abccgcfdba
Nelle adgfcdabf
Nellie abccgdbad, adabbgea, adacebfab, adacffeaa, adadagfba, adadibabe, adbabfbeb, adkddgcad, adkddiaa, bbbfhbxcb, bebhbfice, bcbhdbh, bcbhddcbb, bcdgdabfb, bcdgdaffdd, bcfifhg, gaaxaxj
Nellie A ahbabaeab, ahbabjja, bcbebigd
Nellie Addie adaidagfa
Nellie Augustine ahgciga
Nellie B adkeabaf
Nellie Blanche adabbgbcae
Nellie C bcdeddbh
Nellie E adgfdh, bcdebgaaf
Nellie Eleanor bcfiffc
Nellie Emma ahbgbahb
Nellie F adabbgaicd, adaidbfb
Nellie Gertrude adhcbbfe
Nellie H adkgdegc
Nellie J abccgbabc
Nellie L adgfbka
Nellie M adaceafka, adhafdib, adkgddgcc, aeeaeccb, bbbffcea, bcbehdda
Nellie M H bifiibae
Nellie Maria adaceddbb
Nellie May ahbgbeba
Nellie Richardson adabbgagdb
Nellie S bcfifo
Nellie Sophia adggegdb
Nellie W bbbfhjf
Nelson adacgfeba, bcdgdabe, fcee
Nelson A gbefa
Nelson H adabbgaga, gbefa
Nelson L adhafdie
Nelson Lucius adaabdaeg
Nelson P adgxfadf
Netta Helen adacffeeb
Nettie adaabacaak, adaceddbc, bcbebbbdc
Nettie C adgfcdacac
Nettie H adgxffbbb
Nettie J adadagfbb

Nettie L ahchfecb
Nettie May abbegbdfdd
Nettie W ahbcabfec
Nevers S bcdgdakf
Newell adadiea, adaimbb, adkddfa, adkddg, adkddge, bcbcbbaff
Newell F adkddfaa
Newell H adacffeb
Newman J bcdebgdb, bcdebgdba
Newton bcdgdaiea
Newton Calvin adaceaada
Newton Russell adbabfeg
Newton S bcdgdaiea
Niles adaceaaeca
Nina ahbaacxa, ahbabahfa
Nina Adelaide adacgfach
Nina Celeste abbegbebbd
Ninelle D bbbfhcfeea
Ninette May bcbhddbcbe
Nith bcdge
Noah abccg, abccgda, adag, ahbabfb, ahbabk, ahbac, bcdeaeda
Noah E G abccgch
Nora Ruth bcfifjjac
Norbert Orrin adhafgcbda
Norma Ansten bcdgdbaaacb
Norma Elizabeth bcdedbecab
Norman C bcbhdqacx
Norman E abccgcfdcc
Norman Francis aeeacaaaab
Norman L bcdgdafka
Norman McGregor bcdedbccbc
Norman R abccgcfcab, abccgcfcaba
Norman Robbins bbbebcdaaca
Norman Russell adaimbbeac
Norris Fitz adadabcfaf
Obed H adahdbb
Oceana bcbhdehe
Octavia adaaaiea, bcbhddag
Octavia J adaaaiebb
Octavia W eaabd
Odbur bcdgdeadi
Odbur T bcdgdaffg
Odessa Della bcdebgagg
Ola Frances bcfifhhea
Olif bcdbab
Olin bcdgdeaaff
Olin Heney adaceagcf
Olive abbeaca, abccgchb, adacgfbd, adgfcb, adgfcdaceg, adgfcdb, adgfcdh, adggdaae, adkddd, adkebgc, ahchfb, ahdm, bcdhdeha, bcbhdeka, bcdgdaad, bcdgdafaab, bcdgdagb, bcdgdah, bcdgdee
Olive A bcficand
Olive Cobb adacgfgd
Olive H bcdeddba
Olive Lissett ahbcajga
Olive Sarah bbbffbab
Oliver abbeacaa, adbabfd, adgfdc, adgfdce, adgfdf, adgxfbd, adkgddg, bcdeb, bcdebg
Oliver Buffum adbabfdde
Oliver Kimball bcdedfk

845

305

Oliver L bcdebgaae
Oliver Lawrence bcdeabda
Oliver M bcbhdhda
Oliver Parker bcdebgaa
Oliver Smith bbbfabm, bbbfabmg
Olivia H ahgdhdb
Olla bcdecdba
Olli bcdecc
Olwyn Warland abbegbic
Omar Washburn adbabfdeb
Ora L bcfiffdcd
Ora M bbbebcdada
Orange C bcfifjal
Orator adacebfb
Orchard C abccgcfd, abccgch
Orelena ahghd
Oren adadibaba
Oren Frank abbegfcc
Oren J adgfbgeba, ahfcfdac
Orianna J akebdbbib
Oric ahbabkxad
Orin Moses adaceaah
Orinda Frances ahchfea
Orion David ahbcabaea
Orlando adgfbfde
Orman P ahbabahgb
Ormand Clair abccgcfdea
Orpha bcdecdba
Orpha L adaceage
Orra ahchha
Orren John adabibcae
Orrin adgcadafd
Orrin A adacedfh
Orrin B adaiecab
Orrin Boardman bbbebcdae
Orrin C bcfifjal
Orrin Duane adhagbca
Orrin Ernest abbegbdfch
Orrin H adhafgcbd
Orrin May bcdedbbcd
Orville C bcbhbgg
Orville Howard adabbgagcx
Orville W bcdgdafaac
Osborn Curtis abbeebcaad
Oscar adaabacaaf, bcbhddfaae
Oscar B abccgcfde
Oscar Caswell ahbgbacaa
Oscar Chase adabibccd
Oscar E ahgdhbb
Oscar Everett adabibccda
Oscar R ahbabajg
Oscar Samuel bcbebbbdd
Osman bcdedci
Oswald adgwbgeac
Otis adabbgdg, bcdgdeaced
Otis Little adbabfb
Otis R bcbhdekca
Otis W bcdgena
Otto M gaaxaxm
Owen C ahbcajbb
Owen Oscar adkgdefba
Ozilous J ahbcajba
Packard ahbabaeaaa
Pacola bcdgdafqb

Pamelia adgfcdi
Parker B bcdebgaacf
Parker Tandy adgcacbk
Parna bcfifffa
Patience abdcg, abdf, adbabx, adbae,
adgh, wife ahbabkxe, ahbgbi, dab
Patience T bbbebdaaa
Pattie adacfg
Patty abceaba, ahfck
Paul adbabh, adbag, ahgdg, ahgdgac,
bcdgdabdda, bcdgem
Paul Eugene bcdedbbbjc
Paul L adaceafgeb
Paul Le Baron ahgdhbbf
Paul Lionel ahgdgbac
Paul N bcdgdbaagac
Paul Vincent ahgdhbce
Paul Wielding adkggddgab
Paulina ahggbe
Paulina Smith adkfbba
Pauline abbegbicda, adaimbaib
Pauline Annie bcdgdaalcb
Pauline Augusta adkgddgaa
Pauline Della adgxfaaccba
Pauline Isabel adabibcccc
Pauline M bbbffcbajb
Pauline Merrill adadhacabb
Pauline Wentworth bbbfabmc, bbbfa-
bmf
Peace Chase adhafdh
Peace Neal adhcbba
Pearl adaceaaiba, adkfbeddb, ahbcajgj,
bcdgdaacfa, bcdgdaked
Pearl C adaigbbada
Pearl Elinor adaceafgeb
Pearl Emeline bbbebgabb
Pearl H adabbgbcaac
Pearl L bcdgebc
Pearl P bcdgdbaaab
Peasle bcdbad
Peaslee Moody bcfiibd
Peasley B adaabcje
Peggy ahbgde, bcbcbbdc, bcbcbbf
Pelatiah adbaba, ahgg
Pembroke Sutherland ahbabahg
Percie M bcbhdfagi
Percival abccgcfdab
Percival Barton bcbhdqaa
Percy bcdbad, bcdgdafob, bcdgdeaaba,
bcdgepa
Percy A fceaea
Percy A R adbabgada
Percy Duncan adhafgcbg
Percy E adgfdh
Percy Glover adaimbhcbe
Percy James bcdebgagb
Percy La Forest adbabfeia
Perkins adgfca
Perkins Hews adadhcb
Perkins S ahbcabba
Perley adgcaf, adgcagaa, adkebdh, bcd-
gdaijg, bcdgdeafa
Perley A adkfbbjbg
Perley Albert adkfbbcid

Perley Alvah bcdeaedaab
Permelia abccdgcc
Perrin B abbegfca
Perry Hobbs adkebaac
Persie F adkfbbcdad
Persis L bcbcbbad
Peter abbegfc, adaabcj, ahbgbxd, b, bc-
  bebcc, bcbh, bcbhd, bcbhdb, bcbhdda,
  bcbhddcb, bcbhdeb, bcfifa, bcfifjd
Peter S fcead
Peter Staub bcdbeceeb
Peter Wolf ahchfij
Phebe adabbghi, adggefcc
Phebe A ahdade
Phebe Ann adahdda
Phebya bbbebd
Phene bcdebh
Philena adacffec, adacgff, adaimbca,
  adgfbeec, ahbchda, bcdeddf
Philena Andalusia adacffec
Philena M adaidbg
Philene A adadagaaa
Philetus ahdadae
Philip adad, adadha, adaf, bbbfabmia,
  bcdgdaije, cbbca
Philip C adgxfada
Philip G adabbgaijf
Philip Huse adgfcdacab
Philip McCook adgfbgdcaab
Philip Rice abbegfjadb
Phillis adabbgqdba
Philura M bcfifjjc
Phineas adadaa, adadabb, adadg, adaig,
  bcbhdh, bcdbaa, bcdbecb
Phineas A adaimbda
Phineas B adaimbd
Phineas E adadabbdb
Phineas Kimball bcfifj, bcfifjai, bcfif-
  je
Phoebe abccgaa, abccgad, adahde, adbh,
  wife adggefc, adhcba, ahbche, ahbgia'
  bbbda, bbbebcc, bbbfabibc, bbd, bcd-
  ead, bcdeba, bcdecaj, bcdedfg, bcdg-
  ddf, bcdgdeae, bcdhb, bcfifhe, bcfihb
Phoebe A wife adadiad
Phoebe Amanda bbbfabj
Phoebe Cobb adbabgc
Phoebe E adacgfee
Phoebe Jane Wilson ahbgika
Phoebe M adkehbd
Phoebe O bcdedbbbd
Phoebe P adkgdega
Phoebe Smith bbbfabia
Phoebe Wells ahbgeh
Phyllis adggegbace, bcdgdakfd
Pilusa bcfifjjc
Pliny adacgl
Pliny Augustus adacgla
Ploomy adaaaid
Plummer adgcaca
Polina adaceddea
Polly abbeedb, abbegfi, abdcebb, adaab-
  ca, adaabfec, adabbbdf, wife adacebb,
  adacfdd, adacffb, adaabffia, adadhx,

adaie, adgfbea, adgffa, adggdg, ad-
  hafx, adkdbd, adkdg, adkdga, adkee,
  ahbabce, ahbabi, ahchec, ahdaaa, ah-
  ggbf, bbbebca, bbbffh, bcbebba, bc-
  bebfb, bcbebh, bcdbecd, bcdeaee, bc-
  dedbe, bcdedga, bcfifab, bcfifb, bc-
  fifha, bcfihg, cbaae
Polly Boyd bcdbadh
Porter adaabci, adaceaed
Prentis adggdcc, adggdccaa, adggdcibd
Prescott Robinson adhcbbhbbb
Priscilla abceabbf, adacfe
Priscilla E adabbgaijd
Priscilla M adkecbae
Priscilla Russell adkebaacda
Prudence bcdgdafkd, bcdgdeaib
Ptolemy ahbcabaee
Purcell L ahgdcagd
Purcell Lorenzo ahgdcag
Rachel abbf, adaceddf, adbg, adgcaa,
  aeeab, aeeacd, ahbad, ahchfg, bcbhl,
  bcficae
Rachel Ayer adkgddc
Ralph ahbabajk, bbbfabmh, bbbfhbxc-
  gf
Ralph E bcbhdna
Ralph Elom abbegbdfcd
Ralph Getchell bcdebeeab
Ralph H fceaba
Ralph Harold bbbffcdfc
Ralph K adgfbhadab
Ralph M adgfbgebbe
Ralph P adgfcdacaa
Ralph Percy abbeebbbd
Ralph Philip bcbhddfabh
Ralph S adbabfdhaa
Ralph W adgfbhada, bcbhbfiae, bcdgd-
  baaad
Randall Fuller adacffeeeb
Randolph Clement adaimbhcbg
Rankin bcdgdafki
Rawson bcdebejcb
Ray Elson adaceafgg
Ray Storrs ahgfbdae
Raymond adgfbfbaaa, bcdgddey
Raymond Aaron ahchfija
Raymond C adadhacaaf
Raymond Everett ahgchebbb
Raymond F abccgdfcc
Raymond J adabibcaaa
Raymond Parker adkecbaaci
Raymond Perley adkfbbcidb
Raymond Scott bcbebbcdacb
Raymond W adabbgzd, adabbgzdb
Raymond Wesley bcdgdsaac
Reba adacgfebab
Rebecca adaaba, adabdc, adaceab, adai-
  gac, adggbi, adggdk, adkebb, ahbg-
  dh, ahce, ahchc, ahdaaa, ahdaai, ahg-
  chb, bbbfabmb, wid bcbcb, bcbegi,
  bcbhdbf, bcbhddaj, bcbhddm, bcbh-
  df, bcdbada, bcdbaddb, bcdbeceec,
  gbah
Rebecca B adggeif

Rebecca Elizabeth ahdaagd
Rebecca J adaimaae
Rebecca Maria adkdecb, adkdecee
Rebecca Reed bcdeabbda
Rebeckah ahbcx
Rewth xa
Relief adgcagah, bcficam, bcficap
Reginald bedgdafmba
Reginald B ahbabaeadi
Reginald Edwin adgfbgfaabe
Reginald Webster adaimaaabca
Rena A gbakfa
Retire Parker bcdbedc
Reuben abbeed, adaaafd, adaaai, ada-
aaic, adabbgia, adaila, adailaa, adke-
dk, adkehf, ahbgbxa, bedea, bedeaad,
bcdedbca, bcdedbd, bcdgddf, bcdg-
deac, bcdgdeace
Reuben A adabbghh
Reuben Billings adabbgbcb
Reuben Ernest adabbgbcab
Reuben Smith adaaai
Rex ahchfieb
Rhoda adadied, adaiib, adaija, adgcadc,
adgcae, adgcafa, adgxf, adgxfak, ah-
bgdi, wife ahbgee, ahbgg, bcdgdabc,
bcdgdac, bcdgdage, bcdgddae, bcdgd-
eaaca, bcdgdg
Rhoda A adaceagb
Rhoda Ann adaieaaa, adaimbbd, adgx-
ffba
Rhoda E adgxfbec
Rhoda Little adbabfg
Rhoda R adaimcb
Rice ahbabcdg
Rice S ahbabfaa
Rice Swan ahbabch
Richard abccc, abccdd, adabia, adadh-
acae, adbabbc, adbabi, adhafdgeca,
adkddc, adkddcebc, adkde, ahbcac,
ahbcaje, bede, bedec, bcdecac, bede-
ded, bcdedf, bcdgdia, bcfiffdcca, ga-
axa
Richard Arthur adgfbffcb
Richard B ahbcajce
Richard C abccgeff
Richard Donald ahbabaeadda
Richard E adabbgagcy, adaiiabaad
Richard Frank bcdebgbbc
Richard Furber adkdea
Richard Furber Hamilton adkdead
Richard Godfrey adaabffddb
Richard Harvey ahgdgbaab
Richard Henry ahgdgba
Richard Henry Sylvester bcdebejc
Richard Herbert adadhcaibb
Richard Lane adadabcfae
Richard Phelps adkedjdb
Richard Poole adhcbbgdad
Richard Thompson adhcbbhbba
Richard Weare adkdecc
Richard Whitmore abccgcfcaba
Richard William adkdecehb, adkeecen
Richard Worthen adkddcebf

Richardson Olin adaceagc
Richardson Wallace adaceagcci
Rinaldo E adkeabbaaa
Rinaldo H adkeabbaa
Riou Duane ahgcheb
Riou Leslie ahgchebb
Riou Nelson ahgchebba
Robert xafa, adacgfaci, adgda, adgdaa,
adgfbgbb, adgxfa, adgxfaf, adkfbe-
dec, ahbabajie, ahbgff, ahggbbbc,
bbbfhba, bbbfhbac, bbbfhbx, bbbfhd,
bcdeddhdbc, bcdgdafmb, bcdgdo, be-
dgenaa, g, gbac, gbc
Robert Beebe adggdcgaa
Robert Bradish bcfifjad
Robert Bruce adhafgcdab
Robert Byron adabbgbccca
Robert Carlton adabbgbcag
Robert Clark bbbfhch
Robert E bcdedbacb
Robert Earl bbbfhbxcg
Robert Edgar adgxfafe
Robert Edward Merchant adbbbgva
Robert Elmer adabiggdac
Robert Emery bbbfhcfge
Robert F adgfbgeb
Robert Frederick bcdgdaacg
Robert Guy abbegbibea
Robert H adaimcdga, bbbfhbxcgd, bcd-
eddbb
Robert Harold abbegbdfbaa
Robert Irving adadabbdba
Robert Kimball adggdcca, adggdccaec
Robert M bcbcbaaabe, bcdedbac, bcdg-
dbaaa
Robert McLean bcbcbbgbac
Robert Morrison bcbcbbgbb, bcdeddb
Robert Oliver bbbfabmjb
Robert Myron adaceal
Robert P bcdgdbaaaa
Robert Percy bedged
Robert Piercy adggdccab
Robert R adaieca
Robert S bcbhddcefb
Robert T bcdebgaacba
Robert W ahbabjeca, bcdgdaacd
Robert Wilbur adgfbgebbc
Robert William abbegbibec
Roberta V bcdgdaiie
Robin Russell bcdgdanea
Roderick Thomas bbbfhcfla
Rodney adabbgaieb
Roger bcdgdanej
Roger Wilson adggeilc
Rogers adhcbbjaa
Roland Beeman adhcbbhbb
Rollin bcdecaib
Romanzo E bcfifjaib
Ronald adabbgbebba
Ronald Edward bbbfabmhc
Ronald Morton adabbgbebbb
Rosa Evelyn bcbhbfiac
Rosa E adgxfbec
Rosalie Blanche bcbhddfaea

Rosaltha Addie adaceali
Rosamond Ellen adhafdieaa
Rosamund B ahgciacab
Rosanna ahbgbhb
Rosanna W adkebda
Rosannah bcbhdbl, adaabacah
Roscoe F adaimbbga
Roscoe Greenleaf adbabfeh
Roscoe H bcdgdbacc
Rose adgfbgdbd, bededkad
Rose Caroline adgfbgfdaa
Rose Edna bebcbaabab
Rose Ella ahbcabaed
Rose Lanna bbbffbaac
Rose M bbbfhjg
Rose Mary ahbcabejbb
Rosetta ahbgic
Rosilla abccgaci
Rosilla H adkebdc
Rosina adaabcfbd
Rosina B bcdebgbdca
Rosina W adaabacah
Roswell adaabdeb, ahgfbda, ahgfbdaca
Roswell G adaabcjg
Roswell W adgfbla
Roxana adaabacah, adaabd, wife adacedd, ahbcabef
Roxanna bbbffac
Roxy adaceaha
Roy adhadccdb, bcdgdaidb, bcdgdeaafd
Roy LaVaughn bbbfhjbk
Roy M bbbfhcfgg
Roy O ahbabaeadd
Roy Winthrop adhadcecc
Royal adggeff, ahdadaa
Royal S fcek
Rozilla ahbabajd
Ruanna adaabfdb
Ruby adabbgbccd, bcdgdaida
Ruby B abccgdj
Ruby Louise adhadceha
Ruby Mae bcdgdaacde
Ruel ahbabdae
Ruel A bcbhddaaa
Rufus adaaaif, bcdedce
Rufus B bbbebgb
Rufus F E adaaaiefe
Rufus Frank adaaaifaa
Rufus Franklin adaaaifa
Rufus P abbegfcad
Ruhamah bca
Ruis Elnora abbegbdfdf
Russell Congdon adhccbbi
Russell Leroy bcdgdabeaa
Russell Wright adfcdcaaaa
Ruth abbege, abccdc, adaaab, adfe, adgfbhadac, adhafcb, adhccc, adkecf, wife ahbabcc, ahbabeaeah, ahbabjecd, ahcfi, ahchfijd, bcba, bebegf, bcbei, bcbhddkbxd, bcdgdaace, bcdgdad, wife bcdgdafae, bcdgdafh, bcdgdafeeb, bcdgdanei, bcdgddb, bcdgddea, bcdgdeag, bcdgdf, bcdgdi, bcdib, gbap
Ruth A bbbfhjha

Ruth Alden abbeebcaab
Ruth Bessie adhadceg
Ruth Challis adhaddc
Ruth Dallas bcdgdakbaa
Ruth E adaceafgec, adgxffbde, bcdgdafh
Ruth Ella adacealj, adaidaed
Ruth Ellen adadabcfaa
Ruth Ellsworth adkfbeiba
Ruth Estella adadhcaiaa
Ruth Ethel adgcacbjda
Ruth Evelyn abbegbibed, adadhaaada
Ruth Gage adhahd
Ruth Harodine adhcbbfga
Ruth M adabbgpaab
Ruth Mary adggdadac
Ruth Mildred abccgdfbab
Ruth Nancy adhafdgdb
Ruth Owen bebehdc
Ruth V adacffehb
Ruth Walker ahbgeb
Ruth Wallace gbeaa
Ruth Williams bcbehaa
S Harlow bcbhbgd
S Morton adabbgbeb
Sabrina adadha
Sadie adaiiaafa
Sadie C adkebccb
Sadie Marion ahgchecb
Sadie May abbegbebbc
Sallie adaceaaa, adacead, adacgfc, adacgh, adaidc, adggeeca, ahbabajic
Sallie E abccgdcka
Sally abbegfh, abcfld, adaaafg, adaabck, adabibh, adadagb, adgcaga, adggej, wife adaijc, ahbaaae, ahbabcg, ahbabfb, ahbabh, ahbabjd, ahbabke, wife ahbabkxf, ahbaca, ahbgbc, wife ahbgbh, ahcbba, ahfcd, ahfcff, ahfcid, bbbebcf, bebcbbdb, bebebib, bcbhdbj, bcdeaeb, bcdedbf, bcfifm, bcfiia, cbaac
Sally A adgxfdac, bcdeabea
Sally Ann ahdaadda
Sally A T bcfifjg
Sally B adkebca
Sally G abccgace
Sally W G adahca
Salmon ahgfb, ahgfbg
Salmon Azro Bush ahgfbgc
Sam E adaiiabaac
Samantha adaabdag
Sampson bcdgdaba
Samson M bcdgdafag
Samuel abb, abbe, abbea, abbeacb, abbeaf, abbega, abceabbc, adaaa, adaaafa, adaabd, adaabfa, adaabfx, adabbgd, adabbgs, adabbgsd, adabibl, adaceaae, adaceaaec, adaiec, adaiecb, adadag, adadage, adfc, adfcc, adgcac, adgcacba, adgcacbc, adgcacg, adgfbd, adgfbdea, adgfbgg, adgffca, adk, adkf, adkfba, adkfbbd, adkgab, adkgb, aedaab, Jr ahbaacxca, ahbcha,

ahdf, ahfcab, ahgdc, bbbffc, bbbffcb,
bcb, bcbc, bcbcb, bcbcbaaa, bcbcbb,
bcbcbba, bcbcbbaaa, bcbcbbac, bcb-
eb, bcbebbb, bcbebc, bcbebfa, bcbh-
dgad, bcbhdp, bcdhdpb, bcbhj, bcdg-
daf, bcdgdafmbc, bcfifhi, c, cbaaaa,
cbaaaaa, cbbcb, ccb
Samuel **A** adabbgdaaa
Samuel **Allen** bcbhbgj
Samuel **Alvus** adgcacbab
Samuel **Alonzo** adkebabb
Samuel **B** ahbaacxc
Samuel **Bertram** bbbffcbah
Samuel **Billings** bcdbecee
Samuel **C** adhadcej
Samuel **E** adgxffaa, ahgdcafb
Samuel **Gilman** adaabfaaj
Samuel **H** ahbaacxca, bcbcbaaad
Samuel **Haley** ahbabjj
Samuel **Hall** adgfgab
Samuel **Harris** bbbebga, bbbebgaca
Samuel **Harvey** bcbebbbd
Samuel **Henry** abbeacbd
Samuel **Howard** bcdgdafm
Samuel **J** bbbffcba
Samuel **K** abccgacn
Samuel **Knight** adgfbggb
Samuel **L** adabbgpa
Samuel **Leonard** bcdgdagc
Samuel **Melvin** adgxfafd
Samuel **Moffatt** ahbcabcbb
Samuel **O** bcbebbfac, bcfiib
Samuel **Otis** adaaba
Samuel **P** adabbhed, adaiiaag, adaiia-
agb
Samuel **Phippen** adkdeca, adkdecel
Samuel **Plumer** ahbaaaaa
Samuel **R** ahbgbab
Samuel **Russell** bcdbececa
Samuel **S** adahdc, bbbfhjd
Samuel **Spofford** bcfiib
Samuel **Stillman** cbaaab
Samuel **T** adaaadagfb, adabbgda, ahch-
hc, bcfiib
Samuel **Tilden** adkfbbjeb
Samuel **W** ahgdca
Samuel **Waite** abdceda
Samuel **Whittlesea** ahgdcaf
Sanford ahggb
Saphroneus adacgfac
Sara **Martha** adgfbgebbb
Sarah xac, abbd, abbeacc, abbead, ab-
begbb, abbeh, abc, abcca, abccdcfb,
abcd, abcfd, abdcebee, abdcebh, ab-
dcib, adaaae, wife adaabacaa, adaab-
cba, adabbc, wife adabbgdc, adabbg-
de, adabbgk, adabbgl, adabigb, wife
adacebfa, adacebc, adacfc, wid
adacfe, adadabd, adadaf, adaig-
ah, adailaac, adbf, adfca, adfcdb, ad-
gcab, adgcaccab, adgcagcc, wife adgda, adgfbdec, adgfbecc, wife adgfbfb, wife adgfbha, adgfbi, wife adg-
fdfb, adggbec, adggbh, adggdaad, ad-

gxfaa, adka, adkda, adkfa, adkfbdb,
adkgc, adkgg, aedaaa, ahbaacfe, ah-
baag, ahbabaf, ahbabkxff, wife ahbac, Mrs. ahbb, ahbcaf, wife ahbcx,
ahbgc, ahbgbhc, wife ahbgbx, ahbgig, ahcbeac, ahcbfh, ahchj, ahdd,
ahgdf, ahgdgab, bbbdb, bbbffae, bb-
bfaxc, bbbffadc, bbbfhbxb, bbbfk,
bcbehdba, bcbehg, bcdeaab, bcdecaa,
bcdecahc, bcdece, bcdgdaab, bcdgdabb, bcdgdafah, bcdgdaiica, bcdgded,
bcdgdpe, bcfifjed, bcfifjje, bcfigc,
bcfihdc, ca, cbaaaab, cbaac, cbaag,
wife d, fceaeb
Sarah **A** abccgdh, adaabejc, wife adacgja, adacgjaa, adgfdd, adgxfaaab,
adgxff, adhcdaee, bcdeabea
Sarah **Abigail** adadicca
Sarah **Ann** abccgdcg, abceabed, adada-
bcb, adgfbeja, adkdecm, adkehcc,
ahgfdf, bcdedgc, bcfigfab
Sarah **Augustella** ahgchhbb
Sarah **B** adkebca, ahbabame, bcbegbc
Sarah **Barber** adkdeg
Sarah **Bartlett** adkebac
Sarah **Bradley** bcbehhf
Sarah **Browne** bcfg
Sarah **C** adadabbe, adgfcjbh, adggeig,
adhadca
Sarah **D** bcbhdpe
Sarah **E** wife adabbgabc, adadabbdc,
adadagad, adadhceb, adadibad, adai-
mcdbh, adgfbdbc, adgfbi, adhafaea,
adkddgf, bcbebbcac, bcbeggb, bcde-
bfga, bcdeddac, bcfifhhc
Sarah **Elizabeth** adkdeeg, adkfbebb, ad-
kfbeh, bbbfabmd, bcfigfdb
Sarah **Elizabeth Louisa** bcfifhhg
Sarah **F** abdcebld, adgfbecbd, adgfbf-
ccb, ahgfdai
Sarah **Felch** adaimaf
Sarah **Frances** abdcicaa, adaiebad, ad-
aiiabb, adbabfdeaa, ahgfdagb, fceaa
Sarah **G** adabbgagcb, adadiaa
Sarah **Georgianna** adgcadaaab
Sarah **H** abbegfcb, abccgcfg, adabbgad
Sarah **Helen** adacebba
Sarah **Helena** adhafdgda
Sarah **Holder** adhafdga
Sarah **J** adacedfg, adbabga, adgxfadh,
adhafabd
Sarah **Jane** adbabfbb, adbabfdc, adba-
bfdda, adhafaba, adhagbb
Sarah **L** adkfbbdba, bcfifffh
Sarah **Leah** adaidaef
Sarah **Leona** bcbhdbndc
Sarah **Lincoln** adbabfj
Sarah **Lizzie** abdcebeaa
Sarah **M** adaceaaj, adaceafi, wife ah-
bgea, fceb
Sarah **Marden** adgcacad
Sarah **Melvina** bcbhdbne
Sarah **Mehitable** bcdeabbba
Sarah **Mills** adkfbbf

850

Sarah O adaaaiea
Sarah P adgxfafc
Sarah Peabody adkdbea
Sarah Rebecca gbakb
Sarah T H adaimaaac
Sarah Walker ahbgdfda
Sarepta ahbabada, bcdgdaag
Saul H bbbfhbacb
Savilla A ahbabamh
Scott A adgxfdab
Scott F bbbffafa
Scott J abccgdcfe
Schuyler ahbcabei
Selden Lovett adgfboab
Selenda bcdgdeaaf, bcdgdeada
Selenia adgfbeef
Seraphina Larned bcbcbbgi
Serena adgfbfdb
Seth ahbabkxcc, bcbhddac, bcdgdabddc, bcdgdabgaa
Seth Hinckley adkgae
Sewall abdceba
Sewall B adaimbc, adgxfbg
Sewall E bcbhddceb
Seward ahfcg, ahfcga, ahfegb
Seward H gaaxaxdb
Sewell adacgj, adacgjab, adadhc, adgfbfdc, gaaxaxc
Sewell Lawson adacgje
Sewell Watson adadagaa
Seymour G adacedfi
Sheldon Page abdceblfaa
Shelton Edward adadagabf
Sherburn adhafabb
Sheridan adaabacaah
Sherman adaceddec
Shirley Cheney bcdedbccaa
Shirley Ethel adkgaebfa
Shubal adabbgbeb
Sibbel bededi
Sidney A bcbhdehfb
Sidney Jerome adaabffd
Silas adacebb
Silas Newcomb ahggcd
Silas Wright adadiabc
Simeon abbeee, ahbce, bbbebc, bbbebcda, bcdebfb, bcdebf
Simeon A bcdebfbg
Simeon E adgxfad
Simeon J adgxfdag, adgxffcc
Simeon Low adabbgaii
Simon abce, abccb, abccdg,, abccga, abccgab, abcfh, adgfcdab, adgfcdd, adgfcid, adgfch, aeeac, aeeaea, ahgcia, bbbebcda
Simon B abccgach
Simon Black adgfdaaa
Simon Chase adggegb
Simon Harvey bbbebcdad
Simon Henry adgfcdgab
Smith adadhaab, ahbcabb, bcdgdafee
Smith Emery bcdgdbaada
Smith Glidden adadhabb
Snow H gaaxaxd

Socrates ahbgbe
Solomon adgfbec, ahgci, bcbcab, bcdeca, bedgdaa
Solomon Clement adggdcfb
Solomon G adabbgy
Solon bcfifhka
Sophia adgfbggc, adgfde, adkdde, adkfbbe, ahbgxf, bcbcbbaa, bcbcbbde, bcdgddaad bcdgddad
Sophia Amelia bbbfabbc
Sophia Ann adaimae
Sophia E adgfcih
Sophia Eliza bbbfabhc
Sophia Janet adacgfge
Sophia P adhafgab
Sophia S adabbgxc
Sophronia adacffg, adggefh, ahgdcae, bbbffda
Sophronia Bell bbbffbaae
Sophronia C adggdaab
Sophronia H ahbgbfe
Sophronie bcdgdagcb, bcdgdagk
Spurgeon bcdgdaij
Squiers adadibc
Squire adhafga
Stanley bcdgdeacef
Stanley James bcdgdaalb
Stanley L ahbabaeaed
Stanley M fceafb
Stella adggdade
Stella Willetts adaidaeh
Sterling bbbfabbe, bbbfabbeaa
Sterling Tucker bbbfabbea
Stephen adabbgc, adabbgce, adacebe, adacebf, adgfbdd, adgfbee, adhcbb, adhcbbf, adkdba, adkehba, ahbabjb, ahbcabi, ahcfa, ahcfg, ahfac, bc, bcbehi, bcbhddfaa, bcd, bcdeaa, bcdeab, bcdeabb, bcdecde, bcdecf, bcdee, bcdgdu, bcdi, bcdid, gaa
Stephen Arlon adhafdgcc
Stephen B adabbgddb
Stephen Bean abbegbea
Stephen Franklin adgfbeeg
Stephen H adkgaed, ahbgbxaa
Stephen Henry adhcbbff
Stephen Hinckley adkgaedda
Stephen P adaaba
Stephen Ricker abbegbebbb
Stephen Webster abbegbead
Stephen Y fcei
Stevens M bcbebid
Stewart bcdgdaacf
Stewart Harold bcdgdeafc
Stewart Leitch adaigbbadd
Stillman bcbhddae
Stilson H ahfcfdb
Stilson Hilton ahfcfg
Sumner adgfcjbg, bcdbeccc
Sumner A bcdbeceea
Sumner Adams abbegbib, abbegbibeb
Sumner E adabbgaigi
Sumner W adaabfaacc
Surilla adacgfaa

851

311

Susan wife abbcgfk, abccgcaa, adaabac-
ad, adadhx, adaiiab, wife adgfbga, ad-
ggdaaa, adgxfadcb, adkehi, adkfbab,
adkgdbb, adkgdeb, wife ahbaaab, ah-
baaac, ahbaacdc, ahbaacxa, ahbaah, ah-
bghb, ahcfjc, ahchfee, ahdabb, ahf-
cfccc, wife bbbfhba, bbbfhbxcc, bb-
bfhcda, bcbhddfae, bcdebgad
Susan Adams bcdedfh
Susan B bcdebfgc
Susan C adhadcda, adkehbd
Susan Celia adaabfxb
Susan Clough ahbaee
Susan E adaimf, adgxfad, adkecbai
Susan Emma adbcicac
Susan F adkehbd
Susan Frances adggdccaf
Susan Gilman adgfbfca
Susan H bcficalg
Susan Hammond ahfcaad
Susan Hines bcbcbbgb
Susan Huntington adkdbee
Susan J adaimea, adgxffc
Susan Jane adaimaag, adaimca
Susan Jeannette adgxfadi
Susan Lydia adhafdgcb
Susan M abccgaeb, adgfbejg, adkgdbab
Susan Maria adkdeab
Susan Perkins adgfbeh
Susan R adaimf, bbbfhjba
Susan Rena bbbfhjba
Susan Rockwell adkdecei
Susan S bbbfhag
Susan Viola abccgacaaaa
Susan W adabbbba
Susan Watson adkfbee
Susan White adacgia
Susanna abbegba, adaaba, adggaa,
wife ah, bbbebb, bbbfff, bcbebeb,
bcbebia, bcbehf, wife bcdb, wife bcd-
hc, bcdie, bcfic
Susanna Hoyt bcficaj
Susannah adabbgi, adfd, adkgda, ahc-
fh, ahgfa, bcbhdbk, bcbhh
Susia M adaabfd, adgfdaaae
Susie B adkfbbjdg
Susie Beckman adkfbbjdd
Susie Ethel adadagfab
Susie Etta adaigaaad
Sweet G adahdd
Swett G adahdd
Sybil adacebd, adacee, ahbabaefc
Sybil Ellen adaabdabeab
Sybil Marian adabbbdcec
Sygnoria adabbghba
Sylvana adaimeab
Sylvanus ahbgidb, bbbffagb
Sylvanus P adabbbhb
Sylvester ahggbd, ahggbbba
Sylvester E ahbgbxba
Sylvester J adgcadaff
Sylvester M ahggbba
Sylvester N ahbabcfa
Sylvester W bcdgef

Sylvia adaigbbd
Sylvia Chase adggegbad
Sylvia Lincoln bcbhdbnaca
T George bcdgej
Tabitha abbef, abdcebf, adgxe, ahghf,
wife bbbffcd, bbbffcda
Tabitha Blake abdcebcc
Talbot J adiambiac
Talmadge bcdgdaijaa
Talmon bcdgdaah
Taylor abccgae
Terence Powderly bcbhddkbxa
Thaddeus Ladd bcfifjh
Thaddeus Mason abdcedd
Thankful bcbhddcx, bcbhdde
Thankful P bcdgdaic
Thayer bcdebga
Thelda S bcbhddkbxj
Thelma bbbfhcfka
Thelma A adaigbbacd
Thelma Dorothy bcbhddccbh
Theodate adaidba
Theodora gbakh
Theodore ahgchjc
Theodore B bbbfhcfk, bbbfhcfkc
Theodore Burt ahbabamgb
Theodore E adabbgabdd
Theodore H adaceam
Theodore Moses adadabca
Theodore W bcdebfbad
Theodosia B adadabbdbc
Theophilus bcbhddd
Theophilus S adgfbdba
Theresa adacffef, bcdgdakbc
Theresa C bcdgdaiad
Theresa E bcdgdaiih
Theresa M ahbabajade
Theresa V bcdgdafl
Thirza Leavitt adkebdb
Thirza Richards ahgfbdaa
Thomas x, xa, xaae, xab, aa, adabbgab,
adabbhd, adaimad, adgfbm, adi, ah,
ahbabaedb, ahbca, ahbcab, ahbcab-
fd, ahcbe, ahd, ahdaba, ahdad, ahdg,
ahfcfc, ahfcfcb, b, bb, bba, bbbd,
bbbfhb, bbbfaxd, bcbehdbc, bcbhd-
ba, bcbhddfab, bcbhde, bcbhdec, bc-
dgdaaea, bcdig, bcfica, bcficaa,
(Capt.) cca
Thomas A bbbfhcfl
Thomas Arnold adgxfaaa
Thomas Augustus bcdebeh
Thomas B bcfifjag
Thomas E bcbhdgagf
Thomas H bbbfaxbc
Thomas Henry Clay ahbcabae
Thomas J bcdgdaalce
Thomas Jefferson abccgchad, abceabde,
ahbcabe, ahbcabea, ahbgee, ahdadg,
bcdeaef
Thomas K bcbhdga
Thomas Kalapon ahcbef
Thomas Kempis bcbhdb
Thomas Kennedy bcbhdb

Thomas Leavitt adkdej
Thomas M bcbhddfaaa
Thomas Russell bcbhdgagfg
Thomas Sargent ahgfbf
Thomas Saunders adabbga
Thomas Shepard adacfe
Thomas Usher adkdeaf
Thomas Wellington ahbcajd
Thomas Wooster adadhcc
Thompson Faxon adgfbgfaad, adgfbgfaada
Thornton adabbghf
Thurlough adabbgbe
Thursa bcdgdeade, bcdgdaiad
Thurston adabbghf
Thurston Willis adabbgya
Tilotus adfcdcb
Timothy abccdgc, adbabgad, bcbe, bcbebb, bcbebbc, bcbebbca, bcbef, bcbegh, bcda
Tirza ahgcac
Tirzah Ann Robinson abbegbie
Tobias G bcdgdea
Tom bcbhddfacg
Tressa bcdgdafed
Tressie Emma adaiiabaaa
Tristram adaimb, adaimba, adgxfd
Tristram Coffin ahbaed
Tristram E adgxfdad
Tristram L adgxfda
Tristram T ahbaedc
True Langley adkeabb
True M adgfcdacg
True Perkins adkecba
Truman M adgfbejd
Tryphena adgfbeee, ahbgbfg, ahgffd
Turner Fairbanks bcdeddhdca
Tyler E adaimaaabab
Tyler T bcfiffdcb
Tyrus bcdedb
Udolphus ahcbfc
Ula bcdebgagbb
Ula May bcdebgage
Ulysses abgfde, ahgha
Ulysses G adgfbfbaa
Umadilla ahbcabaeb
Urban bcdgen
Urbana ahgdcac
Uzziel ahcfja
Valentine P abceabcb
Van Rennsalear ahbabajab
Van Renssellear ahbabajb
Varis adaceaaia
Vata adggdccaf, bcdgdeafc
Vaughn bcdgdafece
Velma bcdgdabgg
Vera E adkgdbadb
Vera M gaaxaxia
Vera Madeline adabbgaicba
Verlie Veldine bcbhddccbea
Vermelia C bcdeddaa
Verne Elmer adaceafged
Vernie adaceahfb
Vernon bcdecdbab, bcfiffdcbb

Vernon T bcdecdbaea
Vernon Thayer bcbhdbndhb
Victoria bcbhddaf
Victoria Jane ahbabaje
Victor Eugene adgfcdabd
Victor W ahbabahfc
Victor W T adabbgaje
Vienna adaieaad
Villa adaimaaab, adaimbbda
Villa Gertrude adbabfecb
Vinal Curtis gbefaaa
Vinal Williams abccgchabe
Vinton bbbfhcflb
Viola Maud bcdebgaga
Violet bcdeaefadaa
Violet O bcdgdaiif
Vira abccgachc
Virgil ahbabajaga, ahcbca, bcdedfd
Virgil Maro ahcbcca
Virginia adaiiaaeda, bcdedbccbb
Virginia Alice adkgddgae
Virginia Grace adabbgtaca
Virginia Irene bcbhdbndmb
Virginia Lathrop abdcebeaja
Virginia Madeline bbbfhcfgh
Virginia Seaton adaceafgej
Viva L ahbabajgac
Vivian bcdgdafkib, bcdgdeacfb
Vivian Jennie abccgcfcaab
Vivien Arline abccgcfdeb
Von Carl adadhacad
Vona bcdgdafga
W Newton ahchfeca
Wadleigh adkddh
Waldo Hayward ahbaacfba
Wallace ahbabeafb
Wallace E adaaaaccac
Wallace Edwin adadhcahcb
Wallace Eugene adaceagce
Wallace Gilmore bcbhddccbg
Wallace H bcdbececbb
Wallace Hanscom adbcebcabb
Wallace L adkfbede, bcdbaddda
Wallace Lee adkgaebca
Wallace Luther adaabdaeb
Wallace Silas adggegbaf
Wallace T adabbgaigba
Walter abbegfjbc, adacefa, adadibabb, bbbfhbxce, bcbhdhhb, bcdedkae
Walter Abraham befifjjaa
Walter Amsden abdcicad
Walter B adaimcdbf, adkfbbjaa
Walter Brooks bcdbeced
Walter Curtis bcfiibadb
Walter E adadibcad, adgfdabba, adhafagba, ahbgilia, bcbebbfaaa, bcbhddaab
Walter Earl ahchfecf
Walter Edward adkgaeddb
Walter Emerson adaceafgga
Walter F ahbaacdac
Walter Francis ahbcacbac
Walter George bcbebbcdaxa

Walter Gillingham bcbhddecbj
Walter Guy bcdgdakbb
Walter H adgfgaba
Walter Hay bcdgddah
Walter John adaceafga
Walter Jonathan adhafgcea
Walter K bededkdad
Walter L ahbcabead, bbbfhbxc
Walter Philips adhcdac
Walter Raleigh abbegbeae
Walter Scott bbbfhcf, bbbfhcfc, bbbf-
  hcfkd, bcbebbcdaf
Walter S bbbfhcffa
Walter Simon adggegbae
Walter Talbott ahbgimb
Walter Ware abdcicada
Walter Wheeler Bell ahbcacbabe
Wanda adacgfebaa
Warren adaceaadb, adacedd, bcbhddab,
  bcdecahb
Warren C adaceddcb
Warren H adabbgabde
Warren Hoyt bcbebbbdb
Warren Kinsman adadagabba
Warren L adaceddb
Warren MacLennan adaceddcba
Warren O adabbgaija, ahbabajid
Warren Preble bcfiibada
Warren Quincy ahbaaaac
Warren Roland adabbgaiid
Warren Woodbury adaimbbd
Washington bcdgddaaa
Waterman L bcbhddib
Wayne Burchard ahbgbfabba
Wealthea bcdedke
Weare adhcdaaa, adkdbb, adkdbc, ad-
  kddga
Webster adgfdacd, bcbebbcdae
Webster M bcdedbad
Weber Beach ahchfeba
Wellington ahbabkxaa, bcdgdabg, bcd-
  gdeaj
Welthy ahgfbc
Welthy J ahccgcfa
Wesley Carlos bcbhdbndha
Wesley E bcdgdsab
Wesley J bcdgdbj
Wesley S ahbabjiea
Wesley Summerfield ahgdhbc
Wesley W adhafaga
Westley adabibccca
Weston W adbabfbgb, bcbhddbb
Weston Wesley adbabfbf
Weymouth F adaigbbadc
Whitcher ahbcabd, ahbcabf
Wilbur A bcdbadddb
Wilbur Edgerton bcbehhgbc
Wilbur Edward bcbhbfiad
Wilbur F fceabb
Wilbur O adgfdabbc
Wilda Persis bcbhddaabb
Wildemina adaimcdbc, adaimcdbd
Wilder B bcdeaaaaa
Wilfred bcdgdaieaa

Wilfred B bcdgdnd
Will C ahbcabeab
Will Corning bcdedceaa
Will S adkecbad
Willard ahfcic, bcbhdbnacc, bcbhdbnh,
  bcbhdbnhb, bcdgdafac
Willard Alfred adhcbbfbb
Willard Alvin adaimbil
Willard B bcdgdafecc
Willard C adacedfe
Willard Clare adggeile
Willard Elbert adkfbbciba
Willard Elbridge bcdeddhd
Willard Frank adkfbbcib
Willard H ahbabahcc
Willard Hall bcdeabbb
Willard Henry abbeebcaac
Willard Jefferson adbabfdea
Willard Sawyer adabbgbcc
Willard W bcdeddbc
Willard Wellman bcbhdbnac
William x, xaah, abccgdca, abccgcfka,
  adabbgax, adabbgsf, adabbgt, adab-
  bgtacc, adaceaadc, adaceafd, adacea-
  hfa, adacedf, adadibabc, adadibd, ad-
  aigab, adaigaj, adaiiaaeb, adaimc,
  adgcacb, adgcad, adgfbegg, adgfbfd,
  adgfdaa, adgfdd, adggeb, adggefg,
  adggefgb, adhafdih, Jr dakehbb, adkehe, ahbabaedc, ahbaedc, ahbcabac,
  ahbcacf, ahbcachb, ahbgbh, ahbgbxh,
  ahcbbb, ahfa, ahfcc, ahfcf, ahfcfa,
  ahgdh, bbbebcdaaab, bbbfac, bbbfhbx, bbbfhcga, bbbfhjca, bcbcbaaaaa,
  bcbcbbd, bcbcbeh, bcbebb, bcbcbbec,
  bcbebbf, bcbhddfaaf, bcbhddk, bcbhdn, bcdbadddba, bcdgececc, bcdeae-
  aa, bcdeaeca, bcdecdfb, bcdgdaaec,
  bcdgdafea, Jr bcdgddab, bcdgdma, bcdgds, bcdgel, bcdhd, bcfifag, bcfiff-
  ga, bcfifhi, cbaaaad, cca, (Dowe)
  cca, f, fc, gbaib, gbb
William A adabbgv, adadagfc, adaiia-
  aga, adkecbaca, adkecbacab, ahbgild.
William Albert adkfbbdfa, adkgaeddc
William Alfred adgfbgfdab
William Allen adabbgtac, adgfbeggab
William Arthur adkfbbdfaa
William Auburn bcdbaddaa
William B adacgle, adhafag, ahbcajgc,
  ahgdhdf
William Boynton abbegbdb
William Bradford adgcacbj
William Bryce ahbgbfaab
William Burns adaidaeb
William C abccgcfk, ahgfbdgcb, bbbfa-
  xg, bcbhdbnab
William Cary bcficanb
William Chase adggeha
William Chenery adhcbbgda
William Chester ahchfec
William Clark ahbgbbeaaa
William Cobb adbabga
William D adabbgagce, ahchfigb

William **Deming** adggdcib
William **Dexter** bcdeabbc, bcdeabbd
William **Dwight** adaabdabea
William **E** adaabclc, adhafgcbb, adha-
hedd, ahgciaca, bcdgeha, gaaxaxg-
gbai
William **Edward** bcbebbcaa, bcbhddec-
fa
William **Edwin** adaabfdi
William **Everett** adhaheb
William **F** adaceaeba, adaceaebaa, ad-
gfbn
William **Farmer** bcbehdb
William **Franklin** bcbhddccbe
William **G** adaabfg, ahbgbadea
William **Gilman** adaabfaa
William **Gould** adkfbebch
William **H** abccdgcaaa, abccgchab, ad-
abbgbc, adabbgdb, adgcadaaaa, adg-
fbe, adgfbea, adgfbgdc, adgfcdaca,
ahbaacxac, ahbabjecac, ahbabkbb,
ahbcabcbc, ahbcabeg, ahgcibcb, bbb-
ffcdf, bbbfhcfg, bcbebbfab, bcdebef,
bcdebgah
William **Hammond** adhccbbeb
William **Harrison** adaabfd
William **Harry** adhcbbjdc
William **Henry** abbegbeab, abccdgdc,
adabbgqd, adabbgqdh, adbabgaa, ad-
hafabg, adhafdge, adkdech, adkecb-
aac, bcdedgg, bcfigfbd, gbaicb
William **Henry Harrison** adkfbbce, bc-
fifjak
William **Hervey** ahbabjec
William **Hilton** ahbabjcf
William **Holker** adgxfaaecb
William **Hunt** bcbhddcc
William **J** bcdgdaaac
William **James** adgfcdacbb
William **K** ahbgbxac, ahbgbxaca, bcb-
cbaaaaa
William **Kingsley** bcbcbaaaa
William **L** ahgdcagc
William **Lawrence** adkgddgad
William **Lawton** adkecbad
William **Leonard** bcdedceaab
William **Leslie** adacffice, bcdgdaaaba
William **Little** ahbchga
William **Lovett Walker** abdcebeh
William **Lowell** bcfiibch
William **M** adbabgaad, adgfdg, Jr adg-
fdh, adkecbaac,, bbbebcdaacb
William **McAdam** adhcbbgdab
William **Mellvill** adbabfeb
William **Mitchell** adgfcdac
William **Montgomery** adhafag
William **Moody** bcfiibcib
William **Morrison** abdcicae
William **N** bcfifhi
William **Newton** bcbhdbn
William **North** bcbhdbndb
William **P** ahbcajj, bbbfhac
William **Pease** adggdccb
William **Prescott** bcdeaefb

William **Robert** abbegbdbg
William **S** bbbfhjd, bcbhddja
William **Salley** ahbgbbe
William **Sampson** adgcacbac
William **Sargent** bcbcbaaagaa
William **Segee** bcdgdabda
William **Sheridan** bcdgddalb
William **Snow** abdcebead, abdcebeaj
William **Stanley** adaceagcd
William **Seele** adhaheab
William **Swett** adaimaac
William **Thurman** ahbcabeac
William **V** adabbdcee
William **W** adabbbdcw, adabbgaif, ad-
babgaa, ahgfdaf, ahgfdaj, ahggbbb,
bcbcbaaabc, bcdeaefad
William **Wales** ahbgii
William **Wallace** abceabdj, adabbgaigb,
ahbgii
William **Ward** adaiebae
William **Wellman** bcbhdbna
William **Wilder** adaabfaac
William **Winship** adaimaaaba
Willette adabbhn
Willie bcficalcc, gaxaxa
Willie **M** adabbbdcg
Willie **N** adkddgca
Willie **T** abccgaeab
Willie **Warren** bcdgdnc
Willis **E** adabbgdda
Willis **M** adgfbgeaf
Willis **O** adabbgdd
Wilmot **A** bcdgdbaag
Wilmot **Edwards** bbbfabmaa
Wilmot **Sewall** bbbfabma
Wilmot **Stevens** bbbfabmaaa
Wilsie adaabdabcd
Wilson adkgdba, ahbabahcb, ahbabk-
xea
Wilson **Eliot** bcdedbbdh
Wilson **Everett** adkgdbacb
Wilson **J** ahbabajl
Wilson **N** abccgdfb
Winfield **M** adabbgx
Winfield **Scott** adabbgabdf
Winifred **Elizabeth** bcbhdbndhd
Winnie **Robbins** adgfgabd
Winnifred gbfeaaf
Winnifred **Etta** bcbhddcbc
Winona gbfeaag
Winona **Louise** bcbhddiaabb
Winslow adaabfe
Winthrop adadab, adha, adhab, adhadc,
adhafa, adhafae, adhah
Winthrop **Griffin** adadabcfab
Winthrop **Norris** adadabcf
Winthrop **Phila** adhadce
Winthrop **Sanborn** adadabce
Winthrop **Y** abccgacj
Worrall **C** ahbaeddbd
Worthford **L** adacedhc
Zacchaeus adahda, adaime
Zachaeus adaiiaac, adaim
Zada adacffeac

Zada Mary bcdebgagc
Zadick bbbebcd
Zaida M adaimbhbc
Zebediah Barker bcdbadd
Zebulon adaabce, adaij, adaijb, ahba-
aa, ahbaacd, ahbabaed, ahbabje, bcd-
gdabf
Zelinda Josephine adabbgbch
Zelliah bcficac, bcficag
Zelpha adaik, adaimbe, adkehj
Zelpha Ann adaimbab, adhedaea
Zelphia adgxfdb, adkfbbb, adkfbbba
Zenas adacgk
Zera adgfcdada
Zetta A bedebgbf
Zillah bcdbac, bcdbadf
Zilphana bcfifjae
Zimri bcbhddad
Zopher adail
Zula bcdgdaijc
—— bcdeaa, (Miss) geb
DOWLING Edgar gbaiab
Ida May gbaiab
DOWNE Johannah adadagabc
DOWNER Betsey adkfbb
—— ade
DOWNEY Archibald W ahbabalc
Aurora E ahbabalc
Florence E ahbabalc
George bcdgdafba
Henry E ahbabalc
Herbert A ahbabalc
John ahbabalc
John A ahbabalc
Stella A ahbabalc
Stella A ahbabalc
William B ahbabalc
DOWNING Bessie E adhafdic
Betsey L adhafae
Clarence Victor Blossom abbegbda
Ellen Antoinette abbegbda
Elsie T adhafdic
Fred O adhafdic
Fred S ahbaaheab
Herbert A adhafdic
John C abbegbda
Joseph Henry abbegbda
Katherine W adkdeceb
Lydia Ann ahbaahaeb
Mabel P akebdbbfe
Olive F adhafdic
Oscar adhafdic
Thomas adkdeceb
DOWNS Betsey adkfbb
Daniel adaceaebb
Elzada H wid ahbabaed
Harriet B adaceaebb
Henrietta aeeaecc
Margaret adaieb
DOWEST Henry abcead
Isaac abcead
John abcead
John H adgfcdh
Martha J abcead
Ozem J abcead

DOYLE George W adaabacah
Katherine Elizabeth adbabfeaa
Sarah adgfbgfaa
DRAKE Abra A akebdbbgc
Abraham (Capt) abccd, (Col) akebc
Almira akecafk
Alpheus adgfcda
Bradley akecafk
Cotton W abceaba
Data abceabe
E C ahgff
Deborah wife abbegbi
Edward J ahgfbdb
Hannah abbeaa
Hannah Goss abbegbi
Harriet adgffa
James (Maj) akecb
John abceaba
Jonathan abceabe, akecb
Martha adkgaef
Mary L B adadicd
Nathaniel (Dea) abbegbi
Phillipe akebdbbgc
Sarah Emeline akecafk
DRAPER Levy M bcdeaedb
Lucy P bcdeaedb
Thomas J bcdeaedb
DREW Angie abccgcha
Catherine Jane adhahecd
Charles Kenneth adhahecd
Edwin bcfifhe
Isadore abccgchad
James H adhahecd
Joseph adhahecd
Loranah Sanborn bbbfabi
Moses bbbfabi
Richard Earl adhahecd
Robert adhahecd
Sarah adgfdab
Susan M abccdgca
DRINKWATER Etta S ahbabaeda
Katie L ahbabaeda
Lewis J ahbabaeda
Helen M ahbabaeda
Ralph L ahbabaeda
Walter ahbabaeda
Zebulon Dow ahbabaeda
DRISCOLE Frank E ahgcigc
DRISCOLL Catherine M adhafgcbd
Margaret bcbcbaaba
DRUMMOND Charles L bcbhdhhb
Ellery D bcbcbbgf
Edwin F bcbcbbgf
Harvey T ahbcajdc
Henry bcbcbbgf
Horatio adgfbi
John H abccgdfaa
Joshua bcbcbbgf
Mary bcbhddha
Mary Margaret abccgdfaa
Nellie Louise bcbhdhhb
Roy C ahbcajdc
Thomas ahbcajdc
Walter H adgfbi
DRYER Henry adhafcabd

Mary adhafcabd
DUDLEY Augusta M adgfcjbc
Daniel adka
Elvira adacgk
Joseph (Gov) bcbehhi
Lavina adhafb
Paul (Gov.) ahbaa
Samuel adka
Sarah abbege
DUFF Mary adadhcahb
DUFFIELD Anna adkdece
DUN Elizabeth bca
DUNBAR G W ahbchda
DUNCAN Alexander bcdgdakfe
Christy bcdeaba
Henry B adbabgc
Sarah ex
William adaceaaea
—— (Capt) abccdf
DUNHAM Abbie H ahbabadc
Angie ahbabadc
Eben J ahbabadc
Effie ahbabadc
Elizabeth Anna ahbabaefc
Henry Augustus ahbabaefc
Joseph adgfcdi
Levi B ahbabadc
Orin C ahbabaefc
William H ahbabadc
—— ahchec
DUNLAP Cyrene bbbffcba
D M abccgdfba
James bbbffcba
DUNN Addie Mary bcbcbbgf
Carrie A ahbcajdc
DUNNING George F bbbfabbd
Mary Elizabeth bbbfabbd
DUNPHY Burton L bcdgdanb
DUNSTER Caleb Emery adgfbeh
Eliza Annie adgfbeh
Edward Swift adgfbeh
Jason adgfbeh
Mary Susan adgfbeh, adgfbehb
Samuel adgfbeh
DUNTON Lucy adadage
Samuel bbbfhg
DUPUY Elsa adggdcca
John adggdcca
DURANT Emma F bcdeaebba
Mary adhccbb
Sallie Robinson adaabfxa
Sophia adaabde
DURFEY Clarissa wid adhaff
DURGIN Betsey adadagf
Eliza abbegfgada
Gardner adadaba
Gardner D adadabf
Hannah bcbcbbga
Harriett T adadaba
Henry G adkddcaa
Jonathan adadaba
Mary A adadaba
Mary D adadabf
Nathaniel adadaba
Olive J adadaba

Samuel adadaba
Sarah adadaba
DURKEE Bartholomew (Capt) adggdc, (Col) adkfbeb
Benton Storrs ahgfbdg
Eda Dowe ahgfbdg
Elisha ahgfbdg
Elton Silas ahgfbdg
Ethel Hayes ahgfbdg
Samuel T ahgfbdg
DUSHANE Josephine adabbgaigb
DUSTIN Hannah Mrs. bcc
Nabby bcdedh
Sarah adaiiaba
Simeon bcdedh
Thomas bcfifk
DUSTON Elizabeth bb
DUTTON Alice ahbgbfabb
Carrie adaabclc
Edward W adkebgh
Jacob S adkebgh
John W ahbgbfabb
Lucinda Jane adkebgh
DWELLEY Mary bbbffdb
DWIGHT Clara M adkehcc
Henry L adkehcc
DYER Caroline adgfbgfd
Emily N bcdebfbe
George adbabfbd
Mary D eaabb
EAGAN Rose adgcaccag
EAMES Lydia exa
EASTKOOT ahfca, ahfci
EASTMAN Alpheus bcdeabda
Betsey wife bcdeabda
Ebenezer ahbgf
Elias adggeig
Hannah bcbea
Helen M adgfcicdc
Jane Ambrose bcfiffc
Jehemiah adkfbbde
John L adgfcicdc
Jonathan befifjac
Joseph F bcdeabe
Mary Ann adaigaacb, bcdeabda
Nathaniel C bcfihdd
Otis adaimbae
Sarah bcdeabe
William adgfbb
—— bcdeaeh
EASTON Mary abc
Sarah abb
EATON Abbie adgcaccaf
Abbie V adgxfaaca
Abner L adgxffcb, adhchaaa
Adeline adgxffbba
Alice J adhchaaa
Almon adgxffag
Amos bcbehaa
Benjamin adgca
Betsey adkfbd, bcbehaa, bcficc
Betsey A adgxfaacb
Betsey J wife adkfbbja
Caleb adgxfaaca, adgxfaacb
Caroline bcbhddiaa

857

317

Charles E adgxfaaccb
Charles W adaimcdf
Charlotte adgxfab
Christina adgxfdaba
Climena adgxfdab
Cora E abccgdck
Dorothy adkfba
E F bcdedbbbi
Eben bcfifk
Eliza wife adgxffcc
Elsie adhafdia
Elvira Jane adhahf
George bcbehaa, bbbffaga
George B adaimbcbd
George F adkehk
Gilman adaimcdd
Hannah adail
Hattie akebbce
Helen adgfboa
Hiram abccgdfb, bcfifjb
Izora adabbbcce
Jabez adgxfaa
Jacob adaaai, adhahf
Jacob F adgxffcc
James adgfboa, bcbehg
James L adaimcdg
Jedida adkfba
Jeremiah adgxfada
John adaimcc, b
Jonathan adabbb, adabbd, **adgxfaa**
Joshua M adaimcf
Judith adkfba
King bcbehaa
Lillian M adgxffcc
Liona D adkfbbja
Lola M adaimbbeb
Louisa J wife adgxfaaca, **adgxfaacb**
Lucinda ahgfdd
Lulu A adgxfaaccb
Lydia A adaimcd
Lydia M adgffa
Mariam adkfbd
Mary adadhaa
Mary A adgxfdab
Mary B adaimbhc
Mary E adaimbiad
Mary L adgxffag
Mehitable wid adgx
Mehitable Williams bcbehaa
Melissa Dow adgxfadh
Moses Williams bcbehaa
Nancy adkeh, adkehk
Nancy E abccgdfb
Oliver adkehd
Philena R wife adgxffcb
Rhoda adgca, adgxfada, **adgxfb**
Ruth adgxfab
Ruth Ann bcbehaa
Sally A adgxfdab
Samuel adgxfae
Samuel C adgxfdab
Sarah wife adgxfaa
Sarah A adgxfaa, adaimc
Sarah M adgxffcb
Simeon L adgxfaj

Sophronia ahbabcd
Susia M adgxfdab, adgxfdaf
Thomas adgx, adhal, Jr. adhal, adkfbb-
 ja
Wells H adkehbg
William (Maj) adabb, adkfbd
William C adhccbbec
William E adgxfadh
William True adgxfadh
ECHERT C A adhafdge
ECKLEY Betsey bcfihec
EDDY F B adacgfc
 Jonathan (Col) bcdg
 Nellie R ahbabeada
EDE Antoinette *adaceaaf*
 Clayton adaceaaf
 Elizabeth adaceaaf
 Leland adaceaaf
 Richard adaceaaf
EDGAR John bbbebcf
EDGCOMB Sarah H adgfdd
EDGERLY Carroll D ahbabajm
 Judith adadaba
 Kathryn E ahbabjm
 Reuben E ahbabjm
EDGERTON Wales L bcbehhga
EDMANDS Cora adkedl
EDMUNDS Elsie wife adaieca
 Gardner adaieca
 Nancy F adaieca
 Polly akecb
 —— ahbcabeh
EELS Cynthia ahgdh
EDWARDS Arlene bcdgdafed
 Bessie bcdgdafed
 Blanche bcdgdae
 Eliza bcdgdae
 Elizabeth A bbbfabma
 Ella Watson bcdebeea
 Frank Elmer ahfcfdba
 George H ahfcfdba
 Helen bcdgdafed
 Hepzibah adabibca
 Hurd M bcdgdabdd
 James bcdgdae
 James A ahfcaaaf
 Jessie E bcdgdafed
 Joseph abccgchab
 Lena bcdgdad, bcdgdae
 Lillie ahfgbdg
 Lucinda A abccgchab
 Mabell bcdgdafed
 Robert bcdgdae
 Russel bcdgdafed
 Theophilus bcdgdae
 Thomas bcdgdae
 Walter bcdgdae
 Wilmot bcdgdafed
EGGLESTON —— ahchfij
ELBERSON —— bcdgdaidd
ELBRIDGE Frank Lowe abbegbdd
ELDRED Charles adacedha
ELDRIDGE Betsey D ahbabai
 Charles W ahbabajadb
 Ensign ahbabai

Fred adkfbbjbe
Helen M adkfbbjbe
Henry S ahbabai
Job Dow ahbabai
Lucinda ahbabai
Luther E ahbabai
Mabel adkfbbjbe
Rebecca abccgdce
Wallace J adaabdaba
Warren ahbabajadb
Willard Samuel adaabdah
Wilson E ahbabai
—— adgfcja
ELKINS Henry (Capt) abccd, adkde,
akebb, bcdb
Mary abccac, akecafh
Nellie E abccgacl
ELIOT Bertha bcdedbbd
ELLIOTT Alice M adabibcae
Bessie bcbhdbndm
Eliza Jane bbbffcf
George W bbbffcf
Hannah adkebb
Ida S abccdgcbb
Jane bcdeaeae
James bcfihf
John adabibcae
John James bcfihf
John Sawyer bbbffcf
John W abccdgcbb
Joseph bcfihb
Mary Maria bbbffcf
Maty A bcfihf
Myrtle bcdgdagf
Olive bbbebfj
Priscilla A bcbebbfab
Rachel bcdeaef
Sarah F bbbebdaca
William Plummer bcbebbfab
—— (Com) ahcbfeb, bbbdb
ELLIS Adaline adgged
Beatrice bcdgdanee
Carrie Swift adhcbbfb
Chase Dow adgged
Dyer adgged
Ellen wid abbegbeab
Frank (Rev) bcbhdbnh
George Frank adhcbbfa
Harriet adgged
Harty ahdaaf
Lydia adgged
Mabel Thompson adhcbbfa
Mary Ann adgged
Matthew adgged
Noah adgged
Rachel adgged
Richard adacealc
Sabra adgged
Sarah Ann adgged
Thomas bcdgdanee
Warren adgged
William adabbhh
ELSMORE Adella C ahbgbeb
John ahbgbeb

ELLSWORTH Caroline adkfbei, ahbg-
bjx
Isaac N ahbaahdd
Levi ahbgbjx
Lydia Stoughton adaceaada
Pinckney Webster ahcbccb
—— adkfbej
ELLWELL Ellen Augusta bcbhdhha
Frank bcbhdhha
EMERSON Abigail adgfe
Adaline Martin adaceafa
Addie S akebdbbga
Alice A bcfigdcb
Anna adgfe
Annie abceabed
Arthur Mahlon bcfiibca
Betsey bcfifjj
Catherine adgfe
Charlotte adkebe
Daniel adaceafa, bcfiibca
Daniel (Capt) bcdeaa, bcdeb
Eliphalet adadagb
Ernestine bcdgdaacda
Evelyn bcdedcaa
Fenner H bcbebba
Frances Martin adaceafa
Frank W bcfiibca
Hannah Eaton bcfihed
Harriet bcdedcaa
Harvey Webster bcdedcaa
Henry adadabbda
James bcfifhe
Jeremiah abccgcfh
Jesse adgffa
John adaceafa
John L adgffa
Joseph adgfe, befih
Lizetta adadabbda
Louisa Maria adhaff
Mahala D bcdbaddl
Marden, Marden Jr. adgffa
Mary abccgae
Mary Jane adgffa
Mary P bcbebcbc
Myron E bcfiibca
Moses bcdedcaa
Phoebe bcfih
Ralph W bbbfabmf
Samuel adgfe
Smith (Capt) bcbeg
Solomon adgfe, adgffa
Timothy bcfihed
William Alonzo bcfiibca
William Philander adaceafa
EMERTON Augusta abccgdcec
John I adadhcbb
William Warren adadhcbb
EMERY Abigail akecah
Ada Flagg akecahhe
Annie Laurie abbeebbca
Benjamin abbeh
Charles bbbfa
Daniel abbeh
Eliza Ann bbbfa, bbbfh
Ella May abbeebbca

859

Florence L ahbabajae
Frank M bcdeaedba
Henry Warren abbeebbca
Isaac abbeebbca
Jonathan Rounds adhafabe
Judith bbbfa
Laura A adhafabe
Mary bbbfh
Russell J ahbabajae
Samuel T akecahhe
Willard (Lieut) akecah
EMMONS Caroline wife adgfbfde
Eliakim adgfbfde
Sadie G adgfbfde
ENGLAND Margaret xa
ENGLISH Albert G adkfbbdba
George W adkfbbdba
ENRIGHT Sarah bcdgek
ERSKINE Abbie Rebecca bcbhddn
Alexander bcbhddn
Alexander Edward bcbhddn
Caroline Dow bcbhddn
Clara Belle bcbhddn
Cyrus Henry bcbhddn
Edward Alexander bcbhddn
Fairfield bcbhddn
Isaac Austin bcbhddn
John bcbhddn
John Franklin bcbhddn
Julia Maria bcbhddn
Lloyd Quimby bcbhddn
Mary Ellen bcbhddn
Rebecca Abbie bcbhddn
Sewall Rogers bcbhddn
ERVING Edwin bcfifffe
ESTES Dana Jr. adggdadaa
Lucius D adabiggdc
William H adgfbeca
ESTEY George bcdgdeadc
Levda ahbaacdad
—— bcdgdef, bcdgdi
EVANS Adeline adgfbea
Ann adgfbea
Belinda adgfbea
Benjamin adgfbea
Benjamin Endicott adgxfbeb
Daniel adgfba
Eliza adgfbea
Emmogene adgfcdacaa
Estwick adgfbea
Jeremiah adgfbea
Joseph adgfbea
Josiah abdcebl
Lorenzo adgfbea
Lydia adgfba, adkeac
Mary adgfbea
Mary Ann abdcebl
Nathaniel adgfbea
Orrin L adgfbggb
Samuel Dunster adgfbea
Sarah F adadha
Sarah O wife adaaaiea
Stephen bcfifjb
Susan adgfbea
William H adaaaiea

EVARTS Mary Ann abdcebl
EVELYN Cora E bcfifhhhb
Samuel J bcfifhhhb
EVERETT Cornelia W ahgfdd
Daniel bcbhddaab
Edward bcficada
Harriet R bcbhddaab
Hattie adkgaeddb
Mary Adeline adhafagb
Rebecca ahgf
Thomas Huse bcficada
EWER Rose ahbabadc
EYRES Nicholas (Rev.) edy
FABENS Lydia abceabb
FABYAN Elizabeth abceabd
Lydia abceabb
FAIRBANKS Alice Heath bcdeddhd
Charles ahbghfab
Charles Dow bcbegbd
Elizabeth Philena bcbegbd
Ella M ahbgbfab
Frances Mellisant bcbegbd
Joseph adacfg
Lorenzo Sayles bcdeddhd
Lowell bcbegbd
Mary Ellen bcbegbd
Sybilla adgfcda
FAIRBURN J B bcbcbbeef
FAIRMAN Lillian adaabdaeb
FALCONER Allen bcdecahbb
Eleanor Janet bcdecahbb
FALES Sarah J wid eaab
FALLINGTON Jonathan adkee
Polly adkee
FARLEY Annie M adabbgbcaa
Charlotte bcdeaea
Clinton J adaceaeab
Henrietta bcdeaedac
Mary adhccfha
Thomas adabbgbcaa
William C bcfigfbba
FARMER Betsey bcbehd
Charles adacebfba
Dorcas abccd
FARNHAM James E bbbffbaad
Louise Adelia bbbffbaad
Noah bcbhdbb
—— wid bcdgdaib
FARNSWORTH Alden bcbcbaaaa
Eliza bcfiffc
Huldah Maria bcbcbaaaa
Mary adaabdd
Mary Ann bcfiffc
Polly adaabdd
Simeon bcfiffc
Simeon Dow bcfiffc
FARNUM Abner R bbbebcbca
Betsey ahbge
Edward P ahbgdcb
Hepzibah ahbgh
Hannah ahbge
Joseph (Capt) ahbge
Susan ahbge
FARR Almira P adgcacbj
Caroline bcfiibae

Cynthia Maria adbabfg
Lincoln Dow adbabfg
Mary Ellen adbabfg
Mercy adhadcb
Thomas adbabfg
FARRAR Debonair adabiba
Flora A ahbgbfaa
George Brigham adkdeab
Hiram adabif
Israel, Israel 2nd adabif
Ira adabif
Joseph adkdeab
Josiah adaabad, adabiba, adabif
Julia adabif
Lucinda A adgfcdgc
Nathan adgfcdgc
Perley adabif
Sally adabif
—— xaa
FARREL Amanda bcdgdaab
Caroline bcdgdaabb, bcdgdakb
David bcdgdaab
Elmer bcdgdaab
Emery bcdgdaab
Stephen bcdgdaab
William bcdgdaab
FARRINGTON Abigal J ahbgik
Abbie Louisa adkfbeib
Daniel Jr. adhci
Harriet bcdedbada
Nancy Elizabeth ahgchf
Theodate adhce
Zenas adkfbeib
FARRELL Jane adabbgz
Jennie M adabbgz
FARWELL Benjamin O bcbebcgb
Frank E adkecbaf
FAULKNER Clyde adbabfbgd
Thomas W adbabfbgd
FAULT Catherine bbbffafb
FAY Mary ahgcibd
FEARING Alfred G adgfbfda
FELCH Adeline J adaimea
Daniel adaima, adaimbe
Edward F adgxfdae
Elias adaimbd
Enoch E adgxfdc
Ernest F adgxfdae
Frederick F adaimbbg
Harold C adaimbae
Ida May adaimbbg
Jacob adaim
Mary Ann adaima, adaimbd
Mary Anna bcdcbk
Myron B adgxfdae
Nancy L wife adaimbbg
Ralph F adgxfdae
Samuel adkfbab
Sarah J adgxfadc
Sewall adhcdacd
Thomas adaimea
FELL George W adaidaeb
Hannah Welding adaidae
Mary Emma adaidaeb
Samuel adaidae

FELLOWS Abigail adgcac
Alice M bbbffcbaf
Charles H bbbffcbaf
Deborah adaia
Flora C bbbffcbaf
Frank F akebdbbie
Jeremiah adkdd
Laura A adadhacc
Mary akebdbbie
Ruth adkdd
Sarah adgcac
FENN Angie wid adaabdaba
FENNELL Maria A ahbaacda
FENNO John bcbehhi
Margaret bcdgdeaaf
Mary Ann bcbehhi
—— bcdgdeafc
FENTON William bbbebcf
FENWICK Alberta Amelia bcbhdpaa
Michael bcdhdpaa
FERDONE Maria ahgciac
FERGESON Ivory adkecbad
Sadie adkecbad
FERGUSON Jennie bcdgej
FERNALD Eliza A abccgaccaac
Samuel adaidaa
FERRELL L ahcmfiea
FERREN Abigail bcfigfa
Calvin bcfifae
FERRIS Content adacgfd
FESSENDEN William Pitt (Sen) adh-
ccbb
FIELD Frank adaimaag
Mary C adggdada
FIELDING Anna adhafcj
FIELDS Lizzie abccgchab
FIFE Alfred ahbaee
FIFIELD John K adabibcf
William a
FINK Edward G bcbhddccg
Inez N bcbhddccg
FISH Caroline ahbcajd
Elisha ahghd
FISHER Addison Edward bcbhbge
Albert S adhafad
Irving bcdebgad
Russell A ahbcabejd
—— bcbhbge
FISK Abi P adkebgb
Charlotte bcbebbfa
Jeremiah adkebgb
FISKE Betsey ahbabjc
William ahbabjc
FITCH Abner ahgdf
Addie M adggdcfb
Alma bcdgdafo
Arsinoe ahgdf
Diantha ahgdf
Ebenezer Root ahgdf
Elvira Booney bcbcbbgb
Mariamne ahgdf
Phoebe ahgdf
Solomon bcbcbbgb
Statira ahgdf
FITTS Elizabeth adaaai

Jonathan adbafaa
Ruth A adadabcfa
Sally adaaaif
—— adabib
FITZGERALD Donald bcdgdafef
Elva bcdgdafef
Eugene bcdgdafef
Francis bcdgdafef
George bcdgdafef
Henry ahbabaeb
Horace bcdgdafef
FITZPATRICK Edna May bcbcbaaba
Florence bcbcbaaba
Henry bcbcbaaba
FLAGG Adeline S adbabgda
FLANDERS Andrew Jackson bcdedbcd
Andrew Perry bcdedbcd
Arthur C ahbcaji
Arthur Eugene bcdedbcd
Benjamin adhafgaa
Betsey adaaaieb
Charles Robert bcdedbcd
Collins bbbebfi
Edwin bcbebbbe
Etta Frances bcdedbcd
Frederick M bcdedbcd
John adabb, adkecf, ahggbf
Joseph Jr adabibda
Martha bcbcbaaag
Mary adabb
Mary Esther bcdedbcd
Sarah, Sarah wife adabb
Seth adgxffe
Strowbridge ahbgaba
Thomas adaimbg
Wallace W adkfbbcf
Walter H adhafgaa
Walter W adhcdace
—— adhafgcbf
FLEMING Hugh bcdgdeaic
John M adaaaiec
FLETCHER Annie ahfcaaac
Arianna ahfcaaac
Carrie F abbegbead
Carrie Viola bcbebcgaa
Charles G bcbebcgaa
Charles Horace ahfcaaac
George I bcdeabde
Gilman P bcdeabde
Mary wife abbegbead
Orianna ahfcaaac
Samuel abbegbead
FLICKENSTINE C W ahchfeh
FLIGHT Charlotte G bcdgdaacb
John bcdgdeaabc
Rebecca G bcdgdbaad
FLINT Ella V bbbffbaad
Irene adaabce
Nellie G wid adbabfbgc
Orrin adaceddf
Thomas bbbffbaad
FLITNER Arthur Dow abdcebed
Joseph Henry abdcebed
Mary Elizabeth abdcebed
Zachariah abdcebed

FLOID Annie A abccgacca
FLOOD Ada adkgddga
Andrew adabbgdc
Elizabeth adaf
Miranda wife adabbgdc
Orphia E adabbgdc
FLOWER Charles E abccgaeb
FLUDE Elizabeth abbegbdcb
FLY Gilman adabbgk
Harriet wife abbegbdcb
FLYNN Elizabeth abceabd
Lois akebdb
FOGG Abigail adkeech
Anne adaigaac
Clara adaimbcb
David S akebiv
Ebenezer abccgach
Elizabeth abdb, ahbaaaaa, akebiv
Elizabeth C abccgach
Ellen adaigaac
Greenleaf adadha
Hannah ahbabcf
Hannah E adkeaba
Huldah abbeab, abbeacc
Ida E adkebgc
Israel Dow adkebgc
Jeremiah (Rev) adai, adkdd, adkddb,
    adkebb, akebbc
Joseph adkebgc
Joseph H adkebgc
Katherine C adkech
Katie Marian bcdecdia
Lavina B bcdedggba
N Mary adkebgc
Ruth A adkech
Samuel adkech
Samuel D adkech
——adaimbcf
FOLGER Archie Leonard abbegfgai
Charles H abbegfgai
Mary E bcdgdakba
Wilfred abbegfgai
FOLLANSBEE Daniel B adaimci
Edward E bcbhdeg
Edward F bcbhdeg
John W beficali
Lucy J bcbhdeg
William adhaff
FOLLETT Clara C J adhcbbja
Elizabeth Edith wife adhcbbja
Joseph H adhcbba
FOLSOM Abigail B adadabf
Almira adadiea
Benjamin adadabf
David (Maj) ahbac
Ellen S ahbabdad
Hannah ahbac
Lucinda adadaba, adadabf
Mary adadabg
Mary A adadieab
Mead adadabf
Nancy ahgfdd
Rufus ahbabdad
Sarah wid abceabcb, wife ahba
William ahbac

William H bcdbecae
FOOTE Alonzo bcbcbbacd
Lauretta E adaigaaac
Maud H wid adgxffbd
FORBUSH Mary Ann adgfbgea
FORD Anna (Mrs) bcbhddae
John abbeebc, ahbca, (Capt) ahbch
Maria adhcbbg
Susan K ahbaahd
FORESTER Martha Josephine adacea-
  ebba
FORGATE Grace Lillian wife adaabf-
  fdb
FORSAITH Ursula R bcdeabf
FORTIER Bernard ahbgbxaaa
Mary Ella wid ahbgbxaaa
FOSS Abigail abccgae
Daniel adbabfc
Isaac adkebb, akebdbf
James bcficao
John adadae
Jonathan adadae
Lucy A C bcficao
Mary Jane wid adaabfdf
FOSSETT Francis bbbfhcfi
Linwood bbbfhcfi
Madeline bbbfhcfi
FOSTER Anna bcdgdaab
Arthur G adggdcfbb
Card adff
Caroline adacedf
Charles bcdgdang
Charlotte W wid adaigbbad
David adaigbbad
Dexter N bcdedgd
Elizabeth G adggdcfbb
Ellen (Smith) ahgfdea
Estelle A bcbhdfagf
Fred G adggdcfbb
George E adggdcfbb
J Pierrepont fceka
Jacob (Rev) bcdgg
Jessie Pratt bcdedgd
Joseph adacb
Julia E adacedf
Lydia adacedf
Mabel A adggdcfbb
Mabel Dow bcdedgd
Mary bbbffcbad, bcbhddcc
Nathaniel abcce
Nellie bcdgdaab
Rachel bcbhdna
Raymond H adggdcfbb
Robert bcdedgd
Thomas bbbffcbad
Thomas D adggdcfbb
William Stoddard bcdgdang
Zeralda adggeic
—— befiffda
FOWLES George bcbhddcb
Neota bcbhddcb
FOWLER Abraham adaimb
Adna B adaimbhca
Alice M adgxfdaba

Asa abbeebc
Augusta adaimbg
Bessie C adaimbhca
Betsey adaimbg
Charles A adgxfdaba
Clara bcdgdeadc
E M wife adgxffbb
Hannah ade
Helen F adgxffbb
Ida E bbbebcdaeb
Jacob 3rd adaimbf
Jacob Salonius adaimaabc, adaimbf, ad-
  gxfccd
James, James Jr. adaimbg
Jane bbbe
John adaimcdb
Joseph ade
Josiah ade
Lizzie M adgxfdaba
Lizzie May bcbhddbb
Lowell adgxfdaba
Margaret Ann adaimbf
Margaret E wife adgxfdaba
Maria wife adaimcdb
Martin Luther abbegba
Martha adggeib
Mary ade
Mary E bcbhddbb
Mary F adgxfaacab
Micajah ahbchf
Mima Jane adaimbf
Miriam R adaimaabc
Philip ade
Phylena adhchaaa
Rachel adaimb
Richard adgxffbb
Ruby B adaimaaabc
Sarah fc
Sidney A adaimcdbc
Thomas ade
Tristram adaimbg
Viola F adgxfaacaa
William, William Jr. ade
Zelphia A adaimcdb
FOWNES Martha adkeabba
FOX Elizabeth Marie bcdbeceee
Ernest R bcdbeceee
Freeman bcdgdah
George adaceaag
Oliver (Capt) adacfe
Susan adadai
—— bcdebeec, bcdgdeag
FOYE Ann Cecilia abceaea
Elizabeth abceaea
Ellen Ruthdian abceaea
Fidelia E abceaea
James Nathaniel abceaea
John abceaea
John Harrison abceaea
Lois bcficadb
Martha Abby abceaea
Mary Elizabeth abceaea
Nathaniel abceaea
Orion Leavitt abceaea

Sarah Ann abceaea
Sophia Jenness abceaea
FRANCOIS Sarah bcbhdbn
FRANK Jessie Cecilia ahggbdaac
FRANKLIN B E adgfcjc
Elizabeth xad
FRASER Alexandria bcdgdabdd
FRAWLEE John ahdaaa
FRAZER John ahfd
FREDERICK —— bcdgdeag
FREDERICKSON Frederick akecaabb
FREDRICK Dean Russell adggegbag
Howard William adggegbag
Lura Mae adggegbag
FREEMAN Abbie bcdedbbda
Daniel adggdf, adggdg
George adggdf
Hannah adggdf
Lena M wid adabbgaigb
Lucinda adggdf
Mary adggdf
Mattie B bcbhddccb
Minerva adggdf
Norman L adggdf
Truman adggdf
FREESE Gilbert Warren bcbhddcea
Harriet bcbhddcea
Sarah akecac
FREEZE Jonathan adad
Sarah wid adad
FREMONT John C (Gen) adhccbb, bc-
bhdbnd
FRENCH Abbie C bcbebig
Addie May adacedhg
Addie S adkfbede
Alpha E adacedhg
Asa bbbebcb
Brewster bcbebigb
Burdette E adacedhg
Charles H adacedhg
Dorothy bcbebcbb
Edna M adacedhg
Edward (1) bc
Elias adgxfag
Elihu adabib
Elizabeth adabib, adgfcj, aedaa
Elizabeth Ham abceabdj
Enoch adaidag
Erwin B adacedhg
F F abdcebld
Fannie M wife adhahedd
Francis E adaaaifba
Francis Ormond akecahd
Frank Newell ahbabjid
Fred B adabib
Freddie L adacedhg
George W adacedhg
Hannah adgxfafa, ahbabcdba, (wife)
ahgfda
Hannah F bbbebcb
Henrietta S adaidag
John bcbebiga
John H bcbebiga
Jonathan (Rev) abbeebc, akebij

Joseph adggbaa, bc
Josiah adgxfafa
Lizzie E adkdgbad
Lomacy adggegdb
M Abigail abbeebc
Mabel Etheline adhahedd
Margaret S bcbebig
Mary wid bcbebcbd
Miriam adada
Miranda akebbf
N S adkfbede
Polly adkda
Rachel E adgxfag
Ralph S adhcbbgf
Samuel adada, ahghf
Sarah abbegfa, adadh, ahgfda
Thomas abceabdj
William H adgxfafa
William Hook adgxfafa
Winfield adhahedd
—— ahbcaca
FRETSON Mary A adaimaa, adaimbba
FRIEND Emma adabbghgb
Nathaniel bcbcbbaa
FRINK Margaret ahcfj
FROST Arthur W abccgcfia
Edward adkgaa
Elihu B bbbfaeaa
Geneva Kimball bcdedggb
James adkgaa
Lucy Viola abccgcfia
Mabel Ethel adbabfecb
Mary Elizabeth akebcg
Mary Susan adkgaa
Nathaniel akebif, akebcg
Newton bcdgdaiig
Rachel Ann akebcg
Simeon Ford abcdedggb
—— adkgaa
FROTHINGHAM —— (Capt) adaaah
FRYE Alice adbf
Benjamin adbf
Francis bcdedfa
Fred J adaabcjb
George H adaabcjb
Hannah E bcdedfa
James (Col) abdci, bcbcaa
John C adaabcjb
Jonathan adbf
Judith adbf, adbfh
Mary A adhccgab
Orrin F akecahd
Rowland adbf
Ruth adbf, adbfh
Silas adbf
William adbf
FULLENTON Abigail akecb
FULLER Adele J adgfbfda
Benjamin adgfbfda
Benjamin Franklin adgfbfda
Charleston E ahbcajdd
Charleston S G ahbcajdd
Claude E ahbcajdd
Elizabeth ahb

H A adgfcdh
Jack ahbcajdd
Jessie Idaline adacffeee
John S akebcfab
Liona D wid adkfbbja
Lizzie bbbfhcfc
Melville E adgfbggb
Nabby akebiib
Robert C ahbcajdd
Susan bcbcbbgb
Theodore abcce
William ae
FULLFORD Mandanah bcbcbaaad
Milo E bcbcbaaad
FULTON Arthur D adgfbgdceb
Mary Esther adkddceb
FUNKEY G A bcdeaaaaa
FURBER George W bcfifl
Mary adhafdf
Thomas G abceabda
FURNESS George adacffg
Herman adacffg
Herman Jr. adacffg
Jane adacffg
Lavinia adacffg
Margaret adacffg
Nettie adacffg
Orlando adacffg
FURROW Gertrude Emma bcdgdeafd
GAGE Benjamin adhccc
Anna wife bce
Hannah adhccc
John adhccc, bce, bcfi
Josiah bce
Mary adhccc
GAGNON Gideon bcdgdabfc
GALLAGHER Alice M bcdgdma
Alice W bcdgdma
Ann bcbhddf
Mary E adaabcjfb
Patrick adaabcjfb
GALE Francena A adaaaifb
Georgia C adabbghg
Jacob (Col) adadab, adaie
Maria R adkfbdxc
Susan ahbabje
GALLUP David Dow ahdac
George adabbgba
Isaac ahchha
Jonathan ahdac, ahggd
Simon ahdac
GAMBLE Hamilton R (Gov) ahchfdc
Mattie adggdcic
GAMBRELL Alice W abdcebk
GANNETT Sophia adkfbdx
GARABEDIAN Agavine A adgcacbka
Agnsh A adgcacbka
Susan wife adgcacbka
GARCELON Lucy ahbgbe
GARDINER Abigail wid adaaaf
Albert Green abdcebeac
Benjamin abdcebeac
Jethro adaaaf
Joseph (Capt) ab

Mary adaceaaib
GARDNER Dennis adgcacbc
Louisa adaabdc
Lucinda bcdbede
—— (Col) adhccbb
GARFIELD Marietta adgcacbc
Samuel bcdbeag
GARLAND Abigail abbf, abca, akece
Anne abbf
Charles F adkecebag
Daniel M bcdebgda
Elizabeth wife abbf
Fred J adhafgca
George gbaic
Gladys gbaic
James abbf
John abb, abca
John L adhafgca
Jonathan abbf, Jonathan Jr. abbf
Joseph abbf
Lizzie E adkecebag
Lydia akecb
Mattie M adhafgca
Mary abbf (bis), adaiebab
Peter abb, abbf
Rachel abbf
Samuel abbf
Sarah abbeace, abbf, abca
Simon abbf (bis)
GARMAN George adabbgya
Hattie M adabbgya
Mary G wife adabbgya
GARNETT Nettie gbaic
GARVIN J Howard adkdecebb
John H adkdecebb
Josiah Dow adkdecebb
GASKELL Amy E abbegbebbb
Tyler B abbegbebbb
GATCHELL Mary E adkddix
GATES Diantha wife bcdecaib
Eliza Ann bcdecai
Fannie Minerva bcdecai
Jonathan bcdecaib
Medea Elizabeth adhcbbjc
Nellie E bcdecaib
GAULT Andrew bcbebb
Margaret bcbebb
Phoebe bcfifa
GAUTIER Elizabeth adkeabbad
GAUTRO Leonie M adadhcaia
GAZETTE Joe bcbhdbd
GEARY Kate adadieab
GEDDING Mary E ahgdcag
GEDDIS Martha bbbfhbacb
GELATT David Clifford adacgfaea
Harry B adacgfaea
Judson L adacgfaea
Vivian adacgfaea
GELDART John W adgxfdabb
Sadie L adgxfdabb
GELDERT John A bcbhddfacd
Nina J bcbhddfacd
GENTLEMAN Isabella akecahhec
Robert akecahhec

GEORGE Angus bbbfhcfi
Anna bbbfd
Alice bbbfd
Austin bbbfd
Azor O W adggbb
Betsey adggbb
Catherine abccgdfa
Cora Estella adaabdah
Ebenezer adggbb
Ellis bbbfd
Flora Felicia wid bededch
Henry bbbfd
Hester bbbfd
James adggbb, bbbfd
John, John Jr. bbbfd, bbbff
Joseph bbbffh
Mary bbbfd, bbbffcbag
Mina Minerva adaabdah
Miriam adggbb
Nathaniel adggbb
Polly adggbb
Sam adhch
Sias B adaabdah
Stephen adaabdah
Susanna bbbfd
Thomas bbbfd
—— adggbb
GERRISH Betsey adadabb
Jacob (Col) adkfb
GETCHELL Abigail bcdgdbaadb
Benoni adah
Clementine Augusta bcdedgg
Daniel W bcdedgdakba
Eleanor adah
Eva A adah
Mary A adhafb
Nehimiah Jr. bcdebee
Philomela Ann bcdebee
Lewis H ahgdeead
GIBBES Lewis H ahgdeead
Robert H adgccad
GIBBS J M bcbhdebb
GIBSON Anna adgfcib, bcdgdaieb
Arthur bcdgdaieb
Caroline adgfbecbd
Donald bcdgdaieb
Douglas bcdgdaieb
Frances Louise adgfcicf
Harvey Dow adgfcicf
James Lewis adgfcicf
Margarette bcdgdaieb
Mildred bcdgdaieb
William T adacedhg
GIERS Kate G bcdedkc
GILBERT Arthur Wallace adaabfaad
Benjamin bcdgdafc
Enoch bcdgdafc
Francis Dowe ahgfdad
Hannah ahcbc
Helen adaabfaad
Herman bcdgdafc
James (Dea) ahcbc
Lunna adhafdj
Mary A ahgfdad

Samuel ahgfdad
Stephen adaabfaad
Thomas F adhafdie
GIFFORD Marmaduke adbac
GILE Daniel bcbei
Ebenezer bcc
Ezekiel (Capt) bcbeb, bcbeg, bcbhf, bcdig
Nathan bcbei
GILES Augustus A ahfcfcea
Nolan E ahfcfcea
Walter M ahfcfcea
GILFORD Almira ahbaacd
Jonathan ahbaacd
GILISPI Sarah fcei
GILKEY Rose adgfcdh
GILL Elizabeth bcdgdaiea
Perney bcbebbe
GILLAN John L adadabbdaa
Sadie Agnes adadabbdaa
GILLARD Nettie K bcdgdbacc
GILLCHRIST John (Dr) befifb
—— bcbhdhbb
GILLINGHAM Dexter Davis bcbhddccbc
Gordon Dow bcbhddccbc
Thomas bcbhddccbc
GILMAN Alice adaabf
Amasa ahbabade, ahbabadf
Augustus bcdgdh
Deborah adaabaca, adgfbfc
Dorcas adaabcd
Edgar A bcdebgaea
Edgar Dow bcdebgaea
Edward O abbeebbbb
Elizabeth wid ahbaa
Esther adaabc
Ezra bcdedbag
Frank L bcdedbag
Gertie bcdedbag
Hannah ahbac
Herod S ahbac
Ida E wife bbbfhcfad
James ahbaa
Jeremiah (Capt) ahbab, befica
Joanna adaabf
John akebdbbib
Joshua Jr. adaaba
Judith ahbaa
Leila O bcdebgaea
Leroy Sutherland abbeebbbb
Lettie M ahbabadf
Martha A ahbabadf
Mary adhaf
Nettie T bcdedbag
Polly adgfbfc
Ralph Edward abbeebbbb
S F ahbaedca
Samuel adaabf, Jr. ahba
William adgfbfc
—— (Sheriff) adkfbb
—— (Col) ahbg
GILMORE D abbegbdfc
Elizabeth ahbaadbf

Ellen J hedbaddda
Hannah ahbaadb
James ahbaadb
Jane ahbaadb
John (Lieut) ahbaadb; Jr. ahbaadb
GILPATRICK Frank adgfbgded
GILSON Emma Louise bcdeaecc
GINN Adelaide T abccgcfb
Frances abccgcfb
Justina abccgcfb
Lester H abccgcfb
Percival M abccgcfb
Rufus A abccgcfb
Sarah ahbabaed
Samuel (Capt) abccgcfb
Thomas ahbabaed
Wealthy adccgcfb
Washington adccgcfb
William H adccgcfb
GLASS Mary E bcdeddabe
GLAZIER Nancy adhccf
GLEASON Augusta bcfifffa
C H akebcfe
Eliza eaab
Emeline bcfifffa
Julia adhafgcbg
Louisa bcfifffa
S adgfcja
Samuel bcfifffa
GLIDDEN Abel adaaba
Charity ahbabaefc
Eliza adadhab
Rebecca bcbhdd
Smith adabiga
GLINES George A abbegfgaf
Hannah ahbcaa
Henry akebdbbfd
Ira ahbcaa
James ahbcaa
Louisa ahbcaa
Lucretia Ann abbegfga
Martha adgcadad
Mary ahbcaa
Moses S ahbcaa
Nancy adaabda, ahbcaaa
Samuel ahbcaa
Sarah Elizabeth akebdbbf
Stephen Barker ahbcaa
—— akebdbbi
GLOR Jean ahgdgbc
GLOVER Carrie adkfbbjbf
Mary adkfbebg
F R bcbcbaaaaa
Minnie A bcbcbaaaaa
Victoria A bcdgdaaab
William bcdgdaaab
GLOYD Edwin bcdecdc
Jesse bcdecc, bcdecdb
Jessie bcdecdc
Justin bcdecdc
Mary bedecdb
Mary A bcdecdc
GODDARD Hannah adbac
GODDING Adelbert J ahbabale

Clara A ahbabale
Euphrasia ahbabala
Walter ahbabale
GODFREE Sarah akebij
William a
GODFREY Abigail abbegb, bcbb
Charles D adbabfbgd
Deborah abb
Everett L adaieaad
Grace Iva adaabffdd
Hannah abdccb, akecafi
Jacob D abd
Jacob T akecae
Jennie Ruth adbabfbgd
John (Capt) bcdedf
Jonathan abccdaa, abcd
Joseph abbegb
Simon, Simon Jr. abccdaa
William M a
GODSOE —— bcdgdake
GOFF Burns adaidaea
Elton Mills adaidaea
Katherine Welding adaidaea
Lela B bcdgdafec
Mary E ahbaabdab
Ruth adaidaea
Samuel ahbaacdab
Simeon Becker adaidaea
William R adaidaea
GOFFE John bbbff, (Capt) bcde
GOLDING Henrietta adkfbbdfa
GOLDMORE Mary F wid adkfbbja
GOLDSMITH Abigail akebid
GOOCH Isabel B adgfbp
Lydia adgfbm
William H adgfbp
GOODALE George H adgfbk
Jonathan adhafag
Mary akebbf
Mary Elizabeth adgfbk
Mary Jane adhafag
GOODCHILD Elizabeth ahgchhc
John ahgchhc
GOODENOUGH Darwin E ahbcai
Hiram bcfifjg
GOODING Gertrude adgfcdacab
GOODRICH Arthur E adaigbbae
Clarence E adaigbbae
Doris Elinor abdcebk
Elizur (Rev) ahcbf
Hannah B bcdbee
J Fred adaigbbae
James B abdcebk
Lois bcbcbbc
Marion adaigbbae
Ransom E adaigbbae
William F adaigbbae
GOODWILL Charlotte bcdecahfa
Eleanor bcdecahfa
Fletcher bcdecahfa
GOODWIN Abigail E adaigbb
Agnes D adaaaie
Ada adaaaie
Ada Maria adaigaaa

867

Ann W adaiga
Elizabeth adkfb
Etta Francina adkfbbci
George W adaaaie
Henry adkfb
Jane adhahf
Joshua C adhafdfb
Lizzie J adhafdfb
Lucy adgfbn
Marion E adgfbgfia
Martha adgfb
Mary C adkebabba
Reuben ahbge
Samuel adaigaaa, ahbge, bbbd, bcdcb
Sarah bbbd
Sarah H bcbhdqa
—— bcdcbk
GOOGINS Fred C adkgdegc
GOOKIN Sarah abdcebk
GORGAS Gladys adgfbgfaae
GOSS Ellen A adgxfaacca
Frank M adgxfaacca
Frank P adgxfaacca
John B ahdaaddc
Raymond adgxfaacca
GOSSON Frances bcbhddbba
GOTT Margaret bcbebb
Mary bb
GOUCH Franklin I bcbcbbge
GOULD Alice Maynard adhccbbc
Allen B adgcacbg
Arthur bcdgdafad
Conrad Wieser adhccbbc
David ahbabcdba
Emma F ahbabaeb
Estelle ahbabaeb
Everett H adaidbfb
Edward adhccbbc
Frederick A bcbebbca
George A adaceaeaa
Gilman F ahbabaeb
Grace bbbfabmac
Hannah adaha
Hartford J ahbabaeb
Henry R adaidbfb
Herbert Chase adhccbbc
Isaac ahchbc
Josiah adkdei
Judeth adfb
Lucius ahchbc
Lucius Dow ahchbc
Margaret McClellan adhccbbc
Mary adfb
Mary A ahchbc
Mary R adbabfia
Mussey adfb
Nancy Amelia ahchbc
Neal Dow adhccbbc
Nelson ahbabcdba
Samuel, Samuel Jr. adfb
Sarah adfb, adhe
Silas adkfbeb
Sophronia adaabd
Wallace J ahbabcdba

William Edward adhccbbc
GOULDEN Juley adacfe
GORDON Agnes ahchb
Andrew bcdedcga
Ann Maria abbegbib
Betsey adgfdb
Daniel (Capt) adadab, ahbaaa
Daniel S abbegbib
David abbegfh
Eben C abbegg
Eliphalet abbege
Ellen J adadhacaa
Fred M adhafgca
Hannah adadhaca
Hannah J bcdedcga
Helen bcbhddbaa
Henry D ahcfjf
Jennie bcdedcga
John abbegbf, Jr. ahchb
John Calvin abbegba
Lewis abbegd
Loisa L adgfdaaa
Lucinda Day adgfdaaa
Martha A adgfbg
Mary befifj
Melinda abbegfe
Polly abbege
Samuel (Capt) adadh
Thomas ahcfjf
Tirzah G abbegba
Viva M wid bcbhddbaa
—— abbegd
GOVE Aaron adaha, adahad, adhaff
Abial adhagbf
Abigail adadia
Abijah adadiaa
Abner akex
Abraham akebbf
Abram Alson adadieab
Adalia adahd
Albert adaimbbe
Albert F adhadca
Albert N adaijbb
Andrew Allen adggega
Anna adbabd, adgxb, adhadb
Anna C adhaff
George Mark adadieab
Annie Lummus adggbaa
Annie M wid adgcaccaf
Belle adggega
Benjamin Franklin akebbf
Bennie Guy adadieab
Betsey akebbf
Charles adaiic
Charles C adhaff
Charles Dow adbabd
Charles Alson adadieab
Charles Frederick bcfifb
Clara Adaline adadieab
Clarissa bcfifb
Curtis adggega
Daniel adhcbb
David, David Jr. adbabd
David Dow adhaff

Delia adhae
Dolly adhae
Dolly P adhaff
Ebenezer adada. adha, akebbf
Edith Marion adaijbb
Edward abbd, adaha, adhad
Edward A adkehcca
Edward F akebbcbaa
Edward L adhahd
Edward S adadieab
Elijah adgxe, adadicc
Elijah Dow adhaff
Elinor adabib, adahag
Elizabeth abbd
Enoch, adggbaa, adgxb
Enoch Jr. adggbaa
Enos Sanborn adggega
Ernest L adaimbbea
George L adaijbb, adaimbbe
Hannah adbab, adgxb, adbabd, adhcda, akex
Harold Albert adaijbb
Harriet E adaimbhb
Helen E adaijbb
Henry bcdeaae
Henry Garfield adadieab
Hiram adbabd
Huldah Jane adggbaa
James adaha
Jemima akebbf
Jeremiah adkda
John adaha, adahd, adfa, adgxb, adhadca, adhadda, adhae, adhaff
John Jr. adaha adhadda
John C adkda
John H adhcdb
Jonathan adaha, adbab, adhadd, adhaddb, adhae, akebbf, bcfifb
Jonathan Dow adhaff
Joseph adkda, bcdeaae
Joseph N bcdeaae
Joshua R adhci
Josiah adhae
Judith adaha, wife adhad, adhadca, adhae, adhak
Julia A abceabed
Juliette adggega
Laura adhadca
Levi adaiic
Levi Dow adaiic
Lucretia bcfifb
Lucy adggbaa, adhae
Lucy Ellen adggega
Lydia adhad, adhcbb, akebbf
Lydia Dow adggbaa
Martha adhaff
Mary adahc, adhcba, adfa, adgxb, adgxbb, adgxbba, akebbf
Mary Dow adhadca
Mehitable adahdb
Mehitable P akex
Moses adadia, adaha, adhadb
Nancy adaimbai, adaimbbe, akebbf
Nathan adggbaa, adgxb

Nathan Dow adggbaa
Nellie F adkehcca
Obediah, Obediah Jr. adgxb
Patience adbb, adgxb
Rachel adha
Rhoda Breed adhaff
Richard adhaddb, adhae, Jr. adhae
Ruth adbabd, adgxb
Samuel akebbf
Sarah akebbf
Sarah Abbie adhcdb
Sarah Emma adhaddb
Sarah S adadicc
Simon Green adhadb
Solon Chase adggega
Squiers adhaff
William akex
William Clark bcfifb
William Ellsworth adgcaccaf
William N akebbcbaa
Winthrop adhadca, 2nd adhadca, adhae, adhaff, adhcda
GOWEN Edgar J adabbgagde
Lydia Ann bbbffbaa
—— bcbhbc
GRAHAM David bcdgdaab
Maria abdcebeah, bcdgdad
Sarah Jane adadhcaf
GRAFFAM Clinton Wesley adkgaeda
GRAFTON Ann Fawcett bcbehhi
GRANGER Anna Margaret bbbfabba
GRANT Ada M bcdgdagb, abner, bcdgdagj
Alfred bcdgddf
Allan bcdgdad, bcdgdagj
Alfred Smith adggegbb
Alfred Smith Jr. adggegbb
Angie ahbabaeaa
Arthur Dow adggegbb
Charles bcdgdam
Daniel adabbgpa
Dorothy bcdgdeadc
Edith bcdgdagb
Edna bcdgdaic
Edna Lois adggegbb
Effie bcdgdagb
Evelyn F adabbgpa
Estelle bcdgdeadc
Florence I bcdgdanb
Frederick bcdgdagb, bcdgdagca
Frank bcdgdagha
George bcdgdagb
George Harrison adggegbb
Gladys bcdgdeadc
Harriet adadhcafc
Harry Carlton adggegbb
Hayward bcdgdaijb
Horatio bcdgddacbm, bcdgdeadc
Horatio Nelson bcdgdeadc
Ida bcdgdeadc
Izona bcdgdagha
Jacob ahbabaeaa
James H adgfbeec
James M adahdea

Jane bcdgdah
Jeremiah bcdgdanf
Julia Elizabeth ahcbec
Laura bcdgdbaag
Laura A bcdgdbaag
Luther bcdgdagi
Mandy bcdgdad
Mandy May bcdgdagb
Martha bcdgdaija
Mary ahbab
Maud bcdgdeaae
Miles bcdgdaijb
Minnie bcdgdagb
Moses bcdgdad, bcdgdanc
Nellie J bcdgdagb
Nelson bcdgdagj
Orilla bcdgdagj
Rankin bcdgdagb
Samuel bcdgdaic
Sarah Ann ahgchea
Ward bcdgdagj
Weston bcdgdagb
William bcdgdagha
Zebulon bcdgdagj
GRASS Adaline K adabbgtac
Maud bcdgdaik
Whitefield H adabbgtac
GRAVEL Alida adkfbbcg
GRAVES Abigail bcdcb
Annie J adaimbha
Arthur B bcfifhhda
David bcdcb
Emerett Sophronia bcdebgaa
George c
Hannah bcdcb, abbef
James, James Jr. bcdcb
Jessia bcdgdaiec
John bbbfi, c
Josiah c
Lester bcdebgaa
Lottie ahgcibcb
Lucy bcdcb
Lucy B wife bcfifhhda
Lucy Parsons bcfifhhda
Lydia bcdcb
Lydia R wid adaabff
Martha adadhaaa, bcdcb
Mary c
Mary Elizabeth bcdcb
Olive bcdcb
Phineas bcdcb
Priscilla bcdcb
Samuel, Samuel 2nd bcdcb
Sarah bcdcb
William bcdcb
GRAY A adgfcja
Alanson ahbcabe
Alice C adkgddga
Augusta bcficaled
Cassie adkgdefb
Caroline adabbgahb
Charles adabbgaig, adaimbik
Chauncey ahbcabe
George abdcedb

Gertrude adabbgaig
Irene adgfbffc
Lena bcbhbgda
Marcia ahbcabe
Mary gaaxaxc
Mary Edna wid abdcedb
Mary G wid adgfbl
Mary Kennedy bcfifb
Rosala bcdgdaalb
Rufus E adkgddga
Susan adabbgaig, ahbcabe
Thomas adhcbbdb
GREASON Julian adggeha
GREELE, see Greeley
GREELEY Abra adkef
Amos Dow bbbffda
Andrew adaa, (Capt) abcff
Charles F bbbffda
David ahbabja, bbbffda
Dennis Payson ahbabja
Henry C bbbffda
Horace adggd
Ilsley adggd
J Harvey ahbabame
James bbbffda
Joseph bd
Josiah Bartlett adaaaifad
Lucy W bbbffda
Martha adhccfh
Mary G bbbffda
Philip bbbffda
Phoebe adhccg
Sarah adggd
Sophronia G bbbffda
GREEN Abraham abdg, ad adbaa, ad-
   aih
Alma ahgdcagb
Angelia E ahbabaefa
Anna adaabdf, adhcbba
Arabell adgfbgdcj
Asa adabbgab
Asahel abdg
Caroline abdcebeac
Caroline Amanda bbbfabj
Clarence E ahbabaefa
Claude bcdgdakf
Comfort abdgc, akeab
Daniel adhcbe
David adhcbe, adhch
David Edson adhafce
Dolly adhch
Dorothy (wife) adbaa, adhch
Elizabeth adhaa, adha
Ella May abbegbdd
Ellen adhafce
Elsie A adadieab
Emma adhafce
Enoch (M D) adhadb
Esther abdg
Esther B bcdeabbb
Frank Wilson ahcbee
Franklin Homer adhafce
George adhafce
George Gardner bbbfabj

870

Hannah (wife) adbafb, adbafc
Henry a, ab
Henry Wilson bbbfabj
Huldah adbaa, adggbaa
Isaac abc
Isaiah adahdb
James A adadhacad
Jeremiah adbaa, adha
John abdg, adhc, bcdgdagf
John Dow adbafc
John Lyman adhafce
Jonathan adaabdf, adaih, adbaa, Jr.
  adbaa
Julia E adbabfbg
Kate (Geary) wid adadieab
Kate Amelia bbbfabj
Levi adbaa
Libbie bcbcbbeee
Louisa bbbfabj
Mary adbaa
Mary E adabbgab
Mehitable abc, adhdb, bcbcaa
Melva adadhacad
Moses adbaa
Nabby adbafc
Nancy adbafc
Nathan abdd, adbafb
Newell adadieab
Polly adbafc
Phoebe adhc
Rebecca wife adhcbe
Ruth abdcebk, adbafc, (wife) adhch
Ruth J abdcebk
Sewall adhafce
Simon adbaa, adhafce
Stephen adbaa, adbafb, adbafc
Susan adfcdcb
Wesley adhafce
William adbabfbg
Winthrop adbaa, adfcdcb
—— adabbgaa
GREENE Asenath adaidc
Calvin adaidc
Emma adaidc
Ernest adkdeceha
Gardner adaidc
Jacob, Jacob Jr. adaidc
Mary A adaidc
Mary Jessie adaim, adgx
Nathaniel adaidc
Samuel Saunders adaidc
Sophia adaceaf
GREENLAW Alta H adabbgaicb
Annie bcdgdaaa
Clara E adabbgaicb
GREENLEAF Carrie A adadabbdaa
Henry aia
Mary adkfbbc
GREENLEAFF Moses bcdeaf
GREENMAN Fannie ahbacabfe
Job ahbcabha
GREENOUGH Alice C bbbfhjbc
Frank G bbbfhjbc
GREGG William Whiting adhcbbk

GREGORY Jonas ag
Nettie L adbabfbga
GREVIS John bbbfi
GRIFFIN Arthur bcbhddfaae
Ethel T bcbhddfaae
Florence E adadabcfa
Hannah adad
John adad
John Hill bcbhdbna
Leroy adadabcfa
Mary Abbie akebcfa
Sarah abceabdj
Stella Jackson abdcicad
Sylvia Antoinette bcbhdbna
Thaddeus adaabcji
GRIFFING Harriet A adgfcdad
GRIFFITH James E bcdgdaaeg
Mary Edith bcdgdaeg
GRIGGS Mary Ellen ahbgbade
GRIMES Lucy bcdgdang
GRINDALL Ichabod bbbfk
GRINDELL Henry bcdgdgagg
Laura E bcdgdgagg
GRISWOLD Josephine abbeebcad
Nelson Dow abbeebcad
Leila Ruth abbeebcad
Phoebe ahgha
Thomas Jr. abbeebcad
GRITMAN Mary adacgfeb
GROCUT John W adkddgcaa
Viola Emily adkddgcaa
GROENDYCKE Asa bcbehhj
Mary Ellen bcbehhj
GROFF Bessie L bcdgdafec
James E bcdgdafec
GROSS Ada Maud adabbgaice
Augustus H adabbgaice
—— (Rev.) bcdeca
GROVENOR Francis adgfcdh
GROVER James Jr. bcbhdi
Lawrence E ahbgile
Mary Ann wid adgfcdg
Mary Ella ahbgfab
Samuel bcdgdaii
GUERNSEY John J bcdecahb
Josephine bcdecahb
GUILD Martha C ahbcai
GUILE Judith be
Clarissa ahggc
Samuel ahggc
GUILFORD Eliza adadhca
Rufus adadhca
GUMERSON William ahbgikca
William Dow ahbgikca
GUNNISON Avriel adgcacbcd
Deborah bcdbaddf
John adaabfb
Henry adaabfb
GURDY Adeline Center abbegbdc
Elisha abbegbdc
GURNEY Carrie J wid adaaaaccac
GUTTERSON Sarah bcdb
GUTTMAN Louise bcdgdafc
GYNAN Anna adgxfax

Elizabeth Lavender adgxfaae
Fannie E adaimaabc
Gertrude F adgxfaacb
John A adgxfaae
Lizzie L adgxfaae
M R wife adgxfaacb
Nicholas adaimaabc, adgxfaacb
Philip R adgxfax
—— adgxfaace
HACKETT Hannah adaila
Leroy adgfbfc, adgfbfcb
Melinda ahbcae
HADDOCK Charles bcfe
—— bcbhdbnf
HADLEY Albert J bbbebgab
Clara G akebip
Esther A bbbffag
Lydia adhcbbe
Richard M akebip
Sidney B beficalc
—— adabiggdd
HAFFINE Ada adacffec
HAGERMAN Charlotte bcdgded
Elbridge bcdgdagj
Thomas bcdgdbaaf
HAIGH Walker bcdedfi
HAINES Benjamin ahbgbf
Eliza ahbgbf
Mehitable befi
Thomas befi
HAIR Robert gbal
HALE Anna ahbcabbad
Charles A bcdeadac
Georgia C adabbghg
Martha bbbfb
Mary Phoebe bcfigfdd
Maud bcdgdafqc
Moses bcbegbb
Nathan (Col) abdci, bcde, bcdec
Nathaniel bcfigfdd
Parker bcbegbb
Phebe Wyman beficaj
Susie C adaceafkc
Syene bcbegbb
HALEN —— adkeda
HALEY Edgcomb adgfdd
Mary ahbabj
Nancy adgfdc
Sarah adgfdc
HALL Abigail adhccb
Abram bcdedbe
Allen adbabfdec
Audry bcdgdaijc
Augustus B bebebbcdax
Beatrice Nathalie adbabfdec
Benjamin F adadhcaa
Betsey wife bcbebif
Betsey Neal adhcbbb
Charles bcdgdaijc
Charles B adkdbeb
Charles Warren adadhcaa
Daniel bcbebif
Daniel A adaidba
Diana ahgfbb

Dodge bcbhdehfb
Elizabeth ahbcai
Ellen abbegbeab
Etta Maria adadhcaa
Frank ahbgig
George ahgfbb
Georgie E bcbhdhd
Harold Everett adhaheda
Hate-Evil adhcbb
Hattie M ahbabaeac
Irvin adadhcaa
Ivory ahbgig
James ah
Jennie ahbgig
John adhccb
John P adhaheda
Laura ahgfbb
Laura Ellen bcbebbcdax
Linwood S adbabfbgd
Lizzie E ahbabami
Lomira E ahgfdaea
Louisa M bcbebif
Marian Frances adhaheda
Martha Jane ahbghj
Mary adgfga, adggdk, bbbfb
Mehitable bcdeabb
Minnie ahbgig
Phyllis bcdgdaijc
Ray Philip adhaheda
Rebecca adabbge
Rena W bcbhdehfb
Sarah adggdce
Seth ahgfbb
Solon Alexander adadhcaa
Spurgeon bcdgdaijc
Walter adadhcaa
William ahbgig
Willis bcdeabb
—— abbeb
HALLENBACK Augustus abbegfijba
Nella May abbegfjba
HALLIDAY Minnie M adhafgcda
HALLOCK —— (Gen) adhccbb
HALLOWAY Jennett fceh
HALSEY Havilah Smith cbbcba
HALVERSTADT William bbbfabia
HAM Cassie bcbhdqac
Elizabeth H ahbaeg
Granville Sylvester adgfbef
Hannah adgfbef
Joel adgfbef
Joel Addison adgfbef
John ahbaeg
Laura adabibcae
Lavina S adbabd
HAMBLETT Alice adggdcib
HAMBLIN Nathan Chipman adhcbb-
  jab
HAMES John akebhd
HAMILTON Edna B bcdeddbe
Edna Dow bcdbeceg
Hattie R bcdeaefbb
Helen V wid aeeaeccc
John adgfcda

872

332

M J bcdeddbe
Mamie bcdeddbe
Mary ahbghg
Mary A bbbfhcff
William H bcdbeceg
HAMLIN Alice M bcfiibca
Emma befiibch
Hannibal (Sen) adhccbb
HAMMER Laura ahgfdah
HAMMOND Abigail befifd
Arthur F adkfbedba
Charlotte L ahbabdada
James C ahbgdge
John C befifd
Julia Dana adhccbbe
Sadie H ahbgdge
Stephen F adkfbedba
William ahbgdge
HAMPTON Amy ahchfi
HANCOCK Ann bcba
John bcbcaa
HANDY Jennie adkgddh
Mary E adkgddf
HANES Eleanor akebha
John akebhd
HANLAN Margaret bcdgdaaaba
HANLEY Peter bcbebbbdbd
William bcbebbbdbd
HANNIFORD David abbegf
Hannah abbegf
John ahbc
Martha ahbc
Peter (Capt) abbegf
HANNIGAN Annie E bcdgdakfb
Helen bcdgdafka
HANSON Asa adhccd
Charlotte A ahbabaed
Cynthia adhagbd
Elisie ahbaef
Eunice bcbhdda
Melinda akebim
Sally P bcfigfb
Winthrop bcfigfb
—— adkfbc, bcbhddag
HAPGOOD Cyrus Howard adadhcaic
Cyrus S adadhcaic
Howard adadhcaic
Lorenzo adhcbba
HARDEY Ruth bcdc
HARDING Frank abccgcfb
George H bbbgabhba
Georgia C bbbgabhba
Nathan abccgcfc
Sarah M baccgcfc
Willard abccgcfc
HARDMAN Albert bbbfhcfec
HARDY Abrah adabigge
Anna D adabigge
Beulah bcdeaa
Ednah bcdbed
Henry adkdbe
John C bbbffcbg
Lydia A adabbgaic
Sally bcbebbb

Scott E bbbffcbg
Silas adkdbe
HARFORD Clara adacedfk
Delia E adkfbdx
Warren adkfbdx
HARIHAN Mary F adkecbaac
HARKNESS Joanna adaaafa
HARLOW Arthur adaabdabec
Gerald adaabdabec
Harmon Leroy adggdcia
Helen adaabdabec
Kenneth adaabdabec
Margaret adaabdabec
William Harvey adggdcia
HARMAN George bcdgdaala
Helen bcdgdaala
Lillian E bcdgdaala
Margaret Isabell bcdgdaala
Ralph E bcdgdaala
Robert A bcdgdaala
HARMON Edith H gbaic
Linwood ahbabaefa
Mildred C ahbabajl
Sarah adhafaf
Silas gbaic
HARNDEN William ahbgbff
HARNDON Edward adkedc
HARNEY Sally bcbebbb
HARPER Gaylord bcdecaf
Harry adacglbb
John H abbegfb
William abbed
HARRIGAN Daniel adkfbbi
HARRIMAN Achsah bcbeg
Annie abccgcfh
Charles abccgcfh
Evander (Capt) abccgcfb
Hannah bcfi
Heslyn abccgcfh
Jennie S adabibcaa
Marion abccgcfh
Robert adhafgab
Sarah bcfi
William adabibcaa
HARRINGTON Ella M ahbgbbeaa
George adhadceb
Phineas abccgbc
HARRIS Abner M adadabbdaa
Alice bcdgdbaadf
Annie A adadhcai
Betsey Noyes adhcbbg
Ebenezer ahc
Edward Doubleday abdced
Frances Maria abbegbea
Jennie A adadabbdaa
Josephine abbegfgaa
Lilly bcbhddfabc
Martha ahc
Nancy bcfigdc
Nicholas H adhcbbg
Noah abbegfgaa
Rebecca wid bbbf
Rufus abbegbea
Sarah bcdgded

Thaddeus Mason (Rev) abdced
HARRISON Bertha Dowe ahgdgbc
Eleanor Bradford ahgdgbc
Helen M adacgfac
John Edward ahgdgbc
Mary Ann bcdgeja
Patrick bcdgeja
Ruby bcdbececa
W H (Gen) bcdedk
HARSHA Catherine adacffd
Eugene adacffd
George adacffd
Hugh adacffd
Marion adacffd
Mary adacffd
Mortimer adacffd
HART Abigail T bcficc
Charity gaaxaxe
Harty ahdaaf
James bcfiffi
James A adadibdg
Lucille ahgdcafd
Susanna L bcdedcl
HARTEN George bcdgddacc
Thomas bcdgdeab
HARTLEY Irene bcdgdbe
Maria bcdgdah
Nettie bcdgdakcd
HARTLY Rebecca gba
HARTSHORNE Aaron ahbca
HARTT Joshua (Rev) cbbcb
HARVEY Abigail bcfifjb
Duncan bcfifjb, bcfifjja
Emeline bcfifjb
Harriet bcfifjb
Julia Plate bcficanba
Louisa bcfifjb
Lucinda bcfifjb
Lucy bcfifjdb
Margaret bcfifjb
Mary Jane bcfifjb
Miriam adbabic
Stewart L bcfifjb
Stuart bcfifjb
Thomas ah
William bcfifjb
William Dow bcficanba
William Plate bcficanba
HARWELL Louise bcfifhk
HARWOOD William D bcbebbfab
HASELTINE Abigail bcba
Abraham, Abraham 2nd bcba
Deliverance bcbhb
Joan wife bbb
John bbb
Jonathan bcba, Jr. bcdh
Joshua bcba
Mary bcdh
Mehitable bcfih
Peter bcba
Ruth bcba
Samuel bcba, bcbad
Timothy bcbad
HASILTON —— ahbgaa

HASKELL Alfred Edwin adkfbeia
Asa G adabbgm
Betsey E adabbga
Dorothy adabbbdce
Eben adabbbdce
Eliphalet ahbabaea
Frank bcdeddabc
Georgie E adabbbdce
Helen E adabbgabd
Ina Belle bcdeddabc
John O ahgbdgb
Jonathan adabbgag
Jonathan (Rev vet) adabbgag
Maria A ahbabaea
Mary Frances adkfbeia
Mary H adabbhe
Nelson adabbgagb
Sally bcfiiba
Samuel C abcc.gad
Sarah adabbgag
Sarah E adabbgagc
Thomas adabbgab
Warren adabbgagb
Washington adabbgagc
William H adabbgagb
HASKINS Lorenzo Dow ahghe
HASLAM Emma Frances adadagabb
HASSAM Josiah ahfcfd
Sarah ahfcfd
HASTEY Warren B adbabixx
HASTINGS Abiagil akex
Dorothy bcdebejed
Edith A adgfcdgab
Henry adgfcdgab
Leslie bcdebejed
Philinda ahgfa
Thomas a
HASTY Daniel adkgda
John adkgddb
William adkgda
HASWELL Philip bcdgdabfc
HATCH Aver bcbhdbea
Clarence bcdgdabgg
Ellen Melissa bcbcbbgj
Harry bcdgdabgg
Jerusha bcbhdbea
Leander O ahbabag
Louisa adgfbk
Nailer (Capt) bcbcab
Philo Scott bcbcbbgj
HATHAWAY Jane bbbfabc
HAUGHTON Alphonso J bcdedgg
HAUXWORTH Mary abc
HAVEN Mary Ellen adkgdeg
HAVENER Jane N adbabfbf
HAVILAND —— adhahd
HAWES Lizzie H ahbabcfa
Emma E adkecbaaa
James M adkecbaaa
Mary F bcbcbbeeba
HAWKEN Anna Josephine ahgdgbaa
HAWKES Russell adggeia
Viola adggeia
HAWKINS Comfort adaidbb

874

334

Hepzibah ahgc
Lydia adaidbb
Mary Charlotte adhahec
HAWLEY Avery Stone bcfiffh
Charlotte bcfiffh
Harvey bcfiffh
Henry bcfiffh
L C ahbaeda
Mary Elizabeth bcfiffh
HAWTHORNE Ruth ahbchda
Sarah F adkfbbdc
HAYDEN Azubah J adaabdab
Helen adacffee
Mary adgxfdabb
William M eaaa
William V adaabdab
HAYES Dudley adabibf
Eliza A ahgfbdf
Florence bcdgdabb
George bcdedfi
George H adgxfaacba
Mary adgfbejb
Ralph L adgxfaacba
Sarah adadhabb
—— bcdebgaaca
HAYNES Ada E wid bbbfabhd
Catherine bcbebcg
Hazel Hester bcfifjjaba
Mary D adadagc
Melinda adadhcc
Thad ahbabajgd
Thomas bcfi
Warren adadhcc
HAYS Emma adgfbeed
HAYWARD Lucy A adadibac
Reuben adadibac
HAZELTINE Abigail ahbcf
Anna adaidc
Hannah adggbf, bbbfg, bcfigf
John bcfiha
Mary Ann bcdbadg
Phoebe Dow bcfiha
HAZELTON Nathan C adaabfda
—— adgfbgdcg
HAZEN Laura ahdada
HAZLETT Alton bcdgdafff
Burton bcdgdafff
Gerald bcdgdafff
Jennie bcdgdakf
Paul bcdgdafff
HAZZENS John (Capt.) bcde, bcdi
HEAD —— (Gov) addabcf
HEAGAN George abccgcfc
HEAL Alice May ahbgbba
Caroyln Barker adaabffdc
Wesley A ahbgbba
William adaabffdc
HEALD Charlotte bcdebej
Frank C abbegbdcaa
Mary Phylura abccdgdc
Susan bcbhddb
HEALEY Annie ahbaacdf
Elizabeth ag
Elvira wife adadhcaha

Frank D adgcagaba
Hannah adkdb
Karl H bcdgdafbf
Mabel May adadhcaha
Nancy abceb, abdcebj
Mary adkdb
Rebecca A adbabfbgc
Sally adkdbd
Robert bcdgdafbf
Sarah wife adkdb
Stephen adkdb
William adadhcaha, ag
HEARN Florence Virginia bcdeaefca
HEART Henry adkebae
HEATH Ann abdcg, adbae
Annie M adgcaccaf
Bessie V adhafgcbg
Betsey E adabibcaa
Charles B abbegbdg
Deliverance bcbe, bcdd
Elizabeth bcdd
Emma adaabacaf
Gannie adaabacaf
George adaabacaf
Green bcdd
Hannah bcdd
Hannah May abbegbdg
Hannah W wid bcficadb
Henry Ayers abbegbdg
Jane adadicfba
Jeremiah bcdd
Juanna bcbei
John bcdd
Joseph, Joseph Jr. bcde, be
Josephine abbegbdg
Marcia adaaa
Mary bbbc, bcdd
Nehimiah adfa
Olive Jane abbegbdg
Phoebe bcde
Rachel bbbg, bcbhddc
Robert abbeghd
Samuel be
Sarah E P bcdeddhd
William bcdd
William Augustus abbegbdg
HEATON Cyrus bcfifc
HECKLER Ella Corliss wid adkfbede
HEDBERG Carl August bcdebgagc
Carol bcdebgagc
Hollis bcdebgagc
James bcdebgagc
HEDDERMAN Margaret adkecbaac
William H adkecbaac
HEDDING Elijah B adaceddd
Frank S adaceddd
HEMINGWAY Antoinette Jane adac-
 ffc
Eliza adacffc
Newell adacffc
Sarah adacffc
HEMPHILL Aurora ahbchda
Irene W ahbchda
Irene W abbchda

James ahbchda
Joseph adgfcibaa
Joshua D ahbchda
Sarah J ahbchda
HENDERSON Abram bedbadj
Harry C ahbabajaa
Hattie Lula ahbabajaa
Wallace bedgdagc
William ahbahajaa
HENDRICK Benjamin Dow adkfbaa
Cyrus Eaton adkfbaa
Dorothy bedc
Israel bedb
Mary bedb
Mary Ann adkfbaa
Samuel Jr. adkfbaa
HENDRICKS Jessie Edwina adadieaa
Samuel Henry adadieaa
HENFIELD Mabel A ahbabajd
HENGHAM Anna wid abbegbdfba
HENISTON George ahbabkf
HENRY Eliza Georgia bebcbaaaac
John Harry bebcbaaaac
John B bedgena
Leona bedgena
Mary D wid adhafcabd
William Dexter bebcbaaaac
HENWOOD May E befiibea
Calista bbbfhcfj
Josiah abbegfgad
Lizzie abbegfgad
Orianna E abbegfgad
HERBERT Annie adadhcaib
HERRICK E Maria adadage
John bbbebcba
Ruth ahggcb
HERRIN A adgfcja
—— (Miss) ahbabk
HERRIMAN Cornelia Suydam adkde-
  ceh
Henrietta A bedeaeafae
Matthew be
HERRING Henry bebca
HERSEY Viola adgxfdae
—— bbbebcdada
HERSHEY Elsie Ruth ahbabadb
Guy ahbabadb
HERVEY Jennie bebhddj
—— ahbgbfab
HESS Alvin adacfficd
Vernon adacfficd
W B adacfficd
HEWES Ellen adkgdbacb
HEWETT Edward A adgxfahaa
Harry A adgxfahaa
HEWITT Ellen adaceagd
Josephine adaceaah
HIBBARD Amelia ahgfbdh
Clarissa adaceaeb
Ellen P ahbabamgd
HICKEL Martha M ahbabalc
HICKEY James adabbgbeba
Mary B adabbgbeba
HICKMAN Elizbeth Brinton adbabgc

HICKOK Grove Lawrence ahgchfea
Florence May ahgchfea
HICKS Amos ahcbbd
Asher ahcbbd
Carrie M abdcebli
Catherine ahgdce
Charles abdcebli
Florence E ahgcibc
Gilbert ahcbbd
Helen ahcbbd
Henry ahcbbd
Henry Laurens ahcbbd
Mary Jane ahcbbd
Royal bededbbd
Sarah T adgfbgdca
HIGGINS Carrie M ahbabamg
Eugene P adabbgbcaaa
Frank A adacedded
James T adadiac
John adkgac
Moses (Ens) ba
Robert B adabbgzd
Sylvia N adabbgzd
Viola S adabbgbcaaa
Wealthea Ann adadagab
Willard Elliott ahbgbfaaa
Willard S ahbgbfaaa
William M adacedded
HIGHLAND Naomi ahgfdae
HIGHT William (J. P.) adbabi
HILDEBRAND Frank adacff
Lewis K adacff
Lizzie adacff
Robert adacffia
HILEMAN Ella B abbegfcb
HILIARD Manuel a
HILL Abbie adaidaa
Alfred Thomas bedeaefba
Betsey adaidaa
Charles H adkebb
Daniel adaidaa
Edson adadaba
Elmer O ahbabaeda
Emily adaidaa
Elsie A adgfdabbb
Ernest adaidaa
Fannie adgfdabb
Fannie O befifjai
Florence Louise akebdbbfeb
Frances befifjag
Frances E adgfbggb
Frank adadabbf
Fred adadabbf
George adaidaa
George W adgfdabbc
Gilbert P adhafcae
Harriet adaidaa, adbb
Ida Martha ahgfbdd
Isaac (Gov) abbeebc
Jennie adadabbf
John adgfbj
John B adadabbf
Jonathan abdcic
Joseph adaidaa

Joseph A akebdbbfeb
Julius adgfbegb
Laura adadabbf
Mary adaidaa
Mary E adgfbgfc
Nancy adaabcea
Nellie Edith adgfbgebb, adgfdabbc
Robert adgfe
Sally abdcic
Samuel, Samuel Jr. adaidaa
Sumner adgfcicc
Thomas bcdeaefba
True akebdbbc
William adaidaa
—— ahbcajbc
HILLIARD Aubrey B bcdeddhdb
Carrie Gertrude bcdeddhdb
Catherine adadha
Clarissa akebbcb
Frank R adadicca
George adadha
Harland adadicca
Huldah abbed
Malinda adadicd
Warren E adadicca
—— adkda
HILLMAN Annie bcdgdaib
Belle bcdgdaib
Beulah bcdgdafeh
Edmund bcdgdaib
Elsie bcdgdaib
Glena bcdgdafeh
Greely bcdgdaib
Irma bcdgdafeh
Jasper bcdgdaib
Jeremiah bcdgdah
John bcdgdah
Judson bcdgdafeh, bcdgdaib
Lottie adbabfdea
Marion bcdgdafeh
Martha bcdgdah
Mary bcdgdah
Moses bcdgdah, bcdgdaib
Neamiah bcdgdah
Nelson bcdgdaib
Phebe bcdgdaij
Smith bcdgdafeh
Sylvia bcdgdaib
Thelma bcdgdafeh
Vernon bcdgdafeh
Warren bcdgdah
HILLS Daniel Dow ahbabja
Josiah, Jr. 3rd ahbabja
Josiah Edward ahbabja
Mary Ann ahbabja
Rufus ahbabja
Sarah Hilton ahbabja
HILTON Charles H ahbabi
Daniel Dow ahbabi
Joseph ahbaaad, ahbabi
Joseph (Capt. Col.) ahbabi
Lucretia D ahbabi
Marcia wife ahbabi
Margaret ahfcf

Polly ahbabi
Sarah ahbabj
Stilson ahfcf
Theodore ahbabi
HILYARD John adgcaa
HINCKLEY Abel R adgcacbc
Addie adaabfaac
Enoch bbbfhcfc
Eva bcbhddceb
Jennie M bbbfhcfc
Martha wid adkga
HINDS Benjamin bbbffdba
Burnham W bbbffdba
Cornelius ahbgdca
Sarah Augusta ahbgdca
Ulmer E bbbffdba
William Amos bbbffdba
HINMAN Blanche adgfgabc
Grover Snow adgfgabc
HINNISON Inez bcdgdafka
HINTON Aldear adgfcijd
HISCOX Euphrasia adacffi
John adacffi
HISS P Hansen adkdecehc
HOAG Hussey adhd
Jonathan, Jonathan Jr. adhd
Judith adhad
Levi adhdbd
Martha adbabd, wife adhd
Miriam wife adhcbd
Nathan adhcbd
HOBART Anson ahbcaba
Byram adaidage
—— adkgb
HOBBS Abbie L aeeacaa
Abigail abb bcbb
Amos adkfbec
Benjamin abdb, bcbb
Comfort abdb
Curtis M adkfbec
Dorillus adkfbec
Esther abcca, abdb
James, James Jr. abdb
John aeeacaa, bcbb, Jr. bcbb
Jonathan abdb
Joseph abbj, bcbb, bcbbc
Lavinia adkebaa
Lucy abdb
Mary bcbb
Morris abb, abdb, bcbb
Morris 2nd abdb
Patience abdb
Samuel bcbb
Sarah abdb
Simon bcbb
HOBERT Byron adaidage
HOBSON Dorcas wife ahf
Helen adhahd
Hephzebah ahf
John ahf
HODGDEN Amy D adaabcl
HODGDON Abigail Breed adhccd
Anna adhccd
Dorcas Neal adhccd

John adhccd
Joseph adgfbeee
Mary adhccd
Mary P abccdgc
Moses adhccd
Moses Austin adhccd
Samuel abbegfcac
Susannah adhccd
HODGE Annettie bcdedbbd
Damon bcdedbbca, bcdedbbd
Dora bcdedbbca
Eliza wife bcdedbbca
HODGES Edmund (Capt) adggdc
HODGKIN Marcellus adgfbed
HODGKINS Emma bcdeaefcda
HODGKINSON —— bcdedbbbb
HODGSON Edwina C adabbgbcc
HOIT Almira adafbed
Anna ahbgd
Augustus adgfbed
David adgfbed
Jedediah Jr. ahbgda
Lafayette adgfbed
Lizzie adgfbed
Nathaniel adgfbed
William adgfbed
HOITT Daniel adadh
John adadagfa
Judith adadagfa
Susan C adadagfa
HOLBROOK Charles adaabdag
HOLCOMB Arthur ahgfbdh
Frank Terry ahgfbdh
George Dowe ahgfbdh
Hiram ahgfbdh
Millie Florence ahgfbdh
Sanford Augustus ahgfbdh
HOLCOMBE Peggy ahghe
HOLDEN Andrew Morgan ahbabjja
Charlotte L adgcacca
Dorothy adgcacca
Edward F adkfbeddc
Elizabeth adkgb
Fannie abccgcfia
Ira adgcacca
Joseph adgcacca
Nathaniel ahbabjja
Nathaniel Dow ahbabjja
Ruth D adkfbeddc
HOLDER Lydia B adhafdg
HOLKER Catherine M adgxfaaec
William adgxfaaec
HOLLIS Charles W bcdedfec
Florence Bertha adbabfaia
HOLLISTER Edson bcdebge
HOLMAN D C bcbhbfc
HOLMES Elizabeth bcbebbcdaa
George Bass bcficana
Grisel bcbebfc
John x
Joseph bbbffdb
Maria bcficana
Mary bbbffdb
Polly bbbebg

Rebecca Briggs bcficana
William (Rev.) fab
—— (Miss) ahdg
HOLT Eva Jennie ahgfbdae
James E bcdgdanb
—— adadaba
HOMANS Mary adacgfab
HOME Mary E aeeacaaf
HONEYWOOD Dorothy adggdcc
John adggdcc
Robert adggdcc
HOOD Benjamin adhcbc
Charles H adgfbgdcj
Nellie B adgfbgdcj
HOOK Dora V adacgfaea
Elizabeth akeca
Sally adhcba
HOOKER Joseph (Capt.) ahfae
Mary ahbabja
HOOPER Harry adkdecei
Mary adgfbgdc
HOPE Content adbafa, adhcbc, adhcd, adhci
HOPKINS Betsey adaceaea
George akebcfaca
Hiram adaceafa
Mary adkfbbdfb
Melissa ahbabjbc
HOPPER Benjamin (Capt.) adkge
HOPSON Rebecca ahgfbdga
HORN Rachel adkdeee
HORR Georgianna Elizabeth adkgaee
Marion L adkgaee
HORTON Benjamin bcdebe
Elizabeth McClure bcdebe
Fann adgfbegf
Sallie L adacffe
—— (Miss) bcfifjjbb
HOTALING Frederick B adacgfaca
HOTCHKISS Ida J bcdebfge
HOUGHTON Elizabeth Taylor bcfihec
Henry bbbfhbxa
Marcellus adkech
Sarah adadiba, adadibac
Thomas Jr. bcfihec
HOULIHAN Honora abccgdfab
HOUSLEY —— bbbfhai
HOUSTON Caroline R ahbabajcca, bb-
bfhcfhb
Cora M ahbabajc
Dell ahbabajc
Eliza A abccdgcba
Frank K abccdgcba
Harry ahbabajc, bbbfhcfbb
Henrietta Viola bbbfhcfeb
James H bbbfhcfeb
Sarah A ahbabai
William ahbabajc
HOVEY Mary bcfiiba
Mercy ai
HOW Abijah ahe
HOWARD A M ahbaahda
Carrol H ahggbh
Clarissa adggdcd

Henry bcdgdnc
Henry A adabbgagdb
John ahbgikc
Margaret wife ahgbikc
Mary A adgfcjbg
Mary J adabbgaij
Mildred bedgdnc
Persis bcficap
Sabrina ahbcajg
Sarah J bcdbeced
HOWE Charles Lee ahbgbaf
George Delma ahbgbaf
Fred bcdebeea
James adhafac
Josephine J adabbgagcx
Julia bcbhddfd
Lavina A adgcaccaf
Lydia bcbhddaaa
Scott ahbgbaf
HOWER Charles ahchfik
Emma ahchfik
John ahchfik
HOWLAND Eliza A adkfbedc
Harrison C abbegfccd
Joseph adkfbedc
Mary J wife abbegfccd
Mary Nellie abbegfccd
Ray C adhfbgdcea
HOWLETT Fred O adgcadaaab
Frederick bcdgdaiae
HOWRY DeForest bcdebeeaa
HOXIE George R ahbabaf
HOY Samuel R bcdgdaiaa
HOYLE Isabella adhafagd
Lucius E adhafagd
Maria adhafagd
Milton adhafagd
HOYT Abigail ahbcf
Amos bcbebbca
Anna bbbfc
Anne adfa
Benjamin bbbfc
Benjamin S adgfbfcb
Betsey bcbebbca
Charles Alfred adaimcc
Charles F adhafcj
Diana adacffg
E abdcca
Elizabeth adadabb
Enoch W bbbebcbd
Enos adhafcj
Ephraim adaimcc
Eunice bbbfc
Flora adhafcj
Francelia M adhafcj
George Stephen adaimcc
Hannah Jane adhafgdc
Hannah Jane adhafgdc
Hannah M ahbabaf
Henrietta bbbebcbd
Jabez ahbcf
James F adgcadaaac
Jemima wife adaimcc
Johanna ahbgd

John adhafcj
John M abbegfcab
Jonathan bbbfc
Joshua adadabb
Judith bbbfc
Lilla F adhafcj
Lizzie abbegbibc
Lucy A abccgaeaa
Martha G akex
Martha J bcbebbca
Martha W adgfci
Mary L adhafgcb
Mary M K bcbhbfic
Mehitable bcfiibc
Micah bcfic
Moses bcbebbbd bcfiibc
Nathan adhafgcb adhafgcd
Oliver ahbgd
Rebecca wife ahbgd
Reuben G abbegfcaa
Richard P abceabbg
Sally bbbfc
Samuel D adaimcc
Sarah wife bbbfc
Sarah E bcbebbbd
Susan wife adhafgcb
Susannah bcfic
Timothy bbbfc
William H adhafcj
HUBBARD Delia M bcbhddbca
George bcbhddbca
Mary bcdedbacb bcfifb
Joanna bcdedch
Samuel bcfifb
—— (Gov.) adhccbb
—— bcdebgad
HUCKINS Abigail abbegfa
Albert D abbegfa
Aurelia abbegfch
Calvin abbegfa
Dana Dow abbegfa
Daniel abbegfa
Daniel B abbegfa
David abbegfa
Fred Peter abbegfcb
Hosea Q abbegfa
James (Dea) abbegfa, abbegfcb
Jonathan Dolloff abbegfa
Joseph C abceabbf
Joseph D abbegfa
Martin Luther abbegfcb
Nathan abbegfa
Robert abbegh
Ruth B abbegfca
Sarah abbegfa
Thomas abbegh
HUDSON Maria Colburn bcdeaeg
HUES Nancy bbbfax
HUFF Edith adgfbeje
Ella adgfbeje
Ethele adgfbgdce
James G adgfbeje
HUFFMAN C E abbegbdfc
HUGHES Annie ahbabajag

Elizabeth Adelaide wid adaabcjg
Ella bcdgdqa
Ellen bcdgdagb
HUGGINS Nathaniel akebhbb
HULL Adelia bcdgdabb
Charles adgxfaab
Edward bcdgdabb
Maria bcdgdabb
Martha bcdgdabb
Mary Edna abdcedb
Maud E adgxfaabb
Minnie bcdgdabb
Nathaniel abdcedb
Nettie Dow adgxfaabb
Nona Winifred adggegbaa
Orie bcdgdabb
Shepard bcdgdabb
Sophia A bcdeabc
Thomas bcdgdabb
William bcdgdabb
HULTZ Nettie bcbhddccf
HUMPHREY Carrie ahbaahdea
HUNKIN Lydia adkeha
—— adkef
HUNKINS George W adkehb
HUNNAFORD Hannah abbegf
HUNT Amanda J bbbebcbc
Anthony C adhae
George bcdbadg
John W bbbfhig
Leonard D bcdbeceg
Maria Corine adkfbedd
Pitman bcdgdafbda
Rachel bcbhddc
Sarah adaf
Sarah A adhae
Sarah Elizabeth adgfbfcc
Zebulon ahbcaa
HUNTER Charles ahbgbaee
Daisy Annie adaceagcb
Mercy Jeannette adaceagcb
Sarah A ahgfdaj
William adaceagcb
HUNTETON, see Huntington
HUNTING William abccdaa
HUNTINGTON Ann bcbed
Arthur adgxfadi
Carrie adgxfadi
Edward G ahghc
Flavius J ahghc
Florence Williams ahgcabaa
George Daniel adgxfadi
George Franklin adgxfadi
Grace adgxfadi
Henry Hyde ahgcabaa
Henry Roswell ahgcabaa
Herbert Ellsworth adgxfadi
Herbert Fitch ahgcabaa
Joseph (Rev.) ahgha, ahghc
Joseph ahghc
Julia adkfbbjbg
Lillian Maud adgxfadi
Louisa Clinton ahgcabaa
Mary bbbdb

Nellie May adgxfadi
Nettie adgxfadi
Olive adaceddec
Thomas bbbdb
Timothy, Timothy Jr. bbbdb
William bbbdb
HUNTLEY Anna adaceag
Benjamin gab
Eliphalet gab
Frederick gab
Grace D gaaxaxn
Oliver gab
Rebecca gab
Richard gab
HURD Albert S ahbabahcaa
Carlton adgcacbc
Elizabeth Ann adgcacbc
Ethel Christina ahbabahcaa
Fanny Melinda adgcacbc
Gladis A wid adabbgaiia
Isaac Bradley adgcacbc
Levi adgcacbc
Nancy adgcacbc
Nancy Maria adgcacbc
HUNTOON Carter bcbcbaaad, bcbcba-
aae
M E ahbchcba
Mandanah bchcbaaad
Mary Jane bcbcbaaae
HURLBURT Richard adkgaeg
Sylvia Castle adgfcdacbb
William E adgfcdacbb
HURLE Lucy Jane ahgfbdd
HURST Anna ahdaaddf
—— ahbcajcc
HUSE Anna wid adhcbba
Elizabeth bcbhd
Lydia adgfc
Sam (Capt.) adkfb
HUSSEY Abigail O adhafdf
Andrew adhak
Christopher ab, adhch
Daniel adhafdf
Jane wid adbabf
Joseph adhafb
Mary ab, adba
Mary Jane adbabfe
Nancy adbabga
Samuel adhak
Stephen adbf
HUSTON Eva E adaigbbab
Samuel adaigbbab
HUTCHINGS Lester A bbbfhcfee
Marion Warren bbbfhcfee
HUTCHINS Ellen M adgcadae
Frances bcdd
Issara adgcadae
Johannah wid bc
John adgcadae
John C adgcadae
John T adhafad
Joseph bc, bcd
Mary bcd
HUTCHINSON Daisy ahbabajgb

Jonathan adfa
Susannah ahcf
Willard bbbfhcfj
William E adabbgxc
William P adabbgxc
Winnifred bbbfhcfj
HUYLER Abbie Helen abccgdbah
HYMAN Helen wid adgfbea
IBLITSON Florence bcdgdaidd
IDE Edward ahbchb
Mary E abccgadb
INGALLS David W adkddi
George B adgfcibb
Jane adkddi
Joseph H adgfcibb
Laura M adgfcibb
Luther ahbgbaa
Matilda abbegbic
Nancy bcfifjab
Nellie adkedl
Polly wife adkddi
Rebecca ahgdca
Solomon adacfe
Stephen ahgdca
INGERSOLL Ella F adabbgaigb
Charles F adabbgaigb
Robert (Col.) ahbaedc
INGRAHAM John bcdgdeae
Nellie G adbabfbgc
Sewall S adadibad
Thomas H adbabfbgc
INMAN Rose bbbfhbxcd
INNESS Abbie Alexander adbabfdf
Carrie May adbabfdf
Eliza Hill adbabfdc
Frank Wentworth adbabfdc
George adbabfdf
Hellie adbabfdc
Henry Harrison adbabfdc
John Alexander adbabfdf
Walter Edwin adbabfdf
IRELAND Calvin ahbabke
Graham bcdgdeadc
Stella M bcdgdeadc
—— adaaaieea
IRISH Edith bcdgdnc
Emily bcdeabdaa
Jane bcdebgae
Mary adaceal
IRVINE Mary bcdgdg
IRVING Lydia M wid bcdgdaii
JACK Jane ahbgbxa
JACKMAN Charles E adaimbdg
Esther adf
Jessie L adaieaafca
Juda adgxfafc
Lavinia adkfbbd
Polly bcfifhf
Royal befifd
Zachaeus adgcadaa
JACKSON Andrew (Pres.) adhccbb
Andrew adkgdbaca
Delia M adfcdcaa
H A adadagb

Hannah wid bbbfhc
Joseph ahghe
Nelson A (Rev.) ahbcae
Ruth P wid adkfbeddc
Susan adgfbfda, aedb
JACOBS Charles ahbabjf
Emma adbabfeia
JACQUES Eliza bcdgdae
JAMES Beniah M adadagc
Elizabeth adaaafd
Eunice G adkdececb
Frances A adadagc
George adadagc
George R ahbgbba
George W bcbhdbndd
H Maria ahbgbfaaa
Jesse adgfcdab
Joshua abbeab
Josiah adaaafd
July A akebbcbc
Katie adhafgcba
Ruth ahbaacfd
Susanna abbeab
Winthrop Dow adadagc
JAMESON Andrew bcdgdbaac
Annie adadabbdaa
Archie bcdgdec
Bertie bcdgdakca
Catherine abbeh
Clarence bcdgdaam
Esther bbbd
Edward bcdgdakca
Elizabeth bcdgdakca
Fay bcdgdakca
George A bcdgdakca
Howard bcdgdakca
Hugh bcdgdec
Hugh E bcdgdaam
John T bcdgdakca
Laura bcdgdakca
Mary Pauline bcdgdaam
Mildred bcdgdaam
Nanetta bcdgdakca
Nettie bcdgdakca
Ray bcdgdakca
Ruby bcdgdakca
Susanna bbbd
Virgie F adabbgaiia
—— bcdgdec
JANNEY Charlotte bcdebgah
JANVRIN C Eugene adkddgcd
Fannie adaimbaf
Frank M adaimcdbd, adaimcdbe
Hattie M adaimbiac
John T adgxfaaae
Maud H adgxffbd
Nancy adaimbia
Walter Edward adaimcdbe
Wesley A adgxffbd
JACQUITH Emma F bcdebfbab
JARVIS Annie bcdgdafmd
Mary J bcdeddbc
Thelma bcdgdafmd
William I adabbghe

881

JELLISON Maria H adbabbbx
JENKINS Abigail akebcf
Charles adaceabgac
Elizabeth adhe
Harriet A bcfifha
Joshua adbabf
Pearl adaceagac
Shirley bcdebeeab
William Jr adbf
JENKS Clara ahbabja
JENNESS Charles Austin abceabeb
Elizabeth abcead
Fannie Wesley aeeaecc
Francis, Francis 2nd abca
Hannah abca, abcce (bis), abceaa, abceb
Henry abceaa
Isaac abceaa, abceb
James abcce
James Henry adaimaf
John, John 2nd abcce
Jonathan abca, abcce, abceb
Joseph abca, abceaa, (Capt.) abceb, Jr. abceb
Joseph Disco abceaea
Mary abca, abcce, abceaa, abceb
Mary Ann akecaabac
Nathaniel abcce (bis)
Noah abcce
Polly abcce
Richard (Capt.) abca, Jr. abca, 2nd abceb
Samuel abca
Sarah abca, abceb, abdcib
Simon abca, abcce
Wesley aeeaecc
JENNINGS Elizabeth ahbaee
Frederick K bcdedbcb
Nancy ahbeaddb
Sadie E adhafgcbd
JENNISON Ella ahgdgab
Homer ahgdgab
—— ahgdgab
JEPSON Benjamin adadid
Daniel adadid
Elijah adadid
Eunice adgfcdgaaa
Isaac adadid
John, John Jr. adadid
Jedediah adadid
William adadid
JEWELL Alice May aeeaecb
Anna abdci
Erastus Bloomer aeeaecb
Susan adgxb
JEWETT Abigail bcdeab
Eliza M adgfcdgab
Elizabeth adaidab, bcdbe
Exercise aha
Hannah bbbfaxb
Howard B adgxffah
Jacob bcdeab
Martha bbb
Mary adkfbbccb, ahbgid

Mehitable bcfie
Nellie M abccgcfdc
Newell M adgxffah
Stephen (Dea) bcdea
JOHNS Nellie Matilda adhadcea
Sanford J adhadcea
JOHNSON Albert Tyler bcbcbbga
Alfhild adacgfacba
Alma May bcdgdabgf
Almeda bcdgdafm
Amos F ahgdf
Anna adhcbbc
Anna M adgxfbeb
Benjamin abbf
Benjamin Lockrem abbegbdfbc
Betsey ahcbfea
Clifford Miles bcdgdabgf
Daisy Dow bcdecahd
Daniel adhce
Edmund adadad
Edwin bcdbadg
Elisha bcbcbbgba
Eliza adabbgaji
Elizabeth adacffa wid ahbaeg
Ella Francena wid bbbffbaa
Esther abcca
Eva E wid adabibeaa
Florence adacgfaeb
Frank adgfbggbd
Frank Phelps befihb
Frederick bcdgdabgf
Grace Dow bcdecahd
Haines bcfiha
Hannah bbbff bcdgdm
Harry bcdgdagb
Isaac adacffa
Isaac W adacffa
James adacffa, akecac
James G bcdecahd
Joe (Gen.) ahbaedc
John abbf, bcb, befi
Julia bcdgdabga
Lizzie M adhafcabc
Lockrem Harold abbegbdfbcb
Lydia wife adhce, Lydia bcc
Lydia Frances adkfbeia
Lucas adacffa
Lucius adacffa
Marc Dow bcdecahd
Marie Dow adgfbggbd
Mary abcca, adbb, adacffa, bcdbadg
Mary A adaabcf, adacglb
Mary Allein bcbcbbgba
Moses, Moses Jr. bcfihb
Nancy bcdgdeo
Nathaniel abbec, akecae
Nellie Myrtle bcdgdabgf
Peter, Peter Jr., Peter 3rd abcca
Rachel aedb
Robert Eugene bcdgdabgf
Ruth abcca, abccdg, bcb, adgxb
Ruth Dow bcdecahd
Sadie B adgxfdae
Sally abbcce, akecae

Samuel (Capt) ahbg, Samuel ahgdf
Samuel W ahgdf
Sarah abbeb, abcca, ahgdf
Simon abcca
Thomas F ahgdf
Vera Belle bcdgdabgf
Wendall Allen abcdgdabgf
William adabbgaji, fed
Willoughby Dow bcdecahd
—— bcbebbba
JOINER Orlando A ahgfbdb
JONES Alice Maude ahbabkba
Alidia bcdea
Anna E bcdedcea
Arthur adaimbag
Betsey ahbaad
Betsey B adabibb
Carroll Nelson adbabfg
Charles adhafaab
Charles E adbafa
Charles F adaimbag
Clara Susie ahbabkba
David ahbaad
Davis ahbgeeb
Dolly adbac
Dora Edna wid bcbhddceb
E L bcdecahf
Edward adbabfa (bis)
Edward D ahcfjbc
Eleanor ahbaa, ahbaad, ahbaadb, bcdecahf
Elizabeth adgxa, adgxb, bcfica
Ella M adaimcdga
Ephraim akebbf
Evan, Evan (1) bcdea
Francis adbabfa
Frank Perry adgfbeggaf
Frank W adaimcdga
George E adkddcab, bbbfhbacb
Hannah abbeace, adadic, ahbaadb
Harriet M bcdebgd
Harvey A abbege
Helen adadiec
Isaac N ahbabkba
Isaiah adbabfa
James Nelson adbabfg
Jasper ahbaadb
John adgxa, Jr. adgxa, ahbaad
John D adbabfa
John Paul (Com) bcdcbk
John Warren adaimcdgc
Joshua ahbaad
Joseph Clark adhafaab
Judith ahbaadb
Leonora adadiec
Leora May adhahaca
Leroy Farr adbabfg
Lois wife adbabfg
Lydia bcdea
M Louisa akebdbbfeb
Mary wife adbabfa
Mary Ann adbabfa, ahbaadb
Mehitable adgxa
Michael bcbhdehb

Nancy akebbf
Otis adadiec
Otis W adadiec
Pamelia abbeace
Phena abbeace
Rosa E ahbgeeb
Ruth B bcbehda
S. C. bcdecaic
Sarah adgxfc
Sarah Ellen adbabfa
Sarah Maria ahbaadb
Silas adbabfg
Simon G adadiec
Susan bcbhdehb
Susanna wife adgxa
Timothy ahbaa
Tobias adbabfa
Viola adadiec
William adbabfa
JORDAN Alva Reynolds bcdeddf
Ann adgfbgdch
Charles E adkgac
Elizabeth Hannah bcdeddf
Hannah adgfcjb
Mary J bcbhddfac
Samuel Carter bcdeddf, bcdgdafn
JORSTED Dagny I ahbabalc
JOSLYN Aristeen adacffj
Augusta adacffj
Cyron bcfiffa
Fillmore L adacffj
Mary adacffj
JOY Albert adaigai
Edwin (Rev) adadagfbd
James F abbeebc
Mary L bcdeddhda
Sarah adaceb
JOYCE Aletha adabbga
Leila Aileen adkdecebc
JUDD Curtis J adggdade
Elias ahgb
Elizabeth ahgb
Hannah ahgb
John ahgb
Juliana ahgb
Lois ahgb
Mary Ann adacffea
Solomon ahgb
Thomas, Thomas Jr. ahgb
JUDKINS Frank W ahbabank
Hiram bcbhddceb
Mamie bcdhddceb
Mary E ahbgec
Rufus Norris ahbabahk
Sarah T ahbged
JUDY Nellie G ahbgiifb
KAHLER Anna bcdedkda
KALLOCH Adam B abbegbibea
Ethel E abbegbibea
KANE Doris adabbgbcca
Elmer adabbgbcca
George adabbgbcca
Newell J adabbgbcca
Rudolph adabbgbcca

Willard adabbgbcca
KEACH Lydia J ahbgil
KEARNEY Albert bcdgdbab
Alexander bcdgdbab
Ambrosine bcdgdbabd
Asa bcdgdbab
Augusta bcdgdbab
Bessie bcdgdaidb
Ella bcdgdbab
Ernest bcdgdbab
Florence bcdgdabf
Frank bcdgdbab
Howard bcdgdbab
Maud bcdgdbab
William H bcdgdbab
KEATUNG William bcdgdabc
KEAY Daniel L adbabib
—— bcbhbff
KEDDY Ethel M adhafgcbg
James U adhafgcbg
KEELEY Mary E wid adggdadb
KEENAGHAN Cecilia adaceafgg
KEENAN Anna adabbgagda, adabbhfa
KEENE Richard T adgxfdg
KEILEY Jennie adhafcaa
Lawrence adhafcaa
Mamie A adhafcaa
Willie L adhafcaa
KEITH Frank adkgaee
George O adkgaee
Voorannus B bcfihdc
KELLEY A G adkebdd
Abigail bcdg
Ada adkebdd
Amy bcdgdafk
Angie adaabdaba
Arthur bcdedbada
Charles adkebbd
Corinne A wife adaieaafc
Daniel abbegfa, adaidbbc
Daniel C abbegfa
Darby abbege
Diana adaiga
Donald bcdgdafk
Dudley abbege
Freeman bcdgdaalb
Flora M gbed
Hannah Jane bcdeddab
Hattie adkebbd
Hattie A adabiggf
Hattie V adacgjae
Irad adggdcc
Jonathan Dow abbege
Josiah B adaieaafc
Judson bcdgdafkb
Linder A bcdedbada
Lizzie L wid adadagfb
M S adkebbd
Martin S adkebbd
Mary adaabdaeg
Mary O adaieaafc
Nancy abbege
Polly Nichols abbege
Rebecca adabbgbcaa

Richard adaiga
Rosa adkebbd
Sarah wife abbegfa
Sarah Dudley abbege
Wilbert bcdgdafk
Winnifred bcdgdaalb
KELLOGG George E adgfbeje
KELLY Betsey bcbebcb
Eunice ahbgab
Harriet adaabfdi
Iantha P bcbhdhb
Moses (Col) abccdf
Nathaniel bcfigj
Phoebe bcdedf
Rhoda J ahbgab
Richard ahbgab, bcdedf
Sybil wife bcdedf
KELSEY John ahbabjb
Mary ahbabjb
KELSY Marion M ahbcabcba
KELTON Clarissa adhaff
KEMP Joseph ahbcabef
—— bc
KEMPTON John (Capt) adabbgi
KENDALL Anna ahgfa
Ebenezer, Ebenezer Jr. ahgfa
Hannah bcdebfa
Henry adhafcj
Joshua adgfcdgd
Lemuel ahgfa, ahgfaf
Lydia ahgfa
Mary ahgfa
Mary A adgfcdga
Mary J adabibg
Nellie adgfcdgd
Prescott V adabibg
Rebecca adggei
William H adabibg
—— bcdebff
KENEFICK Elizabeth bcdeddhf
Louise bcdeddhf
Marion bcdeddhf
Owen A bcdedhf
KENESON see Keniston
KENISTON Joseph abbec
Nancy W adhafcd
Samuel adhafcd
—— abccd
KENNARD Marie J adaaaieb
KENNEDY Alfred ahcfjc
Clayton Leon adggegbab
Gordon Douglas adggegbab
Harold Leon adggegbab
Henry ahcfjc
John ahcfjc
Lenora ahbgbbea
Mabel E adkfbbjab
Margaret wid bcbcbaaba
Margaret A wife adkfbbjab
Mary akebda, bcbhdb
Matthew adkfbbjab
Susan bcbhdehc
KENNEY Almira Pond adadhcahc
Sarah bbbffdb

884

KENNISTON Lavina bcbhddbca
KENT J E ahbabjie
KENYON Betsey A adaceaeb
Fannie bedecdf
J F adggeeb
—— adaceac
KERBY Margaret ahcg
KERRIGAN Alberta M bcdgdbaadc
Charles G bcdgdbaadc
Clifford W bcdgdbaadc
Evelyn L bcdgdbaadc
Florence M bcdgdbaadc
Gladys B bcdgdbaadc
Irvin William bcdgdbaadc
Jennie R bcdgdbaadc
Luther M bcdgdbaadc
Mae L bcdgdbaadc
KETCHUM Charlotte bcdgdaaeg
Hiram ahcbfa
Samuel beficaq
KEVEEN Grace May bcbhbfib
John L bcbhbfib
KEYES Emma F bcbebbbdb
Horace W bcbebbbdb
KEYSER Allen adadhaca
Katie A adadhaca
KIBBER Robert Hitchcock adkfbbcib
KIBLING Ellen adggegd
KIDDER Bella bcdgdaaad
Frank bcdgdaaad
—— adaidc
KIDNEY James bcbhddaaa
Laura bcbhddaaa
KIERNAN John J (Sen) ahcfjbc
KILBOURNE —— adaceali
KILBURN Emily Bonney bcbcbbgj
Josiah bcbcbbgj
KILLBURN John adaimaac
Sarah C adaimaac
KILCOLLINS Azporah bcdgdakca
KILLAM Mercy ahch
KILLEN Mary aeeacaaab
KILPATRICK Charles E bcdgdbaadj
Eugene L bcdgdbaadj
KILROY Gertrude bbbffcbah
KIMBALL Abigail bbbfj
Abraham bbbfg
Almira bcbebbcaa
Amarette abbegfgaa
Benjamin bbbfj
Caroline P wife abbegfgaa
David bbbff, bbbfj, Jr. bbbfj
Dayton ahdabb
Dorcas bb
Elbridge bbbfabmi
Elizabeth adhadd
Elvira adadhaba
Eunice bcbcbb
Fred Willis adgfbgfdaa
Hannah bbbfg
Henry bb, bbbfj
Hiram akebdbb
Isaac bcdbe
James F abbegfgaa

John adgfbea, bbbfj
Johnson G bcdedbac
Joseph bbbfj
Judith bbbfg
Lydia bcdbe
Mary bbbfg, bbbfj
Moody adaabfaah
Moses bbbfj
Nabby bbbfj
Nora E bbbfabmi
Reuben bcdedfd
Richard a, ab, ad, ae, ah, bb, bbbfg
Sally bbbfg
Samuel bcdh
Sarah adacf, adkbde, bbbfj, bcbegb, bc-
  dedfd
Sarah Page akebbcb
Stephen akebbcb
Thomas Jefferson adadhaba
Timothy bbbff, bbbfg, Jr. bbbfg
Walter Horace adgfbgfdaa
William L adgcadaff
Willie bcdedbbdx
—— (Capt) bcbhi
KING Abbie adacgfa
Edwin S ahchfecb
Elmer C adaimbifc
Lauretta M ahchfef
Maria ahbaaheae
Lydia Lawrence ahbcaj
Mary wife bcbhdei
Mary E bcbhdei
Mary Ellen bcbhdei
Moses bcbhdei
Pearl adadieab
Susan B ahbgdge
KINGMAN Emilia ahgfdae
KINGSBURY A E adacgfgh
Burt adacgfec
Charles adacgfec
Daniel ahgcha
Mabel adacgfec, wife abccgdfbb
Thomas adacgfec
KINGSLEY Jennette bcbcbaaa
William bcbcbaaa
KINNEY Anna S ahdad
Betsey adaigc, adgfbhc
James ahbgbfb
Levi ahdaad
Mercy ahdaad
Thomas bcdgdaik
KINSLEY Jane adgfcdab
Sarah adgfcdab
KINSMAN Cassius C ahbabdaa
Charles A adggdk
Edmund Everett ahbabdaa
Ephraim, Ephraim Jr. adhhdk
Francis Burnham ahbabdaa
Francis S adggdk
Gideon Dow adggdk
Helen I adadagabc
Howard L adadagabc
Joseph Charles ahbabdaa
Joseph Charles Thiot ahbabdaa

885

345

Julius A adggdk
Lewis Dow adggdk
Margaret Eliza ahbabdaa
Martha J adggdk
Mary Elizabeth ahbabdaa
Mary L adggdk
Minerva adggdk
Rose A adadagabc
Timothy W adadagabc
Warren Downe adadagabc
William adbafc
William M adggdk
KINSON Mary bcdeaae
KIRBY John Dow adacffeed
Julius Tefft adacffeed
Julius Tefft Jr. adacffeed
KIRKPATRICK Allan H abbegbdbd
KIRKWOOD Lillian adgfccdacc
KITLER Lorin F adaabcbd
KNAPP E N adkebgaa
Matilda E bcdbadj
KNEELAND Edward adgfbef
KNESS Ellsworth adacgfaebb
Hugh adacgfaebb
Hugh Saulisbury adacgfaebb
KNIGHT Agnes Ruth abdcebk
Angelina Townsend bcdgdaiib
Eleanor J D adhccfd
Eliphalet bcfigd
Elizabeth Ann abdcebk
Emma adaabfaa
Frank B bcfigfdb
Frank Herbert adhcbbffc
George A bcdgdaiib
Grace Green abdcebk
Hannah bcfigd
Harvey bcdedcgb
Henry Harrison abdcebk
Jabez M adhccfd
Joseph adggdaad
Lydia adaabdaee
Mildred Frances abdcebk
Nathaniel G adaabck
Sophia adgfbgg
Stephen Tilton abdcebk
Wyman B bcfigfdb
KNIGHTS Agnes wid bcbebbcdaa
KNOWLES Abigail abccb, abdcc
Amos bcdgdal, bcdgddc
Ann wife adgxfdad
Ardesia wife adgxfaff
Betsey abccgac, adkddfa
Charles adgxfaff
Charlotte bcdgddc
Elias bcdgddc
Eliza bcdgdak, bcdgddc
Elizabeth Olive akecahh
Ezekiel aceab
Flora M adgxfafe
George bcdgddc
Hattie M adgxfdad
Henry adadaba
Henry W adaimbaf
James Edgar adhccfha

Japhtha bcdgddc
Jesse abbeebbb, (Dea) akecahh
John abbeacc
Lewis A adaimcdd
Lewis E adgxfdad
Martha J adgxfaaba, adgxfaff
Nathaniel G adkebac
Sallie A adaimbbb
Samuel J adhccfha
Sarah A adkddfa
Smith adadaba
Victoria A abbeebbb
KNOWLTON Alvin adkebb
Caroline E adgcagab
Eben abdh
George H adkebb
John adgcagab
Nathaniel ai
Rebecca ahbaac
Sally wife adgcagab
KUEHN Ada Martina bcdebgab
Elvira Hartson bcdebgab
Frank Watson bcdebgab
Hiram bcdebgab
Marana bcdebgdb
Susan Watson bcdebgab
KYTE Mary Dingman adaidae
LaBELLE Alphonso bcdgdsba
Mabel bcdgdsba
LABOUNTY Margaret Nellie adhadcea
Walter adhadcea
LADD Abigail abbegg, bcfifd
Achsah bcfifd
Asa adgfcih
Bela Orlando bcdbee
Charles bcdbee
Cyrus ahchfc
Daniel bcdbee, bce
George Williamson Livermore bcdbee
Gordon abbegg
Hannah bcfifd
Heman bcfifd
Jedediah P bcfifd
Jonathan abbegg
Levi Dow abbegg
Lewis abbegg
Louisa bcfifd
Lucretia bcfifd
Lydia bce
Mary ahgc
Nabby bcfifd
Nancy abbegg, bcfifd
Nathaniel bcfifd
Permelia bcdbee
Polly bcfifd
Richmond bcfifd
Ruth abbegg
Sally bcfifd
Samuel, Samuel Jr. abbegg
Sophronia bcfifd
Stephen, Stephen 2nd abbegg
Thaddeus bcfifd
Welcome D bcfifd
William H bcdbee

LAFFERTY Luenda M ahchfec
LAIGHTON Sylvanus adbabfh
LAKE Thomas adgcad
William H abccgaeaaa
—— adgcaf
LAKEMAN Maria wid ai
Sylvanus, Sylvanus Jr. ahbe
LAKIN John akebdbbfa
Moody akebbf
—— bcbhdgag
LAMBERT Glencora ahbabajc, bbbfh-
cfhb
Hester bbbf
Nettie abbegfjad
Richard bbbf
LAMKIN Charlotte adaccafa
LAMOREAUX —— adabbgagdd
LAMPREY Anna abccdaa
Austin akecaabac
Benjamin abcd, abcc, Jr. abcd, 3rd ab-
cd, abdb, Jr. abdb
Charles Thatcher akecaec
Charlotte abceaa
Daniel abccdaa, (Lieut) abccdaa, ad-
aimbha
Daniel Perley adaimbha
David J akecaabac
Dudley abbeedc, akecaec
Eli abccdaa
Elizabeth abbeh, abccdaa, abcd, ae, ak-
ecag
Ellen Knight adaimbce
Frank akecaec
Gillyen wife ae
Hannah abcd, abcea
Hannah P wife adaimbha
Henry ae
Hezekiah B akecaabac
Howard E adaimbha
Isaac abcea
James abcea
Jane abcd
Jeremiah Dow abccdaa
John abdccb
John D abbeedc
Jonathan L akecaec, akecaee
Joseph A abbeedc
Lettie J adaimbha
Lewis S adaimbha
Lewis T adaibmha
Marietta adaimbha
Marion Ardelle akecaabac
Martha abcea
Mary abcd, abcea
Mary Abby abbeedc
Mary Ann abbeebb
Morris ae
Moses Swett abc
Oliver akecaec
Oliver Freeman akecaec
Reuben abbeebb, akecag
Ruth abccdaa
Sally abccdaa
Samuel abccdaa

Sarah abcd
Sarah Maria akecaec
Simon abcd, abcea, abdb
Simon Nudd akecaec
Warren Carleton akecaabac
William E adaimbha
William T akecaec
LANCASTER Eliza J bcbhdqa
Mary abcc
Mercy bcbehbf, bcbhbfg
Timothy H bcbhdqa
LANCE Betsey adaabcb
Sally adaabcb
LANCEY Bessie Bertha adaceafgea
William adaceafgea
LANE Abbie Ermina adbabfia
Ada Maude adabbgaih
Anna ahfcaaaf
Austin J ahfcaaaf
Charles akecagaa
Clara adbabfeab
Comfort abbed
Cyrus T adaidaga
David abbed
Ebenezer, Ebenezer 2nd abbeacc
Emily R bcdeddb
Frank T adaidagc
George A adaidagc
Hannah abbed
Hattie A adadicfb
James abbeebbc
Joel abbeab
John abbeab, abbeacc (bis), (Maj)
abbed, Jr. abbed, adbabfia
John Dow abbeacc, aeeaeb
John T adaidaga
Joseph abbed
Joshua abbeab, (Dea) abbed, 2nd abb-
ed
Lilla Jane ahfcaaaf
Mary abbeab, abbed
Martha A abbeacf
Meshech abbeab
Miribah A abbeebbc
Nancy abbeacc, adadabcf
Nancy Leavitt abbeacc
Nellie adaidagc
Olive bcbebbfb
Samuel abbed
Samuel Dow abbeab, abbeacc
Sarah abccdaa, bcbhdpaa
Sarah Ann bcbhhg
Sarah E aeeaeb
Thomas abbeacc
William abbeab, Jr. abbeab, (Dea) ab-
beab, 2nd abbeab
LANG Elizabeth abbed
Dowrst abccgab
Hannah abccgab
Mary Jane abccdgcb
Patty abccgab
LANGDON Mary abceab
Sam (Rev) adaij
LANGLEY Alice bcbhddfaa

Andrew Freeze adkebe
Charlotte adkea
Effie bcbhddfac
H B adkebca
Hannah adkeae
Heuron bcbhddfaab
Isaiah adkebca, adkebe, adkebf
Jacob adkeabb
James bcbhddfaa
James E adgfbfbaa
Jessie ahbgbbc
John L adkebf
Mary A adkebca
Mattie A adgfbfbaa
Meedie wid bcbhddfaa
Mehitable adkebf
Nettie bcbhddfaab
Olive Jane adkebf
Timothy adaigaf
True adkeabb
—— ahbgbbc
LANNING Emma C adaabfdfb
LAPONT Laura Jane adhcbbj
LARCOM Anna wife ahfciba
Mishael ahfciba
Susan ahfciba
LARIBEE Beulah ahgb
LARRABEE Clara adgfbef
Emma W ahbgbfaac
Olivia D adgfcdgc
William adgfbef
LARSEN Caroline Augusta Theodora
  bbbffbaadb
Theodor (Capt) bbbffbaadb
LATHAM Julia Ann adgfbgdcaa
LATHROP Ann bcbehdb
Bethiah bcfifl
Eugene R abdcebeaj
Mary E abdcebeaj
LATTY Phoebe b
LAVO Amanda adacgfc
LAWLER Ada M bbbfabmg
John bbbfabmg
LAWRENCE Daniel Dow ahbabjd
David Merrill ahbabjd
Dorothy M bcdeabc
Elizabeth bcdedkb
Gordon Daniel ahbabjd
Lula bcdgdqa
Lydia bcdeac
Mary Susan ahbabjd
Oliver bcdeac
Roxana adabbgea
Sarah Ann ahbabjd
LAYCOCK John Landon adggeilda
LEACH Benjamin, Benjamin Jr. bcd-
  ebd
Chloe abbeacbb
Clarissa ahbgdg
Cora Jane abdcebcab
Florence bbbfhcfc
Hannah bcdebd
Ira bcdebd
Isabella abbeacbb

Lorin C abbeacbb
Lydia bcfiffa
Martha Jane abbeacbb
Mary Abigail bcfiffa
Robert bcfiffa
Simeon bcdebd
LEAMAN Annie bcbhddba
LEAR Eleanor R adggdcib
LEARY Pauline adabiggda
LEATHE Elijah A bcdeaad
LEAVITT Abigail aeeacab
Benjamin abdd
Betsey adaaai
Betty abbeea, abbj
Caroline F akecahba
Dudley adaaai, akebc
J J akecahj
John aeead
Jonathan akecaea
Luther aeeacc
Mary akeb, bcdgdaace
Mary Ann abccgacca
Miriam abbeebbb
Moses akecaea, abbeaa, (Capt) adgxa,
  akecahba
Rachel akebc
Samuel (Col) adgg
Sarah wid akecad
Sarah A akecaec
Simon abbeaa
Thomas Hale akecahg
—— abbeaa
LE BARNES George ahgdcafc
LE BARON Edna May adgfcdgcc
LE BOSQUET Lydia bcdbecc
LE CLAIR Annie E adhcbbfg
Blanche akebdbbiga
Dennis akebdbbiga
LEE Agnes ahbaacdab
Bertha adacgfeba
Fitzhugh (Gen) adhccbb
Doris bcdgdaiif
Francis bcdgdaiif
Howard bcdgdaiif
Jesse (Elder) ahghe
Joseph adkfbbdfc
Nancy F adhcbc
Nathan Jr. ahfcia
Robert P adkfbbdfc
Seth ahbabaeb
William bcdgdeag, (Rev) faab
LEEHY Joanna adkfbbjd
Mary wife adkfbbjd
Thomas adkfbbjd
LEETE —— (Gov) adggdccab
LEHECKA William F ahbabajgca
LEIGH Eliza J bcbhdeia
LEIGHTON Charles F abccdgcab
Abigail adaha
Daniel W adabbgbebb
Cornelia bcdedbbd
John adhafdf
Lois adadagad
Louise adabbgda

Lucy adaidaa
Mabel Moore adabbgbebb
Mary E adhafdf
LEITCH Martha J adaigbbad
LELAND Christine adgfbgeaea
Walter E adgfbgeaea
LENIHAN Julia beficaled
LENTON Maria fcee
LEONARD Henry ahdade
John A adabih
LE RAY —— ahbcabeaa
LESLIE Frank bcdgdeae
Jonas bcbee
LETTON Anna S adggdada
Theodore W adggdada
LETTRICK Jane bcdgdagh
LEVERMORE Levi adaabd
LEWELLEN Evelyn M bcdeaedaaa
LEWIS Alfred akecaah
Amos bcdgdbb
Betsey ahbabaed
Clark K adabibg
Cyrus adbabge
Edmund Jr. bcfifl
Elizabeth adhe, bcbh
Henry Prentiss bcfifl
Joseph adaabcfbc
Mary bbbfhcf
Priscilla bcdedbad
Sarah adhafgce
Susannah adhe
William adbabge
LEYS Mary Ann abdcebec
LIBBEY Abigail ahbabkb
Francis abbeh
George W adadhaaa
Hannah wife ahbabkb
James adgfcdac
Jonathan ahbabkb
Lydia ahbabkb
Mary abbeh
Mary Octavia adadhaaa
Mehitable Thayer adgfcdac
—— adgfcdacca
LIBBY Charles Albert adgfdcf
Erah adkeabaa
Frank J bcfifhhhb
Frank S adhccfeb
George B adgfdcd
George W akebce
Hannah E bcdgdafec
Isaac Lotan adggea
John Bayles adggea
Jonathen Jr adgfdcd
Lizzie E adkeabaa
Mabel F bcfifhhhb
Miranda adkgdca
Nellie A adkgddd
Olive adkeabaa
LIGHT Ellen adadhcafa
LIGHTBODY Ruth adgfcdgaaa
Samuel adgfcdgaaa
LINCOLN Alice L bcdedcfc
Blanche Estelle bcbhdbnae

Cornelius J (Col) adggeic
Delia Jane ahbcaba
Edward adaceaebba
Ellen R ahbgbxb
George H bbbffbaab
Grace Sarah bbbffbaab
Isaac adbabf
Lewis Perkins bbbffbaaba
Lillian Josephine adaceaebba
Lucia Dolly adggeic
Lucy wife adbabf
Zilpha adbabf
LINDBURG Daisy adabbgaiea
Magnus adabbgaiea
LINDERMAN Eva adacffec
George adacffec
George H (Rev) adacffed
Hubert adacffec
Montie adacffec
S L adacffec
LINDLEY —— adggega
LINDSAY Edmond adadhcbc
Ella adadhcbc
Henry adadhcbc
N W bcdedbbbg
LINGFELTER C T adacgfacd
Helen M adacgfacd
Mildred adacgfacd
LINTON Jane adhccfh
John adhccfh
LISLE William bcdedk
LITCHFIELD Georgietta F bcdeddhdc
William abbegfjd
LITTLE Annie ahbchg
Emma L bcfigfde
Ernest E bcfigfde
Frank Henry bcfigfde
Frank W bcfigfde
George H bcfigfde
Hattie A bcfigfde
Hazen R ahbghjg
Helen J bcgigfde
Henry C bcgigfde
Herbert C bcfiibcg
John C bcfigfde
Joshua Follingsby bcbhdf
Mary L bcfigfde
Mary Poor bcfigfdd
Minnie A bcfigfde
Nathaniel Hale bcfigfde
LITTLEFIELD Albert L adkgaec
Caroline abccgdce
Charles H adkgaec
Daniel H abccgdce
Emma P adaimbbe
Homer bbbebcdaab
Julia A adaceaebaa
S F adadagabd
Sarah abdcebe
LITTLEHALE Edna Dow bcdbeda
Nellie (Mrs.) adgfcdgd
Richard b
Sargent S bcdbeda
LIVERMORE Thomas L (Col) adgfgab

LOCK Harriet akebdbbgc
LOCKE Abbie adaimd
Abigail adaabdf
Abbot A akecahc
Alice Etta bcbebbbdc
Benjamin abdcd
Bethia adacb
Betsey adacb
Betty abccgac
Daniel B adgffcc
Dudley S akecahc
Ednah E adaigaaac
Edward, Edward 2nd adacb
Elnora L adaimbae
Fred W adaigaaac
George A adhcbbffd
George C adaimbae
Henry abceac
Hubbard adaimd
Inez A adaimbae
James adacb
Jeremiah, Jeremiah 2nd abceac
Jeremiah A adaimbae
John adacb
John D akecahc
Joseph abca, Jr abca, abcea, abceac, Jr abceac
Josiah adacb
Laura Jane adaimbae
Luella B adaimbae
Lucy adhafag
Lydia adaimbd, adaimd, adggbdb, adgxfbe, adgxfbf
Margaret Alice adhcbbffd
Mary abceabef, abceac
Mary L adaimbae
Mercy abceac
Miriam abbeedc, akecaec
Samuel abdcd, sr abdcd, abcfk
Sarah A adkddce
Sarah C adkddgc
Simon adacb, adaimd, adggbd
Timothy Blake adacb
LOCKWOOD Nellie adaceagcc
LOFFY A adgxfafg
LOFINCK Clara E ahchfdca
LONEY George adhcdace
LONG Caroline adkfbdx
Mary A adgxfahaa
LONGFELLOW Mary adggeibaa
LONGHORN Elizabeth bcba
LONGLEY (also see Langley)
Fred akebdbbfa
John F adgfcjbf
LONGMORE Elizabeth adgfbgead
LONGSTAFF John bcdgdah
LOOMIS Mary Adele ahgfbdd
Nancy ahghc
Nellie Maude adhcbbgg
Solomon P ahggca
LORD Charlotte Lucia adkdeeca
Christie Leander adkdeeca
Clarissa Alvina ahbgdfd

Elizabeth M bcdebfbd
Eugenia Maud adkdeeca
Fanny akebid
Frank bcdedbcb
Kirke Abbot adkdeeca
Mary Ann adaija
Philena S bcdebfba
Edward S adabbgagcx
Hazel Anita adabbgagcx
Hannah C akebdbbb
LOSINGER Josephine adadabga
LOTT Florence A ahgfbdb
LOVE Fannie Tamar wid abbegbdb
LOVEJOY Caroline S ahgfbdga
Cornelia A bcdeaeh
Daniel bcdeae
Sally bcdeae
LOVERING Annie Dow adkdecei
Arthur adkdecei
Cornelia Herriman adkdecei
Ebenezer abcb
Eleanor adkdecei
Gilbert bcdeaae
James W adkdecei
Joseph adkdecei
Susan Rockwell adkdecei
—— (Col) abbeacb, adaieb
LOVETT Florence adbabfic
Mabel adbabfic
LOVEWELL Abbie bcbebcga
LOVIT Thomas a
LOW Abiel Abbot adkecl
Daniel D bbbfhbaca
Mehitable adgfcdac
Olive bbbfhbaca
Seth adkdecl
LOWD Elizabeth abceabd, abceabdb
Daniel abceabd
LOWE Charles E adkgaeda
Eleanor Dennis adkgaeda
George B adkgaeda
Martha A bcbhddcea
Thomas adabbgac
William adkgaeda
Whitney B adabbhm
LOWELL Ann Russell bcbhdpa
Charles bcbhdde
Charles W bcbhdde
David G adhafdj
Elizabeth adkgaa
Ellen Maria adhcbbg
Harrison adgfbgdc
Lydia A adgfbgdc
Mary L bbbfhcfg
Pauline abbegba
Raciel adkdgg
Sarah A ahbgbeb
Thomas sr bcbhdpa
—— bcbcbbad
LOWRY —— adggdf
LUCE Belle bcfifjjb
Catherine adacffh
Chauncey adacffh

LUCY Lydia D adaabff
LUDDEN Hiram adggeim
La Motte adggeim
LUDLOW Bertha H abbegbiba
Carroll H abbegbiba
Effie L abbegbiba
Emilie E abbegbiba
Maria P abbegbiba
Roy E abbegbiba
Whitten abbegbiba
LUFKIN Asa A adkgaebe
David bcbebd
Ella adkgaebe
Lucy A akecaec
—— bcfifhbb
LULL Jeremiah aia
John, John Jr aia
Mary ahbe
Matressa F adgfbfcc
LUNDY Enen bbbfhi
LUNNELL Laura bcdeaedaac
Walter bcdeaedaac
LUNT Lucia adkdee
LUTWICK Alonzo bcbgdeag
David bcdgddb, bcdgdeag
George bcdgdeag
Izetta bcdgeag
Jane bcdgdl
Jennie bcdgdagh, bcdgdeag
John bcdgddb, bcdgdeag
Laura bcdgdeag
Lorene bcdgddb
Matthew bcdgddb
LYDDEN Ida May ahgcigb
LYDSTON Timothy ahbgfa, ahbgfh
LYFORD Addie Grace adabibcca
Alfred ahbaea
Augustus ahbaea
Caroline ahbaea
Eliza ahbaa
Francis ahbaa
Harriet ahbabaja
John Ham adabibcca
John Pearl adabibcca
Joseph ahbaea, Jr ahbaea, ahbaed
Lydia E ahbabaj
Moses ahbaea
Paul John adabibcca
Ruby Elizabeth adabibcca
Susanna ahbaed
LYKINS Julia ahgfbdc
LYLE Sarah Crandall adgfbgfaa
LYMAN Abner adhafce
Henrietta ahgchj
LYNDE Robert bcdedbag
LYON Eugenia P adgfbgfda
—— adabba
LYONS May E bcbhdekd
Thomas E bcbhdekd
MABAN Evalena bbbffcha
MABBS Fannie bbbfabmg
MACCLYMENT David bcbhbgb
Harry A bcbhbgb
MACE Horace O abbeebbc

Josiah D abbeace
Mary abbeed, akece
Samuel abbeac
Sarah ahbgba
MACK Mary O (Mrs.) ahchfg
MACKIN Anna adkgdbacb
John T adkgdbacb
MACLENNAN Minnie adaceddcb
MACLINN George Darling adgcaccafa
Lester Hobart adgcaccafa
MACREYNOLDS Laura Christina ab-
begbdbf
MACURE Joseph adgfcd
MADDOCK Amy ahchfifa
Lindley H ahchfifa
MADDOCKS Alexander H adgcagag
Willard L adgcagac
MADIGAN David bcdgeka
Ellen bcdgeka
MAGHAN Ellen bcbhdbedaa
MAGNER Mame Wall adacffeh
MAGOON Elizabeth adbabfi
MAGUIRE Charles adhafdgea
Edith Charlotte adhafdgea
Ella Powers adhafdgea
Jean Edna adhafdgea
Katherine Aileen adhafdgea
MAHAFFIE Luvina adacffea
MAHAN Hannah N ahfcfce
MAHANY Hepzibah bcfigfb
MAINE Joel T bbbfhjf
MAKER Bessie M gbakh
Blanche B gbakh
Job gbakh
MALCOLMSON Edna bcdebgaae
MALLORY Mary (Barnum) wid ahche
MALONEY J D (U S N) bcdbeceec
James Dobson bcdbeceec
MALOON Climena ahbgdc
Luke ake
Sarah ake
MALTBIE Albert Lyman abbegbdff
Achsah Adelia abbegbdff
Edna Alice Theodora abbegbdff
MAN Chloe bcficai
MANCHESTER Marie Abigail adgfb-
gfa
MANGAN William H ahbabalb
MANING Ann a
MANK Abbie adhafdgec
MANLEY Olla V bcdecdba
Polly ahggb
Sarah J bcdeaefb
MANN Alice M bcbhddceb
Addie Adeline akebis
Isaac bcbhddceb
Jacob E bbbffafaa
Joseph Merrill bbbffafaa
Mary Catherine adbabfdd
Nathan akebis
MANNING Annie Dell bcbcbbacd
Eunice Kinsman bcfifi
Henry Waldo bcbcbbacd
John Parker bcbcbbacd

Walter Everett bcbcbbacd
MANSFIELD Sarah bcdgdanea
MANSON Catherine Lucretia adgfgab
MANWELL Peter bcdecb
MARBLE see also Marvel
Abigail bcdc
Hannah bcdc
Harriet B wid adaceaebb
Nathaniel, Nathaniel jr. bcdc
Rachel bcdc
MARCH Abigail ahbchcb
David ahbgia
Eldad adhagbc
Eliza A adhagbc
Elizabeth xaa
George ahbgia
Jacob ahbgia
Lydia wife adhagbc
MARCUM —— c
MARCY Samuel adacfe
—— (Gov) ahchfe
MARDEN Ally adbabfea
Ella F adgfbgfi
Hannah adgcada
Judith bcbb
Samuel abceaea
Sarah adgcada
MARLIE —— bcdgdagj
MARRIAN Elizabeth abcb
MARSH Abigail adkdecec
Almond adggeif
Anna ahgcab
Annie bcbhddfaba
Dudley adaaba
Elizabeth ahcb
Ellen bcdbaddaa
George abbegfja
George F abbegfja
Hattie B adgxfaacba
Helen M ahbabahgb
Ida adggeif
Mary akebdbbga, ba, be
Nancy akebdbbga
Olive adggeif
Sarah wife akebdbbga
Stephen D akebdbbga
MARSHALL Annie M wid adabbgbcaa
Clarissa adhagba
George adabbgbcaa
Ida May Heath bcdebgbbc
Lovisa A abccgchc
MARTAIN Alice M adgfcdaceb
Charles adgfcdaceb
MARTEL Charlotte M akebdbbgdb
Zeno akebdbbgdb
MARTELL Phebe adahdx
MARTEN Sarah adkfb
MARVEL David adaaae
Esther wife adaaae
Jonathan adaaae
MASON Adelaide adabbpaa
Adelia D bbbfhja
Caroline ahfcfce
Clara B adkgdbac

Freelove bcdecah
Harriet Newell adgfbff
Ida S adgxfagc
Jerusha abbegba
Julia wife adgxfagc
Louisa abccgdf
Love aeeac
Lutie E bcbcbbgbba
Lydia Ann bcdecah
Mary abcce
Mary Eliza bcdedbcd
Nancy bcdecah
Nicholas W bcbcbbgbba
Rachel adhahd
S Bailey adgxfagc
Samuel abceac
Sarah abccgdc
Wheaton bcdecaa
William E adgfbffa
MASSEY Pashere adhafcabdb
Richard adhafcabdb
MASSY Adeline P bcdeddc
Norace S bcdeddc
Jonathan bcdeddc
Lizzie H bcdeddc
Myra S bcdeddc
Stillman E bcdeddc
MARSTON Abbie S akecafh
Abial abdg, adhc
Abigail abbec, adbccb, aeeaec, akecaa
Abraham akece, bcdgdabb
Albert Jeremiah abbegbdd
Anna akead
Betty adbgca
Clara Hazel bcdgdanea
Comfort akece
Cotton Ward akece
D W adkebda
Daniel abbec, adkebda, akece
David abbeaa, abbf, akece, Cornet
    akece, akg
Deborah abbefe, akec, akece
Edith bcdgdaib
Eliza Hilliard abdbcaf
Emily A adkebabb
Emma Frances abbegbdd
Ephraim abccb, abdcc, (Capt) abdgc,
    akea
G Harvey ahbabi
George adkebda, bcdgdanea
Hannah abbf
Irene gbaiab
Isaac, Isaac Jr akece
Jane abbef
Jennette Eliza abbegbdd
Jeremiah abbegbdd
John abdgc, akeab, ah
John Blake abbegbdd
John Dow abbegbdd
John Melcher abdgca
Jonathan abdbcae, abdgca, (Col) akec-
    ad, (Capt) akecaf
Josiah akecac
Lawrence bbbfhcfb

Lena C adkebda
Louisa Webster abbegbdd
Lucinda aeeaca
Mabbie adkebda
Mary abdcc, akeac
Mary Ellen abbegbdd
Nancy abdgca
Phoebe abccb, akea
Obadiah abbf
Polly abbeebb
Roy R bbbfhcfb
Samuel abdgca, (Gen) ahbabi, akeaf
Sarah abc, akeaa, akecaf, bcdgdeaf
Sarah B adgxfadf
Simeon abbeh
Simon abbef, akec, akece
Thomas abc
Thomas E aeeaeca
William bcdgdbad
—— abca
MARTIN Almina bcdedbcb
Andrew Jr. ahbcah
Annie bcbebbbdbd
Christopher bcdgdea
Daniel akebcf
Edwin Walter bcdedbcb
Ella Gertrude bbbfhbxcd
Emma bcdedbbbc
Emma Josephine bcdedbcb
Eunice ahfcaa
Frances Eliza bcdedbcb
George bbbfhbxcd
Helen Gertrude bcdedbcb
Ira Foster bcdedbcb
Ira Foster Jr bcdedbcb
Jahiel Hale bcdedbcb
Louis Buffum adaabcja
Lucetta bcdgdea
M (Dr) bcdeabc
Mary ad
Mary E abccgacl
Mary Ella bcdedbcb
Meline bcbebbcdax
Mehitable adaabfg
Ninian ahdaaddi
Robert bcbhddbaa
Sarah bcdedbc
Viva M bcdedbc
MATHERSON —— ahbcabcbd
MATHEWSON Charles bcdbecca
MATTESON Jesse ahchfd
—— ahgchha
MATTHES Benjamin, Benjamin Jr. ah-
babjia
Charles Herbert ahbabjia
Ida ahbabjia
MATTHEWS E gaaxaxa
Etta wife gaaxaxa
Janette adgfbef
Lillian adhahedb
Lucinda akebinb
Mary bcbebbfacb
Nancy H gaaxaxa
MATTHEWSON Charles bcfifjaa

Philip bcfifjaa
MAVERICK Dwight D ahbabcdbc
E H ahbabcdbc
Edward E ahbabcdbc
Eliza bcb
Lillian M ahbabcdbc
MAXFIELD Betty adgcac
Elizabeth bcbebf
John bcfk
James adadabbd
Naomi adadabbd
Sophronia G bbbffbaa
MAXIM Flora abccgcfdb
MAXON Beulah bcdgdafn
Ernest bcdgdafj
Farrel bcdgdafn
Hedley bcdgdafj
John bcdgdafj
Maud bcdgdafn
May bcdgdafj
Percy bcdgdafj
Ruby bcdgdaai
Tyler bcdgdaai, bcdgdafj
MAXSON Mary adgfcdab
MAXWELL Emily Judson adbabfde
Isabella D adadhcahd
Sarah adbabfde
MAY Prudence ahbghh
Sally ahfcfd
Sarah abbeac
MAYHEW Annie C ahbabaee
Fred A ahbabaee
Hosea B ahbabaee
MAYNAHAN Hannah adaiiaaed
MAYNARD Frank abbegfgag
John, John (1) adhccbb
Maria Cornelia Durant adhccbb
Mary F wife abbegfgag
Nellie V abbegfgag
Sally bcdedfd
McADAM Grace Enid adhcbbgda
William adhcbbgda
McADAMS Annie bcdgdbaaac
Richard bbbebcf
McALLISTER Esther adaabcjj
Frank bbbfhcfed
Gertrude H adgxffbba
John D adgxffbba
Mary bbbffc
McALPINE Eben bcdedbcg
George Willis bcdedbcg
William Henry bcdedbcg
McARTHUR Jennie ahgdgaa
McBIRNEY Mary bcfiheb
McCABE Mary adhafgcbg
McCAFFREY Belle adaabdabg
McCAIN Harry adggeicba
Harry A adggeicba
McCALL Anne, Anne wife eb
Samuel eb
McCANN Sophronia adaieba
McCARTER Martha bcbcbbaf
McCARTHY John adabigb
McCARTNEY W ahfcfca

William Jr ahfcfca
McCARTY Anna adaceaeba
McCAUSLAND Harold bbbfaxbca
J Merritt bbbfaxbca
McCLAIN Katie bcdgdeaceb
McCLELLAN Geneva bcdgdafda
Clyde bcdgdaijd
Herbert bcdgdafda
Mary bbbfabh
Pauline bcdgdafda
Phyllis bcdgdafda
Robert adgcadad
Spencer bcdgdafda
McCLOSKEY Beatrice bcdgdaijd
McCLOUD Flora R befifjjad
Mel— befifjjad
McCLURE Albert A ahbabaee
Elizabeth Burns bcdebf
James Wallace adbabfdf
Mary ahbaahe
McCONNELL Ellsworth Dow adhahfa
George H adhahfa
Thomas adhahfa
McCOOL Annie adgfcdacb
McCORMICK Frances bbbfhcf
Patrick bbbfhcf
McCOY Bridget adahdc
Daniel adahdc
Lois adgfe
McCRAY Daisy bcbcbaaaga
William S bcbcbaaaga
McCREASE Lydia adgg, adgi
McCRESSON Elizabeth adgfbgfib
McCRILLIS Mary adaidb
Mary wife adaidb
Robert adaidb
McCUBREY Annie bcbhddfaca
McCUE James Anthony abccgdfab
Thomas abccgdfab
McCULLOCH Annie J adbabfbgd
McCURDY Christopher bcdgdpaa
Joanna bcdgdpaa
McDANIELS Elizabeth adgcadad
Henry W adgcadad
Joseph adgcadad
Lucretia adadagfb
Nehimiah adgcadad
Tristram adgcadad
William adgcadad
McDERMOTT Elizabeth C ahgdccad
McDOEL William bbbfh
McDOLE Georgianna akebdbbgda
McDONALD Ainsworth Duncan adbab-
  fdc
Barnes Sibley adbabfdc
Catherine adkgdba
Daniel Donald adbabfdc
Donald Inness adbabfdc
Reed Inness adbabfdc
Sarah Inness adbabfdc
McDOUGAL John Dudley ahchfe
Maria A ahchfe
McDUFFIE Rhoda befifjd
McEACHERN Barbara abbegbdg

McELROY Cecil bcdgddeab
Frank bcdgddeab
Ward bcdgddeab
McFARLAND Maggie gbefa
Murry adaabdaebb
Wesley bcdgdaiia
McFARREN Minnie Dow ahgchm
William H ahgchm
McFREDERICK Annie R bcdgdaka
Mary bcdgdafbd
Rebecca A bcdgdaka
McGEE John ahgcica
McGIBBONY Cassia bcdgdabc
Elizabeth bcdgdabc
Fannie bcdgdabc
Florence bcdgdabc
James bcdgdabc
Mabel bcdgdabc
Martha bcdgdabc
McGIGGEN Hazel bcdgdaalb
McGILTON Margaret bbbfabmaa
McGLOUCHLIN Emma abdceblfa
McGOWAN Janet Crawford adabibicb
McGRAW Bridget bcdebgaag
M A ahchfiga
McGREGOR Charlotte bcdedbccb
McGULLION Nellie L ahfcfcec
McILROY Mary bcdgdafeg
McINTIRE Phoebe L abdcib
Susan adhcbbfbb
—— akebdbbad
McINTYRE Charles W bcdebgaak
James bcdgdafp
McKECHNIE Jeanie Lang ahfcfceh
William ahfcfceh
McKEEN Elizabeth bcdgdakch
Sarah A bcdgds
McKENNA Nora adaabcjfb
McKENNEY Annie B bbbfabhba
Isadore bcdgdk
McKENZIE Benjamin bcdgdeae
Edward adabbgbebc
Eliza Ella ahbcabfa
Hope E bbbfhjbf
Julius Adelbert ahbcabfa
Minnie May adabbgbebc
Oliver W ahbcabfa
Oliver William ahbcabfa
Raymond Havens ahbcabfa
Willie Edgar ahbcabfa
McKEOWN Henry J adabbgbcac
Marguerette bcbhdpaa
McKINNEY Allison bcdgdafbf
Estell bcdgdafbf
Iva bcdgdafbf
Pearl bcdgdafbf
Roy bcdgdafbf
Theodore bcdgdafbf
McLANE Mary bcdebe
McLAUGHLIN Alice May bcdgel
Emily bcdgdanee
Emma abdcebk
Martha adkgda
Mary Ann bcdgdaaad

Myrtle adaceaaec
McLAWN Susan wid bcbhdqaa
McLAY Jane bcdgdeafa
McLEAN Alexander F bcbcbbgba
Donald adbabfefe
Emma Euphemia bcbcbbgba
Margaret wife bcbcbbgba
Margaret Belle adbabfefe
Minnie E bcbcbbgba
Nathaniel (Maj) ahchfig
Sophia ahchfig
McLELLAN Alvina Azubah adaabdaba
Don Thomas adaabdaba
Elizabeth bcdgdafea
Herbert bcdgdafda
Ida Lilla adaabdaba
Jeffie Alvina adaabdaba
Jessie Lydia adaabdaba
John C Dow adaabdaba
Thomas adaabdaba
McLEOD Clara E bcdgdeaceb
John K bcdgdeaceb
Mary F adkfbbja
Norman adkfbbja
Rachel wife adkfbbja
—— bcdgdaib
McMAHON Nathaniel G bbbfaxbd
McMANUS Lucy ahbgbjx
McMONAGLE Cornelius bbbfabk
McMONEGAL Mary bbbfae
McMORRIS Mary adacffeh
McMULLEN James bcdgdeaah
McMURPHY Hiram B bbbffba
McNAB Juliette bcdedbcca
McNALLY Dorothy bcdgdeaif
Grace bcdgdeadc
Roy bcdgdeaif
McPHERSON Rose bcdgdakg
William J bcdgdakg
McRAE Christie adbabfefe
McQUESTION William bcfifb
McQUILLAN Estella adkddgdb
Ira adkede
McQUILLEN Elijah P adaieaad
Estella adaieaad
Mary E adaieaad
McVITTY Cyrus Cook bcdedkc
Elias C bcdedkc
Frank D bcdedkc
Louisa bcdedkc
Willard D bcdedkc
William bcdedkc
MEACHAM Phoebe ahbgi
MEAD Albigence ahbaee
Darius Johnson ahbaee
Darius Johnson ahbaee
Joseph ahbaee
Mary wife ahbaee
Mary Jane ahbaee
Sarah Eliza ahbaee
MEADE Eva J adaceaebaa
Lyman W adaceaebaa
MEADER Abigail bca
Diantha adhaff

Mary adbabbb
MEANEY Charlotte W adaigbbad
James adaigbbad
MEARS George Henry bcbehde
MEDBURY —— ahdadag
MEDLEY Ida ahbaedf
MELCHAM Charlotte Ann adkdeec
Joseph adkdeec
MELCHER Levi abdgcaf
Rhoda abdgca
Samuel abdgca
MELEGLEN —— adiaiaafc
MELLEN Abigail wid bcdedb
MELVIN Hannah S bcdebgbi
Elgin adhafgcbc
Lucy E adhafgcbc
MERCHANT Clifford adabbgqdb
Josephine akebdbbiga
Marian A adabbgv
Olive adabbgqdb
MEREDITH Joseph Henderson ahcbecc
MEREDYDD, King of Powis, ahgdgbb
MERIAN Jo a
MERRIFIELD Rilla bbbfabmac
MERRIHEW Rillia Lizzie bbbfabmac
MERRILL Abigail dcd
Alice S adgfcdace
Amanda Green bbbfabl
Ambrose Dow bcficc
Amos adgfcig
Andrew J adaimcc
Betsey ahbgc
Caroline Elizabeth bbbfabh
Carrie Wall adkfbeia
Charles ahbabadc
Charles Henry bbbfabl
Chester Arnold adhahedb
Daniel Jr (Ens) bcdead
Deborah bcdbad
Dolly adaaaifa
Ebenezer ahbgc
Edgar H adhahedb
Edwin J adkfbbch
Eleanor Amelia bbbfabl
Elizabeth adgfcig
Ella Florence ahbaahea
Ellen Louisa adhccfd
Emily adgfcig
Ephraim ahbcacd
Ethel Jennie adadhacab
Frank adgxfdaa, adkfbbje
Frank Leslie adggegbaf
Frank S adgxffbc
Franklin adgxfaaac
G W ahbaahea
George B adgxfam
George Warren, George Warren Jr ad-
  aimbifa
George William bbbfabl
Hannah adggbe, ahbgc, ahfcfdb, bcbe-
  bi, bcbebiefi bcficc
Hannah A adgxffbc
Harold Wayne adggegbad
Helen F adkfbbje

Henry Green bbbfabl
Henry H adadhacab
Horace adgfcig, adkfbeia
Isaac befifc
Isaac Edwin adgfcicc
John Jr adkc
John Johnson befice
Joseph adaaaifa
Joshua bebehhc, (Maj) befice
Lena bbbffcdd
Louise Dow adgfcicc
Luther C ahbcacd
Lydia adab
Manly V ahbgc
Margaret Dow bbbfabl
Martha J wife adgxffbc
Mary adkehb
Mary Frances bbbcabl
Mary M adaaaifa
Moses ahbcacd, dcd
Nancy ahbgc
Nathaniel, Nathaniel Jr ahbgc
Phebe ahbgc
Raleigh ahbgc
Roxa ahbgc
Sally ahbgc
Sarah adaimc, adgfcig, adkebdb, bcbeh
Sarah A adbabfdeb
Simon adgfcig
Stephen (Capt) adgda
Thomas Leonard bbbfabl
Vienna wife adkfbbje
Wiggins adabic
William bbbfabh
William John bbbfabl
William T ahbabadc
Willis Freeman adaabfdfa
—— adabie
MERRITHEW Benjamin bcdgddf
Emma bcdgddf, bcdgdeae
Frank bcdgdeae
Frederick bcdgdeae
Hannah bcdgddf, bcdgdeae, bcdgdead
Harriet bcdgddae, bcdgdeae
Henry bcdgdeae
Joan bcdgdeac, bcdgddf
John bcdgddf, bcdgdeae
John Allan bcdgdeae
Laura bcdgdeae
Leonard bcdgddf
Nora bcdgdeae
MERRITT Hannah bcdgdeadf
Samuel adacfc
MERRY Eliza M bcbhdeh
Hattie adadabbdb
MESERVE Samuel abbeh
MESSER Abigail bcdecd
Timothy bcdc
METCALF Eli adaabdabe
Ellen adaabdabe
Sally ahbgil
METCALFE Mitchill a
MEW Harriet adaabdabb
MEYERS Jennie M bbbffdba

MICHAUD Deborah J ahbabaeadc
Joseph M ahbabaeadc
MIDGES Leon P ahfcaaag
MIGHILL Thomas (Capt) bcbhda
MILBURN Elizabeth adbabfd
MILES Adeline adkeda
Anna adkeda
Aurilla adkeda
Dorothy adaabdaed
Ida Maude adaabdaed
John adkeda
Julia adkeda
Mabel Augusta adaabdaed
Marcus Tullius Cicero adkeda
Mark Hill adkeda
Miranda adkeda
Orin adaabdaed
Orin Luther adaabdaed
Reuben, Reuben Jr adkeda
Willard W (Hon) adaabdaed
MILLARTON Anna ahgf
MILLBURY Austin A bcdgdbaadd
James M bcdgdbaadd
John bcdgdbaadi
Waldo O bcdgdbaadd
MILLEN Clifford A adkfbbcia
MILLER Agnes bcbhddfaa
Arthur A bbbffagd
Byron ahbaedf
Carroll Bent bcdgdbacb
Eva Ethel adkfbbjba
Hulda bcdgdaal, bcdgdafee
Jacob ahbaedf
John bcbhddfaa
Mary A Wilhelm bcdeaefc
Mary Alice bcdgdbacb
Mary E bhddfaa
Mary G adkfbebi
Mertie ahbaedf
Norman Paul bcdgdbacb
Ralph Davison bcdgdbacb
Samuel bcdeaefa
Sarah ahbcae
Sarah E bcdeaefa wife bcdeaefa
Smith ahghe
Tobias (Rev) akecaeb
Victor ahbaedf
Viola ahbaedf
Westley adkfbbjba
MILLETTE Marie L ahbaabdac
MILLIKEN Ezra C adgfbhadaa
Harriet adabbgbe
Marion Harriet adgfbhadaa
Rebecca E bcdbece
MILLIS Hattie E adabibic
MILLS Amos befied
Blanche Evelyn bcbebbfaca
Charles bcbebbfaca
Elizabeth ahbcabeg
Emma bcdgdeae
Ephraim befied
Marcia C ahgcic
Mary adaabcbd
McLeod bcdgdeae

MILNE Alice Mary bcbebbcdaca
John J bcbebbcdaca
Ruth bcbebbcdaca
MINAN see Moynahan
MINITER John T ahbabjcfa
Milton ahbabjcfa
MINK Susan ahfcfcc
MINOT Betsey bcbehb
Lovina abbegfgaa
MIRICK Benjamin bcdebeg
MISKELL Ella ahbgbfaab
MITCHEL Sarah bcdc
William adabid
MITCHELL Alexander adggdcc
Charles Baker bbbfabbeb
Charles W ahbabaeae
Georgia A adkgdefba
Guy Melvin adaiebad
James K adaaaaccac
Joanna adgfcd
John bcdgdafaf
Lillian G ahbabaeae
Lucy F wife adaaaaccac
Mary A adgfbfbaa
Mehitable bcdeab
Meriba H adabid
Wesley Howard adaiebad
William adaaba
William Dow adaiebad
MOAR Elvira H adaceaea
Timothy adaceaea
MOBURY —— bcdgdae
MOERS Eliza M adabbhg
Levi B adabbhg
MOFFATT —— (Miss) ahbcabc
MOHR Laurel bcdgdafqb
Philip bcdgdafqb
MOHUN Bridget ahbabjbfa
MOIR Elizabeth Dow adgcacbadb
James adgcacbadb
Nancy Jean adgcacbadb
MOLYNEUX Fannie adacea
—— (pere) adacea
MONAHAN Ella ahchfijb
Mary abbegfgaf
MONBLEAU Eveline I adkecbaca
Oliver adkecbaca
MONK Edward bcbhdee
MONROE James (Pres) p 4, adkdb
MONTGOMERY Annie bcdedbbbj
Jane adhafad
Maria adhafdgb
Martin bcdecad
Sarah adhafa
MOODY Addie Sarah adgxfafc
Alden True adgxfafc
Angeline M adhahec
Elizabeth ahb
Eva F bbbfhcfa
Frank adaimbhg
John adgxfafc, (Capt) adaabc, (Capt) ahbaac
John Wesley adgxfafc
Joseph adgxfafc

Martha wid bcbhdgbeaa
MOON Blanche adaceaaia
Eugene adabbgtab
Lizzie O adabbgu
Madge Hazel adabbgtab
Mary E adabbgpa
Mary S adabbgpaa
Stillman adabbgu
MOONEY Hercules (Col) ahbgb, akebh
MOORE Anna R adacgfd
Berdelia wid adabbgdab
Catherine ahbabjcf
Clarista ahchfh
Cynthia bcbcbbacd
Edmund (Capt) bcd
Frank P adhafgbb
Guy B adhafgbb
Joseph adadhac
Martha adaabff
Mary Ann bcbebbb
Mary Jane adadhac
Polly akebh
Robert W abbegbg
William abbegba
—— adkeabbaa
MOORS Agnes wife bcdgdafdb
Alice Maud bcdgdafdb
Edith bcdgdafj
Eugene bcdgdafdb
Jessia wife bcdgdafdb
John bcdgdafdb
Kenneth bcdgdafdb
Neal bcdgdafdb
Nellie bcdgdafdb
MORDHOFF George adacffeg
MORE Addis E adacgffe
Fannie J abccgacha
Fred abccgacha
George I abccgacha
Hannah J adkcabba
John H adacgfc
Mabel L abccgacha
MOREY Susie B adabbbdce
William adabbbdce
MORGAN Lydia ahbchc
Martha adgfcib
Netie Clark ahbaacfba
Sarah adggeffa
Stephen adgfcib
William C ahbaacfba
MORRELL Annie E bbbfaea
Asa adbabhb
Hannah wife adbabhb
Peter adbabhb
MORRILL Aaron, Aaron Jr. adfa
Abigail wife adkehe
Abraham adhe
Abraham Dow bcdeda
Benjamin adkehe, ahb
Charles adkfbbda
Charles Chauncey adkdeae
David adadib
Elijah adfa
Esther adadib

897

357

Etta R bbbebcdae
Frank adgxfdaa
Hannah wife adfa, adfe, wife adhe, ad-
kehe
Henry adfa
Isaac Jr. adg
Jacob ad, adadib, adfa
Jedediah adhe
John adfe, adhe, Jr. adhe, 2nd adhe,
befi
Joseph (Maj) bcdeda
Josiah adhe
Judith adfa
Keziah adfe
Lena E ahbabaefe
Martha adkebb
Martha M adggf
Mary abdcebe, adfe, adggf, adkehb
Mary F wid adhafaab
Mehitable adfa
Miriam adfe, ahbaba
Nahum (Hon) abdcebe
Peace adfe, adhe
Pelatiah adfe
Sarah wife adadib, adgca, adggd
Smith adggefh
Susanna adfa, adfe
Susannah abbegb
Theodate adfa, adfad
W abbegbdfc
William Pepperell adfe
Winthrop adhe
MORRIS Albert Dowe ahgdgbb
Henry Burling ahgdgbb
Hilda Bertha ahgdgbb
Joel ahggh
MORRISON Abraham adkecj
Alexander Clark adkecj
Alfred adkecj
Alva bcdeda
Asa bcdeda
Anna bcdeddhdb
Benjamin bcdeda
Daniel abbegg, adkecj
Eben abbegg
Edward Gove adkecj
Elizabeth bcdeda, bcdedd
Eva adadagfc
Ira bcdeda
John adadagfe
Leonard bcdeda, bcdedfe
Lizzie bbbffadbb
Maria Elizabeth bcdedfe
Mary bcdeda, Mary wife adkecj
Mary Ann adkecbaa
Nancy bcddea, bcficc
Robert bcdeda, bcdedd
Samuel adhaff, bcdeda
Sarah adhaddb
Sarah Ann Bagley adkecj
Susan Evans abdcica
—— bcdgdpe
MORSE Aaron ahgfbdf
Ada bcdeaeafc

Albert adacebfc
Annie B adhafgcba
Aura A adhagba
Blanche V adacebfc
Bylon L adhagba
Carleton bcbhddfa
Charles L bcbcbbeeba
Chester E bcbcbbeeba
Ellen gaaxaxd
George F ahbaaaaab
H R Adella bcbhddfa
Hannah J ahbgbxb
Henrietta P wife ahbaaaaab
Herbert adhafgcba
Isaac ahgfa
Jane adhafcab
Jeremiah adhagba
John H adkebaad
John W adabibcac
Julian abbegfgaf
Katherine J adkfbbcib
Laura adgfbhadaa
Louise bcdeddh
Lucinda Burdick bcfihed
Lydia D ahbaaaaab
Martha A gaaxax
Mary bcdeaad
Mary A wid adaaaaccab
Mary Bliss adggegb
Mary Jane adadhac
Mattie Hall adgfbdf
Robert, Robert Jr. ahbabaac
Ruth wid adgcacb
William T adhagba
—— adaaaifb, adaiiaafb, bcdeaefdb
MORTON Elva D bcdedbbbc
Florence adabibif
Judith ahgcibb
Mary B bcdedbbb
William bcdedbbbc, bcdedbcb
MOSER William J ahbabalc
MOSES Andrew J bcdgegb
Frank L adadibdk
Helen bcdgdaii
Margaret V abdcca
William Rufus bcdgegb
MOSHER —— bcdgdabc
MOSHIN Julia ahbcajc
MOSS Hannah J ahbgbxb
Moses ahbgbxb
MOTT Amelia A fcec
MOULTON Abigail abbj
Alice V adadhaaad
Alvah (Dr) abbegfja
Amos abccgcfi
Betsey bcdedba
Caleb adkehg
Charles F. adkehg, ahgciga
Daniel abbeh, bcdedbf
Daniel Y adhcdaeaa
Eli bcdedbbc
Elizabeth abccgb, bcbhbc
Enoch adabibi
Frances Ann adabibi

Hannah abbeeb
Harry abccgcfi
Henry adadha
James Madison bcdedbcc
Jeremiah abbeebb, aeeb
Jessie A adhcdaeaa
John abbeeb, abbeh, abdcebd, bcdedba
John Arthur adhcdaeaa
John S adkehg
Jonathan (Sgt) abbeh, Jr. abbeh
Joseph abbeh, adkehg
Josiah abbeeb
Jotham adgfbl
Laura bcdedbbc
Leonard abccgcfi
Lewis B abccgbc
Lucy abbeh
Lydia abbf
Martha adhcdaeaa, aeeb
Mary abbeeb, abbeh, ad, bbbfb, wife bcdedba
Mary B bcdedbbb
Mary G adgfbl
Mehitabel abbeh
Nathan abccf
Phebe L bcdedbbb
Robert aeeb
Sarah abbeh
Sarah B abccgbc
Sarah Elizabeth abbegfja, bcdedbcc
Susan A adkehg
William abbb, abccf
Wyatt abccgbc
—— akebdbbfeb, bcdgdpd
MOUNT Eva E (Mrs.) ahbabja
MOUNTFORD Addie adhccc
Fanny adhccc
Jennie adhccc
Joseph adhccc
Wallace adhccc
MOWATT Charles H adaaaifaa
MOWER Martha adhcbba
Nathan adbabh
MOWERS Delia adgfbgea
Thomas P adgfbgea
MOYNAHAN Hannah adaiiaae
MUDGE Eliza Brewer adadhcbb
MUDGETT John Philander bbbebcbb
Mary abbegfcb
Nathan bcdbeaf
Sarah bcdeaa (bis)
—— adabib
MULFORD Belle bcdedkd
MULHEREN Martha adgfgabc
MULLEN Catherine Elizabeth bbbfa-bib
Frank bcdgdand
Rebecca M adabbgb
MULLER Ezza adadhaab
MULLET Rufus ahbabale
MUMFORD John adff
Sarah adff
MUNCH Delia Ann adggegbac
MUNN Charles R adacgfach

Marion Margaretta adacgfach
MUNROE Agnes adaigaac
MUNSELL Dorothy adgfcdadd
E A adgfcdadd
MUNSEY Abigail adadibd
Ann Elizabeth bbbfhcg
David bbbfhcg
Henry adadibd
MUNSON Clinton De Witt adgfbegb
Delia gab
Helen Phemy Paulina adgfbcgb
Homer Castellan adgfbegb
Nellie bcdgdmab
Reuben L adgfbegb
MURCH Martha adggeilc
MURDOUGH Elizabeth M adgcadaaa
William adgcadaaa
MURPHY Agnes abbegbifa
Arthur abbegbifa
Catherine bcbeggab
J W abbegbifa
Joshua adabbgdd
Mary J adgfbp
Michael adaimbif
Nellie adkddgcaa
Norman abbegbifa
Pearl abbegbifa
Rhoda A adabbgdd
Sadie A adaimbif
Sarah J wife adaimbif
William abbegbifa
MURRAY Abigail abccdg
Edward Alden bcdedbcf
Edward Rolloff Classon bcdedbcf
Gilbert Herbert bcdedbcf
James abccdgb
MUSCLOUGH se Murdough
MUSSEY Lydia adh
MUZZEY Fannie E adgaacbg
George S adgcacbg
Joseph adf
Mary adf
—— wid adf
MUZZY John ahbaacdad
Lele E ahbaacdad
MYERS Gertrude fcea
NADEAU Alphonsine bcdgena
NAGLE Mary Julia bcbcbbgl
NANCE Bessie Lenore ahgfbdcb
Clarence Leroy ahgfbdcb
Dow Willard ahgfbdcb
Fern Eulalia ahgfbdcb
Norma Alberta ahgfbdcb
Rose Augustus ahgfbdcb
Serigna Edgar ahgfbdcb
NASH Walter C bcbhbgdb
—— adkgaa
NASON Adelia D bbbfhja
Alicea F adaimbaia
Catherine McDonald adkgdba
Daniel bcbhddccb
Deborah adhadda
Frank adaimbaia
John bbbfhja

Julia wife adaimbaia
Maud L bcbhddccb
Robert adkgdba
—— bcdeaad
NATTER Addie wife adgxffbf
Anna adaabfdf
Jacob adaabfdf
Joseph abccdgd
Mary Clough abccdgd
Mildred E adgxffbf
Nancy wife adaabfdf
Otis adgxffbf
NAYLOR Herbert Oscar adhcbbgf
James adhcbbgf
NEAL Andrew adhcc
Dorcas adhcc
Dorcas wife adhcc
James adbabh, adbag
James L bcbebbcaf
Jennie C bcbebbcaf
Lydia adbabh
Mary adgfbea, adkccba, bcfifb
Minnie W ahbabajadc
Peace adhcbb
NEALE Mary Sargent adbabd
NEALLEY John adadaba
Loanna adadaba
Rouetta adadaba
NEALOR Mary A aeeaeccc
NEEDHAM Levi J adaceddbb
Matilda ahgfbh
NEILL Anna adhafcc
NELSON Amy Richardson adgfcibc
James adacgh
Joseph adadhacd
Julia Ann adkccbaa
Moses adkccbaa
Sally adgfbdb
Samuel adgfcibc
Stephen adadhacd
William Rufus akecahd
NESTER Mary aeeacaaaa
NETTLETON Aaron bcdbeb
Jeremiah bcdbeb
Joel bcdbeb
NEWCOMB Alfred adkgddhd
Martha Elfrida adkgddhd
Hannah ahggc
NEWELL Anna wid adkbbebk
Edwin S ahbabajaf
Florence bcdgdabfc
Frederick bcdgdabfc
Joseph (Lieut) adacfe
Ralph A bcdgdabfc
Ralph T ahbabajaf
T Henry ahbaacdg
NEWHALL Isaiah bbbebcdad
Kenneth bcdgdafah
Mary wife bbbebcdad
Mary A bbbebcdad
Sarah adggdad
NEWLAND Rose bcdgdafmb
Sarah bcdecdba
NEWMAN Abigail akebbf

Betsey wid abccgac
Lillie ahbgilb
Mary Ann abccgacm
Samuel K bccgacn
NEWSON —— bcdgdabc
NEWTON Asa bcdeaec
Matilda Sophronia bcdeaec
Sarah adfcd
NICHOLAS E P bcdecaibb
NICHOLS Anna aia
Charles abccgdbac
Clara N bbbfhcfa
Elizabeth abdcicab, adaaaaccab, ahba-
   adbfc
Esther, Esther 2nd bcbcaaa
Eunice ahcbc
Garrise abbeacba
George abbeacba
Harriet bcbcaaa
Helen abbeacba
Henry adhafcab
John adac
Laodicea bcbcbbgj
Levi abbcacba
Lucy abbeacba
Martha bcbebg
Mary adac, ahbaadbfc, bcbebg
Moses (Col) adgxca, ahbae, bcdeaa, bc-
   deab, bcdeb
Phineas bcbebg
Polly adadhcc
Phoda ahbaadbfc
Sarah adgxb, adhe
Sarah Jane adhafcab
Thomas ad, bcbcbbgh
William G ahbaadbfc
William Wight ahbaadbfc
NICHOLSON Jennie Alice bbbebcdaa-
   ab
Thomas bbbebcdaaab
NICKERSON Ella adkgaa
Helen Davis abbcgfa
—— adkgaa
NICOLSON Doris bbbfhcfca
Lora bbbfhcfca
Matthew bbbfhcfca
Norman bbbfhcfca
NILES Alphonso R bcdgdbaadh
Betsey A adaabfaal
Lida (Mrs) adaabfaaa
Mary Ann adkdecf
W W (Bishop) adggdcc
NIXON John (Col) ahbab
Thomas (Col) bcdhc
NOBLE Cyrus bbbfabhc
Cyrus L bbbfabhc
Georgianna adkgded
Louis H adkgded
Molly ahbabe
Queenie bbbfabhc
Ralph bbbfabhc
Sias ahbaec
Thomas ahbaabfd
Willard C bbbfabhc

900

—— befifhf
NOLAN Henry J ahfcfceeca
Robert ahfcfceeca
NORCROSS John Calvin ahbgbba
NORMAN Philip adhafdgeb
—— adhafdgeb
NORRIS John (Capt) adadh
Theophilus adadabf
NORTH Lucy E bcbhdbnd
William bcbhdbnd
NORTHASSE William adkdebb
NORTHEND Allan Platt ahgchebab
Frances Caroline ahgchebab
NORTHROP Mary ahgchfe
NORTHY Austin B bcdedcgaa
NORTON Carrie adhcdach
Dorr adaceaade
Elverdo adabbgqd
Jennie May adabbgqd
John bcdgd
Mary F adabbgahe
Michael bcbhb
Nina bcdebgagb
Ruth bcdgd
NORWOOD John adabbgba
Lydia M bcdgdali
NOURSE Harvey p 4
Rebecca p 4
NOYES Albert adhcaca
Gilbert H bcdedcgab
Hezekiah H bcbcbbgi
Leon E bcdedcfb
Russell Dow adadagfah
Samuel bcbehc
Sarah bcbehc
Sophia Page beficap
William B adadagfab
NUDD A E akebix
Abbie Emma akebdbbfea
Abigail akebbe, akebg, akebhc, akex
Abigail M akecaabc
Abraham akecaga
Ada Isabella akecahhee
Addie Adeline wife akebis
Adeline akebih
Albert Willis akebieb
Almira abbeebb, akebdbbd, akecafd
Alvin F akebinbb
Alice M akebdbbgde
Amos akebbcbc
Andrew J akebdbbf
Andrew T akebdbbgc
Ann Bowers akebdbbbi
Ann Clarissa akecafj
Annie E wife akebdbbge
Archie H akebdbbgdd
Arthur akebdbdb
Arthur Edward akebdbbigc
Benjamin akebc, akebi, akebj, akecah-bbd
Benjamin B akebdbbg
Benjamin F akebit
Benjamin Leavitt akebcfa
Bertha akebcfaca

Betsey akecaeb
Betsey B akebbcbb
Betty akecad
Carleton H akebdbbihh
Carlos akebdbda
Caroline akecahc
Caroline Belle akecahbad
Caroline Tappan akebdbbigab
Catherine akebccb
Celia Augusta akebcfab
Charles akebjc
Charles F akebdbbii
Charles Grover akebdbbgdba
Charles H akevdbbgdb, akebhab, ake-bhba, akebinaa, akebiw
Charles W akebiaa
Charles William akecagab
Clara akebdbbad
Clara G wid akebip
Clara Maria akeceebac
Clarence William akebdbbigd
Clarissa akebdbbh
Clarissa Ann akecafi
Clifton W akebinba
Daniel akebcc, akebccc, akecaaf
David akebbb, akebij, akebik, akebim, akecah
David Franklin akecahbb
David Kimball akebdbbi
David P akebiq, akebiqa
Deziah akebj
Dora W akecaababb
Edna May akebdbbigac
Ednah akecaabad
Elgie Scott akebdbbih
Eleanor F akebdbbihe
Electa Wilder akecahhb
Eliza akebcg, akecaah
Elizabeth akebdbbbg, akebdbbfb, wid akebiv
Elizabeth Frances akecahe
Elizabeth M akebif
Ella F akebbcbaa
Ellen Amanda akebdbbie
Elmer Russell akebdbbfec
Emeline akecafk
Enos H akebdab
Erastus akebdbba, akebdbbfc
Ethel Maty akebdbbigb
Ethel Mae akecahbaaa
Eugenia Minerva akebbcbac
Eugene Frank akecahbba
Everett Lewis akecahbaab
Finette akebdbg
Flora Belle akebdbbgh
Florence Lucy akecababc
Florette akebdbbfg
Forest L akebiz
Francelia akebbcbad
Frank Everett akebiea
Frank Herman akebbcbab
Frank Horace akebdbbgdaa
Fred J akebiy
Fred W akebdbbgaa

George akebbcbca
George Emery akebcf
George F akecagba
George I akebirb
George Van Buren akebcfc
George Warren akebdbbfeb
Georgianna L akebbcbcb
Georgiette S wife akebiu
Gladys akebdbbihi
Gracie Leavitt akecahbac
Guy Leon akebiya
Haley akecafca
Hannah akebbcc, akebi, wid akebi, akebk, akecb, akg
Hannah T akebdbbbe
Harold Douglas akebdbbige
Harriet Ann akecagaa
Harry E akecahbbb
Hattie Marie akebdbbgdae
Helen Louise akebdbbgdad
Helen M akebdaaa
Henry akebcb, akebic
Hiram akebdbbgf
Horace G akebdbbgd
Howard M akebje
Hosea L akebdbbbb
Ida L akebbcbaf
Ira P akebhba
Isaac P akebdbd
Isabelle akebdbbfa
Ivory akebii
Jacob akecai
James akeb, akebd, akebdb, Jr akebib, akecaac
Jemima akebbce
Jeremiah Smith akecafb
Joan wid xaaf, wid a, wid ak
John ak, akebbcb, akebe, akebfb, akebima, akecaag
John A akebja
John Adams akecahh
John B akebdbbgda, akebir, akebjd
John H akebira
John K akebdbbgg
John Leavitt akebcfac
John Philip akecaabaa
John S akebbca
Jonathan akebdbi, akebi, akecaff
Joseph akebdd, akebinb
Joseph H akebdbbgb
Joseph L akecahbaa
Joseph Ward akecahg
Joseph Warren akebdbb, akebdbbb, akebdbbba
Josephine akebdbbfd
Josephine C akebiac
Josiah akecaaa
Julia akecaabb
Julia Ann akecaabae
Katherine Louisa akebdbbfeba
Leon Peaslee akebiyb
Levi akebda
Levi C akebdaa
Lewis Philip akecahba

Louisa akebiib, akecaabd, akecafa
Lucretia akebca
Lucy akebca
Lydia akecafc
Mabel Josephine akecaababa
Manson Harlan akebdbbif
Marcia A akecahj
Margaret akebdbbbh
Marietta F akecahha
Marion Philbrook akebdbbihc
Martha akebdbbac, akebhd, akebj
Martha A akebjb
Martha E akecahi
Martha T akecahf
Mary abdgc, akea, akeba, akebbf, akebdbbab, akebdbf, akebib, akecaaga, akecac, akecaed
Mary A wife akebdaa
Mary Abby akebcfaa
Mary Ann akebch
Mary D akecafg
Mary Ella akebdbbic
Mary Jane Loring akebdbbbd
Mary M akebiab
Mary Melissa akebcfc
Maude akecahbbc
May akebdbbc
Molly akece
Moses akecaae, akecaf
Moses Paul akecahhd, akecahhec
Nancy akebee, akecaabe, wife akebia
Nicholas ak
Olive Annette akebdbbid
Olive Etta akecahhea
Oliver akecaaba
Oliver F akebdbbbc, akebdbbbf
Oliver W akecaabaf
Orren Clark akebdbbff
Otis W akebdbbaa, akebdbbge,
Peabody akebie
Pollia wife akebda
Raleigh Martel akebdbbgdbb
Raymond George akebdbbfebb
Richard ak, akebha
Richard T akebhaa
Robert ak, Junr ak, akebdbc
Robert Louis akebdbbgdbc
Roger xaaf, ak
Ruth akecaea
Ruth M akebinbc
Ruth P akebhbb
Sally akebcd
Samuel ake, akeba, akebba, akebhb, akebia, akebig, akecaad, akecag, akecc
Sarah aeeacab, akebbcc, akebdbh, akecaec, akecagb, akecd
Sarah Abbie akebcfb
Sarah Ann akecafe, akecahd
Sarah P wid akebil
Simon akebiia, akeca, akecab, akecae, akecafe
Sophronia akebib
Stacy L akecahhc

Stacy Leavitt adhcdad, akecaha, akec-
  ahhe
Stephen akebfd
Stephen W kebfda
Susan akebita
Susan E wife akebit
Thomas ak, akebdba, akebf, akebfc, Jr
  akebfc, akec, akecaa, akecaab
Thomas Hale akecaabab
Thomas L akebid
Virginia akebdbbihh
W ak
Wallace akebdbbiga
Walter akebdbbigaa
Walter Elbridge akebdbbig
Warren akebdbbfe, akebdc
Warren Alfred akebjda
Warren Benjamin akebdbbga
Weare akebbc
Willard Emery akecahb
William ak, akebbcba, akebbd, akebd-
  ba, akebh
William E akebix
William H akebina, Jr akebinb
NUTE Mary E akecaec
Paul akebch
Thomas akebih
NUTTER Anna adaafdf
NUTTING Benjamin bcdecab
Charles P bcdeaefb
Daniel B adaimbcf
Etta H adaimbcf
Lillian J bcdeaefb
Sarah Lillie Josephine bcdeaefb
NYE Arthur bcdedfg
OAKES Herbert adhafagc
OATMAN —— adggdcdc
OBRIEN Henry adgfbeef
O'BRIEN Annetta bbbfabbd
Frances M adgxfax
Minnie bcfiibci
Robert gbaf
OBRION Preston adhccgad
ODELL Eber Ellsworth adbabfddg
George (Dr) akecad
Maud adacgfacf
ODIORNE Abigail ahbgfib
O'DONNELL Ellen aeeacaaa
OESTERREICH —— bcbhdndk
OGDEN Cornelia adacgfe
O'KEEFE —— bcdedbbdaa
OLCOTT Thomas c
OLDRICKA Johanna adhafdgca
OLIVER John (Maj) ahghe
—— bcbhddah
ONSTOTT Roxana adhcbbge, adhcbbgg
ONTHANK Lucetta wife adggefeb
Sarah S adggefeb
William B adggefeb
OPDYKE Jennie M bcbegbd
ORBETON Frank ahbgbbd
Jane ahbgbbd
Joseph ahbgbbd
—— ahbgbbd

ORDWAY Edith Belle bcfiibcg
Eleazer bbbfff
Elizbeth wife bcbed
Frank W adaimbdi
French adkebad
George T bcfiibcg
James adgcac, Jr. bcdea, bcded
Lydia bcdea
Moses bcded
ORMSBY Richard b
ORNE Sally bbbfhd
ORONO Frank Lewis bcdgdaalb
Louisa Lewis bcdgdaalb
ORPHAN Izetta bcbhdgage
ORR Melissa J bcbhddceb
Osborn Ann adked
Jacob adked
OSBORNE Anga V adgxfaacab
Alice Maud adkdecebc
Elizabeth M adhafdf
George W adgxfaacab
Lindley H adhahd
Sarah A adhafdig
OSGOOD Betsey adaabfc
Celestia adabibe
Charles H adadicf
Clara Ann adgfgaba
David (Capt) adaabfc
Dudley adaabff
Edwin S adaabfc
Frances Ann adabibe
Henry W adaabfc
Hiram P (Rev) adggehd
J Frank adaabfc
John (Capt) bcd
John C adggehd
Joseph (Capt) adacffg
Josiah adacffg
Julia A adabibe
Luther adgfgaba
Martha adacffg
Martha A adaabfc
Mary Ann adaabff
Mary E adabibe
Nathan B adabibe
Nathaniel B adabibe
Polly ahbaeg
Samuel (Dea) adacffg
Samuel W adacffg
Sarah adfa
William C adaabfc
OSTRUM —— adaceddea
OSWALD Magdalen bcdbecee
OTIS Maria adaigbbac
Moses bcdbeceda
Nellie J bcdbeceda
OUTHOUSE Frances bcdgddac
OWEN Charles Fred adkgaedda
Daniel P ahgfdc
Daniel Perry ahgfbdb, ahgfdc
Esther ahgfde
Franklin Dodge ahgfdc
George adhccfd
George Cushman adhccfd

Gertrude adkgaedda
Lemuel Dowe ahgfdc
Thomas F adgxfaaada
Timothy ahgfde
—— (Admiral) adgfed
OWENS Elijah ahchfg
Lena adacedded
PACKARD Alice B ahbabaeaa
Angie (Grant) wid ahbabaeaa
Fred A ahbabaefd
Henry B ahbabadc
Joseph bcdbadde
Sarah J eaab
PADDOCK Elizabeth B ahgchfd
Emma Dow ahgchfd
Samuel B ahgchfd
PADMAN William (Rev) abceabba
PAGE Abigail abbj, abbja, abccf, bc-
  bb, bcfifc
Abner abbj
Abraham bcfifc
Albert W adhahd
Almon O ahbgilh
Anna abdd, akecad, akg, akgf
Asa H ahbgilh
Benjamin Jr bcbh, bcfiibae
Blanche ahbgilh
Catherine bcfican
Charity akg
Charles T adhahd
Christopher abbe, abbj
Clarence W adhahd
Cornelius bcba
Cynthia adhafga
Daniel M adkeci
David H adkeci
Deborah abccgac
David (Capt) bbbffafb
Ebenezer be
Edwin bcfiffe
Elisha akg
Eliza abccgad
Eliza Ann abccgad
Elizabeh bcfiffe
Ellen A bcbhdek
Emily Alberta adggegbae
Ezra A abdceblfa
Francis akg, (Dea) akg
Frank adkfbbjbg
George adkecbac
Hannah ab, adb, adbaa, adbabd, adg-
  fbf, akg, bed, bcfifc, bcfifhe
Harrison B ahbgilh
Helen bcfifc, bcfiffe
Helen T adhahd
Isaac bcfifc
Isaac J bbbffcbac
James A abccgad
Jane wife adkecbac bcfifc
Jennie S wid adabibcaa
Job bcfifc
John adga adgbb, ba, be
John M bcfiibae
Joseph, Joseph Jr be

Josiah abbj, akg, bcfiffe
Judith adbbd, adhag
Lillian bcdgdsaa
Lillian Hannah abdceblfa
Lottie bbbffcbac
Lucy wife ab
Margaret M adkecbac
Marion H adkfbbjbg
Martha bcfifa, bcfifc, be
Mary abbe, abc, abbj, abceb, abdc, adb-
  aa, wife adhag, akg, ba, bcfiffe
Mary Sherburne abccgad
Meribah akg
Micajah adbaa
Nathan bcfifc
Nathan Barker bcfifc
Nathaniel abbj
Noah abccgac
Onesiphorus abc, ba
Oneysiphorus, Oneysiphorus Jr adgh
Otis bcdgdafl
Phebe be
Phoebe abccgad, bcdf
Reuben abbj, abccgad
Robert a, ab, ah
Samuel abbj, abccgad
Sarah abbj, adgh, akg, bcficad
Sarah A adaiebac
Sarah Sherburne abccgad
Septimus (Rev) adkdeba
Shubael abbj
Sophia H bcbebbbdb
Stephen abdd, aeeacb
Susannah bcbh
Taberthy adaig
Theodate abdb
Thomas ab, be
William bcfifc
Wilson M adhahd
Winthrop adgh
Wright bcfiffe
PAIGE Amos adbb
Daniel adbb, adhai
Edward D abbegbiba
Eliphalet adbabd
Enoch adbb
Hannah wife adbb
John adhai
John H adhcbba
Judith adbb, adhag
Mary adhafaa, adhafcj
Nathan adbb
Samuel adbb
Theophilus adbb
Van R adhafgcf
PAINE Anna E adgfcjbd
Elizabeth ahb
Ichabod adacebg
Samuel (Capt) bcdeca
—— bcbhdndj
PALLEN William adkfbdxa
PALMER Aaron, Aaron Jr adkfbc
Abigail wife ahgca
Almira B adkddgd

Angie M adadagfbd
Anna adahdc
Asa abccgacd
Benjamin abcflb
Betsey bcbebbbd
Daniel abbeedc
Elizabeth abccg
Etta wid abccgbada
John ahgca
Joseph adgfba, adkdeac
Marguerite adkecbaac
Martha Moore adkdeac
Mary J akecaec
Mehitable ahgca
Orrin A adadagfbd
Peter bcdecda
Phebe ahbch
Phoebe abccg
Sadie M abccgbada
Walter B adhadcea
—— adkedl, ahgcf
PARCHER Lucia Morse abccdgcbba
Sumner C abccdgcbba
PARFITT Maria Emma adaabdaeba
PARK Abel adgfcih
Ella Celeste ahgchhb
Frank adgfcih
Hiram adgfcih
Luella adgfcih
Mary adgfcih
Myron adgfcih
Simon adgfcih
William adgfcih
PARKE Hannah adgfbee
PARKER Abigail adhcbbfc
Anna abca, abceb
Asa ahgb
Cardie (Dr) ahgha
Diantha bcbcbaaae
Ebenezer Batchelder bcdeabba
Edwin J adaigaac
Edna bcdbed
Elizabeth adaiiaacc
Ethelene Ruth adaigaac
Eveline M adggdccae
Fannie Elvira bcdeabba
Frank S ahggbh
Henry F ahggbh
James B bcdgdakbb
Jeannette abccgcfca
John bcdgdaida
John R bcdeaedac
Joseph bc
Joseph E akebdbbc
Larestine B bcdedbac
Lena bcdgdakbb
Maria ahdgbh
Marion Elizabeth ahggbh
Mary ahggbh
Nellie H bcdeaedac
Ralph H ahggbh
Rovenia adgfbgeah
Retire Hathorne bcdbed
Samuel D bcdedbac

Sanford ahggbh
Sarah adgcacba, ahggbh
Sarah J adaiiab
Sherman J ahggbh
Susie Evelyn bcbcbbaffa
Tabitha ahgh
Thomas bbbff
Wilber K adkddgcc
Willard bcdeabba
William T bcbcbbaffa
PARKHURST Edith M adkddceb
PARKIN Frederick bcdgdaga
PARKINSON George E bcdedcfb
PARMALIE Sarah D bcdeddf
PARMENTER Obed bcdbaddk
PARNELL Bessie bbbffafb
PARRIS Albion K (Judge) adhccbb
PARSONS Almira abceaba
Amos Seavey (Col) abceaba
Anna Seavey abceaba
Charlotte abbegfj
Eliza abceaba, ahbgea
Elizabeth adggeild
Eunice ahbaba
Isaac Dow abceaba
James Monroe abceaba
Job ahbabb
John ahbabal
Joseph 2nd abceaba, Dr abceae, abceaba,
  (Capt) adkdb
Joseph Warren abceabed
Leta M ahbabajad
Lovina abceaba
Martha abceaba
Mary abceae, bcdcbk
Mary H adkfbeddc
Mary J adggdcda
Polly Dow abceaba
Samuel abceaba
Susan adkdea
Thomas adkdea
Warren (Dr) abceabed
William Irving abceabed
—— ahbabb
PARTRIDGE Electa bcbhddfa
PATCH Betsey adhafah
Mary Jane bcdeaeda
Richard bcdeaeda
PATTEE Asa (Capt) bcfie, Jr bcfie
Daniel bcfifha
Daniel D bcfifha
Dorcas wife bcdeb
Enoch Dow befifha
Hannah bcdeb befif
Jesse befifha
James bcfifha
John befifha
Judith ahbabja
Mary wife befifha
Moses bcfie
Peter bcfie
Seth bcdeb
William B bcfifha
PATTEN Ann E akebdbbga

Dora bbbfhcgb
Emeline bcbehhe
Jesse akebbf
Mabel F adhafabaab
William adhafabaab
PATTERSON Alonzo bcdgdaga
Archibald bcdgdegi, bcdgdeaaca
Archie acdgdagi
Burton bcdgdafea
Ella M bcdgdbaaga
Emeline L ahbabaja
Eva bcdgdeaai
George abccgdbad
Hattie bcdgdane, bcdgdbaf
Hosea bcfifjjc
James ahgcabb
John bcdgdaga
Leon M bcfifjjc
Leona bcdgdeae
Letha bcdgdaib
Lewis ahbabaja
Lydia B bcdgdagi
Marion bcdgdaga
Mary bcdgdaga
Nathan bcdgdbaf
Mina bcdgdagi
Nathaniel bcdgdane
Neal bcdgdaga
Roland A bcdgdeaaca
Susie bcdgdaga
Verna bcdgdafea
—— Miss bcdgded
PATTISON Everett W adhccbbc
PAXTON Catherine E bbbffadbb
Melville bbbffadbb
PAYNE Miranda adadieaa
Robert bcbhbgk
PAYSON Andrew bcbebbbdb
Charlotte, Charlotte wife bcbebbbdb
PEABODY Allen adadibdg
Emily adkdbe
Frank adadibdg
Gertrude adaabcef
Louise adadibdg
Stephen (Col) bcdif, (Rev) bcfic
Susannah adkebaac
PEACOCK Eliza A abdcebca
Elizabeth adaceafg
PEAK Betsey A adaceaai
PEALE Polly ahbaacxc
PEARL Cora Ethel ahbabamgd
David ahbabamgd
William H adaidaa
PEARSON Alice M adhccga
Arthur Lincoln bbbffcha
Bessie adaabfdfb
Edward G adgxfam
Elizabeth ahfcaaba
Hattie Ella bbbffcha
Henry F ahbgdcc
Jacob adaabfdfb
John bbbffcha
Joseph bbbffcha
Lizzie Evalina bbbffcha

PEASE Annabel abccgcfde
Ebenezer, Ebenezer Jr. adggdcc
Fred V adabibccd
George adggdcc
Gertrude Frances wid bcbhddbba
Hannah C bbbfhcfga
Hulda adggdcc
Lucretia Martha adggdcc
Lucy adgfcdgab
Zilla N adabibccd
PEASLEE Abigail adadabf
Abner adhafah
Abraham adhcba
Amos adadica
Anna R adhafgc
Daniel bcdba
Elijah adadiaa
Franklin H bcdbaddb
Hattie M akebiy
Henry Wheeler adadiaa
Humphrey, Humphrey Jr. adhcba
James adhafgc
John, John Jr. adgffb
Jonathan adhcba
Keziah adhcba
Lucy Dow adgffb
Lydia Anna adaica
Lydia Ann adadica
Mary wife adadiaa, adadic, adbb, adhcba
Mary Agnes adkfbbdba
Mary E adgffb
Moses adhcba
Nancy adhcba, adhcbai
Obadiah adhcba
Patience adhcba
Phoebe adhcba
Rebecca wife bcdba
Rebeckah bcdba
Ruth adbb
Samuel adadiaa
Sarah adadica, adhafah
Stephen adhcba
Susan C adgffb
PEASLEY Jane bca
John ad
Peter ahbcag
PECK Lydia ahdaadd
Samuel ahgfc
PEERSON Charlotte bcebbbdb
PEET Eber ahgdhe
PELCK Severene bbbffbaadb
PELON Joseph J adgxffae
PELTON Emma A bcbhbfib
PENDERGAST George Sherburne akebbce
PENDLETON Florence akebdbbih
Frank akebdbbih
PENN Philip adkdec
PENNELL Clara W adgfcdaca
Frank Adams adhcbbgf
PENNOCK Elizabeth bcdgdagf
PEPPER Hannah adacgj
Isaiah adacfa

John adacfa
Rebecca adace
Sarah adacg
PERAM Hannah ahfcfce
PERCHER Leroy adkecbad
Rhoda B wife adkecbad
Sadie F adkecbad
PERCIVAL Margaret M adahx
PERKINS Abigail adbaa, wid adbaa
Abraham a, ab, ad, adg, bcdcb
Abraham Jr. ad, adg
Albert S akecahbaa
Augusta adaimbbe
Benjamin adgg, adgi
Bertie Lee adaimbij
Betty adacb
Charles G adaimbai, adaimbbe
Christiania adkebabba
Corydon N adaimbbe
Daniel adhe, adkebge
Elizabeth adg, adgfbe
Ellen adaieaaff
Elmira Abigail adaabffe
Flora adaimbbe
Frank A adaimbij
Freeman adgxffbba
George W D adkebge
Glidden bcdgdabgab
Graydon bcdgdabgab
Hamilton P adabibcf
Hannah Ann abbeebbb
Harriet bcfifha
Henry C adaimbij
Henry J akecahbba
Irving N adaimbij
James abbeebbb, abcea
James abbeebbb, abcea
James H adkebabba
Jonathan abceac, adkfbc
Jonathan O adaimbij
Joseph adgi
Joshua adgfbe
Lewis L abceaba
Lillian adaimbbe
Lillian S adaimbai
Lucy adgxfaaccb
Lydia adgg
Martha abcea
Martha A adgxffbba
Mary adkecb, adkfbc
Mary F wid adgcadaf
Mary Ida akecahbaa
Minerva A akecahbba
Myrtle adaimbbe
Nancy akebhb
Otto W abbege
Patience adacb
Peleg D adgfbdbc
Percy L adaimbbe
Polly adggeh
Raymond adaimbij
Rebecca C akebdbbg
Richard bcficanc
Ruth adahdca

Sarah bcdcb
Sarah Dudley abbege
Sarah M J adgxfdae
Silas bcdgdabgab
Solomon adgfbe
William adgffcb
—— adaidc
PERLEY Charles M adaijbd
Ellen C adgxfaacca
Helen adaijbd
Lawrence adaijbd
Putnam adkdbea
Sam (Rev) adaia, adaic, adggf, adhab, akebbf, akebc
PERRINS Rue adaceafa
PERRY Charles W bcbhdehfd
Helen ahgdgbab
Henry ahgdgbab
Mary J bbbebcbb
Patrick Henry ahgdgbab
Varnum bbbebcbb
Woodward A bcbhdehfd
PERSONS Melinda adacfe
PETERSON Lula wid bcdgdda
PETTIBONE Lucy ahgdca
PETTINGELL Cutting bcdcbk
Frank Hervey bcdebk
Hattie S adkebf
Johanna Morse ahbabaa
Nathaniel Henry bcdcbk
PETTITT Alma Winnifred ahchfija
J D bcbhdbndc
Joseph H bcdeddc
Muriel bcdeddc
PEVEAR Euphemia Coffrin adaabdaeba
Frank W adaabdaeba
PEVERE Susanna adkda
PEVERLEY George Dow abbegbicb
John abbegbicba
Lucy Jane ahfcaaac
PHELPS Alexander ahgff
Alonzo ahgff
Betsey E adgfbej
Burnham ahbabja
D Alexander ahgff
E H ahdaadd
Frances A adkedj
George adgfbeg
Lorenzo ahgff
Lydia ahgff
Orris Spencer ahbabja
Parnel E adgfbeg
Polly ahgff
PHERSON —— bbbfg
PHILBRICK Almira P adkebcc
Andrew adahdca
Anna Sarah akecafi
Ara abbeea
B Frank adhafde
Belle Aurora adhafdj
Benjamin abbj
Benning aeeaccb
Carrie Nudd akecafi

907

367

Cynthia abdccb
Daniel abdccb
David abbef, adbccb, adhafdj
Dorothy abbeea
Elias M ahbabamga
Elizabeth abce
Ezra B aeeaccb
George Oliver aeeaccb
Hanah akeba
Harrison adhafdj
Hattie Emily adhafdj
Isaiah abbeea
James abbeea, abbef, Jr. abbef, ah
Jennie May aeeaccb
John abdccb, adhch, akecafi
John Ezra aeeaccb
John Leonard akecafi
John Warren akecafi
Jonathan abdccb, Jr. abdccb, abdccbe,
  aeeaec, akecafi, bcdeaa
Joseph abbeea, (Dea) abbef, 2nd abb-
  ef, aeb
Josephine Marjorie aeeaccb
Josiah adkebcc, akecahbb
Judith abbed
Judith abbed
Laura M adahdca
Martha Ann akecafi
Mary ah
Mary Abby akecafi
May Esther aeeaec
Mehitable akex
Mina abccgach
Nathan abbj
Polly abdccb
Rosina E akecahbb
Samuel abbef
Sally bcdeaa
Simeon abbeea, abdgca
Simon abbeea, abbef
Sylvia Celestia adhafdj
PHILLIPS Abigail adbafa, adhci
Abraham Dow adhci
Anna adhci
Anna Dow adhcbc
Benjamin, Benjamin Jr. adhci
Content adhci
Frances bcdgdane
George adbabfdda, adhcbc
Hannah adaceae, adhcbc, adhcd
John, John Jr. adhcbc
Jonathan adhci
Jonathan Dow adhcbc
Judith adhcbc
Matthew bcdgdee
Mary adhci, ahgdc, bcdgdba
Mary Jane bcdgdba
Phebe adhci
Ruth Ann bcdedfda
Sarah ahbabag, ahbb, da
Stephen adhcbc
Walter adbafa, adhcbc, 2nd adhcbc, ad-
  hcd, adhci, Jr. adhci
—— bcdebgaaa, bcdgdx

PHILP V E abbegfjcaa
PHILPOT Rhoda adkecbad
PHINNEY Hannah adkgddg
PHIPPEN Mattie Mildred wid adabb-
  gra
Rebecca Maria adkdec
Samuel adkdec
PHIPPS Emily bcdebei
William (Sir) ab
PICKARD Annie May bbegbicd
Elias akebdbbi
Nancy M akebdbbi
PICKERING Anne adkfbbdfc
Harry Edward adhcbbfe
Herbert Dow adhcbbfe
James William Churchill adhcbbfe
James Jr. adhcbbfe
Josie Belle adhcbbfe
Lydia abceabc
Nellie Gertrude adhcbbfe
Sophia adabbbdc
Thomas S adabbbdc
PICKETT Mary adkfbbjba
PIERCE Annie adkgg
Annie L adabibccd
Calvin bcdeaeae
Carrie E adabbgaie
Dolly adgkk, adkgge
Franklin (Pres) ahgfdah
George S adhafdj
Ira T adaabdaeg
Isaac bcdeaeh
Jane Ann bbbffcbad
Jane E adaigbbab
Jonathan O adacffg
Juna adggeija
Lawrence W adgxfadi
Lillian B adaabdaeg
Lydia bcbhddh
Mattie Mildred adabbgra
Mattie Mildred adabbgra
Phoebe S bbbebdaa
Richard adkgg
Samuel adkgg
Sarah B wid acfifff
Sarah J bcdeaeae
Susan adkgg
William adkgg
PIERCY Alexander adggdcca
Jacob adggdcca
Susan Frances adggdcca
PIERS James ahdaaddg
PIERSON Charles Dow adacffehb
Charles M adacffehb
Frank ahbabjh
Herman Dow adacffehb
Levi ahbabjh
PIKE Amasa adkfbbcg
Daniel abbegfa
E abbegfcc
Ednah adgxfag
Elmer E adkfbbcg
Ezekiel abbegfa
George C adaimbbeab

George A bcbebbbdb
Hattie adkdeeb
Hattie P bcbebbbdb
Helen M ahgfbdga
James H adaimbbeab
John (Rev) adc, ahgfbdga
Lizzie M abbegfcc
Louisa adgxfah
Mary L D adaimbbeab
Otis adgxfag
Philip adkdeeb
Robert (Maj) ab, ba, (Capt) adggf
S wife abbegfcc
PILLSBURY Betsey ahbcacg
Celia A ahbgbeb
Cynthia adkbcacg
George W adaaaig
Jonathan bcdbac
Joseph ahbgbeb
Merrill ahbcacc ahbcacg, Jr ahbcacg
Sylvester Isaac ahbcacg
PILSBURY Betsey akebbcb
PINFIELD Elizabeth adgfcdaa
PINGUE Rebecca bcded
PINKHAM Abigail adbabd
Abigail S adadagb
Clarence bcdgdabfb
Fannie Beulah bcdgdabfb
Franklin bcdgdabfb
Harold bcdgdabfb
John adbabfee
Madelin bcdgdabfb
Maurice bcdgdabfb
Oshea bcdbedd
Polly bcbhdp
Robert bcdgdabfb
William E adbabfee
—— akebdb
PIPER Arthur Bennett adaabcjf
Dorothy A adaabcjf
Hannah D akebfda
Helen Frances adaabcjf
Joseph F abdcebcb
Mary A ahgfbgc
Sarah J eaab
—— (Lieut) adaaah
PIPPIN Louisa J wid adabigge
PITMAN Oscar V adabibig
Susan adadhea
PITTS Huldah Coleman adaaaf
N A adaidagd
Susan abbeebbea
PLACE Alfred Griffin adhcbbfba
Edith Dow adhcbbfba
Edith Marion adhcbbfba
Everett Eugene adhcbbfba
Everett Griffin adhcbbfba
Gertrude adhcbbfba
Griffin adhcbbfba
Naomi bcbhddia
PLUMER Harriet ahbaacxa
Nancy ahbaaaa
Samuel (Gov) ahbaaaa
PLUMMER Albert ahbabamgc

Florence E ahbabamgc
Laura E bcbhddiaa
Mabel P bcbhdehg
Mary A bcbhdef
Polly bcdedg
Rhoda Ann bcdeddh
Sally adhafg
Samuel bcdeddh
Sarah bcfifhi
Silas bcdedg
William bcbhddiaabd
PLUNKET Gerald bcbebaaa
PLUNKETT Esther bcfiibca
POAGE Edwin Flye bcbhbgdb
POLAND Mary akebdbbih
Roxana adkdeac
POLHAMUS Sarah fced
POLHEMUS Arthur adggeii
POLLARD —— adaabdaba
POLLOCK Elizabeth June adhcbbfc
W S abbegbdfc
POMEROY Wright bcfihf
POND Annie Moriarty dhcbbk
Benjamin adhcbbk
Benjamin Fetty Place adhcbbk
Charles Choate adhcbbk
Clara Baldwin adhcbbk
Emma Sumner adhcbbk
Enoch (Rev) ahcbc, ahcbf
Hiram adhcbc
Lucius Augustus adhcbbk
Washington Gregg adhcbbk
William Whiting adhcbbk
POOLE Elizabeth bbbfhcg
Louisa M adhcbbgda
POOLER Abbie F adgfcjc
Coolidge adgfcjc
John F adgfcjc
Joseph W adgfcjc
Leslie adgfcjc
Philena adgfcjc
Sidney L adgfcjc
Willis adgfcjc
POOR Benjamin Kimball bcfica
Charles Augustus bcfica
Charles Herbert bcfica
Ellen R bcfica
Emeline bbbffch
Enoch (Col) akebb
Hannah bbbebeda
James bcficap
Jonathan, Jonathan 2nd bcficap
Mary Phoebe bcfigfdd
Nathaniel Hale bcfigfdd
Persis H bcficap
Sarah hbabahk
—— (Col) adadh (Enoch)
POPE Pamelia F ahbcacb
William W adhadcb
PORTER Carrie May bcbhbgd
Ella bcdgdafk
Emery E adgcacbjc
Esther bcdgdg
George bcdgdg

Gertrude bebhdna
Jacob C bcdgdg
Jennie A abbegbdcac
John adkdb, bcdgdg
John Dow bcdgdg
Marjorie
Mary ahggcc, bcdgdg, bcdgdgg
Sarah ahbabahk
—— (Col) adadh (Enoch)
PORTER Carrie May bcbhbgd
Ella bcdgdafk
Emery E adgcacbjc
Esther bcdgdg
George bcdgdg
Gertrude bcbhdna
Jacob C bcdgdg
Jennie A abbegbdcac
John adkdb, bcdgdg
John Dow bcdgdg
Marjorie
Mary ahggcc, bcdgdgm, bcdgdgg
Robert bcbhdna
POST George M abdgcafacb
Hanford Palmer abdgcafacb
Maria wife abdgcafacb
Millie bcbhddfa
Owen abdgcafacb
POTTER Eudora R bbbfhcgb
Floretta ahgdcag
Henry Linberger bcbhdbcdab
John Clarkson bcbhdbcdab
Parmelia bcdedfc
Samuel bcdedfc
Sarah bbbfhbx
POTTLE Richard adkgad
William adkgad
POULIN Rose ahbgbxaaa
POWEL Charles Pise Carr ahgdgbc
Dorothy Alice ahgdgbc
Edith Adaline ahgdgbc
Florence ahgdgbc
Florence Dowe ahgdgbc
Harvey Dowe ahgdgbc
Katherine Lorenz ahgdgcb
Robert Harvey ahgdgbc
Samuel Wilberforce ahgdgbc
POWELL Jane wife bcbebfea
John bcbebfea
Laura E bcbebfea
POWER Mary A adgfbgfa
John adgfbgfa
POWERS Daniel bcfifc
Catherine Aileen adhafdgea
Ellen bcbcbaab
Ella P adhafdge
Frances A bcdebgbdc
Hiram adggeffa
Jean Edna adhafdgea
Jonathan ahgfa
Laura Weeks bcdedbca
Lura bcdbaddd
Martin E bcdedbca
Mary E adggeffa
—— adabbgaik

PRATT E A ahbcabea
Edna Maud ahbabahcd
Jane adggehd
L E abbeebcaac
Lucy bcfiffdc
Martha L abbeebcaac
W W ahbabahcd
Wallace ahbabaeadd
Wilda Jane ahbabaeadd
PRAY James Jerome bbbfabie
PRENTICE Asenath wife ahdae
David ahdae
Ephraim ahdae
John ahdadae
Luania adacgfg
Manassah ahdadae
PRENTISS Abigail Bigelow bcfifl
PRESBY Florence adhafgcbc
Henry bcdedbaf
George W bcdedbaa
Lucinda bcdedbac
Rodney E adgffb
PRESCOT Samuel abcfc
PRESCOTT Abigail adgxb
B F (Gov) adadabcf
Daniel Marshall adkebdb
Eben P bcbhddba
Edwin Augustus adkebdc
Emma Foster adkebdc
Erasmus D adkebdc
Faith McKinley adaimaaad
Frank adadabgb
Gladys adaimaaad
Helen adaimaaad
Herbert L abbegfgada
Izoza Z bcbhddba
Jane bcdgdaae
Jedediah Jr adkebdb
Jennie S adaimaaad
John (Capt) ahbcx
John Dow adaimaaad
Joseph Pernham adkebdb
Josiah F adkebdb
Lennox adaimaaad
Mary abdcebc
Mary Ann abbegfc
Mary Dow abbegfb
Mary E wife ahbabjd
Mildred abbegfgada
Rachel ahbabjb
Reuben A ahbabjd
Rhoda adgxb
Robert adkdd
Rufus abbegfb
Sarah Frances ahbabjd
Susan wife bcbhddba
William adaimaaad
—— (Col) bcdea
PRESSEY John bbbd
Melvin adabbhb
William bbbd
PRESTON Aaron ahdaf
Bathsheba adggea
Elizabeth adhaa, ahdadag

910

Joseph adggea, ahdadag
Mary ahdadag
Rebecca ahdadag
PRIBLE Abial befiiba
Betsey abccgc
Elinor Lancaster befiiba
PRICE Adeline Elsie ahbcai
Annie M bedgdaaed
Benjamin bbbffcdc
Charles R ahbcai
Grace Agnes ahbcai
James Harvey ahbcai
Lucy bedgdw
Malvina F ahbcai
Martha Caroline ahbcai
Orlando H ahbcai
Stephen ahbcai
William ahbcai
William Henry ahbcai
William J adaimbik
PRIEST Hatie L bedgddahc
Marshall G bebcbbad
PRINCE Anna De Bevoise adkdece
Christopher adkdece
Matilda abbegbda
PRINDLE Flora A adgcacbad
PRIOR Helen adgxfbeb
Lucy bedgdw
PRITCHETT Kate Julia adaimaf
PROCTOR Jonathan bedcb
Moses bedeaei
Sally bedebdc
PROUTY Clarissa bededfc
PULLEN Belle C bbbfhcfh
PUNDERSON Lydia adggdcc
PURCELL Mary Ellen adhcbbjd
Thomas William adhcbbjd
William feb
PURDY David fcc
Vera M ahbgbadea
PURINGTON Abigail adaic
Elizabeth wife adh
James ad, adh
John adbc
Joseph abccgace
Joshua ad
Lydia adahd
Mary adh
PURRINGTON Harriet adhcbbg
PUSHARD Charles adabibk
Mary wife adabibk
Mary J adabibk
PUTNAM Alice adhafage
Arthur ahbabjk
Betsey W bbbebcbe
Eugene adkebgc
Frank adhafage
George W adhafage
Mabel True wife abccgdbaf
Robie adgfcdgab
Thomas Lord ahbabjk
PUTNEY E G adabiggx
Eva Gee bedebei
PYE Simeon (Capt) ahggbe

RACKLIFF Charles befifhe
RADCLIFF Isadore adbabgad
RADCLIFFE Charles B adbabgda
Christine F adbabgda
RADDIN Lena B adaimbbdcc
Rhoda Augusta adaimbbdcd
RADOUT Mary A wid adgfbgfa
RAINES Mary Ann adgfcdg
RAMSDELL James bedgdafp
Jane Maria adaieaaf
RAMSEY Fannie bededfb
RAND Alphonso abccgchb
Charles D ahfcaaaf
Emily R bbbebga
Elizabeth Martha abceabf
Emma L adkgaede
Isaac Dow abceabf
James Alba abccabefa
John Tuck abceabf
Lucinda ahbabaeaa
Martha bbbebcda
Mary Tuck abceabf
Octavius Theodore bededbcb
Oscar L bbbebgaa
Sarah abbeebbb
Thomas abceabf
William (Rev) ad
RANDALL Almira R adgfbei
Arthur W adaimbdk
Betsey J adgfbei
Daniel bedgddd
Elijah bcbhddfac
George B adabige
Hannah M adabige
Morace adgfbei
Jeremiah adgfbei
Lillian M adaimcdga
Mary A adgfbei
Nathaniel adgfbei
Sadie M bcbhddfac
Sarah ahbcabed
—— adkebgc
RANDOLPH Elizabeth abbegbdcb
William F abbegbdcb
RANGER George W ahbgbba
RANKIN Hannah bcbhdec
—— adkddia
RANLIT Lydia adgf
RANSOM Ammi C adaabfd
Beulah befic
Fannie F adaabfd
RASMUSSAN —— bedgdaieab
RATLIFF Dick ahbcabeb
RAWLINGS Nicholas (Capt) akebc
Milton abbegbdff
RAWSON Abbie Jenness bedebejc
Edward ahbcai
James F bedebejc
Sarah wife fo
William Barron ahbcai
RAYBOLD Harry abdcebk
RAYMOND Edward S bededdc
Ellen A bedebgbi
Howard bededdc

Jennie Van Loan adhafcac
John adhafcj
John H bcdeddc
William bcdebgbi
READ James Neal adhccgac
REARDON Catherine akebdbba
Dennis akebdbba
RECORD Clara bcdeddabc
RECTOR Esther adhahea
REDDELL Frank bcdebgab
REDICK Daniel adgfbgfab
William adgfbgfab
REDMAN Charles eaaba
John akecaaba, akeed
Mary adaimaf
Sarah Elizabeth akecaaba
REGAN John adgfbef
REID George (Col) abdci
REILEY Hattie D adaimbifa
REMEY Sarah bcdeddab
REMICK W A abcegcfcb
REMINGTON Nellie J bcfifjjaa
REMMOND Lydia adadibba
REED Albert bcdedbab
Anson bcdbadg
Chauncey adaabcj
Cynthia adkfbbcib
Darius bcdbadg
Ella L bbbfhbxcg
George W (Capt) adkgdegd
Hamlin bcdbadg
Hannah bcdbadg
Joshua Curtis bcdedbcac
Laurilla adaabcj
Laurinda adaabcj
Lulu Belle abbegfgaf
Marion Antoinette adkgdegd
Nancy wife adaabcj
Olive Scott Weston bbbfhjbk
Philansa adaabcj
Roswell C abbegfgaf
Roxie bcbhdh
Sarah bcdbadg
Thomas Bracket adhccbb
William bcdbadg
William Authur bcdedbcac
William Edsel bbbfhjbk
RENDALL Abigail wid akebcf
RENEAU Carrie Ann adgfgabc
James Polk adgfgabc
REYNOLDS Calvin adbabfa
Edith M wid gbaic
Joseph adbabd
Mary bcdedbbc
Nettie E adgfbege
Samuel (Capt) adbabd
—— ahbcabb a
RHINES Alva Dow bcdeddaa
Ella Mary bcdeddaa
Nelson bcdeddaa
Sadie Bell bcdeddaa
RHOADES Rebecca J bcdaddg
RHODES Phoebe ahbabja
RICE Belina ahgdhb

Charles bcdgdg
Mary Agnes abbegfjb
Lizzie adgfcdh
Phoebe Lillian ahbgiif
RICH Anne L adkgdca
Luke adkgdca
Wealthy ahbaacdf
RICHARDS Abigail bcfiib
Alexander, Alexander Jr. ahgdcab
Alice adggdcc
Edna Earl adgfbeje
Edward K adgfbeje
Emeline Mead adhccfe
Evelyn abcegcfg
Fred ahgdcae
George ahgdcae
Hattie ahgdcae
James abcegcfg
John bcfifb
Mary adbabd
Philip W adaijbb
Samuel ahgdcae
Seth bcdbeag
Solomon Nash ahgfbda
Theresa Emilia ahgfbda
William adc
RICHARDSON Alford bcdbeccd
Alford Sumner bcdbeccd
Alice M adaigbbae
B M adabibcab
Carrie B adabbgbcaaa
Charles bcdbeccd
Charles Brooks bcdbeccd
Clarissa D adaidbf
Cynthia M bbbfaxbc
Edward H adgfbejg
Esther abd
Flora J adabibcab
Georgianna Dow bcdbeccd
Hannah ahgch
Jane adhafdfb
John Wesley adaimaf
Jonathan bcfifjab
Josephine E bcdebeeb
L E adgfcibc
Lucy adgfcibc
Malachai Langdon bcfifjab
Rachel adacedd
S J bcdedbbbe
Sarah bbbffb
Sarah Ann adailaa
Susan adadagfbc
William ahchfif
—— adaaaieeb
RICHEY Edna bcdedbacb
Joseph bcdedbacb
RICHIE Todd bcdgdagi
RICHMOND Abiah adacgf
Abigail adkebd
Charles ahgchl
Emilie ahgchl
Nathan adkebd
RICHTER —— adadabgab
RICKER Isaac Wenworth ahgfdab

Sarah Mitchell abbegbebb
RIDEOUT Ellen wife adbcebcaa
RIDGEWELL Ella May bcbhdgage
Stephen bcbhdgage
RIDLEY Abigail adgfbea
Caroline P abccgcfd
RIDLON Clara A bcbhbfia
Eliza ahbgbf
Wesley bcbhbfia
RIFENBURG Lucy E ahbcabba
RILEY Annie wife akebdbbii
Mary akebdbbii
Michael akebdbbii
RINES Albert adaimbbga
Alberta adaimbbga
Edward bbbfhcfl
Ella bbbfhcfl
Maggie bbbfhck
Rachel bbbfhcfl
Rosilla bbbfhjb
RING Elizabeth adhcda
Helen B adaaaieb
Page adaaaieb
Rhoda adgcad
Warren H adgcadae
William bcdcb
RIPLEY Rookie T wid adhafgcbe
RISLEY Elizabeth ahggbh
RITCHERSON —— adaiiaafa
RIX William a
ROBBINS Abbie L adaceaah
Alta S adabbgx
Asa adaceaab
Carrie ahbgbaeb
Clara A adabbgbeb
Clarence bcdgdmaa
Edwin bcdecaiba
Elizabeth xaag
Emma adaceaab, bcbhdn
Eunice adhafd
Hannah adabbgaig
Isabella adabbgzd
Jemima adhafc
Jonathan daabbgbb
Loraine adaceaab
Maud Elizabeth bbbebcdaac
Roana adaceaab
Vernice adaceaab
Wilbur adaceaab
William bcdgdmaa
William S bbbebcdaac
Wilmot adacenab
Wilson adaceaab
ROAF —— akebiib
ROBERDS Lynne adgcadaffa
ROBERTS Ann bcdc
Eliza ahfcib
Ellen A bbbfabmab
Ephraim bcdc
David bcdc
Gertrude Lavinia abbegbdbf
Hannah L ahbcai
Harriet bbbfabbea
Harriet B bcdedfdb

Harriet Dow abbegba
Harriet Ellen abbegbdbf
Henry C adhafce
Irving Henry abbegbdbf
Idella Theresa adhcbbgd
Isaac Leavitt abbegba
J R ahbabjbb
James bcdedfdb
Jane ahbgba
Jennie adkebb, bcdgdaace, bcdgei
John adhcbba
John adhcbbhb, ahbabh
John A ahbabjbb
John Knox abbegba
John William adkebabba
Jonathan abbeaa, adadabcf, adadage
Joseph ahbabh
Josiah abbegba
Joseph Dow abbegba
Judith Ellen adadabcf
Keziah, Keziah wife adhcb
Leavitt abbegba
Lewis A adaimeab
Lora adacgfc
Lorenzo B adbabfeab
Luther B adhcbbgd
Lydia adbabh, adbag
Mary ahbabjb
Mary Ann abbegba
Marion Elesa abccgdbah
Nancy adadhaac
Nancy Dow abbegba
Nellie M adbabfeab
Richard bbbfabmab
Ruel Ambrose abbegbdbf
Rufus Lewis abbegba
Sally abbegbdc
Sally ahbabi
Sally Tilon abbegba
Samuel ahbgba
Sarah ahbca, bcdc
Sarah Elizabeth ahbcabae
Stephen adheb
Susannah abbegba
Thomas akebcfe
Timothy Jr. adbf
Vanie Buck adhcbbhb
Washington Irving abbegbdbf
William adkda
William H adkgaa
—— ahbcabcca, bcbhddaj
Zetta bcbhddbcb
—— (Capt) abdci
—— adkddca
ROBERTSON Bessie Viola akebdbbgde
Elizabeth bcdbee
Jessie ahfcfceh
John T akebdbbgde
Martilda ahdaag
Mary Estelle adggegbac
ROBEY Lydia aeda
ROBIE Abigail abdc
Bathsheba abbed
Carrie E adkddgf

913

Charles adkddgf
Huldah abcea
Lydia adggdaa
Mary abcb, adggdaac
Norris adkddgf
Samuel abcb, abdc, akebg
ROBINSON Abigail ahbabd
Abigail Dow abbegba
Albert Joseph adbabfic
Alice Emily abbegbdbf
Almira P adaimbc
Amanda ahbgbae
Angeline abbegba
Anna Davidson bcdebgb
Belinda Rose adadage
Betsey adkeab, ahgfbdd
Benjamin abbegba
Beulah adggeile
Burton Henry adbabfic
Burton Willard adbabfic
Catherine ahbabc
Chester Garfield abbegbdbf
Cornelius Irving abbegbdbf
David bcdebgb
Dolly adabibi
Eliza Dow abbegba
Francis Willard adbabfic
Frederick William abbegbdbf
George E ahbabjbb, bcdgdaace
George F (Maj) adggeeca
George W abccgdhah
Gertrude Eliza adkebabba
ROBY Henry a
Jonathan adggdaa
Josiah akecaaga
ROCKWELL Constance adggdccah
Henry Lewis adggdccah
Horace Ensign adggdccah
Horace Lewis adggdccah
ROCKWOOD Mary bbbfhceff
RODGERS C E ahbcacbaa
ROES Carsten adkgdda
ROGERS Abbie akebdbbd
Abigail bbbfb
Albert Nash ahgfbdaa
Artemus adhcbbj, ahgfbdaa
Amaziah bcbhddaa
Burton Stowell ahgfbdaa
Charles Byron adbabfh
David bcdbede
Dorcas wife adbabfh
Ellen A adbabfh
Elsie Lurancy ahgfbdaa
Emma F adbabfh
Ethel C bbbfhjbk
Fannie adaabdabed
George Ensign ahgfbdaa
Hallett J adaieaafca
Hannah adbabc
Isaiah P (Rev) adbabfh
Jeff adhafdie
Jeremiah adbabfh
John Wesley adbabfh
Judith Richardson adhcbbj

Laura bcdcaedaac
Leonard M adaieaafca
Lizzie ahbabahg
Lizzie J adhafdie
Luther akebdbbd
Lydia wife adhcbbj
Manlius ahgfbdaa
Martha A adbabfh
Mary adbabfh
Mary E bcbhddaa
Mary R adaabdabd
Nabby ahcba
Nellie adhafdif
Nettie Dowe ahgfbdaa
Olive ahcbb
Robert West ahgfbdaa
Roswell Dowe ahgfbdaa
Sarah bcdbede
Wesley adaceahb
—— akebdbbgh
ROGERSON Minnie bcdbaiic
ROLLINS Amanda Jane abbegbdc
Anna Dow bcdecdbac
Georgianna bbbfaxbc
Gilman abbegbdc
John R bcdecdbac
Joseph F abbegbdc
Sarah P bbbfaxd
Wilbur akebdbbfd
William bbbfaxbc
ROLPH Jane ahbgdf
ROOSEVELT Theodore bbbfabm, bbb-
   fabma
ROOT Abbie adacgle
Cassius D ahbcachca
Mabel adaceagca
Mary Elizabeth ahbcacbab
Rufus R bcfifffc
Sarah F adadagacca
ROPER Edward F ahbgaa
ROPES Caroline E ahbaacfb
ROSE Catherine ahgg
ROSS Amos H adaimeab
Bessie Marston akecaabae
Charles W akecaabae
Elvira adhcdach
George Levi adaimbifc
George W Jr. adaimbife
Hiram ahbgfi
Mary E bcbhdhh
Nellie G adaimeab
Vina Hall ahgfdea
—— bcdgdabb
ROUIX James R adbabfdcb
Mary Geneva adbabfdcb
Matilda bcdgdea
ROUNDY —— adbabfa
ROUNDS Alice Beulah adkgaedb
Arthur Harold adkgaedb
Catherine adkgdd
Edgar Dow adkgaedb
Edgar E adkgaedb
Gertrude Alester adkgaedb
Gertrude Mary adkgaedb

914

374

ROW Ruth adkdd
ROWAN Andrew, Jr. 3rd bbbc
Betsey bbbc
Elizabeth bbbc
Henry bbbc
John, John 2nd bbbc
Joseph bbbc
Margaret bbbc
Phoebe wife bbbc
Sally bbbc
Thomas bbbc
ROWE Ella F adkfbeib
Elwin M ahbabadd
Flora F ahbabadd
Jerry adaieaafl
John S adaieaafl
Jonathan abdca
Mazie adaimbbb
Nellie A adabibccc
Orison V ahbabadd
W S adgxfafc
William H ahbabadd
—— adfe
ROWELL Anna akebbf
Dora adaababb
Gertrude F adaabdabd
Herbert D ahbabaefd
Joshua adaabdabb
Madeline B ahbabaefd
Orra S adaabdaba
Philip ad
Sarah adfb
Sybil H ahbabaefd
ROWLAND Sophronia adggdaa
ROWLEY Madison adhafgce
Roxy L adhafgce
RUDD Alice adaceaad
RUDDOCK Ida adaimbhf
RUDLONG Olive S ahbabjbd
RUGGLES Paul (Dr.) adabid
Rebecca bcfifjb
RUMNEY Sarah bcdedda
RUNDLETT Anna adhaa
Sarah akecagb
True adadabe
RUNLET Lydia adgf
RUNNEL Elmira B cbaahfa
RUNNELS Roxanna bbbffdb
Samuel (Capt) akebh
RUSSEL Beecher abdgdeacea
Daniel adacfg
RUSSELL Adolphus adacffb
Alphonso adacffb
Amanda adacffb
Amy adacffb
Aurora adggebi
David adacffb
Edna F adkehaa
Eliza adacffb
Gideon adacffb
Gustavus adacffb
Helen adacffb
Jeannette adacffb
Joseph adacffb

Joseph S adadagb
Leon bcdeddabe
Lucy M ahcfjbc
Martha abdceebeb
Mary J adadagb
Minnie O adfcdcaaa
Miriam adacffb
Peter ahbcag
Raymond bcdgdafad
Ruthven adacffb
Sophia adkebaacd
William Ellsworth bcdeddabe
William O bcdeddabe
—— bcdeabba
RUST Daniel ahghe
RYAN Eliza Bruce abdgcafa
Eliza Marston adbgcafacb
Elizabeth Bond abdgcafac
Esther Bradbury abdgcafac
Isaac abdgcafa
Henry Bruce abdgcafa
Jabez Spicer abdgcafa
Nellie F adkehbh
Norman William abdgcafac
Theodore A adggeila
William Spicer abdgcafac
RYERSON Christina adabba
Abenezer adabba
Esther adabba
Howell adabba
Joseph adabba
Luke adabba
Marten adabba
Nancy adabba
Nathaniel adabba
Nehimiah adabba
Reading adabba
Osgood adabba
Sarah adabba
Simeon adabba
QUIGG Abel G bcbehdd
Mary G bcbehdd
QUIMBY Albert H bcbcbbgl
Carrie Etta ahgfbdgbb
Catherine Alice bcbcbbgl
Frank Albert bcbcbbgl
George F adggdcie
Jemima adkddc, akebbcb
Lewis J adggdcie
Mary A bbbebcdaaa
Ruth I adggdcie
Sarah adkebcc, bbbebda
QUINN Michael aeeacaaab
Thomas aeeacaaab
QUINT George adaabfd
Mary wife adaabfd
Orren adgfbea
SABINE Jennie bebhdq
SACKETT Julia E adadagac
Minnie adggeil
SAFFORD Helen ahgcabcaa
Mark abccdaa
SALISBURY Caroline Lydia adacgfae
Vesta E gaaxaxc

SALLEY Mary Love ahbgbb
SALTER Titus (Capt) akebbb
SALTONSTALL (Capt) ade, bcb
SAMBON Apphia ahbcaba
SANBORN Abial akea
Abigail P akebdbd
Abner abbeb
Abraham abbd
Alice H akebdbbgaa
Alice L abdceblf
Amanda S bebebbfab
Amelia Barber bebcbbga
Anna adadabc, aeb
Apphia ahbcaba
Arthur W adkddgda
Comfort Dow abbegh
Daniel abccda, abdb, (Dea) abdb
David adabigc
David Page bebcbbga
Dolly adadag
Eliza adgfgaba
Elizabeth bcdebef
Ellen Josephine bebcbbga
Emma Electa bebcbbga
Ezra bbbebdaca
Frances wife abdceblf
Francis Davison bebcbbga
Hannah abccdaa
Harriet abbegbe, adkgae
Henry adadag, Jr ahbaacxaa
Hiram akebdbd
Jack abdcebk
Jacob D ahbaahe
Jennie Lindsey bebcbbga
John abbec
Josiah abbeb
Judith adha
Julia Ann adabige
Laura Burnham bebcbbga
Levi abdceblf, bebcbbga
Lucy abbegbea, adkgd, adkgdb
Luther Dow bebcbbga
Martha aee
Martha E ahbabjie
Mary abbecf, ad
Mary E bbbebdaca
Molly abbeb, ahbabja
Moses ahbgbc
Nancy adadabc
Nathan E akebdbbfg
Nathaniel abbegh, adabige
Permelia ahbgbbe, ahbgbc
Peter ahbaaac
Rachel aeea
Richard (sr) adk
Ruth A adaidbf
Sally M adadhaaa
Samuel abbeb
Sarah ahfcaaa
Sarah E ahbaacxaa
Steu a
Theodate abbeaa
Thomas Lowell abdcebk
William abcb, ad

Winthrop abbeb
SANBORNE B H bcdgdbaal
SANDBERG John bcdebgagd
SANDERMAN Isabella akecahhec
SANDERS A H adacffia
Isaac L adaabdaec
John a
Nathaniel bbbeb
Phoebe bbbeb
SANDERSON John ahdade
Turner ahbabjcd
SANDS Mahala Jane bcbhddfa
Stephen bcbhddfa
Zola E ahbabaeda
SANDSTEIN Marcus, Marcus Jr. bcd-
edceab
SANFORD Carola Helena adkdeceh
Charles O bcdeddhcb
Edgar Joseph adacgfgd
Fred adacgfgd
George adaabdaec
George Kittridge adaabdaec
Greta Marie adacgfd
Mabel Peasley adacgfd
Lynn Edgar adacgfgd
Sally adacgi
Viah adacgl
Zena adacgl
SANGER Margaret bcbebbc
SANSOUCIE Camille bbbffcbacb
Cordelia bbbffcbacb
SANTAU George adbadcee
SARGENT Abigail adac
Amos adgfbegc
Annie adkfbedba
Calvin bcbebcb
Charles adggegbb
Charles P adgcaccai
Darius bcbebcb
Daniel Dow bbbebcbea
David bcbcaa
Edith M L adkebcca
Edmund P bcdgdaaee
Ethel G adkebcca
Erastus bcbebcb
Ezekiel, Ezekiel Jr. bcbebcb
Eugene W adkebcca
George Ernest adkebcca
John Herman bbbebcbea
Joseph bcbegg
Lena M bbbebcbea
Lettice bbbebcbea
Louisa B adgxfdab
Martha L bcdgdaaee
Mary ada
Mehitable bcbcaa
Nancy adgcadaf
Neal A bbbebcbea
Owen Perry adgxfdab
Phebe adbaa
Rebecca W adgfbegc
Ruth bbbebdac
Sarepta adgffca
William ada

916

William D adabige
Woodbury Quimby adkebcca
—— akebdbbab
SARTELLE Charles bcdeaeafaa
SARTOR Katie E adaceaaia
SARTWELL —— (Capt) abccdf
SATTERLY Susanna adfa
SAVAGE Carrie Porter bcbhbgdb
Elizabeth Means bcbhbgdb
Frances bcbhbgdb
Harlow Dow bcbhbgdb
Jane abdgcaf
Patty Shelby bcbhbgdb
Samuel S bcbhbgdb
Samuel Stephenson bcbhbgdb
Sarah A bcbhdi
Sarah Margaret bcbhbgdb
Virginia McCready bcbhbgdb
SAVELS John akebii
SAUNDERS Betsey adabbg
Betty adabbg
Eben adabbgn
Thomas adabbg
SAUNDERSON Mina bcdgdafq
SAVORY Elizabeth S bcbebfe
Fred A bbbebgad
Fred H bbbebgad
Jasper J adacgfd
Miriam E bbbebgad
Thomas bcbebfe
SAWIN Ervina O ahbabjbd
Isaac (Dr) addadjbd
SAWTELLE Dean bcdgdafp
SAWYER Abigail O abbegfcad
Albert L adhafdfb
Alexander Dow adkgaefa
Anna bcdecaia
Archelus W adkgaefa
Archie W adkgaefa
Caton adkfbbjbf
Clara adkfbbjbf
Clara E adkgaefa
Daniel adhccd
Ebenezer adaceafj
Edith J adkgaefa
Edward adhafdga
Eliza adgfbgeaea
Elizabeth adhce
Emily A adkgaefa
Emma Alice bcbhbfgb
Flora E adkgaefa
George L adkgaefa
Helen Blanche ahbabjiba
Jacob bbbffagc
James (Capt) bcbcaa
Jessie adhafdfb
John E ahbabjiba
Lizzie Merwin bbbffagc
Louisa adabibca
Mable Florence adkgaefa
Margaret bcbebbc
Martha adkga
Mary wife bbbffagc
Mary L abccgaea

Myrtle Gertrude adaabcefa
Nathan adhccd, bcdecae
Nellie L adkgaefa
Percy G adkgaefa
Samuel Herman adaabcefa
Samuel Rufus adaabcefa
Smith abbegfcad
Thelma Allen adaabcefa
Wilfred A adkgaefa
William abccgaea
—— adaidc, (Miss) bcficanb
SAXE —— ahbcabcd
SCELLEY Mehitable adhab
SCARRET Atkins bcdedcb
Charles bcdedcb
Cynthia bcdedcb
Ellen bcdedcb
Emma bcdedcb
Erasmus bcdedcb
George bcdedcb
Harriet bcdedcb
Josiah (Rev) bcdedcb
SCHENCK Daniel Dow ahgchfc
Lewis Richardson ahgchfc
Margaret Lucia ahgchfc
Mary Elizabeth ahgchfc
Schuyler G ahgchfc
SCHEUERMAN Norma Augusta ahg-
  dgbc
SCHLESSINGER Auguste bbbfabbf
Emily bbbfabbf
SCHLEY Annie adggeibab
SCHULTZ Mabel B ahbgile
William B bcdebgaaj
—— ahbgile
SCHWARTZ B F bcdedkaa
Mary E ahbabalc
SCOLLAY Evalina wid bbbffcha
SCOTHERN —— adacffib
SCOTT Arnold bcfihecb
Christopher bcbhddbba
Delia F ahbcacba
Delia Frances ahbcach
G W R (Rev) bcfihecb
George Dow bcfihecb
Gertrude Frances bcbhddbba
Jennie L bcdgdakb
Joseph bcdgdg
Margaret bcdgdafeb
Mary Elizabeth bcfihecb
Mary J adabbgaij
Samuel A adabbgaij
Sarah adaabaak, bcdgdafaa
—— adabbgac, adabbgaib
SCOVILL Ada bcdgdagc
Lena bcdgdagc
Mabel bcdgdagc
May bcdgdagc
SCRIBNER Elizabeth bcfie
SCRIMENGER Agnes bcbebbcdaa
Andrew bcbebbcdaa
SCRIPTURE Persis ahbabae
SCRIVER —— bcdgdbd
SCROLLINS Nellie F bcbcbaaba

917

SCULLY Nancy bcdeda
SEAMANS Henry C adgxfaaae
—— bcdbac
SEAMONS Clayton ahchfih
Nora ahchfih
SEARLE Lillie V adggega
SEARLES Cordelia adkfbedc
SEARS Adelaide ahgchfg
Eliza wife adbabfdha
Frankie May wid adbabfdea
George adbabfdha
Hattie adbabfdha
Isaac H ahbaeddb
Lydia adaceaee
Nancie ahbaeddb
—— adkedc
SEAVERNS Abigail adhafaab
SEAVEY Almira H adgfcicd
Ann Elizabeth abceabec
Cornelia akecahj
Elizabeth abceab, abceaea
Hattie M wife adabbgqa
James W abceabec
John H abceabec
John Langdon abceabec
Lyman abceaba
Mary abceaba, abceabec, abceae
Mary P adaidagf
Polly abceabeb
Sidney abceabec
William abceab
—— adabbbhada
SECOR William J fceb
SEEBACH Oscar adhahece
SEELEY Linsay E bcdgdanb
Mary A adgfcjc
SELLERS Anna M adabbgaic
Sally adabbgc
SELLEY Eleanor (Getchell) adah
Mehitable adhab
SENTER Thomas bbbff
—— (Col) adkdb
SERVIN Abraham A ahggbba
Catherine Ann ahggbba
SERVIS Sally bcdgdaalc
SESSIONS Kesiah adggdc
Resolved adggdc
Simeon adggdc
SEVERANCE Alice wife adaaaiebc
Dinah adab
Elizabeth adgfbee
Elsie bcdgdabda
Ephraim adab
SEWARD Arthur gbakda
Mary E gbakda
William H adhccbb
SEWALL Pauline Wentworth bbbfabm
William W bbbfabm
SEWELL Dearborn abdcib
SEYMOUR Abner F ahgdf
Albert L ahgdf
Albert P ahgdf
Alfred R ahgdf
Bradford ahgdf

SGOBEL Paolo adgfbegb
SHACKFORD Albion C adhafahb
Charles adhafahb
Edith M abccdgcaa
Lydia A abccdgca
Seth adaidaa
William dab
William J adhafahb
SHACKLEY Abigail adgfbecb
SHAFFER Carrie adacgfea
SHAILER Cora ahbgbadd
SHANNON Abigail abdcca
Dolphena bcdgdafeba
Nathaniel, Nathaniel Jr. bcdgdafeba
Nathaniel Vaughan bcdgdafeba
Thomas bcdgdafeba
SHAPLEIGH Marion Dow bbbebcdada
—— bbbebcdada
SHARP Lucy abbegbdcb
SHATSWELL Theo b
SHAW Abby adaija
Asa adaija
Benjamin abd, adabi, aeeacab, akecagb
Bertha L bbbfabha
Elizabeth adaija
Elsie bcdgdane
Emma Ann abbegfgaf
Esther abd
Hannah adabi
Harriet adhccba
Hiram adaija
Jeremiah F adaija
Jerusha abdcd
John abdgca
Jonathan adgcadaa
Josiah adaija
Lydia adgcadaa
Mary wife adabi
Mary Ann wid adaija
Moses aeeacab
Neal D adhccba
Polly K abbegfl
Rhoda adhafab
Sally adkecd
Sarah akecb
Stephen bcdgdane
—— bcbhddaf, bcdgdabgc
SHAWPENNY Eugene adaigaacb
Evelyn Davis adaigaacb
SHEA Charles adabbgaige
Edna L bcdgdaaaba
Eli bcdgdaaaba
Eva M adabbgaige
Johanna bcdgeja
Kate akebdbba
Mary Magdalene adabbgagda
SHEAME Melliceka adhafcabdb
SHEAN Henry bcdgdeaia
SHEARER Dora bededefcc
SHELDON Frances A bcdecahe
George A bcdecahe
Margery wife bcdecahe
SHELLEY Bessie Istell ahgfdaga
Burton Istell ahgfdaga

918

378

Florence William ahgfdaga
Helen Florence ahgfdaga
Lena Alice ahgfdaga
Marjorie French ahgfdaga
Percy Rickley ahgfdaga
William Stearns ahgfdaga
SHELMAN Nina ahbgimd
SHEPARD Abbie Eliza abdcebk
Allie Minetta adkdeecb
Almira S wife adaabcjg
Aurelia bcfifhe
Benjamin adbabfc
Charles adaabdda
Comfort abcd
Elizabeth bcf
Elizabeth Adelaide adaabcjg
Elizabeth Merrill bcfifhe
Eugene H adkebdc
Florence Louisa abdcebk
Frederick Knight abdcebk
Grace Madeline adadhaaac
Hannah bcdi, bcfifhe
Helen Beatrice abdcebk
Helen Patterson abdcebk
Henrietta D bcfifhe
James adadhaaac
Jesse bcfifhe
Jesse Turner bcfifhe
John abdb
John F abdcebh, abdcebk
Leah adabibcad
Lewis F abdcebh
Lewis Frederick abdcebk
Mary P bcfifhe
Moses bcfifhe
Phoebe Almanza bcfifhe
Samuel adk, ba, (Lieut) bcdi
Sarah adk, ba
Sarah Lizzie abdcebk
Theresa Louise bcfifhe
—— adaieaad, (Miss) bcbhddc
SHERBURN A D adgfcjbb
Betsey bcfigfa
Josiah bcfigfa
Sarah adkddi
SHERBURNE Frances abdf
Hannah akebbc
Sarah abbj, abecgad
Sarah E adaabcje
William B adaabcje
SHERMAN Annie E bbbfabmh
—— bcdbac
Arabella bcbhdekc
Clara gbaq
Florence I adaidaa
Isora adhadca
Mary P adacedhc
Mary T bcdedbada
Mildred Roselle adkgdefba
Orra E adkgdefba
Samuel bcdedbada
W T (Gen.) abbeebbc, adhccbb
SHIBLES Lucinda Ann bcbhdbeaa
SHIPLEY Elizabeth wid abca

SHIPMAN Alfred Dow adhcbbba
Caroline adhcbbba
Frederick William adhcbbba
Isabelle adhcbbba
John adhcbbba
SHORES Hannah wife adaigaaa
Maria Bartlett adaaaacc
Matthew adaaaacc
Nettie adaigaaa
William adaigaaa
SHOREY Alice M ahbabadbb
Alton C ahbabadbb
Doris I ahbabadbb
Edwin B ahbabadbb
Estella J ahbabadbb
Helen E ahbabadbb
Herbert E ahbabadbb
Maurice E ahbabadbb
Oscar O ahbabadbb
Ralph O ahbabadbb
Sarah R ahbabadbb
Thelma I ahbabadbb
Verne Leighton adbabfecb
SHORT Alfred C adgxffb
Daniel Bailey adkeeb
SHORTRIDGE Richard (Capt) akebb
SHOTWELL Amy Titus adhahd
SHOVE Hannah wife adaak
Josiah adaak
Nathaniel adaak
SIAS Joseph ahbaa, (Capt) ahbae
Sarepta bbbffda
—— adgfbea
SIBLEY Atlanta adhcbbffd
Benjamin adkda
Fannie J ahbgbxac
Hannah adkda
Josiah Dow adkda
Mary adkda
Nancy adkda
Richard adkda
Samuel adkda
Sarah adkda
SIDELINGER Charles bcbhded
SIDWAY Thomas W adkfbebd
SIGGINS —— bcdgdeafc
SILLMAN Sarah cbaa
SILSBEE Elizabeth adhcbc
SILSBY Caroline S adhcbbb
Hannah wife adhcd
Harriet adhcd
Henry adhcd
SILVER Sarah bcbeb
SIMMONS Addie L bcbdeceda
Arthur bcdgdafdb
SIMONDS Elizabeth wid adab
Helen M adabiggd
John adab
Louisa adhade
Nathan ah
Richard bbbff, bbbfg, Jr. bbbfg
—— abccgaca
SIMONS Asa Jr. (Capt) bcdeabdb
Mary bcdh

SIMPSON A adacedfi
Annie E beficaled
Charles bcdgdafl
Della bcdgdafl
Dennis beficaled
Joseph adgcadafg
Marie ahfcfda
Samuel W adgcadafg
Susannah akebfc
Thomas E adgcadafg
—— adadibd, adgfbfa, bcbhdi
SINCLAIR Sarah ahbcaa
SINGLETARY Lydia bce
SINGNEY Eugena akebdbbgdb
SINJOHN Mary abbegfcce
SINKERSON Joseph Dawson adhafagc
SKIDMORE Gertrude akebie
SKILLIN Dora Edna bcbhddceb
Lester E bcbhddceb
SKILLIINGS Lucy Ellen ahbgbad
—— befifhe
SKINNER, Carrie Dow ahgdccaa
Henry O befiffh
Lewis H ahgdccaa
Mary ahcix
Maud Melina adhcbbfdb
Samuel cbaae
SLATER Hazel bcbhddcca
SLEEPER Abigail abca
Elizabeth adg
Moses adbabi
Sarah Ann akecaga
William akecaga
Thomas a
SLOCUM Hiram ahgciac
Jane Ann ahgciac
SMALL Avesta S adkfbbjb
Bertira E adggeffaa
Dorcas M bcdgdpaa
Edith May adkgaee
Flora A adkgaee
George abccgchad
George G adaimbib
Hilda A wife adkfbbcda, adkfbbjb
John C C adkgaee
Lemuel adabbggac
Luella Mary abccgchad
Martha Maria adkgagaee
Mary bcbebbbdb
Mary Frances adkgaee
Nellie M adkfbbcda
Perley adkfbbcda, adkfbbjb
Rebecca A adkgaee
Walter S adkgaee
William adkgaee
William M adkgaee
SMART Asenath bcdbadd
Josiah T ahbabcdf
T C adbabfa
—— (Mrs.) ahbabc
SMILLIE John bcbcbbga
SMITH Abbie M abccgbaba
Abigail abbegfa, wife abccgbad
Absalom bbbfabi

Addie B adgbfagb
Addie Dow adgfcicb
Albert adgfdabba
Alice adabbgabdf, adabbgagd, adacffic
Alton L bbbfff
Amy R adadhacab
Ann abbd
Ann F adkehbd
Asenath Dow bcdbaddb
Augusta wife abccgbaba
Augusta A abccgbad
Belinda adhcdac
Benjamin adgfcicb
Bertha Eldora abdceble
Betsey adabb, adkehc
Byron befifjaa
C H W ahgfbdacc
Caroline bcbcbbga
Carolyn adggegbai
Carrie E adkgaebf
Charles bcdgdafbe
Charles E adgcaccab, bcdbecef
Charles Horace abdceble
Charles O adaimaaac
Charles Willard adhcbbhbb
Charlotte bbbfha
Chauncey bcdbaddb
Christopher (Dea) abbj
Clark adaabfaal
Clarence bcbcbbgf
Cyrus adaaaica, adggdci
Daisy adggeik
Daniel ahb
Ednah bcdbedf
Edwin adadhace
Edwin Hilton abdceble
Elbridge adkehi
Eldora Lockwood adgfcdacc
Eliza adaimaaac
Eliza H adkfbedc
Eliza M abbegbifc
Elizabeth ahb
Ella L bcbhdgag
Ellen B bcdedbae
Elmer H abbegbifc
Esther bcbebff
Flora J wid adabibdab
Frank befifhe
Frank A adaabfaal
Frank Edwin adgfcicb, adggeilb
Frank French T abdceble
Frank T bbbebcdaeb
Frederick adacgfc
George adaceali, ahbgbaea
George W adhafad, (U S. N.) akebbce
Georgiette S akebiu
Gladys A adabbgaiia
Grace xab, adgfcicb
Hannah G bcdedcga
Harriet bbbebcdaeb
Harriet J adkgaebfc
Hattie A adgfbhada
Herbert adaceagaa
Hester J abccgcfcaa

920

Isabel C bedbaddb
Isaiah bcbhdgag
Jacob (Capt) ahci
Jacob B abccgbad
James abbegfcce, adaabd, (Capt) ahbg,
    akebi
James Chase adkfbee
Jeremiah abbegfga
Jesse adggeik
John abbegbie, adabbgbca, adkehbd,
    bcdcbk, Jr., bcdcbk
John Dow abccgbaba
Jonathan abbegbie
Joseph (Capt) ad, bbd
Joseph E adabbgaiia, adgfbeh
Josie L adacgfc
Justus Jesse adkfbee
Lemuel bedcbk
Linie Etta adgfbgeae
Lizzie E adgfbgfdaa
Louisa Frances abbegbif
Louisa L abceacb
Lucilla A adggdci
Lucinda I adgfdabba
Lucy adaabfa, aeeb, bcdcbk, bcdeaea
Lucy W adabbgu
Luther Thomas adaabdaee
Lydia bedcbk
Lydia E adkehi
Lydia A bedgdp, bedgdpa
Lyman befifd
Mamie befiffdcd
Marguerite adhcbbhbb
Martha C abbegfcc
Martha J bcbhdpa
Martha O akebiv
Mary akece
Mary A adadagfb, wife akebiu
Mary Ann Frances abbegbda
Mary D adadhacab
Mary Emily adggdcca
Mary Geneva wid adbabfdeb
Mary Helen adgfcicb
Mary J adhafad
Mary Love wid ahgbb
Mehitable wife ahgfdea
Meribah akg
Melinda Knowles adkfbed
Michael bcbhh
Moses ahgfdea
Nathaniel ahb
Nathaniel Brown bcdbaddb
Nelson adaceagaa
Olivia A bcbegga
Orin adaabdaee
Osman adaabfaag
Phoebe bbbfab, bbd
Priscilla bbd
Rebecca H adabbgbca
Reuben adhafad
Richard ad, adkehi
Robert ab, (Dr) adggdcca
Roland Q adacffehb
Roy bedgdafbf

Sabrina H adgfcdaa
Sadie A adkehbd
Sadie Dow adaimaaac
Samuel bbd, Jr. bbd
Samuel Garfield bcdbedf
Sarah akebbb
Sarah A adgfbhad
Sarah Abby abbegfgaa
Sarah L adhafad
Seba H adhccg
Silas bcfifffb
Solomon bbd
Stella ahbabaeda
Stephen T bcdeaeg
Susan abcfb
Susan Dow abbegbie
Susanna wife ab
Susannah bbd
T Frank adaabdaee
Theodore abbegbie
Thomas a, adaabdaee, bcdgdpa
Wallace Edmund ahgbdacc
Wallis L adgcaccaj
Wilbur bcdgdafbe
William adhafad, adhafb, bcdgdafbb
William C akebiu
William H adhafde
Winthrop Hilton abdceble
—— adaimbbb, adaimbcc, adggeif, ah-
    fd, ahggeb, bcbcbbde
SMITHERMAN Clyde adgfcdabe
Earl adgfcdabe
Roy adgfcdabe
SMULLEN Burns bcdgdafkc
Cecil bcdgdafkc
Ella bcdgdafke
Fred bcdgdafkc
Freda bcdgdafkc
Thelma, bcdgdafkc
Violet bcdgdafki
SMYTHE Agnes M ahgdhbb
SNELL Clarinda S adkgaef
Eleazer (vet) adkgaed, adkgaef
Martha A adgkaed
SNELLEN Charles adgfbef
James adgfbef
SNETHEN Nicholas ahghe
SNOW Almira ahgche
Annie M abccgcff
Ernest abdcebeaf
Ethel abdcicac
Gertrude abdcicac
William N abdcebef
Windsor L abdcicac
SNOWMAN Eunice Caroline adabbgai
SNYDER Mary ahbabai
Ward bcdecaibb
—— bcdeabdaa
SOLE Benjamin T adabbhe
SOMES Flossie A bcbhdekc
Kiah B bcbhdekc
SOMERBY Abel bebha
Abiel, Abiel Jr. bcbha
John bcbha

921

381

Rebecca bcbha
SOMERSBY (see Somerby)
SOULE Dora Louise bcdgddahc
A P bcdgddahc
SOUTHER Annie Lowell adgxffbdc
Charles A adgxffbdc
Charles H adaimcdgc
Ella H adaimcdg
Esther A adgxffbba
Hannah adkehd
Ida B wife adaimcdg
Martha F adaimbi
Robert adaimcdg
SOUTHERLAND —— bcbhddfa
SOUTHMAYD Elizabeth Starr ahbcach
SOUTHWICK Anstriss adadic
SOUTHWORTH Alice Carpenter adg-
gdcc
Edmund ahgfbb
Myra bcdeda
SOWTER John xac
Katherine xa
Susan xa
SPACKMAN Ethel A adgcacbjd
William J adgcacbjd
SPALDING Joseph adaceaada
Martha Stoughton adaceaada
Silas M bcdeaeg
SPANDO Theresa adaidaba
SPANGE Mary bcficadbb
SPARKS Jared abdced
SPAULDING Adna Parsons ahbabag
Albina ahbabag
Asher ahbabag
Cynthia ahbabag
Deborah Dow ahbabag
Edward abbeebc
Eliza Ann bcdeabc
Eva M wid bcbebbcdab
Gilman ahbabag
Hannah C bcdeabc
James G bcdeabc
Joseph adbac
Josiah Dow ahbabag
Lucy M bcdeabc
Lydia L bcdeabc
Martha Ann ahbabag
Mary A E bcdeabc
Mary Annette bcdeabc
Melvin L bcdeabc
Randall H ahbabag
Simeon bcdeabc
Simeon Dow bcdeabc
SPEAR Charles F adgfbege
Clara E adgfbege
Eva M adabbgaige
George E adgfbege
Jacob Cummins adgfbege
M Warren ahbcajbc
Minnie E adgfbege
Sarah adgfdabbd
William H adgfbege
SPEARS Clara E bcbhdehf
SPECHT Minnie bcdebgaae

SPENCER Barbara bcbhddcea
Burgess adacgfc
Emma J adkgaeg
Eva M adkgaeg
Harriet adaceaff
Ida M adkgaeg
Lucretia adggdcd
Vaughn bcbhddcca
Velma bcbhddcca
Walter A bcbhddcca
Walter W bcbhddcca
William adkgaeg
William R bcbhddcca
Winfield bcbhddcca
SPENGLER Lydia M adacffeha
SPERRY Anson Martin bcdbeac
Bela J bcdbeac
SPILLER E C adabibe
SPINNEY Alexander bcdbadf
Charles, Charles Jr. adabbgbcd
Chandler abccgaca
SPITNER Laura bcdgdaald
SPOFFORD Abram bcficb
Betsey bcficb
Daniel Webster adgxfaae
Ellen D adgxfdabb
Florence H adabbha
Isaac bcficb
John, John Jr. bcficb
Sarah bcficb
Thomas bcficb
SPOONER Alden adaceaeg
Clara E bcbhdgaa
Marilla adhcbbffb
SPRAGUE Bertha bbbfhcgbf
Dexter bcdgdaiid
Frank bcdgdaiid
Garafilia Mohalby adggehb
Isaac adggehb
Marcella ahbabjed
Rebecca Stillman adggehb
Sarah adabbgqd
Walter B bcdgdaiid
SPREY Hattie A abbegbdbe
SPRING —— adkgded
SPRY C ahghe
SQUIER Clara adgxfam
SQUIRES —— bcdedbada
STACE (see Stacy)
STACY Ann bc
Elizabeth wife bc
Sarah bc
Simon, Simon Jr. bc
Susannah bc
Thomas bc
STACKPOLE John akebcg
Peter M adbabhc
Sarah wife adbabhc
Thomas adbabhc
STAIRS Celeste bcdgdafc
Lura M abccgcfcaa
Nathan Y abccgcfcaa
STALBIRD Aaron bcdedbbbc
Benjamin bcdedbbd

Cynthia bcdedbbd
Douzetta bcdedbbbc
ST. AMANS Melvina ahbabaeadc
STANDISH Miles (Capt) bcbhdbeda
STANFORD Mary bcdedbc
William (Lieut) abdf
STANIELS Charles adgcadae
Josiah Prentice adadiabb
Lizzie T adadiabb
Martha A adadiabb
STANLEY Mary adkfbede
Mercy Maria adaceagc
Sumner adhafcb
STANTON Abigail adabc
Julia A adacgff
Paul H adkda
STANWOOD Susan bcdcbk
STANYAN Elizabeth abccda
James ad
John ad
STAPLES Caroline adgfbgea
Caroline T abbegbibea
Clara A adkgaee
Harriet J adkgdea
John adabbgf
Joseph adgfbgeb
Nancy abccgdfb
Sarah A adgfbgeb
Sarah F bcbhdqab
William adabbgf
STARBIRD Nancy Murray adaabfb
STARBUCK Sarah bc
STARK Charles bbbebcbd
George H bcdeaefbb
John (Col) abbeg, abccd, bcdb
Lucius E bcdeacfbb
STARLING Octavia Ann adhahed
STARR Annie W bbbffcbaj
Charles F ahgchla
Margaret Theresa bbbffcbah
Thomas bbbffcbah
START George bcdf
Julia K adbabfbg
ST. CLAIR Katy bcdgdafab
STEARNS Elizabeth Marshall ahgfdag
George W bbbfabmd
Horace bbbffcf
Pauline bbbfabmd
Rosewel bbbfabmd
Susan abbegbie
Thomas adhafcg
STEELE Jane Adeline adhahe
STELL Julia akecahd
STEPHENS Alexander H adhccbb
Charles bcdgddad
John bcdgddad
STEPHENSON Catherine akebbce
STERLING Julia ahcbceb
Lela bcdgdafc
STERNBERG Henry bcdgdafo
Minna Catherine bcdgdafo
STETSON Eliza ahcbfe
Sally Barstow adhcbbgd
Zilpha adkddh

STEVENS Abby ahbabjbb
Albertine M ahfcfceg
Alice Maud bcdeaefcd
Anna abdcebi
Barbara Susie adbabfeaaa
Bertha A adgfcdgcb
Charles Dolloff abbegbb
Charles H bcdedbbbj
Clara Jane adkgaedd
Edward C abdcebi
Eleanor Ford bcfihb
Elizabeth adgfcb, ahbaedd
Fernando adaabacad
Fred W bcfigfbca
George B ahgff
George E adgfcdgcb
Helen A bcdedbbbj
Henry bbbg
Henry Coleman bbbfabmaa
Herbert adbabfeaaa
Hiram P bcdeaefd
Horace bbbffcf
Jennie adkecbaaaa
Jerusha bbbg
Joanna adbabi
John W adhcbbje
Joseph bcfifhi
Katherine M bbbfabmaa
Kenneth Walter adhcbbje
Lester C bcdebgafa
Lovina bcbcbaaa
Lucy A ahbgdc
Lucy O bcdecaha
Marcia E adgcacbk
Martha bcfifhi
Mary bbbffaf
Mary A bcdedfg
Mary Ann adgcacca
Melvin A ahgff
Minnie adhafdiea
Minnie E befiibca
Nancy ahbaacxaa
Owen adgfcdgcb
Parmelia bcdedfc
Phoebe bbbebc, bcdbecea
Samuel, Smuel Jr. bbbg
Sarah adkfbeia, akebbcba, bcbcbbac
Ward J adgfcdgcb
William N ahgff
—— abbegbb, aeeaeb, (Capt.) ahbcaj,
    ahgchfd, bcbhdbnaa
STEVENSON Mary bea
STEWART Anna ahcfe
Charles E ahbabamgb
H Edna ahbabamgb
Ida bcdgdagf
Ira bcdgdagf
John adaaaib
Lois wid bcfiff
Lovina befifff
Marion adaimaabe
Mary adabbgd
Moses bcfiff
Vera bcdgdaghb

ST. GEORGE Arthur J adhadceeb
Ruth Elizabeth adhadceeb
STICKMAN Ida May abccdgcbba
STICKNEY Arthur bcfifffa
Joseph abcfld
Orinda bcdedbb
Ruth wid bcba
Sarah akebir
Susanna akebbf
Thomas (Lieut-Col.) ahbaac, bcdeb
STILES Henry M cb
STILLING Annettie wid bcdedbbd
ST. JOHN A gbao
George bcbebbcdax
Lillian bcbebbcdax
STIMPSON Edith Chaney bbbfhjba
Edward Stearns ahbabjf
Elwell William bbbfhjba
Lillian E bbbfabmj
Sarah Ellen ahbabjf
William Elwell Parks bbbfhjba
STIMSON Edward ahbabjf
STINSON Addie E wife adabbgaighb
Bradley V ahbgfib
Herbert W adabbgaighb
Ida M abbegbif
Joseph C adabbgi
Julia Alice adabbgaighb
Julia B adabbgaii
Lettie A ahbgfib
Otis adabbgca
STITHAM Charles bcdgdeaic
Cora bcdgdeaic
Florence bcdgdeaic
Vera bcdgdeaic
STOCK Mary A adaceafgg
Thomas adaceafgg
STOCKMAN Ida May abccdgcbba
STODDARD Albert bcdebgaga
Albert A bcdebgaga
Carol bcdebgaga
Delia bcdebgaga
Eugene O ahbabajada
Frank bcdebgaga
Gladys bcdebgaga
Hollis bcdebgaga
Ida bcdebgaga
James bcdebgaga, bcdebgagag
Lawrence bcdebgaga, bcdebgagah
Lola bcdebgaga
Margaret ahbabajada
Mary bcdebgaga
Oralenna adgfbei
Ula bcdebgaga
STONE Anna bcdeaefb
Charles Burton ahbcacg
Charles Dow abbegbdca
Ellen Susan adaabcefa
Eva adaceagca
Frank bcdeaefb
Grace E bcdedcfcb
Henry adacedff
Joseph abccgacf
Kate bcdeaefb

Melvin adadieab
Oliver adacga
Silas bcdeaefb
Uriah bcdedcfcb
——(Capt.) ahbca
STOODLEY Thomas E adaiebaa
STORER William bc
STOREY William adkfbbf, bc
STORMANN Merle L bcbhddceba
Clyde Dow bcbhdderba
Corinne Doris bcbhdderba
Eugene Elmer bcbhdderba
Florence Mae bcbhdderba
Merle Leon bcbhdderba
Lawrence Wesley bcbhdderba
Phyllis Frances bcbhdderba
STORRS Augustus ahgfbd
Charlotte ahbaaha
Polly ahgfbd
STORY Ann bc
Elizabeth ahf
Maria A bbebfg
Seth (Dea) bc
William bc
STOTT A bcbcbbeea
Amelia B bcbcbbeeb
John bcbcbbeeb
STOVER Abbie F ahbabkbb
Matilda bcbhdek
Sarah bcbhdek
STOWE Mary bcdeaec
STOWELL Mary wid bcdeabb
ST PIERRE Joseph ahbaaheae
Josephine ahbaaheae
STRAIGHT Christian fa
STRANAHAN Fitch James ahgdf
James S T ahgdf
Mary ahgdf
STRAW Daniel bcdbeae
STREETER Bailey adgcacad
Martin V B adgcacad
Mary adkebd
STRICKLAND Jared (Col) cca
STRINGHAM Kate (Geary) adadieab
STROBECK Amy L adacedfd
Arthur W adacedfd
Byron K adacedfd
Charlie C adacedfd
Julius B adacedfd
Laura L adacedfd
Oland H adacedfd
STRONG Sylvester fcf
STROUT Betsey ahbgb
Eva Eulalia adhcbbfb
Joshua (Capt) ahbgb
Melville adhcbbffb
STUART Caroline adhafgcdc
Hannah gbam
John adaaaib
STUBBS Frank bcdgdcfdb
STUDHOLME Donald Mitchell adace-
    ddbc
J Mitchell adaceddbc

924

384

Janet May adaceddbc
Jeannette Dow adaceddbc
Raymond Collyer adaceddbc
STUDLEY Olive Marion abbegfjac
STURTEVANT Asa ahbabaf
Edith M adhafgcdb
Ellura ahbabaf
Hattie M wife adhafgcdb
Herbert adhafgcdb
Lewis L ahbabaf
Sarah ahbabaf
Savilla ahbabaf
William L ahbabaf
STYLES Augusta adgfbhad
Nicholas adkdeaca
Sabrina L adkdeaca
STYRING Margaret adacealk
SULLIVAN Albert bcdgdbaadg
Celia L bebebbfaad
Etta adgfbefh
Eva M bcbebbcdab
Frank adgfbef
George adgfbef, adgfbefh
Ida May adgfbef, adgfbefh
James D adgfbef
Jennie A bcdgdbaadg
John H bcbebbfaad
Lozetta adgfbef, adgfbefb
Lydia adgfbec, adgfbef
Lyman Sylvester adgfbef
Nancy adgfbef
Nellie akecaabeb
Sanie Belle adgfbef
Sarah adgfbef
Stephen adgfbef
Stephen Frank adgfbef
Susan adgfbef
William adgfbcfh
William Henry adgfbef, adgfbefi
SUMNER Charles adhccbb
Lucinda adhadca
Mary ahcbea
SUTHERLAND Frances adggegbaf
Mary ahbabah
SUTTON Anna ai
Ebenezer ai
Elizabeth wid ai
Joseph ai
Richard ai
Susannah wid ai
SWAIN Aris Maria bcfifl
Hannah abca
Lydia adadha
Phineas adadagf
Rhoda adadagf
Sarah adgfbdb
William adgfbdb, adgfbdb
SWALLOW Nancy bcdgdakbb
SWAN Brenda adaigbbae
Elizabeth abbegfk
Polly adgfbeb
SWAZEY Addie E bbbfhbxcg
John F bbbfhbxcg

SWEAT Theophilus adacec
SWEATT Alice Etta wid bcbebbbdc
SWEENY Theresa adkfbbdf
SWEET Lizzie J adhafdfb
SWEETZER Frank Eliot bcdbecca
SWENSON S M adggdch
SWETT Lizzie bcdedbada
Moses ad, adba
Patience adba
Sarah abdb, bcbb
SWIFT, Arthur Howard adgfgabcd
Bradford Elmer adgfgabcd
Charles Richard ahbcaji
Edith Gertrude ahbcaji
Edwin Joseph ahbcaji
Elmer adgfgabcd
Fred E adgfgabcd
Lucretia adgfgabcd
Margaret A bbbfabj
Mary Otis wid adgfgaba
Zebria J D ahbcaji
SWINTON Agnes bcdebgab
SWITS ahgdccb
Harmon D ahgdccb
Jennie, ahgdccb
William J. ahgdccb
SWITZER Mary adaigaa
SYKES Eva M bcdeddhca
Harry adadibdh
William bcdeddhca
—— adadibdh
SYLVADA Clara Bernice adaijbb
SYLVESTER Elizabeth Charlotte bcd-
  ebej
Samuel bcdebej
TABBITTS Sara E gaaxaxl
TABBUTT Louise M adabbgbebb
TAFT Sidney adahdbc
TAGGART Jonathan, Jonathan Jr. bc-
  fifm
Rachel ahbabaeae
TALLMAN Alanson Benjamin adacgff
Christopher Palmer adacgff
Darwin Washington adacgff
Edwin Ephraim adacgff
Eudalia Josephine adacgff
Olive Lucretia adacgff
Philena Jane adacgff
TANDY Lucy adgcaeb
TAPLEY John S bcdgdv
TAPLIN Sulliman adggdaaa
William adkfbbdd
TAPPAN Ada Bingham adkdecec
Amy M abbegbeaf
Ann ahgha
Daniel (Rev.) adkdecec
John W adggdcc
Mary adkgac
TAPPEN Gladys adkdecei
TARBELL Arthur Elwood adbabfecb
Earle Norton adbabfecb
Eva Gertrude dababfecb
Gladys Elmira adbabfecb

925

Jacob Norton adbabfecb
Ruth adbabfecb
Sterling Dow adbabfecb
TARBOX John bcbcb
Jonathan bcbcb
Olive N adgfbgdch
Orlando adgfbgdch
William bcbcb
TARLTON Alfred W ahgfdae
Hannah akebb, akebba
Julia A ahgfdae
Mary wid abcce
TARR Sarah ahbgfi
TARRANT Frederick William adkedja
Mildred Frances adkedja
TASH —— (Col) adadab, adadh
TASKER Lemuel C adadagfbc
Nathaniel adadagfbc
TATE Catherine Bertha ahgdcagc
TAYLOR A G adadagaca
Abbie bcdeabc
Alba C bcdbecea
Alicea F adaimbaia
Amos adgfdc
Annie Clark bcdbecea
Annie E wid adabbgea
Arabella Stevens bcdbecea
Arthur bcdebgde
Belle bcdbecea
Barnabas bbbffce
Berdelia adabbgdab
Bethia abbf
Charles Everett bcdbecea
David ahgfdaj
Duane S bcdeabc
Ednah Dow bcdbecea
Ella M bcdbecea
Elois bcdgdafag
Frank A bcdeaedaaa
George Dow bcdecea
Hannah C akebdbbb
Harriet adgfdc
James H bcdeabc
James M bcdeabc
Jesse adgfbca
John abb, abcb, bcdbecea
John W adabbgdab
Lizzie adacffib
Lucella bcdeabc
Mabel E bcdeaedaaa
Mary J ahgfdaj
Nettie M bcdeabc
Pauline bbbffce
Mary J ahgfdaj
Nettie M bcdeabc
Pauline bbbffce
Phoebe ahgd
Purney E bcdgdbaadk
Raymond bcdeabc
Romaine K bcdeabc
Samuel D bcdbecea
Samuel D Jr. bcdbecea
Sarah abb, akeba

Sarah J wid adhafab
Susan adacffib
Susan F adaigaaa
Willaim akecaeb
—— adacffib
TEDFORD Earle bcdgdafkj
Evelyn bcdgdafkj
F C bcdgdafkj
Kenneth bcdgdafkj
TEFFT Emory N ahchfeg
TEED Ann bcdgdd
Anna bcdgdd
James bcdgdad
TEMPLE Annie bcdgdafeb
Eva A bcdedcfd
TENNANT Caroline bcdbadg
Charles William bcdbadg
Henry bcdbadg
John bcdbadg
William bcdbadg
TENNEY Arthur John ahgfdah
Caroline bcfifhf
Cleora ahgfbdga
Elizabeth adaidab
John Sr. (Capt) ahgfdd, Jr (Capt) ah-
    gfdd
John Frances ahgfdd
Julia Flynn ahgfdah
Lovina M adgcacba
Lemuel Dowe ahgfdd
Orittie bcfifhf
Reuben ahgfbdga
Samuel bcfifhf
Samuel Stillman Jackman bcfifhf
Samson adgcacba
Susanna ahbga
Thomas adaidab
Ulysses Dowe adgfdah, ahgfdda
—— adkfbdx
TERRELL Charles bcdgdakch
Fay bcdgdakch
Gray ahbcabfec
TERRY Ephraim adggdcc
Lester bcdeaeafe
Mary adggdcc
TETUALT Judith ahbaahaea
TEWKSBURY Almira bcfigfdd
Naomi adhafce
Nettie M abccgbada
Rosanna ahbgecb
THACKREY Harold A bcdebgagh
THAW A Blair adgfcdaab
THAXTER Nancy bbbfax
THAYER Betsey adgfcdac
Charles G adhafcj
Elizabeth G bcdhdbndh
Margaret A bcdebel
Rebecca ahgfbdg
Susan bcdebg
Tileston ahcfje
——abdgca
THERIAULT Mary bcdgdn
THOMAS Abigail akeb, bcfife

Adeliade J bcbhdehfg
Annie Lloyd adggeibab
Benjamin (Capt) akeb, bcfife
C E bcbhdehfg
Caleb bcfife
Charles A ahgfbdgb
Charles P ahgfbdgb
Deborah bcfife
Edna C ahbabajadc
Edward Emerson ahgfbdgb
Emma adadhacad
Enoch bcfife
Francis M ahbcai
Frank D ahgfbdgb
Hannah Dow bcfife
Hugh ahbabajag
Job bcfife
John bcfife
Lena M adabbgaigb
Lloyd adggeibab
Lois Nelson ahbabcdb
Marion Nellie ahbabajag
Mary adhccga, bbbfabmab
Mehitable bcfife
Nathaniel adabbgaigb
Thomas Whittemore bcfife
William adadhcahd, bcfife
—— bcdgdbf
William S adadhcahd
William Moody bcfife
—— bcdgdbfl
THOMPSON Aaron. Aaron Jr. ahcbfea
Abijah adhcbbff
Amorilla adadhadae
Agnes bcdhbfiaa
Anthony adggdcc
Augustus B (Rev) adgfbgfca
Celende adhcbbf
E N adbabfbe
Elizabeth adgfcif
Elizabeth I adkehbha
Emma Tryphena adhcbbff
Esther adggdcc
Frances adkgde
Frances Evelyn bcfifhhhb
Frank D (Hon) adaabdaed
George A adkehbha
Gideon adggdcc
Helena wife adggdcc
Henry adggdcc
Jennette wid adhcdab
John adggdcc
John F bcdcaie
Josephine adbabfbe
Julia E adadhcbda
Lois ahfc
Lulu W adgfbgfca
Luther bcbcbbg
Lydia bcbcbbg
Margaret adadagabba
Mary adabbgl
Melissa abbegbb
Melvill adabbgaid
Nathaniel adgfcb

Nathaniel Jr. adgfcb
Nora bcdedbbcc
Samuel adggdcc
Sarah Lillian adhcbbhbb
Seth W bcdecai
Stephen adggdcc
Thomas, Thomas Jr. adggdcc
Thomas J bcfifhe
—— adaigad, (Gen) adhcbbf, ahggf, bcdgdafdb
THRASHER Jonathan adgj
THRESHER Gertrude May adkedjd
THROOP John (Capt) adggdc
THORNDYKE Charles W adhafdig
Julia eaac
William adhafdig
THORNE Cora H bcdedbab
Susan bcdecahb
—— bcdedbab
THORNTON Anne E adkfbdxa
THURBER Mary Ann adbabd
THURLOW Edna Day adkfbbcib
Justus adkbbcib
THURSTON Caroline ahbcajh
Sarah ahbabi
—— adgfbea
TIBBETS Florence Alice bcbebcgabb
Henry Eugene bcbebcgabb
—— ahggbh
TIBBETTS Emma E adaimbhbc
Hattie F bcdgdbac
Leonard adkdeac
Lucy Ann adkdeac
Silas akebhc
TICHENOR Halsey Taft bcdedfdbb
Marion Pruden bcdedfdbb
TID Mary bcdgda
TIDD James bcdgdia
Julia bcdgdia
TIDLEY Mary bcdgda
Salaveras bcdgda
TIFFT Charles Arthur ahbcabcbe
Charles Henry ahbcabcbe
Minnie Lurena ahbcabcbe
TILDEN Abigail ahbabjea
Anna ahgha
TILLETT Magnes bcdedb
Mary bcdedb
TILSON Arvilla adgfcdgb
TILTON Abigail abbe, abbj, abdcic
Abraham 3rd aia
Ada May bcbhddceb
Charles adaceagf
Elbridge abdcieb
Eldridge abdcebcc
John D akebdbbga
Joseph badcebj
Margaret adain
Mary Ann akebdbbga
Mary M abdcieb
Mary Otis adgfgaba
Otis adgfgaba
Peter G adhcdaeb
Samuel abdcebcc

Samuel P abdcebf
Weare D abdcebj
—— abccgbada, akebbcd
TINNEY Elizabeth abccgdba
TITCOMB Charles ahbabke
Elias ahbabke
Hannah M bcficadba
Louis Frederick bcbehhf
Mabel L ahbabaefb
Pierson bcbehhf
Sarah Elizabeth bcbehhf
Tirzah bcdea
TITUS Bertha C bcdgdbaaa
Calvin bcdedbci
Edwin Calvin bcdedbci
Ernest Dow bcdedbci
Ernest Dow bcdedbci
Martin bcdedfc
Mary A bcdedfc
Sarah bcdedbcc
Sarah Elizabeth bcdedbci
Solon Rufus bcdedbci
TOBIE —— bcbhddag
TOBIN Cora adaigaaac
TOBINS Eva E adabibcaa
Norman B adabibcaa
TODD Frederick adkgdec
TOMPKINS Adelaide bcdgdafe
Agnes bcdgdaghb
Alda M bcdgdaik
Arvid bcdgddae
Coy bcdgdaik
Domie H bcdgdaik
Eldora bcdgec
Frank bcdgddae, bcdgdeae
Gertrude bcdgdafea
Herbert Smith bcdgdaik
Ira bcdgdaik
Jacob bcdgdaii, bcdgddae
Joel bcdgdaik, bcdgddae
Mary ad
Olive bcdgdafa
Sarah bcdgdah
Tressa bcdgdaii, bcdgddae
William bcdgddb
—— bcdgdaib, bcdgddae
TOPPING Caroline M adkgac
Dolly adkgac
Elias adkgac
Elizabeth adkgac, adkgace
Luther adkgace
Lydia adkgac, adkgaci
Martha D adkgac
Mary adkgaci
Nancy adkgac
Samuel adkgac
Sybil adkgac
TORR Sarah ahbabjj
TORREY Lester bcdeaefbe
TOURTILLOT Charles F ahbabjbc
Fred abdcebk
Jesse ahbabjbc
TOWLE Abigail abbeaa, akecaab
Alice R adaiebab

Amos abbeaa, Jr. abbeaa, akecaab, ak-
ecd
Anna B adaiebab
Anthony abbeace, abdd
Arthur C ahbgbi
Belinda adadai
Betsey akecahd, akecd
Betty akecd
Benjamin abdd
Caleb abdd, ahddb
Charles abbeace
Charles Lewis abbeace
Comfort abbeaa, akece
Daniel akecd
David adaiebab, akecad
David Amos adaiebab
Dolly abbeaa
Eliza Hook akecad
Elizabeth Frances abbeace
Esther abdd
Eva Lewella ahbgbi
Ezekiel abdd
Francis abdd
Gardiner ahbaaaaa
Hannah abbeaa, akecac
Jabez abbeace, Sr. abbeace, abdd
Jeremiah abdd, abddc
John Darling ahbgbi
John Dow abbeace
John Nelon ahbgbi
Jonathan abcca, ahbgbi
Joseph ahbgbi, akecd
Lydia akecd
Lydia Hale akecad
Levi ahbabi
Mark adgcaccaa
Martha Melissa ahbgbi
Martin Richardson ahbgbi
Mary abbef ahbgbi, akecad
Mary A adhcdaed
Matthias abdd
Maud A adaiebab
Molly akecahj
Nancy akecad
Nancy L adadagaa
Nathaniel abdd
Oliver abbeaa, ah
Patience abdd, akecad
Patience J akecadh, akecahb
Philip abdd, Jr. abdd, 2nd abdd, akec-
ad, (Ens.) akecad, Jr. akecad
Priscilla abbef
Rebecca adadagfbd
Sally akecd
Sally Bartlett akecad
Samuel abbeace, abcca, abdd
Sarah abbeaa
Sarah Josephine ahbaaaaa
Simon adadai, akecad
Thomas J abbeacf
Zacharias abdd
TOWLES Julia A ahbgbafbb
TOWN Ellen M bcdbeceda
TOWNE Abigail bcdedl

Eli ahbabae
Joseph bcdedl
Olivia adadibab
Sybil ahbabae
TOWNEY Sarah bcbhdehfb
TOWNSEND Abigail bcdeabbe
Julia Ann ahcbcc
Margaret J adabbgu
Rufus E bcdeabbe
Stephen Dow bcdeabbe
TRACY Amos S adacebba
Etta adaabacae
Isabella M adggdci
Wallace adaabacae
TRAFTON Amanda N bcdgdaiib
Charles bcdgdg
TRAIN Ansel adhafaaa
Arthur H adhafaaa
Henry adhafaaa
TRASK Abbie Swazey adaigbbac
Amasa adgfcdgb
Ancil adaigbbac
Clara bcdecaca
Lucy A adgfcdgb
Rosena bcbhbfi
TRALL Charles adacealh
TRAPP Sally ahghche
TRAVERSE Roxa Jane adkebabba
TRAVIS see Traverse
TREADWELL Joseph bcbhh
Nathaniel Jr. aia
Sarah abdg
TREAT Sara adkgdegd
TREFETHAN Charlotte Ann bcdedbcb
Mannie ahbabahcc
TREMBLE —— wid bcdgded
TRICKEY Abigail adadagb
Charles T adadagb
Dorothy A adadagb
Frank E adadagb
Fred adadagb
George B adadagb
Henry D adadagb
Joseph M adadagb
Joseph S adadagb
Mary Ann adadagb
Nellie A adadagb
—— adgfbei
TRIGGS Georgie A abccdgccc
William abccdgccc
TRIPP Mary A adgfbfba
Warren adgfbfba
TROTT Mary Elizabeth abdcebea
TROWBRIDGE Amos, Amos Jr. ahcbbd
Ira ahgca
James ahcbbd
Laura ahcbbd
TRUAX Caroline M ahgdcca
Lillian adacgfgg
TRUE Amanda adggdd
Amelia Fifield adggdj
Andrew Clement adgxfam
Annie L adgxfafd

Charlotte S abccgdb
Daniel adggdd
Ezekiel, Ezekiel 3rd adggf
George adggdd
Hannah ahbabji
Henry, Henry (Capt) adggf
Jacob adggf
Joahan ahbabaea
John adggf
John A adgxfam
John E adgxfam
Julia bbbfabm
Lydia adggdd
Mary adka, adggf
Moses adggdj
Nancy adggdd, adggdj
Osgood adggdd
Ploomy A adgxfam
Ruth adgxfaf, adgxfam
Stella M adggdj
William Jr. adka
Zelpha adkebdb
TRUELL Ella bcdedfda
Ira Whitcomb bcdedfda
TRUESDELL Sam adaimbhg
TRUFTON —— wid gab
TRUMBULL Mary ai
TRUNDY Agnes M adabbgdda
Henry E adabbgdda
Mary O adabbgaice
TRYON Andrew Jackson ahbgbai
Mellen ahbgbai
TUBBS Anjenet Ella Augusta May ab-
  begbdfd
TUCK Abby Elizabeth akecahd
Amos akecahd
Amos Otis akecahd
Benjamin abbf
Carrie M adbabgaa
Charles, Charles Jr. akecahd
Edward abbed, abcfb, akecahd
Ellen akecahd
Hannah abbed
Isabella akecahd
John (Dea) abb, abcfb, Jr. abcfb, ak-
  ecahd
Mary abceabf, abcfb, wid ah
Nathan abcfb
Sarah abbea, abbec
TUCKER Blanche adacgfed
Charles Henry adhcdaee
Charlotte Mary adhafde
Daniel bbbfabbe
Edna A adhadccb, adhadcea
Edna Anna adhadcec
Edward adacgfed
Eliza Jane adhafde
Elizabeth ahfcgb, bcdf
Eugene M adhadccb, adhadcee
Ezekiel bcbehb
Greeley Dow adhafde
Gurdeon adhadccb
Hannah bcdf

929

Henry bcbehb
Horace adhafde
Ida F adacgfed
James Monroe S adhcdaec
John Smith adhafde
Joseph bcdf, Jr. bcdf, be
Joshua (Rev) adhadccb
Lucy Maria adhafde
Lydia adhaff
Maria adhaff
Mary abceabd, adkfbe, bcdf, bcdfa
Mary Manning bbbfabbe
Morris be
Moses, Moses Jr. bcdf
Parker bcdf
Phebe bcdf
Orlando Horace adhafde
Reuben bcdf
Sarah bcdf
TUFTS Nancy bcdeaefd
TULLOCH Polly bcdedb
TULON Mary ahfcfceea
TUPPER Edwin Lombard ahbabjef
Jennie Elizabeth ahbabjef
TURCOTTE Joseph adabiggda
Nellie J adabiggda
TURG Bennet abcegdba
Milicent abcegdba
TURNENLIFFT John W ahchbb
TURNER Azro bcdeddhdc
Clara A wife bcdeddhdc
Cora May bcdeddhdc
Eliza F bbbffdc
James bcbhdda
Mary Elizabeth bcbhdda
Mary F adhccbbeb
Sally adkgb
William M adgfbcja
—— ahbabje
TUTTLE Addie F accacaaf
Catherine adadhcb
Doris A bcbcbfiaa
Harry E bcbcbfiaa
Jacob B aeeacaaf
Nancy B adaijbb
Ruexbie George abbcgbdb
Sarah adaidaa
William W adgcaf
TWISDEN Lydia adgfbece
TWOMBLY Charles adaabcja
Emma C adaimbcb
John adaimbe
John Hanson adaabcbb
Orrison adaabcja
Tobias adaabcbb
—— adgfbei
TYLER Ellis adacgfd
Ezra adgfdd
Mary ahgdcaf
ULSTER Richard, Earl of, eb
UNDERSTOCK David ahgfbdd
UPHAM Timothy (Rev) adacea
UPTON James ahbcaca
URIE Jennie E bcfiffdb

Robert bcfiffdb
USHER —— adkgaa
UTLEY Sarah ahgfd
VALENTINE Abram E adgcadaffb
Melvin Dow adgcadaffb
VALLIE Hattie adaiiabaa
VANCE Susie E bcdedfb
VANCUREN SUSAN fca
VANDERCOOK Frank E adgkaeg
VANDUZEN Eliza adaceaae
VAN DUZER Jsephine fccaf
VAN HORNE M J adacgff
VAN NAME Mary adadagab
VAN OCKER Roselette adaceahf
VAN VRANKEN Emma Carrie ahgdc-
  cad
Stephen Gates ahgdccad
VAN WICK Jane Ann bcficanb
VARNER Annie Laura akebdbbig
Joseph akebdbbig
Sarah L akebdbbig
VARNEY Aaron adbabc
Lydia adhae
Rhoda adadica
Simeon adbabc
Solomon adhae
Wallace adhadccc
VARNUM Joel acdaac
Margaret bcfifjb
VARTY Clara ahgfbdh
VAUGHN Edith Longfellow adggeibaa
Richard Fairfax adggeibaa
VEAZEY Robert a
VEAZIE Frances R bcbhdqaba
VEDDER Helen adgfgabc
VERRILL Alice Gertrude bbbfabbea
Byron D bbbfabbea
C H bcdcdbbbh
Caroline bcdgdalb
VESEY E adadhaaad
John ahfad
Marion (Mrs.) ahbcaa
Verdie V adadhaaad
VICKERY Elizabeth ahbabcfa
Flora bcdgeja
VINING George A bbbffcbab
John bbbffcbab
Timothy ahbgbfg
VITTUM Abbie M wid abccgbaba
Almira wife abccgbada
Alpheus abccgbada
Etta abccgbada
VOGEL William H abdgcafac
VOORHEES Philip abdgcaf
—— (Adm.) abdgcaf
VORHIS Martha adaidacd
VOSE Amarilla ahbabjec
Harriet bbbfabbe
VRIE Charles adgfbffb
VROMAN Geraldine adacgfacb
VROOMAN Elizabeth ahbcaca
Hannah ahbcaca
Jacob ahbcaca

Richard Dow ahbcaca
WADE Catherine P eaab
Fannie adabibcab
John bcdbecc
Kate Turner adhccbbeb
Leander A adhccbbeb
Mary ahggbb
Sarah Brooks bcdbecc
WADLEIGH Ann adkf
Benjamin bbbb
Hannah adgfbd, bbbb
Gustavus B adgcaccaf
Ida Belle adgcaccaf
Joseph adkd
Mary adkd
Nancy bcbhdqa
Peter akebik
Ruth bedcb
WADLEY Phebe bcbcbaab
WADLIN. See also Wadleigh
Jeremiah adgfbn
Mary Frances adgfbn
Miriam adgfbbdg
WADSWORTH Burton adhafde
Solomon cbaag
WAHR Mary adggcicb
Gottlieb adggeicb
WAITE Aurora M adhafdi
Cook adaceaac
Louisa Amelinette adaceaac
Mary abcf, adaceaac
Thomas adhafdi
WAITT Hannah abdced
WAKEFIELD William a
WALDECK Arnold Otto bcbehhh
O bcbehhh
WALDO Carrie bbbffafaa
WALDRON Charles adgfbhadb
Maria E ahbabahf
Mary G bcfifl
Nellie May adgfbhadb
WALES Hannah ahgfdah
Kate befiffdcb
WALKER Alexander bcbhdbnde
Charles bcdeaefb
Freeman (Maj) adggeg
G R adgfbggb
Jennie M bcbebbbd
Levi T abccabei
Lucy adggeg
Philene ahdaadde
Ruth ahbge
Stillman adaabcjh
Susan S adbabia
WALL Elizabeth ah
Hannah ah
James ah
Mary ah
Rachel bbbfhjba
Richard B ahgha
Sarah ah
WALLACE Elmer adaabdabcd
Gertrude abccgbada
Iola adaabdabed

James Henry adhafaea
John gbag
John B gbaka
Josephine gbea
Mary akebbf
Thomas J adaabdabed
Victoria M akebdbbig
WALLIN Mortimer Fiske Dow ahbabjcb
Reuben ahbabjcb
WALLINGFORD Elizabeth abdceda
George W abdceda
Thomas (Col) adgfg
WALLIS —— adgfbef
WALLS Bentley bbbfabmac
Rilla bbbfabmac
WALTER Mary adggdcc
WALTON A (Capt) ahbgbfe
Abigail adaimbh
Alice Mary adaimaabb
Cora abccgcfda
Cyrus adaimbai
Daniel adaimbb, adgxfaaa
Edwin adgxfdae
Emily J adaimbbd
Fank Royce adgxfdae
Helen M adabbhd
James L adaimaabb
Jennett adaiiaa
John N adaimeg
Jonathan L adgxfdae
Josephine M adaimbai
Lydia Ann adgxfaaa
Mary adaicaafl, adgxff
Miriam bcbegg
Nancy adaimbb
Rebecca adaaaacca
Rosanna wife adaimbai
Samuel adgxff
Susan J adaimaa
Tristram Heyes adgxfdac
William adaimaa, adgxfdac
William H adgxfadd
William Stacy adgxfdae
—— adaceagb
WARD Alphonso E bbbfabhab
Clinton adaabfaacb
Cotton akecb
Daniel Harvey adgfcica
Deborah akecb
Dow ahgdgaab
Eva May abccgcfdb
Florence ahgdgaab, ahgdgaabc
George P abccgcfdb
Hannah akecb
Louise abccgdfaa
Mary aeb, bcbcbbeeb
Mary Ann bcdgddg
Mary Adeline ahgdgaab
Mary E wid bcbhddfaa
Noah akecb
Rachel abbeab, akecb
Roy ahgdgaab

Sarah abceabe, akecb
Simon (Capt) akecb
Sophronia adgfbhadb
Susan adhafgcd
Theron ahgdgaab
Thomas akecb
Thomas Otis abbeebbbc
—— ahbcajca, bcdgdagj
WARE Amos N beficai
Daniel beficai
Daniel Leonard beficai
Elizabeth Jones beficai
Horatio beficai
Melatiah beficai
Susan L beficai
William beficai
WARK Rachel Jane bcdgdsa
William bcdgdsa
WARNER Inya adacgfggb
WARREN Abby wife adadibab
Abby L adadibab
Barbara J bbbfhcfee
Joseph (Gen) bcdea
Mary akebd
Oren O adadibab
—— ahbgbbeb
WARRENER Mary bcbebbcaf
WASHBURN George ahbabaf
Levi (Rev) bcdbcdf
Lyman adggdab
Sarah E adgxffah
WASS Bertha Eliabeth befifhhg
Fred Leslie befifhhg
George Raymond befifhhg
Gertie May befifhhg
Harry befifhhg
Ida Belle befifhhg
Henry befifhhg
Roy Carlton befifhhg
WASSON Clara bcdgea
WATERBURY Mary Emma adggegba
WATERHOUSE Julia abccgdfc
WATERMAN Celia J ahbabag
Ford ahgfbh
Jerusha S ahbgii
John befiffa
Lucy adbabfbgd
Maria E befiffdc
W. ahgfbh
WATERS Jane adggde
WATSON Abijah bbbebda
Betsey adadaga
Caroline Eaton ahbcabcb
Charotte bcdgddad
Chick bcdgddad
David bcdgddab
Elijah bcdgdg
Essie bcdgdagf
Fred (Dr) bcdgddad
Gertrude bcdgdagf
Hannah bcdgdagf
Harry bcdgbagb
Henry bcdgdagf, bcdgddab

James bcdedcff
Lottie bcdgdagf
Lydia wife adadagaa
Lydia A adadagaa
Mabel D bcdedcff
Manzer bcdgddad
Martha adhcbbdc
Mary bcdgddad, bcdgdf
Mary J wid ahgfdaj
Miriam bcbegg
Norris bcdgddab
Polly bbbebda
Roy bcdgdagf
Sally adgfdd
Sewell adadagaa
Stephen adkeg
Susan A ahbabjj
Walter bcdgddad
William adadaga, bcdgddab
—— bcdgddaa, bcdgddab, bcdgdh
WATTS Mary bcbebfa
WAUGH James bcdebgdbb
Joseph bcbcbbab
WAXAM Edgar ahgfdaca
WAY Mary R bcdgdda
WEALE Marie Elizabeth abbegbebbb
WEARE Alice Sarah adaimaf
Annie Laura adaimaf
Charles Austin adaimaf
Eliza bcdedbacb
Elizabeth abdc, adkdb
Ella Maria adaimaf
Hattie B adkddgca
Jemima akebb
John abdch, adhadde, Jr. adhadde
Joseph T akeaa
Joseph Taylor adaimaf
Josephine adaimaf
Lydia wife adhadde
Mary abdcg
Meshech (Gov.) adaf, adkdb
Nathaniel abcf
Rosie Bell adaimaf
Sarah abcf
Taylor adaimaf
WEATHERHEAD Paul Elton abbegb-
dfbc, abbegbdfbca
WEAVER Josie adkebgbaa
Sophia wid adabibj
WEBB Maud M abccgcfde
William abccgcfde
—— bcdgddad
WEBBER Annie Peters adacedfj
Celia Jennie bcbcbcgabb
Emeline ahbgbxa
Emily A adhafcad
George E befifhhh
Hannah adhe
Mary F adhcbbjac
Mavis Eloise adacedfj
Raymond Sullivan adacedfj
William ahbgbxa
William Greenleaf adacedfj

William W adacedfj
WEBBERLY Eliza bcdgdaacc
Martha E bcdgeg
WEBER Eliza ahchfe
Eunice Mary ahchfij
Lois wife adaii, adgxf
Sarah ahchfd
WEBSTER Abigail abbegg
Adelbert C adkecbaaaa
Anne adfcdca
D Louise bcdeddhcb
Daniel adggd
Delia bcbebbbdc
Ezekiel F adggbeb
Flavilla adabbgtab
Frank D bcbebbbdc
Hattie M adadagff
Jacob (Capt) abceab
John adabbgaig, bcdbade, bcfi
Lanville adgfcdacd
Louisa bcdgdaaee
Lucy J bcbebbbdc
Martha E ahbgbfa
Mary Frances adabbgaig
Mary Gott adabbgy
Maud M adkecbaaaa
Noyes adggbea
Stark bbbfhbxb
Stephen bbbfhh
Thomas ah
Viola ahgfbdacb
WEDGEWOOD Jonathan (Capt.) abce-
 abe
WEED Elizabeth bbbd
Hattie adabbgaja
Mary adabbbd, adgcadaa
Mary A ahbabkb
Wealthy bcbhdbnd
WEEDON Lucy ahgfbdca
WEEKS Ada ahbaacdae
George Warner ahbaee
Joshua abca
Leslie bcbhddcf
Lucy akebce
Martin R bbbffda
Mary W bcdedbca
Minot bcbcbbga
Salchell adkdeeg
WEEMAN Mary adkgdef
WELCH —— ahbcajcb, (Col.) bcdb
WELD Hattie A adggdcib
Hiram A adggdcib
WELLEBY Martha E bcdgegb
WELLINGTON Dolly ahbabjc
Ebenezer ahbabje
Sally ahbabje
WELLMAN James bcbhdbn
Lucy M bcbhddkbxa
Sarah bcbhdbn
O A bcbhddkbxa
—— bcdgdpc
WELLS Abigail bcbcbbca
Bessie bcfiffdcc

David adggej
Eleazer bbbffa
Emma adkdeae
Ethel Maud adadhacaa
Etta N adadagacca
Eunice adhcdb
Ezekiel (Capt) ahbgi
Hannah Phillips adhcdb
John adadagacca
Lyman B adadhacaa
Mary bbbffa
Minnie M abdceblia
Moses adhcdb
Phoebe ahbgi
Ralph ahbghh
Sarah wife bbbffa
Sarah Phillips adhcdb
Webster adaabffb
William ahbghh
WENDELL Auburn adceabecb
Charles abceabecb
Olive abceabecb
WENTWORTH Abra adbabb
Alexa adbabb
B F adadhaabb
Clark adaigbba
Ephraim adadhcf
John adbabb
Lois adaabcbb
Mary E adadhce
Sarah E adaigbba
WERN Perry bcdebgaec
WESCOTT David bcdebgab
WESSON Almon Frank adacglb
Charles adgfbef
Edwin A adacglb
Elizabeth adacglb
Ellen M adacglb
George McClellan adacglb
Lysander B adacglb
William Pliny adacglb
WEST Adeline W adaidagf
Clara E bcbcbbgc
George W adaidagf
Hugh bcbhddha
Jabez (Capt) bcdg
Luther akebcg
Mary A bcbhddha
Ralph (Mrs.) adaabfaak
WESTLAKE Henry adkfbbdfb
Thomas H adkfbbdfb
WESTON George S bcfigfda
John W adhcbbdc
Margaret ahbabda
WETHERBEE Mary T ahbgbaed
Sarah Paine bcficap
WETMORE David adaceagb
Ellen Jeannette adaceagb
WEYMOUTH Grace C adgfciea
Hattie abbegbifc
WHALEY Emma J ahbgidb
Ephraim ahbgidb
Sarah wife ahbgidb

933

WHARFF Albert J ahbabadb
Stella Arline ahbabadb
WHARTON Mary adaaaf
WHEATON Berle bcdgdeaia
Frederick bcdgdeaia
Ruth bcdgdeaia
WHEELDON Eliza Freelove adabbgpaa
Levi adabbgpaa
WHEELER Abigail bcdbaddb
Alice Lillian adhafdgd
Alice M adhafdgc
Amos abccgadb
Angie bcbhddcca
Augustus bcbhdpaa
Benjamin (Rev) abccgadb, bbbffd, bc-ded
Benjamin Ide abccgadb
Bertha T bcdhdpaa
E H bcfigfbc
Eliza Ann bcfigfbc
Ethel May bcdedfg
Flora Belle adggdccae
Genevieve adadabbdb
Hannah bbbffd
James P adggdccae
Joanna wife bbbffd
Johanna Crosby bbbffdba
John A bcdedfg, Jr. bcdedfg
Jonathan ahchg
Mary bcded
Mary Azilla bcdedfg
Oliver adggdccae
Rena bcfiffdeba
Sarah bbbffbaad
Sarah Bender ahgchh
Silas bcdedi
Walter P ahbcachd
William Rust bcdedfg
WHEELOCK Eleazur (Rev.) ahgff
Theodora ahgff
WHELPLEY Bertha Elsie adkfbbdfa
Wilmot adkfbbdfa
WHIPPLE Catherine bcdebe
Ezra ahdb
Gertrude ahgdcaa
John (Capt.) ahfca
Josephine ahgdcaa
Kate ahgdcaa
Lois M bcdbaddda
Stephen ahgdcaa
Thomas (Capt) adacg
WHIDDEN Eliza Freelove adabbgpaa
Pauline Avey abbegbeaa
WHIPPS William O bcbcbaaaac
WHITACAR Louisa J akebbcbaa
WHITAKER Rebecca adggdaac
William bcbhdbedc
WHITCHER Abner ahbcb
Eleanor adadhc
Isaac ahbcb
Malinda akebik
Mary Celende adhcbbffa
Melinda akebdbbg

WHITCOMB Benjamin (Maj.) bcdeca
WHITE Adonijah ahgchg
Arthur M adhafdiea
Beulah bcbcbbg
Bridget bcdgeka
Clara Louise bbbfhcfe
David bbbfhcfe
Cornelia Murray ahgdgba
Eliza bcdedfdb
Ellen adhcbbjd
Fannie Tamar abbegbdb
George bcdgeja
Gladys L adhafdiea
Grace Fletcher adaidaba
Grace J bcdgeja
Hannah adacfe, bcdedca
Joan bcdgdafj
Joanna bbbfabi
John (Capt) bc
Margaret ahbgd
Mary bcdgdakg
Mary E bcdebfa
Nicholas bcd
S adggdadac
Sophia adaceaf
Sophronia wife bbbfhcfe
Wallace adgcacbc
Zelma bbbfhbxd
—— ahbaacfc
WHITEHILL Frank adacgfea
WHITEHOUSE Eliza bcbhdeb
WHITHAM Sarah Glendora ahbgim
WHITING Elizabeth bcfe
Hannah bcfe
John, John Jr. bcfe
Jonathan bcfe
Joseph bcfe
Judith bcfe
Sarah bcfe
WHITMAN Julia ahggccb
WHITMORE Augusta abccgcfcab
Richard A abccgcfcab
WHITNEY Frederick akebiib
George D akecahj
Henry akebiib
Joseph akebiib
Kate akebiib
W W bcbegbd
—— ahbcabia
WHITTAKER William bd
WHITTEMORE A T adhafdj
Eben adkfbba
Nancy adkfbba
WHITTEN Nancy Frances akebig
WHITTIER Anna adaca, adacac
Betsey bbbebcbe
David A adaimae
John adaca
John Greenleaf ab, adhcdb
Lydia bcdedfa
Mitchel adaca
Moses adaca
Susan adfa

Thomas bcdbadh
William adaca, (Dr) adaca
WHITTLE Fanny adhebbd
—— wid adgfedg
Joseph J adhafcabd
WHITTON Annie M adhafcabd
WHOLLEY Blanche M adadhcaib
Dennis adadhcaib
WHYTE Oena May adhaheda
WICKLOW John fcg
WIGGIN Betsey akebfc
Chase adadhaa
John abdcca
Lora A adadhacd
Lovina adkgddfc
Nancy adadhaa
Stephen adadhacd
Zoa Olive adadhacd
—— akebfd
WILBER Mary adai
WILBERTON George adkfbebb
L G (Dr) adkfbebb
WILBUR Lizzie A adkgaedda
Louisa ahchg
WILCOX Dorcas bcdedka
Hudson bcbhddfaa
Tony bcbhddfaa
Warren bcdgdeaaa
—— bcbcbbeb
WILDE Caroline Elizabeth adggbf
Harriet H bcfigfddc
WILDER Abel bcdecag
Delia E bcdecag
Helen T bcdecag
Henry Fayette bcdecag
Lovisa adaabdaec
Mary bcdecag
Mary Eva ahbgiifa
Sarah D bcdecag
Thomas bcdecag
Thomas Eugene bcdecag
WILDMAN Frank C ahbgbfaab
Harriet E ahbgbfaab
WILES Albert bcdgdagf
WILEY Cora adacglb
Hazel ahbabajgaa
WILFORD Gilbert bd
Martha bd
Mary bd
Nathaniel bd
Ruth bd
WILHELM Mary bcdeaefb
WILKINS Alonzo adkebf
Arthur bcdgdeaie
D W adgfbggb
Freeman bcdgdeaid
Henry bcdgdeag
Lillian bcdgdeaie
Mary E bcdgdt
Oscar bcdgdeaie
Theodora bcdgdeaid
WILKINSON Rachel R akebip
WILLARD Charles ahgfbdb

Charles Ernest ahgfbdb
Curtis A ahgfbdca
Daniel M adadhacae
Etta May adhebbffa
Henry A adadagc
Joel W adhebbffa
Oliver ahgfbdca
Susie H adadhacae
WILLEY Edna Maria adggdccab
Effie adabbgdaae
Martha akebdbbi
Tomson bbbffcd
William bbbffcd
—— akebdbbac
WIGGLESWORTH —— (Col) ahbg
WIGHT Charles L ahbaadbf
Margaret ahbaadbf
William H ahbaadbf
William H G ahbaadbf
—— bcbcbbei
—— bcbhbgb
WILLIS Charles adaabdaej
Glen Charles adaabdaej
Jack Edgar adaabdaej
Katherine J D adkgaebfa
WILSON Abigail wid adacfe
Alfred ahbabjbb
Amelia R bcdbaddl
Anna D adhahd
Charles ahggcb
Elizabeth ahbg, ahbga, bcdgem
Ella bcdebgad
Ella V wid bbbffbaad
Ellen J bcbhbgb
Elmer E adbabfddb
Experience adaabfb
George A ahbabjbb
Henry adhahd
John, John Jr. adhahd, ahggcb
Laura B bcbhddfacd
Lillian J abdcebcaba
Lorenzo ahggcb
Louisa ahbcacf
Lucy P adhahd
Lucy S adhecgaa
Mary adhahd
Mary Dow adhahd
Mary Elizabeth bcbhbgb
Matthew bcdgdakd
Roxanna ahggcb
Ruth bcba
Samuel ahggcb
Sarah wife ahbabjbb
Sumner bcdebgad
Susan E bcficale
Thomas Thorndyke adhahd
Wilson adhahd
WINANS Jennie ahgcibb
WINCH George adkfbbe
George Francis adkfbbe
WINCHESTER Helen Gove adaimbhbc
James A adaimbhbc
John Allen adaimbhbc

WINDSOR Mary C adggdcca
WING Abby wife bcbebcgab
Arthur Wilford adhaheef
Ivan adhaheef
Jabez bcbebcgab
James bcbebcgab
Sarah P bcbebcgab
WINGATE Elizabeth adaaaaa
John Jr akebefb
Joshua (Col) bcdec
WINN William adhcbbfc
William H adhcbbfc
William Henry adhcbbfc
WINNER Ollie Kate adadabbdbb
WINSLOW Colcord adbabic
Elijah adbabfc
Elizabeth A adbabic
Henry adbabfh
Phoebe wife adbabfc
William adbabfc
Zilpah Jane adbabfc
WINTER Helen bcdeddhca
WINTERS Mary bcdgdaalb
WILLIAMS Albert ahbcae
Alice J bcdgeb
Anna Madge adaigbbaa
Annie bcdgdafqd
Christian ad
Delia A bcdebef
Fernald Johnson (Col) bcdebef
Dorothy adkehbh
Eliza M adkgaebc
Ephraim gbxxa
Ezra T adkgaebc
Fannie bcdgdaacj
Franklin akecahe
Guy adacebfba
Hannah bcfiibc
Hiram gbefa
Isaac ahbcae
Isaac H ahbcae
Josephine M gbefa
Mary ahbcae, bcc
Rose adhcdach
Ruth ahgchl, bcbeha
Thomas ahbcai
—— (Col) ahfae
WIRTH Sybilla ahbabaji
WISE Humphrey adg
Mary adg
WISER Clara B adabibcaa
WITHAM Clifford adabbgaigb
Hattie adabbgaigb
WITT Augusta ahbgdca
Hollis adbadb
WITTER Polly bcdedfb
WOBBLY Eliza bcdgdi
WODLEY Moses bbbebe
WOLCOTT Polly adacff
WOLEBEN Maryette ahgdhdhda
WOLF Mary J ahchfi
WOLFF Scott adacffec
WOOD Abraham bcfifjja

Dorothy adkg
Edna Stanhope bcbhbgdb
Effie G ahbabajga
Eleanor adgfbfb
Florence adggdcfba
Grace M bcbebbfac
Hiram akecad
Inez gaaxaxg
John bcbhdbeaa
Lavina bcbhdbeaa
Martha bcbhdbeaa
Maryanne bcfifjja
Rebecca ahgdca
Permilley wife bcfifjja
W N ahchfed
WOODARD Ella Mabel bcbcbbgbb
George F bcbcbbgbb
James Horace ahbgbxc
WOODBRIDGE John (Rev) bcbehhi
WOODBURY Benjamin bcdbac
Benjamin Jr. bcdbac
Daniel bcdbac
Delia bcdbac
Ernest Roliston adgfcicf
Ira bcdbac
Jonathan bcdbac
Jonathan Jr. bcdbac
Lucie adgfbffc
Manley Gates bcdbac
Olive bcdbac
Phineas bcdbac
Roxana bcdbac
Ruth adaimbbdbcb
Susanna C abbegfcad
Zillah bcdbac
WOODERS Lloyd adhahecc
Marie Adeline adhahecc
Neal Dow adhahecc
WOODLEY Hannah bcbehhm
WOODMAN Josephine bcdgdsba
Sally adkedl
WOODRUFF James Daws abbegbdd
WOODS Adeline Mercy adaceagca
Albert adaceagca
Alberta adaceagca
Carter Richardson adaceagca
Eliza bbbffag
Ellen adacgfc
Elroy Russel adaceagca
Eve Jennette adaceagca
Grace M bcdbeceada
Henry W bcdbeceada
John M akecafk
Mary A adbafab
Stella M bcbebbfaad
Thomas B (Rev.) adadagea
WOODSIDE Margaret Shepard bcdcd--
dd
WOODWARD Augustus ahggca
Charles D adgfcdgab
George A bbbffagc
Robie A adgfcdgab
WOODWORTH Cynthia bcdecac

Sarah D bbbffba
WOOSTER George adgfbea
Georgia gaaxaxb
WORCESTER Judith gaa
Susannah bc
William (Rev.) bc
WORK Eliza B bcdeabc
WORRALD Susan Lydia abccgaeaaa
WORTH Anney adgd
M Mark adabbgbcf
Margaret adabbgbcf
WORTHEN Addie I wid adadagad
Deborah wife adgffc
Eliphalet ahbcf
Enoch adkddc, akebbcb
Ensign adbabfeca
Eunice wife adbabfeca
Ezekiel ad, Maj. adkddc, bcbe
Hannah adbab, adgffc, adhae
Jemima adkddc
Jessie Mabel Connor adbabfeca
Judith bcbe
Mary akebbcb
Samuel adgffc, bcbe
—— (Capt.) (see Ezekiel) ahbgb
WORTHING Hiram adbabfea
Mary G adbabfeb
Mary Roxana adbabfea
WORTHLEY James, James Jr. ahbgbbb
Jesse adgxfak
Robert Dow adgxfak
Thomas bcfifi
WRAY Lillian ahgdhbc
WRIGHT Adelaide bcdgdaba
Alfred bcdgdeab
Allen S adaccaebd
Ambrose bcdgdeab
Annie bcbhdehb
Bertha bcdgd—p
Charles Edward bcbcbbgl
Clara bcdgdakfa, bcdgdeah, bcdgdq
David adkebabbf
Edmund bcficae
Elva bcdgdaijf
Eva M adgfbgead
Frank D ahbabjecd
George bcdgdeah, bcficae
George Edmund bcficae
Gordon bcdgdaijf
Grace I adkebabbf
Hattie bcdgdeabb, akdebabbf
Henry F adfcdcaaa
Henry P bbbebgac
Herbert bcdgdeah
Howard bcdgdeah
Hugh bcdgdad
Irene B ahgfdae
Israel bcdgdeah
James adaimbbb
James H adgfbgead
John adgfcdgca, bcdgdeab
John Elliott abbegbdd

Jonathan bcficae
Julia bcdgdaaca, bcdgdeah
Laversa bcdgdaijf
Lillian M adfcdcaaa
Maria bcdgdaijf
Martha bcdgdaa
Mary adgxffag, bcdgdeab, bcdgdf
Millard bcdgdaijf
Philip bcdgdaijf
Ruth wife bcficae
Sanders bcdgdeaafg
Saunders bcdgdeah
Sheldon Carpenter bcbcbbgl
Stella M bbbebgac
Susan bcdgdan
Walter H ahbabjecd
Walter T ahbabjecd
—— wid adkehg, bbbfhag
WRIGHTON George, George Jr. bcdebgad
Jessie bcdebgad
WYATT Mary bb
WYMAN Alice J bcbhddkbx
Ann bcdbaa
Calvin ahbgbfa
E W adaaaifac
Elvira ahbabaj
Lot bcdeabf
Ruth bbbffeb
Samuel O ahbabadc
Sarah bcdcae
Stephen Dow bcdeabf
Timothy, Timothy Jr. bcdeabf
William bcbhddkbx
—— bcbcbb
YATES Andrew adacedfc
Charles L adkgded
Charlotte adaigbbad
Fannie Etta adkgded
Frances gbefaa
Frank E adkgded
John Abner adkgded
Sylvanus R adkgded
Vivian bcdgdafdb
William H adkgded
YEATEN Enoch Dow adkdeg
Samuel, Samuel Jr. adkdeg
William Barber adkdeg
YEATON Alvin S ahfcaaac
Cora A ahfcaaac
Dolly Maloon abccgaccaa
Dorothy abccgaccaa
John Jr. adadagfb
Joseph H adbabfbb
Laury A adadagfb
Louisa wife abccgaccaa
Martha wife ahfcaaac
Mary abcca
Nathaniel abccgaccaa
YELVERTON Fanny Belinda fce
YERXA Amaziah bcdgdafc
Elias bcdgdafc
Ella bcdgdafc

937

Fannie bcdgdab
Henry bcdgdafc
Mahala bcdgdaf
Norman bcdgdafc
Samuel bcdgdafc, bcdgddg
YORK Augusta akebbcbb
Bertha May gaaxaxea
Daniel akebbcbb
Etta J adkgddfc
John akebbcbb
Mellen A adkgddfc
YOULIN Samuel ahfcad
YOUMANS A ahgfbg
YOUNG Aaron ahbchcb
Abbie bcdgdbaal
Abby L adgfbgae
Augusta A bcbebbbdd
Charles (Mrs) adaabfaab
Charles Woodbury akebcb
Clara gbaic
Daniel akebbcbb
Delight bcbhdh
Dolly abbegg
Electa M abbegbibd
Elizabeth bcdgdeaaa
Elizabeth J abbegbibd
Ella Francena bbbffbaa
Elmer abbegbibd
Elmer W ahbabadf
Enoch P akecaabab
Ermina V adhcbbffa
Ernest E abbegbibd
Eunice abbecbb
George N abccgad
Gideon bcbhdh
Hale akebib
Hannah abbegg
Harold bcdgdafaf
Harriet A adhafabb
Harry Hill ahbaaaaad
Helen S abbegbibd

Henry Newton adaidaed
Henry Newton Jr. adaidaed
Hezekiah bcdgded
Holly bcdgdafaf
J W Saunders bcdgded
Jacob Suydam adaidead
James, James Jr. akebce
Jane B adbabfb
John bcdgdafaf, bcdgdeaaa, bcdgded
Joel bcdgdeaaa, bcdgded
Lucretia akebce
Lucy Hatch bcdebfb
Lydia adgfbh
Lydia B ahbchcb
Mary ahgb
Mary J ahgdcaga
Maud S adbabfeaaa
Myrtle bcdgdafaf
Nancy adgfbgf
Nathalie May adaidaed
Phoebe adgfbgf
Rachel akebce
Robert adhafcj, bcbebbbdd
Roxana wid ahbabi
Sally bcfihd
Sarah bcfii
Sarah Elnora akebce
Sarah M akecaabab
Saunders bcdgded
Solomon bbbffbaa
Stanley bcdgdafaf
Susan abbegg, bcdedla
Susannah E adbabgada
William D abbegbibd
ZANTS Doris ahggbd
ZERBE (Miss) adggdega
ZEINAANTZ Charles S ahbabale
ZIHN Andreas bcfihedb
—— Bertha E adaceagada
—— Christopher adhecga
—— Jacob adaceefc

938

SUPPLEMENT

ADDITIONS AND CORRECTIONS

IN August 1927 the Dow Book was handed to the printers. The type was set rapidly and with no delay the work passed into the page proof stage. From this point it was impossible to add new matter to the body of the Book and especially to the index.

As soon as the Author received his galley proofs, a set was sent to Herbert B. Dow for comparison, to eliminate as many errors as possible and to add such new matter as had been discovered. Proofs were sent elsewhere as widely as possible to the many who have contributed information to this Book. Simultaneously, there seemed to spring up a country wide interest in Dow genealogy and more letters of inquiry and information were received than ever before in the same span of time. It seems unfair to the Dow family, of whom over 20,000 individuals are now alive in this country, to omit this great mass of supplemental information. The only way to include it was to hold a supplement open, to index it, and to send it to the printer at the latest possible moment.

The Author has in his possession about 10,000 items, Dow names which so far are unconnectible with the family trees. At times he considered printing this enormous disconnected chapter. But that is too great a task. Instead, he includes in this Supplemental Appendix those disconnected items which seem most important or most easily provable when readers of the published work begin correspondence with the Author.

No genealogy has ever been completed. Most Authors say nothing about their disconnected items and no one else knows how proportionately large they are. This Author has been frank on this subject. He hopes to live many years to add almost daily to the connected family trees.

This supplement is arranged in the strictly alphabetical order prevailing in the main body.

Henry Dow a. A very interesting item has been dug out by Wm. G. Nichols, who notes incidentally that John Huggins of Dedham disappears from that town simultaneously with the appearance of John Huggins in Hampton, where he remained permanently. The record of Suffolk deeds notes that 23 (10) 1643 Richard Cole late of Hampton for 5£ sells to Henry Dove (or Doue) of Watertown his lott and appurtenances in Hampton, provided that if said Richard Cole shall return to this country within three years and will satisfy the said 5£ and other charges he shall have his lot back again.

We remember that Margaret Cole came from Ormsby with the Metcalfe family as a servant, the usual custom. It is clear that some connection exists between Margaret and Richard Cole. If he were her father one might suppose that they would come to America together and that no homesickness for old England would induce Richard to return without her. It is more likely that he was her brother and had come on a later vessel. It is evident that he acquired his Hampton property long before Henry Dow decided to move to Hampton. Richard had gone to England before September 1643. Perhaps Henry Dow drove a sharp bargain with his brother-in-law. Perhaps, however, he acted in all kindness, advancing money to Richard in full expectation that the latter would redeem his lot. As Richard did not come back at all, Henry Dow added a rare bargain to his land holdings. We note that Henry did not use this lot, but bought a place when he came to Hampton in 1644.

Abigail Dow abbeaa m Mch 19, 1775, Amos Towle b May 6, 1749, d Aug 29, 1825, son of Amos and Hannah (Drake). Death dates of children:

Amos Apr 7, 1855; Sarah Feb 21, 1852; Comfort Aug 4, 1832; Oliver May 1855; Hannah Apr 25, 1866; Abigail Sept 1857

Helen Dow abbeebcaaa m Feb 17, 1917, William J Hale M D of Ann Arbor.

Polly Dow abbeedb m (his 2nd) after 1838 John Drake Lamprey.

Mary Floretta Dow abbegbeba m George Hall; 2nd William H Barker.

David Elwyn Dow abbegbebba in 1921 was resident manager of Tremont Theatre, Boston. His wife was known on the stage as Rae Elwyn. They starred together as Mr and Mrs David Elwyn.

Stephen Ricker Dow abbegbebbb; div; returned to Boston, resumed business, and has lived down his misfortunes. It is now realized that his acts which were questioned were not done for personal gain, but rather to uphold the credit of the corporations in which he took great pride.

Leonora M Dow abbegbig b 1847, dau. of Levi, is untraced

Albert Woodbury Dow abbegfjca d Glendale June 27, 1913.

Levi Dow abbegfk. His m date is June 3, 1832.

Sarah Dow abbeh had children (Moulton):

g Elizabeth bap Mch 27, 1768   h Comfort bap Apr 22, 1770

Mary Dow abca d Jan 2, 1755.

George W Dow abccdgcaa. N H official rec, doubtless correct, give him as son of John abccdgcb.

Lillian Lucy Dow abccdgcaad b Concord Oct 11, 1905.

Simon Dow abccdg. No trace of his 2 dau. nor missing son. The Barnstead farm descended by way of the 3rd son.

Jeremiah Dow abccdgb may have been 1stborn, surely b by 1791; served in Legislature representing Barnstead in 1819; moved soon after to New Durham, farmer. He m about 1825 Mary Hall, both of New Durham. He d of old age at the home of his dau Sarah in New Durham. Children:

a Sarah Hall d New Durham, life long resident, Jan 18, 1899, ae 73-9-16
b Samuel Hall b New Durham Dec 1827
c (this and subsequent not in order of birth) Lorenzo b Nov 1835
d Timothy. He lived to comparatively old age, unm.
e Abigail m —— Wentworth; children Benjamin and Rosanna
f Mary m —— Welch; children,—John, Benjamin, Mary, Addie
g Betsey m —— Sargent; children,—Grace, Hattie, Cora, Edmund, Florence. All these d without children. Grace m George Cosson of New Durham. Hattie m George Elwell of Gloucester, Mass. Edmund m Mattie Buzzell of Compton, N H; d at his desk in Boston Post Office, 44 years a supt there. Cora unm of Medford, Mass

Sarah H Dow abccdgba m Daniel Burnham. Only child:

a Emma F m 1874 —— Coburn. A son George G later took the name of Burnham; m 2nd John Walker; 4 children; living 1928 in Farmington, N H

Samuel Hall Dow abccdgbb and his posterity are fully traced in this Book sub adgfgab (q v)

Lorenzo Dow abccdgbc d at his sister's home two days before her, Jan 20, 1899. He m Emily Myrick; no children. He had followed many trades in many places.

Winthrop Y Dow abccgacj d in Boston, rec giving him as son of Simon of Hampton. This seems error. Simon Dow is abccgab.

Lucy Dow abccgdceb m Amos Adelbert Colcord, son of James and Abbie (Lamphor).

Eleanor Dow abccc m Samuel Brackett b Nov 13, 1721, son of Anthony, immigrant from Wales 1769; m 2nd Sept 8, 1770, Jeremiah Berry b about 1724.

Hannah Dow abcfe. It is not improbable that she was the Hannah m Feb 14, 1768, Jacob Barnard, son of Samuel and Elizabeth (Connor) and that their son Samuel was the one mentioned in Jonathan Dow's will.

Abigail Dow abdca m Jonathan Rowe b Sept 30, 1710. N H rec give her b Kensington June 22, 1727. Jonathan son of Robert and Mehitable (Leavitt).

Comfort Dow abdcb and Josiah Batchelder had children:

a Ephraim b Oct 5, 1752   b Simon b Oct 17, 1753
c Betty b Nov 30, 1755   d Josiah b Apr 16, 1758

Tabitha Dow abdcebf d unm Aug 10, 1818. Her niece Tabitha Blake Dow abdcebcc m Samuel P Tilton.

401

James Jewett Dow abdcebeg.   Date death probably error.   He m Almira C Marble and lived Bedford, Mass.   Rec bid him as James W b Sanford, Me, and Laura C Marble.   A son:

a   John W b about 1863, farmer of Kingston, N H, m Aug 21, 1884, Mary L Bowley b 1866, dau of Eben and Sarah E (McDaniels)

William L W Dow abdcebeh must be the W L W Dow who m Dec 24, 1872, Helen Chase.

Henry W Dow abdcicab.   Apparently a child;—for:

a   Harry E b Somerville Oct 27, 1886; d Somerville June 29, 1913

Elijah Dow adaaaaa left an only dau.   Jacob Dow, given as his son, is adaaaha.

Samuel Dow adaaafa was living Nantucket in 1814; m about 1793 Lydia Coffin, dau of Paul and Ruth.   Nantucket records all the children:

a   George b Apr 26, 1794   b   Lydia b Nov 24, 1795
c   Alexander b Aug 19, 1797   d   —— ——
e   Mary b Apr 4, 1811   f   Susan b Mch 25, 1814

The Samuel Dow, Quaker, who m Joanna Harkness is most likely son of Judah Dow adaaaj; cf adaaacf in book.

George Dow adaaafaa m Nancy Long; 2nd Jane Fisher, dau of Abraham.   One child by 1st wife:

a   Samuel H; unt
b   Susan Fisher b May 1832; m David Stanton of Nantucket, son of Giles
c   Ann Maria b Aug 1836

Lydia Dow adaaafab m Timothy M Gardner, son of Eliakim and Pamela.

Alexander Dow adaaafac m Charlotte Cobb, dau of William and Charlotte.   Friends rec never give maiden names.   Children:

a   Mary C b Nov 7, 1821; m Albert Easton, son of George and Sarah
b   Charlotte b 1823; m William Foster Mitchell, son of William and Lydia
d   Alexander Cobb b Oct 5, 1830; m Brockton, Mass, Chloe C —— b 1838; unt
     By this time the children of the Nantucket Quakers were scattering widely, impelled by business opportunity
c   Phebe Ann b July 1827; m Melvin B Macy, son of Edward W and Elizabeth
e   Emily F b Nov 26, 1832   f   Reuben b May 3, 1835
g   George C b Apr 30, 1841; unt

Reuben Dow adaaafacf moved to Fitchburg, Mass, dealer and manufacturer of tin plate; m Dec 29, 1863, Carolina Augusta Robbins b Leominster Feb 15, 1840.   Children b Nantucket:

a   Walter Gilman b Dec 30, 1769; unt   b   Charlotte Rebecca b Apr 4, 1873,

Susan Dow adaaafaf may be she who m Charles Billings, Quaker, pioneer of Billingsbridge, Ont.   A considerable Quaker colony came from Cape Cod and Nantucket into Ontario.

Elizabeth Dow adaafb, in Nantucket rec b Sept 8, 1770, m William Googins of Me.

Ruth Dow adaafc m Thomas Marshall of Nantucket.

Reuben Dow adaaafd m Elizabeth Bunker, dau of Joshua.   Perhaps only child:

    a Rebecca b Nantucket May 24, 1801; m Francis Folger, son of Francis and Susan

Rebecca Dow adaaafe b Nantucket Dec 28, 1776, is the missing dau of Henry.

Sally Dow adaaafg b Nantucket; m Israel Brightman; 2nd Thomas Paddach (sic), son of Abishai.

James Dow adaaafx. The Author has never yet been able to ascertain the origin and identities of the Quakers who made a settlement in New York State, around Lyons and Sodus. A rather remarkable narrative is placed here. It was dictated by a grand daughter, then at advanced age, too much from memory alone, earlier parts from hearsay wholly, but it is too definite, too circumstantial not to have a large basis in fact,—even to be almost entirely correct, some one salient fact lacking.

The father of James lived Cambridgeport, Boston, or both, a tanner and currier, who made in various ways a very substantial fortune for his time. There were 7 sons, 2 dying young. No daughters are mentioned. They included Moses, Aaron (one of these the first born), John, Sidney and Joseph, 25 years younger than the oldest. This firstborn conducted a coastwise shipping business from Boston, becoming prominent and successful. But his fondness for worldliness loomed large in the mind of the simple Quaker-bred narrator. Nominally a Methodist, he gambled and swore, even drank. James lost his mother at an early age and was brought up by friends of the family, who were Quakers. He is said to have married a Boston lady, who bore him two sons, dying soon after. He then, about 1828, married 2nd Loving Berry, who had been nurse to his first wife. This match displeased the rich and very aristocratic family and there was thereafter little or no communication. The father dying intestate, the brothers offered to James as his share of inheritance a shoe factory in Claremont, Mass (there is no such place). He took it, but later developed the idea that he had been taken advantage of and that his share should have been much larger. Attacked by tuberculosis, he sold out and bought a farm near Lyons, N Y, where he and his wife are buried in the Quaker cemetery.

Altho imaginary fortunes always grow with the passage of years, it is quite certain that no American Dow family fits the requirements given above. A simple hypothesis which would make everything plausible is that James was not a Dow but the family which brought him up was a Quaker Dow one and that in later years James took their name, his own having no associations dear to him. What makes the matter most interesting here is the Quaker connection. The children of James, two older being unknown:

c Jane Abigail b Boston 1829   d Lucinda Flavilla b Boston 1831
e Henry Kimball b 1833   f Alzina Elizabeth b 1835, both Cambridgeport

Jane A Dow adaaafxc living 1917 Wagon Mound, N M; m 1847 Jacob Absalom Bright. Children:

a George Washington   b Thomas Jefferson   c Elvira H
d Lucinda   e Elizabeth   f Emma   g Charles
h William   i Ellsworth   j John

Lucinda F Dow adaaafxd d 1784; m Oshawa, N Y, Jan 1849 James Monroe Cooper. Children:

a Alzina E b Dunkirk 1851; d 1857
b Medora b 1853; m 1871 Frederick G Heights of Dunkirk; has 1 surviving son
    and 1 grand dau
c Agnes E b 1861; d 1875

Henry K Dow adaaafxe d Lima, Ohio, 1903; m 1855 Elizabeth Hungerford b Killarney, Ire, 1841; d Dunkirk Oct 15, 1899. Carpenter and pattern maker, mechanical skill being an inheritance of the whole family. Ardent prohibitionists, studiously inclined. Children:

a James Maurice b Smithport, Pa, 1856   b Henry b Smithport 1858
c Neal Hill b Dunkirk 1874

James M Dow adaaafxea owner and manager of Kenton (Ohio) Engineering Works, m 1883 Nellie Fleber d Buffalo 1895; m 2nd Kenton 1898 Tillie Steiner. Child:

a Maurice (dau)

Henry Dow adaaafxeb d North East, Pa, June 6, 1902, freight agent for the Nickel Plate; m Dunkirk Dec 31, 1884, Agnes Quigley. Children:

a Charles J b Dec 9, 1885: accountant and Spanish translator, m Coneaut, Ohio,
    Oct 28, 1914, Ruth B Chapman
b Maria Agnes b Dec 25, 1890; in 1915 jewelry engraver of Los Angeles, her
    mother with her

Neal Hill Dow adaaafxec, draftsman with American Locomotive Co, Dunkirk, m 1902 Kate Neal of Dunkirk. Child:

a Marlin b 1905

Alzina E Dow adaaafxf d Houston, Tex, 1883; m Dunkirk 1851 Samuel Hill McElroy.

Elijah Dow adaaah. The account in Stearns Hist N H is correct, derived from family rec. Salisbury rec seldom give parents' names and necessitate wholesale guessing at identities. Elijah's 1stborn, and perhaps only child:

a Jacob b Nov 18, 1780 or 1781; m Judith Bartlett. Their posterity in this **Book**
    is under adkeba, in error; it belongs to adaaaha

Sarah Bartlett Dow adaaahac (adkebac in the main text of the Book) m (her name given as Dow) Bradford, Mass, Apr 17, 1848, Albert S. Hardy Jr widower b 1829, son of David. Her m rec of 1846 to Nathaniel G Knowles of Northwood may or may not be correct.

Judah Dow adaaaj. Vital statistics have not been found of a large proportion of the line of adaa, although they must have lived long in or near Hampton Falls. One branch went to Nantucket and are rediscovered in the records of that island. Another appears by 1748 in Epping but without a single datum of a whole generation.

It is evident that Judah Dow married young and remained until 1787 in Hampton Falls. His name appeared regularly in the tax lists, but then drops out. Nevertheless his name reappears in Hampton Falls in 1790 with wife, two daughters and three sons, two sons being born before 1774. The inference is that Judah sold his farm in 1787 and three years later was temporarily in Hampton Falls with his family. All this family is untraced. We believe that some of them went to Vermont; that one son was Samuel Dow, a Quaker, who set up a trip hammer in 1796 in Danby, Vt., but who died in 1805, leaving two daughters, one of whom married Charles Billings, Quaker, of Billings Bridge, Ontario.

Alton F Dow adaabceab. His wife Nellie J d Winthrop, Mass, ae 63, Oct 2, 1921.

Frederick Dow adaabcead is surely he of Lowell m Rosie Smith, who m 2nd Lowell in 1908. Children of Frederick:

    a Edith M m Oct 28, 1908, Roy Varnum, son of George W and Jennie (Bartlett)
    b Stella M b Sept 24, 1895; d Lowell Oct 26, 1901

DeWitt Clinton Dow adaabcjfb. Possibly the rec now under adabiggda belong to him. If so, the latter is untraced.

Ira Dow adaabdd b Feb 16, 1803. A family rec, much open to doubt, gives him as the untraced Ira Dow ahbgdd. His family is correctly given sub adaabdd.

The more one has delved into the involved and disconnected records of the two Dow families who for many generations remained closely associated in Epping, then in Gilmanton, finally in Walden, Vt, the more do obscure points seem clarified and proved, the more also get into the tangle. There is a record, not proven by the Author, that James Gilman Dow ahbaai had a son Ira b about 1788. Some Ira (Author thinks this one) d N H 1830. There is also a rec, proof not seen by Author, that James Gilman Dow ahbaai had a 6th child,—Samuel b 1805. This Samuel fits perfectly him who m Walden May 4, 1831, Sophronia Gould. If so, it was ahbaai who was deacon of Walden church in 1805. If our train of calculation be correct, it is likely that Alice Dow and Dolly Dow, now considered sub adaabd, m Oct 11, 1827, James Smith and Levi Levermore, respectively, are daughters of James G ahbaai.

Winslow Dow adaabfe. It is absolutely proven that he was brother of Harrison Dow and Darius Jerome Dow, all being sons of Jonathan b 1776 and Joanna (Gilman). Jonathan is placed in this Book wholly for convenience as adaabf, which cannot possibly be true. A letter from Winslow's son written in 1903 has just come to light. This states positively that Winslow Hermon Dow b Fairfax, Vt, Aug 17, 1808, d Fairfax 1890, son of John Dow of Gilmanton. This fits perfectly the John or Jonathan b Epping 1776, son of Capt Noah Dow ahbac. The owner of the name seemed to vacillate in preference between John and Jonathan. and we can no longer doubt that the lines of ahbac, ahbgd, adaab were represented in the exodus from Gilmanton to Walden before 1800.

Winslow Dow m 1835 Adeline L Chamberlain b 1810, d 1895, dau of Ebenezer of Walden. There were 7 children, of whom the 1850 census gives 5 more or less carelessly:

a George W b Fairfax 1838
b —— —— dau (presumably Betsey) m W H Lamberton
c William E b about 1842 (family rec)
d Lydia b about 1844. This leaves Polly, Eveline and Edward, mentioned in census but not in family rec

Eva C Dow adaabfeb, properly ahbacbeg, b Barnet 1850, m Mch 11, 1866, Wiman H Lamberton, ae 23, farmer of Marshfield.

A disconnected rec which belongs in this group:

Sophia B Dow b Walden or Groton, of Hardwick m Mch 8, 1842, Samuel G Cheever of Hardwick. Two children, by own rec:

a William H m Nashua, N H, 1869
b Eunice R m Nashua 1872 Thadeus B Mason

Sarah Dow adabbc m Josiah Crockett. Their dau Sarah m William Webb. Mrs. Merton T Goodrich of Monson, Me, descends from these three lines.

Dinah Dow adabbd m Jonathan Eaton. Their dau Hannah m Samuel Webb and had a son William.

Mary Dow adabbge m Joseph Colby Stinson b 1782, d 1849. Their son Edmund m Bethia Webb, dau of William.

Nelson Haskell Dow adabbgaga reappears as Nelson A Dow of Waite, Me; m Mary Davis b Wellington, Me; 2nd Josephine M Williams. Became mill operative of Harmony. State rec indicate 9 children:

a Edward H (also as Edgar) b about 1873
b Myrtle L b May 9, 1875; d Dexter Feb 16, 1901
h —— —— son b Waite Feb 27, 1892

Edward H Dow adabbgagaa, laborer and guide of Princeton, Me, m Ada Crosby. Children:

a Vinal Curtis b July 30, 1903   b Doris E b Aug 29, 1904
c and d twins b May 30, 1909   e Margarite Williams b Sept 6, 1915
f and g Winnifred and Winona b Aug 19, 1917

Lydia Dow adabe. Some Lydia of Salisbury d May 8, 1731, perhaps she. She would be rather young to marry Michael Brooks in 1739.

Charles F Dow adabibca d Ashland Jan 24, 1908. His son Daniel Buswell Dow had 4th child:

a Gladys Belle b Nov 28, 1899

Jonathan Dow adabih. Almost certain it was he who m June 3, 1803, Mary Dicy, both of Gilmanton. Of their children:

b Melinda b Dec 15, 1808; d Jan 24, 1893; m Sept 1831 David Huckins abbegfab; had a family
c Jonathan; unt
d Dorothy m Nov 26, 1836, Jonathan Dolloff Huckins abbegfac; d without children

Lafayette Dow adaceafe had a son Willard b about 1846. His two dau were living in Chittenden 1910.

Wallace E Dow adaceagcc d Pittsford, Vt, Sept 6, 1927, survived by widow, sisters Mrs Woods of Brandon, Mrs Hunter of Holden; brothers William S and Olin H of Holden, Jay A of Rutland. Every one of his children survives and there are 13 grandchildren. His Children,—Mrs Raymond Brunkee, St Joseph, Mich; Mrs N L Bushey, St Joseph; Mrs O L Hall, Chicago; Mrs Ernest Lackard, Pittsford; Miss Marguerite Dow, Pittsford; Albert J Dow, Pittsford, Richardson W Dow, Boston; Frederick E Dow, Rutland.

Isaac Dow adacef had also:

c Clementine m Joseph Blazo; had 4 sons, 2 dau
d Adaline b May 23, 1809
e Elvira b Apr 10, 1811; d Apr 22, 1879
f Isaac b May 23, 1813; d Nov 5, 1881; m Sept 12, 1837, Maryetta Dodge of Brandon; no children
g Horace b Feb 22, 1815; d July 3, 1882
h Azubah b July 15, 1817; d July 28, 1884; m Charles Sullings; 2 dau
i George W b Dec 15, 1826; d Jan 13, 1856; m Lucy Sumner; a dau Lillie A b Aug 19, 1853

Horace Dow adacefg m Elizabeth Sullings. Children:

a Lorain Elizabeth b Nov 22, 1840; m Wakeman J Mead; 1 son, 2 dau
b Charles Horace b Sept 24, 1847; d June 12, 1852
c Wilbur Horace b May 16, 1853

Wilbur H Dow adacefgc m Dec 22, 1881, Emma Alice Hall b Apr. 18, 1859. Children:

a Horace Nelson b Dec 3, 1884   b Paul Audrey b May 1, 1886
c Ruth Viola b Jan 26, 1888   d Hazel Lillian b Mch 9, 1893
e Chester Sullings b Sept 30, 1896

Horace N Dow adacefgca m Oct 10, 1906, Bessie E Hunt b Oct 31, 1884. Child:

a   Juanita b Mch 25, 1908

Martha Dow adacfb m Feb 26, 1782, Amos Mills d Oct 25, 1795; moved 1834 from Hampstead to Dunbarton. Child:

a   Ephraim b Jan 8, 1790

Sarah Dow adacfc m Mch 30, 1790, Samuel Ezekiel Merritt of Warren, Mass.

Isaiah Dow adacfd of Warren, Mass, had also:

x   Foster b Sept 16, 1795; unt

Sarah C Dow adadabbe m Samuel B Cilley b Mch 20, 1816, d May 26, 1874, son of Abraham B and Rebecca (Dow) Cilley adkecf.

Ruth Ellen Dow adadabcfaa m Sept 26, 1925, Erskine H Childers, son of Erskine and Mary Alden (Osgood). Erskine Childers, Irish patriot, executed Dublin Nov. 24, 1922.

Winthrop G Dow adadabcfab m June 12, 1926, Ann Merrill, dau of William B of Newton Center, Mass.

Louisa Dow adadabgb m L M Blake.

Smith Dow adadhaab. His wid m 2nd B F Wentworth. His son b Aug 31, 1856, is untraced. His dau Sarah A m Mch 21, 1875, Moses Elon Clark.

Warren Hazen Dow adadhcec b Woburn Dec 19, 1851; not now living; m Annie J Crawford. Our informant recalls his two older sisters but gave no data of them. Our informant mentions two children, but coincidence of name and place indicates three:

a   Oscar Wentworth b 1874 (parents named in m rec)
b   Warren A b 1875; m Woburn Sept 21, 1899, Annie (Crawford) McElroy, ae
    18. M rec does not give parents of either party
c   Bertha Emmaline b 1877; m Feb 7, 1895, William A Harvey; live Cambridge,
    Mass

Oscar W Dow adadhceca of Cambridge m Oct 22, 1908, Guenn Howard Blair, ae 25, dau of James and Jessie N (Pagan). In 1925 he a manager in Belmont, Mass. Children:

a   Arnold Forbes b Aug 21, 1913   b   Gordon Blair b Apr 1915

Forest A Dow adadiabf used this name when he married Myra P Foster b Ipswich and consequently eluded the genealogist. His wid living 1925 in Attleboro, Mass. Four children:

a   Martha Pearl, m and has children   b   Ruth, m a clergyman
c   Florence Lida b Saugus, Mass, Sept 4, 1901
d   Almys Forest b Saugus Oct 18, 1905. He was saved from the genealogist by the
    clerk's entry as Almira Foster

Arthur B Dow adaigaaae and Edith M Campbell had:

a   Bernice May b Pembroke Oct 7, 1916

Betsey Dow adgcacd m Oct 1808 John Hurd of Dunbarton.
Annie Stearns Butterfield Dow adgfbfcc d Boston Dec 28, 1916;
bur Tamworth.   Her dau Sarah F Dow m Lewis A Crossett.

Beniah Dow adgfcdg had children:

e   Elvira A b Jan 16, 1843   f   Ada J b May 13, 1854

John Dow adgcadaa.   To him a son twin with Horace M:

b   Wallace b May 2, 1832

Wallace Dow adgcadaab, in 1850 in census as laborer of Newbury;
in 1857 stage driver of Hopkinton; m Nov 27, 1857, Emily Ann Sawyer b
Henniker.   He d injury from lifting Sept 8, 1870.   Children:

a   Ada E b Henniker Nov 26, 1860; m July 30, 1879, Frank J. White of Hop-
      kinton; 2nd Nov 14, 1903, George W Sargent of Henniker; lives Henniker
b   William H b Henniker Jan 27, 1867; d in childhood
c   Myron W b Henniker Feb 26, 1868

Myron W Dow adgcadaabc, farmer of Hopkinton, moved to Henniker; d Henniker 1925; m Hopkinton Jan 5, 1898, Nettie M Shattuck,
wid, dau of Jonathan and Elizabeth (Howe) Vitty of Weare.

Abraham Dow adgfbfb.   Letters received Nov 1927 from his
grandson, James C Dow, make matters clear.   He d 1877 at the home of
his son Henry in Saco.   His 1st wife was Sarah ——; m 2nd Jan 19, 1817,
Elinear (McDonald) Wood b McDonald Isles, Scotland, both of Saco.
Children, dates authoritative for a and c:

a   Tristram Storey b 1824   b   Charles W b 1826
c   Albert b Sept 11, 1828   d   Martha b 1830
e   James S b 1832   f   Lizzie b 1835   g   Henry b 1838
h   Ellen b 1843; m Capt —— Langley; a son Nelson

Tristram S Dow adgfbfba d Feb 16, 1885; m No Providence, R I,
1865 Sarah Anna Caswell b 1836, d June 9, 1909, dau of James and Mehitable.   He was a pioneer 1850 to Calif, crossing the plains, but returned
via the Isthmus some years later.   A high grade of mechanical skill
characterizes this whole line.   Child:

a   James Caswell b Warwick, R I, Feb 12, 1866

James C Dow adgfbfbaa, grad High School and Commercial Col-
lege, was a newspaper man until he became an etcher on steel; m 1890,
Emma Victoria Andrews b Coventry, Conn, 1861; m 2nd June 19, 1914,
Anna (Lanson) Tillson of Wrentham b Boston, 1882, dau of Charles and
Christine Lanson.   Children:

a   Mehitable S b Sept 25, 1892; m Harold L Arnold of Providence; dau Madolin
      Tristram b Jan 31, 1926
b   Tristram M b Warwick Apr 18, 1895; d Providence Jan 27, 1924; joined U S
      Naval forces Boston Oct 19, 1917; hon disch Sept 30, 1921; 32nd degree
      mason, St John's Commandery

Charles W Dow adgfbfbb, ship carpenter of Biddeford, d Stoneham Mass; m 1855 Mary E Goodale b Wells, Me, Dec 1839, d Kennebunk Jan 31, 1913, dau of George H and Louisa (Hatch). Dau:

    a   Ellen L b June 15, 1857; d Melrose Sept 9, 1901, unm; a stenographer in Boston

Albert Dow adgfbfbc carding overseer of Biddeford killed Oct 2, 1897, while walking on railroad track; m 1855 Mary A Tripp b Westport, Mass, 1831, d Saco Sept 24, 1911, dau of Warren and Celia (Bliss). Children:

    a   Lydia b abt 1856
    b   John b abt 1859; at one time postal clerk of Fall River, Mass
    c   Ulysses Grant b Saco abt 1826

Ulysses G Dow adgfbfbcc moulder of Saco m Jan 20, 1894, Mattie A Langley b 1870, dau of James H and Mary A (Mitchell). Children:

    a   Raymond b Sept 27, 1894   b   Ned Emerson b Nov 9, 1895

Martha Dow adgfbfbd m James Mitchell. Only son,—Fred.

James S Dow adgfbfbe d Valley Falls, R I; m Lucy ——. No children, but adopted 2 dau:

    a   Izzie; not now living   b   Emily

Jeremiah Dow adgfga is properly abccdgb (q v). That he was akin to Moses Dow, who figures in this book as adgfg is very improbable. Moses Dow, as the 1790 census shows, was then in New Durham with wife and no children. Presumably he was newly married and inferentially born 1760-68. If he had posterity we do not know. His identity is wholly a guess.

Lydia M Dow adgfcig m Horace Jefferson Merrill of Irasburg b Nov 5, 1812, d Mch 26, 1901, son of Abner and Mary (Carpenter). Lydia Maria Dow, not possibly identical, b Wheelock, m Thomas Cox; a dau Mary E m 1861 Horace M Pattee of Sanbornton.

Lucy Dow adgffb and John Peaslee had 1stborn:

    a   Hannah E b Oct 7, 1799; m Oliver Barnard (Ipswich rec)

Daniel Dow adggbcb. A Salisbury rec seems to place him: William Dow Jr ae 22, teamster of Newburyport, son of Daniel and Elizabeth of Seabrook, m Nov 5, 1844, Mary Abigail Dow of Salisbury.

Nicholas Depuis adggdcca, Huguenot of Artois, was among the many who fled into Holland to escape a prolonged persecution by the French catholics. These Huguenot refugees, altho welcomed by the Dutch and given Civic and other rights, found it difficult to compete in material prosperity with the inherited strength of their new neighbors and many of them welcomed the opportunity to emigrate to New Amsterdam. Nicholas had married Catherine (Reynard) De Vos and three children had come to them, when, in Oct 1662, they sailed in the Pemberton Church to New Amsterdam. The French spelling of their name quickly became Hollandized; it was often spelled Dupuy but a century later had become more or less firmly Depuy (pronounced as pew, of a church).

Moses Depuy, 2nd son of Nicholas, b presumably about 1655, m about 1680 Maria Wyncoop of Albany, dau of Cornelius, probably already being a resident of the Kingston district.   Of their large family:

Jacobus Depuy eleventh child, b Kingston 1703, m 1725 Sarah Schoonmaker, dau of Joachem of Kingston.   Probably he was the founder of the large number of Depuys of Rochester township, somewhat inland from Kingston, a fine farming country.   They had many children:

Benjamin Depuy of Rochester was about the tenth child, b 1744 or later.   He m about 1775 Jane Miller.

Henry Miller Depuy was twin with Sara b Jan 31, 1783.   His marriage to Catherine Brink occurred not later than 1808 and was probably at Shawangunk Church, that being the second oldest in the Kingston district.   They made their home in Ulsterville, being the only members of the family thereabouts.   Eltsje was their third child, the older being:

a   Henry Brink b Feb 11, 1809   b   Sarah Jane b Mch 20, 1811

A little delving into the archives carries the line of Catherine Brink back.   Lambert Brink and wife were immigrants to New York about the same time as Nicholas Depuis.   A son was born to them on the voyage,—Cornelis Lambertson Brink.   Cornelis m 1685 Marietie Egbertson of New York, a strange occurrence of a purely Anglo-Saxon name.   The couple were early settlers in Ulster Co and their child Lammert Cornelison Brink was bap Kingston 1689.   He m 1723 (perhaps earlier) Rachel de Mon bap Kingston June 5, 1688.   Cornelis Lambertson Brink bap Kingston 1724 m 1748 Elsie van Brentschooten bap July 11, 1725. Solomon Brink bap Kingston 1755 m about 1781 Sarah Van Keuren. The Van Keuren family settled near the river across from Poughkeepsie, and Sarah's baptism probably was not at Kingston.   Catherine Brink bap Shawangunk Church 1788, m Henry Miller DePuy.

Walron du Mon m Grietjen Hendrickson and their son Walron bap Mch 13, 1667, m 1688 Catharyn ter Bos of New York.   Rachel de (sic) Mon m Lammert Cornelison Brink.

Solomon Van Brentschooten m 1715 Elsjen Schoonmaker; their dau Elsje bap Kingston July 11, 1725; m Cornelis Lambertson Brink. Elsjen Schoonmaker bap Apr 14, 1689; m Solomon Van Brentschooten. She was the daughter of Hendrik Hendrikson Schoonmaker, son of Hendrik of Albany, and Geerthrug de Witt.   Geerthrug de Witt m 1688; bap Kingston Oct 15, 1668, dau of Tierck Claessen de Wit and Barber Anderieson, both of New York.

George H Dow adggefgx and Ida had:

x   Eda E b Strafford Mch 1, 1872; m (Eda M) Orford, N H, June 1, 1889, William
     N S Claflin. She now of Claremont, N H. Children, Strafford rec: Esther
     Irene b July 31, 1891, and Ida Mae b May 28, 1895

Miriam Dow adgxb m (int pub Seabrook 17: 11 mo: 1757) Jonathan Gove d 1784. If this were a town rec, it would appear as Nov 17,
1757. Apparently it was a Friends' rec. Gove Gen gives Jonathan
Gove m Miriam Norton with inexact date 1751 and gives the children,
all with inexact dates. In no Seabrook rec can we find a Miriam Norton,
and we do not find any Norton among the Friends. We believe the Gove
Gen wholly in error and all of its dates about 6 years too early. The
marriages of two children are outside the Friends:

a   Jacob m —— Fogg   b   John   c   Ruth m Joseph Jones
d   Mehitable m Isaiah Green
e   Hannah m Benjamin Clark. Their son Edward Gove Clark akexa m Mehitable
     Philbrick Gove
f   Jonathan   g   Elihu, half witted   h   Miriam, d unm

The Gove family was always disposed toward giving children first
or middle names indicating maternal ancestry. Here the name Elihu
presumes the correctness of our identification. Isaiah Green reappears
as adahdb of Weare, Quaker.

Joseph Dow adgxca. Herbert B Dow identifies him with our
Joseph Dow adgcad, who m Sarah Berry and d Pittsfield before 1805.
This seems partly correct and it surely accounts for the two Josephs of
Pittsfield or Chichester. However, Sarah dau of Joseph, who m William
McDaniel, is proven correct as we have it. Herbert B Dow identifies
Jonathan Dow who m Dec 14, 1775, Annie Worth, as adgxcb. This is
wholly conjecture. A family legend gives to Joseph Dow adgcad a
cousin Jonathan, not a brother Jonathan. At least six different Dows of
the sixth generation located in or near Pittsfield and to identify them
all has so far been impossible.

Francis Byron Dow adgxfaaf. He is properly the Frank B Dow
adaaaccaa, but remains unt.

William Dow adgxfagba. He seems to be the William, son of
Edwin, d Seabrook Nov 6, 1864, ae 3 mos.

George A Dow adgxfahb. Little doubt of correct identification.
He m Oct 18, 1866, Eleanor Frances Eaton b Feb 12, 1844, dau of James
and Hannah (Greeley). Children:

a   Louisa P b July 9, 1868; d Nov 12, 1884   b   Lizzie M b Aug 7,1871
c   Nellie M b Jan 18, 1878
d   Grace Gardner b Jan 14, 1881; m May 10, 1906, Frederick Walter Libbey (his
     2nd) b Gray, Me, son of Charles E and Elizabeth (Crocker)
e   George E b Aug 7, 1887

George E Dow adgxfahbe presumably he who m Annie M Clancy and had:

a   Ellen Gardner b Salisbury Aug 4, 1910

Albert F Dow adhafagb.   Mary E wife of Albert F Dow d Fall River Apr 8, 1920.   Only child:

a   Walter Everett b Lawrence Nov 30, 1871

Walter E Dow adhafagba m Nov 30, 1893, Mary T Reed b May 4, 1870, dau of Benjamin T and Mary E (Clark).   A child:

a   Carleton William b Fall River June 8, 1894; m Miriam B —— b Dec 6, 1898; child,—Mary Louise b June 27, 1923

George Alvin Dow adhafcabd.   His 1stborn and fifth child:

a   Hazel Marie b Jan 1891   e   Guy Alvin b Jan 5, 1898

Annette Dow adhcbbdb d Apr 15, 1884; m Thomas M Guy.

Mary Dow adhcbbdd was living 1924 in Los Angeles; b July 6, 1846; m 1866 Gordon B West.   Children:

a   Mary b 1867   b   Guy B b Jan 1869   c   Lulu T b Aug 27, 1871

Marie C Dow adhcbbgga m Oct 10, 1908, Stacie Robert Heath b July 22, 1883, son of George Clinton and Anna Fernald (Stacie).   A child:

a   Lois Maradine b Sept 6, 1909

Nadine Dow adhcbbggb m Aug 10, 1907, Jacob Ernest Davies b Oct 3, 1874, son of Jacob Poure and Margaret Hanna (Hoar).

Rogers Dow adhcbbjaa m June 1, 1918, Clara Munroe Veit.

Frederick A Dow adhcbbjab has children:

c   Samuel Lester b Nov 26, 1894   d   Kenneth Carman b Oct 10, 1900

Jennie A Dow adhcbbje.   This is mistaken identity, perhaps one of the Seabrook Dows.

Jedediah Dow adhcc.   His younger children:

d   Dorcas Neal b Nov 8, 1770   e   Abraham b Dec 31, 1774
f   Jedediah b Apr 26, 1777   g   Jonathan b Oct 31, 1782

Meshech Weare Dow adkdbf gets no mention in any family account, except the facts of his birth and death.   There is a strong presumption that he married.   There is a record, so far inexplicable: Weare Dow of Boston m Aug 3, 1801, Sally Washburn Keith.   Weare Dow adkdbc, if married at all, continued to pass as a bachelor in Hampton Falls.   The benedict could not have been adkdbf, unless his birth date is very wrong in rec.   However, there was a Meshech Weare Dow b 1810.

Meshech Weare Dow adkdbfa m, ae 25, Nov 22, 1835, Rachel

Johnson, both of Loudon. No rec of children. He lived a few years at Northfield, maker of linen wheels and shuttles; an odd character known as "Old Shuttle Dow."

Charles H Dow adkddceb b 1870. His son:

a   Charles Howard b West Somerville, Mass, Oct 31, 1897; d Exeter Apr 6, 1898

Newell Dow adkddfa had four children by 2nd wife:

b   Sarah A   c   Almira G   d   Mertie M, not now living
e   Servander Crosby

Servander C Dow adkddfae, shoemaker of Newburyport, m Delia Kelley b Ire. Children b Newburyport:

a   Ethel Mildred b June 18, 1901   b   Lillia Edith b Apr 17, 1902
c   Newell Francis b Feb 26, 1903   d   Servander N d Aug 15, 1905, ae 1-7-11
e   Sewander C b Jan 31, 1906   f   Lillian Delia b Feb 29, 1908

Furber Dow adkddgb of Kensington m Oct 1856 Margaret Ellen Safford b Mch 31, 1833, dau of William Brazier and Dolly N (Bott). He d 1863. Children:

a   William   b   George; both d young

Charles Chase Dow adkddgc d Kensington Sept 26, 1885; m Nov 16, 1857, Sarah C Locke, b May 1, 1826, d Feb 12, 1911, dau of Daniel and Elizabeth C. Two children besides those already mentioned:

a   Frederick Howard b 1858   b   Henry S b 1861

Frederick H Dow adkddgca, expressman of Kensington, m Sept 13, 1879, Clara Isabella Austin b 1861, dau of James and Louisa. Children:

a   Sarah L b Kensington Aug 31, 1882   b   Ethel A b Salem, Mass, 1884

Sadie Louise Dow adkddgcaa m Aug 26, 1905, Chester Garfield Perley b Nov 13, 1881, son of David T and Elizabeth A (Lavallette).

Ethel A Dow adkddgcab m Oct 26, 1904, Oscar S Hutchinson, div, ae 26, son of Arthur and Rhoda A (Kneeland); live Haverhill.

Henry S Dow adkddgcb m Dec 25, 1885, Addie F Janvrin b 1866. He d Brookline Feb 10, 1918. No rec of children.

William N Dow properly adkddgcc m Hattie B Weare, ae 19, dau of Jonathan E and Irene S (French).

Charles Forrest Dow adkddgcca m 1st Sept 27, 1903, Lottie M Villas, ae 16, dau of William and Hattie (Phillips).

Nellie Dow adkddgcce m Henry Dickinson.

Joseph Napoleon Bonaparte Dow adkfbbcd. Out of the tangle of imperfect Salisbury and Seabrook records there comes just before the forms of this supplement are closed a little clearing. Called by his birth

record Napoleon Bonaparte, he married as Joseph N, and his children
have been credited to his uncle Joseph Warren Dow adkfbbj, who is
untraced and possibly did not exist. Joseph N B Dow m 1859 Mary E
Beckman and moved from Salisbury into Seabrook. A veteran of the
Civil War, his wife d 1872 and he m 2nd —— ——. His children:

a Henry H b 1860; appears in Book as adkfbbja
b Joseph Allen b 1861; appears as adkfbbjb
c Mary E d Mch 18, 1868; as adkfbbjc
d Frank P b 1869; appears as adkfbbcda
e John W b 1872; appears as adkfbbjd
f Charles S b Oct 25, 1872; appears as adkfbbje
g Samuel J Tilden b 1876

Samuel T Dow adkfbbcdg has been for over twenty years a shoemaker of Newburyport; a Methodist; m Lillie H Brown, both of Seabrook. Children, all b Newburyport:

a Katherine Stanley b Feb 17, 1908   b Edna May b July 6, 1909
c Samuel b 1910; not living   d Alfred Nason b 1912
e Rollin Topan b 1915   f Lillian G b 1917   g Ethel R b 1919
h Howard F b 1922   i Marion b 1925

Cyrus Dow adkfbda m about 1842 Caroline Long. She divorced
him; he moved away. The son Cyrus P was only child and was cared
for by a loyal friend of the family.

Elizabeth Dow aeeaa b about 1751; m Reuben Gore Dearborn of
No Hampton.

Lucinda E Dow aeeacaae m Nov 25, 1873, Artemus Bradford
Edmands (Draper Gen). Children:

a Frank b June 29, 1874   b George b Feb 19, 1876
c Arthur Bradford b May 18, 1878   d Fanny b Feb 3, 1887

George A Dow aeeacac d No Hampton 1855; m 1852 Julia M Hobbs
b Nov 3, 1835, dau of Morris and Nancy (Perkins). She m 2nd June 29,
1856, Benjamin Perkins of Seabrook.

Benjamin Dow ahba. If he died at 65, the date should be 1777.
The Plumer ms. is blurred badly here. There is an undated rec of
Benjamin Dow, a cordwainer of Durham, N. H. The identity is extremely
unlikely. A cordwainer has little chance to accumulate money and the
real estate deeds prove that Benjamin Dow ahba was a wealthy man on
his arrival in Epping 1748. There is, however, a record, the date un-
certainly given as 1734, of Benjamin Dow of Rowley m Hannah Follett.
This last name is certainly correct.

Benjamin Dow ahbaaab. Place and name of child indicate that
there was either a second child or a niece:

Emma J Dow ahbaaabb b Jan 8, 1832, of Joliet, Ill, m Lee, N H,
Aug 14, 1873, Albert Luther Comings, son of Albert Gallatin. Children:

a Albert b May 21, 1874   b Mary Elizabeth b Lee Nov 16, 1875
c Carrie Lydia b Sept 17, 1877   d Ben Dow b Jan 27, 1879

e Nellie Maud b Apr 14, 1884. Dates from Comings Gen. Mother was, then, 52 at this time. If birth date in error, she would still be a member of this line, but perhaps a grand niece.

The 1790 census of Epping, N H, shows a Josiah Dow with wife and young son, of whom no trace has yet been found. The identity of Josiah is uncertain. When the missing records of Epping 2nd church from 1772 onward are inspected, it is possible but not at all certain that his children will appear. It is certain, however, that the Dow family of Lee, N H, came from Epping. It is equally certain that the Dows of Lee bore names which follow closely those of the ahba family. Two sons of Daniel Dow ahbab moved to Lee, but both married too late to be parents of the disconnected Dow of Lee. Nevertheless, the kinship is reasonably certain. For indexing convenience we call Josiah Dow ahbax, altho he was just about the same age as Josiah Dow ahbae, and he is almost certainly identical. The Josiah Dow of Canterbury ahbae in this book was of Quaker ancestry.

Judith Dow ahbaaad m Joseph H. Hilton, had a dau:

a Lucretia b July 15, 1809

Sarah Dow ahbaaae. Her m to —— Creighton of Lee may be error. Sarah Dow of Exeter m James Brackett b Sept 19, 1789, d Aug 11, 1882.

Daniel Dow ahbab. Some Daniel Dow m about 1762 Katherine —— of Newbery b 1742. To them:

x Molly b May 24, 1763; m (int pub Feb 21, 1789) Joseph Todd

Lyford Dow ahbaba. One of his missing dau by 1st wife:

b Charlotte b 1787; untraced

Julia P Dow ahbabale and Adelbert J Godding had also:

c Ralph d in infancy   d Dora M b Nov 8, 1883
e Arthur C b July 17, 1885   f Roy H b Sept 8, 1887

Josiah Dow ahbax may have married 1788 or a little earlier. Constructively, we shall allot to him three children:

a Josiah b N H 1789; lived and d in Lee
b Benjamin. He is certainly ahbaaab, who appears in census as born 1805 (almost obvious error) with wife Susan b N H 1798. Lee rec gives Benjamin Dow of Epping m Lee Aug 27, 1818, Sukey Lawrence of Lee. No further rec in Lee
c Lydia of Lee m Lee 1813 Spencer Wentworth; no further rec

Josiah Dow ahbaxa was evidently a poor man, for in 1850 his farm was assessed at only $100. His wife, according to census, was Eliza Grant b N H 1796. We recall that Daniel Dow ahbab m 2nd a Grant of Exeter. Family rec gives Elizabeth Grant, who d in Dover. Another rec calls her Louisa Grant b Meredith. Their children are proven by family rec, but the order is apparently arbitrary:

a Daniel   b David   c John N   d Orren (Orin, family rec)
e Stephen   f Emily Ann   g Jane   h Susan   i Abbie

Daniel Dow ahbaxaa, unknown except that family rec says he had a son Frank moved many years ago to Calif.

David Dow ahbaxab appears in the Book as adbabia, that position being guessed as he married in Berwick, Me, adbabi being the only known Dow of that time and place.   He was a stone mason and after marriage moved to Mass, for many years foreman or superintendent of mill construction, mostly in Lawrence.   He m Berwick (int pub Aug 1, 1840) Susan S Walker, dau of Edward.   She of Berwick, but b Waterville, held a certificate granted by act of Congress as a real daughter of the Revolution.   She d Feb 28, 1902, ae 81 by family rec.   Census gave her b 1819.   A Saugus rec names their children correctly and dates them, but credits them to David Mason Dow and Martha (Grover).   Andover 1850 census finds them with 3 children, with realty assessed $810, and with them brother John b N H 1824 and sister Susan b N H 1830.   David and Susan had two more sons than here given, both dying in infancy:

 a John O b July 12, 1841; d Apr 27, 1845
 b Emma Anne b N´H May 21, 1843
 c Mary Frances b Apr 12, 1845; d Sept 12, 1846
 d Charles Edwin b Feb 8, 1847
 e Nellie Frances b July 4, 1862

Emma A Dow ahbaxabb b Lee d Oct 30, 1882; m July 4, 1864, George Caleb Prince.   Children:

 a George Leonard b Sept 16, 1865; d Feb 10, 1866
 b Arthur Dow b July 5, 1867; well known in masonic circles; his firm is G C
  Prince & Son, stationers, Lowell, Mass; m June 18, 1890, Mabel Winslow, d
  1892; 2nd Waterville Oct 17, 1894, Bertha Inez Bass; no children
 c Mabel Irvette b May 3, d Oct 1, 1870

Charles E Dow ahbaxabd d 1904; m Susan Frances Kennard, a 1st cousin, b Lee 1850, living in 1928.   To them an only son:

 a Walter Edwin b Apr 15, 1875; m June 15, 1899, Marie Elmire Lemieux; live
  Lawrence; no children

Nellie Frances Dow ahbaxabe d 1891; m Dr Edward Butler of El Paso, Tex, and Canon City, Colo.   Two sons, Edward and Harry, d young.

John N Dow ahbaxac stone mason d Epping Apr 13, 1895.   Census 1850 found him in Andover, with wife and children in Lee.   Wife Susan b N H 1820; d wid Lee June 10, 1909, cause old age.   More children born after 1850:

 a Albert b 1843; moved with his sister to Brockton, Mass; his family there a
  few years ago
 b Elizabeth A b 1846

Orren Dow ahbaxad b Lee Sept 25, 1834, lived many years in Newmarket; farmer and laborer, m Maryanna Smith b Newfields June 25, 1844; d Newmarket Apr 21, 1905, dau of George and —— (Marshbank) b Scotland.   Grieving at wife's death, he took to drink and d delirium tremens July 19, 1906.   Had previously lost his 2 sons and a dau:

a George M, shoemaker, d Manchester Feb 26, 1895, ae 24-5-8, unm
b Josiah L d Newmarket May 6, 1885, ae 2

Stephen G Dow ahbaxae stone mason lived Bridgeton, Me;   m Emma L Johnson.   Perhaps more than one child:

a Roy J b Boston 1859; hotel employe of Bridgeton, m Aug 9, 1901, Daisy Benson, ae 21, waitress, of Littleton, dau of Alfred and Anna J (Thompson)

Emily Ann Dow ahbaxaf must be the Emeline Dow d Lee 1877 (no other data).

Abbie Dow ahbaxai.   Rec gives Mary A Dow, 4th child of Josiah and Louisa (Grant), m Dudley Rowe of Epping and had a dau m 1869. There is a garble here.   Mary A (Dow) —— of Lee m 2nd 1869 Francis C Bartlett.

Albert G Dow ahbghg, tanner and harness maker, moved 1830 to Attica, N Y; thence 1842 to Chatham, Ohio, and to McKeen, Ill, in 1866.   Altho of quite mature years and with a large family, he enlisted in 129th Ohio; disch 1864 but immediately re-enlisted.   July 3, 1864, while on sentry duty he was captured and was confined in Lynchburg, Danville, Andersonville and Florence prisons.   Exchanged Nov 27, 1864, he reached home more dead than alive from hunger and abuse.

Isaac W Dow ahbghga d May 7, 1876, presumably unm.

Ada Salisbury Dow ahbghgb d Feb 16, 1879; m Feb 24, 1859, John Riley of Chatham b Apr 28, 1831; d Apr 25, 1866.   Children:

a Julia Buckingham b Apr 28, 1860   b Albert John b Mch 5, 1862
c Maggie Hamilton b Oct 20, 1863; m 1871 Mike Motter; 3 children
d Charles M b 1871   e Roy Boyer b Nov 26, 1873
f Myrtle Allace b June 27, 1878

Mary Ann Dow ahbghgc m June 20, 1865; **Maria Hepzibah Dow** ahbghgd m Mch 29, 1859; **John Rogers Dow** ahbghge m Nov 8, 1868. Unfortunately our informant gives no names or further tracing.

Albert Gallatin Dow ahbghgf of McKeen, Ill, m Feb 7, 1868, Caroline Loser b July 2, 1846.   Children:

a Dora Hamilton b Apr 28, 1869   b Maria Maholm b Sept 10, 1870
c Albert Gallatin b Jan 5, 1872; unt
d Benjamin Franklin b Oct 7, 1874; unt

Lydia Metcalf Dow ahbgiic of Denmark, Ia., d Jan 20, 1919; m 1st —— James; 2nd —— Bass; 3rd —— Henderson.   Children by 1st husband:

a Clara Dow b Oct 2, 1869; m June 10, 1885, John McDonald Wilmans; 3 children
b Irma E b Aug 4, 1890, San Francisco
c Frederick S b Seattle July 28, 1893

Frank Wells Dow ahbgiid d Logan, Iowa, Mch 22, 1926; m Aug 22, 1869, Catherine Elsie Copp b Tioga Co, Pa, Feb 11, 1852. Children, elder 3 b Saunders Co, Neb:

a Nellie b July 6, 1872   b Frank b Mch 4, 1874
c Milton H b Oct 19, 1876   d Cecil E b Apr 30, 1882
e Leola G b Aug 27, 1889   f Lisle Warren b May 23, 1896

Nellie Dow ahbgiida m Sept 25, 1890, Gale Mills b Nov 25, 1871, real estate dealer of Lincoln, Neb. Children b Logan:

a Eva b July 4, 1891   b Harry b Dec 3, 1892; d July 12, 1914
c Leona b July 26, 1896   d Leslie b Aug 6, 1898
e Ada b May 6, 1903   f Morrell b Jan 17, 1905
g Donald b June 29, 1910; d Feb 14, 1916

Frank Dow ahbgiidb m Feb 18, 1894, Florence E Servis b Harrison Co, Ia, Feb 18, 1876. Children:

a Valeria b Mch 6, d Aug 12, 1895
b Elzina b June 7, 1898; m —— —— Dec 31, 1917
c Thele b Feb 2, 1899; m —— —— June 26, 1917
d Evelyn b Dec 13, 1900
e Wyman L b Oct 20, 1901; d Sept 30, 1907

Milton H Dow ahbgiidc and **Cecil E Dow** ahbgiidd are married and live Logan, Iowa.

Leola G Dow ahbgiide m Mch 12, 1910, Fred Her an Cook b Laport, Ind, Apr 7, 1891. Children b Logan:

a Esther b Jan 15, 1911   b Nellie b Oct 5, 1912
c Doris b Sept 15, 1915   d Edna b Jan 10, 1918

Wyman Everet Dow ahbgiie moved from Logan to Buffalo Gap, S D; m Feb 2, 1881, Mrs Sarah Isabelle (Cloud) Stigler b Peoria, Ill, Jan 3, 1853, d Logan Dec 23, 1907. Children:

a Arthur Vivian b Jan 10, d Apr 1, 1883
b Sidney Glenn b Dec 7, 1887
c Guy Wigston b Oct 3, 1891   d Kenneth Bryant b Apr 2, 1894
e Ira Benton b Dec 1, 1896; d Jan 20, 1908

Sidney G Dow ahbgiieb of Sioux Falls and Park Rapids, Minn, m Dec 4, 1914, Leda Cleo Gates b Edgarton, Minn, May 25, 1884. Children:

a Frances Irene b Aug 31, 1916   b Ilda Eulalia b Jan 27, 1918
c Wyman Edward b Aug 21, 1923

Guy Wigston Dow ahbgiiec of No Dak m Sept 16, 1914, Amanda Johnson b Clark, S D, Nov 20, 1890. Children:

a Everett Johnson b Nov 15, 1916
b Eunice Isabelle b Aug 26, 1918
c Joyce Cavella b Aug 19, 1921   d Gale Warren b Aug 7, 1923

Mary Eunice Dow ahbgiig of Reeder Mills, Ia, m Jan 5, 1881, Fred L Borden b Lyme, N H, Sept 1, 1859. Children:

a John W b Sept 22, 1882   b Edward A b Apr 4, 1889

Arthur W Dow ahbgiih m Jan 1, 1890, Mary E LaFollette d West Sioux Falls Aug 23, 1910, dau of Joshua Usual and Susannah (Underwood) Children:

a Bessie Alice b Jan 10, 1892; d in infancy
b Harrie Arthur b Feb 25, 1894

Isaac Wilson Dow ahbgik was a coach-maker; moved to Ohio in 1843 and in 1854 to what is now Denmark, Ia. In 1858 he pioneered to Kansas to help make it a free state. The great drought of 1860 drove him back to Iowa. As he was both a Latin and Greek scholar, he was able to open a private school but the remuneration for a full term was only about $100. This sum, however, enabled him to hold on to his Kansas lands. His 2nd wife d Sept 30, 1858; he did not remarry and the care of his children prevented his serving during the War except in defense of Ft Lincoln against the Confederates under Price. Justice of the Peace, Universalist, Free Soiler, teetotaler, he lived and died greatly respected.

Phebe J W Dow ahbgika d Iills, Okla, Mch 2, 1902; m June 6, 1867, William Franklin Griffey b Ia Oct 10, 1844, d Nov 29, 1924, served in 12th Ill until July 1865. Children:

a Clara E b Aug 24, 1869; m John C Hilton
b Charles Franklin b Oct 18, 1871; m Laura M Streeter; 2nd Mrs Mary M Alexander
c Anna Augusta b Sept 6, 1873; m Delafayette Fanning
d James Leroy b Apr 13, 1886; m Maude T Dunsmore; 2nd Malena Della Downey

Howard Wilson Dow ahbgikcb of Pond Creek m Aug 2, 1924, Pearl Crisswell b July 2, 1902, dau of Samuel B and Florence L (Beshare). Child:

a Betty Loraine b Oct 2, 1925

Nancy Waterman Dow ahbgike of Corvallis, Ore, d May 24, 1906; m Mch 14, 1879, George Washington Smith b N Y July 1, 1828, d Corvallis Oct 6, 1916. Children:

a Emma Jane b Dec 22, 1879; m William Campbell
b Frank Wells b Aug 15, 1881; d Mch 20, 1924; m Ocea Seriena Taylor
c George Washington b Feb 4, 1886
d Flora Eunice b June 27, 1888; m Bert Laun Taylor
e Fannie Carria Frances b May 12, 1900; m Alexander Stewart
f Bertha L b Mch 5, 1892; m Henry M Stanley Stewart

Joseph Dow ahbgil moved 1877 to the Black Hills near Deadwood, Dak; at first a miner. Was next a storekeeper and postmaster at Bakersville. He with sons Edward B and Jose K took up homesteads and timber claims and established the Bar W ranch in Custer Co, which proved very successful.

Edward Buchanan Dow ahbgilc m 1st July 5, 1884, ———— ———; 2nd Apr 18, 1898, Estelle M Ferguson. No children.

William Adams Dow ahbgild m Sept 3, 1881, Mary Anna Smith of Littleton, N H; killed in auto and train collision Nov 8, 1915. No children.

Lillian Jane Dow ahbgile m July 15, 1886, Charles Schultz of Joliet, Ill. She d Apr 4, 1899. Her dau Mabel B m Lawrence Grover. They live with several children at Southern Pines, S C.

Frank Scott Dow ahbgilf̦ m May 11, 1887, Mary A Haney, dau of John and Mary Jane (Edwards). Went 1877 to Calif, thence to Dak, a gold hunter. Returned to Vermont farming 1882, back to Spokane 1889. No children.

Dexter Dean Dow ahbgilg m —— Sept 21, 1890. At the time of the San Francisco earthquake and fire of 1905 he disappeared, probably lost in the ruins. No children.

Jose Keach Dow ahbgili m Aug 3, 1887, Minnie Dean, dau of Ephraim of Spearville, Ind, and Frances J (Watson) of Richmond, Va. Going to Dak 1882 he was organizer of the Bar W ranch. He d there Oct 22, 1902.

Walter E Dow ahbgilia b Jan 4, 1889; m July 26, 1912, Carolyn Louise Cowalski of La Cross b Sept 9, 1897. Child:

a Louisa Laverna b Dec 30, 1913

Laverna Frances Dow ahbgilib b July 26, 1894; m May 28, 1919, Henry Lee Erwin b Nov 1, 1892. He served as engineer in France 22 mos. Child d 1920 in infancy.

Nancy Dow ahcbfa m Hiram Ketchum. Davis Gen gives a son:

a Edmund b Mch 1, 1843; m Adelaide R Lathrop

Stephen Dow ahcfg m Abigail ——. In 1810 living in Marion, N Y. One son, 9 dau:

a Augusta; grew up   b Atlas Emma Dolph; m and d in Jackson, Mich
g (order uncertain Alphia Hutchins b Marion 1810

Alphia H Dow ahcfgg practiced medicine in Utica, but moved 1850 to Iowa. It may be noted that almost every Dow who went west at this period joined heartily in the anti-slavery and free-soil movements. Alphia Dow moved in 1866 to Kansas, founding the town of Ottawa. He d 1892; m two sisters named Ross; 1 child by 1st m:

a Lavenda m —— Higgins. Their dau Lennie and Millie now of Elmira, N Y
b (by Fannie Ross, order of birth not stated) Caroline m —— Starr; d Oelwine, Iowa
c —— d in infancy
d Newton d Wellsville, Kan; presumably married
e Elisha Rhoades Wright d La Crosse, Kan, unm
f Alphia Chapin b Marion June 23, 1848; d La Crosse Mch 2, 1912

Alphia C Dow ahcfggf m 1st —— Jones, 1 child; 2nd at Barclay, Kan, Olivia Eliza Smith.   Children:

a   Emma m —— Whiteman; now of La Crosse
b   James Elton, now oil operator of Tulsa, Okla
c   Fannie m —— McDaniel of Great Bend, Kan
d   Morrill Thornton; grad Harvard; now with General Electric Co, Elmira

Clarissa Dow ahchba m Feb 11, 1808, Robert Benedict b July 11, 1776, d Nov 6, 1855.   She d Philadelphia Apr 27, 1868.   Children:

a   Sarah b Feb 23, 1809   b   Harriet b July 10, 1811
c   Nathan Dow b Apr 7, 1815

John Dow ahche m 2nd wid Tempa Leake.   Child by 1st wife:

c   Mary Barnum b 1796; d May 6, 1823

Lucy Dow ahchea m Feb 12, 1812, Greeley Davis of Reading, Pa. Twelve children, of whom:

a   Lott b Dec 19, 1812; m Oct 4, 1837, Susan Sencepaugh; 2nd Julia Woodruff Hudson

Polly Dow ahcheb m —— Dunham.   Children:

a   Andrew Jackson b 1815; d June 25, 1904
b   Amy m —— —— Foote. A son A J Foote of Hornell, N Y, 1908

Nettie Lucinda Dow ahchfecb m Edwin S King.   Children:

a   Beatrice Ella   b   George William   c   Ethel Maud
d   Earl Edwin   e   Helen Margaret

Gertrude Lucetta Dow ahchfecc b Apr 14, 1870; m Sept 27, 1892, George R. Murray of Mo.   Child:

a   Florence Alberta b Oct 7, 1894

Mary Eliza Dow ahchfed m William Norris Woods b Dec 8, 1829. Children:

a   Carrie Eliza b July 26, 1861; d East Otto Mch 20, 1865
b   William Chester b Feb 14, 1862 (?); d Aug 16, 1865
c   Milicent Irene b Nov 9, 1877; of Burnside, Ky

Gertrude Malvina Dow ahchfeg m Emery Nathaniel Tefft.   Only child:

a   Gertrude Irene b June 16, 1870; m and in 1893 lived East Otto with 3 children

Maria Isabelle Dow ahchfeh m Charles Henry Fleckinstine b Dec 8, 1853.   Children:

a   Etoile Esther b Mch 5, 1881   b   Nellie Belle b Mch 9, 1884
c   John Charles b July 16, 1886   d   Daisy Susetta b Jan 18, 1890

Benjamin Dow ahchff lived Pulaski and Palermo, N. Y.   Children:

a   Malvina C b May 24,1837; d Oct 27, 1852
b   Isabelle b Dec 13, 1838   c   (2nd wife) Martha W b July 7, 1866

Isabelle Dow ahchffb m July 4, 1857, William Henry Doane.
Children:

a Viola M   b Benjamin F   c George W   d Susan B
e Florence M

Martha W Dow ahchffc m Sept 26, 1888, Benjamin L Zufeld.
Children:
a Harold Benjamin b June 14, 1891   b Oliver Norman b Feb 3, 1894

Elisha A Dow ahchfid m July 28, 1879, Barbarita McAfee d May
20, 1896. Their family now mostly in New Mexico:

a Louisa M b Apr 26, 1875   b Anna Amy b Apr 19, 1877
c Carolina b May 12, 1878   d Ellen b Feb 15, 1880
e Clara b Aug 12, 1881   f Elizabeth Ioa b Aug 2, 1884
g Daniel M b Oct 30, 1886   h Elisha A b July 31, 1890
i Frank R b Mch 19, 1892   j James M b May 23, 1894
k Mary Barbarita b May 8, 1896

John G Dow ahchfie m Sept. 2, 1882, Severa McAfee b Nov 8,
1866, d Dec 31, 1883; m 2nd Sept 28, 1886, Addie Cora Bennett b Nov
1, 1860. Children:

a Severa McAfee b Dec 15, 1883
b Amy Gertrude b Dec 19, 1888; d June 10, 1889
c Grace Eleanor b July 9, 1890   d Rex

Milton Dow ahchfig b Kansas, lived Chilili, N M; m July 28,
1874, Isabella McAfee b July 4, 1861. Children:

a Margarita b May 4, 1875   b William D b Mch 18, 1877
c John b June 4, d July 31, 1879
d Susanna b Jan 1, 1881; d May 22, 1882
e Mary b Nov 19, 1883; d Mch 17, 1884   f Dora b Aug 23, 1885

g Edith b May 7, 1888   h Bessie b June 11, 1890
i Lillie b Mch 4, 1893   j Lizzie b May 20, 1895

Margaret A Dow ahchfik d Mch 14, 1893; m 1880 Henry Hower.
Children:

a Charles b Mch 15, 1881   b Emma b July 6, 1888
c John H b July 5, 1891

Lucy Dow ahchg and Asa Brown had eleven children:

a Lucy b Oct 25, 1795   b Deborah b Apr 9, 1797
c Mercy b Nov 19, 1798   d Sarah b Jan 3, 1801
e Asa b Feb 14, 1803   f Wheeler b Apr 9, 1805
g Rebecca b May 14, 1807   h Maria b Nov 4, 1809
i Benjamin b Oct 31, 1810   j Martha b Mch 9, 1813
k Emeline Marilla

Benjamin Dow ahchh m 2nd 1824 Lucy Gallup b May 1, 1786, d
Mch 1, 1855. Gallup Gen gives his 2nd child Calista

Orra Dow ahchha d Plainfield Mch 14, 1883; m Nov 10, 1824,
Isaac (?; Gallup Gen gives John) Gallup b Jan 13, 1799, d Feb 1867.
Children:

a Sarah b Mch 2, 1826   b Benjamin Dow b May 22, 1828
c Albert b May 28, 1830   d Isaac b Nov 11, 1835
e Lucy E b Nov 27, 1838   f Martha E b Feb 7, 1843

Elisha Dow ahdaab m Mch 21, 1811, Thankful Davis. Of their 9 children:

   b   Olive Smith b Nov 22, 1813   c   Penelope Davis b Feb 21, 1815

Nathan Dow ahdaag had younger children:

   i   William P b May 30, 1840   j   Sally Ann b Oct 3, 1842

Rebecca Dow ahdaai m Dec 24, 1847, Nehimiah Stevens; 2 sons, 2 dau

Elizabeth Dow ahdac m Jan 3, 1788, Jonathan Gallup; always lived Plainfield. Children:

   a   John b Jan 4, 1789   b   David b Mch 26, 1790; d Jan 7, 1848
   c   Thomas b Mch 12, 1792   d   Simon b Sept 27, 1793; d Apr 13, 1851

Martha Dow ahdfa. There are surely no extant records by which to trace Samuel Dow ahda or his brother Thomas. Census 1790 indicates that, unless Samuel were a widower, he had no daughter,—only two sons. However, in this family somewhere belongs Martha Dow b Plainfield 1770, m Oct 30, 1794, Jeremiah Kinne b May 27, 1764. The Plainfield Dows and Kinneys often intermarried. Martha d Plainfield Apr 16, 1813. He m 2nd Cloe Wilcox.

George E Dow ahfcfcba of Manchester m Georgia A Emery of Waterville, Me, b 1853, d Manchester Nov 16, 1901, dau of Daniel and Abbie.

Ephraim Dow ahgce always lived Sou Coventry; m Dec 1, 1785, Alice Davenport. Children:

   a   Harry b 1786; d June 28, 1834   b   Samuel b 1788
   c   Fanny m —— —— Castner; children,—Rufus and Calvin
   d   Allecia m —— —— Coleman; lived Cooperstown, N Y
   e   Anna   f   Orrin
   g   Charles d June 27, 1813; bap on deathbed

Harry Dow ahgcea d Coventry June 28, 1834; m Sept 24, 1807, Sally Sprague b about 1783, dau of Samuel and Elizabeth (Cook). He was bap Mch 10, 1817, but evidently fell mildly from grace, for he was excommunicated for drunkenness Feb 8, 1828. Children, Coventry rec:

   a   Rufus b Feb 12, 1808; d Apr 27, 1851
   b   William b Sept 20, 1810; m 1835, Abiah Gowdy.
   c   Fannie b Mch 9, 1812, m Jan 5, 1834, Miles C Dexter.
   d   Charles b May 1814
   e   Olive b Sept 17, 1816; m May 8, 1853, Austin D Perkins
   f   Oliver b Apr 1822; d Mch 2, 1832   g   Orrin b Oct 10, 1827; d Oct 1855
   h   Phebe b 1829; d Feb 14, 1833

Rufus Dow ahgceaa m Nov 25, 1831, Betsey Fuller. Children:

   a   Mary E m May 4, 1853, George H Dexter; a dau Nettie
   b   Emma Maria m May 30, 1853, Addison L Metcalf
   c   Lucien B   d   Jane b about 1838; d Dec 9, 1853

Samuel Dow ahgceb m Apr 10, 1816, Eliza H Albro; lived Coventry. Children:

a Eliza bap May 18, 1817   b Nancy bap June 21, 1818
c Eunice bap Aug 21, 1819; d Feb 15, 1878; m 1840 John Albro b 1820, d Dec 19, 1877
d Ephraim bap June 10, 1821

Lavina Dow ahgcf m Uriah Palmer; a dau Diantha b 1780

Hepzibah Dow ahgcg m Oct 12, 1786, Bildad Curtis b Aug 10, 1765, d July 16, 1832, son of Samuel and Joanna (Dimock). Children:

a Samuel b 1787   b Marvin d Sept 14, 1866
c Joanna d Aug 22, 1793
d Augustus b 1792; d May 4, 1801   e Roderick d June 10, 1878
f Lucy d July 20, 1875   g William A d 1862
h John d Oct 19, 1803
i Mary b Dec 25, 1803; d June 4, 1804   j Emily d Mch 21, 1875
k Caroline b June 4, 1808; d Aug 16, 1862   l Julia b 1810

Eunice Dow ahgcha m Feb 9, 1825, Nathaniel Kingsbury b Apr 9, 1796, d July 12, 1843. Children:

a Joseph b May 4, 1826; d Apr 15, 1839
b Henry P b Feb 25, 1827; d June 6, 1853
c Mary F b June 28, 1829; d June 29, 1833
d Dwight L b Oct 30, 1832; d July 15, 1833

Hannah Dow ahgchc m Mch 10, 1825, Joseph Dorman b June 4, 1805, d Apr 7, 1836, son of Joseph and Lucy. Children:

a Lucy Maria b Apr 2, 1827; d May 13, 1862
b Richard Augustus b Aug 7, 1829

Hezekiah R Dow ahgchf m 1st Aug 26, 1835, Harriet Patch b Apr 22, 1817, d Dec 18, 1841. Two children by 1st wife.

Hezekiah F Dow ahgchfe m Mary Northrop b Nov 21, 1852. Children:

a William Bradford b Jan 19, 1874
b Hezekiah Farrington b May 29, 1876; d Aug 2, 1877
c Charles Farrington b 1878

Augustus F Dow ahgchh m Aug 1, 1838, Jane M Tremain b Apr 16, 1820, d Sept 11, 1845, dau of Augustus and Sally (McKinston); m 2nd Mch 26, 1850, Sarah Bender Wheeler b Dec 10, 1826, d May 7, 1894, dau of Zenas and Mary (Low). Children:

a Jane Augustella b Jan 10, 1843
b Augustus Francisco b Sept 4, 1851; d June 8, 1895
c Joy Wheeler b Jan 18, 1860   d Ada Louise b Mch 11, 1862
e Frances Augusta b Jan 29, 1866; d Apr 22, 1867

Jane A Dow ahgchha m Sept 26, 1866, William H Matteson, son of Horatio G of Scituate, R I. Children:

a William Henry b July 7, 1867   b Laura Ethel b Feb 21, 1873
c Alexander Tremain b Apr 8, 1879

Joy Wheeler Dow ahgchhc m June 20, 1904, Elizabeth Goodchild b Oct 5, 1873, dau of John and Mary (Crowley). Second child:

b Joy Wheeler b June 5, 1909

Edward Huntington Dow ahgchj m Nov 25, 1840, Henrietta Cutter Lyman, dau of Martin.   Children b Coventry:

a   Lyman White b Jan 31, 1842   b   Theodore E b Nov 19, 1843
c   Emmet A b Sept 6, 1847; d July 18, 1848
d   Mary Josephine b Jan 26, 1851
e   James B b Sept 26, 1856   f   Grace M b Apr 22, 1861; d Jan 3, 1863

Theodore E Dow ahgchjb m Feb 11, 1869, Nancy Ellen Sewell b Feb 27, 1840.   Children:

a   Frederick Sewell b May 27, 1870   b   Robert Edward b Feb 25, 1872
c   George Bidwell b Nov 24, 1873
d   Josephine Martha b Oct 20, 1875

James Richardson Dow ahgchl was the first president of the Metropolitan Life Insurance Co. of N Y.   His dau Emilie Genevieve m 2nd Edward M Farnsworth; in 1928 living Brookline, Mass.

Solomon Dow ahgci m Tirzah Dow ahgcae, a half niece.   An eighth child:

h   Frederick Houghton b Oct 11, 1817

Simon Dow ahgcia d Jan 2, 1852; m Sept 16, 1819, Almira Johnson b Jan 10, 1802, d Sept 26, 1876.   Children:

a   Charlotte A b Jan 23, 1822   b   Cornelia Johnson b June 13, 1824
c   Johnson S b Sept 20, 1827; d May 19, 1875
d   Sophia E b Oct 4, 1831   e   Amanda L b Mch 30, 1834

Cornelia Jane Dow ahgciab m Dec 10, 1848, Maxon Palmer Lewis of Norwich.   Children:

a   Emma J b Mch 29, 1850
b   Carrie Amanda b Jan 4, 1861; m Henry Leslie Huntington

Amanda L Dow ahgciae m Norwich Nov 30, 1852, Samuel S Hopkins.   Children:

a   Alice L b Mch 2, 1857   b   Jessie D b June 21, 1867
c   Louis A b Dec 24, 1875

Cyrus Dow ahgcib m Charity A Chapman, dau of Parley.   A child, twin:

c   Augusta b Oct 9, 1841

Beverley A Dow ahgcif m Elizabeth A Cole of Norwich b Sept 14, 1823, d May 28, 1863.   They moved to Vt.   Children:

a   Edgar A b May 25, d Sept 7, 1855
b   Annie E b Aug 21, 1858; d Aug 8, 1861
c   Frostine A b Jan 5, d Feb 6, 1863

Nellie Augustine Dow ahgciga.   One son was Benjamin F Moulton b May 13, 1876.

De Witt Canfield Dow ahgcigb had a dau:

b   Nellie Leone b Mch 2, 1876

Frederick Houghton Dow ahgcih m 1840 Henrietta Safford. Children:

a   Henry G b Nov 24, 1842; d July 7, 1871
b   Jeannette b July 4, 1847; m Nov 22, 1866, William C Lyman, son of Emmet
c   Frederick Dwight b Apr 27, 1849; m June 19, 1878, Carrie J Pearl, dau of Charles
d   Winslow L b Jan 14, 1851   e   Ludlow E b Mch 15, 1855

Henry G Dow ahgciha m Mch 31, 1866, Almerida C Lawrence, dau of Charles. Child:

a   Herbert H b Mch 2, 1870

Daniel Clark Dow ahgcj m Mch 28, 1805, Melinda Dimmick. Coventry rec say no further.

Betsey Dow ahgck m June 16, 1803, John Mead b Nov 6, 1776, d June 15, 1857, son of John and Elizabeth. Children:

a   Mary b Oct 28, 1804; d Sept 24, 1837
b   John O b Oct 14, 1806; d Nov 27, 1874
c   Sophronia b Dec 14, 1808; d Feb 14, 1836
d   Matilda b Jan 27, 1811; d May 5, 1777
e   Rufus Francisco b Apr 6, 1813; d July 4, 1868
f   William A b Oct 12, 1815; d Apr 13, 1845
g   Lucy b July 28, 1817; d Dec 26, 1835
h   Julia b Nov 6, 1819; d May 31, 1855
i   Charlotte E b Sept 29, 1821
j   Abby A b Jan 3, 1824; d Jan 3, 1842
k   Louisa J b Mch 8, 1829; d Dec 10, 1833

Kate E Dow ahgdcce m May 22, 1873, Lucas Witbeck.

Francis Dow ahgfdae had children:
b   Frank b Concord 1850   c   Harriet F b Concord 1854

Frank Dow ahgfdaeb d Lowell Aug 14, 1916, survived by sister, widow and two sons; in 1887 was bookkeeper in U S Navy Yard; later member of Bartlett & Dow, Lowell.

Harriet F Dow ahgfdaec m Albert Wilson; 4 children; m 2nd Paul Connell; of Billerica and Malden; spent her second widowhood with her aunt in Manchester, N H,—Mrs Tenney ahgfdah.

Tryphena Dowe ahgfdd and Capt John Tenney had also:
d   Roswell Algernon b June 17, 1844

Lizzie Allan Dow ahggbdaaa m —— —— Wade. Two children:
a   Elizabeth Wentworth   b   John Melmoth

Hannah Dow ahggf m Aug 28, 1800, James Thompson of Lebanon, Conn.

Joseph French Dow bbbebcbb m Nov 8, 1845, Martha Thompson. Maria T in official rec, careless error.

George Lovejoy Dow bbbebcbd had two children older than Josephine B. Names not found.

Simon Dow bbbebcda had a fifth child:

e   John E b 1850

John E Dow bbbebcdae m Caroline E Ropes and lived Danvers, Mass.   Perhaps other children:

a   Waldo Hayward b 1882

Waldo H Dow bbbebcdaea m Aug 21, 1907, Nettie Clark Morgan, dau of William C and Susan A (Clark) of Beverly.   One child:

a   Lydia b 1908

Ladd Dow bbbebch.   According to a letter from his brother written many years ago, Ladd Dow, free soiler, reached Kansas by 1855; his son Asa b about 1830 was the first man killed in the border troubles by pro slavery raiders.   Ladd m a Miss Dustin, according to the same authority, but it is possible that he has confused names with Asa bcdedha (q v). The Author believes himself correct,—that the son of Ladd was Andrew J and that the wife was not a Miss Dustin.

Daniel Dow bbbebci m Cinderella Noble b Apr 6, 1834, d May 26, 1913, dau of Eli and Annie H (Wheeler) of Stoneham.   Two children:

a   Annie m —— —— Green   b   Charles lived Washington, D C

Cyrus B Dow bbbebdac.   His 1stborn probably did not die young; his 3rdborn was:

c   Flora P b Aug 1, 1871; m 1895 Joseph W Johnson, both of Warner

Lorenzo G Dow bbbebfg had also:

b   Annie b Contoocook 1852; dau of Lorenzo and Mary Ann of Hopkinton, m
     Feb 12, 1872, William P Bailey

Frances Currier Dow bbbebgaa m Oscar L Rand.   Children:

a   Oscar S b Bristol Dec 3, 1873   b   Blanche E b Canaan Mch 22, 1876
c   Herman S b Canaan Oct 15, 1879; d Apr 1, 1881

Harold Wright Dow bbbebgacb m 1925 Alice B Hill

David Dow bbbffad.   His wife was Lucretia Alcock.   His sister Sarah m Hiram —— ——

Freeman Dow bbbffaf had 4 children, the 3rd untraced.   Mary was 4th, b May 12, 1858

Harry E Dow bbbffcbae m Aug 30, 1900, Annie B Aldrich; in 1917 living in Bedford, N H

Augusta Mary Dow bbbffcbaf m Charles H Fellows b Jan 2, 1851, son of Richard and Mary (Collins).   Children:

a   Alice Mary b June 19, 1897   b   Flora Cyrene b Jan 22, 1899

William H Dow bbbffcdf had 5 children:

a Ray Gordon b Goffstown Oct 16, 1885   b Mildred b Feb 15, 1889
c —— —— son b Dec 13, 1890   d Ralph Harold b Nov 16, 1894
e Esther Belle b Jan 11, 1899

Eliza Dow bbbffcg m May 6, 1841, Horace Stearns d Aug 9, 1895; lived Goffstown, Manchester, Bedford.   Children:

a Charles H b July 12, 1844   b William H b Dec 26, 1845
c Harriet, twin   d Sarah E b Feb 24, 1848
e Arthur E b Dec 21, 1852   f Harriet J b May 24, 1854

Margery Dow bbbfg m Aug 1, 1805, Josiah Allen; lived Deering

John Dow bbbfhcd.   The m rec of one son and d rec of another show his wife was Mary Hastings.   Same rec gives both sons b Sidney, probably careless error:

b George W b 1834   c Benjamin F b 1835

George W Dow bbbfhcdb, joiner of Sidney, m Portsmouth Mch 29, 1859, Lysena S Linscate, ae 18 b Bangor, dau of William and Caroline

Benjamin F Dow bbbfhcdc enlisted 1861 from Sidney; m Lizzie Wellman b Washington; painter d married Augusta Mch 18, 1905. Second child guessed:

a Owen W b Sidney 1871   b Charles b about 1875

Owen W Dow bbbfhcdca, hostler of Augusta, m Oct 31, 1896, Blanche E Leavitt, ae 19, of Augusta, dau of Israel and Emma (Gowen).   Children b Augusta:

b —— —— dau b July 11, 1898   c Gladys M b July 3, 1900
d Pearl Elizabeth b Nov 13, 1901; d (Beryl E) Feb 3, 1902
e —— —— dau b Oct 19, 1906 (father now a farmer)
f Ruth Blanche b July 14, 1909

Charles Dow bbbfhcdcb fireman of Sidney m Effie Richards b Augusta.   Child:

a —— —— son b Sidney May 12, 1904

James Dow bcbcbaa.   We learn 1928 from a great grand dau that James came to Barnet from "down country" after his marriage.   He m 1st a Scotch woman.   She was presumably one of the large Scotch-Irish migration to Londonderry, N H.   She d in Barnet or Greensboro and he m 2nd, by whom 2 children.   He m 3rd his deceased wife's sister and for this both were excommunicated from the Presbyterian church.   Our informant gives the older children as William, Samuel, James and Amos and children by 2nd wife as:

e Sargent lived many years at Greensboro; left 3 children
f Frank (Benjamin Franklin) who "can give a great deal of information." Unfortunately he has never replied to letter after letter seeking information

Flora E Dow bcbcbaacd is wife of G J Plunkett merchant of Barton, Vt.   Our 1928 informant gives a member of this family, identity not given:

Howard Ransom Dow b West Glover, Vt, Sept 30, 1889, m Jan 14, 1918, Corine Vancour b Richford, Vt, 1892, d Berlin, N H, Aug 8, 1923. Children b Berlin:

a   Robert James b Mch 6, 1921   b   Flora Anita b Feb 26, 1922

Sophia Dow bcbcbbda m Feb 19, 1819, Samuel Smith of Londonderry

Annie Elvira Dow bcbcbbgbaa m Charles Hayes Elliott of Somersworth; lived Lynn. A dau:

a   Harriet Louise b Lynn Sept 9, 1906

Moses Dow bcbeba d Plaistow Sept 3, 1754, ae 3-5-17

Samuel Warren Dow bcbebbbdbc d Warner Nov 5, 1906, unm

Samuel Oscar Dow bcbebbbdd and bcbebbfac are probably identical and first key is correct.   If so, he m twice, with no children by Augusta A Young and 5 by Grace M Wood.

Lorenzo Dow bcbebbfb does not belong here.   His various records are duplicated in Salisbury, Mass, b Jan 11, 1821. Amesbury gives some Lorenzo Dow d unm, perhaps a careless error

Henry E Dow bcbebbfa had a dau, in addition to those previously found:

c   Jeannette D b Concord Oct 17, 1856; m Sept 9, 1874, Frank D Webster. She
    d May 30, 1879. A dau Della or Delia b 1876 m Harvey M Dow bcbebbbdc

Sally Dow bcbebib m June 9, 1816, Amos C Clement.   June 11, 1899, a memorial window to them was placed in Newburyport Baptist Church

Jesse Bradley Dow bcbehhe m Apr 11, 1841, Emeline S Patten, Cambridge rec:

a   Jerome Bradley b Apr 1842; d ae 3 mos
b   Jesse Bradley b Apr 27, 1847; unt

John Calvin Dow bcbehhib (Capt), returning from Liverpool, enlisted in U S Navy; transferred to U S Geodetic Survey as nautical expert; stationed many years at Manilla; d at sea Aug 24, 1913

William Abner Dow bcbhddagf has children:

c   Doris Muriel b 1901   d   Abner Gilmore b 1903

Jeremiah Dow bcbhddc m Sarah Glidden and had 9 children b presumably from about 1826 onward. A paragraph belonging here in the text has disappeared.   The children:

a   Rebecca   b   Rachel   c   Emily   d   Isaiah   e   Margaret
f   Adeline   g   Elmira   h   Jeremiah   i   Joseph

430

The Author is under the impression that the two younger sons left no issue.

Isaiah Dow bcbhddcd m Naomi Place. Their 6 children correctly given, but as children of Jeremiah Dow bcbhddc. Harry F Dow b 1850, m in 1883

Mary A Dow bcbhdeg m 2nd about 1852 Zenas Rodgers of Braintree

Mahala Esther Dow bcbhbdfgba b Boston about 1887; m No Attleboro, Mass. Dec 25, 1907, Morton A Hardy, son of Marcellus A and Ellen Louise (Fuller)

Rebecca Dow bcdbaddb and Rev Nathaniel Brown Smith had other children:

   a Lucette m Lyman Cheney of Henniker
   d Edgar b 1846; m Mary J Gould   e Alice L
   f Herbert m Emma Farnum of Francestown

After Rebecca's death Nathaniel Brown Smith m 2nd Susanna P Collins

Edward Dow bcdbaddf b July 11, 1820. He left a dau:

   a Ella F b Auburn 1850; m 1867 —— Johnson. Their dau Lola M b 1869 m
      1887 William F Currier

Lorenzo Dow bcdbaddj d Concord Feb 20, 1886, ae 58-6-21. He has occasionally been confused with Lorenzo Dow of Croyden m Rhoda Sanborn with a large family. This latter was not a Dow at all. He assumed this name legally from admiration of the famous preacher

Leonard M Dow bcdbececb has also:

   c Charles Leonard b Louisville about 1890; machinist of Plainfield, N J

Peter Staub Dow bcdbeceeb is a member of the faculty of Dartmouth College; unm.

   b Lucy A b Hancock Sept 27, 1855

Oliver Lawrence Dow bcdeabda had also:

Hattie E Dow bcdeabdab m June 18, 1879, Charles Reid.

Ellen Dow bcdeaedbb m Joseph E Ober.

Thomas J Dow bcdeaef m Rachel Elliott, dau of David of Pepperell. Firstborn:

   a Jefferson b 1825; not found in 1850 census

Charlotte Augusta Dow bcdebed m Winslow, Me, July 13, 1831, David F Ring.

Marion Dow bcdebejcc and James G Blaine 3rd had also:

   b James G (4th) b Feb 1915; d June 1917

Elsie Dow bcdebejce m June 6, 1925, Edwin Seccomb Wallace, **son** of Frederick W, of Waterbury, Conn.

John R Dow bcdebfa. He m Hannah I Kendall of Milton, Mass. A John R Dow of Gardiner, Me (see bbbfhcd) m Mary E White b May 12, 1820.

Sarah Dow bcdecaa became the 3rd wife of Wheaton Mason and step mother to his 6 children. Her own children were:

a John   b Laura   c Cyrus

Mary Dow bcdecab m Benjamin Nutting. Among their children were Solomon and James

Eliza Dow bcdecad m Martin Montgomery, who is mentioned in the Albert Gallatin Dow autobiography as a substantial business man. A son Clarence succeeded him.

Caroline Dow bcdecae m Nathan Sawyer. They had a family but separated.

Nancy Dow bcdecaf m Gaylord Harper. Children:

a   Levant m Olive Welch
b   Leverett m Alice —— ——; 2nd Delilah Briggs, by whom a large family
c   Jane d 1927, ae 93; m Henry Judd; 2nd —— —— Dusenbark
d   Eliza lived and d Lockport; thrice m
e   Oliver m Cordelia Harper; his cousin
f   Caroline Dow m Darwin Lyman Geer. A dau is Mrs Jessie Dow Purviance of Evanston, Ill
g   Albert Gallatin m Mary Murtaugh
h   Amos d ae 2
i   Emma Elvira d 1922; m De Los Wood; 2nd John L Davis
j   Laura Amelia m Robinson Sheldon; 2nd Samuel T Littleton. One child by 2nd husband. In 1828 living Balboa, Calif, only survivor of her generation Children,—Charles, Emma, Robinson, Melvin Albertus

Chester Perry Dow bcdecaca m Clara Trask, dau of Casper and Grateful (Ellis).

Hannah Dow bcdedbab d Oct 6, 1854; m James Whipple. It was their dau who m —— Thorne, having Cora H m Eugene E Dow bcdedbbaa.

Webster M Dow bcdedbad m Priscilla (Chamberlain) Lewis wid and had five children:

a   Albert Webster   b   Julia A b 1858   c   Corett; unt
d   Charles A b Apr 18, 1861; d, Apr 7, 1862
e   Earty (sic) b Aug 13, 1865; d June 23, 1872

Albert Webster Dow bcdedbada had a dau b 1881.

Julia A Dow bcdedbadb d Feb 4, 1926; m 1878 Ora Violett; a dau Ida b 1880, m 1900 James Connery of Lisbon.

Asa Dow bcdedbae m Ellen B Smith, nee Aldrich; had 2 dau.

a Minnie B b Oct 7, 1869; d Jan 24, 1872
b Jennie V b June 17, 1872; m Joseph H Bond; d Nov 23, 1890 in child birth

Errold Norman Dow bcdedbbdbb; but further untraced.

Reuben Dow bcdedbd d 1819; unm.

Richard Dow bcdedcd had a son:

a Newton b Providence 1839; d Dec 9, 1863

Jonathan Dow bcdedcf. Cole Gen gives him m Abigail Towne b Oct 20, 1817, d Mch 25, 1897, dau of Joseph and Mehitable (Cole).

Alice Lincoln Dow bcdedcfcbb m Jan 1, 1927, Winfield Fairbanks Robinson of Newton Highlands.

Ethel M Dow bcdedcfdb m Frank Raymond Stubbs. Children:

a Joseph   b Eleanor, grad Smith College 1925   c Frank Raymond

Asa Dow bcdedcg. His wife d 1868; he m 2nd 1870 Eunice Oakes.

George Harvey Dow bcdedcga had 3rd child:

c Herman b 1873; m Maud McLuces; dau Leafy Maud b Lisbon Apr 19, 1910

Sarah E Dow bcdeddac m Nov 7, 1868, W J Burnett of Marseilles. Children:

a Alida B   b William T   c Lizzie M

Elizabeth Dow bcdedgh m Sept 20, 1842, Charles Bingley Hall b June 28, 1815, d May 8, 1883, son of Richard.

Sibbel Dow bcdedi m Silas Wheeler, who m 2nd Oct 8, 1846, Elizabeth Larkin. Two children by Sibbel.

Belle Dow bcdgdagi was bap Ann Isabelle. She and Archie Patterson have two children more than given:

a Roland A b 1889   x Lydia B m Henry Kelley

Ernest B Dow bcdgdbaaga m Ella M Patterson. Three children:

a Meredith M b Sept 12, 1914   b Muriel M b Dec 13, 1916
c Paul N b Apr 8, 1919

David Dow bcdgddaab b Canterbury 1856 (rec gives N H, but N B?), farmer of Canterbury, m Annie F Cummings. Children:

a Bert b Canterbury 1885. Note the strange interval now
c Earl Chester b Wentworth, N H, Apr 10, 1907
d Ernest b Sept 6, 1910   e Alice b Nov 14, 1912

Bert Dow bcdgddaaba laborer of Wentworth, moved to Orford; m Nov 18, 1909, Ethel Downing, ae 17, dau of Willie E and Luna M (Poor). Children:

a Roland E b Mch 10, d Apr 16, 1910
b Willie Bert b Oct 18, 1912
c Aletha L b Apr 9, 1915   d Bessie Mabel b Nov 3, 1916

Lydia Dow bcfiffb m 1812 Jonathan Bell. Children:

a   Frederick b June 28, 1814; m Betsey Warren
b   Almira b Aug 22, 1817   c   Mary b Aug 4, 1821
d   Margaret b May 12, 1823
e   James Russell b June 8, 1825; m Saloma Gordon
f   Ira b Oct 6, 1834

James E Dow bcfifff was named James Colony Dow

Fostean Dow bcfifffb left a dau Dolores (Smith) of Aurora, Ill.

Ellen Augusta Dow bcfifhhf m 1865 Obediah B Besse b Nov 27, 1834. One dau:

a   Nellie Louisa b Dec 11, 1867

Solon Dow bcfifhka d Melrose Apr 15, 1919. D rec did not name wife. Three children:

a   Louisa A   b   Grace Louisa b Manchester, N H, 1871
c   Lillian

Louis A Dow bcfifhkaa is an architect; m Lillian H Crowthers. Children:

a   Paul Crowthers b Feb 18, 1902; m June 10, 1926, Helen Cushing, dau of
      Edward Harmon
b   Phyllis A b Sept 3, 1903

Grace Louisa Dow bcfifhkab m June 1, 1897, Charles H Bugbee; in 1919 living Clarendon, Tex.

Elizabeth Dow bcfifi. Some other Elizabeth m Robert Danforth. Elizabeth bcfifi m Thomas Worthley and had:

a   Jemima m James H Buxton   b   Samuel m Lydia Manning
c   Hannah m Andrew Kidder   d   Sally m John Blake
e   Mary m Hiram Kidder   f   Susanna m George K Bagley
g   Thomas Dow m Matilda Hyde
h   Betsey m Peter Lougee, 2nd John Crocker

Peter Dow bcfifjd d Neb July 11, 1886; m June 22, 1828, Rhoda McDuffee b May 6, 1801, d Apr 29, 1843. Children:

a   Nancy   b   Lewis b 1830   c   Elisha M b May 6, 1832
d   Charles Phineas b July 9, 1835   e   Cynthia F b Oct 27, 1838
f   Alonzo E b Apr 25, 1843; lived Elk Point, S D; left 4 sons, 5 dau
c   Sarah b 1835; date of marriage clearly wrong; she m 2nd Carl Ansorge
d   James b Mch 8, 1839; d Aug 3, 1852

Elisha M Dow bcfifjdc d Mch 1902; m Juliet Shaw. They left a son:

a   Julius E b about 1862; living 1903 in Vernonia, Ore

Charles Phineas Dow bcfifjdd of Beaver Dam, Wis, d Sioux City Sept 28, 1903; m Nov 18, 1857, Elizabeth Heath. Children:

a   Lelia b May 5, 1859; d May 7, 1897
b   Ioa Jeannette b Oct 15, 1860; m June 5, 1876, Austin Guthrie Kingsbury d
      May 7, 1897; a son Hugh Roblee b Ponce Oct 7, 1889
c   Frank b Apr 7; d Aug 30, 1863   d   —— dau b Sept 9; d Sept 30, 1864
e   Minnie b Jan 12, 1866; living Sioux City 1903 with widowed mother

f Kate b Oct 8, 1867; m June 3, 1889, James Frederick Haney; lived Minneapolis;
   children,—Willis James b June 5, 1890, Alice Irene b Dec 23. 1891
g Luella b Dec 11, 1872   h Edith b Aug 29, d Sept 17, 1876

Cynthia F Dow bcfifjde m Feb 4, 1862, William F Wade d Jan 11, 1893; lived Calliope, Ia; left 7 sons, 1 dau.

Walter Abraham Dow bcfifjjaa; living 1924 Keene, N. H.   A dau:

a Inez N b Ryegate June 23, 1890; d Franconia Apr 11, 1896

Myrtle Dow bcfifjjbc m Sept 29, 1900, Walter V Barrett; of Landaff, N H.

William Henry Dow bcfigfbd lived N H; m Jan 18, 1872, Hannah E Davis, ae 25, dau of John C and Hannah (Mudgett).

Frank Edward Dow bcfigfddc had also:

b Richard b Lynn 1912

Mehitable Dow bcfiha had also:

b Martha (Hazeltine) b 1796; d 1884; unm

Phoebe Dow bcfihb d Aug 16, 1830; m Moses Johnson b Feb 29, 1768, d May 17, 1840.   Children:

a Cynthia b Mch 20, 1791   b Phebe b Feb 9, 1793; d Jan 8, 1894
c Moses b Dec 5, 1799; d Dec 20, 1812   d Frank Phelps
e Hiram b Oct 16, 1807; m Sarah Kimball
f Nancy b Aug 28, 1813   g Moses b Mch 28, 1815

Moses Dow bcfihd d Nov 27, 1839; m Sally Young b 1807; d July 6, 1866.   Children:

a Moses Franklin
b Ann Katherine b 1828; m Nathaniel Coggswell Eastman d 1859

Joseph Emerson Dow bcfihe.   A sixth child Joseph Emerson b 1826, d in young manhood.

Emma J Dow bcfihecc and Leonard Francis Cutter had children:

a Lillian Arnold b 1870   b Lucy Elizabeth   c Leonard Francis
d Charles Winthrop   e Irving Taylor

Polly Dow bcfihg d Feb 8, 1840.

Hannah Dow bcfihi d Dec 6, 1853.

Of the great mass of disconnected records accumulated during the twenty years of study of Dow Genealogy, a majority are of value only when some additional data permit establishing a connection. Those collected here are either the earlier or have some individual interest. As each must be indexed, we continue alphabetical order and begin with h, the symbols in g referring to a connected family in the main part of the Book.

Norman N Dow ha, meat cutter of Bangor, Me, d in service France 1919, ae about 23, unm.

Samuel Dow haa of Belfast, married, enlisted 20th inf Oct 11, 1862; d July 3, 1863, ae 45

Daniel Dow haaa m Mary R ——; lived Belfast, Children, by own rec:

a   Hannah b G July 20, 1851   b   Margaret E b Sept 20, 1861

George Dow haaaa of Belgrade, veteran of Civil War. Recent directory gives Isaac Dow and Wesley Dow farmers of Belgrade Lakes.

Samuel Dow haaab of Bucksport, b Me 1808, mill man, no realty, wife Irene b Me 1810. Children, by census, all untraced:

a   William b 1834   b   Mary b 1836   c   Lavinia b 1837
d   Henry b 1840   e   Laura b 1845

Samuel Dow haaac, teamster of Bucksport, b Me 1820, no realty; wife Mary b Me 1827. Child:

a   Howard b Mch 1850; unt

Joseph Dow haaad seaman of Bucksport, b Me 1821; no realty; wife Sarah. Child:

a   Edwin b 1849; unt

Homer Dow haaae was Justice of the Peace Canton 1839.

Enos Dow haaaf of Clinton enlisted 1863.

John Dow haaag of Corinna owned a litigated pig in 1828.

Harris Dow haaah m Matilda M Marsh b Dixfield, d Farmington Feb 22, 1904, ae 75-8-19, dau of Daniel and Annette (Park).

Hannah Dow haaai m Mch 10, 1753, Joseph Irish of Falmouth b Apr 12, 1728.

Lyman O Dow haaaj b Farmington, m May 1, 1863, Sarah E Lewis, both of Roxbury, Mass. She d Somerville Mch 2, 1905, dau of Thoːas and Elizabeth (Mitchell).

Mary Dow haaak of Portage Lake b N H 1774; no realty in 1850. Next three names in census presumably her children, b Me:

a   James b 1799, laborer   b   David b 1819   c   William b 1805

William Dow haaakc appears Portage Lake as laborer, no wife, no realty. Surely his children:

a   Mary b 1833   b   Eliza b 1834   c   Eunice b 1836
d   Alexander b 1841   e   David b 1843   f   Ellen b 1845
g   George b 1847

Alexander Dow haaakcd, presumably identical, b 1837, farmer of Portage Lake, parents not in rec, m Ashland Mch 31, 1864, Clara Drake, ae 22, dau of Nelson, farmer.

George Dow haaal m Hattie P Libby b Feb 15, 1817, dau of Edwin Ruthven (cf adkfbebl) and Margaret (Rice) of Porter.

George Gordon Dow haaam b Portland, son of Alfred (we doubt father's name), d Shrewsbury, Mass, Dec 18, 1903, ae 81-0-16.

Charles L Dow haaan of Howland int pub Oct 30, 1831, to Fidelia G Labree of Corinna.

Fanny Dow haaao b Me 1823 of Kilmarnock in 1850 census; presumably children:

a   William b 1844   b   Charles b 1846

George W Dow haaap had brothers and sisters; m Addie Garville. Only child:

a   Richard O b Lewiston 1883

Richard O Dow haaapa m Lynn, Mass, Oct 3, 1904, Emma M Hubner ae 18 dau of Oscar and Amelia (Fleisher). He d; she m 2nd L G Arnold. Children, b Worcester, Mass:

a   Kenneth H b Sept 20, 1905   b   Marjorie C b Nov 25, 1906; d young

Benjamin Dow haaaq b N H 1808, blacksmith of Gardiner in 1850; realty $2,800; m Gardiner Oct 10, 1835, Eliza Ann Lincoln b Me 1812. Children, census and Hist Gardiner coinciding:

a   George Lincoln b July 10, 1837; d Sept 10, 1851
b   Abby Frances b Feb 25, 1841; d Haverhill 1901; m Alonzo W Cram
c   Ann Maria b Jan 7, 1844   d   Mary Eliza b Apr 23, 1848

Joseph Dow haaas of township 33, Hancock Co, b Me 1820, farmer, realty $300; wife Lovinia b Me 1815; no children in census.

John W Dow haaat and J S Dow were Civil War veterans of East Livermore.

Jonathan Dow haaau b Me 1820; wife Lucenda b Me 1828, in census of Newburgh, no occupation, realty or children.

Thomas Dow haaav bap Nobleboro June 18, 1808. Mrs. Sarah Dow m Dec 1, 1814, Samuel Hussey.

Moses M Dow haaaw (surely adbabbb line) b Palermo, shoemaker, then farmer of Palermo, m Annie M Evans b Brooks. Children, by own rec:

a   Sarah M b 1865; d Alna Jan 28, 1902   b   Wilbur N b 1869
c   James M laborer of Alna d Mch 7, 1908, ae 31-3-10, unm

Wilbur N Dow haaawb laborer of Bath m Nov 21, 1917, Mary C Davis ae 45, nurse, b Culpepper, Va, dau of John J and Annie M (McCord). Presumably identical with Wilber N Dow b Palermo Aug 4, 1871, in 1906 farmer of Liberty.

Charles Fulton Dow haaax d Portland Feb 26, 1865; was in 1847-9 directory, business not stated.

Justin Sylvanus Dow haaay, farmer of Minnesota, m Naomi Moore; came from Portland, Me, his parents from a Me coast town. His 1stborn brought up by friends in Minneapolis; he himself went to Seattle; m 2nd and had a family, of whom 1 found:

    a Wilber Olin b Minneapolis Sept 1, 1860   b Frank, of Compton, Calif

Wilber O Dow haaaya came to Los Angeles in 1875, well known in land speculation and local politics; d 1920; m Santa Cruz Dec 26, 1886, Irene Eladsit Bowen of a Sou Car family.   Children:

    a Tisdale Justin, of Los Angeles 1923, unm   b Wilber Olin
    c Naomi A d young   d Ione E m Philip S Low
    e Adelaide m Paul Stassforth

Orlen S Dow haaaz, ship carpenter of Robinston, d widower Oct 28, 1898, ae 75, 6 mos.

David Smith Dow haaba b Sandford Dec 26, 1819, later of Waterloo, Me; cordwainer of Hampstead, N H, m May 16, 1842 (both then of Danvers) Eliza Welch Osgood b Jan 1821, dau of Daniel of Hampstead and Sarah (Stevens).   Presumably an older child:

    b Sarah Eliza d Mch 13, 1847   c George A b 1848; living 1850

James C Dow haabb (Lieut) enlisted 1861 from Sheepscot.

William Dow haabc m Isabella Libby b Jan 13, 1803, dau of Capt Moses and Elizabeth (Libby) of Scarboro.

Emma F Dow haabe, m Feb 6, 1877, Alden Doe, farmer of Washington.

Nathaniel F Dow haabf enlisted from Vienna 1861. These two items suggest bcbhd line.

Samuel Dow haabg b Me 1804, farmer, realty $1,000; wife Hannah b Me 1810; children by 1850 Waterville census:

    a Olive b 1828   b Lucinda b 1832

William Dow haabh m Sarah T Kimball. A dau, by own rec:

    a Julia R b Waterville, d Lewiston Feb 23, 1894, ae 59, unm

Asa Dow haabi b Me 1815, farmer of Wellington, realty $200; wife Elizabeth b Me 1822.   One child by census:

    a Franklin b 1846; unt

As New Hampshire was settled much earlier than Maine, one expects many more items in the disconnected mass.

Polly Dow haabk m Belmont Nov 1, 1807, Thomas Proctor, both of Alton.

Livona Dow haabl m Wolfboro June 30, 1846, Levi Glidden, both of Alton.

Thomas S Dow haabm m Nancy —— b Gilford.   First and last child proven, others conjecture:

  a   Justin b Alton 1851   b   Eugene b Alton 1851
  c   Alvin (no date)
  d   Ira b Alton June 11, 1858 (son of Thomas L); unt

Justin Dow haabma, shoemaker of Farmington, m Jan 20, 1872, Belle Pinkham ae 18, dau of Samuel and Lucy of Dover.   This family Quaker, but not found in Pinkham Gen.

Eugene Dow haabmb, teamster of Farmington, m Etta E Davis ae 41.   A child:

  a —— son b Sept 4, 1902

Alvin Dow haabmc b Alton m Flora Hill b Canada.   A child,—rec missing.

Ivory Dow haabn m Hannah A ——.   A child:

  a Frederick A b Oct 25, d Nov 8, 1858, in Alton

Mehitable Dow haabo m Maj John Johnson; a son John m Dec 25, 1813, Betsey Poor b Apr 8, 1794, d Aug 25, 1853; had a family; of Atkinson (Poor Gen.—Name Mehitable probably wrong; if Dow at all must be befi line).

Susan C Dow haabp of Canterbury (Clough? ahbae?) m Dec 10, 1818, Dearborn Johnson of Concord.

Benjamin Dow haabq m Feb 17, 1825, Nancy Mooney (Moore, Hist Canterbury) b Canterbury 1802, dau of Capt Joseph and Elizabeth (Whidden).   A son:

  a Lycurgus; lived Durham; unt

Catherine Dow haabr b Oct 1, 1807; d Nov 21, 1878; m June 20, 1830, Biley Lyford, son of John (ahbae indicated); moved to St. Albans, Me.   Children:

  a Mary A b Apr 27, 1832   b   Caroline b May 7, 1833
  c   Daniel Calvin b Feb 23, 1836; m Lododiski Maria Fletcher; 2nd Josephine N
      Harmon
  d   Henry Harrison b Oct 14, 1844; m Violetta Rollins

Records of Chichester are mostly unidentifiable but must belong to the adai, the aedaab, adgcac or adgcad lines. Rec is clear that Samuel Dow b 1760 was there, a Rev pensioner in 1850.

Sally Dow haabs m Chichester Nov 17, 1796, Obediah Marsten.

Mary Esther Dow haabsx b Chichester m Stephen G Marston b Pittsfield. A dau Angeline J m Pittsfield 1868 Albert C Marston. A series of marriages of same names are almost invariably connected.

Samuel Dow haabt b Chichester, farmer of Chichester, d Loudon Apr 18, 1870; m Apr 3, 1840, Eliza Gale b Loudon 1818; census 1850 gives them farmers of Loudon with 3 children:

    a Malvina b 1840   b Jacob b 1845   c Samuel b 1846

The same Samuel Dow had children by own rec, lettered for convenience:

    d Joseph b Loudon Jan 16, 1836   e Samuel b Loudon 1838
    f William b Barnstead 1842

Jacob Dow haabtb married farmer d Barnstead 1883. Some Jacob E Dow farmer of Loudon, living 1915 off Pittsfield road, m Betsey Wilson. Directory 1909 gives (presumably) his children:

    a Jennie m —— Drew
    b Melvina (note recurrence of name); probably of Concord by 1915 directory

Samuel Dow haabtc, haabte. Two candidates for them: Samuel Dow d Loudon Apr 27, 1902, ae 52. Age does not fit. Samuel Dow b Loudon about 1856 (date wrong; cf m date) m Loudon Apr 14, 1871, Abbie A Little b 1856. Children:

    a Fred S b Loudon 1880
    b Florence M m Mch 17, 1900, William J MacKenzie, both of Epsom

Fred S Dow haabtca engineer of Raymond m Apr 4, 1903, Clarissa A Fitts ae 19, dau of George and Clarissa (Ross) of Canterbury; div; m 2nd Ida M York ae 19, dau of Frank and Jane. Children:

    a George Raymond b Dec 1, 1909   b Charlotte Frances b Mch 25, 1914
    c Flossie Lenayne b Oct 25, 1916

Joseph Dow haabtd. His 2nd m rec specifies parents Samuel and Eliza (Gale). Of Bow he m 2nd (ae 65) Dec 24, 1902, Rosa J (Holt) Beadslee ae 42 (her 2nd), dau of Enoch and Sarah D Jenkins. Her dau by 1st m Susan C m —— Potter of Providence; she herself living in Lancaster by fairly recent directory. Presumably same Joseph Dow section hand of Concord m Apr 9, 1859, Ann F Glines b Canterbury Aug 10, 1834; d Bow Sept 20, 1900, dau of James Carpenter and Sarah (Heath) both b Canterbury. State rec says 5 children:

    a Warren P   b Nellie b Canterbury July 8, 1865
    d and e —— —— twins b and d Concord July 11, 1871

Warren P Dow haabtda, gardener of Bow, appears as an itinerant Second Adventist evangelist; m Aug 15, 1895, Ida Louise Lake b July 4, 1872, dau of Moses Rowell and Mary Jane (Batchelder).

William Dow haabtf shoemaker of Concord m Littleton July 6, 1878, Sarah A Locke ae 26, b New Lisbon, of Barnstead. A Concord item cannot be identical, unless 1850 census has a duplication: Samuel Dow b N H 1817, farmer without realty. Name following is William Dow b N H 1839. Age fits William Dow laborer of Loudon d Boscawen almshouse May 30, 1914, ae 75.

Only hereditary Dow families of Concord are ahbg and bcbebb. Few others remained more than one generation.

Hannah Dow haabu m Apr 4, 1820, Eleazer Davis, both of Concord.

Andrew A Dow haabv b N H 1818 farmer of Concord m Maria L W b N H 1820. Children by census:
a   Mary b 1842   b   Ann Maria b 1843

Susan H Dow haabw b N H 1783, presumably wid in 1850 census. Next name presumably her son:

Francis Dow haabwa b N H 1824, blacksmith; wife Mary A b N H 1825. Firstborn:
a   Francis b N H 1850; unt

Ruth Dow haabx b N H 1795 alone in 1850.

Benjamin F Dow haaby of Cornish m Nov 30, 1829, Loisa Adams of Plainfield; perhaps identical,—Benjamin Dow of Anoro, Ohio, m Apr 19, 1848, Betsey G Morrill of Plainfield. Maybe this is the missing adggdi.

Hannah Dow haabz of Deerfield m Epsom Mch 17, 1827, Samuel Bartlett of Northwood.

David Dow Jr habaa b Mass sailor m Nancy Gould. One child sure:
a   Mary Roxana b Deering June 16, 1800; d Enfield Nov 10, 1883, a Shaker
b   (guess) Lucy b Newburyport; Shaker, d Canterbury May 30, 1882

Daniel Dow habab b N H 1815; wife Ruth b N H 1825; shoemaker of Derry, 1850 census.

Thomas Edward Dow habac, said in son's rec b Dover (Quaker line indicated), m Mary Irving Burbeck. Sons b Lowell, found by own rec:
a   Louis Henry b Apr 1, 1872   b   Ralph Noyes

Louis H Dow habaca, grad Harvard, m July 16, 1896, Rebecca Rumrill of Springfield, Mass; in 1923 professor in Dartmouth; never replied to repeated letters of genealogical inquiry.

Ralph N Dow habacb, architect of Cambridge (not in recent directory), m Aug 10, 1897, Edith Weston Moreland ae 20, dau of John H and Maria (Stone)   Children:

a Louis Irving b Mch 4, 1903   b Dorothy b Apr 19, 1906
c Margery b or d Feb 11, 1909

Hannah Dow habae m July 24, 1820, James Patterson, both of Dunbarton.

Susan C Dow habaf m (Durham and Newmarket rec) Nov 21, 1826, Daniel Emerson, son of Joseph and Temperance (Dame) of Northwood. Epping rec gives her of Epping, him of Lee.

Sally Dow habag m Durham (date lacking) Jonathan Drew b 1770, son of Lieut. Zebulon and Sarah, blacksmith; moved from Dayton, Me, to Tuftonborough. adgfb line indicated.   Children:

a Hezekiah   b Mary   c Chandler   d Daniel   e John
f Lydia

Sally Dow habah of East Kingston m Nov 7, 1796, John Sanborn of Meredith.

Mrs Abigail Dow habai of Epping m Lee May 21, 1795, Benjamin Barker (ahbab).

Hannah Dow habaj m Epping June 19, 1777, James Rundlett 3rd.

Sally Dow habak m Jan 17, 1815, Asa Norris, both of Epping.

Hannah Dow habal m Epping 29: 12: 1798, Chase Stevens.

Deborah Dow habam of Epsom m Samuel Chapman b Apr 18, 1797. Ten children b Epsom.

Nancy Dow haban d Exeter Jan 30, 1875, ae 88.

Parker Dow habap b Me 1807, farmer of Franklin assessed $500 in 1850; wife Clarissa b N H 1802; no children in census.

Rebecca Dow habaq m Belmont Dec 8, 1796, Abel Glidden, both of Gilmanton. He b 1774, Free Will Baptist clergyman ordained Nov 9, 1810, pastor in Gilford and Gilmanton.

Lydia Dow habar m Belmont Jan 19, 1825, Stephen C Ladd, both of Gilmanton.

Lydia Dow habas m Belmont Feb 5, 1789, John Boynton of New Hampton.

Susanna Dow habat m Belmont Oct 15, 1795, Joshua Gilman Jr.

Susanna Dow habau m Belmont Apr 25, 1799, Dudley Marsh, both of Gilmanton.

Elizabeth Dow habav b N H 1770 appears in Gilmanton 1850 census alone. Wid?

Samuel Otis Dow habaw (known only from d rec of son) b Gilmanton, m Jane C Allen b Gilmanton. A son:

   a Simeon G b Gilmanton Feb 21, 1809; d widower Laconia Oct 11, 1887; no
      other rec

Nancy Dow habax b Gilmanton Jan 27, 1795; d Dec 25, 1877; m Sept 22, 1824, Jacob Copp, carpenter of Sanbornton; moved to Laconia (cf names sub bbbb). Children:

   a Malinda b Oct 7, 1825; m William H Rowan
   b Stephen Ladd b Sept 25, 1827
   c Julian Philbrick b June 1, 1830; m Henry Seaverns
   d James Madison b Aug 27, 1833

Henry P Dow habay of Gilford, veteran of Civil War.

Masa (Amasa?) **Dow** habaz d Greenland Aug 5, 1818, ae 23. We recall that Amasa Dow aeda came from Greenland.

Elizabeth Dow habba of Hampton Falls m Nov 26, 1818, John Hasty (also spelled Hersty) of Berwick, Me.

Nancy Dow habbb once of Hampton Falls d Newbury July 16, 1839, ae 74.

Rhoda Dow habbc m (int pub Salisbury Mch 17) Hampton Falls Mch 29, 1783, Charles Chase.

Philo Dow habbd b N H 1802; shoemaker, realty $1,200; wife Harriet b N H 1800. He d widower Hampstead Aug 25, 1884. Children, if any, gone by 1850.

Jane Dow habbe m Hopkinton Jan 4, 1812, Gideon Newton.

Hannah Dow habbf b Webster, d Hopkinton Mch 8, 1881, ae 85 unm.

Nancy Dow habbg of Hopkinton m Henniker Nov 19, 1795, Timothy How of Methuen.

Clarissa Dow habbh m Dec 28, 1843, Isaac Merrill, both of Hopkinton.

Eliza Dow habbi d Kensington Aug 28, 1800, ae 80.

Molly Dow habbj m Lee (Kensington rec) 1807 John Doe of Newmarket.

John Palmer Dow habbk m Dorothy Brown, both of Kensington. At least 1 child:

   a Almon P b Kensington Apr 10, 1831; d widower Exeter Nov 16, 1913, unt

Nancy Dow habbl m Exeter July 29, 1818, David Prescott, both of Kensington. Children:

a H Gilmore b 1844   b Marilla b 1857

Hannah Dow habbm m Lebanon May 14, 1795, James Fuller.

Nancy Dow habbq m Bow Mch 14, 1813, Isaac Johonnet.

William Dow habbr had:

a Betsey b Bow Feb 13, 1791; presumably identical with Betsey Dow m Bow Oct 1808 John Hurd of Dunbarton

Charlotte Dow habbs of Bow m June 10, 1811, William Perkins of Kittery, Me.

Charlotte Dow habbt m Edward Silver of Bow. A child:

a Laura Ann m 1840 Squier Felch of Weare

William Dow habbu m Bradford Dec 1811 Susanna Collins.

Amos Webster Dow habbv m Sept 22, 1803, Dorothy Gerdy, both of Bridgewater.

Deborah Dow habbw of Loudon m Nov 27, 1806, Ebenezer Bean of Barnstead.

Lois Dow habbx b Moultonborough Jan 6, 1782 (Weare rec).

Mrs **Sarah Dow** habby d Moultonborough July 28, 1899, ae 86.

Daniel Dow habbz m Moultonborough Aug 10, 1810, Polly Chadbourne (Chandler, State rec).

Mary Dow habca married d Moultonborough Jan 3, 1874, ae 84.

Asa Dow habcb m Aug 19, 1821, Abigail Picker, both of Moultonborough.

Stephen Dow habcc of Moultonborough m Jan 4, 1828, Hannah Cram of Weare b about 1787, 4th child of Thomas and Sarah (Mudgett). There is a long series of Cram-Dow intermarriages in Weare in the bcdeaa line (q v). A child found by own rec:

a Joseph L b Moultonborough 1834 by m rec, 1836 by d rec; d Pelham, Mass, Dec 28, 1899; overseer of Manchester, m Oct 28, 1854, Sarah G Willey d Manchester Mch 17, 1882, ae 49-9-19, dau of John and Sarah G of Campton

Josiah Dow habcd of Moultonborough b N H 1801, was 1850 farmer of Concord assessed $3,000; wife Betsey b 1805. Census gives 2 children:

a Mary E b 1843
b Sarah F b 1848; m Oct 9, 1895, George K Brown of Moultonborough

Kezia B Dow habce m Nov 1833 Sylvester Gordon, both of Moultonborough.

Heman Dow habcf b N H 1824; wife Harriet b N H 1828:

Moses Dow b N H 1826; wife Augusta b N H 1831; were sash and blind manufacturers in Nashua 1850.

Levi Dow habcg m June 3, 1823, Elizabeth Swan, both of New Hampton. Cannot be abbegfk.

Melinda Dow habch m Mch 14, 1843, Levi Carter, both of New Hampton.

Lyman N Dow habci b 1827, in 1850 carpenter of Concord, m Mch 8, 1848, Abigail G Gordon, both of New Hampton. Firstborn:

  a Nathan L b June 1849

Dennis J Dow habcj b N H 1813; wife Lydia D b N H 1816; cabinet maker of Newmarket in 1850. Children by census:

  a Martha b N H 1840   b Daniel T b 1846
  c Althie M b 1848. Next name in census is M C L Dow b Vt 1843

Sarah Dow habcj m No Hampton Allison Libby b Apr 6, 1757, son of Allison and Sarah (Skillings).

Elizabeth Dow habck of Ossipee m Tamworth Feb 5, 1793, Israel Folsom of Tamworth.

Mary Dow habcl b Ossipee July 8, 1797, d Alton Dec 24, 1887, dau of Aaron Hanson b Lebanon, Me. Clue here to disconnected Alton Dows?

Mrs **Surviah Dow** habcm m Feb 3, 1799, Robert Johnson, both of Pittsfield. Surely some of these Pittsfield items are of lost adai lines.

Nancy Dow habcn (Anna in 1850 census, b N H 1794), not a Quaker, m Jan 18, 1816, Jeremiah Dow adadie.

Susan Dow habco b N H 1792, no land, in 1850 census.

Elizabeth Dow habcp b Mass 1788; realty $2,000 in 1850. Both widows?

Nancy Dow habcq of Pittsfield m Dec 31, 1818, Jeremiah Berry of Epsom.

Jacob Dow habcr m July 24, 1825, Lydia Chase, both of Pittsfield.

John Dow habcs b Pittsfield m Abbie —— b Barnstead. A child:

  a Charles W b Barnstead 1854; m Brookfield Aug 18, 1877, Emily Berry, ae 22, dau of Benjamin and Paley

John Dow habct of Plaistow conveyed (deed rec at Exeter) Apr 8, 1765, to his son John Dow Jr one half of the farm "where I now dwell in Plaistow."

Mary Dow habcu m Plaistow about 1761 John Cooper. Plaistow dates are often hopelessly garbled in an official re-transcript.

Mary Dow habcv m Plaistow about 1784 John Harriman.

Abigail Dow habcw int pub Plaistow Apr 8, 1748, m (Kingston rec) June 2, 1748, Joseph Harriman Jr b Apr 18, 1726, son of Joseph and Lydia (Eaton).

Thomas Dow habcy b 1820, **John Dow** b 1822, **Derby Dow** b 1824, all b N H , appear in Raymond 1850 census, farmers but without land.

Mary Dow habcz m July 13, 1780, Isaiah Foss, both of Barrington.

Lucy Dow habda b Salem Mch 7, 1763, dau of —— and Mehitable (Bayley). Salem has a lot of hopelessly garbled rec. Lucy Dow m Apr 3, 1783, Herman Amy (rec both in Salem and Bath, M H).

James Dow habdb of Salem m Mch 20, 1794, Mary Smith of Londonderry. Rec gives a child to James and Anna:

a Rebecca Clendennin b Salem July 18, 1795

Elizabeth Dow habdc, apparently wid b Wheeler, will dated 1822 mentions brothers Sampson and Abijah, sisters Molly Wheeler and Molly Dyke.

Henry D Dow habdd m Nov 21, 1793 Abigail Ellingwood (Salem rec).

Ruth Dow habde housewife d Sanbornton Aug 12, 1850, ae 65.

Almira Dow habdf of Sanbornton m May 29, 1832, Albert Marshall of Weare, son of Benjamin and Lydia (Cilley); at some time lived Dunbarton. Children:

a Ansel H m Helen Ham; 2nd Mary Jameson
b Almus b 1833; m Sarah E Follansbee; 2nd Abbie E Osborn
c Allen W b 1839; unm
d Anna M m (Anna J) Weare 1864 Dr Robert B Carswell
e Martha A m Weare 1866 Charles O George
f John C of Lyme m 1879 Kate Gertrude Perkins

Moses Dow habdg m Dec 11, 1813, Miriam Tewksbury, both of Sandwich.

Several volumes of Seabrook vital records are extant but many years ago were playthings for children and are much defaced.   About 66 per cent of all Seabrook records were in the disconnected list of this Book until Miss Mary Jessie Greene of Hampton Falls undertook a systematic clearing up,—a work in genealogy as fine as ever done in America.

Jane Dow habdh is said by official rec m Feb 14, 1769, Daniel Felch, both of Hampton Falls. This is error. Daniel, the fisherman and first of his race to come to Seabrook, m Jane Page. About 60 of their posterity intermarried with Dow.

Lydia Dow habdi m (int pub Nov 17, 1770) Samuel Eaton of Seabrook. Children:

a Amanda   b George   c Lydia   d Daniel   e Nancy

Levi Dow habdj prisoner of war d Halifax between Nov 23, 1776, and Dec 26, 1767. Name Levi is all that suggests Seabrook.

Polly Dow habdk m Seabrook 1803 Samuel Eaton.

Zelphia Dow habdl m Seabrook Dec 4, 1818, Moses Jones. If adaik, would be 56.

Jane Dow habdm m Seabrook May 10, 1813, Benjamin Brown.

Daniel Dow habdn m Elizabeth ——, both of Seabrook. He i, almost surely adggbcb. Some Daniel d tuberculosis Dedham, Mass. Mch 31, 1848. Children of Daniel and Elizabeth:

a Stephen S m Oct 29, 1840, Betsey E Brocklebank, both of Georgetown, Mass.
   She d wid Georgetown Mch 21, 1906, dau of Samuel and Mehitable (Emerson)
b William b 1822   c Nancy T b 1824

Levi Dow habdo of Seabrook m Feb 4, 1821, Nancy Eaton. At least ten contemporaries of these names in Seabrook. He b 1798, d 1840. Children:

a Joseph French b July 29, 1821   b Mary b Sept 13, 1822
c Lois b Oct 10, 1824   d Lydia b July 7, 1829
e Charles Edward b Aug 26, 1834; d May2, 1842

Joseph F Dow habdoa mariner m Oct 29, 1846, Laura Ann Lake of Salisbury, d Salisbury Feb 13, 1901, ae 74-1-13, dau of Joseph and Ann (Hoyt). Child:

a Georgianna b Oct 15, 1847

Mary Dow habdob m Salisbury Dec 20, 1846, Nicholas P French Jr b Aug 26, 1821, son of Josiah and Hannah (French). Children:

a Augusta b Aug 8, 1850   b Caroline b Jan 27, 1856; m Thomas Ronan
c Luther William b Feb 7, 1861

Lois Dow habdoc (in rec, dau of Henry) m Oct 24, 1844, Andrew Eaton, seaman of Seabrook, son of Christopher and Lydia.

Lydia Dow habdod m Apr 17, 1848, William Roberts of Amesbury shoemaker ae 19, son of William and Sarah.

Hannah Dow habdp m Seabrook Oct 1, 1816, Benjamin Brown.

Sarah Ann Dow habdq m July 3, 1839, Henry L Dwight; moved to Raymond. A dau:

a Clara m Aaron M Dow adkehcc

Hannah Dow habdr m by Rev Sam Perley June 4, 1774, Jacob Jones of Salisbury.

Phoebe Dow habds b Seabrook 1798; m Feb 18, 1819, Job Jenness b 1795, d Canaan, son of Richard and Mary (Page) abcecd; lived Hampton, Exeter, Lynnfield, Canaan. Children, Hampton rec:

a Rosina d Feb 24, 1844, ae 23, unm   b ——— d Aug 16, 1833
c Lucinda b Dec 27, 1833

Jane Dow habdt b Seabrook Jan 2, 1765 (parents not mentioned in rec). Some Jane Dow in rec as wid had children (possibly she became wid later, rec notwithstanding):

a ——— dau b Sept 1, 1790   b Jane b Apr 1, 1792

Eda Dow habdu d Springfield July 27, 1860, ae 75. Presumably wid with son Joseph P b N H 1813, shoemaker, no wife; realty $400 in 1850.

Miriam Dow habdv of Tamworth m Mch 24, 1825, George Frost Folsom b July 7, 1797. Children:

a Clarissa Augusta d married Lowell, Mass   b George Frost d young

Ann P Dow habdw m Tamworth Oct 12, 1827, Elisha Hines.

Ruth L Dow habdx of Wolfboro int pub Oct 27, 1825, to William Towle.

Samuel Dow habdy of Groton, Vt, b Me 1785, laborer. One child in census:

a William b N H 1811

William Dow habdya blacksmith of Groton, assessed 1850 at $500; m Feb 13, 1834, Lydia Richardson b Topsham 1815. Children, 1860 census giving each a year later than 1850:

a George b Vt 1839-40
b Lucinda b 1841-2; m Nov 3, 1866, Abner Sanderson, ae 40, farmer of Waltham, Mass
c Charles b 1844-5; unto   d Emma b 1846-7

George Dow habdyaa teamster of Groton, assessed 1870 at $1,500; m Minnie ——— b 1843. Children, 1870 census:

a Belle b 1868   b ——— son b 1870

Daniel Dow habdy m Dec 5, 1801, Lucy Russell, both of Hartland; apparently moved late in life to Jericho. Children:

a Lucetta b June 13, 1802   b Augustus Wolston b Apr 28, 1804

Augustus W Dow habdyb farmer of Underhill, Vt, taxed 1850 on $4,000; m Hannah Abbott b Vt Oct 30, 1814, d July 1872. Children:

a Jane b 1833; m June 13, 1855, Elon Prouty of Jericho
b Ellen b 1838; m May 10, 1855, Hiram B Fish, lawyer of Jericho. Children,— Bertha, Addie, Grace

Lewis Dow habdz of Peacham m Dec 15, 1822, Pamelia Beal of Cabot.

Eliza Dow habea of Peacham m Dec 1, 1825, Allen Russell of Danville.

Darius Dow habeb of Royalton m Dec 7, 1839, Jerusha Skinner of Roxbury

Alexander B Dow habec b St Albans 1818, farmer of Ryegate assessed 1850 at $2,400; wife Jennie C (Jane C) b St Albans 1827. A Child:

    a   James Crawford b Ryegate Sept 21, 1849

Eben Dow habed b Vt 1821, farmer of Sharon, assessed 1850 at $2,000; wife Julia b N H. Children, by census:

    a   Alma b Vt 1844   b   Harvey b 1846   c   Albert b 1848

John Dow habee m Dec 8, 1843, Judith Fuller, both of Vershire. Census 1850 shows him farmer of Orford, assessed $1,500; wife Judith b Vt 1822. Children:

    a   Miranda b Vt 1846   b   Daniel b 1847; unt
    c   Harriett b N H 1849-50

Henry Dow habef of Weybridge m Mch 1, 1805, Sukey Baker.

Nancy Dow habeg of Windsor m July 20, 1829, Marvin Smith.

Olive A Dow habeh int pub Amesbury Mch 9, 1844; m Kingston Mch 25, 1845 (sic rec) John H Currier, both of Amesbury.

Nancy Dow habei of Amesbury m (int Aug 11, 1828) Charles B Osgood of Salisbury and Newburyport b Jan 3, 1806. Children, Osgood Gen:

    a   Charles E b Nov 20, 1831
    b   Annie H b Jan 12, 1836, m Edward T. Wallace of Wolfboro

David Dow habek m Apr 10, 1844, Polly Partridge, both of Auburn.

Mrs Jane Dow habel int pub Aug 30, 1809, to Jacob Williams, both of Beverly (ahfc line).

Philip B Dow habem b Me 1811, carpenter of Billerica m Sept 5, 1832, Hannah L Carr b Mass 1808. No children. He m 2nd of Lawrence June 23, 1852, Charlotte Rice b Mch 4, 1816, dau of William and Charlotte (Whitman) of Sudbury.

Sarah Dow haben of Billerica m Jan 17, 1782, Ebenezer Newman of Woburn.

Official rec of Boston give no Dow birth prior to 1800.

Obediah Dow habeo surveyor of boards Boston 1772.

Nathan Dow habep tailor of Ship St, Boston 1796 directory.

Weare Dow habeq of Boston m Aug 3, 1801, Sally Washburn Keith.

William Dow haber paid two sewer assessments Boston 1805.

James M Dow habes of Boston m (int pub Dec 1, 1844) Martha T Noyes of Haverhill.   Child:

a —— infant d Haverhill July 9, 1846

Joseph Dow habet of Boston m Caroline Amelia Humphrey b Dec 13, 1821, dau of Benjamin and Oreins (Turner).   Children, Humphrey Gen:

a Benjamin   b Caroline L   c Joseph; all untraced

Theodore H Dow habeu m Nancy C —— b Jan 10, 1817.   Children b Cambridge:

a Theodore d Sept 7, 1849, ae 7, 7 mos
b John b June 18, 1844; unt   c Joseph R b Nov 7, 1848; unt

Jonathan R Dow habev b N H 1810, blacksmith m Cambridge Feb 8, 1844, Mary R Hall of Chelsea, b Me 1826.   Children:

a Alphonso b Jan 8, 1845; d Nov 7, 1848
b Sarah M b Mass 1847   c Ella B b Oct 30, 1848

James Dow habew b N H 1807, carder; wife Eunice b Mass 1816. Children, census:

a Austin b Mass 1838   b Eugene L b Mass 1847; both unt

Elizabeth Dow habex b Mass 1777, in family of Sylvanus Swan Danvers 1850.

Zeruiah Dow habey m Haverhill before 1743 John Straw.   Children:

a Anna b Dec 28, 1743   b Lydia b Nov 23, 1746

Miriam Dow habez of Haverhill int pub Mch 24, 1792, to Joseph Stewart of Newburyport.   Possibly, but improbably identical is: Miriam Dow m Haverhill Aug 8, 1792, Enoch Pierce of Newburyport b Jan 13, 1753, son of Samuel and Mary (Brown).

Elizabeth Dow habfa of Haverhill m Oct 16, 1749, David Foster, presumably he b Boxford, of Pomfret, son of Timothy and Martha (Dorman).

Hannah Dow habfb m Haverhill May 10, 1808 (his 2nd) Sherburn Shaw.

Eunice Dow habfc b Mass 1791; Susan K Dow b Mass 1825 (mother and dau?) in Ipswich 1850 census.

Lynn, Mass, being the seat of Quarterly Meeting, has some early Quaker rec.

Mary Dow habfd ae about 19 d Lynn 3 mo: 1739.

Nancy Dow habfe m Apr 1, 1818, John Lummus.

Miriam Dow habff m Sept 1, 1818, Charles Adams.

Lydia C Dow habfg m Aug 27, 1820, David Bowler.

Sarah Dow habfh m Feb 17, 1825, Benjamin Homan.

Daniel Dow habfi d at sea 11 mo: 1833; m Dec 17, 1826, Susan B Hallowell. She m 2nd Aug 16, 1838, John Porter; 2 children by him. Daniel's children:

> a Susan Jane b Dec 19, 1827   b Daniel b July 25, 1830
> c Mary A b 1833; in 1850 census

Daniel Dow habfib m Harriet Wiles of Swampscott. Child:

> a Hattie Charlotte m Oct 2, 1883, William Cune Boynton; child Arthur Cleveland d in infancy

Dolly Dow habfj m Lynn before 1827 David Buffum (surely adbab line from Me).

Joseph W Dow habfk d Nov 28, 1843, ae 29; m Feb 19, 1837, Dorothy M Hunt. She m 2nd (int pub Mch 2, 1845) Daniel S Lewis.

Rebecca Dow habfl m Lynn Apr 23, 1835, Benjamin Cook.

Betsey Dow habfm int pub Lynn Feb 3, 1839, to David Pherson.

Henry W Dow habfn wheelwright had:

> a George Henry b N H; unt   b Mary Jane b Me May 12, 1848

William N Dow habfo cordwainer m Sarah ——. Children:

> a Melissa H   b Jacob Lovering d Sept 2, 1845, ae 10 mos
> c Roland H b Lynn Oct 3, 1845; unt

John C Dow habfp cordwainer of Lynn d consumption Feb 1, 1847, ae 40; m Oct 5, 1843, Mary Eliza Glover dau of Peter and Mary. She m 2nd Oct 6, 1847, William H Demerritt, ae 40, cordwainer, son of John and Abigail.

De Witt C Dow habfq of Lynnfield had wife Mary d 1922, ae about 63; bur Windsor, Vt.

Mary Dow habfr of Roxbury m Malden Dec 27, 1829, Benjamin Gates.

Isaac F Dow habfs of Methuen in 1850, shoe cutter, m July 31, 1843, Elizabeth A Glines b N H 1827. He b N H 1827. Children, by census b N H:

> a Lucien R b 1846   b Albert L b 1847; both unt

Elizabeth Dow habft m Newbury Feb 16, 1769, Daniel Hale 3rd.

Mrs **Susannah Dow** habfu b 1756; d Newbury Apr 11, 1839.

Mary Dow habfv m Newbury Feb 26, 1778, Enoch Moody; presumably the Enoch b Apr 3, 1754, son of Moses and Elizabeth.   Children, Newbury rec:

a   Enoch b Feb 12, 1780; int pub Apr 11, 1801, to Salley Pillsbury
b   Esther b June 29, 1781; m Apr 7, 1807, Michael Sumner
c   David b Feb 8, 1787   d   Mary b Apr 26, 1792
e   Sally b Aug 27, 1797; m Sept 21, 1816, Moses Newell

Mrs **Mary Dow** habfw int pub Aug 27, 1774, to Jonathan Rogers.

Chloe Dow habfx m Newburyport Feb 21, 1785, Milo Freeman.

Molly Dow habfy int pub Feb 21, 1789, to Joseph Todd of Newburyport.

William Dow habfz had wife Anna.   Newburyport rec gives children:

a   Ann b July 2, 1794   b   Mary b Feb 1, 1797
c   William bap Nov 3, 1799; bur Dec 31, 1801
d   Henry Kimball b Mch 16, 1802; unt   e   William bap Dec 28, 1807; unt

William Dow habga d Newburyport Oct 7, 1800; no other data.

Betsey Dow habgb m Oct 28, 1793, Joseph Tyler.   Children, Newburyport rec:

a   Joseph b Apr 21, 1795; d on voyage from S A June 1817
b   Elizabeth b June 29, 1797
c   John b Dec 29, 1799; m June 20, 1834, Ann Coffin Dutton
d   Rebecca b Aug 19, 1802; m Feb 3, 1831, Joseph Morss Jr

Israel Dow habgc int pub Dec 7, 1805, to Jane Davis of Salem (Newburyport rec).

Edward Dow habgd b 1783; d Dec 14, 1825.

John Dow habge b 1786; d Mch 1802.

Jonathan Dow habgf drowned Sept 22, 1830.

Jonathan Dow habgg stranger d Apr 4, 1831.

Rhuany C Dow habgh int pub Newburyport Apr 1, 1842, to **David T Clark**; lived Amesbury.

John B Dow habgi farmer and shoemaker m (int pub Newbury Mch 7, 1835) Betsey Bickford b Barnstead, N H, d Rochester, N H, June 2, 1883, ae 81-11-3, dau of Charles.   A child:

a   John Bickford b Newburyport May 14, 1838; unt

Abigail Dow habgj admitted to Roxbury 4th church Oct 8, 1769.

Zilpah Dow habgk b Me 1804 at Salem hotel 1850 census; presumably wid with children b Mass:

a Helen b 1834   b Edwin b 1836; unt   c Anna b 1838

habgl. Six names in Salem rec, no parents given, but suggestive of a single family:

a Lucy F b Jan 9, 1826   b George W b May 9, 1830
c Olivia A b Feb 18, 1833   d Ocsar L b June 8, 1841
e William b June 18, 1843   f Nancy Melcher b Dec 18, 1848

David Dow habgm son of John b Sept 7, 1731 (names presumably garbled).

Joseph Dow habgn son of Joseph bap Aug 25, 1759.

Joseph Dow habgo d Dec 8, 1780 (no other data).

Hannah Dow (Mrs) habgp d Salisbury Dec 8, 1780 (no other data).

Hannah Dow habgq b Mass 1777; Lucy Dow b Mass 1811, presumably wid and dau, living Salisbury 1850 with Moses and Lucy Merrill.

Joseph Dow habgr b Salisbury Aug 22, 1788; m Apr 9, 1815, Ruth Gibson b 1795, d Aug 11, 1850, dau of Ensign James and Anna (Forrest) of Northfield. In 1850 they of Sanbornton; he living 1877 Sou Danbury. Children:

a Hazen b 1816; d Nov 5, 1820
b Polly G b Mch 21, 1821; m (Mary) of Sanbornton Dec 1844 Alpheus S Bean farmer of Belmont and Gilmanton; d without children Sept 1846

John G Dow habgs b 1790 in Salisbury 1850 census; no wife but next names presumably his children:

a Eunice b 1826   b Stephen b 1827; unt

Hannah Dow habgt int pub Salisbury, m Newburyport Dec 16, 1834, Thomas Jordan of Newburyport.

Sarah Dow habgu m Salisbury June 30, 1801, Abel Bagley; left a son John.

Reuben Eaton Dow habgv drowned Salisbury Beach Mch 23, 1810, ae 20.

William Dow habgw b Mass 1801, farmer without land; wife Margaret b Me 1800. Children b Mass, 1850 census:

a Mary b 1834   b Charles b 1840

Joshua Dow habgx b Mass 1800; farmer, realty $1,200; wife Abiah b N H 1798. Children, census:

a Amos b Mass 1833, laborer, unt   b Smith b Mass 1835; unt

Rebecca B Dow habgy of Salisbury int pub Sept 18, 1835, to Eli B Howard of Amesbury.

Walter Dow habgz b Mass 1810, stone mason; wife Mary b Mass 1811. Children b N H, 1850 census:

a   Henry b 1832, laborer, unt   b   Hannah b 1836   c   Lucy b 1838
d   Lewis b 1840; unt   e   Mary b 1842   f   Elvira b 1844

Meriam Dow habha m Oct 19, 1818, Stephen Fellows, both of Salisbury.

Mary Dow habhb of Coventry, Conn, m Mch 23, 1785, Isaac Roberts

Frances Dow habhd m Joseph Chandler. A child:

a   Lydia m Harmon Herrick of Southampton, L I, vet of 1812, d 1840. This
     suggests c Dow family

Lydia Dow habhe of Lyme m Jan 13, 1780, Roswell Beckwith. c line?

Lydia Dowe habhf m Mansfield May 25, 1773, Benjamin Agard.

Sarah Dow habhg of Middleton m Nov 14, 1781, William Warner, widower.

Susanna Dow habhh b Pomfret 1761; m July 16, 1775, Nathaniel Grow b May 25, 1753, d July 9, 1838, Rev veteran; moved to Guilford, Vt, later to Henderson, N Y, where she d July 31, 1814. Children b Windham, Conn:

a   Timothy b Oct 28, 1775; d Jan 9, 1779
b   Rebeckah b May 4, 1777; m (Conn rec Joel or John Bigelow) by Grow Gen
     John J Atwell; 2nd Hubbard Randall
c   Lucinda b Dec 12, 1778; m Elisha Chase of Guilford
d   Sally b Mch 27, 1781; m John Barney of Guilford
e   Abigail b Feb 18, 1783   f   Alva b Feb 13, 1786
g   Eaton b July 16, 1788

A number of Dow appear early in New York City but they are probably for the most part of the Dutch family of Douw, they themselves often spelling it Dow. Its best known is Abraham Dow, later of Albany, licensed Sept 24, 1761, to Catherine Lansinge. A genealogy of this family has been published.

Katherine Dow habhi owned land 1709.

George Dow witnessed a will Mamaroneck Oct 3, 1737.

Phebe Dow licensed to Benjamin Oakley Feb 7, 1773.

Sarah Dow licensed to Henry Inness July 15, 1777.

Rachel Dow licensed to Henry Van Renselaer Sept 18, 1786.

Isaac Dow m Margaret Angeoine, dau of Zachariah of New Rochelle; was executor of Zachariah's will Oct 26, 1739.

Mary Dow m Peter Chatterton. A child by own rec:

a   Hannah b Clinton, Dutchess Co, Jan 1, 1795; m Troy Aug 29, 1813, John Urann
    b Harlem Heights June 29, 1791

Henry Dow (three items possibly for one individual) in 2nd N Y reg, Capt Jonathan Holmes; licensed to —— Marsshalk Sept 13, 1780; witnessed (with John Dow) will of a Mr Siegler May 14, 1783.

John Dow in 1779 a mason; witnessed Siegler will 1783.

John Dow licensed to Elizabeth Dow July 5, 1781. John Dow witnessed (with William Dow and James Dow) will Oct 23, 1779, of George Willis of Newark.

James Dow licensed to Sarah Lewis Apr 11, 1775.

Moses Dow habhj private 1812, Capt John Hinchman.

Samuel Dow habhk enlisted N J for 5 years from May 11, 1812, Capt H H Van Dahlem.

Elijah Dow habhl of Northern Liberties, Pa, 1790 census 1a, 1b, 2c.

Alexander Dow habhm of Southwark, Pa, shoe manufacturer Front St, 1790 census, alone.

Samuel Dow in lodging house Philadelphia 1790.

Parthenia Dow, sister of Ann Morrison, mentioned in latter's will Philadelphia 1833.

James Dow habhn 2nd Lieut 3rd Pa reg Sept 25, 1775, to Oct 1776.

William Dow habho ensign 1st Md reg Apr 17, 1777; resigned Dec 1, 1777.

Peter Dow habhp of Fairfax Co, Va, in census list 1790; 1 dwelling, 3 other buildings, 1 white soul, 4 whites, 6 blacks. Perhaps the negroes and the four whites had no souls.

The British fleet off Sou Car 1783 was headed by H M S Perseverance, Capt Dow.

Robert Dow of Camden Dist, Sou Car by 1790 census 3a, 5b, 2c, 3d. Perhaps identical with ¡Robert Dow original grantee, May 16, 1791, of 1,000 acres Cole's Creek, La. He owned this land Oct 17, 1795.

Jose Dow habhq appears in a Spanish census of Natchez dist, Miss 1792.

Index to Supplement

The letter key, which readily identifies any of the more than 40,000 persons mentioned in this Book, and which, as the Book is alphabetically arranged, obviates the necessity of numbered pages, is continued in this supplemental index. A symbol beginning with a denotes descent from the first Dow immigrant,—Henry Dow of 1637. A symbol beginning with b denotes descent from the second Dow immigrant, —Thomas Dow immigrant,—Thomas Dow of 1639. There are seven Dow immigrants to America prior to 1775. A symbol herein beginning with h (eighth letter) denotes the collection of the more important Dow Items not yet connected with the genealogical main lines. If a symbol contains eight letters, the individual attached to it is of the eighth generation. A denotes a firstborn, b a secondborn, and so on—

ABBOTT Hannah habdyb
ADAMS Charles habff
Loisa haaby
AGARD Benjamin habhf
ALBRO Eliza H ahgceb
John ahgcec
ALDRICH Ellen B bcdbae
ALEXANDER Mary M wid ahbgika
ALLEN Jane C habaw
Josiah bbbfg
AMY Herman habda
ANDERIESON Barber adggdcea
ANDREWS Emma Victoria adgfbfbaa
ANGEOINE Margaret habhi
Zachariah habhi
ANSORGE Carl befchdc
ARNOLD Harold L adgfbfbaaa
L G haaapa
Madolin Tristram adgfbfbaaa
ATWELL John J habhh
AUSTIN Clara Isabella adkddgca
James adkddgca
Louisa wife adkddgca
BAGLEY Abel habgu
George K befifi
John habgu
Bailey William P bbbebfgb
BAKER Sukey hebef
BARKER Benjamin habai
William H abbegbeba
BARNARD Jacob abcfe
Oliver adgffb
Samuel abcfe
BARNEY John habhh
BARRETT Walter V befifijbc

BARTLETT Francis C ahbaxai
Jennie adaabceada
Judith adaaaha
Samuel haabz
BASS Bertha Inez ahbaxabb
—— ahbiic
BATCHELDER Betty abdcb
Ephraim abdcb
Josiah, Josiah Jr. abdcb
Mary Jane haabdta
Simon abdcb
BAYLEY Mehitable habda
BEADSLEE Rosa J wid haabtd
BEAL Pamelia habdz
BEAN Alpheus S habgrb
Ebenezer habbw
BECKMAN Mary E adkfbbcd
BECKWITH Roswell habhe
BELL Almira befiffb
Frederick befiffb
Ira befiffb
James Russell befiffb
Nathan befiffb
Margaret befiffb
Mary befiffb
BENEDICT Addie Cora ahchfie
Harriet ahchba
Nathan Dow ahchba
Robert ahchba
Sarah ahchba
BENSON Alfred ahbaxaea
Daisy ahbaxaea
BERRY Benjamin habcsa
Emily habcsa
Jeremiah abcec, habcq

997

Loving adaaafx
Paley wife habcsa
Sarah adgxca
BESSE Nellie Louisa bcfifhhf
Obediah B bcfifhhf
BESHARE Florence L ahbgikcb
BICKFORD Betsey habgi
Charles habgi
BIGELOW Joel (or John) habhh
BILLINGS Charles adaaafaf
BLAINE James G bcdebejcc
BLAIR Guenn Howard adadhcecb
James adadhcecb
BLAKE John befifi
L M adadabgb
BLAZO Joseph adacefc
BLISS Celia adgfbfbc
BOND Joseph H bcdedbaeb
BORDEN Edward A ahbgiig
Fred L ahbgiig
John W ahbgiig
BOTT Dolly N adkddgb
BOWEN Irene Eladsit haaaya
BOWLER David habfg
BOWLEY Eben abdcebega
Mary L abdcebega
BOYNTON Arthur Cleveland habfiaa
John habas
William Cune habfiaa
BRACKETT Anthony abcec
James ahbaaae
Samuel abcec
BRENTSCHOOTEN family adggdcca
BRIGGS Delilah bcdecaf
BRIGHT Charles adaaafxc
Elizabeth adaaafxc
Ellsworth adaaaxfc
Elvira H adaaaxfc
Emma adaaaxfc
George Washington adaaaxfc
Jacob Absalom adaaaxfc
John adaaaxfc
Lucinda adaaaxfc
Thomas Jefferson adaaaxfc
William adaaaaxxfc
BRIGHTMAN Israel adaaafg
BRINK family adggdcca
BROCKLEBANK Betsey E habdna
Samuel habdna
BROOKS Michael adabe
BROWN Asa, Jr. ahchg
Benjamin ahchg, habdm, habdp
Deborah ahchg
Dorothy habbk
Emeline Marilla ahchg
George K habcdb
Lillie H adkfbbcdg
Lucy ahchg
Martha ahchg
Maria ahchg
Mary habez
Mercy ahchg
Rebecca ahchg
Sarah ahchg
Wheeler ahchg

BRUNKEE Raymond adaceagcc
BUFFUM David habfj
BUGBEE Charles H. bcfifhkab
BUNKER Elizabeth adaaafd
Joshua adaaafd
BURBECK Mary Irving habac
BURNETT Alida B. bcdeddac
Lizzie M bcdeddac
W J bcdeddac
William T bcdeddac
BURNHAM Daniel abccdgba
Emma F abccdgba
George D abccdgba
BUSHEY N L adaceagcc
BUTLER Edward (Dr.) Jr. ahbaxabe
Harry ahbaxabe
BUXTON James H bcfifi
BUTTERFIELD Annie Stearns adgfb-
  fcc
BUZZELL Mattie abccdgbg
CAMPBELL Edith M adaigaaae
William ahbgike
CARPENTER Mary adgfcig
CARR Hannah L habem
CARSWELL Robert B (Dr) habdf
CARTER Levi habch
CASS Jonathan habig
CASTNER Calvin ahgcec
Rufus ahgcec
—— ahgcec
CASWELL James adgfbfba
Mehitable wife adgfbfba
Sarah Anna adgfbfba
CHADBOURNE Polly habbz
CHAMBERLAIN Adeline L adaabfe
Ebenezer adaabfe
Priscilla bcdedbad
CHANDLER Joseph habhd
Lydia habcr
Polly habbz
CHAPMAN Charity A ahgcib
Parley ahgcib
Ruth B adaafxeba
Samuel habam
CHASE Charles habbc
Helen abdcecceh
Lydia habor
CHATTERTON Hannah habhi
Peter habhi
CHENEY Lyman bcdbaddb
CHEEVER Eunice R adaabfex
Samuel G adaabfex
William M adaabfex
CHILDERS Erskine adadabcfaa
Erskine H adadabcfaa
CILLEY Abraham B adadabbe
Lydia habdf
Samuel B adadabbe
CLAFLIN Esther Irene adggefgxx
Ida Mae adggefgxx
William N S adggefgxx
CLANCY Annie M adgxfahbe
CLARK Benjamin adgxb
David T habgh
Edward Gove adgxb

998

Mary E adhafagba
Moses Elon adadhaaba
Susan A bbbebcdaea
CLAY Jennie adbabiax
CLEMENT Amos C bcbebib
CLOUD Sarah Isabelle ahbgiie
CLOUGH Charlotte adaaajb
COBB Charlotte adaaafac, wife adaa-
  afac
COBURN George D abcedgba
—— abcedgba
COFFIN Lydia adaaafa
Paul adaaafa
Ruth wife adaaafa
COLCORD Amos Adelbert abcegdceb
James abcegdceb
COLE Elizabeth A ahgcif
Margaret a
Mehitable bededef
Richard a
COLEMAN —— ahgced
COLLINS Mary bbbffcbaf
Susanna habbu, habie
Susanna P bcdbaddb
COMINGS Albert ahbaaabb
Albert Gallatin ahbaaabb
Albert Luther ahbaaabb
Ben Dow ahbaaabb
Carrie Lydia ahbaaabb
Mary Elizabeth ahbaaabb
Nellie Maud ahbaaabb
CONNELL Paul ahgfdaec
CONNERY James bcdbedbadb
COPP Jacob habax
James Madison habax
Julian Philbrick habax
Katherine Elsie ahbgiid
Malinda habax
Stephen Ladd habax
COOK Benjamin habfl
Doris ahbgiide
Edna ahbgiide
Elizabeth ahgcea, habhc
Esther ahbgiidde
Fred Herman ahbgiide
Nellie ahbgiide
COOPER Agnes E adaaafxd
Alzina E adaaafxd
James Monroe adaaafxd
John habcu
Medora adaaafxd
COSSON George abcedgbg
COWALSKI Carolyn Louise ahbgilia
COX Mary E adgfcig
Thomas adgfcig
CRAM Alonzo W haaaqb
Hannah habcc
Thomas habcc
CRAWFORD Annie adadhcccb
Annie J adadhcec
CREIGHTON —— ahbaaae
CRISSWELL Pearl ahbgikcb
Samuel B ahbgikcb
CROCKER Elizabeth adgxfahbd
John bcfifi

CROCKETT Josiah adabbc
Sarah adabbc
Crosby Ada adabbgagaa
CROSSETT Lewis A adgfbfcc
CROWLEY Mary ahgchhc
CROWTHERS Lillian H bcbfhkaa
CUMMINGS Annie F bcdgddaab
CURRIER John H habeh
CURRIER Wm Jr.
CURTIS Augustus ahgheg
Bildad ahgheg
CURTIS William F bcdbaddfa
Bildad ahgcg
Augustus ahgcg
Caroline ahgcg
Emily ahgcg
Joanna ahgcg
John ahgcg
Julia ahgcg
Lucy ahgcg
Marvin ahgcg
Mary ahgcg
Roderick ahgcg
Samuel, Samuel Jr ahgcg
William A ahgcg
CUSHING Edward Harmon bcfifhkaa
Helen bcfifhkaa
CUTTER Charles Winthrop bcfihecc
Irving Taylor bcfihecc
Leonard Francis bcfihece
Lillian Arnold bcfihecc
Lucy Elizabeth bcfihecc
DAME Temperance habaf
DANFORTH Robert bcfifi
DAVENPORT Alice ahgce
DAVIES Jacob Ernest adhcbbggb
Jacob Poure adhcbbggb
DAVIS Eleazer haabu
Etta E haabmb
Greeley ahchea
Hannah E bcfigfbd
Jane habgc
John C bcfigfhd
John J haaawc
John L bcdecaf
Lott ahchea
Mary adabbgaga
Mary C haaawc
Thankful ahdaab
DEAN Ephraim ahbgili
Minnie ahbgili
DEARBORN Reuben Gore aeeaa
DEMERRITT Abigail wife habfp
John habfp
William H habfp
DE MON family adggdcca
DE PUY family adggdcca
DE VOS (Reynard) Catherine adggd-
  cca
DE WITT family adggdcca
DEXTER George H ahgceaaa
Miles D ahgceac
Nettie ahgceaaa
DICKINSON Henry adkddgcce
DICY Mary adabih

999

DIMMICK Melinda ahgcj
DIMOCK Joanna ahgeg
DOANE Benjamin F ahchffb
Florence M ahchffb
George W ahchffb
Susan B ahchffb
Viola M ahchffb
William Henry ahchffb
DODGE Maryetta adaceff
DOE Alden haabe
Franklin haabia
John habbj
DORMAN Joseph, Joseph Jr ahgchc
Lucy wife ahgchc
Lucy Maria ahgchc
Martha habfa
Richard Augustus ahgchc
DOW Aaron adaaaafx
Aaron M (adkehce) habdq
Abbie ahbaxai, wife habcs
Abby Frances haaaqb
Abiah wife habgx
Abigail abbeaa, abccdgbe, abdca, hab-
  ai, habcw, habgj, habig
Abner Gilmore bcbhddagfd
Abraham adgfbfb, adhcce
Ada E adgcadaaba
Ada J adgfcdgf
Ada Louise ahgchhd
Ada Salisbury ahbghgb
Adeline adacefd
Adelaide haaayae
Adeline bcbhddcf
Albert adgfbfbc, ahbaxaea, habbpaa,
  habedc
Albert F adhafagb
Albert Gallatin ahbghg, ahbghgf, ah-
  bghgfc
Albert L habfab
Albert Webster bcdedbada
Albert Woodbury abbegfjca
Aletha L bcdgddaabac
Alexander adaaafc, haaaked, habhm
Alexander B habce
Alfred haaam
Alfred Nason adkfbbcdgd
Alice adaabdd, wife bcdccaf, bcdgdda-
  abe
Alice Lincoln bcdedcfebb
Allecia ahgced
Alma habeda
Almira habdf
Almira G adkddfac
Almon P habbka
Almys Forest adadiabfd
Alonzo E befifjdf
Alphonso habeva
Alphia Chapin ahcfggf
Alphia Hutchins ahcfgg
Althie M habcjc
Alton F adaabceab
Alvin haabmc
Alzina Elizabeth adaaafxf
Amanda L ahgciae
Amos habgxa

Amos Webster habbv
Amy Gertrude ahchfieb
Andrew A haabv
Andrew J bbbebcha
Ann habfza
Ann Isabelle bedgdagi
Ann Maria adaaafaac, haaaqc
Ann Katherine befihdb, haabvb
Ann P habdw
Anna ahgcee, haben, wife habfz, habgze
Anna Amy ahchfidb
Annette adhcbbdb
Annie bbbebcia, bbbebfgb
Annie E ahgcifb
Annie Elvira bcbcbbgbaa
Arnold Forbes adadhceeba
Arthur B adaigaaae
Arthur Vivian ahbgiiea
Arthur W ahbgiih
Asa bbbebcha, bcdedbae, bcdcdeg, haa-
  bi, habeb
Augusta ahcfg, ahgcibc, wife habef
Atlas Emma Dolph ahcfgb
Augusta Mary bbbffcbaf
Augustus Francisco ahgchh, ahgchhb
Augustus Wolston habdyb
Austin habewa
Azubah adacefh
Belle habdyaaa
Beniah adgfcdg
Benjamin ahba, ahbaxb, ahchff, ahchh,
  haaaq, haabq, haaby, habbn, habeta
Benjamin F bbbfhedc, haaby
Benjamin Franklin ahbghgfd
Bernice May adaigaaaca
Bert bcdgddaaba
Bertha E adadhcece
Bertha Emmaline adadhceea
Beryl E bbbfhedaf
Bessie ahchfigh
Bessie Alice ahbgiiha
Bessie Mabel bcdgddaabad
Betsey abccdgbg, adaabfeb, adgeacd,
  ahgck, habbr, habcd, habfm, habgb,
  habib
Betty Loraine ahbgikcba
Beverley A ahgcif
Celista ahchhb
Carleton William adhafagbaa
Carolina ahchfidc
Caroline ahfcggb, bcdecae
Caroline L habetb
Catherine haabr
Cecil E ahbgiidd
Charles ahgcead, ahgceg, bbbebc, bbb-
  bfhedcb, haaacb, habdyac, habgwb
Charles A bcdedhadd
Charles Chase adkddgc
Charles E adbabiad, habejb
Charles Edward habdoe
Charles Edwin ahbaxabd
Charles F adadibca
Charles Farrington ahgehfcc
Charles Forrest adkddgcca
Charles Fulton haaax

1000

Charles Horace adacefgb
Charles Howard adkddbeba
Charles J adaaafxeba
Charles L haaan
Charles Leonard bedbeceebe
Charles S adkfbbcd
Charles Phineas befifjdd
Charles W adgfbbbb, habesa
Charlotte adaaafaeb, ahbabab, habbs, habbt, habie, habid
Charlotte A ahgciaa
Charlotte Augusta bedebed
Charlotte Frances haabteab
Charlotte Rebecca adaaafaefa
Chester Perry bedecaca
Chester Sullings adacefgce
Chloe habfx
Clara ahchfide
Clarissa ahehba, wife habap, habbh
Clementine adacefe
Comfort abdeb
Corett bededbade
Cornelia Jane ahgeiab
Cornelia Johnson ahgeiab
Cynthia F befifide
Cyrus adkfbda, ahgcib
Cyrus B bbbebdae
Cyrus P adkfbdaa
Daniel ahbab, ahbaxaa, bbbebei, haaa, habab, habbz, habdn, habdy, habeeb, habej, habfi, habfib
Daniel Buswell adabibeaa
Daniel Clark ahgej
Daniel M ahchfidg
Daniel T habejb
Darius habeb
David ahbaxab, bbbffad, bedgddaab, haaakb, haaakec, habaa, habek, habgm
David Elwyn abbegbebba
David Mason ahbaxab
David Smith haaba
Deborah habam, habbw
Dennis J habej
Derby habey
DeWitt C habfq
DeWitt Confield ahgeigb
DeWitt Clinton adaabejfb
Dexter Dean ahbgilg
Dinah adabbd
Dolly adaabdd, habfj
Dora ahchfigf
Dora Hamilton ahbghgfa
Dorcas Neal adheed
Doris E adabbgaganb
Doris Muriel bebhddagfa
Dorothy habaebb
Earl Chester bedgddaabe
Earty bededbade
Eben habed
Ebenezer adadhee
Eda habdu
Eda E adggefxx
Edgar adabbgagaa

Edgar A ahgcifa
Edith ahchfigg
Edith M adaabceada
Edward bedbaddf, habgd
Edward Buchanan ahbgile
Edward H adabbgagaa
Edward Huntington ahgehj
Edna May adkfbbcdgb
Edwin adgdfagba, haaada, habgzb
Eleanor abcee
Elijah adaaaaa, adaaah, habbl
Elisha ahdaab
Elisha A ahehfid, ahchfidh
Elisha M befifide
Elisha Rhodes Wright ahefgge
Eliza ahgceba, bbbffeg, bedecad, haaakeb habbi, habea
Elizabeth aeeaa, ahdae, bededgh, bcfii, wife haabi, habav, habba, habek, habep, habde, habdn, habex, habfa, habft, habhi
Elizabeth A ahbacaeb, habbpab
Elizabeth Ioa ahchfidf
Ella A bedhaddfa
Ella B habeve
Ellen adgfbfbh, ahchfidd, bedeaedbb, haaakef, habdybb
Ellen Gardner adgxfahbea
Ellen L adgfbfbba
Elmira bebhddeg
Elvira adacefe, habgzf
Elsie bedebijee
Elvira A adgfedge
Elzina ahbgiidbb
Emelie ahbaxaf
Emilie Genevieve ahgchla
Emily adgfbfberb, bebhddee
Emily Ann ahbaxaf
Emily F adaaafaee
Emma adbabiab, ahefggfa, habeja, habdyad
Emma Anne ahbaxabb
Emma F haabe
Emma J ahbaaabb, befhiece
Emma Maria ahgecaab
Emmet A ahgehje
Enos haaaf
Ephraim ahgcee, ahgceebd
Ernest bedgddaabd
Ernest B bedgdbaaga
Esther Belle bbbffedfd
Ethel A adkddgeab
Ethel M bededefdb
Errold Norman bededbbdbb
Ethel M bededebdb
Ethel Mildred adkddfaea
Ethel R adkfbbedgg
Eugene haabmb
Eugene E bededbad
Eugene L habewb
Eunice ahgcebc, ahgcha, haaakee, habfe, wife habew, habgsa
Eunice Isabelle ahbgiieeb
Fannie ahefggfe, ahgceac
Fanny ahgcee, wife haaao

Flora Anita bcbcbaacd
Flora P bbbcbdaca
Florence Lida adadiabfc
Florence M haabtcb
Flossie Lonayne haabtcac
Forest A adadiabf
Fostean bcbffb
Foster adacfdx
Frances habhd
Frances Augusta ahgchhe
Frances Currier bbbcbgaa
Frances Irene ahbgiieba
Francis ahgfdae, haabwa, habwaa
Francis Byron adgxfaaf
Frank ahgfdaeb, ahbaxaaa, ahbgiidb,
  bcfifjddc, haaayb
Frank Edward bcfigfddc
Frank P adkfbbed, dkfbbcd
Frank R ahchfidi
Frank Scott ahbgilf
Frank Wells ahbgiid
Fred S haabtca
Frederick adaabcead
Frederick A adhcbbjab, haabna
Frederick Augustus adhcbbjab
Frederick Dwight ahgcihc
Frederick Houghton ahgcih
Frederick Howard adkddgca
Frederick Sewell ahgchjba
Freeman bbbffab
Frostine A ahgcifc
Furber adkddgb
George adaaafa, adaaafaa, adkddgbb,
  haaaa, haaakcg, haaal, habdyaa, hab-
  hi
George A adgxfahb, aeeacac, haabac
George Alvin adhafcabd
George Bidwell ahgchjbc
George C adaaafacg
George E adgxfahbe
George Edward ahfcfcba
George Gordon haaam
George H adggefgx
George Harvey bcdedcga
George Henry habfna
George Lincoln haaaqa
George Lovejoy bbbebcbd
George M ahbaxada
George Raymond haabtcaa
George W abccdgcaa, adaabfea, adac-
  efi, bbbfhcdb, haaap, habglb
Georgianna habdcaa
Gertrude Lucetta ahchfecc
Gladys Belle adabibcaad
Gladys M bbbfhcdcac
Gordon Blair adadhcecbb
Grace Eleanor ahchfiec
Grace Gardner adgxfahbd
Grace H adbabiadb
Grace Louisa bcffhkab
Grace M ahgchjf
Guy Alvin adhafcabde
Guy Wigston ahbgiiec

Hannah abcfe, ahgchc, ahgff, bcdedbah,
  bcfihi, haaai, haabg, haabu, haabz,
  habae, habaj, habel, habbf, habbm,
  habdp, habdr, habfb, Mrs. habgp, ha-
  bgq, habgt, habgzb
Hannah G haaaa
Hannah A wife habbd
Harold Wright bbbebgacb
Harrie Arthur ahbgiihb
Harriet wife habbd, wife habcf
Harriet F ahgfdaec
Harriett habeec
Harris haaah
Harry ahgcea, habhc
Harry E abdcicaba, bbbffcbac
Harry F bcbhddcda
Harvey habedb
Harvey M bcbebbbdc, bcbebbbfac
Hattie Charlotte habfiaa
Hattie E bcdeabdab
Hazel Lillian adacefgcd
Hazel Marie adhafcabda
Hazen habgra
Helen abbeebcaaa, habgka
Helen Gertrude adaabceaaaa
Henry a, adaaaf, adaaafxeb, adaabceaa,
  adgfbfbg, haaabd, habef, habgza, ha-
  bhi
Heman habef
Henry D habdd
Henry E bcbebbfa
Henry Eugene adaabceaaa
Henry G ahgciha
Henry H (adkfbbja) adkfbbcd
Henry Kimball adaaafxe, habfzd
Henry P habay
Henry S adkddgcb
Henry W habfn
Henry Ware abdcicab
Hepzibah ahgcg
Herbert H ahgcihaa
Herman bcdedcgaa
Hezekiah Farrington ahgchfe, ahgchfeb
Hezekiah Richardson ahgchf
Homer haaae
Horace adacefg
Horace M adgcadaaa
Horace Nelson adacefgca
Howard haaaca
Howard F adkfbbcdgh
Howard Ransom bcbebaacd
Howard Wilson ahbgikcb
Ilda Eulalia ahbgiiebb
Inez N bcfifjfaaa
Ioa Jeannette bcfifjddb
Ione E haaayad
Ira adaabdd, haabmd
Ira Benton ahbgiiee
Isaac adacef, adaceff, haaaa, habhi
Isaac F habfs
Isaac W ahbghga
Isaac Wilson ahbgik
Isabelle ahchffb
Isaiah bcbhddcd
Israel habgc

Ivory haabn
J S haaat
Jacob adaaaha, haabgh, haber
Jacob E haabtb
Jacob Lovering habfcb
James adaaafx bcbcbaa, haaaka, habdb,
　habew, habhi, habhn
James B ahgchje
James C (Lieut) haabb
James Caswell adgfbfbaa
James Crawford habeca
James Colony befifff
James Gilman adaabdd
James Elton ahcfggfb
James Jewett abdcebeg
James M ahchfidj, haaawc, habes
James Maurice adaaafxea
James Richardson ahgchl
James S adgfbfbe
Jane ahbaxag, ahgceaad, habbe, habdh,
　habdm, habdt, habdtb, habdyba, wife
　habel
Jane Abigail adaaafxc
Jane Augustella ahgchcha
Jane C wife habec
Jeanette ahgcihb
Jeannette D bebebbfac
Jedediah adhcc, adhccf
Jefferson bcdeaefa
Jennie haabtba
Jennie A adhcbbje
Jennie C wife habec
Jennie V bcdedbaeb
Jeremiah abccdgb, adgfga, bcbhddch,
　(adadie) haben
Jerome Napleon Bonaparte adkfbbcd
Jerome Bradley bcbchhea
Jesse Bradley bcbchhe, bcbchheb
John abccdgcaa, abccdgcb, adaabfe, ad-
　babia, adgcadaa, adgfbfbcb, ahche,
　ahchfigc, bbbfhcd, haaag, habcs, Jr
　habct, habcy, habee, habej, habeub,
　habge, habgi, habgm, habhi
John Bickford habgia
John C habfp
John Calvin bcbehhib
John E bbbebcdbe
John G ahchfie, habgs
John N ahbaxac
John O adbabiaa, ahbaxaba
John Palmer habbk
John R bcdebfa
John Rogers ahbghge
John W abdcebega, adkfbbcd, haaat
Jonathan adaabfe, adabih, adabihc, ad-
　gxca, adhccg, bcdedcf haaau, habgf,
　habgg
Jonathan R habev
Johnson S ahgciac
Jose habhq
Jose Keach ahbgili
Joseph adaaafx, adgxca, ahbgil, bcbh-
　ddci, haaad, haaas, haabtd, habet, ha-
　bete, habgn, habgna, habgo, habgr
Joseph Allen (adkfbbjb) adkfbbcd

Joseph Emerson bcfihc
Joseph French bbbebcbb, habdca
Joseph L habeca
Joseph P habdua
Joseph R habeuc
Joseph W habfk
Joseph Warren (adkfbbj) adkfbbcd
Josephine Martha ahgchjbd
Joshua habgx
Josiah ahbax, ahbaxa, habcd
Josiah L ahbaxadb
Joy Wheeler ahgchhc, ahgchhbc
Joyce Cavella ahbgiiecc
Juanita adacefgcaa
Judith ahbaaad
Julia wife habed
Julia A bcdedbadb
Julia P ahbabale
Julia R haabha
Julius E bcfifjdca
Justin haabma
Justin Sylvanus haaay
Kate befifjddf
Kate E ahgdcce
Katherine habhi
Katherine Stanley adkfbbcdga
Kenneth Bryant ahbgiied
Kenneth Carman adhcbbajd
Kenneth H haaapaa
Kezia B habce
Ladd bbbebch
Lafayette adaceafe
Laura haaabe
Lavenda ahcfgga
Laverna Frances ahbgilib
Lavina ahgcf
Lavinia haaabc
Leafy Maud bcdedcgaca
Lelia befifjdda
Leola G ahbgiide
Leonard M bcdbececb
Leonora M abbegbig
Levi abbegbig, habeg, habdj, habdo
Lewis bcfifjdb, habdz, habgzd, habhi
Lillia Edith adkddfaeb
Lillian bcfifhkac
Lillian Delia adkddfaef
Lillian G adkfbbcdgf
Lillian Jane ahbgile
Lillian Lucy adccdgcaad
Lillie ahchfigi
Lillie A adacefia
Lisle Warren ahbgiidf
Livona haabl
Lizzie adgfbfbf, ahchfifj
Lizzie Allan ahggbdaäa
Lizzie M adgxfahbb
Lois habbx, habdcc
Lorain Elizabeth adacefga
Lorenzo abccdgbc, bcbcbbfb, bcdbaddj
Lorenzo G bbbebfg
Louis Henry habaca
Louis A beffhkaa
Louis Irving habacba
Louisa adadabgb

1003

Louisa Laverna ahbgiliaa
Louisa M ahchfida
Louisa P adgxfahba
Lovinia wife haaas
Lucenda wife haaau
Lucetta habdya
Lucien B ahgceaac
Lucien R habfsa
Lucinda haabgb, habdyab
Lucinda E aeeacaae
Lucinda Flavilla adaaafxd
Lucy abccgdceb, adgffb, ahchea, ahchg,
  habda, habgqa, habgzc
Lucy A bcdeabdab
Lucy F habgla
Ludlow E ahgcihe
Lycurgus haabqa
Lydia adaaafab, adaaafb, adaabfed, ad-
  abe, adgfbfbca, ahbaxc, bbbebcdaeaa,
  befiffb, habar, habas, habbo, wife ha-
  bcj, habdi, habdod, habhe, (Dowe)
  habhf
Lydia C habfg
Lydia M adgfcig
Lydia Metcalf ahbgiic
Lyford ahbaba
Lyman N habci
Lyman O haaaj
Lyman White ahgchja
M C L habcjc
Mahala Esther bcbhbdfgba
Malvina haabta
Malvina C ahchffa
Marea Agnes adaaafxebb
Margaret bcbhddce, wife habgw
Margaret A ahchfik
Margaret E haaab
Margarita ahchfiga
Margarite Williams adabbgagaae
Margery bbbfg
Margey habad
Maria Hepzibah ahbghgd
Maria Isabelle ahchfeh
Maria L W wife haabv
Maria Maholm ahbghgfb
Marie C adhebbgga
Marion adbabiadxa, adkfbbcdgi, bcd-
  ebejcc
Marjorie C haaapab
Marlin adaaafxeca
Martha adacfb, adgfbfbd, ahdfa, habcja
Martha Pearl adadiabfa
Martha W ahchffc
Mary abca, abccdgbf, adaaafe, (adab-
  bgc) adabbd, adkfbbcd, adhebbdd,
  ahchfige, bcdecab, haaabb, haaak,
  haaakca, haabva, wife habca, wife
  habcl, habcu, habcv, habcz, habdeb,
  habfd, wife habfq, habfr, habfv,
  (Mrs) habfw, habfzb, habgwa, wife
  habgz, habgzc, habhb, habhi
Mary A ahbaxai, bcbhdeg, wife haab-
  wa, habfic
Mary Ann ahbghgc
Mary Barbarita ahchfidk

Mary Barnum ahchec
Mary C adaaafaca
Mary E adaabccaab, ahgceaaa, habcda
Mary Eliza ahchfed, haaaqd
Mary Esther haabsx
Mary Eunice ahbgiig
Mary Eloretta abbegbeba
Mary Frances ahbaxabc
Mary G habgrb
Mary Jane habfnb
Mary Josephine ahgchjd
Mary Louise adhafagbaaa
Mary Roxana habaaa
Masa habaz
Maurice adaaafxeaa
Mehitable befiha, haabo
Mehitable S adgfbfbaaa
Melinda adabihb, habch
Meleissa H habfca
Melvina haabtbb
Meredith M bcdgdbaagaa
Meriam habha
Mertie M adkddfad
Meshech Weare adkdbf, adkdbfa
Milton ahchfig
Milton H ahbgiidc
Minnie befifidde, wife habdyaa
Minnie B bcdedbaea
Miriam adgxb, adgxd, habdv, habeea,
  habez, habff
Miriam B wife adhafagbaa
Molly ahbabx, habbj, habfy
Morrell Thornton ahefggfd
Moses abccdga, adaaafx, bcbeba, habcf,
  habdg, habhj
Moses M haaaw
Muriel M bcdgdbaagab
Myron W adgceadaabc
Myrtle befifjjbc
Myrtle L adabbgagab
Moses Franklin befihda
Nadine adhebbggb
Nancy ahcbfa, ahgcebb, bcdecaf, be-
  fifida, wife haabm, haban, habax, ha-
  bbb, habbg, habbl, habbq, haben, ha-
  bcq, habeg, habei, habfe, habia
Nancy C wife habeu
Nancy Melcher habglf
Nancy T habdc
Nancy Waterman ahbgike
Naomi A haaayac
Nathan ahdaag, habep
Nathan L habcia
Nathaniel F haabf
Neal Hill adaaafxec
Ned Emerson adgfbfbecb
Nellie adkddgece, ahbgiida, haabtda
Nellie Augustine ahgeiga
Nellie Frances ahbaxabe
Nellie J wife adaabccab
Nellie Leone ahgcigbb
Nellie M adgxfahbc
Nelson A adabbgaga
Nelson Haskell adabbgaga
Nettie Lucinda ahchfecb

1004

464

Newell adkddfa
Newell Francis adkddfaec
Newton bcdedcda, ahcfggd
Noah (Capt) adaabfe
Norman N ha
Obediah habeo
Olive ahgceae, haabga
Olive A habeh
Olive Smith ahdaabb
Oliver ahgccaf
Oliver Lawrence bcdeabda
Olivia A habglc
Orlon S haaaz
Orra ahchha
Orren ahbaxad
Orrin ahgceag, ahgcef
Oscar L habgld
Oscar Wentworth adadhceca, adadhceeb
Owen W bbbfhcdca
Parker habap
Parthenia habhm
Paul Crowthers befifhkaaa
Paul Audrey adacefgcb
Paul N bcdgdbaagac
Pearl Elizabeth bbbfhcdcad
Penelope Davis ahdaabc
Peter befifjd, habhp
Peter Staub bcdbeceeb
Phebe ahgceah, habhi
Phebe Ann adaaafacc
Phebe Jane Wilson ahbgika
Philip B habem
Philo hbbd
Phyllis A befifhkaab
Polly ahcheb, befihg, haabk, habdk
Polly G habgrb
Rachel bcbhddcb, habhi
Ralph Harold bbbffidfd
Ralph Noyes habacb
Ray Gordon bbbffedfa
Raymond adgfbfbcca
Rebecca adaaafda, adaaafe, adaaabbe,
  ahdaai, bcdbaddb, habaq, bcdbaddb,
  bcbhddca, habfl
Rebecca B habgy
Rebecca Clendennin habdb
Reuben adaaafacf, bcdedbd
Reuben Eaton habgv
Rex ahchfied
Rhoda habbc
Rhuany C habgh
Richard befigfddcb, bcdedcd
Richard D haaapa
Robert habhp
Robert Edward ahgchjbb
Robert James bcbcbaacd
Rogers adhcbbjaa
Roland E bcdgddaabaa
Roland H habfoc
Rollin Topan adkfbbcdge
Roy J ahbaxaea
Rufus ahgceaa
Ruth adadiabfb, haabx, wife habab,
  habde
Ruth Blanche bbbfhcdaf

Ruth Ellen adadabcfaa
Ruth L habdx
Ruth Viola adacefgcc
Sadie Louise adkddgcaa
Sally haabs, bcbebib, habag, habah, ha-
  bak
Sally Ann ahdaagj
Samuel adaaafa, adaaaja, adaabdd, ad-
  kfbbcdgc, ahgceb, haa, haaab, haaac,
  haabg, haabs, haabt, haabtc, haabtc,
  habdy, habhk, habhm
Samuel H adaaafaaa
Samuel Hall abccdgbb
Samuel Lester adhcbbjabc
Samuel Oscar bcbebbbdb
Samuel Otis habaw
Samuel J Tilden adkfbbcdg
Samuel Warren bcbebbbdbc, bbbffae
Sarah abbeh, adabbc, adacfc, ahbaaae,
  bcdecaa, befihdc, wife haaav, hab-
  ckj, habcx, haben, habfo, habfh, ha-
  bgu, habhg, habhi
Sarah A adadhaaba, adkddfab
Sarah Ann habdq
Sarah Bartlett adaaahac
Sarah C adadabbe
Sarah E bcdeddae
Sarah Eliza haabab
Sarah F adgfbfcc, habcdb
Sarah H adgfgad
Sarah Hall abccdgba
Sarah L adkddgcaa
Sarah M haaawa, habcvb
Sargent bcbcbaae
Servander C adkddfae, adkddfaec
Servander N adkddfaed
Severa McAfee ahchfiea
Sibbel bcdedi
Sidney adaaafx
Sidney Glenn ahbgiib
Simeon G habawa
Simon abccdg, abccgab, abccgacj, ahg-
  cia
Smith habgxb
Solomon ahgci
Solon befifhka
Sophia bcbebbda
Sophia B adaabfex
Sophia E ahgciad
Stella M adaabceadb
Stephen ahcbg, habcc, habgsb
Stephen G ahbaxae
Stephen Ricker abbegbebbb
Stephen S habdna
Susan adaaaff, adbabia, wife ahbaxac,
  ahbaxah, habco, habej, wife habej
Susan C haabp, habaf
Susan Fisher adaaafaab
Susan H haabw
Susan Jane habfia
Susan K habfc
Surviah wife habcm
Susanna ahchfigd, habat, habau, habhh
Susannah (Mrs) habfu
Tabitha abdcebf

Tabitha **Blake** abdcebcc, abdcebf
Thele ahbgiidbc
Theodore habeua
Theodore E ahgchjb
Theodore H habeu
Thomas haaav, habcy
Thomas Edward habac
Thomas J bcdeaef
Thomas L haabmd
Thomas S haabm
Thomas W adbabiadxd
Timothy abccdgbd
Tisdale Justin haaayaa
Tirzah ahgci
Tristram **Coffin** adaaajb
Tristram **M** adgfbfbaab
Tristram **Storey** adgfbfba
Tryphena ahgfdd
Ulysses **Grant** adgfbfbcc
Valeria ahbgiidba
Vinal **Curtis** adabbgagaaa
Wallace adgcadaab
Waldo **Hayward** bbbebcdeea
Wallace E adaceagcc
Walter habgz
Walter **Abraham** bcfifijaa
Walter B adaabceaab
Walter Ed adbabiadx, ahbgilia
Walter Edwin ahbaxabda
Walter Everett adhafagba
Walter **Gilman** adaaafacfa
Warren A adadhcecb
Warren Hazen adadhcec
Warren P haabtda
Weare habcq
Webster **M** bcdedhad
Wesley haaaa
Wilber **Olin** haaaya, haaayab
Wilbur **Horace** adacefgc
Wilbur **N** haaawb
Willard adaceafea
William adkddgba, adgxfagba, ahgceab,
  haaaba, haaakc, haaaoa, haabc, ha-
  abh, haabtf, habbr, habbu, habdnb,
  habdya, haber, habfz, habfzc, habfze,
  habga, habgle, habgw, habhi, habho,
  habib, habie
William **Adams** ahbgild
William **Bradford** ahgchfea
William **D** ahgchfigb
William E adaabfcc
William H adgcadaabb, bbbffcdf
William **Henry** bcfigfbd
William L W abdcebeh
William **N** adkddgcc, habfo
William **P** ahdaagi
Willie **Bert** bcdgddaabab
Winnifred adabbgagaaf
Winona adabbgagaag
Winslow **Herman** adaabfe
Winslow L ahgcihd
Winthrop **Griffin** adadbcfab
Winthrop Y abccgacj
Wyman **Edward** ahbgiiebc
Wyman **Everet** ahbgiie

Wyman L ahbgiidbe
Zelphia habdl
Zeruiah habey
Zilpah habgk
DOWNEY Malena **Della** ahbgika
DOWNING Ethel bcdgddaaba
Willie E bcdgddaaba
DREW Chandler habag
Daniel habag
Hezekiah habag
John habag
Jonathan habag
Lydia habag
Mary habag
Sarah wife habag
Zebulon (Lieut) habag
—— haabtba
DUNHAM Amy ahcheb
Andrew Jackson ahcheb
DUNSMORE Maude **T** ahbgika
DUPUY see Depuy
DUSENBARK —— bcdecaf
DUSTIN —— (Miss) bbbebch
DUTTON Ann **Coffin** habgb
DWIGHT Clara habdq
Henry L habdq
DYKE Molly habdc
EASTMAN Nathaniel Coggswell bcfih-
  db
EASTON Albert adaaafaca
George adaaafaca
Sarah wife adaaafaca
EATON Amanda habdi
Andrew habdoc
Christopher habdoc
Daniel habdi
Eleanor Frances adgxfahb
George habdi
Hannah adabbd
James adgxfahb
Jonathan adabbd
Liona **G** adaabceaa
Lydia habcw, habdi, wife habdoc
Mabel **Elizabeth** adaabceaaa
Margaret **A** wife adaabceaaa
Metthew adaabceaaa
Nancy habdi, habdo
Samuel habdi, habdk
EDMANDS Artemus Bradford aeeac-
  aae
Arthur Bradford aeeacaae
Fanny aeeacaae
Frank aeeacaae
George aeeacaae
EDWARDS Mary Jane ahbgilf
EGBERTSON Maritie adggdcca
ELLIOTT Charles Hayes bcbcbhghaa
Harriet Louise bcbcbbgbaa
David bcdeaef
Rachel bcdcaef
ELLINGWOOD Abigail habdd
ELLIS Grateful bcdecaca
ELWELL George abccdgbg
ELWYN David abbegbebba
Rae abbegbebba

1006

EMERSON Daniel habaf
Joseph habaf
Mehitable habdna
EMERY Abbie wife ahfcfcba
Daniel ahfcfcba
Georgia A ahfcfcba
ERWIN Henry Lee ahbgilib
EVANS Annie M haaaw
FANNING Delafayette ahbgika
FARNUM Emma bcdbaddb
FARNSWORTH Edward M ahgchla
FELCH Daniel habdh
Squier habbt, habid
FELLOWS Alice Mary bbbffcbaf
Charles H bbbffcbaf
Flora Cyrene bbbffcbaf
Richard bbbffcbaf
Stephen habha
FERGUSON Estelle M ahbgilc
FISH Addie habdybb
Bertha habdybb
Grace habdybb
Hiram B habdybb
FISHER Abraham adaaafaa
Jane adaaafaa
FITTS Clarissa A haabtca
George haabtca
FLEBER Nellie adaaafxea
FLECKINSTINE Charles Henry ahch-
feh
Daisy Susetta ahchfeh
Etoile Esther ahchfeh
John Charles ahchfeh
Nellie Belle ahchfeb
FLEISHER Amelia haaapa
FLETCHER Lododiski Maria haabr
FOGG —— adgxb
FOLGER Francis adaaafda
Susan wife adaaafda
FOLLANSBEE Sarah E habdf
FOLLETT Hannah ahba
FOLSOM Clarissa Augusta habdv
George Frost habdv
Israel habck
FOOTE A J ahcheb
FORREST Anna habgr
FOSS Isaiah habcz
FOSTER David habfa
Myra P adadiabf
Timothy habfa
FREEMAN Milo habfx
FRENCH Augusta habdcb
Caroline habdcb
Hannah habdcb
Irene S adkddgcc
Josiah habdcb
Luther William habdcb
Nicholas P Jr habdcb
FULLER Betsey ahgceaa
Ellen Louise bcbhbdfgba
James habbm
Judith habee
GALE Eliza haabt
Warren ahbgiiecd
GALLUP Albert ahchha

Benjamin Dow ahchha
David ahdac
Isaac, Isaac Jr ahchha
John ahchha, ahdac
Jonathan ahdac
Lucy ahdac
Lucy E ahchha
Martha E ahchha
Sarah ahchha
Simon ahdac
Thomas ahdac
GARDNER Eliakim adaaafab
Pamela wife adaaafab
Timothy M adaaafab
GARVILLE Addie haaap
GATES Benjamin habfr
Leda Cleo ahbgiieb
GEER Darwin Lyman bcdecaf
GEORGE Charles O habdf
GERDY Dorothy habbv
GIBSON Ensign James habgr
Ruth habgr
GILMAN Joanna adaabfe
Joshua Jr habat
GLIDDEN Abel habaq
Levi haabl
Sarah bcbhddc
GLINES Ann F haabtd
Elizabeth A habfs
James haabtd
GLOVER Mary wife habfp
Mary Eliza habfp
Peter habfp
GODDING, Adelbert J ahbabale
Arthur C ahbaable
Dora M ahbabale
Ralph ahbabale
Roy H ahbabale
GOODALE George H adgfbfbb
Mary E adgfbfbb
GOODCHILD Elizabeth ahgchhc
John ahgchhc
GOODRICH Merton T adabbc
GOOGINS William adaaafb
GORDON Abigail G habci
Saloma bcfiffb
Sylvester habce
GOULD Nancy habaa
Mary J bcdbaddb
Sophronia adaabdd
GOVE Elihu adgxb
Hannah adgxb
John adgxb
Jonathan adgxb, Jr adgxb, adgxd
Mehitable adgxb
Miriam adgxb
GOWDY Abiah ahgceab
GOWEN Emma bbbfhcdca
GRANT Eliza ahbaxa
Elizabeth ahbaxa
Louisa ahbaxa
GREELEY Hannah adgxfahb
GREEN Isaiah adgxb
—— bbbebcia
GRIFFEY Anna Augusta ahbgika

1007

Charles Franklin ahbgika
Clara E ahbgika
James Leroy ahbgika
William Franklin ahbgika
GROVER Lawrence ahbgile
Martha ahbaxab
Susan ahbaxab
GROW Abigail habhh
Alva habhh
Eaton habhh
Lucinda habhh
Nathaniel habhh
Rebecca habhh
Sally habhh
Timothy habhh
GUY Thomas M adhcbbdb
HALE Daniel 3rd habft
William J (MD) abbeebcaaa
HALL Emma Alice adacefgc
Charles Bengley bcdedgh
George abbegbeba
Mary abcedgb
Mary R habev
O L adaceagcc
Richard bcdedgh
HALLOWELL Suan B habfi
HAM Helen habdf
HANEY Alice Irene befifjddf
James Frederick befifjddf
John ahbgilf
Mary A ahbgilf
Willis James befifjddf
HANSON Aaron habel
HARDY Albert S adaaahae
David adaaahae
Marcellus A bcbhbdfgba
Morton A bcbhbdfgba
HARKNESS Joanna adaaaf
HARMON Josephine N haabr
HARPER Albert Gallatin bcdecaf
Amos bcdecaf
Caroline Dow bcdecaf
Cordelia bcdecaf
Eliza bcdecaf
Emma bcdecaf
Gaylord H bcdecaf
Jane bcdecaf
Laura Amelia bcdecaf
Levant bcdecaf
Leverett bcdecaf
Oliver bcdecaf
HARRIMAN John habev
Joseph, Joseph Jr habcw
HARVEY William A adadhcece
HASTINGS Mary bbbfhcd
HASTY John habba
HATCH Louisa adgfbfbb
HAZELTINE Martha befiha
HEATH Elizabeth befifjdd
George Clinton adhcbbgga
Lois Maradine adhcbbgga
Sarah haabtd
Stacie Robert adhcbbgga
HEIGHTS Frederick G adaaafxd
HENDERSON —— ahbgiic

HENDRICKSON family adggdcca
HERRICK Harmon habhd
HERSTY John habba
HILL Alice B bbbebgacb
Flora haabmc
HILTON John C ahbgika
Joseph H ahbaaad
LUCRETIA ahbaaad
HINCHMAN John (Capt) habhj
HINES Elisha habdw
HOAR Margaret Hanna adhcbbggb
HOBBS Julia M aceacac
Morris aeeacac
HOLMES Jonathan (Capt) habhi
HOLT Enoch haabtd
Rosa J haabtd
Susan C haabtd
HOMAN Benjamin habfh
HOPKINS Alice L ahgciae
Jessie D ahgciae
Louis A ahgciae
Samuel S ahgciae
HOW Timothy habbg
HOWARD Eli B habgy
HOWE Elizabeth adgcadaabc
HOWER Charles ahchfik
Emma ahchfik
Henry ahchfik
John H ahchfik
HOYT Ann habdca
HUBNER Emma M haaapa
Oscar haaapa
HUCKINS David (abbegfab) adabihf
Jonathan Dolloff (abbegfac) adabihc
HUDSON Julia Woodruff ahchea
HUGGINS John a
Lennie ahcfgga
Millie ahcfgga
—— ahcfgga
HUMPHREY Benjamin habet
Caroline Amelia habet
HUNGERFORD Elizabeth adaaafxe
HUNT Bessie E adacefgca
Dorothy M habfk
HUNTINGTON Henry Leslie ahgciab
HURD John adgcacd, habbr
HUSSEY Samuel haaav
HUTCHINSON Arthur adkddgcab
Oscar S adkddgcab
HYDE Matilda befifi
INNESS Henry habhi
IRISH Joseph haaai
JAMES Clara Dow ahbgiic
Frederick S ahbgiic
Irma E ahbgiic
—— ahbgiic
JAMESON Mary habdf
JANVRIN Addie F adkddgcb
JENKINS Sarah D haabtd
JENNESS Job habdr
Lucinda habdr
Richard (abeccd habdr
Rosina habdr
JOHONNET Isaac habbq
JOHNSON Almira ahgcia

1008

Amanda ahbgiiee
Cynthia befihb
Dearborn haabp
Emma L ahbaxae
Frank Phelp, befihb
Hiram befihb
John haabo
Joseph W bbbebdaca
Lola M bedbaddfa
Moses befihb
Nancy befihb
Phebe befihb
Rachel adkfbfa
Robert habem
—— bedbaddfa
JONES Joseph adgxb
Moses habdl
JORDAN Thomas habgt
JUDD Henry bedecaf
KEITH Sally Washburn adkdbf, habeq
KELLEY Delia adkddfae
KENDALL Hannah I bedebfa
KENNARD Susan Frances ahbaxabd
KENNEDY Mabel Elizabeth adaabce-
aaa
Matthew adaabceaaa
KETCHUM Edward ahebfa
Hiram ahebfa
KIDDER Andrew befifi
Hiram befifi
KIMBALL Sarah befihb
Sarah T haabh
KING Beatrice Ella ahchfeeb
Earl Edwin ahchfeeb
Edwin S ahchfeeb
Ethel Maud ahchfeeb
George William ahchfeeb
Helen Margaret ahchfeeb
KINGSBURY Austin Guthrie befifjdd
Dwight L ahgeha
Henry P ahgeha
Hugh Roblee befifjdd
Joseph ahgeha
Mary F ahgeha
Nathaniel ahgeha
KINNE Jeremiah ahdfa
KNEELAND Rhoda A adkddgeab
KNOWLES Nathaniel G adaaahac
LABREE Fidelia G haaan
LACKARD Ernest adaceagce
LADD Stephen C habar
LAFOLLETTE Joshua Usual ahbgiih
Mary E ahbgiih
LAKE Ida Louise haabtda
Joseph haabtda, h
Laura Ann haabtda
Moses Rowell haabtda
LAMBERTON Wiman H adaabfeb
LAMPHOR Abbie abecgdceb
LANGLEY James H adgfbfbce
Mattie A adgfbfbce
Nelson adgfbfbh
—— (Capt) adgfbfbh
LANSON Anna adgfbfbaa
Charles adgfbfbaa

Christine wife adgfbfbaa
LARKIN Elizabeth bededi
LEAKE Tempa wid ahche
LEAVITT Blanche E bbbfhcdca
Israel bbbfhcdca
Mehitable abdca
LEMIEUX Marie Elmire ahbaxabda
LEVERMORE Levi adaabdd
LEWIS Carrie Amanda ahgciab
Daniel S habfk
Emma J ahgciab
Maxon Palmer ahgciab
Priscilla bededbad
Sarah E haaaj
Thomas haaaj
LATHROP Adelaide R ahebfa
LAVALLETTE Elizabeth A adkddgcaa
LAWRENCE Almerida C ahgciha
Charles ahgciha
Sukey ahbaxb
LIBBEY Charles E adgxfahbd
Frederick Walter adgxfahbd
LIBBY Allison, Allison Jr habej
Edwin Ruthven haaal
Elizabeth haabc
Hattie P haaal
Isabella haabc
MEAD Abby A ahgck
Moses haabc
LINCOLN Eliza Ann haaaq
LINSCATE Caroline wife bbbfhcdb
Lysena S bbbfhcdb
William bbbfhcdb
LITTLE Abbie A haaabtc
LITTLETON Melvin Albertus bedecaf
Samuel T bedecaf
LOCKE Daniel adkddgc
Elizabeth C wife adkddgc
Sarah A haabtf
Sarah C adkddgc
LONG Caroline adkfbda
Nancy adaaafaa
LOSER Caroline ahbghgf
LOUGEE Peter befifi
LOW Mary ahgchh
Philip S haaaya
LUMMUS John habfe
LYFORD Biley haabr
Caroline haabr
Daniel Calvin haabr
Henry Harrison haabr
John haabr
Mary A haabr
LYMAN Emmet ahgcihb
Henrietta Cutter ahgchj
Martin ahgchj
William C ahgcihb
MACKENZIE William J haabtcb
MACY Edward W adaaafacc
Elizabeth wife adaaafacc
Melvin B adaaafacc
MANNING Lydia befifi
MARBLE Almira C abdcebeg
MARSH Daniel haaah
Dudley habau

1009

Matilda **M** haaah
MARSHBANK —— ahbaxad
MARSHALK —— habhi
MARSTEN Obediah haabs
MARSTON Albert C haabsx
Angeline **J** haabsx
Stephen **G** haaabsx
MARSHALL Albert habdf
Allen **W** habdf
Almus habdf
Anna **J** habdf
Anna **M** habdf
Ansel **H** habdf
Benjamin habdf
John **C** habdf
Martha **A** habdf
Thomas adaaafc
MASON Cyrus bcdecaa
John bcdecaa
Laura bcdecaa
Thadeus **B** adaabfex
Wheaton bcdecaa
MATTESON Alexander Tremain ahgch-
ha
Horatio **G** ahgchha
Laura Ethel ahgchha
William Henry ahgchha
MCAFEE Barbarita ahchfid
Isabella ahchfig
Severa ahchfie
MCCORD Annie M haaawc
McDANIEL William adgxca
—— ahcfggfc
McDANIELS Sarah E abdcebega
McDONALD Eleanor wid adgfbfb
McDUFFEE Rhoda bcfifjd
McELROY Annie adadhcecb
Samuel Hill adaaafxf
McKINSTON Sally ahgchh
McLUCES Maud bcdedcgaa
MEAD Abby A ahgck
Charlotte **E** ahgck
John, John Jr ahgck
John **O** ahgck
Julia ahgck
Louisa **J** ahgck
Lucy ahgck
Mary ahgck
Matilda ahgck
Rufus Francisco ahgck
Sophronia ahgck
Wakeman **J** adacefga
William **A** ahgck
MERRILL Abner adgfcig
Ann adadbcfab
Horace Jefferson adgfcig
Isaac habbh
Lucy wife habgq
Moses habgq
William **B** adadabcfab
MERRITT Samuel Ezekiel adacfc
METCALF Addison L ahgceaab
MILLER Jane adggdcca
MILLS Ada ahbgiida
Amos adacfb

Donald ahbgiida
Ephraim adacfb
Eva ahbgiida
Gale ahbgiida
Harry ahbgiida
Leona ahbgiida
Leslie ahbgiida
Morrell ahbgiida
MITCHELL Elizabeth haaaj
Fred adgfbfbd
James adgfbfbd
Lydia wife adaaafacb
Mary **A** adgfbcbd
William adaaafacb
William Foster adaaaacb
MONTGOMERY Clarence bcdecad
Martin bcdecad
MOODY David habfv
Elizabeth wife habfv
Enoch, Enoch Jr habfv
Esther habfv
Moses habfv
Mary habfv
Sally habfv
MOONEY Joseph (Capt) haabq
Nancy haabq
MOORE Nancy haabq
Naomi haaay
MORELAND Edith Weston habacb
John **H** habacb
MORGAN Nettie Clark bbbebcdaea
William **C** bbbebcdaea
MORRILL Betsey G haaby
MORRISON Ann habhm
MORSS Joseph Jr habgb
MOTTER Mike ahbghgb
MOULTON Benjamin F ahgciga
Comfort abbeh
Elizabeth abbeh
MUDGETT Hannah bcfigfbd
Sarah habec
MURRAY Florence Alberta ahchfecc
George **R** ahchfecc
MURTAUGH Mary bcdecaf
MYRICK Emily abcedgbc
NEAL Kate adaaafxec
NEWELL Moses habfv
NEWMAN Ebenezer haben
NEWTON Gideon habbe
NOBLE Cinderella bbbebci
Eli bbbebci
NORRIS Asa habak
NORTHROP Mary ahgchfe
NORTON Miriam adgxb
NOYES Martha T habes
NUTTING Benjamin bcdecab
James bcdecab
Solomon bcdecab
OAKES Eunice bcdedeg
OAKLEY Benjamin habhi
OBER Joseph E bcdeaedbb
OSBORN Abbie E habdf
OSGOOD Annie H habei
Charles **B** habei
Charles **E** habei

Daniel haaba
Eliza Welch haaba
Mary Alden adadabcaa
PADDACH Abishai adaaafg
Thomas adaaafg
PAGAN Jessie N adadhceeb
PAGE Jane habdh
Mary (abceed) habdr
PALMER Diantha ahgcf
Uriah ahgcf
PARK Annette haaah
PARTRIDGE Polly habek
PATCH Harriet ahgchf
PATTEE Horace M adgfcig
PATTERSON Archie bcdgdagi
Ella M bcdgdbaaga
James habae
Lydia B bcdgdagi
Roland A bcdgdagi
PATTEN Emeline S bcbehhe
PEARL Carrie J ahgcihc
Charles ahgcihc
PEASLEE Hannah E adgfbb
John adgffb
PERLEY Chester Garfield adkddgcaa
David T adkddgcaa
PERKINS Austin D ahgceae
Benjamin aeeacae
Kate Gertrude habdf
Nancy aecacae
William habbs, habic
PHERSON David habfm
PHILLIPS Hattie adkddgcea
PICKER Abigail habcb
PIERCE Enoch habez
Samuel habez
PILLSBURY Salley habfv
PINKHAM Belle haabma
Lucy wife haabma
Samuel haabma
PLACE Naomi bcbhdded
PLUNKETT G J bcbcbaacd
POOR Betsey haabo
Luna M bcdgddaaba
POTTER John habfi
—— haabtd
PRESCOTT David habbl
H Gilmore habbl
Marilla habbl
PRINCE Arthur Dow ahbaxabb
George Caleb ahbaxabb
George Leonard ahbaxabb
PROCTOR Thomas haabk
PROUTY Elon habdyba
PURVIANCE Jessie Dow (Mrs) bede-
caf
QUIGLEY Agnes adaaafxeb
RAND Blanche E bbbebgaa
Herman S bbbcbgaa
Oscar L bbbebgaa
Oscar S bbbebgaa
RANDALL Hubbard habhh
REED Benjamin T adhafagba
Mary T adhafagba
REID Charles bcdeabdab

REYNARD Catherine (De Vos) adggd-
cca
RICE Charlotte habem
Margaret haaal
William habem
RICHARDS Effie bbbfhcdcb, haabdbb
RICHARDSON Lydia habdya
RILEY Albert John ahbghgb
Charles M ahbghgb
John ahbghgb
Julia Buckingham ahbghgb
Maggie Hamilton ahbghgb
Myrtle Allace ahbghgb
Roy Boyer ahbghgb
RING David F bcdcbed
ROBBINS Caroline Augusta adaaafaef
Roberts Isaac habhb
Sarah wife habdcd
William habdcd
ROBINSON Winfield Fairbanks bcdcd-
cfebb
RODGERS Zenas bcbhdeg
ROGERS Jonathan habfw
ROLLINS Violetta haabr
RONAN Thomas habdcb
ROPES Caroile E bbbebcbde
ROSS Clarissa haabtca
Fannie ahcfgg
ROWAN William H habax
ROWE Dudley ahbaxai
Jonathan abdca
RUMRILL Rebecca habaca
RUNDLETT James 3rd habaj
RUSSELL Allen habea
Lucy habdy
SAFFORD Henrietta ahgcih
Margaret Ellen adkddgb
William Brazier adkddgb
SANBORN John habah
Rhodes bcdbaddj
SANDERSON Abner habdyab
SARGENT Cora abcedgbg
Edmund abcedgbg
Florence abcedgbg
George W adgcadaaba
Grace abcedgbg
Hattie abcedgbg
SAWYER Emily Ann adgcadaab
Nathan bcdecae
SCHOONMAKER family adggdcea
SCHULTZ Charles ahbgile
Mabel B ahbgile
SEAVERNS Henry habax
SENCEPAUGH Susan ahchea
SERVIS Florence E ahbgiidb
SEWELL Nancy Ellen ahgchjb
SHATTUCK Nettie M wid adgcadaabc
SHAW Juliet befifjdc
Sherburn habfb
SHELDON Charles bcdecaf
Emma bcdecaf
Robinson bcdecaf
SILVER Edward habbt
Laura Ann habbt
SKILLINGS Sarah habej

SKINNER Jurusha habeb
SMITH Alice L bedbaddb
Bethra L ahbgike
Edgar bedbaddb
Emma Jane ahbgike
Dolores befiffb
Ellen B bededbae
Fannie Carria Frances ahbgike
Flora Eunice ahbgike
Frank Wells ahbgike
George ahbaxad
George Washington ahbgike. Jr ahbgike
Herbert bedbaddb
James adaabdd
Lucette bedbaddb
Marvin habeg
Mary habdb
Mary Anna ahbgild
Maryanna ahbaxad
Nathaniel Brown bedbaddb
Rosie adaabcead
Olivia Eliza ahefggb
Samuel bebebbda
SPRAGUE Sally ahgcea
Samuel ahgcea, bebebbda
STACIE Anna Fernald adhcbbgga
STANTON David adaaafaab
Giles adanafaab
STARR —— ahefggb
STASSFORTH Paul haayae
STEARNS Arthur E bbbffeg
Charles H bbbffeg
Harriet bbbffeg
Harriet J bbbffeg
Horace bbbffeg
Sarah E bbbffeg
William H bbbffeg
STEINER Tillie adaaafxea
STEVENS Chase habal
Nehimiah ahdaai
Sarah haaba
STEWART Alexander ahbgike
Henry M Stanley ahbgike
Joseph habez
STUBBS Eleanor bededcfdb
Frank Raymond bededefdb
Joseph bededcfdb
STINSON Edmund adabbd
Joseph Colby adabbd
STRAW John habey
STREETER Laura M ahbgika
STONE Maria habacb
STIGLER Sarah I wid ahbgiie
STUBBS Eleanor bededcfdh
Frank Raymond bededefdh
Joseph bededcfdh
SULLINGS Charles adacefg
Elizabeth adacefg
SUMNER Lucy adacefi
Michael habfv
SWAN Elizabeth habeg
Sylvanus habex
TAYLOR Bert Laun ahbgike
Ocea Seriena ahbgike
TEFFT Emery Nathaniel ahchfeg

Gertrude Irene ahchfeg
TENNEY John ahgfdd
Roswell Algernon ahgfdd
TER BOS family adggdcca
TEWKSBURY Miriam habdg
THOMPSON Anna J ahbaxaea
James ahggf
THORNE Cora H bededhad
—— bededhad
TILLSON Anna wid adgfbfbaa
TILTON Samuel P abdecbce
TODD Joseph ahbabx
TOWLE Abigail abbeaa
Amos abbeaa
Comfort abbeaa
Hannah abbeaa
Oliver abbeaa
Sarah abbeaa
William habdx
TODD Joseph habfy
TOWNE Abigail bededef
Joseph bededcfdb
TRASK Casper bedecaea
Clara bedecaea
TREMAIN Augustus ahgchh
Jane M ahgchh
TRIPP Mary A adgfbfbc
Warren adgfbfbc
TURNER Oriens habet
TYLER Elizabeth habgb
Joseph, Joseph Jr habgb
John habgb
Rebecca habgb
UNDERWOOD Susannah ahbgiih
URANN John habhi
VANCOUR Corine bebebaaed
VAN DAHLEM H H (Capt) habhk
VAN KEUREN family adggdcca
VAN RENSELAER Henry habhi
VARNUM George W adaabccada
Roy adaabceada
VEIT Clara Munroe adhcbbjaa
VILLAS Lottie M adkddgcca
William adkddgeaa
VIOLETT Ida bededbadb
Ora bededbadb
VITTY Jonathan adgcadaabc
Nettie M adgcadaabc
WADE Elizabeth Wentworth abggbd-aaa
John Melmoth abggbdaaa
William F befifjde
—— ahggbdaaa
WALKER Edward ahbaxab
John abeedgba, adgfgad
Susan S ahbaxab
WALLACE Edward T habei
Edwin Seccomb bedebejee
Frederick W bedebejee
WARNER William habhg
WARREN Betsey befiffb
WATSON Frances J ahbgili
WEARE Hattie B adkddgce
Jonathan E adkddgce
WEBB Bethia adabbd

1012

472

Samuel adabbd
William adabbd
WEBSTER Delia bcbebbfac
Frank D bcbebbfac
WELCH Addie abccdgbf
Benjamin abccdgbf
John abccdgbf
Mary abccdgbf
Olive bcdecaf
WELLMAN Lizzie bbbfhcdc
WENTWORTH Benjamin abccdgbe
Rosanna ahccdgbe
Spencer ahbaxc
WEST Gordon B adhcbbdd
Guy B adhcbbdd
Lulu T adhcbbdd
Mary adhcbbdd
WHEELER Annie H bbbebci
Molly habdc
Sarah Bender ahgchh
Silas bcdedi
Zenas ahgchh
WHIDDEN Elizabeth haabq
WHIPPLE James bcdedbad
WHITE Frank J adgcadaaba
Mary E bcdebfa
WHITEMAN ——- ahcfggf
WHITMAN Charlotte habem
WILCOX Cloe ahdfa
WILES Harriet habfia
WILLEY John habcca
Sarah G habcca, wife habcca
WILLIAMS Jacob habel
Josephine M adabbgaga
WILLIS George habhi
WILMANS John McDonald ahbgiic
WILSON Albert ahgfdaec
Betsey haabtb
WINSLOW Mabel ahbaxabb

WITBECK Lucas ahgdcce
WOOD DeLos bcdecaf
Elinear adgfbfb
Grace M bcbebbbdd
WOODS Carrie Eliza ahchfed
Gertrude Malvina ahchfed
Milicent Irene ahchfed
William Chester ahchfed
William Norris ahchfed
WORTH Annie adgxca
WYNCOOP Cornelius adggdcca
Maria adggdcca
WORTHLEY Betsey bcfifi
Hannah G bcfifi
Jemima bcfifi
Mary bcfifi
Sally bcfifi
Samuel bcfifi
Susanna bcfifi
Thomas bcfifi
Thomas Dow bcfifi
YORK Frank haabtca
Ida M haabtca
Jane wife haabtca
Young Augusta A bcbebbbdd
Sally bcfihb
ZUFELD Benjamin L ahchffc
Harold Benjamin ahchffc
Oliver Norman ahchffc

—— Abigail ahcfg
—— Chloe C adaaafacd
Ida adggefgx
Irene haaab
Katherine ahbab
Lucy adgfbfbe
Mary haaac
Mary R haaa
Sarah adgfbfb, haaad

www.ingramcontent.com/pod-product-compliance
Lightning Source LLC
Chambersburg PA
CBHW050328270326
41926CB00016B/3362